The Life and Work of
GERARD NOODT

Gerard Noodt and his wife, Sara Maria van der Marck van Leur, 1692, both by Willem van Mieris (Private collection, the Netherlands). Photo: Han Meyer.

The Life and Work of

GERARD NOODT

(1647–1725)

Dutch Legal Scholarship
Between Humanism and Enlightenment

G. C. J. J. VAN DEN BERGH

CLARENDON PRESS · OXFORD
1988

Oxford University Press, Walton Street, Oxford OX2 6DP
Oxford New York Toronto
Delhi Bombay Calcutta Madras Karachi
Petaling Jaya Singapore Hong Kong Tokyo
Nairobi Dar es Salaam Cape Town
Melbourne Auckland
and associated companies in
Berlin Ibadan

Oxford is a trade mark of Oxford University Press

Published in the United States
by Oxford University Press, New York

British Library Cataloguing in Publication Data
Bergh, G. C.J.J. van den
The life and work of Gerard Noodt (1647–1725) : Dutch legal scholarship between humanism and enlightenment.
1. Noodt, Gerard 2. Lawyers—Netherlands —Biography I. Title
340'.109 [LAW]
ISBN 0–19–825602–7

Library of Congress Cataloging in Publication Data
Bergh, G. C. J. J. van den.
The life and work of Gerard Noodt, 1647–1725: Dutch legal scholarship between humanism and enlightenment
G.C.J.J. van den Bergh.
p.cm. Bibliography: p. Includes indexes.
1. Noodt, Gerard, 1647–1725. 2. Law teachers—Netherlands —Biography. 3. Roman-Dutch law. I. Title.
KJA2128.B47 1988
340'.07'11492—dc19
[B]
ISBN 0–19–825602–7

Set by Wyvern Typesetting Ltd, Bristol

Printed in Great Britain
at the University Printing House, Oxford
by David Stanford
Printer to the University

PREFACE

This book describes the life and work of Gerard Noodt (1647–1725) and tries to fill a major gap in the history of European civil law scholarship. The study of the Dutch Elegant School, in its time the leading school in Europe, has been greatly neglected over the last century. I have put Noodt's work in the context of his personal experiences and general intellectual background. Civil law scholarship, a well-established discipline from the Middle Ages, developed close relations with classical scholarship in the humanistic tradition, and towards the end of the seventeenth century came under the influence of rationalistic natural law theory, which marked the beginning of the era of Enlightenment. Noodt played a crucial role in this development. His address on the freedom of religion (1706) assured him a place in the history of Enlightenment and the making of a legal theory of human rights, but up to now it has been seen too much in isolation. A detailed analysis of Noodt's work places it in context and allows for an assessment of his contribution to the development of civil law as well as to Roman law scholarship.

Archives and libraries are the laboratories of the historian, and I have made use of them as much as I could. It would be impossible to name all the persons and institutions that in some way or other have been helpful in the making of this book, but some of them must be named here. I thank, in the first place, the staff of the library of the Instituut voor Rechtsgeschiedenis in Utrecht, Marianne Roelofs-Hendriks, Simone van den Berg, and Corrie Zwanenberg. Without this superb library and their help I could never have completed this book as it is now. I also would like to thank John Sibbald of the Advocates Library, Edinburgh, as well as Willem Meeuwissen, director of the municipal archives in Nijmegen and his staff. Some others who have helped me on special points are mentioned in the relevant notes.

The manuscript was read in various stages by Robert Feenstra, Bernard Stolte, and Theo Veen. I am very grateful for their interest in the work and their critical remarks. Corjo Jansen also read the manuscript and helped me in various ways in preparing it for the press. Finally Peter Stein, Queens' College, Cambridge, read it and corrected my English. I thank him for the help and encouragement he gave me in a most generous way. I thank Els van Tol for typing and correcting the manuscript with great care and loyalty.

Taking the trouble to get to know someone else is always an exploration of oneself, and making the acquaintance of Gerard Noodt was never dull. It has greatly enriched my life. But, however painstaking our research may have been, or however honest our *fides historiae*, we can retrieve no more than a very small part of reality. And the story as told by the historian will always remain his selection and presentation of the available facts. So I cannot help having created, in a sense, my own Noodt. Quite an agreeable chap, I must say. I hope many readers will agree. I also hope to convince them, as Noodt did when publishing the first part of his commentary on the Digest, that civil law is not sad, austere, dull, and trifling, but a beautiful account of what is essential for human society. But in this respect I have no great expectations, I confess.

I dedicate this book to the memory of my teacher and promoter Adriaan Pitlo.

G.C.J.J.v.d.B.

Nijmegen
9 April 1987

CONTENTS

LIST OF ILLUSTRATIONS

ABBREVIATIONS

1. Works of Noodt

Opera omnia 1713	G. Noodt, *Opera omnia, cum ante edita, tum adhuc inedita, quorum index et ordo est post praefationem*. Leiden: Johannes van der Linden jun., 1713 (Ahsmann–Feenstra: 1984, nr. 464).
Opera i, ii	G. Noodt, *Opera omnia, recognita, aucta, emendata multos in locis atque in duos tomos distributa. Huic novae editioni inter alia accessit Joannis Barbeyracii Historica vitae auctoris narratio*. Leiden: J. A. Langerak, 1735 (Ahsmann–Feenstra, 1984: nr. 466).
Register	Register van het geslagt van Noodt (Noodt's autograph) ARA Coll. Van Tets van Goudriaan, inv. nr. 101.
Register Biesman	Register van het geslacht van de Bijesmans en eenige andere daer aen verwante familien (Noodt's autograph) ARA Coll. Van Tets van Goudriaan, inv. nr. 107.

2. Works of reference

v. d. Aa	A. J. van der Aa, *Biografisch Woordenboek der Nederlanden*, 21 vols. Haarlem, 1852–78. Repr. in 7 vols., 1969.
v. d. Aa, Geogr.	A. J. van der Aa, *Aardrijkskundig Woordenboek der Nederlanden*, 13 vols. Gorinchem, 1836–51.
AGN	*Algemene Geschiedenis der Nederlanden*, 15 vols. Haarlem, 1981–2.
Ahsmann–Feenstra	M. Ahsmann and R. Feenstra, *Bibliografie van hoogleraren in de*

	rechten aan de Leidse universiteit tot 1811. Amsterdam, Oxford, and New York, 1984.
Album scholasticum	C. A. Siegenbeek van Heukelom-Lamme and O. C. D. Idenburg-Siegenbeek van Heukelom, *Album scholasticum academiae Lugduno-Batavae MDLXXV-MCMXL*. Leiden, 1941.
AS Amsterdam	*Album academicum van het Athenaeum illustre en van de universiteit van Amsterdam*. Amsterdam, 1913.
AP Franeker	Th. J. Meijer (ed.), *Album promotorum Academiae Franekerensis*. Franeker, 1972.
AS Franeker	S. J. Fockema Andreae and Th. J. Meijer (eds.), *Album studiosorum Academiae Franekerensis*. Franeker, 1968.
AS Groningen	*Album studiosorum academiae groninganae*. Groningen, 1915.
AS Harderwijk	D. G. van Epen, *Album studiosorum academiae gelro-zutphanicae 1648–1818*. The Hague, 1904.
AS Leiden	*Album studiosorum Academiae Lugduno Batavae 1575–1875*. The Hague, 1875.
AP Utrecht	*Album promotorum Utrecht 1636–1815*. Utrecht, 1936.
AS Utrecht	*Album studiosorum academiae rheno-trajectinae 1636–1886*.
ARA	Algemeen Rijksarchief (General state archives, The Hague).
Barbeyrac, *Vita*	*J. Barbeyrac, Vita V. C. Gerardi Noodt, Jurisconsulti et Antecessoris celeberrimi*, in *Opera* I (pages not numbered).
Dekkers	R. Dekkers, *Bibliotheca belgica juridica: Een biobibliographisch overzicht der rechtsgeleerdheid in de Nederlanden van de vroegste tijd af tot 1800*. Brussels, 1951.
FIRA	*Fontes iuris romani antejustiniani*. i.

	Leges. Florence, 1941; ii. *Auctores*. Florence, 1940; iii. *Negotia*. Another edn., Florence, 1972.
GA	Gemeentearchief (municipal archives).
Gebauer–Spangenberg	*Corpus Juris Civilis*, collected by Georgius Christanus Gebauer and after his death ed. Georgius Augustus Spangenberg. i. (Institutes and Digest) Göttingen, 1776; ii. (Codex and Novellae) Göttingen, 1797.
HRG	*Handwörterbuch zur Deutschen Rechtsgeschichte*, ed. Adalbert Erler and Ekkehard Kaufmann. i- . Berlin, 1971– .
Kernkamp	G. W. Kernkamp (ed.), *Acta et decreta senatus: Vroedschapsresolutiën en andere bescheiden betreffende de Utrechtse academie*, 3 vols. Utrecht, 1936–40. (The memorial volume of 1936 is cited as Kernkamp, 1936; for references see the bibliography.)
Kleine Pauly	Der kleine Pauly; *Lexikon der Antike*. Auf der Grundlage von Pauly's Realencyclopädie der classischen Altertumswissenschaft unter Mitwirkung zahlreicher Fachgelehrten bearbeitet und herausgegeben von Konrat Ziegler und Walther Sontheimer. 5 vols. Deutscher Taschenbuch Verlag, 1979.
Lipenius	M. Lipenius, *Bibliotheca realis juridica post Friderici Gottlieb Struvii et Gottlob Augusti Ienichii curas emendata, multis accessionibus aucta et locupletata*, 2 vols. Leipzig, 1757. Supplementary volumes by Schott, 1775; v, Senkenberg, 1789; Madihn 1816, 1823. Anastatic repr., 6 vols., Hildesheim and New York, 1970–1.
Mo	Digesta Iustiniani Augusti

	recognovit adsumpto in operis societatem Paulo Kruegero Th. Mommsen. Vol. i–ii. Editio altera lucis ope expressa, Berlin, 1962. Cited by volume: page: and line.
Molhuysen	P. C. Molhuysen (ed.), *Bronnen tot de geschiedenis der Leidsche universiteit*, 7 vols. The Hague, 1913–24. (Rijks Geschiedkundige Publicatiën Nrs. 20, 29, 38, 45, 48, 53, 56.)
NNBW	*Nieuw Nederlandsch Biografisch Woordenboek*, 10 vols. Leiden, 1911–37.
RA	Rijksarchief (state archives in each province).
RE	Pauly's *Realencyclopädie der classischen Altertumswissenschaft*, neue Bearbeitung von G. Wissowa *et al.* 80 vols. Stuttgart, 1893– .
Roberts	A. A. Roberts, *A South African Legal Bibliography being a bio-bibliographical survey and law-finder of the Roman and Roman-Dutch legal literature in southern Africa*. Pretoria, 1942.
UL	University Library.

Unless otherwise indicated texts from the Corpus Juris are cited from the *edito stereotypa* of Mommsen, Krüger, Schöll, and Kroll. I used the edition of Berlin, 1895. For citation of legal sources I followed Feenstra–Rossi, *Index adbreviationum et de modo citandi fontes* (Ius Romanum Medii Aevi, Pars I, 1 a–d), Milan: Giuffrè, 1961, pp. 109–18.

I

Introduction

Scientific biography is a branch of historiography which Dutch historians, unlike their British colleagues, do not seem to cultivate assiduously. This is true even more for history of law. Let me give a random sample. When J. M. Kemper (1776–1824) tried to urge King William I in 1814 to make a national codification, instead of copying the French one, he said, among other things, that he wished 'to save us the disgrace that we, living in the native country of De Groot, Van Bijnkershœk, Noodt, and Schulting, would take a foreign model as a lead'.[1]

Now, undoubtedly very much has been written about Hugo de Groot (1583–1645), who is a class of his own, but the only biography of Cornelis van Bijnkershœk (1673–1743) dates from 1869,[2] and for all its qualities it must be regarded as out of date now, if only because of the many materials which have come to light since, for instance his diary as a supreme court judge[3] and sixty-two letters to his 'pater spiritualis' Cornelius van Eck (1662–1732).[4] The two others, both born in Nijmegen, fared even worse. Neither Gerard Noodt (1647–1725), who in his time was known all over Europe, nor Anton Schulting (1656–1734), who once was called the Dutch Cujas,[5] has a modern biography.

1. J. M. Kemper to William I, The Hague, 22 Dec. 1814, Voorduin I. 1, p. 32. Compare already the opinion of Heineccius, an outstanding scholar, dating from 1737. When asked to take a chair in Leiden, he replied in the negative, but he added: 'This one thing I acknowledge, that there is in me an untiring zeal to do something for legal studies. But the outstanding example of your Dutchmen Bijnkershœk, Noodt and Schulting first incited this to me. I try to follow their tracks, but with hardly equal footsteps.' Molhuysen v: 1920: 60*.
2. Star Numan, 1869.
3. Van Bijnkershoek, 1926–62.
4. UL Utrecht, MS 1000. Van Bijnkershœk calls van Eck his 'pater spiritualis' in his letter of 16 June 1707, in which he announces the birth of his first son, who is called Cornelius after Van Eck.
5. Vitriarius, 1734; Saxe, 1789; Haubold, 1809: 142. According to Palazzini Finetti, 1953: 333, Noodt was given this epithet too, but he gives no source and I have not been able to find one.

Naturally it might be questioned whether the four men named by Kemper really formed the peak of Dutch legal scholarship during the Republic, but he does not seem to be very far off the mark. A sampling from the *Novissimo digesto italiano* (which appeared 1968–75),[6] although not representative in every respect either, does seem to indicate fairly adequately which Dutch jurists from the Republic are still remembered. The number of lines devoted to each gives some indication of their relative importance; I have added it in brackets. Of course, Grozio (82), the only one with an Italianized name, is easily at the top. He is followed by Van Bijnkershœk (21) and Schulting (18). But only because the well-known advice of the Leiden law faculty to King Vittorío Amedeo II of Savoy[7] is mentioned under the name of Schulting, who (accidentally?) signed it first, Noodt has eight lines. The other Dutch jurists mentioned are Henrik Brenkman (8), Ulrik Huber (8), Paulus Vœt (7), Simon van Grœnewegen van der Made (7), Johannes Vœt (6), Antonius Matthæus I, II, and III (together 4, each 6), and Cornelis van Eck (5). The overall picture does not seem to have changed greatly over the last hundred and fifty years. No doubt the order in the *Novissimo digesto* is based mainly on merit in legal scholarship. If importance for legal practice had been the criterion, we would have a totally different list, in which e.g. Johannes Vœt and Simon van Grœnewegen van der Made would rank high above Noodt.[8]

Recent studies do not seem to change our picture of the state of legal biography greatly. Vinnius (1599–1657), who, by the way, is not mentioned in the *Novissimo digesto*, and Johannes Vœt (1647–1713) have been the subject of mainly bibliographical studies recently.[9] Only to Ulrik Huber (1636–1694) and Henrik Brenkman (1681–1736) have more comprehensive studies been devoted.[10]

Considering the state of biographical studies, it will hardly come as a surprise that Noodt's fame in our time is very unbalanced. As an example, I note what the new General History of the Netherlands (*AGN*) has to say about him. A chapter on the history of religion names him as the author of a speech on freedom of religion dating from 1706, without mentioning that he was a law professor, and a

6. This is a specialized legal encyclopaedia. In the recent biographical dictionary of Simpson, 1984, apart from Grotius and Van Bijnkershœk only Vinnius is named.
7. See below, p. 287.
8. See Roberts, 14–15.
9. Roberts, 1933; Feenstra and Waal, 1975.
10. Veen, 1976; Stolte, 1981.

very famous one at that.[11] In a survey of legal scholarship in the Republic he is named as a true representative of legal humanism, but no mention is made of his two most famous speeches, one on the power of the sovereign, the other on freedom of religion.[12] Both passages are echoes of an appreciation which petrified long ago and has not been challenged by independent research ever since.

Noodt's fame has been divided in this way for a long time. The two addresses of 1699 and 1706 have assured him a place in the history of Enlightenment.[13] Very soon after appearing, they were translated into French and German, and even twice over into English and Dutch (the original publication being in Latin, of course). They were reprinted several times during the eighteenth century and, significantly, in 1784, at the high point of the patriotic revolt[14] a new Dutch translation of the address on the power of the sovereign was published, with a lengthy, high-pitched introduction stressing its relevance, from a patriot point of view, in contemporary political conditions.[15]

It might seem that the two speeches stand more or less isolated from the rest of Noodt's work. His fame as a jurist is mainly of interest to specialists. He is regarded as a great jurist and a great scholar, one of the best experts on classical Roman law of his time.[16] His name as a jurist is highlighted, among other things, by the fact that he and Vœt are cited as authorities by the county court of Hertogenbosch as late as 1914.[17]

This state of opinion about Noodt suggests what the first aim of a modern biography should be: to reconstruct the unity of the man and his work. Noodt consciously spoke about freedom of religion as a jurist, and for his listeners it was clear enough, for that matter, that orthodox theologians would disagree with him. Moreover, the way he argued in this case did not differ greatly from the method with which he interpreted texts of Roman law. He always combined the tradition of humanistic philology in law, which from its beginning had been critical in both senses of the word, philologically as well as

11. S. B. J. Zilverberg, *AGN* ix: 323. According to him Noodt's address was the first fundamental publication on the subject of toleration in the Republic.
12. G. van Dievoet, *AGN* vii: 315.
13. Zwager, 1980: 84 f., 100; Hazard, 1973: 346.
14. See Schama, 1977.
15. See below p. 205.
16. See Haubold, 1805: 136 and below Ch. IV at note 5.
17. See below 261f.

politically, with the newly emerging rationalism of natural law thinking, which was characteristic of the early Enlightenment and laid the basis for modern ideas about the rule of law and human rights. While being anything but a revolutionary himself, he thus contributed to the making of that explosive mixture of critical philology and natural law rationalism which brought so many jurists to the van of bourgeois revolutionary movements between 1700 and 1848.

Noodt's work is related, moreover, to social experience. The links between scholarly work and his life story, between ideas and experience, can in fact be demonstrated with singular clarity in his case. As a son of a family of Remonstrant merchants in Nijmegen, where the battle between civic freedom and absolutist ambitions began early in the seventeenth century and persecution of Remonstrants was very heavy, he knew from family tradition the bitter experiences which incited the desire for civil and religious freedom. According to family tradition there had already been a Gerard Noodt who had to fly his country for Alva,[18] and there were many other incidents. In all these instances there is, in the minds of the sufferers, the notion of a breach of well-established rights and it is to this notion that Noodt was to give legal form with the help of humanistic philology and rationalistic natural law. This form marks a transition in several respects: transition from humanism to Enlightenment, transition from the period in which civil freedom was focused on the city and its privileges to that in which the focus is on the state, the constitution, the rule of law, and fundamental human rights.

This biography is another proof of the fact that historical research is difficult to plan and hardly feasible as team-work. On 14 December 1971 a small group of scholars assembled in the Law Institute of the Catholic University of Nijmegen—in alphabetical order, G. C. J. J. van den Bergh, J. A. H. Bots, J. J. Brinkhof, J. Schimmel, and B. H. Stolte—to plan joint studies on Noodt, which were to be published in 1975 for the two hundred-and-fiftieth anniversary of his death. Tasks were parcelled out and first steps were taken to get an impression of available materials. Bots collected data on Noodt's correspondence, Brinkhof studied the autograph of Noodt's lecture notes on the Pandects,[19] Stolte made a provisional bibliography and a list of collections in various archives. I began to study the printed works and the main collections in the archives, with which I was greatly

18. Roukens, 1767: 4. 19. UL Leiden, MS BPL 575.

helped by the much regretted Jan Schimmel, then director of the city archives of Nijmegen, as well as by the data collected by the others. This study incited in me a keen and lasting interest in Noodt, but the group soon disintegrated. Everyone had much to do of his own, and after all writing history remains a one-man job. By that I do not want to deny, of course, that every historian is dependent on many specialists, in ever growing numbers, in fact. I too could never have written this book without the inspiration, hints, and advice of innumerable people, of whom only a few could be mentioned in the Preface.

Naturally, I underestimated the writing of a biography, as so many have done before. Whoever wants to say something about a scholar of the past without repeating existing accounts, must read a lot besides his own works. Only when one has a rough picture of what happened in legal scholarship, say, between the middle of the sixteenth century and the middle of the eighteenth, can one place Noodt's life and work in its time and in the proper historical perspective. But that is not all. In order to be able to assess the—always relative—originality of Noodt's contribution, one has to be oriented in many other fields: political history, history of philosophy and political theory, history of universities, etc. Not to mention the study of numerous documents, the repeated visits to archives, the correspondence.

So the year 1975 passed without the contemplated publication, and many more. In 1977 I was able to present the first results of my research in lectures in Amsterdam and Leiden. The main lines of the picture that I had formed by then have not changed essentially, although since then much new material has been studied, which corrected, amplified, and deepened the picture in many points. Part of the pleasure of making a biography consists in some sort of detective work. Combining details from various sources, one may find proof for connections that had been long conjectured or, on the other hand, may have to accept as untenable what had seemed almost certain. And naturally 'il faut faire la part des séductions de l'érudition'.[20]

For the story of Noodt's life two sources are essential. The first, to which in fact all biographies go back, is an obituary written by his son-in-law Jan Ham van den Ende, apparently shortly after Noodt's

20. Simonnet, in Eyssell, 1860: p. xviii.

death, of which Barbeyrac made a French translation.[21] Barbeyrac used it as basis for his life of Noodt, which first was published in French in 1731,[22] and then, revised and translated into Latin, in the edition of Noodt's *Opera omnia* of 1735. It is found in most of the later editions, and is used by all biographers.[23]

The second source is much less known. It is a panegyric on Noodt which Theodoor Leonard Roukens pronounced on 27 August 1767, as best alumnus of Nijmegen grammar school for that year.[24] It was published in Nijmegen in a limited edition, and probably hardly circulated outside the city. It became more widely known when Henricus Johannes Arntzenius, born in Nijmegen, made extensive use of it in his inaugural address in Utrecht, pronounced on 22 September 1788 and entitled: 'About Nijmegen's Gerard Noodt as the perfect model of a professor of Roman law'.[25]

For the first part of Noodt's life, Van den Ende made use of an autobiographic fragment, forming part of the 'Register of the family Noodt' that Noodt wrote with his own hand, but unfortunately left unfinished.[26] This fragment, which gives a very detailed account, must have been drafted in Franeker around 1680, shortly after the death of both parents, which is described in great detail. As far as Noodt himself is concerned, the latest fact mentioned is the inauguration in Franeker. Apart from that, Van den Ende as well as Barbeyrac must have made use of some of the papers which are found now in the Van Tets van Goudriaan collection in the Algemeen Rijksarchief in The Hague. Roukens furthermore adds some information from family papers and tradition which is not found in other sources. The truth of some of his anecdotes may be doubted.

Barbeyrac's life of Noodt is an excellent piece of work and very sympathetic, but it has one major disadvantage. By training Barbeyrac was a theologian. He taught natural law in Lausanne, but only received an honorary law degree *in absentia* at the age of 43 from Basle before his departure to Groningen, because he or the faculty considered this a formal requirement for his nomination as ordinary

21. Both are found in ARA Tets van Goudriaan, inv. nr. 119.
22. Barbeyrac i, 1731: pp. xxxiv–xc. On this see his letter to J. v. d. Ende, Groningen 26 May 1731, ARA Tets van Goudriaan, inv. nr. 92.
23. e.g. Nicéron xvi, 1731: 303–20; Paquot i, 1760: 181–92; Jugler ii, 1775: 365 ff. Additions in v, 1780: 153 ff. and vi. 2, 1780: 355; J. van Kuyk in *NNBW* ii, 1912, cols. 999–1001.
24. Copies are in ARA Tets van Goudriaan, inv. nr. 120 and UL Leiden.
25. Arntzenius, 1788.
26. Register Noodt, ARA Tets van Goudriaan, inv. nr. 101.

professor of private and public law there.[27] Though a most erudite man, in a technical sense he was not much of a jurist and certainly not a first-class Romanist.[28] Therefore, he was unable to make an adequate assessment of Noodt's scholarly work and its place in the tradition of Romanistic scholarship. This is what must be supplemented in the first place.

The framework of the book more or less presented itself. Chronology, of course, determines the main line of the story of Noodt's life, which is told in the second chapter. Here one naturally also finds the main data about Noodt's publications and other scholarly activities. For convenience, the detailed discussion of Noodt's work, its background, and its influence on the development of legal scholarship is given in the third chapter. A biography, after all, must be readable for people with various interests. As a result, some things will have to be said twice, and more cross-references are needed, but the alternative would seem much less attractive. In the fourth chapter, criticism of Noodt's work will be discussed and the final chapter summarizes results and tries to round off the picture of Noodt as a man and a scholar.

Some appendices are added, but I do not intend to edit sources at any length. A list of materials in archives is added. The most important collection—the remainder of Noodt's personal papers—now forms part of the Van Tets van Goudriaan collection. Other materials are found in the municipal archives of Nijmegen and in archives and libraries all over Europe. For an exact bibliography of Noodt's works I can refer now to Ahsmann and Feenstra's excellent bibliography of Leiden law professors.[29]

27. See *NNBW* i, 236, and the more detailed and somewhat different account in Meylan, 1937: 117ff.
28. He acknowledged this himself, more or less, in a letter to Turrettini of Apr. 1717. But the task of a law professor, he said, was to give good principles to youth (on the basis of natural law), not to show erudition and sagacity in the explanation of perplexed legal texts; see Meylan, 1937: 117f. In earlier publications he even expressed himself rather critically about Roman law, as many natural law scholars used to do, see Meylan, 1937: 60. In the first instance, the law faculty of Basle gave him a cold shoulder: the candidate should first specify his publications in civil law. That was asking too much. Barbeyrac was annoyed, and not without reason. After all, he was already professor in the law faculty of Lausanne.
29. Ahsmann–Feenstra, 1984: nrs. 419–80. The following corrections should be made. As far as Book I is concerned, nr. 422 is a reissue, with new title-page, dedication and index, of nr. 421. Nr. 424 is only a title-edn. of nr. 423, and nr. 468 of 467. The bibliographical data concerning Noodt's works in Coing's *Handbuch* ii.1 (Coing, 1977) are incomplete and absolutely unreliable.

2

Life and Career

1. Nijmegen 1647–1679

Birth, youth, social, and political background

Gerard Noodt was born in Nijmegen on Saturday, 4 September 1647.[1] At his birth, says Noodt in an autobiographical fragment, his mother had a bad time because he was big and fat; for a time she was in danger of her life.[2] Gerard was the fifth child of Peter Noodt[3] and Gijsbertje Biesman.[4] The Noodts were a fairly well-to-do family of merchants and artisans. Noodt's great-grandfather was a wine-merchant,[5] his father a goldsmith.[6] But his father's main functions apparently lay in the city administration. He was auditor of the city,[7] administrator of the citizens' children's orphanage from 1652, and 'gemeensman' from 1646.[8]

This meant that he belonged to the 'gemeente', the merchant and

1. Nijmegen still had the Julian calendar at that time, so according to the present calendar it would be 14 September.
2. Register.
3. Born in Emmerich (where his parents had fled because of the dangers of the war) on Friday, 6 January 1606, died in Nijmegen on Sunday, 23 May 1680; Register. Peter Noodt and Gijsbertje Biesman had six children, but apart from the eldest, Johan (born 1 April 1642), and Gerard none survived the parents. Most of them lived only for weeks or months. See Appendix 1.
4. Born in Nijmegen on Thursday, 22 August 1605, died there on Monday, 26 July 1680. Register. She was a daughter of Gerard Biesman (died on Friday, 23 April 1647); Register Biesman.
5. See Appendix 1. Noodt's great-great-grandfather bought in May 1542 the house 'De gulden hoirn', on the corner of the Grote Straat and the Platenmakersstraat, with a back entrance on the Arminiaanse Plaats, see Van Schevichaven, 1896: 80, 155.
6. *Catalogus*, 1983: 48; *Gelders zilver*, 1955: 110. Peter Noodt was commissioned by the city to make a silver cup in 1649 and silver ornaments for the burgomaster's caps in 1655. See also n. 40, below.
7. As such he is mentioned in the city accounts from 1673/4 until 1680/1, GA Nijmegen, OAN, inv. nrs. 889–97.
8. Chosen 11 February 1646, Register. In the city accounts, he is mentioned as such in Raadsignaten of 22 and 25 February 1675, GA Nijmegen, OAN.

artisan class, and was a member of the board of 'gemeenslieden', successor to the guild of St Nicholas,[9] which represented the guilds and the merchant population and had to be heard by the city's government on all important matters. In Nijmegen, the most important power of the board was the 'keur', that is, the election of city magistrates, which took place every year.[10] Peter Noodt must have been an important man. He lived with his family in a big house, right in the centre of the city, at the corner of the Grote Markt and the Grote Straat.[11] The house bore the name 'The golden ring(s)'.[12] These seem to be the same rings that appear in Peter Noodt's coat of arms,[13] which he most likely took at his marriage with Gijsbertje Biesman. It was the emblem of the Biesmans, and apparently the house as well.

In order to understand the social setting in which Gerard Noodt grew up, something must be said about the political and social background of the time. Nijmegen, once a Roman city, later royal domain and imperial city of the Holy Roman Empire—nominally until 1274, when the emperor-elect pawned the city to the duke of Guelders, but in fact and sentiment much longer[14]—regarded itself as some kind of semi-autonomous city republic. The 'keur', the annual election of magistrates on 2 January, symbolized civic freedom.[15]

That freedom had been at issue ever since 1591, when Prince Maurice captured Nijmegen from the Spanish. In the treaty of capitulation it was provided that temporarily—until a peace was to be signed—Maurice would appoint magistrates himself, from two recommended for each post.[16] At that time this provision must have

9. Kolman, 1952.
10. Kolman, 1952.
11. The centre is marked by the 'blue stone', still lying there in the pavement.
12. Van Schevichaven, 1896: 323. Cf. Roukens, 1767: 7. The house has disappeared; the one standing there now dates from 1880 only.
13. The coat of arms is on the tombstone (see below, Fig. 3). The weapon is halved, with on the right half a walnut tree, on the left three rings around a small scutcheon. Noodt used his mother's seal (three rings around a scutcheon) after her death, e.g. for sealing letters to Van Eck, 26 Mar. 1689, 3 Oct. 1693, and 9 Mar. 1716 (UL Utrecht, MS 1000). It has above the weapon the initials G[ijsberta] B[iesman].
14. As late as 1561 Nijmegen was summoned before the Reichskammergericht for unauthorized mintage. The court did not declare itself incompetent and Nijmegen accepted its jurisdiction. The custom to seek judgment in difficult cases in Aix-la-Chapelle, Nijmegen's mother-city as far as privileges were concerned, came to an end only in 1746, see Nève, 1972: 314 f. and *passim*.
15. Kolman, 1952: p. iv.
16. Kolman, 1952: pp. iv, 59–68; Geurts and Janssen, 1975: 27.

seemed understandable enough. Considering the fact that the majority of the population still must have been Roman Catholic, the risk that, as soon as Maurice left, the city would side with Spain again, was far from imaginary.[17] And from a strategic point of view the possession of Nijmegen was of vital interest. Nijmegen was a strong fortress and right below it lay the Mookerhei, where the Oranges often started their military campaigns.[18]

The peace, anticipated by the provision of 1591, was long in coming, but Nijmegen did not forget its former freedom. During the truce with Spain (1609–21) Nijmegen, opposing the other quarters of Guelders, was strongly Arminian, and in politics sided with Holland and Oldenbarnevelt.[19] In 1617 the city government made an effort to get the election of magistrates back. The movement was led by burgomaster Christoffel Biesman (1573–1628),[20] a forceful personality. According to the family tradition, as recorded by Gerard Noodt,[21] he had already played an important part in repelling the attempt of Maarten Schenk on Nijmegen in 1589. He is said to have been the first to beat the alarm and organize defences. In 1603 he was nominated burgomaster for the first time. His brother Lambert Biesman was a hardly less formidable man. He was the first citizen of Nijmegen to sail to the East Indies. Later, he took part, as sailor and subsequently as captain, in Olivier van Noort's expedition around the world. He was captured by the Spanish in Philippine waters and executed with the garrotte, being the only member of the Dutch crew that refused conversion before dying. A Franciscan witnessing the execution wrote that he was 'the most insolent heretic I saw in my life'.[22]

Gerard's mother, Gijsbertje Biesman, was Christoffel's niece and, after the premature death of her father Gerard Biesman, she was brought up in his house.[23] Her first marriage was linked to his political associations. Biesman, deputy of the States of Guelders at the decisive session of the States-General of 11 November 1617, was one of the two deputies from Guelders who were the staunchest supporters of Oldenbarnevelt.[24] The other was Hendrik van Brienen, burgomaster of Wageningen, and member of the nobility of

17. Poelhekke, 1973: 190.
18. Poelhekke, 1975: 176.
19. Poelhekke, 1975: 167.
20. On him Kolman, 1952: 135 f.; Poelhekke, 1975: 168.
21. Register Biesman.
22. Rietbergen, 1983: 18 ff.
23. Register; Register Biesman.
24. Kolman, 1952: 135; Poelhekke, 1975: 169.

the Veluwe, who stood out till the end against the calling of a national synod.[25] His son Jan van Brienen, 'gemeensman' and lieutenant of the citizen soldiery in Nijmegen, was Gijsbertje's first husband.[26]

On New Year's eve of 1617 Maurice personally led some of his troops to Nijmegen to change the city government.[27] The town council was purged, and, violating the treaty of 1591, Maurice this time appointed the new members himself. But the Arminians proved stubborn. They simply refused to take a nomination from the hands of the prince.[28] Christoffel Biesman kept refusing any nomination until much later, long after Maurice died and was succeeded by Frederick-Henry.[29] A delegation of the city government that was removed by Maurice, led by Biesman, was received by the States of Holland with as great distinction 'as if it concerned a friendly nation overrun by the enemy'.[30]

The newly appointed city government immediately started prosecution of the Arminians with unprecedented fierceness. Gerard Noodt's maternal grandmother, Willemken van Wanrade[31] was arrested twice, in 1619 and 1622, for allegedly organizing services in her house, and she was heavily fined.[32] The brothers Jacob and Peter Noodt, 19 and 16 years of age, sailed in 1622 from Amsterdam to Danzig, to settle in Poland, where their half-brother was a well-to-do merchant in Warsaw.[33] Some years later Jacob, a goldsmith, settled in Frederikstadt in Schleswig, the town that received so many Arminian *emigrés* and still has a Dutch minister as well as a typical Dutch look to its architecture. He became a burgomaster there, and founded the German branch of the family Noodt,[34] which still survives and which has also produced some distinguished academics.

25. Poelhekke, 1975: 169.
26. Register Biesman.
27. Kolman, 1952: 153 f.; Poelhekke, 1975: 168 ff.
28. Kolman, 1952: 153–7; Poelhekke, 1975: 169. And see below, n. 53.
29. Register Biesman: 'Nademaels is hem wel sijne vorige weerdigheit in de Regeringe tot Nijmegen door Hooggedagte Prins Maurits en oock door prins Frederik Hendrik weder aengeboden; doch hij heeft het selve 't elckens geexcuseert.'
30. Poelhekke, 1975: 169.
31. On her SA 30. 9. 1628; Graadt Jonckers, 1897: 168. I thank Mr N. A. Hamers for this reference. On her own account of her arrest (GA Nijmegen, Coll. Biesman, inv. nr. 12) see below, p. 229 ff. And see Janssen, 1983: 70 ff.
32. GA Nijmegen, Biesman, inv. nr. 12.
33. Register. It concerns Wilhelm Noodt, born in 1590 from the first marriage of Rijk Noodt with Wendel van Steenbergen (see Appendix 1): 'Wilhelm Noodt heeft gewoont tot Warschouw in Polen, en is geweest een koopman van seer goede gelegentheijt aen het hof van de koning, en van grote middelen.'
34. W. Noodt, 1921. There is a copy in GA Nijmegen.

Peter stayed seven years in Poland,[35] and then travelled to Vienna and through the imperial heritage lands,[36] Germany and France.[37] In 1636 he was back in Nijmegen, but because the plague was raging there he soon left again, this time for Hamburg.[38] In 1640 he finally settled in Nijmegen and a year later he married Gijsbertje Biesman, the still young widow of Jan van Brienen.[39] In February of the same year (i.e. 1641) he got permission to work as a goldsmith and was admitted to the guild, on the condition that he made a piece of goldwork to prove his skill.[40] Apparently, the guild was reluctant to accept him, because he was not apprenticed in the city. Most likely he did his term of apprenticeship together with his brother Jacob in Warsaw.

The marriage of Peter Noodt, member of the 'gemeente', to the niece of the late burgomaster Biesman, who belonged to the city patriciate,[41] must have meant something of an advance for the Noodt

35. According to a notification of citizenship, issued by burgomasters and aldermen of Nijmegen in 1626/7, the brothers were in Poland at that time. Latin text on parchment, with hanging seal, dated 8 Mar. 1626, ARA Tets van Goudriaan, inv. nr. 102. Dutch text, dated 9 June 1627, ibid.
36. The countries included in this term have varied in different periods, see *HRG* i: 967.
37. Register.
38. Register.
39. The marriage took place 10 Jan. 1641; Register (this has 9 Jan.); GA Nijmegen RBS 1173, 10 Jan. 1641. Johan van Brienen died 11 Oct. 1636 from the plague. Of the four children he had with Gijsbertje (Joanna, 1631; Gerard 1632; Christoffel, 1634; Christoffel, 1635) only the last one survived. He is named in Gijsbertje's will of 30 July 1670 (GA Nijmegen Coll. Biesman, inv. nr. 56). Christoffel van Brienen, like his father, was lieutenant of the citizen's soldiery of Nijmegen. He married Elisabeth Baccart, but died childless 11 Dec. 1677 (Register Biesman).
40. *Catalogus*, 1983: 48.
41. Her ancestors were councillors (ministeriales?) of the dukes of Guelders. One Theodorus Biesman was invested by Duke Arnold in 1441 with the tithe of Eijckenhorst ('in de kerspelen van Nijmegen en Wijchen'). He bore the title Lord of Eijckenhorst. His son Gerard was appointed chief forester (waldgraaf) of the lower Rhine forest and curator of the judgeship in Nijmegen (Register Biesman). In 1636 the tithe of Eijckenhorst was invested on Jan van Brienen, as husband and guardian of Gijsbertje Biesman. In 1642 Peter Noodt took the oath as feudal tenant in the same capacity. Gijsbertje willed the tithe 30 July 1670 (GA Nijmegen Biesman, inv. nr. 56) to her sons Johan and Gerard Noodt, with the duty to pay her son by previous marriage, Christoffel van Brienen, for life, one third of the tithe due each year. To the will is added in transfix a disposition, in which Gijsertje before the feudal court of Guelders wills the usufruct of the tenancy to Peter Noodt for life. Should one of the children seek investiture in violation of this disposition, he is disinherited. In 17 Aug. 1680, after the death of both parents, Johan and Gerard Noodt were invested with the tithe (ARA Tets van Goudriaan, inv. nr. 106).

family. Although the 'gemeente' cannot be regarded as a lower class in the modern sense,[42] there certainly was some difference. Peter Noodt did not keep his Arminian or Remonstrant beliefs. Evidently he could not have obtained a public office if he had. Some time between 1642 and 1644 he became a member of the Reformed Church. His eldest son, Johan, born 11 April 1642, was baptized in the Remonstrant church of Nijmegen.[43] But from the second (Hendriksken, born 24 January 1644 and died three months later) all were baptized in the Reformed church of St Steven.[44] If we want to assess this change of religion, we must keep in mind that, while some people, like Gerard Noodt's maternal grandmother Willemken van Wanrade, sacrificed much to remain true to the Remonstrant Church, for others in Nijmegen to side with the Arminians had always been more of a political than a religious choice. In the forties prosecutions had stopped, but Remonstrants still were barred from public office. And anyway, Peter Noodt may still have felt 'Arminian' in his heart and passed this on to his son Gerard, who remained a member of the Reformed Church all his life, but certainly never belonged to the orthodox side.[45]

In the meantime Nijmegen kept yearning for its former freedom. In 1647, the year of Gerard's birth, and well before the peace of Munster was a fact, the city council conferred with the board of 'gemeenslieden'—of which Peter Noodt was a member—on how to get back the election.[46] After the peace treaty had been signed, they took the young Prince William II by surprise, while he was staying in his hunting-lodge in Dieren, and simply told him that in the future they would elect the magistrates in the old way again. William, taken aback at first, was certainly not the man to accept the message with equanimity. He brought the matter before the Landdag of Guelders, which happened to be meeting in Nijmegen. He went there in person, with a military following. In the deliberations that followed, the city council soon gave in,[47] but the 'gemeenslieden' stood four-square on their rights. In the end, naturally, the stadholder had it all his own

42. But see Poelhekke, 1973: 193.
43. Register.
44. GA Nijmegen, OAN, Doopboeken Ned. Herv. Gemeente.
45. Curiously enough, F. Confortius, the Italian censor of Noodt's *Opera omnia* (Naples: Fratres Terres, 1786; Ahsmann–Feenstra, 1984: nr. 472), said that Noodt was an Arminian, see below, p. 225.
46. Kolman, 1952: 175 f.; Poelhekke, 1975: 201; Jenniskens, 1973.
47. Kolman, 1952: 183 f.; Poelhekke, 1975: 201.

way, again not without some sabre-rattling. Here, in Nijmegen, the monarchical and absolutist ambitions of the prince were revealed for the first time, without so much as an excuse.

But only a few years later William died prematurely, at the age of 24,[48] and so the tide turned. The first stadholderless period (1650–72) began, the period in which Gerard Noodt grew up and came of age. In Nijmegen the political scene changed drastically. As in 1617 the city, opposing the other quarters of Guelders, sided with Holland and the 'Lœvesteiners', the party of 'true freedom' whose leader was to be Johan de Witt.[49] Nijmegen immediately restored its election.[50] But inside the city a new alignment began to reveal itself, which was to dominate future developments until the days of revolution at the end of the eighteenth century. The magistrates, who did not stand out against Prince William in 1647, quickly developed into a ruling aristocracy, with all the characteristics of the regent class. While in 1648 the city council promised the 'gemeenslieden' the election as of old, to win them for concerted action, in 1651 they made their first effort to do without them,[51] that is, replace election by co-optation. Naturally the 'gemeenslieden' protested fiercely. At that time, with great difficulty, a compromise could still be reached. But in 1672, when the tide turned once again, the magistrates sided with the Orange party, and flatly opposed the claims of the 'gemeenslieden'. This laid the seed of a conflict that in the first years of the eighteenth century was to lead to a bloody revolt, and played a role in the Batavian revolution. But, for the time being, the power of the city aristocracy only increased. Especially after 1675, when William III ruled absolutely and filled the seats of the city's government with his creatures, the 'gemeente' was shut out from political power for many years. The old freedom was never forgotten, however.

In the board of 'gemeenslieden' Peter Noodt, as we will see presently, bore for as long as he could the banner of civic freedom which his wife's uncle Christoffel Biesman had held in 1617. Twice he was offered a nomination as burgomaster, a considerable advance. But, according to his son Gerard's account, he refused, the second time after careful consideration, 'because he believed that his becom-

48. 6 Nov. 1650, see *AGN* viii, 1979: 266 f.
49. Poelhekke, 1975: 207. Nijmegen supported Holland in the 'Grote Vergadering' of 1651, see Poelhekke, 1973: 205 f. In later years Nijmegen grew more critical of de Witt's policy, see Poelhekke, 1975: 202.
50. Kolman, 1952: 192; Poelhekke, 1975: 202.
51. Kolman, 1952: 183; Poelhekke, 1973: 193; 1975: 202.

ing a magistrate would turn the minds of his children and divert them from their studies'.[52] Here we find the traditional theme of the republican hero, refusing to take a nomination, just as the classical jurists Labeo and Aulus Cascellius refused nomination as consul from the hands of the tyrant Augustus.[53] Consul and burgomaster are usually identified in the seventeenth century and in fact the Latin word is often translated by the Dutch one. In his son's description, Peter Noodt's gesture has something of a last stand against the irresistible ascendancy of the regent oligarchy. But perhaps we must take Gerard's account with a pinch of salt. From a letter of Peter Noodt to his son it appears that, in 1679 at least, the father—who was 73 by then—was not loath to get nominated as burgomaster, but rather thought he did not stand a chance of election without the right patrons.[54]

In 1702 the history of 1650 repeated itself. Within weeks of the death of William III (19 March) the States of Guelders repealed the despised 'Regeringsreglement' of 1675. But they decided at once that the nomination of magistrates would remain with the regents, that is, would continue to be done by co-optation. The decision immediately provoked a bourgeois revolt, which in fact started in Nijmegen.[55] The primary demand was the restoration of the election of magistrates by 'gemeenslieden'. It was, in fact, the first democratic revolt of the eighteenth century, the first chord in an age which was to end with the great Revolution.[56] In Nijmegen, where the board of 'gemeenslieden' was not filled during the reign of William III and as a result was, in fact, nearly extinct,[57] the 'gemeente' succeeded in

52. Register: '. . . met wel voorbedagten rade . . . omdat hij geloofde dat het bekomen van magistrature zijne kinderen soude doen andere gedagten nemen, als hij wel wenste, ende haer vervolgens in haer studien nadelig zijn.' The notion that studying was bourgeois and below the dignity of nobility is illustrated by Scaliger, who believed he was an aristocrat and, trying to act like one, 'refused to let himself be seen reading or working'; cf. Grafton, 1983: 162.

53. *Pomp.* D. 1. 2. 2. 45 and 47; cf. Cannegieter, 1770; Regtsgeleerde, 1770.

54. Nijmegen, 30 Oct. 1679 (ARA Tets van Goudriaan, inv. nr. 110): 'De heer Koerman [cf. n. 80] . . . heeft mij vorders vertrouwder wijse versekert dat hij sijn Hoogh[ey]t, voor wenich dagen tot Dijeren van mij had gesproken, om mij inde magestraet te brengen maer sijn Hoogh[ey]t hadde geseyt dat voor dit mael het niet konde weesen, maer ten naesten als het weer gebeurde, soude hij hem te wille daer in sijn. Maer als ick U de waerheyt sal seggen, so beslaet mij dat wenich plaets, also ick weet dat andere meer sullen daer konnen te weeg brengen als sijn Ed. hoe wel dat hij geern wat goets doen wilde, . . .'

55. Wertheim-Gijse Weenink, 1972: 61.

56. Wertheim-Gijse Weenink, 1975: 231 f.

57. Peter Noodt had died in 1680.

forcing the nomination of new members, but regent opposition soon caused the movement to escalate. On 23 June the 'gemeenslieden' even removed the complete city government, a plainly revolutionary act. The Landdag of Guelders did not accept this, and on 4 August Nijmegen was occupied by a military force and the regent's order restored.[58] The revolutionaries fled and, as in 1618, they sent a delegation to Holland. From a letter of Perizonius to Van Eck we learn that by the end of September a delegation of *tribuni* (= gemeenslieden) from Nijmegen was in Leiden, and was to go on from there to Haarlem and Amsterdam to advocate their cause.[59] They did so very skilfully and many wondered why the States of Guelders pursued such an odious affair to such extremes, but this time they could hardly expect support from the regent magistrates, who in the intervening years had developed political as well as family ties with the regents in Guelders. In 1705 the tide turned and the bourgeois revolutionaries were in power in Nijmegen again for some time. By then the conflict had hardened. After the failure of a conservative attack on the city hall, some of its leaders and ex-burgomaster Roukens, who did not take part in the raid but was suspected of inspiring it, were executed without any form of trial,[60] a fact discrediting the revolt in the eyes of many.

The background just sketched determined Noodt's life and work to a great extent. This does not mean, by the way, that he took an active part in all the tribulations himself. Quite to the contrary. He always remained in the first place a scholar, and the demoralizing belief in action as the only true faith had yet to be invented. As Perizonius wrote to Van Eck about the trouble in Guelders, he might have said: 'But this does not concern us.'[61] In 1672, when Nijmegen's citizens bravely held out for nine days against the overwhelming French forces besieging the city, Noodt seems to have remained with his books. He only temporarily migrated to the house of the Roukens family in the Platemakersstraat, in order to be less disturbed by the French artillery bombardment, which apparently was aiming at St

58. Wertheim-Gijse Weenink, 1975: 238.
59. Perizonius to Van Eck, Leiden, 30 Sept. 1702, UL Utrecht, MS 1000: 'Fuerint plurimis diebus heic loci Neomagensium Tribunorum delegati et egerint cum nostris magistratibus, profecti hinc hodie Harlemiae, unde Amstelodamum cogitant. Videntur multis causam suam satis bene agere. Et mirantur plerique, ordines Geldriae rem tam invidiosam usque adeo persequi. Sed haec nihil ad nos.'
60. Wertheim-Gijse Weenink, 1975: 263.
61. See the letter quoted in n. 59, above.

Steven's, near the paternal home.[62] He utterly rejected the revolutionary movements in his home town between 1702 and 1708. Already before 7 August 1705, the revolution's bloody Tuesday, he had turned away. He had friends and family on both sides and did not want to be drawn into the conflict. From that time he never again spent a vacation in Nijmegen, as he previously had done regularly.[63]

Now we may have some doubts about the truth of the facts just mentioned. They come from Roukens, a son of a regent family and a descendant of the best-known victim of 1705. In 1767, when patriot sentiments were beginning to stir, a hero for regent circles certainly was expected to abhor revolutionary movements and violence. But, nevertheless, I believe that for Noodt intellectual pursuits and violent action were worlds apart. On another occasion (admittedly again reported by Roukens) he is reputed to have said 'Marti cum musis nihil commune'.[64]

Education and first appointment

Gerard must have been a bright boy. From his youth he had been inclined to studies; before his fifth year he could read Dutch proficiently.[65] Before his seventh birthday, that is in 1654,[66] he entered Nijmegen grammar school, then headed by master Werichius.[67] The school seems to have had seven classes.[68] Gerard was an excellent student. He won the prize five times and the rector used to point him out as an example even to much older students. As he says himself, this made him feel embarrassed, but also stimulated his application.[69] As the best of the final year in grammar school he was chosen to speak the valedictory address. The subject was the disadvantage of travelling much.[70] Perhaps his father, who spent half his life abroad, inspired the choice of subject, but it was not

62. Roukens, 1767: 7.
63. Roukens, 1767: 7.
64. 'Mars and the Muses have nothing in common.'
65. Register.
66. We do not know when exactly the school year began, but if it was on 1 Sept., as usual, Noodt was still 6 in 1654.
67. He was succeeded in 1659 by Isaac Gruter and in 1662 by Henricus Grevenbroeck, see Bastiaanse, Bots, and Evers, 1985: 46–71.
68. Bastiaanse, Bots, and Evers, 1985: 51.
69. Register.
70. Register; Roukens, 1767: 6; Barbeyrac, 1731: XXXVII; Barbeyrac, *Vita*, fol. 2; Jugler ii, 1775: 365. The title was *In vituperium peregrinationis*.

unusual.[71] And Gerard does not seem to have liked travelling; indeed, as far as we know, he never went abroad. The *peregrinatio academica* after his university studies remained within the borders of the Republic, and all offers for a professorship from abroad were turned down. After grammar school, presumably in 1662,[72] academic education was to follow, and for this Nijmegen's own short-lived university, founded in 1655,[73] was an obvious choice.

The foundation of Nijmegen's first university[74] can be explained also by the political background just sketched. It is a counter-stroke of the quarter of Nijmegen against the other quarters of Guelders, and a direct attack on the position of the university of Harderwijk, founded in 1648, which was meant to be the university of Guelders. The establishment of a university, an act believed to be the prerogative of the sovereign power,[75] clearly expressed the aspirations towards autonomy then found in Nijmegen. No wonder the other quarters of Guelders regarded it with disfavour. The Court of Guelders in Arnhem did not acknowledge the diplomas of Nijmegen jurists who applied for admission to the bar.[76]

In the first two and a half years at the university Noodt studied history and letters under Johan Schulting[77]—whose son

71. John Locke delivered a lengthy case against the institution of the grand tour: Dialogues on the use of foreign travel, see Kelly, 1975: 29. According to Barbeyrac (1731: XXXVIII) it was a usual subject for rhetoric.

72. Van den Ende gives the year 1663 (he left an open space in the manuscript, in which the year was written later) in the obituary (ARA Tets van Goudriaan, inv. nr. 119), and he is followed by all later biographers. But this can have been no more than guesswork; around 1680 Noodt himself did not remember the exact date; in the autobiographical fragment (Register) he left it open. The year 1662 may be more probable, considering the fact that he studied *artes* (mathematics, philosophy, and letters) for over 2½ years before doing law. Then he would have been eight years at grammar school (the normal period for someone preparing for university) and six at the university (1662–8). If he entered university in 1663 he would have done his law studies in 2½ years as well. In itself, this no doubt is possible, but Noodt says that he studied three years with De Greve (Register).

73. On this university see Sassen, 1955; 1962; Brinkhoff, 1969; Lindeboom, 1969; Hermesdorf, 1970*a*; 1970*b*; 1971*a*; 1971*b*; Brinkhof, 1972; Van den Bergh, 1972, all with further literature. Boom and Driessen, 1983, is very unreliable, even for a provisional edition.

74. Nijmegen has had a Catholic University since 1923.

75. Coing, 1977: 23.

76. Brinkhof, 1972: 14–17.

77. 1630–66; on him see *NNBW* iii: 156; v. d. Aa xvii: 536; Sassen, 1962: 110. Schulting was a favourite pupil of J. F. Gronovius. His teaching must have been fairly good, and, in fact, at least part of the praise that Grævius later gave Noodt, calling him the only law professor not unschooled in letters (see below, p. 46) may be due to him. There are several elements in Noodt's work which may be traced

Anton,[78] 'the Dutch Cujacius', was later to become Noodt's colleague in Leiden—and mathematics and philosophy under Theodoor Craanen.[79] Craanen taught in Nijmegen until 1670, when he was appointed in Leiden with the strict order to teach only Aristotle. When he nevertheless began to propagate strongly the philosophy of Descartes, he lost his chair of philosophy and his chairmanship of the Staten Collegie (college for poor students of theology). From 1673 he taught only in the medical faculty. In 1685 he went to Berlin as court-physician to the Great Elector, Frederick William of Brandenburg (1640–88). Nijmegen may have been opposed, but the quality of its professors was not in doubt.

Noodt liked the study of mathematics and philosophy, but changed his subject on the advice of his father's friend Arnold Cœrman (died 1688).[80] Cœrman acted as justice from the quarter of Nijmegen in the Court of Guelders. He told Noodt 'that mathematics and similar sciences might well please and adorn a man, but that life was too short to learn everything equally well, and that therefore it was better to direct one's studies to matters being more useful and necessary for society'.[81] In fact, Cœrman is expressing a

back to a training in classical philology, e.g. his knowledge of Latin, his very extensive reading in the classics, the use of inscriptions and abbreviations. Like Gronovius, Schulting and Noodt were mainly Latinists.

78. Nijmegen, 15 July 1659–Leiden 1734 March 12, *NNBW* i: 1462. Date of birth from GA Nijmegen, OAN, Doopboeken Ned. herv. Gem. The dates of birth in *NNBW* are not correct; it has for Anton (i: 1462) 23 July 1659, for his brother Cornelis (iii: 1156) 15 July 1659, that is, eight days earlier! See also Sassen, 1962; 111, who, for convenience, leaves out the date of birth of Cornelis. In fact, Cornelis was baptized 1 Dec. 1660. The widow of Johan Schulting, Catharina van den Berg[h], daughter of a burgomaster of Nijmegen, fled with her children to Dordrecht in 1672, and afterwards settled in Leiden, where Anton did his studies. According to A. v. Haller, who visited Leiden and met him in 1725/7, Anton suffered from gout and was no longer in function by then: 'ein gelehrter, aber ausgedienter Mann. Er hat noch by Hrn. Jenner am Schmauss gewest. Izt ist er gichtig und ausser Brauch.' Lindeboom, 1958: 95.

79. On him see v. d. Aa iii, 1852: 806; Molhuysen iii: 274–7; Sassen, 1962: 114–15. He was a Cartesian and possibly stood in contact with Spinoza.

80. On him see Maris-Driessen, 1978: 301. Noodt dedicated a disputation to him in 1668 (Ahsmann–Feenstra, 1984, nr. 419), as well as book I of his *Probabilia* (1674), see below, p. 138. UL Utrecht, MS 1095 (2 vols. in folio), contains an extensive collection of legal material made, or at least used, by Coerman. It contains transcripts of the privileges and city ordinance of Nijmegen and other cities and of various laws, charters, treaties, all with annotations in Coerman's hand, an alphabet of legal adversaria by Coerman, etc. There are additions in various other hands. Apparently this was Coerman's working collection, which remained in use with other jurists well into the eighteenth century.

81. Register.

traditional opinion here;[82] the social usefulness of mathematics and science was not a well-established fact by then.

No doubt Noodt was influenced by his two and a half years of study in mathematics and philosophy as well as his training as a jurist. Although already in grammar school the *Logic* of Burgersdijk had been taught,[83] Noodt will have the academy to thank for a degree of philosophical training unusual among jurists, a feeling for logical subtleties,[84] and the rigorous method of argumentation demonstrated masterfully in his 1698 treatise on interest and usury. In his Utrecht inaugural address of 1684 he stresses the importance of a training in geometry and philosophy for jurists, pointing to the example of Sextus Pompeius, 'who had supreme knowledge of civil law and perfect mastery of geometry and stoic philosophy'.[85] Unfortunately, we know next to nothing about Craanen's teaching in Nijmegen. He was already regarded as a Cartesian there, so he will have introduced Noodt to the new philosophy,[86] and may thus have laid the foundation of Noodt's critical rationalism, his relativistic attitude concerning the authority of Antiquity[87] and of Roman law in particular. Whereas most jurists—conservative, as they usually are—stuck to Aristotelianism or adapted only some elements from Cartesianism,[88] Noodt must have been more open to the new philosophy, though he did not become a true Cartesian. There is another point of interest here. Craanen was a militant man, who took special delight in battles with theologians.[89] Likewise Noodt, while being a much more peace-loving man who avoided literary debates as much as possible, did not hesitate to discuss subjects on which orthodox theologians had strong and quite different opinions.[90]

Craanen was not the only Cartesian in Nijmegen. Like most young universities Nijmegen seems to have had a preference for the newest ideas. When Noodt studied there, the chair of theology was held by Wittichius, who later, when he was professor in Leiden, was involved

82. The necessity to combine theory with practice had often been stressed since the Middle Ages, and law and medicine were regarded as the model for this, see Herberger, 1981: 161 f.
83. Bastiaanse, Bots, and Evers, 1985: 56.
84. See below, Ch. 5, at n. 16.
85. *Opera* i: 618.
86. On this, in general, Thijssen-Schoute, 1954; McGahagan, 1976.
87. Cf. Gerretzen, 1940: 4 f.
88. Cf. Campegius Vitringa, as cited by Veen, 1976: 185 n. 89.
89. McGahagan, 1976: 11.
90. See especially his speech on freedom of religion, below, p. 233.
91. On him, see *NNBW* x: 1233–4; Sassen, 1962: 105–8.

in many debates with the orthodox theologians.[91] Wittichius's best pupil in Nijmegen was Abraham Gulichius,[92] also reputed a Cartesian and Coccejan, who later in 1679 was inaugurated, together with Noodt, as professor in Franeker. And there was yet another Cartesian in Nijmegen whom Noodt must have met as a student, although he does not say as much: Johannes Braunius,[93] from 1661 minister of the Walloon church in Nijmegen and later professor of theology in Groningen. Being regarded as a Cartesian and Coccejan, he there came under the suspicion of heterodoxy, and was involved in bitter literary debates with his faculty colleague.

Between 1679 and 1682 Noodt corresponded regularly with Braunius in Groningen,[94] and his letters have a rather amicable tone. Thus, in a letter of 18 February 1681 Noodt asks in a postscript, apparently jokingly, whether Mrs Braunius is already taking lessons in Hebrew and theology, 'because it would be nice for you, if you had such a diversion. Whenever I take a wife, I will stipulate the same in the marriage-settlement.' That Noodt must have been rather fond of Mrs Braunius is evident from another letter, written from Franeker on 6 November 1681:

If your wife would give me the honour of visiting me sometime in my loneliness and displacement, and you would be so kind as to accompany her, you can be sure that we will find opportunity to have fun and that I will be greatly honoured. And if you can manage, please do me the favour of using this professor's kitchen, to punish him for not taking a wife. I will give you many beautiful things and will let Mrs Braunius give the orders herself. In the morning we together will take care of the chocolate, which I expect one of these days from Holland. If the presentation is not correct, nevertheless accept the invitation.[95]

92. 1642–79. On him, see Boeles ii. 1, 1879: 284–6; *NNBW* vi: 652. He studied and taught in Nijmegen and subsequently was professor in Hamm and Franeker.
93. 1628–1709. On him *NNBW* vi: 189; Sassen, 1962: 116–17.
94. Noodt to Braunius, Franeker, 18 Feb. 1681 (UL Amsterdam, 16 Cf. 1); April 27 (UL Leiden, BPL 246); Nov. 6 (ibid.); 18 Oct. 1682 (RA Gelderland, Van Steen, Van Ommeren en Waijenstein, inv. nr. 94; copy UL Leiden, BPL 1961).
95. UL Leiden, BPL 246: 'Indijen me juffrouw UEd. Lijefste mij de eere wilde doen van mij in mijne eensaemheijt en peligrimmage eens te komen sijen, en UEd. wilde so veel goetheijt hebben van haer Ed. hijer te conduiseren, so kan UEd. neffens haer verseeckert zijn, dat wij evel sullen konnen stof vinden on vrolijck te zijn, en dat mij veel eere soude geschijeden. Ende indijen UEd. het kan bijbrengen, so doet mij de vrijntschap en valt desen professor eens in de keucken tot straf dat hij egeen wijf en neemt. Ick sal U veel vraeije dingen geven, en sal Juffrouw de Bruyn selfs laten ordineren. Wij sullen alleen onder ons beijden des morgens sorgen voor de chocolate, die ick metten eerste uijt Holland verwagt. Is het qualijck gepraesenteerd, so doet het evenwel.'

However, if Noodt does not count Braunius among his teachers, it is for a good reason. Braunius did not hold a chair in Nijmegen university[96] and as a philologist he cannot have influenced Noodt very much. As was not unusual among classicists in the seventeenth century,[97] Noodt's main interest was in Latin; he was much less versed in Greek, and knew virtually nothing of oriental languages. In 1678 he wrote to Marcus Meibom[98] that he preferred to abstain from a judgment of his emendations in the Old Testament, 'because that study is far removed from the praetorian edict. Moreover I never studied Hebrew'.

On Cœrman's advice, Noodt changed to law. His teacher in this field was Petrus de Greve (1621–77) from Arnhem, member of a family which had produced several distinguished lawyers.[99] De Greve studied in Harderwijk, and under Wissenbach in Franeker.[1] After practising for some years at the bar of the Court of Friesland in Leeuwarden, he became a professor in Harderwijk, and subsequently in Nijmegen. He had a great reputation as a teacher, especially as in his lectures he referred to contemporary law and legal practice to a much greater degree than was usual in his day.[2] When in 1655 Nijmegen bought him away from Harderwijk for the substantial salary of 1,200 guilders, many students followed him there.[3] The names of some of them are known from three volumes of *disputationes anniversariae*,[4] as far as we know, all that he published. Unfortunately, we do not know very much about his scientific ideas. Through Wissenbach, who was also the teacher of Ulrik Huber, he must have received some training in the methods of humanist

96. Sassen, 1962: 116.
97. Cf. Gerretzen, 1940: 1 f.
98. Noodt to M. Meibom, Nijmegen, 14 Dec. 1678 (Forschungsbibl. Gotha Chart. A 413): 'Meum autem [judicium] eo exspectatis minus, quia id opus ab edicto praetoris recedit plurimum. Deinde sanctum linguam nunquam attigi.' On M. Meibom (1630–1711) see v. d. Aa v: 164. After years at the court of Christina of Sweden and as librarian to the king of Denmark, he came to Amsterdam, where he was professor (1668–70) and then lived as 'Privatgelehrter' in rather poor conditions.
99. Vorsterman van Oijen iii, 1890: 407 f.
1. 1607–63, *NNBW* iii: 1440.
2. Van den Bergh, 1972: 20.
3. Sassen, 1962: 108.
4. On these, see Hermesdorf, 1971*b*: 161 f. They were a series of disputations spanning one academic year, and following the *ordo legum*, the order of titles in Digest or Codex. This was a traditional form of teaching by that time. In the 16th century e.g. Duaren published *disputationes anniversariae* in Bourges; cf. Eyssell, 1860: 159.

philology, but in this respect he has left no proof of his scholarship. I tend to assume that he can hardly have had a decisive influence on Noodt's formation.

In 1668, at the age of 20, Noodt concluded his law studies in Nijmegen with two disputations, the first taking place on 8 April,[5] the second on 27 June.[6] He did not take a degree, most likely because a Nijmegen degree would not be of much use for a future career in law;[7] therefore, when he arrived in Franeker some months later, he was formally an undergraduate student. But, whether he had a degree or not, Noodt was very well trained indeed. The first disputation was written by his teacher as was usual,[8] but the second was by himself.[9] It already stands out because of its richness in citations from classical authors, which is quite unusual in this type of literature[10] and is not a feature of the disputations written by his teacher De Greve. In both disputes De Greve gave full credit to his excellent pupil by keeping silent and adding nothing to the defence.[11]

In September 1668 Noodt left Nijmegen for a very limited *peregrinatio academica*, during which he was to take his doctor's degree in law. First, he went to Leiden, where he stayed until shortly after the Easter (11 April) of 1669.[12] According to his own account he heard only public lectures by the law professors Daniel Colonius,[13] A. Beeckerts van Thienen,[14] A. Rusius,[15] and S. Marchant,[16] as well as of the classicist Gronovius[17] and some others, but did not attend private courses.[18] From Leiden he proceeded to Utrecht, where he stayed some six weeks. He attended public lectures of the jurists

5. Ahsmann–Feenstra, 1984, nr. 419.
6. Ahsmann–Feenstra, 1984, nr. 420.
7. The academy claimed to have the *jus promovendi*, but it did not have a charter from the Court of Guelders in Arnhem and this did not admit *doctores juris* from Nijmegen to the bar, presumably for political reasons in the first place, see Brinkhof, 1972: 16. So, for someone hoping to enter the legal profession in Arnhem, it would be a waste of money to take a degree in Nijmegen. However, the court did not have a monopoly on admission of advocates for all Guelders.
8. See, in general, Schubart-Fikentscher, 1970.
9. Register. Noodt signed the dedication as 'auctor'.
10. Cf. Canoy-Olthoff, 1983: 20.
11. Register.
12. Register.
13. 1608–72, professor 1648–72, *NNBW* iv: 446.
14. 1623–69, professor 1654–69, *NNBW* iii: 76.
15. 1604–78, professor 1659–78, *NNBW* v: 1243.
16. *c.*1630–70, professor 1658–70, v. d. Aa viii.
17. 1611–71, professor 1658–71, *NNBW* i: 989; Gerretzen, 1940: 2.
18. Register.

Cyprianus Regneri ab Oosterga,[19] Antonius Matthaeus III,[20] and Lucas van de Poll,[21] as well as of the philologist and historian J. G. Grævius.[22] Again he did not hear anybody *privatim*. In Leiden Noodt enrolled on 5 October 1668 as student of letters,[23] in Utrecht we have no enrolment. At the end of May or in the first days of June he left for Franeker. On 7 June after an examination he was enrolled in the rotulus as *juris candidatus* and admitted to the final examination.[24] Two days later he was created *doctor juris* by Taco van Glins.[25] At the age of 21 Noodt thus completed his academic training. As is stated in his diploma, he first passed an examination and then gave lectures on D 3. 3. 51 and on *Decretum Gratiani* C 3 q. 6 c. 18, that is, on the adage 'Whoever accuses someone else of a crime must prove his accusation'. Finally he defended a disputation without *præses*, that is, all by himself.[26] If Noodt wrote this thesis himself, he must have done so in Leiden or Utrecht, because he hardly had enough time to write it in Franeker. Possibly Noodt simply defended a thesis written by someone else, as was not unusual. Neither about its authorship, nor about its contents, has he left a word.

From Franeker Noodt travelled to Leeuwarden, where he met the famous Ulrik Huber. Huber apparently had business to do in the Frisian capital and did not attend the promotion. Noodt asked him to put his signature on the diploma.[27] Via Groningen, Harderwijk, and Deventer, Noodt returned home, visiting the local university or academy in each place; quite a useful excursion for someone contemplating an academic career.

On his return to Nijmegen he settled there as attorney. He did not

19. Prof. Institutes 1641, primarius 1671, *NNBW* ii: 1179.
20. Lector 1667, extraord. 1670, ord. 1674, *NNBW* ii: 1115.
21. Collegia privata 1659, extraord. 1660, ord. 1662, *NNBW* vii: 846.
22. *NNBW* iv: 669; Gerretzen, 1940: 18–27; Zwager, 1980: 27. Noodt and he became friends later, see below, p. 59.
23. AS Leiden, 1875: 550: Gerardus Noodt, Neomagensis 21 L.
24. AS Franeker, nr. 7100: 1669 jun. 7 G. Noot, Neomago-Gelrus Jur. Cand.; Boeles, ii. 1, 1879: 280. RA Leeuwarden, Franeker Universiteit, inv. nr. 18, fol. 108^{v}: 7 June 1669: D. Gerhardus Noot Neomago Gelrus ad Examen juridicum admissus est.
25. 1619–73, ord. 1667, Boeles, ii. 1, 1879: 241–3. Cf. RA Leeuwarden, Franeker universiteit, inv. nr. 18, fol. 108; AP Franeker, 1971, p. 45. Van Glins' main publication was a book in Dutch on maritime law, which for a long period remained a standard work on its subject. The first edn. appeared in 1695, the last in 1753.
26. All this is mentioned in the diploma, ARA Tets van Goudriaan, inv. nr. 108.
27. Register.

seek admission or take the oath at the Court of Guelders and Zutphen in Arnhem,[28] so one might suppose that he only acted as consultant advocate. But we know that he actually acted as advocate before the aldermen's court in Nijmegen. His own account is confirmed in detail by the Nijmegen archives. Although we have no trace of it, we must assume that Noodt was also admitted by that court. The Court of Guelders had no monopoly on admission of advocates in the province.

One might not expect very much from a bookworm like Noodt, but in fact he seems to have been fairly successful in the *nobile officium*. On 10 July 1670 he delivered an opinion in a criminal case together with Petrus de Greve.[29] On Friday 17 February 1671 the aldermen's court called him as advocate for the defence for two men suspected of manslaughter, against whom the death penalty was demanded. One Johan Barten, former horseman in the cavalry company of Captain Verschoor, was accused of killing in 1666 Dirk Renes, lieutenant of Sir Weede, Governor of Grave. Antonis van Tricht, sergeant in the company of Engelbert Beeckman, which lay in garrison in Nijmegen, was accused of killing on 26 October 1670 Artus Grisart, citizen of Nijmegen. Noodt defended both so ably that neither was sentenced to death. The indictment against Johan Barten was dismissed on a plea of self-defence and Antonis van Tricht, who was absent, was sentenced for excess of self-defence to banishment from the city for only two years.[30] The case brought Noodt such fame that another man, suspected of manslaughter and on the run, wrote to him that he would pay him a big fee and give himself up to await sentence, if Noodt were prepared to take up his defence. But Noodt flatly refused, believing it to be a reckless plan for someone who was still free.[31] Legal practice was Noodt's major occupation only for a few years. On 27 December 1671, at the age of 24, he was appointed professor of law in the university of Nijmegen, to assist Petrus de Greve, who could no longer cope with the

28. The verso of the doctoral diploma (see n. 26 on p. 24), where the date of admission and oath used to be noted by the court clerk, is blank and I found no traces of Noodt's admission in the Appointements-boeck of the Court, RA Arnhem, Arch. Hof., inv. nr. 1161–1200. On the various types of advocates, see Frijhoff, 1981: 247 f.

29. Barels ii, 1778: 4–7.

30. Register; GA Nijmegen, ORAN, inv. nr. 966, Crimineel schepenprotocol, fols. 6–9.

31. Register.

numbers of students on his own. Noodt got a salary of 400 guilders a year.[32] In fact, his was the last appointment in the university,[33] which was to meet its doom only half a year later.

The first university of Nijmegen really perished before it could strike roots. Political events intervened drastically. The disaster of 1672 and the ensuing economic crisis, which fell on all universities in the Republic, proved fatal to Nijmegen. The university closed temporarily, never to be reopened again. If there was some regular teaching between May 1674, when the French left,[34] and 1679, when the university ended with the departure of Noodt as the last professor,[35] hardly a trace of it remains. After French occupation and looting Guelders was reduced to utter poverty.[36] Under the direction of the French commissar Methelet, Nijmegen was plundered systematically; Braunius published an eyewitness account of the episode.[37] The professors, whose pay could not be secured, left Nijmegen one by one, and only very few students remained. Towards the end of 1677 Noodt was, in fact, the only remaining professor; on 12 February 1678 he presided over the last promotion that was to take place.[38]

From the period of French occupation there is an anecdote which throws some light on Noodt's character. When Nijmegen had surrendered and King Louis XIV was in his headquarters at the castle of Oosterhout[39] across the Waal, the senate of Nijmegen university (some five professors) decided to pay its respects to the new master,

32. GA Nijmegen OAN, inv. nr. 111, RS Wednesday 27 Dec. 1671: 'Op Rapport van den Hr. Curateuren van de Academie binnen dese stadt heeft een Eerb. Raadt geapprobeert ende geconfirmeert der voorraam bij Haar Ed. tot beneficeringe en voortsettinge van de Academie alhier gedaan ende vervolgens tot een tweede professor in den rechten laten beroepen Gerardus Noodt der beyden rechten doctor, van goede studie en reputatie, ende sulx op een tractement van vier hondert gls. s'jaars.' *NNBW* ii: 999, following Barbeyrac, erroneously gives the date as 25 Dec. The autobiographical fragment and Van den Ende's necrology have the correct date.
33. Sassen, 1955: 63.
34. Wertheim-Gijse Weenink, 1975: 223.
35. Sassen, 1955: 65. A formal decision abolishing the university is found nowhere. In fact, the city magistrate kept hoping for many decades that it would be possible to reopen the university. When Noodt, the last professor, left for Franeker in September 1679, the university simply ceased to exist.
36. Wertheim-Gijse Weenink, 1975: 223.
37. Braunius, 1675. At the request of advocate Gijsbert Mooringh, who was also mentioned in it, the city council prohibited further sale of the pamphlet, Sassen, 1962: 116.
38. Sassen, 1955: 65.
39. In the village of Valburg.

as was the old custom.[40] They agreed to go there in full academic dress, preceded by the beadle with his rod, and to welcome the king with an address in Latin. Only Noodt disagreed. Mars and the Muses have nothing in common, he said; in the bustle of military activity they could hardly expect to get admission to the king in person. The French are known to be insolent and mocking, the court personnel in particular are notorious for their conceitedness. They have no respect for learning and mock scholars. When these arguments made no impression, Noodt gave in and promised to participate. But he predicted that such an ill-considered mission could bring nothing but shame.

And so they went, across the Waal and over the dyke, the professors in academic dress, the beadle with his rod. The young French noblemen and officers looked with amazement at the queer procession, surrounded it and mocked it. The professors did their best to get access to the king, but because no one knew French well enough, they did not understand the officers and could not make themselves clear. Turned away and full of shame, they had to return without having seen so much as a glimpse of the king. To avoid further abuse they told the beadle to wrap his staff in his coat. Noodt alone had shown more sense than all the professors combined, Roukens concludes.[41] He had certainly shown himself to be a chip off the old block, though not as uncompromising as the Biesmans had been.

About Noodt's legal activities after the French occupation we know only very little. Apart from legal practice and teaching (if that continued) he must have spent much of his time in studies. On 2 July 1677 he delivered with W. Water and J. Verstegen an opinion, in fact the concept of a judgment, to the Noble Court of Elst in the Overbetuwe, which the court actually followed in its decision.[42] Noodt stayed in Nijmegen until September 1679. Thus he experienced at close hand how the 'liberated' city was punished for its resistance and suffering and how William III imposed the autocratic 'Regeringsreglement' of 1675,[43] which at once put an end to the traditional autonomy and influence of the board of 'gemeenslieden'.

40. The senate of Utrecht had the same intention, but the city government formally prohibited it from doing so, Kernkamp i: 507 n. 5; 512.
41. Roukens, 1767: 7.
42. Van den Berg iii, 1784, nr. 135, pp. 339–46.
43. Read by the prince on the Landdag, 1675 Feb. 29. Wertheim-Gijse Weenink, 1975: 230. And see Maris, 1981: 130 ff.; Maris, 1984.

Formally the board was maintained, but only to let it die out in a natural way. During William's rule no new members were appointed, and in 1702 there was in fact hardly a 'gemeensman' surviving.

Gerard Noodt must have had first-hand information about all this, because his father, reinstated as 'gemeensman', was chosen as the board's speaker in 1675. It was Peter Noodt who 'as chairman and in the name of the *gemeente* formally protested against the imposition of the Government Regulation, and declared it utterly null and void'.[44] His words, though of no effect, honoured the memory of Christoffel Biesman.

In the meantime Noodt waited in vain for the back pay of his salary, which grew to a considerable amount. The exhausted city, which remained poverty-stricken well into the eighties,[45] could not pay. On 17 April 1679, when the money owed to the widow of Petrus de Greve and Professors Teyler and Noodt together had mounted up to 14,000 guilders, an agreement was made.[46] The three were to get 8,000, of which 1,678 was due to Noodt. But from an account drawn up in 1684 it appears that after five years little over half of the sum due to the widow of De Greve had been paid. The others will hardly have fared better. In those days arrears of payment were not unusual, however. On 4 July 1693 Perizonius wrote Van Eck that he had already waited fourteen months for his annual salary.[47] Whether Noodt ever received the whole sum we do not know, but very soon he was to get a new and well-paid job elsewhere.

2. Franeker, Utrecht, Leiden 1679–1686

From Nijmegen to Franeker

Although Noodt stayed in Nijmegen until September 1679, he must already have been hoping for an appointment elsewhere. It can hardly be an accident that his first publications, which appear when his own university is very nearly closed, coincide with vacancies at

44. Register. Cf. GA Nijmegen, OAN, Raadsignaat 1675 Febr. 25, where Peter Noodt is named as chairman.
45. See Bots, 1978: 170. A traveller in 1678 noted that the city looked very old and delapidated.
46. GA Nijmegen, Gymnasium, inv. nr. 951. The paper, in which the agreement is mentioned, dates from 1684. Unfortunately, only the first leaf has survived. For the city government the matter was treated by Willem Water, jun., as auditor of the city; on him see below, p. 190.
47. Perizonius to Van Eck, Leiden, 4 July 1693, UL Utrecht, MS 1000.

other universities. This is nothing unusual. It is no shame to try to draw attention to oneself by a publication, when there is a vacancy somewhere.[48] Apart from Cujas, the Dutch poet Bilderdijk did so twice, but in vain, when trying to get a nomination in the Leiden law faculty.[49]

In 1674 there were vacancies in Utrecht and Franeker. The first was already of long standing. The French occupied Utrecht on 13 June 1672. All the students fled, and the survival of the university was in jeopardy for some time, and, in fact, not for the last time in its existence. Antonius Matthaeus III, son of the founding law professor in Utrecht, wanted to be in before the rain, and by 20 October 1672 had accepted a chair in Leiden. This time he would not get the 1,400 guilders offered him in 1670 but only 1,200. As times were worse, and he was willing enough, his price dropped accordingly.[50] He departed for Leiden immediately, and for the time being even had to leave his books and furniture behind, because the French had prohibited all carriage of freight to Holland behind the inundation line. Only after the French had left—on 13 November 1673—did university life gradually revive, to be formally resumed with an address by J. G. Grævius at the beginning of 1674.[51] In Franeker Noodt's promoter Taco van Glins died on 11 February 1673.

So there were good reasons for publishing something as soon as possible. Considering the date of the dedication—1 July 1674[52]—Book I of the *Probabilia* came too late for the vacancy in Utrecht. On 11 May Johannes Vœt, only a month younger than Noodt, was appointed there.[53] Now this is quite understandable, and could

48. See on Cujas, Volterra, 1978: 306. Cf. *Regtsgeleerde*, 1772: 58. Commenting on the fact that H. Cannegieter has dedicated a book to the great pensionary Van Bleiswijk, governor of Leiden university, to thank him for appointing his brother, the author writes: 'Wij zouden uit dit gezach van den Heer van Bleiswijk wel haast mogen opmaken, dat de Leidsche Curatoren den Heer Cannegieter zelve wel eens Hoorgleraar te Leiden, bij voorvallende gelegenheid deed worden, zo hij dit zou ambiëren . . .'

49. Bilderdijk, 1806; 1819–20; 1829.

50. Kernkamp i: 511 n. 1; Molhuysen iii: 263. I follow Kernkamp but, according to the acta of Leiden, the governors and burgomasters offered Matthæus the same as in 1670.

51. 24 Apr. 1674. *NNBW* iv: 670 erroneously dates the reopening to 1675, confusing two addresses by Grævius; cf. Kernkamp ii: 22.

52. In fact, Noodt could only have sent the copy to the printer, Felix Lopez in Leiden, after the French had left Nijmegen in May 1674.

53. Kernkamp ii: 16. Vœt is appointed on the condition that he will get no pay during the first two years!

hardly have surprised Noodt himself. Johannes was a member of the powerful local Vœt-clan, a son of Paulus and a grandson of Gisbert, who still dominated the university.[54] Moreover, Johannes was professor at the famous Nassauische Gymnasium in Herborn,[55] a position more important and—from the point of view of the Orangists who had just returned to power—more respectable than Noodt's professorship in the young, questionable, and ill-fated university of recalcitrant Nijmegen.

In the meantime Professor Noodt must already have had some reputation as a scholar, at least in Nijmegen. On 10 May 1674 the Italian scholar G. B. Pacichelli (1641–1702) sent a report about his visit to Nijmegen to the Roman antiquarian G. P. Bellori.[56] Among other things he wrote: 'There is an academy there, which has turned out a man of reputation, but has not the rights of a university.' If by 'man of reputation' Noodt is meant—we cannot be sure of that, but there certainly are not many candidates for the title[57]—Pacichelli will have heard about Noodt from Noodt's friends Gisbert Cuper[58] and Johannes Smetius the Younger,[59] whom he said he had met. The *Probabilia* were not yet published at that time, but they certainly will have circulated in manuscript form among Noodt's learned friends in Nijmegen.

The vacancy in Franeker was to remain for many years and Noodt did not stand a chance there either. As a result of the war, the States of Friesland were forced to cut the university budget considerably. On 30 March 1672 they decided to reduce the law faculty to two professorships. As there were still three then, the vacancy left by the death of Taco van Glins was not filled. Only after the resignation on 16 June 1675 of Danckelmann, who had actually been on leave for some years, was there a vacancy.[60] But Noodt was not on the list of candidates and, after several others had refused the post, on 10

54. Gisbert died 1676. Johannes' brother Paulus Vœt van Winssen (*NNBW* vii: 1279) was a member of the Utrecht city council. See, in general, McGahagan, 1976: 27 f.
55. Coing, 1977: 31, 60.
56. Begheijn, 1981: 108.
57. Another possible candidate, though not very famous, is Abraham Gulichius, see § 1 n. 92, and below, p. 39.
58. G. Cuper was professor at the Athenaeum of Deventer from 1668. Later, he was burgomaster there and deputy to the States General. Noodt and Cuper corresponded practically all their lives, though at great intervals. The last letter we have dates from 1713. On Cuper see *NNBW* iv: 486 and Veenendaal, 1958: 78–94.
59. Noodt's relation with Smetius junior is highlighted in his letter to Cuper, Nijmegen, 25 May 1678, KB, 72 G 20.
60. Boeles ii. 1, 1879: 255, 274.

January 1678 Sebastiaan Schelkens was appointed.[61] There can be no doubt that Ulrik Huber, the only surviving professor in the law faculty and a headstrong man at that, will have had a big say in the appointment. There is no evidence, however, which might suggest that Noodt was wilfully ignored, although it does not seem possible that the publication of the *Probabilia* could have escaped Huber's attention and the attitude to Roman law studies expressed in it is not likely to have appealed to him.[62] We know nothing about the circulation of the book, and anyway Noodt's 'discovery' only came some years later. Maybe Noodt already coveted a professorship in Leiden by then, although for the moment there was no vacancy there. In Book I of the *Probabilia*, published in 1674, there are extensive laudations of two Leiden law professors, G. C. Crusius[63] and J. F. Böckelmann.[64] These are occasional phrases, which will be suppressed in later editions.[65] The praise of Böckelmann is especially notable here, because ten years later, in his inaugural address in Utrecht, Noodt launched a sharp attack on the use of compendia in law teaching, a method introduced into the Netherlands precisely by this same Böckelmann.[66] Small wonder that the praise was suppressed in the next edition of the *Probabilia*!

Noodt owed his breakthrough partly to political developments. In 1675, after many *pourparlers*, the parties in the Dutch war chose Nijmegen as the scene for the peace negotiations. They took place there from 1676 to 1678. Among the diplomats sent to Nijmegen were several lovers of letters and some scholars.[67] As members of the international republic of letters, they were interested in many things besides the actual negotiations, which took only a small part of their time. Noodt, a local professor of some repute, will have interested

61. Boeles ii. 1, 1879: 274. After studies and various travels Schelkens (1634–1700) was professor in Hertogenbosch from 1663 to 1672. When nominated to Franeker, he had not yet obtained a doctor's degree in law. This he took a year later. Schelkens acted as promoter of Van Bijnkershœk, 1694 May 17; Van Eck had already left Franeker by then, v. d. Aa vi. 79.
62. See below, Ch. 4, at n. 64.
63. *Probabilia* 1. 4. 2, *Opera* i: 56 f.
64. *Probabilia* 1. 9. 7, *Opera* i: 122.
65. Crucius is left out in the edn. of the *Opera omnia* of 1713, Böckelmann already by the edn. of 1691.
66. Cf. Feenstra, 1985*a*.
67. Apart from those mentioned in the text, mention must be made of Sir William Temple, the first English ambassador. He had a training in various languages, had travelled much, and was fairly well schooled in history and philology, see Van 't Hooft, 1978: 116.

them hardly less than the cabinet of Roman antiquities of Smetius father and son.[68] The city did not have much else to offer.

Two of the diplomats Noodt met in Nijmegen had a decisive influence on his career, but many were interested in him. One of the very rare copies of the first impressions of Noodt's *Probabilia*, which was published in Leiden in 1674, is now in East Berlin.[69] It comes from the library of the diplomat and scholar Ezechiel Spanheim,[70] who was envoy of the Count Palatine in Nijmegen and visited the cabinet of Smetius on 21 March 1677 and on 27 February 1678.[71] Most likely Spanheim met Noodt in Nijmegen, and acquired the book there. We already know that Noodt and Smetius junior were friends. The government in Kleve of the Great Elector, Frederick William of Brandenburg, moved the fastest. The permanent envoy of Brandenburg in the Hague, Werner Wilhelm Blaspeil,[72] arrived in Nijmegen with full powers of the government council in Kleve to offer Noodt a professorship in Duisburg. The honourable offer, made in October 1677, was graciously turned down by Noodt.[73]

During the winter of 1677–8 social-life in Nijmegen was at a high-point and in this the young and learned professor had an unexpected role to play. His teacher and senior colleague Petrus de Greve did him the inexpressible favour of dying then.[74] In February or March 1678 there was a solemn academic session, when Noodt pronounced the obituary speech 'in the presence of Ambassador Van Beverningk, the city government of Nijmegen and a great number of people'.[75] The speech made a great impression on all present.

68. Bots, 1978: 170 f., with a postscript by Brinkhoff.
69. Ahsmann–Feenstra, 1984: nr. 421. There is also a copy in the Advocates Library, Edinburgh, nr. A 67–3. Like the other copies of the *Probabilia* in that library, it belonged to the library of Lord George Douglas. Douglas visited the Republic 1686/7, see below, n. 19 on p. 78.
70. On him see Bots, 1978: 179, with n. 32, who gives further literature. See *Allg. deutsche Biogr.* 35, 1893: 50–9; *Biogr. Wörterb. z. deutschen Gesch.* iii, 1975: 2692–3. The copy of the *Probabilia* in the Staatsbibliothek in East Berlin has nr. Gb. 11701. The blank facing the title-page has a slip pasted in, reading: 'Ex. bibliotheca Ezech. Spanhemii'.
71. Bots, 1978: 179. In the *praefatio ad lectorem* of his *Antiquitates Neomagenses* (1678) Smetius junior expresses his esteem for the numismatist E. Spanheim, 'hoc tempore legatus Noviomagum missus ad pacificum tot caduceatorum conventum'; Brinkhoff, 1978: 182.
72. On him see *Allg. deutsche Biogr.* 2, 1875: 696–8; Van 't Hooft, 1978: 119, 124, 135.
73. Register.
74. 31 Dec. 1677, Sassen, 1962: 108.
75. Register. The speech is printed with Roukens, 1767. See Ahsmann–Feenstra, 1984: nr. 426. The general title-page of Roukens, 1767, gives the date of the speech as III Cal. Mart. (= 27 Feb.), the title-page of the speech III Id. Mart. (= 13 March).

Hieronymus van Beverningk,[76] just named, was a diplomat with a brilliant though not undisputed record. As ambassador to England he is believed to have played a major role—which he emphatically denied later—in the making of the Act of Seclusion of 1654, the secret protocol attached to the peace-treaty of the first Anglo-Dutch war which aimed to exclude the Orange family permanently from the office of stadholder. Later, he disassociated himself more or less from De Witt and the Lœvesteiners, which of course benefited his career under William III. Among other things, he was 'deputy in the fields', representing the States-General with the army in Guelders, in 1672.[77] On 10 August 1678 he and the French envoy d'Estrades signed a separate peace between the Republic and France, at the instance of the States-General, but much against the wishes of William III, who saw his schemes for a European policy thwarted. William, in fact, still went into battle against the French on 14 August, to prevent them from taking Mons,[78] pretending that he had not yet received word of the signing of the peace-treaty. Van Beverningk was also a lover of letters. As we will see presently, he was very interested in Noodt's *Probabilia*, and on 4 January 1678 he visited the cabinet of Smetius with an extensive following.[79] In 1673 he was appointed a governor of Leiden university, and this became his main concern after his retirement from politics.[80]

Another important man whom Noodt met in Nijmegen was the second ambassador of the Republic at the peace-conference, the Frisian statesman and diplomat Willem van Haren,[81] head of the 'grietenij het Bildt' and ambassador for the Republic on many missions. In 1679 he was appointed a governor of the Frisian university at Franeker, but even before this he was already trying to win Noodt to this university.

In 1679 a new impression of Noodt's *Probabilia* was brought out, this time in three volumes.[82] As far as Book I is concerned it was a reissue, with a new title-page, dedication, and index. Books II and III

76. 1614–90. On him see *NNBW* iii: 127; *Numaga* 25 (1978) nr. 4, *passim*; *AGN* 8, 1979: 272, 289.
77. Wertheim-Gijse Weenink, 1975: 218.
78. Van 't Hooft, 1978: 129.
79. Bots, 1978: 178.
80. *NNBW* vii: 128.
81. 1626–1708, v. d. Aa vi: 57; *Encyclopaedie van Friesland*, Amsterdam and Brussels, 1958, i.v.; *Numaga* 25 (1978): 4, *passim*; de Wal, 1825; Boeles i. 1, 1879: 280. Noodt dedicated to Van Haren the first impression of *De jurisdictione et imperio*. The dedication is dated 7 Oct. 1690.
82. Ahsmann–Feenstra, 1984, nr. 422.

form, in fact, a separate book.[83] Once more, it is tempting to connect the date of publication with vacancies. This time there was one in Leiden, which came up twice. On 19 December 1678 A. Rusius died; his successor, S. Cœman died on 28 September 1679, shortly after having pronounced his inaugural address.[84] Both times there remained only two professors in the law faculty (Böckelmann and Matthaeus III) and therefore the nomination of a successor was an urgent problem. In the fall of 1679, however, after the premature death of Coeman, Noodt was no longer in the running, because he had been appointed to Franeker only weeks before (4 September). At the beginning of 1680 Johannes Voet got the Leiden job—perhaps because Noodt was no longer available.[85] Noodt was regarded by some as a possible candidate: in October 1679 Van Haren told Noodt in public that he had heard this from the best sources in Holland, adding 'that he hopes that Noodt will not be so disrespectful to the province of Friesland, where he has been received with so much love, as to depart immediately or very soon'.[86] Apparently Van Haren was well aware that Noodt might have preferred Leiden to Franeker, and that powerful people were interested in him.

But what about the earlier period, after the death of Rusius (late 1678, early 1679)? It is exactly in this period that the *Probabilia* in three volumes were published in Leiden.[87] The book was brought

83. I have inspected the copies in Deutsche Staatsbibliothek, East Berlin, UL Basle and Advocates Library, Edinburgh.

84. *Album scholasticum*, 1941; Molhuysen iii: 345–6, 349. For the inaugural address see Ahsmann–Feenstra, 1984: nr. 110.

85. Molhuysen iii: 350–1; Kernkamp ii: 47. Actually, Van Beverningk played a decisive role in the nomination of Vœt.

86. Noodt to father, Franeker, 25 Oct. 1679, ARA Tets van Goudriaan, inv. nr. 105: 'Sijne Excell. seijde mij in praesentie van verscheijde luijden, dat hij in Holland hadde gehoord, dat ick tot Leijden tegenwoordig in consideratie quam tot de plaetse van de Heer Koemans zalr., en dat hij het selve hadde uijt de mond van Heren, die daer van kennisse, en misschijn, seijde hij, oock daer in te seggen hadden. Doch voegde daer bij, Mijn Heer ick hebbe oock al wat tegens U gesolliciteert, en hope, dat ghij de provincie van Frijsland, daer je met so veel lijefde bent gekomen, en ontfangen, het affront niet sult aendoen van aenstonts of so haest te vertrecken, en voorts seijde sijne Excell. veel andere vrijndelijckheden, die ick geerne hoorde.' The talk took place 'voorleden donderdag', that is, on 23 Oct., about two months before the nomination of Vœt took place. Most likely, Van Haren got the information from Van Beverningk himself. This might explain why Van Beverningk proposed Vœt as a successor for Coeman and did not say a word about Noodt; see above, n. 85.

87. Register: 'In het begin van het jaar 1679 heeft hij met den druck uitgegeven sijn tweede en derde boeck van sijn probabilia juris, en sulx op versoeck van hoogstgedagte sijne Excellentie de Heer van Beverninck, die het eerste boek hadde

out, so the dedication says, at the instance of Van Beverningk, who, as we already know, met Noodt in Nijmegen and, after reading the first book of the *Probabilia*, assured him 'that he was very eager to read more of this kind of speculation'.[88] The dedication of the book to Van Beverningk, the governor of Leiden, is even made part of the title: *Probabilia juris civilis . . . ad Hieronymum Beverningium.*[89] A less disguised application for the chair in Leiden can hardly be imagined. Nevertheless, we cannot be sure that the publication was provoked directly by Rusius' death. If a book is published during a vacancy, this naturally does not imply that it was written for the occasion. That is simply impossible with this type of work, and moreover Noodt does not seem to have been a very fast writer. From a letter to Cuper of 25 May 1678 we can gather that at that time Noodt was already preparing the second book of *Probabilia*;[90] he sent some samples with his letter, asking for Cuper's comments. And only five days after Rusius died in Leiden, Noodt wrote from Nijmegen to Marcus Meibom that he intended to send him Books II and III of the *Probabilia* soon.[91] This might mean that they already were in the press by then, though not necessarily.

But, as we know, on 11 May 1679 not Noodt but Cœman was appointed. We cannot know whether this happened because Van Beveringk was absent or because Van Haren outwitted him.[92] For that matter, Noodt's position then was fairly advantageous. While

gelezen, en hem betuigt, dat hij seer begerig was om meer van die slag van speculatien te sien.'

88. Dedicatio: '. . . repetii et virtutis et honoris iter velut auctoritate et suasu tuo, animumque denuo ad scribendum adjeci . . .'
89. In the third impression, appearing towards the end of 1690 or the beginning of 1691, the dedication has disappeared from the title (see Ahsmann–Feenstra, 1984: nr. 423), although the book is still dedicated to Van Beverningk, who, by the way, died towards the end of 1690.
90. Noodt to Cuper, Nijmegen, 25 May 1678: 'alterum probabilium meorum librum brevi edere institui, in eo praeter caetera emendationes ex siglis, notisque aliquot. Ex his exemplum ad te unum, atque alterum mitto; rogans serio, de istis ut arbitrii me tui certiorem facias. Qualecunque id fuerit, mihi gratum, acceptumque erit.' The pieces annexed to the letter are concerned with D 7. 1. 15. 4 (*Probabilia* ii. 14) and D 12. 4. 15 (*Probabilia* ii. 5). In both cases, Noodt argues on the basis of the so-called 'notae' of Valerius Probus (modern edn. Girard and Senn, 1967: 9 ff.).
91. Noodt to M. Meibom, Nijmegen 1678 Dec. 14, Forschungsbibl. Gotha, Chart. A 413.
92. From Molhuysen iii: 346 it seems correct to conclude that Van Beverningk was absent indeed. Only two other governors are named there as present at the deliberation. Van Haren had asked Noodt for Franeker informally already in March.

the vacancy in Leiden caused by Rusius' death was still open, at the beginning of 1679 a new one arose in Franeker, when Ulrik Huber was appointed councillor in the Court of Friesland (24 February).[93] Only a few weeks later, in March, Noodt was asked privately by Van Haren whether he was willing to accept the chair.[94] Curiously enough Van Haren was not yet governor of Franeker university; his appointment dates from May.[95] Did he act on his own, or on private instructions from the governors? We do not know. It seems likely that Noodt delayed his answer until a decision was taken in Leiden. Only a fortnight after the nomination of Cœman (11 May) the Estates of Friesland sent Noodt their official proposal.[96] On 4 September, Noodt's thirty-second birthday, he was appointed professor in Franeker, on a salary of 1,150 guilders.[97] Barely six months later this was to be raised considerably, after the first proposal from Utrecht. Gisbert Cuper, who had become professor in Deventer in the meantime,[98] wrote to Noodt to wish him luck, and asked him to take care of two relatives who were going to study in Franeker, sons of his brother-in-law, the Deventer burgomaster Arnold van Suchtelen.[99]

In the second half of August Noodt travelled to Franeker to look for rooms, and after returning to Nijmegen he sent Cuper an extensive report of the trip.[1] He had rented four rooms with the clerk of the senate. Furthermore, he would be able to rent rooms for the

93. Veen, 1976: 1. 94. Register. 95. Boeles ii. 1, 1879: 280.
96. The States decided to nominate Noodt on 15 May, see Vriemoet, 1763: 589. Because Friesland still had the Julian calendar, the date is 25 May according to the Gregorian calendar which obtained in Holland. Noodt's reply was dated 21 May, according to the Register.
97. The salary was 1,000 guilders, to which a supplement of 150 guilders was added. This supplement was awarded the professors in 1672 as compensation for the loss of tax immunities, see Boeles i, 1878: 52 f.
98. *NNBW* iv: 486.
99. Cuper to Noodt 31 July [1679] (concept), KB, 72 G 20.
1. Noodt to Cuper, Nijmegen, 31 Aug. 1679, KB, 72 G 20: 'Simul e frisiis reversus fui, nihil tam antiquum mihi fuit, Vir Amplissime, quam ut itineris mei rationem atque eventum tibi, ita ut promisi, exponerem. Hospitii gratia, ut scis, abieram. Hospitem autem eum inveni, qui Senatui Franekerano a secretis est. Apud eum vero cubicula mihi quatuor. Vidi et quintum eadem in domo, sed hoc, etsi non inscitum, minus tamen, ut puto, quam ut binos cognatos tuos caperet. Igitur viciniam circumspexi proximam et in ea cubiculum inveni egregium, quod sufficere utrique possit. Lecti certe in eo more Frisico bini, spatium autem justum et amplum. Si tamen separari malent, cubiculum erit et alterum eadem in domo, sed angustius paulo, quam illud prius. Merces illius majoris, si ab uno habitabitur, nisi fallor, quinquaginta Carolinis monetae nostrae, aut paulo minoris aestimatur,

Van Suchtelen boys with the beadle, who was asking 60 guilders for lodging, food, and service. For himself, Noodt was deliberating as to how his food and drink could be provided for in a way suitable to his situation. His host was prepared to take care of this for 4 guilders a week—wines excluded. But when he was told that the Frisians generally took little trouble over cooking, he also talked to a cook, who was prepared to make his meals for 5 guilders a week. He still had not taken a decision. Apparently Noodt travelled from Nijmegen to Amsterdam and from there by boat to Friesland, an easier and safer trip than overland. In Amsterdam he met the German scholar Marcus Meibom, whom he already knew and with whom he had corresponded before.[2]

In the middle of September Noodt left Nijmegen to take up his professorship in Franeker. Again, the trip went via Amsterdam, where he took the boat to Harlingen on Tuesday, 23 September. He arrived there next morning about 10 a.m., and about 1.30 p.m. he was in Franeker.[3] The first letters exchanged between father and son have

si a duobus, putem sexaginta circumcirca comparari posse. Hoc autem pretium aliquanto minoris aestimatur. Hospes, si eum qui Pedellus noster est primarius, homo, ut mihi videtur, satis modestus. In eadem vicinia domus meae cum domum etiam aliam inspicerem; in ea cubicula repperi duo, quorem singula quadraginta florenis, sive Carolinis taxantur, pretio, opinor, non iniquo, si cogites ab hospite, id est locatore, non cubiculum tantum, sed et lectum et stragula dari, praeterea habitantium lintea ejus cura lavari, vestes item, si qua parte solutae sint, sarciri. Caeterum candelas et ignem, uti alibi passim, conducentium inpensis propriis emi oportet. Cubiculorum conditiones vides. Jam quod ad victum attinet, egi cum hospite meo, et quaesivi, si eum nobis victum et potum meridie et vesperi praeberet, qui hominem deceret conditionis meae, quid ipse, quid cognati tui pro eo debituri essent septimanis singulis. Primum homo vinum excepit, deinde singulis florenos indicavit quaternos. Placebat primum conditio, sed cum deinde audirem Frisios plerosque non valde curiosos artis coquendi esse, cum coquo colloucutus fui, qui pretium singulis per singulas septimanas statuit quinos florenos. Sed ipse nihil adhuc in his definivi, ut ad te rem integram referrem.' From Noodt's letter to his father, Franeker, 25 Oct. 1679 (see n. 39), it appears that only one of the Van Suchtelen boys came to Franeker, and that Noodt gave him one of his own rooms, leaving himself with three: 'Monsieur Van Suchtelen is nu van Deventer oock hijer gekomen. Ick hebbe hem een kamer overgelaeten, en hebbe selfs noch drije gemacken voor mij.'

2. On M. Meibom (1630–1711) see § 1 n. 98. See Noodt to Meibom, Nijmegen, 4 Dec. 1678, Forschungsbibl. Gotha Chart A 413. From this letter it appears that Meibom had visited Noodt in Nijmegen shortly before: '. . . cum nuper adesses mihi . . .'. In Amsterdam, Noodt received from Meibom a book, which he sent on to Cuper. Cuper thanks him for this in his letter to Noodt, Deventer, 5 Sept. 1679 (concept) KB 72 G 20.
3. Register; Noodt to father, Franeker, 5 Oct. 1679, ARA Tets van Goudriaan, inv. nr. 105. The date of this letter is not correct, see n. 6.

a cordial tone. Gerard reported in great detail his arrival and first experiences. People in Franeker had been looking forward to his arrival and in the Academy two letters were waiting for him. On 2 October he travelled to Leeuwarden to collect his commission,[4] and to discuss the date of his inauguration with the governors. They intended to take up the matter with the prince, who was expected to attend the inauguration in person. At 2 o'clock in the afternoon he was received in audience by the prince, who gave him 'a very polite reception'.[5]

Noodt wrote a lengthy letter to his father about his inauguration,[6]

4. The letter of appointment is in ARA Tets van Goudriaan, inv. nr. 109.
5. Noodt to father, Franeker, 5 Oct. 1679, ARA Tets van Goudriaan, inv. nr. 105. On the dating of this letter see n. 6.
6. Noodt to father, Franeker, 9/19 Oct. 1679, ARA Tets van Goudriaan, inv. nr. 105. This letter has a double date, as have the dates mentioned in it. Noodt is marking here the difference in calendar (10 days) between Holland (Gregorian) and Friesland and Guelders (Julian). The letter of 5 Oct. (see nn. 3 and 5) is dated 'Thursday'. This is not correct. 5 Oct. 1679 (Julian) was a Sunday! In fact, the letter must have been written on Thursday, 2 October 1679 (Julian calendar). So the inauguration, taking place on 6/16 Oct., was in fact five days later. '... so dijent desen omme UEd. te adverteren, dat den dach tot de voorsz. introductie is aengesteld geweest tegen voorleden maendagh den 6/16 octob., dat dijenvolgens de Heren Curatoren Ockinga, Rhala en Duijs voorleden Sondach den 5/15 octob. omtrent den avond van Leeuwarden alhijer in de herberg de Valck genaemt zijn aengekomen, en mij dijen selven avond beneffens den heer rector Magnificus en de assessoren van den Academie met de Professor Gulicius bij haer hebben te eten genodigt, ende ons allen seer vrijndelijck en beleefdelijck onthaelt en getracteert. Dat voorts des maendags daer aen volgende zijde den 6/16 octob. omtrent 10 uiren Sijne Hoogheijt den Here Stadhouder van Frijsland alhier mede ten selven eijnde met een karosse van ses paerden en eenige Edelluijden onder het losbranden van het canon is binnen gekomen. Dat de professoren sigh daer op en corps naer sijne Hoogheijt en de voorsz. Heren Curatoren in de Valck hebben begeven, en daer na met de selve van daer gesamentlijck naer de Academie zijn gegaen in volgende ordre. Eerste de Edelluijden van de Prins, daer na beijde Pedellen met de scepters, doen sijne Hoogheijt geleijt tusschen de Heren Ockinga en Rhala; daer na ben ick gevolgt tusschen de Heren Duijs en de Rector Magnificus Blancardus. daer na de professor Gulicius tusschen de Professoren Arnoldus en Witsius, daer na de andere professoren paer en paer. In de poort van de Academie komende zijn wij gegaen in de Senaet, alwaer sijn Hoogheijt door den Rector Magnificus met een korte, dog brave oratie in Neerduijts gecomplimenteert wierde. Uijt de senaet kamer zijn wij naer de kerck van de Academie gegaen op volgende ordre, te weten, Eerst sijne Hoogheijt, daer na de heer Ockinga, daer na ick, daer na de Heren Rhala en Duijs, daer na de Professor Gulichius, en so voort. In de kerck wierd eerste een braef musijck gemaeckt, daer na hebbe ick *de civili prudentia* georeert, en in het eijnde de Curatoren in het generael, en daer na sijn Hoogheijt in het particulier aangesproocken. De forme van de aenspraeck hebbe ick per copiam hijer neffens geleijt. Daer na is wederom gemusiceert, en eijndelijck de oratie van de Heer Gulichius gevolgt. De selve is geweest *de admiranda hominis natura*. Als wij uijt de Valck op straet en in de voorsz. kerck van de Academie quamen, hebben

which took place on Monday, 16 October (Gregorian calendar). On the Sunday the governors Ockinga,[7] Rhala,[8] and Doys[9] came from Leeuwarden to Franeker, where they put up at the Falcon Inn.[10] That night the new professors, Noodt and Gulichius,[11]—incidentally both alumni of the grammar school and university of Nijmegen—the rector Blancardus,[12] and his assessors were invited to dinner by the governors. On Monday at 10 a.m. the stadholder of Friesland and honorary governor of the university Hendrik Casimir II of Nassau (1657–97), rode into Franeker in a coach with six horses and with a following of noblemen, the guns firing a salute. The professors went in procession to the Falcon Inn to greet the prince and governors. Then all proceeded to the Academy in the following order: 'First the noblemen of the prince, then the two beadles with their staffs, then the prince between governors Ockinga and Rhala, then myself between governor Doys and rector Blancardus, then professor

wij t'elckens eenen seer groten toeloop van menschen niet alleen uijt Franeker, maer oock uijt Leeuwarden en de hijer omliggende plaetsen gevonden, en zijn onder andere in de kerck selfs verscheijde dames van conditie praesent geweest. Uijt de kerck zijn wij eerst weer in de senaet gegaen en heeft sijn Hoogheijt met de Curatoren en voorts met de Heren Professoren eerst mij en doen mijn Confrater van Gulick aldaer de hand gegeven, en tot onse professie ons beijde veel gelucks gewenscht. Dit gedaen zijnde, zijn wij met de Prins en Curatoren altemael na de Valck gekeert, ende aldaer uijtsteeckende kostelijck en splendijd getracteert. En mene, datter eene tafel van meer als vijftich menschen geweest is. Sijn Hoogheijt heeft sigh in het geselschap seer familiair en gemeensaem getoont. Invoegen alle de werelt sigh omtrent hem bleef gedeckt houden, en sijn Hoogheijt het verscheijde malen excuseerde, als ijemand om respects halven, wanneer 't hem door sijn Hoogheijt wierde gebragt, bleef over ende staen. Sijn Hoogheijt heeft voor de Professoren in het generael veel aestijems getoont, ende in het particulier elck op sijn rang over tafel een romer toegedroncken. Echter reeckent men voor eene seer particuliere eere, die mij en de professor Gulichius bij desen geschijet is. Welgem. sijn Hoogheijt heeft den selven dagh tusschen ligten en donckeren sijn afscheijt eerst van de Heren Curatoren en daer na van den rector Magnificus en de Professoren, die daer omtrent waeren, gelijck mede van eenige andere Heren genomen, en is doen in sijn carosse en so voort naer Leeuwarden gekeert. De Heren Curatoren hebben mij de eere altemael gedaen van mij te verklaren, dat ick haer ten enemael voldaen hadde.'

7. Hero van Ockinga, governor 1656–82, Boeles ii. 1, 1879: 8.
8. Johannes Rhala (1630–86), son of Professor Rhala, governor 1673–86, Boeles ii. 1, 1879: 8.
9. Gerlich Doys (1625–85), governor 1677–85, Boeles ii. 1, 1879: 9. Apparently, Van Haren was not present at the inauguration.
10. On the corner of Voorstraat and Raadhuisplein, now the Friesland Bank.
11. On him, see § 1 n. 92 above. Gulichius died on 31 Dec. 1679.
12. On him, see Boeles ii. 1, 1879: 147–51; Gerretzen, 1940: 43–5; Scholtens and Feenstra 1974: 201 f.

Gulichius between the professors Arnoldus and Witsius, and then the other professors in pairs.' They entered the gate[13] of the Academy and went to the senate hall, where the rector welcomed the prince with a speech in Dutch.

Then they processed to the academy church[14] in the following order: 'Namely, first the prince, then Ockinga, then me, then the governors Rhala and Doys, then professor Gulichius, and so on.' In the church the session began with music. Then Noodt pronounced his inaugural address on *civilis prudentia*, an appropriate piece for the occasion, expounding clearly his position as a legal scholar as well as his ideas on legal education. After that, there was music again, and then Gulichius's speech. Wherever the procession went many people were gathered and in the church 'even several ladies of rank were present'. After the ceremony the procession went back to the senate hall, where Noodt and Gulichius were complimented by the prince, the governors, and their colleagues. Then they returned with the prince and the governors to the Falcon Inn, where they were 'treated excellently, exquisitely, and splendidly . . . And I believe that there were more than fifty people at the table.' The prince was very informal and familiar, although everybody kept his head down and stood up respectfully when the prince addressed him. At the table the prince proposed a toast to each of the professors individually, according to his rank.

Naturally Noodt regarded the presence of the prince at his inauguration, with all the pomp and circumstance, as a 'very special honour', but whether the stadholder, more a soldier than a man of letters, enjoyed sitting out two Latin speeches on one day, may seriously be doubted. After the prince had left about nightfall, the governors gave Noodt the assurance that they were completely satisfied by his performance. The next day, he was invited to dine with the governors once more. Everybody was very friendly, especially the governors and other gentlemen of rank, as well as most justices from the Court at Leeuwarden. 'So I think this is a good professor's country, because usually they give me much honour.' But nevertheless Noodt kept modest: 'Everybody asks me to have my speech printed, which I actually can do without costs, the province

13. See Karstkarel and Terpstra, 1985: 206 f. The gate, now vanished, was on the Vijverstraat.
14. See Karstkarel and Terpstra, 1985: 206 f. The church has vanished likewise, only a few fragments remain in the present building.

being agreeable to pay for it. But I could not decide to do so as yet, because I believe that I may well be satisfied with the honour I have received already.'[15]

A week later Noodt is still in excellent heart,

> because the air is not bad over here, and the house where I live is very good indeed. The people are very polite, and take good care of me. In the city, wherever I go, I am honoured by people I do not even know. The professors think well enough of me. Last Thursday, that is, eight days ago [19 October] I have started my lectures and on Friday my public lessons. And for the lectures on the Institutes I already have some twenty students, for those on the Pandects eight. I think this will do for a start, especially because rumour was spread here as well as in Groningen and Emden, that I was not to come before the winter. With the result that several students, despairing of my arrival, went to Leiden and elsewhere. Up to now, my public lessons are also of my liking and I think that my colleagues may expect from my activities a success for the Academy, and they are satisfied with me.

Once more, Noodt says that Friesland is a good professor's country.[16] In November, only weeks after his inauguration he

15. Noodt to his father, Franeker, 9/19 Oct. 1679, ARA Tets van Goudriaan, inv. nr. 105: '. . . Een ijegelijck versoeckt mij, dat ick mijn oratie sal laten drucken, t gene ick oock sonder mijn onkosten konde doen, also sulx van de landschap betaelt word; maer ick hebbe als noch daer toe niet konnen resolveren; om dat mij dunckt, dat ick met de eere, die ick bereijts bekomen hebbe, konde vergenoegt zijn.' The address was printed for the first time in the *Opera omnia* of 1713, in the index of which it is announced as 'hactenus inedita'. Nevertheless, most older biographers, as well as Dekkers: 124, have an edn. of Franeker, 1679! Cf. Ahsmann–Feenstra, 1984, nr. 427.
16. Noodt to father, Franeker, 25 Oct. 1679, ARA Tets van Goudriaan, inv. nr. 105: '. . . Want mij de lugt hijer niet quaet is, en het huys, waer ick wone, is seer wel. De luijden zijn seer beleeft, en passen mij wel op. In de stad, waer ick passere, geschijet mij eere van luijden, die ick niet eens kenne. Bij de Professoren ben ick heel wel gesijen. Ick hebbe hijer voorleden donderdagh, te weten van daeg acht dagen mijne Collegien en vrijdaegs daer aen volgende mijne publijcke lessen begonnen. En hebbe in het Collegie over de Istituta al in de twintig studenten, en over de Pandecten acht. Het gene mij dunckt, dat voor een begin wel gaen kan; en te meer, om dat men hijer omtrent hadde uijtgestroijt, gelijck mede tot Groeningen en tot Embden, dat ick voor de winter niet soude komen. Invoegen verscheijde studenten, aen mij desperende, naer Leijden en elders zijn vertrocken. In mijne publijcke lessen gaet het oock tot noch toe seer naer mijn sinn, en mene dat mijne Confraters van mijne affaires voor de academie succes tegemoet sijen, en van mij voldaen zijn. Mij word oock geseijd, datter nogh eenige studenten hijer souden bij mij komen. . . . Invoegen UEd. en mijn Lijeve Moeder mij vrij kond geloven, dat ick hijer in een land ben, daer he mij seer wel aenstaet, en om met een woord te seggen, daer het mij dunckt al een seer goed professors land te zijn; Het gene mij alle mijne Confraters oock eenpariglijck verklaren; . . .'. The governors really were most obliging. On 1 May 1680 Noodt wrote to his nephew Peter in Heidelberg (as

conferred degrees on four students, two from Deventer, one from Kampen, and one from Amsterdam.[17] As it is unusual for a new professor to have promotions of local students so soon, these students will have followed Noodt from Nijmegen to Franeker.

His father warned him not to take too much on his shoulders, nor to work himself to the bone with private lectures.[18] He had heard that the beer in Franeker was bad, but that they brewed a very good one in Sneek. Noodt replied that to his knowledge he never drank Franeker beer, but always the one from Sneek, which was brought in every day at a low price.[19] His father's letters already regularly mention the failing health of Gerard's mother. Both parents died only a few months later.

On 21 May 1680 Peter Noodt arrived back ill in Nijmegen from a boat trip via Kleve to Emmerich, which he had made with some friends. He was so weak that he had to be carried home in a chair. On Sunday, 23 May he died. His wife followed him very soon, as both had wished. On Monday, 16 July 1680 she was taken with a heavy pain in the loins, accompanied by fever, which lasted a week. On Sunday, 25 July she blessed and admonished her sons Johan and Gerard, and commended Gerard 'in her name to say to the friends good night for all eternity'. On Monday, at about 10.30 a.m., she died 'very Christianly and with much resolution'.[20]

We do not know very much about Noodt's life in Franeker. In a letter to Braunius of 6 November 1681, he vaguely allude to some kind of gossip about him: 'As far as I am concerned, I do not know I have done so much wrong. But they say it has never been as

n. 17 on p. 60) that in March, after having been in office only half a year, he had received a full year's salary (1,150 guilders) plus 200 guilders for moving expenses.

17. See AP Franeker. It concerns G. Herweyer from Kampen (7 Nov.), G. Bruyns and E. Aerssen from Deventer (13 Nov.), and F. a Collen from Amsterdam (21 Nov.).
18. P. Noodt to son, Nijmegen, 20 Mar. 1680, ARA Tets van Goudriaan, inv. nr. 105: '... Want ic soude niet raden dat ghij UEd. te veel op de hals haelt en afarbeijdet met private colegien, daer om begeere ick dat ghij niet meer doet als wat met U gesontheijt acordeert, en opdat die niet geforceert wort en daer door mogt verswacken. En om dat ick gehoort hebbe dat UEd. daer slegt bier hebt, maer tot Sneeck soude geheel goet bier gebrouwen worden, en dat is binnen lants, dat daer wel te krijgen is, so legt daer op toe.'
19. G. Noodt to father, Franeker, 2 Apr. 1680, ARA Tets van Goudriaan, inv. nr. 105: '... Wat het bier aengaet, daer ben ick noijt om verlegen geweest, want ick so lang, als ick hijer ben geweest, mijnes wetens noijt noch Franeker bier gedroncken hebbe; maer altijd Sneecker bier, dat hijer voor weinig kosten te scheep al daeg kan gebragt worden, en seer goed is.'
20. Register.

bad[21] as now. Although I did not yet read anything about it in the newspapers.'[22] So it will not have been a very serious matter. A more important fact is that towards the end of 1680 Noodt caught the quartan fever (most likely malaria),[23] which continued for several months,[24] and made it next to impossible for him to do any serious work. On 27 April 1681 Noodt was still unable to write a letter to Braunius with his own hand, and therefore dictated it to a friend. When the quartan fever yielded, there came another fever, even heavier than the first.

> . . . my weakness, with which I am left after my former illness, and which is increased because I had a relapse, makes it completely impossible to do any work. The doctor advised me not to tire my brain with serious thoughts or studies, which he considers very harmful, as in fact I experienced myself. My quartan, which I had for several months, left me on 12 March, to be followed by an even worse fever, which not only continued until the seventeenth without intermission, but also was very heavy with regard to heat, cold, sweat, and vomiting, and exhausted me very much.[25]

21. The translation is uncertain. According to Kiliaen's *Etymologicum teutonicae linguae*, Antwerp, 1594 (repr. Amsterdam, 1972), in Frisian 'naer' means weak or worn out (lassus, languidus), but it can also mean 'unpleasant', 'bad', or 'close'.
22. Noodt to Braunius, Franeker, 6 Nov. 1681, UL Leiden, BPL 246: 'Wat mij belangt, ick wete niet, dat ick noch so veel quaets gedaen hebbe. Evel seijtmen, dat het noijt so naer is geweest, als nu. Hoewel ick er in de courant noch niet van gelesen hebbe.'
23. Information from Prof. de Moulin, Institute for the History of Medicine, Catholic University, Nijmegen.
24. In a letter to Cuper (Franeker, 11 Feb. 1681, KB 72 G 20) Noodt speaks of three months, in a letter to Braunius (Franeker, 18 Feb. 1681, UL Amsterdam, 16. Cf. 1) of four. Which means that he must have fallen ill at the end of Oct., or the beginning of Nov., 1680.
25. Noodt to Braunius, Franeker, 27 Apr. 1681, UL Leiden, BPL 246 (not autograph): '. . . mijn swakheid, die ik van de voorgaende siekte behouden heb, en die nu noch daer bij comt, avermits weer ingestort ben, maekt mij 't selve t'enemael onmogelijk. Ook heeft mijn medicus mij geraden, dat ik mijn herssenen niet veel werks zal geven, met serieuse gedachten ofte studien, als hij 't selve seer schadelijk oordeelt, gelijk ik self mede heb bevonden. Mijn quartain, die mij enige maenden had angehangen, heeft mij op den 12en Maert verlaten, maer daer is een coorts op gevolgt, die tot den 17en niet alleen continuel en sonder enige intermissie, maer ook ten ansien van de hitte, coude, sweten, braken seer vehement is geweest, ende mij seer gematteert heeft.' Noodt also apologizes for not being able to help Braunius in some procedure (with the senate of Groningen?): 'Seer gaern zoude ik Uw. Ed. dienst doen, omtrent het opstellen vande bewuste Duplijck, maer mijn swakheid, die 'k vande voorgaende siekte behouden heb, en die nu noch daer bij comt, . . . maekt mij 't selve 't enemael onmogelijk.' Only in the autumn of 1681, when returning to Franeker from a vacation (in Nijmegen?), did Noodt write to Braunius (Franeker, 6 Nov. 1681, UL Leiden, BPL 246) that he was completely free of fever.

Noodt seems to have recovered completely only in the fall of 1681. It is the only serious illness we know of in the life of the robust scholar. In October 1682 he informed Braunius that he had a good many students.[26] During his first years in Franeker his main correspondents are, apart from his father (7 letters), two old friends from Nijmegen who also have become professors: Gisbert Cuper in Deventer (4 letters) and Johannes Braunius in Groningen (4 letters).

In Franeker Noodt could welcome Perizonius, who was appointed there towards the end of 1681 and inaugurated in 1682.[27] Apparently Noodt played an important part in his nomination. When on 26 October 1681, the senate after a long delay drew up a list of candidates for the chair of history and rhetoric, Noodt—no doubt prompted by Grævius—was the only one to propose the name of Perizonius,[28] and therefore it did not figure on the list presented to the governors. But after intensive lobbying, in which Huber (later Perizonius' opponent) is also assumed to have played a part,[29] Perizonius got the job. In a letter to Braunius of 6 November 1681 Noodt gave a report of the nomination, which was decided only by the narrowest margin.

As far as the vacancy in our university is concerned, it was given last Saturday at 11 to Perizonius, as you may know already. But it was a close thing, because he was very nearly not even put on the nomination. Mr Cœtier[30] was put up for nomination unanimously by all the governors, as was Mr Lomejer.[31] But they were divided about the third nominee. Mr Van Haren proposed Perizonius, but Messrs Rhala and Doys Mr Borgesius[32] of Groningen. Mr Ockinga had him in mind as well, but he changed his mind and sided with Mr Van Haren. Therefore, the votes were two against two,

26. Noodt to Braunius, Franeker, 18 Oct. 1682, RA Gelderland, Van den Steen, Van Ommeren en Waijenstein, inv. nr. 94. The letter is ed., with numerous errors in the transcription, by J. A(rntzenius) in Van Hasselt, 1807.
27. On him, see *NNBW* v: 478; Meyer, 1971. On the nomination in Franeker see Meyer, 1971: 44 f.
28. RA Leeuwarden, Franeker universiteit, inv. nr. 18: Diarium Academicum 1664–1683, fol. 361.
29. There hardly seems to be any solid proof for the assumption.
30. 1647–1723, *NNBW* iv: 442. In 1693 he is nominated to Franeker, as successor to Perizonius. See also below, p. 87.
31. 1636–99, v. d. Aa iv: 179.
32. A son of the principal of the grammar school in Groningen, *NNBW* x: 92; see Meyer, 1971: 44.

and in this form the governors[33] presented the nomination last Friday. But anyway Perizonius has the chair.[34]

Considering the close relations of Noodt and Van Haren it seems likely that the latter was Noodt's spokesman for the discussion in the board of governors and that Noodt, who had proposed Perizonius in the senate, also suggested his name to Van Haren. Perizonius contributed a laudatory verse to Noodt's Utrecht inaugural address (1684), and it was Noodt who procured lodgings for him when he was appointed to Leiden in 1693.[35] In Leiden they seem to have been close friends, although Perizonius, a bachelor, appears to have turned sour in his old age. In his letters to Van Eck he often speaks rather critically about Noodt's work, especially his lust for emendations.[36]

From Franeker to Utrecht

However good a professor's country Friesland may have been, Noodt would never have fancied staying there all his life. It was not unusual for a promising professor to proceed from Franeker or Harderwijk, directly or via Utrecht, to Leiden, but Noodt's progress

33. In the text (see next note) the word 'door' seems to have fallen out. Without it, the text says that the nomination is presented to, instead of by, the governors, which is impossible.
34. Noodt to Braunius, Franeker, 6 Nov. 1781, UL Leiden, BPL 246: 'Wat de vacante professie alhijer aenbelangt, de selve is voorleden Saturdach ten elf uiren vergeven aen de Heer Perisonius, als UEd. misschijn all sal verstaen hebben; maer het heeft schrap gelopen, also het wenig scheelde, of hij was niet eens op de nominatie gekomen. Mijn Heer Coetier is er opgebragt met eenparigheijt van stemmen van alle de Heren Curatoren, insgelijx is dominus Lomejer daer op geraeckt. Maer omtrent de derde persoon van de nominatie is verschil geweest. Mijn Heer van Haeren sloegh voor de Heer Perizonius, de Heer Rhala en Duijs de Heer Borgesius van Groningen. Op deselve had de Heer Ockinga sijn gedagten oock; maar sijn Ed. is gediverteert, en heeft sigh met mijn Heer van Haeren gevoegt; invoegen de twee stemmen tegens twee waeren, en de nominatie op die wijse [door] de Heren Curatoren voorleden vrijdag is voorgebragt. Doch het sij hoe het sij, Perizonius heeft de plaetse.'
35. Meyer, 1971: 89. In *De foenore et usuris* (1698) Noodt calls Perizonius 'amicus meus a multis annis' (*Opera* i: 210).
36. Perizonius' appreciation of Noodt appears from a letter to Van Eck (Leiden, 3 Dec. 1695, UL Utrecht, MS 1000), where he writes that he does not understand Van Eck's question: 'Quaestionem quam mihi ponis, non satis intellego, Pedaneos enim judices fuisse Privatos judices, id ubique jam a Cl. Noodtio est demonstratum et res certa est.' But when Perizonius grew older, he became ever more critical. He wrote to Van Eck from Leiden, 2 Apr. 1706 (UL Utrecht, MS 1000): '. . . quod ad emendationem ejus attinet, audax et dura est . . .'; see further below, Ch. 3, § 1 at n. 69.

was very quick indeed. Utrecht asked him three times.[37] It seems likely that Grævius had a hand in this. His appreciation of Noodt appears from a letter to Heinsius of 27 March 1680, in which he reports the failure of the first proposal:

Witsius[38] from Franeker has taken the vacant chair of Burman. But Noodt could not be persuaded to give us his energy. He is kept and bound by the Frisians with golden chains. Which of course I resent. He is an excellent man and among our law professors the only one who is not unschooled in our letters. Refinement of manners and wit adorn his erudition.[39]

The first proposal from Utrecht already came, when Noodt had hardly been six months in Franeker. On 3 March 1680 the town council of Utrecht decided 'after mature deliberation and on good testimony' to ask Noodt.[40] On Saturday, 6 March a delegation of three gentlemen arrived in Franeker:[41] the councillor Vœt van Winssen,[42] the bailiff Van der Vaart Doeyenburg, and the secretary Quint, offering him the chair left vacant by Johannes Vœt's departure for Leiden. Noodt asked for a delay until Tuesday, and departed for Leeuwarden the same day. On Sunday he spoke with governors Ockinga, Van Haren, Rhala, and Doys. Moreover, he had a separate talk with Van Haren, the man who had won him for Franeker. Noodt decided to turn down the proposal 'without demanding anything in kind of payment, leaving that completely to the discretion and liberality of the States'.[43] That well-considered modesty did him no harm. His salary was raised by no less than 400 guilders, that is from 1,000 to 1,400 plus 150, without any further obligations.[44] He was discharged of the duty to pay to his prede-

37. Mention is made of this in the Utrecht inaugural address of 1684, *Opera* i: 616.
38. 1636–1708, *NNBW* iii: 1445–8. Professor of theology in Franeker, Utrecht, and Leiden. See also Van Genderen, 1953; McGahagan, 1976: 324 f.
39. Burman, iv, 1927: 649: '. . . sed Noothius non potuit persuaderi, ut suam nobis addiceret operam, a Frisiis aureis compedibus vinctus et retentus. Quod sane dolo. Nam vir est egregius et qui solus inter juris antistites apud nos litterarum nostrarum non est rudis; eruditionem ornat morum et ingenii elegantia.'
40. Kernkamp ii: 49.
41. Noodt to his father, Franeker, 15 Mar. 1680, ARA Tets van Goudriaan, inv. nr. 105.
42. He is a son of Paulus Vœt (1619–77) and a brother of Johannes, see *NNBW* vii: 1279.
43. Boeles, ii. 1, 1879: 281. Cf. the letter of Noodt to his nephew Peter in Heidelberg, Franeker, 1 May 1680, ARA Tets van Goudriaan, inv. nr. 111.
44. Noodt to his father (as n. 41): 'Waer mede ick in plaetse van elf honderd en vijftigh Caroli guldens des jaers sal hebben een somma van sesteijnde half hondert guldens jaers, sonder dat ick eenigen meerderen arbeijd, als voren, doen sal.'

cessor Huber 1,200 guilders, the sum Huber had paid in 1672 as a forced loan, 'on his office to the country in the bad times', and which his successor had to repay him.[45] Moreover, he got another 200 guilders for moving expenses. All this really may be called binding with golden chains. 'I think that if I had bargained, I easily could have had some 200 guilders a year more. But on the advice of Mr Van Haren, who honours me much and goes about with me, I thought this the best and fairest by far.'[46]

According to Noodt's own testimony, no one in Franeker had ever had their salary increased so quickly. Quite understandably, he was very proud, and in an extensive postscript he asked his father to greet—and inform, no doubt—all the friends in Nijmegen:

> Please present my good offices to cousin Singendonck and cousin Romswinckel, to Mr Smith. I recommend myself to the favours of Messrs Fagel, Cuper, Mr Verschoor, cousin Reinders and his father, cousin Uirmond, Mr Schivelberg, Mr Kœrman, Mr Smetius and his family, the cousins Tijssen, and all the friends, not forgetting cousin de Haert. Greetings also to cousin De Greve and her brother, as well as Miss Hattenus and her niece.[47]

In his reply the proud father urges his son to inform Van Beverningk and, in fact, goes as far as more or less dictating the letter:

> I think you should write to his Excellency Beverninge on this, and inform

45. Noodt to his father (as n. 41). About these forced loans, see Boeles i, 1878: 52. Civil servants, giving a forced loan to the state, were sometimes given a debenture 'on their name and quality', with the right to cede this to their successor. The successor was to take over the debenture, Boeles i, 1878: 54. The loan, therefore, was not a personal obligation, but one resting on the office, with which it went on to the next incumbent. Apparently, Noodt had not taken over Huber's debenture in March 1680, and now he was liberated from the duty to do so. Huber had lent 1,200 guilders in total, the equivalent of a year's salary. Nowhere in our sources do we find evidence that the States compensated Huber for the loss of his claim on Noodt to take over his debenture. Naturally, Huber kept his claim of repayment on the States.

46. Noodt to his father (as n. 41): 'Ick mene, so ick hadde willen marchanderen, dat mijn tractement noch wel 200 guldens des jaers meer soude geaugmenteert zijn geweest; maer ick hebbe dit op het aenraden van mijn Heer van Haren, die mij veel eer doet, en met mij rond gaat, verre het beste en eerlijxte gehouden.'

47. Noodt to his father (as n. 41): 'Gelijeft mijne dijenst te melden aen Neef Singendonck en Neef Romswinckel, aen de Heer Smith. Ick recommandere mijne gebiedenisse mede aen de Heren Fagel, Cuper, de Heer Verschoor, Neef Reijnders, en sijn vader, Neef Uirmond, Mijn Heer Schivelberg, Monsr. Koerman, Mijn Heer Smetius en zijn familie, de Neven Tijssen en alle de vrijnden. Neef de Haert niet te vergeten. De groetenisse mede aen Nicht ende Neef de Greve. Insgelijx juffrouw Hattenus en haer Nigt.'

him about the proposal from Utrecht, which was very satisfactory, but because you had come there only recently and the Province had spent a great deal on you, and his Excellency Van Haren had been your promoter, whom you did not want to disappoint, which might be resented, or whatever you think best. And I think you should also continue the friendship you have made with burgomaster Verbolt [of Nijmegen]. One never knows where it might be useful.[48]

Noodt wrote to Braunius in Groningen about the refused proposal only a year after the event (18 February 1681).[49] He said he had heard that the chair in Utrecht had been supplemented and given to J. van Muyden, but this information is not wholly correct. Van Muyden, former vice-principal of the Hieronymus-school in Utrecht, was paid only 400 guilders as professor of the Institutes, and had to wait many years for a rise.[50]

But Utrecht did not give up. On 27 December 1682 the town council decided 'unanimously after serious consideration and information' to ask Noodt.[51] Mr Spoor and the secretary De Reuver, who were entrusted with the proposal, reported on 8 February 1683 about their useless trip to Franeker: Noodt had refused again. The town council now was determined to offer him a salary of 1,600 guilders, without taking a formal decision for the moment, however.[52] Apparently, Noodt gave his decision immediately this time, without consulting the governors. But he did not make a secret of the proposal from Utrecht either, of course. On 27 February the States of Friesland wrote to him that they had heard, 'by a sidewind', that Utrecht had offered him a professorship and that he had turned it down, about which they were 'extremely pleased'. In the resolution accompanying the letter, they wrote that they had heard that Noodt

48. P. Noodt to his son, Nijmegen, 20 Mar. 1680, ARA Tets van Goudriaan, inv. nr. 110; 'Mij dunckt UEd. behoore sijn Execellentie Beverninge eens hier over te schrijven en hem bekend te maken met het beroep van Uytrecht, dat wel seer na sin waer, maer omdat ghij so nieuwelings daer gecomen waert ende de Provinsie veel lasten over UEd. angewent hadde en sijn Excellentie Haren Ued. promoteur geweest waer, die ghij ook niet geern wildet desobligeren so dat het mogte qualick genomen worden, ofte so een manier UEd. oordeelt het beste te wesen. En mij dunck UEd. hoorden met de Burgemeester Verbolt [of Nijmegen] ook te continueren de gemaeckte vrijntschap. Men weet somwijlen niet waer het kan te pas komen.'

49. Noodt to Braunius, Franeker, 18 Feb. 1681, UL Amsterdam, 16. Cf. 1.

50. Kernkamp ii: 58. Van Muijden got a rise to 800 guilders only in 1685.

51. Kernkamp ii: 72.

52. Kernkamp ii: 72.

was offered 1,700 guilders by Utrecht.[53] Did Noodt exaggerate, or should we say 'fama crescit eundo'? The States now raised his salary to 1,650 guilders. Together with the 150 guilders, which were granted to professors in 1672 to compensate them for the loss of immunity from taxation, Noodt now had 1,800 guilders a year. With this Noodt, at the age of 36, was among the best paid law professors in the Republic.[54]

But Utrecht kept returning. On 8 October 1683, hardly nine months after their last proposal, the town council decided to offer Noodt a professorship with a salary of 1,600 guilders per annum, the sum they had decided on before.[55] And, curiously enough, this time Noodt accepted the offer forthwith. On 13 October he told the States of Friesland, in person, that he had done so.[56] On 23 October his answer arrived in Utrecht.[57] And what is more puzzling still is that, nominally, the salary Utrecht was offering was much less than what he had in Franeker. Now the nominal salary in itself does not say very much. It was only part of a professor's income. In addition, he got examination fees and graduation fees, as well as payment for private lectures. We do not know exactly what all this might amount to, but it certainly could be a very substantial income.[58] And, as far as we

53. Extract, Res. Staten van Friesland, 23 Feb. 1783; ARA Tets van Goudriaan, inv. nr. 112.
54. Salaries ranged from 400 to 2,600 guilders (E. Otto in Utrecht, a very exceptional case) but the average was about 1,200 guilders.
55. Kernkamp ii: 76.
56. Boeles ii. 1, 1879: 281 f.
57. Kernkamp ii: 76.
58. Some indication can be taken from data concerning Utrecht. In 1675 the senate decided that the professors should receive 5 guilders for a tentamination, 20 guilders for an examination, 10 guilders for a private graduation, and 25 guilders for a public one (Kernkamp ii: 224). Assuming (a hypothetical case, but a moderate guess) that a law professor has every year 20 tentaminations and examinations, 5 private promotions, and 2 public ones, this would make 600 guilders a year. To this must be added the income from private lecturing. The annual fee students paid was 30 guilders or more. (Frijhoff, 1981: 62). Assuming, again, that the same professor has 20 students in his private lectures, this would add another 600 guilders, making a total of 1,200 guilders a year, to which fees for disputations should be added. Our guess is confirmed by data from the eighteenth century. F. A. van der Marck writes to the king of Prussia (UL Leiden, BPL 1160) that he earns 2,500 guilders, while at that time his official salary is 1,400 guilders. P. Bondam writes to M. Tydeman, Kampen, 15 Dec. 1772 (UL Utrecht, MS 1348) that he hesitates to take a chair in Utrecht: in Harderwijk his salary is 1,900 guilders, but there are years that he can make an additional 1,600 to 1,800 guilders from fees. I thank Mr C. J. H. Jansen for these data. These are very substantial incomes, considering the fact that in Utrecht in 1661 the gardener of the Hortus only received 150 guilders a year (Kernkamp i: 360), the riding-master and the

know, Utrecht must have had about two and a half times as many law students as Franeker.[59] Moreover, Utrecht still had some tax-immunities for professors, though not as many as Leiden.[60]

But even if, on the whole, Noodt's income may not have deteriorated on his change to Utrecht, it still seems to demand an explanation why he should accept a chair which he had refused only nine months before. No consultations and no bargaining with governors, this time. Apparently, not even his protector Willem van Haren could keep him. Moreover, he must have realized that by accepting a chair in Utrecht right at the beginning of the new academic year he would cause a lot of trouble for his faculty. But the only concession he was prepared to make was to stay in Franeker for the winter semester. In the senate meeting of 7 January 1684, he handed in his robe and some books he had on loan from the provincial library.[61] It is a collection very characteristic of Noodt's research interests: the Theodosian Code, the works of the humanists Eguinarius Baro and François Hotman, and those of the fathers of the Church Augustine and Ambrosius. Some days later he left Friesland—the good professor's country—for good.[62] On 14 January he enrolled as member of the Reformed Church in Utrecht.[63] Did he have another reason to leave? I think he did and we even know his name: Ulrik Huber.

Noodt had succeeded in Franeker to the chair of Huber. For Huber, it was no doubt a very great honour to be nominated senator

French teacher 100 guilders each (Kernkamp ii: 465). There are no fundamental studies about the proportions of income in the seventeenth century as yet, but the estimate of Frijhoff, 1981: 61, is that the average income of an unschooled workman was not far above 100 guilders a year.

59. According to Frijhoff, 1981: 389, in the period 1675–99, 289 students took a law degree in Franeker, as against 695 in Utrecht. This makes an average of 11.6 degrees a year for Franeker and 28 for Utrecht. Considering these numbers, the story that the student population of Utrecht dropped seriously, because it had no *privilegium fori* and tax immunities were abolished in 1657 (v. Haller, see Lindeboom, 1958: 66; Gerretzen, 1940: 18), stands in the need of qualification. On the revocation of tax immunities, see Kernkamp i: 319.
60. Wine-money was 24 guilders, robe-money 30 guilders. For immunities in Utrecht, see Kernkamp i: 170 f. The professors of Utrecht petitioned several times to get the same immunities as in Leiden, see Kernkamp ii: 55, 484 f., 579.
61. RA Leeuwarden, Franeker universiteit, inv. nr. 19, fol. 18.
62. Boeles ii. 1, 1879: 282.
63. GA Utrecht, lidmatenregister van de gereformeerde gemeente, inv. nr. 411: '71 De heer Gerardus Noot professor woonende bij 't heerensalens-steegje op attestatie van Franeker dato 14 Januari 1684.' The street mentioned seems to be what is now the Zadelstraat. I thank Dr J. E. A. L. Struick and Mrs Riphaagen of the municipal archives, Utrecht, for this reference.

in the Court of Friesland. With this, the grandson of a Swiss mercenary officer reached the top of Frisian society. In fact, becoming a senator in Friesland came near to an elevation to peerage. But Huber did not like the work, and after three years he gave up his chair in the court.[64] Because Leiden was offering him a chair (for the third time),[65] and Friesland wanted to keep him at any price, on 24 February 1682 they gave him an assignment—with the princely salary of 2,000 guilders—which was bound to cause much trouble. And indeed it did.

Huber was not reappointed to the law faculty. Formally, this could hardly be done, considering the fact that there was no vacancy, and no nomination was presented by the senate. And even if these formalities might have been provided for, there remained a social impediment. It would be a degradation for a senator of the Court of Friesland to become no more than an ordinary law professor in Franeker.[66] So Huber got a very special assignment. He was to settle down in Franeker and received all the qualifications of a professor, without being one. He could lecture—in fact, *privatim*—order disputations to be printed, do examinations (from 1684), sit in the senate, and cast a vote in nominations. As ex-senator—the title he was to carry in the future—in the senate he took precedence over all professors, and came directly after the rector.[67]

That this arrangement was asking for trouble became clear soon enough. Many students, only coming to Franeker to hear Huber—who lectured in his home—did not enrol at the university. This implied that they refused to submit to academic jurisdiction.[68] Huber not only permitted, but in fact invited and encouraged such conduct, although later he denied this emphatically. This became very clear in 1688, when one of his students proposed to defend the thesis that students had the choice between the jurisdictions of the Academy and the city's magistrate court. When in a senate meeting a fierce and unanimous protest against the thesis was voiced, Huber made an

64. Boeles ii. 1, 1879: 222; Veen, 1976: 3 f.
65. Cf. Veen, 1976: 3 n. 14.
66. Veen, in: Huber 1978: 12 ff. On the title-page of his *Auspicia domestica*, a collection of speeches on the occasion of his return to Franeker (Huber, 1682), he called the nomination in Franeker an 'otium', and said himself that a return from the judiciary to the academy had never occurred before (Huber, 1682: 4). Since the Middle Ages, the normal career of outstanding jurists had indeed been the other way round. Usually they left the university long before they were forty.
67. Boeles ii. 1, 1879: 222.
68. Boeles ii. 1, 1879: 223.

apology, but a week later a pamphlet defending the same thesis and bearing his own name was nailed to the doors of the Academy and the Exchange.[69] Huber had set up as a competitor to his own university. This might not only have had grave financial consequences, it involved fundamental legal issues concerning the status of universities. Incidentally, it is quite evident that the States of Friesland, who were very cross at Huber when the conflict broke out in the open,[70] had created the conditions for it with their own hands.

The conflict concerning academic jurisdiction which became a public issue in 1688 began, in fact, in 1683, exactly in the period between the second and the third offers made to Noodt from Utrecht. On 18 June of that year the senate—Noodt being present, Huber absent—expressed its anxiety about the considerable number of students that did not enrol and decided that from the beginning of the new academic year no student should be admitted to the private lectures of the professors unless the rector had confirmed his enrolment. When in the senate meeting of 21 June this decision was read—Huber again being absent—the senate decided to add a fine for professors who failed to comply. The decision was to be communicated to Huber.[71] After the rector had tried several times, but in vain, to discuss the matter with him, the senate decided that he should be admonished in a senate meeting and that the decision should be read to him. This was intended to happen on 5 November, but the outcome was such that on 7 November the senate decided to draw up a formal statement about what happened, to be inserted in the Acta (in view of possible legal steps). According to this statement[72] Huber was present at the senate meeting of 5 November in order to examine a student. After this was done the rector tried in a friendly way to discuss the matter with him, but again in vain. Huber replied that he had told his students to inscribe, but he did not want to deny admittance to his private lectures to those who failed to do so. When

69. Boeles i, 1878: 355 ff.; ii. 1, 1879: 223. Huber's attack on academic jurisdiction was not altogether new. His teacher Wissenbach had already defended the thesis that the *Constitutio Habita* of Frederick Barbarossa (1158)—the basis of the *forum privilegiatum* for academics—did not imply criminal cases, but only civil ones. The same view is defended in a disputation held under De Greve (another pupil of Wissenbach). The matter had already been a matter of debate for many years; see Van den Bergh, 1972: 21 f.

70. Boeles i, 1878: 357 n. 2. They even imposed a fine on him.

71. RA Leeuwarden, Franeker universiteit, inv. nr. 19, pp. 6–7.

72. RA Leeuwarden, Franeker universiteit, inv. nr. 19, pp. 15 f.; text printed as appendix in Van Eck, 1688: 116 f.

the secretary of the senate was about to read the decision of 18 June, Huber refused to listen and left the senate meeting before it was closed, saying, 'You must summon me before a higher competent judge. I will appoint you a good day.' The senate then wrote to the Deputy States of Friesland, who were emphatic in their reply of 5 December: all students must enrol and those who fail to do so must be denied admission to the lectures. They specifically ordered the senate to report on Huber's behaviour.[73] With this, apparently, the matter subsided for some years.

The members of the law faculty must indeed have felt Huber's competition—as well as its effect on their income—quite soon. There may be a hint at this in a letter from Noodt to Braunius, dating from 18 October 1682.[74] Noodt says there that the number of his students 'has by no means decreased'. It would not be easy to explain this expression in any other way. After all, it was written at the beginning of the academic year: 'About our Academy I can only say that we now have a considerable concourse of nice and decent students, in law as well as in theology, and that I have the luck not to be badly off as far as the number of listeners, in my public lessons as well as privately, is concerned; in any case my classes have decreased not at all.' On the appearance of it, there was not yet an open conflict then. We cannot conclude much from the fact that on 3 December 1682 Schelkens, Huber, and Noodt signed the confirmation of a legal opinion, written by some advocates in the Hague.[75] But even when Huber criticized a conjecture of Noodt in his *Digressiones justinianeae* of 1688 (the piece itself must have been written before September 1686), the tone still is courteous. Only a few years later did Huber openly resort to invective.[76] But the incident in 1683 was

73. Van Eck, 1688: 120–1.
74. As n. 26 on p. 44: 'Van onse Academie kan ick niets seggen, als dat wij tegenwoordigh in de selve eenen considerablen toeloop hebben van brave en fatsoenlijcke studenten, so wel in jure, als Theologia, en voorts, en dat ick het geluck hebbe van in het getall van auditores so publice als privatim niet misgedeelt te zijn; immers dat mijne collegien in genen dele vermindert zijn.'
75. Van den Berg iii, 1784: 373. This was, in fact, a faculty opinion, so we cannot conclude anything from it as regards the personal feelings between its members.
76. See *Digressiones justinianeae*, Franeker 1688: 551: 'Vir Clarissimus mutuisque amicitiae officiis mihi conjunctissimus Gerardus Noodt Jurisc. et Antecessor Ultrajectinus, ad hunc textum scripsit elegantissimum commentarium . . . Dicam simpliciter, quid mihi videatur, et rationem cur ita visum sit, addam. Lector quod ipsi videbitur eliget, si vacat; et simul ita existimet velim, nihil innocentius, quam ejusmodi permutationes opinionum inter amicos.' But compare *Praelectiones juris romani* iii, Franeker, 1690: 677: 'Ex quibus manifestum est, quam procul a via

telling enough and Noodt, a peace-loving man, will have preferred to avoid strife by taking the chair in Utrecht. He could have expected, moreover, to be appointed rector in Franeker within the next few years, and this would have put him in a central position in the quarrel with Huber. To his successor, Van Eck, befell the unpleasant task of writing for the senate a public refutation of Huber's thesis concerning academic jurisdiction.[77] Huber had a rather violent character and was prone to conflict. The fact that Huber and Noodt, moreover, had totally different attitudes, in their didactic as well as scientific and religious orientations, makes it very likely that there was not much love lost between the two men.

Huber had deeply humiliated Taco van Glins (Noodt's promoter) by demanding that he be submitted to an examination by Huber, before being appointed. No wonder the two men were at odds till death.[78] Huber had already established himself as a polemicist by his debate with Feltman (1675).[79] Later, he was to have violent controversies with Van Eck as well as with Perizonius, who both were Noodt's friends. As early as 1667 he succinctly expressed his idea of law teaching: start with the Institutes and subsequently teach the Pandects, without much humanistic learning.[80] There also was a fundamental difference of scientific orientation between Noodt and Huber in the field in which Huber, one of the founders of modern public law, was a specialist. All his life Noodt taught Roman public (or rather constitutional) law, a subject which Huber regarded as useless for law teaching, because Roman public law had gone down with the Roman state.[81]

In 1684, only months after Noodt had left Franeker for good, Huber made a barely concealed attack on him in a dialogue 'De ratione iuris docendi et discendi'.[82] Böckelmann, Crusius, and

rationis et Themidos absint, qui ut probent . . .'. For humanistic jurists it was a very heavy insult to say that they had departed from the way of reason as well as of Themis. Noodt later especially took exception at the 'irata Themide' in Bijnkershoek's criticism, see below p. 216. For the criticism of Noodt in Huber's posthumously edited *Eunomia romana* (1700) see below, n. 89.

77. Boeles i, 1878: 356; van den Bergh, 1986*b*: 40.
78. Boeles ii. 1, 1879: 241 ff.
79. Veen, 1976: 199 f.; Feenstra, 1982*b*: 107.
80. Boeles ii. 1, 1879: 222 n. 1.
81. Huber, 1978: 38–9.
82. Perizonius to Rijcke, Franeker, 19 Sept. 1684, UL Leiden, BPL 337; cited in Meyer, 1971: 74: 'Huber noster scripsit dialogum inter ipsum et Bokelmannum ac Crusium, in quo per latus Crusii petit Notium, et dum in eum incurrit, plus satis

Huber figure in it as interlocutors but, as Perizonius says and as is clear enough from internal evidence,[83] it was Noodt who was attacked in the guise of Crusius. The immediate cause for Huber's attack was Noodt's inaugural address in Utrecht, given in February 1684, in which he had pointed to the use of compendia as the main cause of the decline of legal studies and defended the place of humanistic philology in the law curriculum. Böckelmann, who had introduced the *methodus compendiaria* into the Republic, was the appropriate protagonist for the compendium. Crusius was a fair enough representative of the elegant tradition, and, moreover, Noodt had praised him in Book I of the *Probabilia*. After criticizing the ideas which Noodt had defended in his lecture, Huber turns against his scientific work in general, and with this—as Perizonius surmised—against all who concentrate on criticism and humanistic philology.[84] This thinly disguised attack on Noodt, shortly after he had left Franeker, confirms our suspicion that Huber was the reason for Noodt's departure to Utrecht. It may even reinforce the suspicion that in 1675 Huber may have prevented Noodt from being a candidate for the succession of Danckelmann.

Evidently, Huber's programme was at odds with the *methodus noodtiana*, which will be discussed later. Huber did not seem to reject Cartesianism out of hand—in fact, he published a work by Descartes for teaching purposes, without authorization[85]—but he strongly believed that Cartesian method was not applicable in law or theology.[86] Noodt, on the other hand, was more open to the new philosophy. Finally, Huber was a religious man with strong orthodox convictions. In October 1686 he raised hell against a student of Rœll,[87] for defending a thesis which allegedly gave reason

iniquum se probat omnibus qui Crisin aliquando exercent, et humaniora profitentur. Titulus est "de ratione iuris docendi et discendi" '. The dialogue was published in 1684, see Veen, in Huber, 1978: 7 n. 43. It was re-edited, with slight changes in title and text, as an appendix to the edns. of the *Digressiones justinianeae* of 1688 and 1696. Feenstra, 1985*a*: 142, seems to assume that Crusius actually has criticized the *methodus compendiaria*, but he gives no evidence. From Perizonius' letter it is clear that the words ascribed to Crusius are in fact Noodt's. There are several literal citations from Noodt's address as well as from his *Probabilia* in the dialogue.

83. See below, Ch. 4, at nn. 64 f.
84. See n. 82.
85. Thijssen-Schoute, 1954: 529 f.
86. Veen, 1976: 183.
87. H. A. Roell (1653–1718), see *NNBW* x: 821 f.

too much authority over Scripture. Huber behaved in such a way that the rector had to order him to sit down.[88] Noodt, on the other hand, had already made it clear in his inaugural address in Franeker that—as far as law was concerned—he would put reason above mere authority. And certainly he did not like polemics or religious zeal.

After all this, it seems quite explicable why in January 1684 Noodt left Franeker. In fact, many years later he still spoke in a very unfriendly way of Huber in a letter to Van Eck. The letter, dating from 1693, concerned a series of disputations[89] defended by students of Huber (and written by him), in which opinions of Noodt were attacked:

> Also, I thank you for sending me the disputes *pro eunomia juris*, concerning those passages which Mr Huber directs against some of my speculations. I have read them, but I think they are very cold and not worth refuting. Because I believe that Mr Huber does not write for intelligent people, nor to promote studies, but only to carp in the presence of youngsters, that know nothing about the matter. In fact, I find that he cites and refutes authors without having read their work. Which appears from the fact that he cites and refutes words that are not there. Also, I find that sometimes, after many contradictions, he makes my opinion his own.[90]

Inciting youngsters who knew nothing about the matter, that was exactly what Huber was accused of having done in the affair of academic jurisdiction.

If we may be fairly certain what the reasons were for Noodt's departure from Franeker, we do not know everything that happened between him and Huber between Huber's assignment (February 1682) and Noodt's departure (January 1684). Is it overinterpreting to read a hint at Huber as early as Noodt's account of his inauguration,

88. Boeles ii. 1, 1879: 224; Veen, 1976: 161 f., 166 f.
89. Later ed. by Ulrik's son Zacharias, *Eunomia romana*, Franeker 1700. On this, see below, Ch. 4, at n. 77.
90. Noodt to Van Eck, Leiden, 3 Oct. 1693, UL Utrecht, MS 1000: 'Oock ben ick UEd. danckbaer voor de communicatie die UEd. mij heeft believen te geven van de bewuste disputen pro eunomia juris, raeckende die passagien welcke de Heer Huber heeft tegens eenige mijner speculatien; welcke ick mede gelesen, doch seer kout en niet refuterens waerdigh gevonden hebbe; immers, bij verstandige luijden, waer voor mijns oordeels de Heer Huber niet en schrijft, gelijck mede niet om de studien te verbeteren, maer alleen om wat te carperen bij jonge luijden die daer geene kennisse van hebben: gelijck ick dan oock bevinde, dat hij allegeert auteuren, ende die refuteert, sonder dat hij se gelesen heeft. Blijckende daer uit, dat hij uit haer citeert en wederleijt woorden die er niet in staen, oock bevinde somtijts, dat hij, na veel tegenspreecken, eindelijck mijne sentimenten de sijne mæckt.'

where he writes that 'most justices from the court at Leeuwarden'—not all—had invited him and offered their friendship and help?[91] We can only guess. However, if Noodt's students were not decreasing by October 1682, this is likely to have been the case a year later. Apart from causing a decrease in inscription fees, Huber directly competed with the law professors for the fees of examinations, disputations, graduations, and private lectures, which, as we have seen, formed a substantial part of their income. So, after all, Noodt may also have had financial reasons for taking the chair in Utrecht. In all fairness it must be added that Huber, for his part, might also have had financial grievances against Noodt. In 1680 the States kept Noodt in Friesland by discharging him of the duty to repay to Huber the forced loan of 1,200 guilders which Huber had paid to the States in 1672. Naturally, the States should have indemnified Huber for this, or repaid the loan. But there is no evidence that they actually did so, and they certainly will not have been too eager to do it after Huber had caused so much trouble.

The wording of Noodt's commission in Utrecht is rather unusual. Whereas before very traditional terms had been used (*professor Institutionum*, *Pandectarum*, *Codicis*) and later 'ius civile' was to become the standard term,[92] Noodt was appointed *professor juris legumque Romanorum* (professor of law and the Roman laws). This is a formula without precedent, which was used never again. Perhaps Noodt himself proposed it. If this is true, it may be taken as a sign of his growing professional and historical consciousness. 'Law' and 'the Roman laws' are no longer identical, as they had been in universities from the Middle Ages.

It is easy to imagine how pleased Utrecht was with the acquisition of the famous professor. One of the burgomasters told Græevius in passing that it would be appreciated if the inauguration took place in the great auditorium (now the aula). The senate was quite willing to concur, but then a new place for the music (balcony) should be made first, because the old one had collapsed recently.[93] On 12 February 1684 Noodt recited in the great auditorium his inaugural address concerning the causes of the corruption of legal science.[94] Although

91. Noodt to his father (as n. 58): '. . . Dat mij oock de meeste Raetsheren van Leeuwarden seer hebben uijtgenodigt, en veel vrijntschap en goede officien en dijensten van selfs ængepræsenteert.'
92. See Van den Bergh, 1986*a*: 12.
93. Kernkamp ii: 76.
94. Ahsmann–Feenstra, 1984: nr. 428.

the ceremony was not quite as splendid as the one in Franeker four years before, it still seems impressive enough:

Preceded by two beadles, followed by two porters he goes from his house to the town hall; from there, he is conducted to the senate hall by the members of the city council Sijpesteijn and Nijpoort, and from there to the lectern by the same. After the speech, they conduct him back to the senate hall, where his colleages congratulate him, and then he is guided home.[95]

That was at a time when professors were still regarded as men of some importance![96]

We do know virtually nothing about Noodt's activities during the five semesters he taught in Utrecht (February 1684 to July 1686). We also have no letters from this period. No doubt the most important fact of it was his marriage, to which we will come presently. Two students followed Noodt from Franeker and lived with him in Utrecht.[97] Only nine times did he confer a degree. For one of these cases we can ascertain that the student in question followed Noodt from Franeker to Utrecht,[98] and for another one this is probable.[99] Apparently, the other law professors kept most of the degree ceremonies to themselves, if only for the fees involved.[1]

The law faculty of Utrecht was rather insignificant at that time. When the governors of Leiden had their eye on Johannes Vœt, and sent their secretary Pieter Burgersdijk to Utrecht to take soundings, he heard that the law faculty seemed to lean on Vœt alone.[2] Cyprianus Regneri ab Oosterga,[3] whose lectures Noodt heard fifteen

95. Kernkamp ii: 76.

96. Lange, 1980: 279 f.; Dionisotti, 1971: 194.

97. In the register of members of the reformed church (GA Utrecht, inv. nr. 411) are inscribed immediately after Noodt, and as domiciled on the same address, two people from Franeker: Johan de Witt, student (nr. 72, 5 March), and Sydske Wijngaerden, j[uris] d[octor] (?) (nr. 73, 4 March). Neither one of them figures in AS and AP Franeker or Utrecht.

98. On 5 July 1684 Matthias Janssonius from Leeuwarden was graduated by Noodt, with a thesis on L.F. 2. 53. In April 1680 he had enrolled at Franeker, see AS Franeker, nr. 7808. The subject, by the way, belonged to a field that Noodt never studied thoroughly. Therefore, it seems beyond doubt that Janssonius wrote the thesis himself.

99. On 21 April 1684 Cornelis Wouters from Emden, East Friesland, was graduated by Noodt. His first inscription in AS Utrecht is in the same year, but we have no inscription in AS Franeker.

1. According to AP Utrecht there were 65 law promotions during the 30 months that Noodt stayed in Utrecht. They were divided as follows: Cyprianus, 22; van de Poll, 18; van Muijden 16; Noodt 9.

2. Molhuysen iii: 350.

3. See n. 19 on p. 24. And see De Wal, 1825: 194 f. His criticisms of Roman Law were

years before, though not a first-rate scholar and rather disputatious,[4] no doubt had some quality. As a young scholar in Leiden he had entered polemics with two local professors, Mæstertius[5] and Salmasius.[6] He was a Cartesian, and took an active part in the battles with Vœtians.[7] He showed a critical–rational attitude towards the authority of traditional Roman law—more or less in the same vein as Noodt did later—in a study on the injustice of some Roman laws.[8] So there must have been some congeniality of mind between Regneri ab Oosterga and Noodt, though they were different in character. But when Noodt came to Utrecht, Regneri ab Oosterga was an old man and had not published anything new for fifteen years or so.[9]

Lucas van de Poll, whose lectures Noodt also attended, had published nothing but some occasional poems and a commemorative speech on the Union of Utrecht since then. During his life, he was to publish but one scholarly work.[10] Johan van Muyden, former vice-principal of the Hieronymus-school, and professor of the Institutes since 1680, perhaps only got the professorship as a consolation prize because he was not considered for the office of principal, vacated in the same year.[11] In 1684 he had not yet published anything, and during his lifetime he brought out no more than two compendia of the sort that Noodt detested.[12] The only congenial spirit and friend Noodt found in Utrecht was the classicist and historian J. G. Grævius, who was eighteen years his senior. The letters Noodt exchanged with him, after Noodt's departure to Leiden, bear witness

very controversial, see Walch, in Eckhard and Walch, 1802: 284. He was also criticized for his Cartesianism. Regneri ab Oosterga's teaching did not appeal to Huber, see Veen, in Huber, 1978: 3: '. . . le Professeur est un homme peu sçavant et peu accomodé à enseigner un homme qui se veut avancer de bons escients'.

4. See Kernkamp, 1936: 242.
5. On him, Feenstra, 1982*a*: 297 ff.
6. 1588–1633, *NNBW* v: 649. He wrote a controversial treatise *de usuris* (1638) and repeated his thesis in *de modo usurarum* (1639).
7. Especially concerning the estate of the chapters of Utrecht, which had come into the hands of powerful families, and of which Vœt urged in vain that it should be restored to its former ecclesiastical use; cf. McGahagan, 1976: 175.
8. Regneri ab Oosterga, 1640.
9. The last part to appear of his *Censura Belgica* was published in 1669.
10. Van de Poll, 1700.
11. In August 1680 the principal Ratingen had died, see Kernkamp ii: 58.
12. *Compendiosa Institutionum Justinianaeorum tractatio*, 2nd imp. Utrecht: Halma, 1694; 3rd imp. Utrecht: Halma, 1737; *Compendiosa Pandectarum tractatio*. Utrecht: Halma, 1695; 2nd imp. Utrecht: Charlois, 1718. For Noodt's opinion on compendia, see *Opera* i: 620, 621, 629. On p. 621: '. . . quod compendium vocatur, sapientiae damnum est'. And see below, p. 161 ff.

to that friendship.[13] Among other things, we can learn from them that the Grævius family was a guest of the Noodts in Leiden. It was also through Grævius that someone from Deventer asked Noodt's advice on a case of marriage prohibitions.[14]

Noodt may have introduced as a new element in Utrecht the teaching of natural law (possibly in private lectures on Grotius).[15] In the meantime, Franeker and Utrecht were not the only universities that made offers to Noodt. Apart from the proposal from Duisburg from 1677, which has already been mentioned,[16] in 1680 there was a proposal from Heidelberg. It was conveyed to Noodt by his nephew Peter Noodt, who was burgomaster there. As an explanation why he could not accept the offer Noodt gave a lengthy survey of all the honours and favours he had received in Friesland.[17] The young

13. Grævius to Noodt, Utrecht, 25 Sept. 1686, 10 Nov. 1686, 18 Oct. 1687, ARA Tets van Goudriaan, inv. nr. 114; Noodt to Grævius, Leiden, 21 Nov. 1686, KB Kopenhagen.
14. Grævius to Noodt, Utrecht, 10 Nov. 1686, ARA Tets van Goudriaan, inv. nr. 114. On this see below, p. 285.
15. So Kernkamp, 1936: 276. Noodt pleaded for the introduction of natural law into the law curriculum in his inaugural address in Franeker, but we only have lecture notes of his *collegium Grotianum* in Leiden.
16. See above, p. 32.
17. G. Noodt to P. Noodt, 1 May 1680, ARA Tets van Goudriaan, inv. nr. 111. His main reason for refusing is that he was treated very generously by the States of Friesland (in reply to the first proposal from Utrecht) only a few weeks before, and therefore could not decently leave (unless the conditions were considerably better!): '. . . dat ick tot Franeker ongeveer voor een jaer eerst beroepen, en zedert omtrent de acht maenden maer daer geweest ben, en effectieve dijenst gedaen hebbe; dat ick voorst het geluck gehad hebbe, dat sijne Hoogheijt de Heere Stadhouder van Frijsland mijne introductie in persoon heeft bijgewoont, dat de Heren Staeten mij daerenboven veel eere gedaen, en in de voorleden maert, ten tijden als ick hijer omtrent 6 maenden geweest was, niet te min eene somma van 1150 guldens, zijnde een geheel jaer tractament, hebben t' huys gesonden behalven eene somma van 200 guldens voor de onkosten, die ick tot het transport van mijne meublen gedaen hadde; en als mij weinig dagen daer na door drije gecommitteerde Heren van Utregt in der selver Universiteit een beroep tot de professie in de rechten gepraesenteert wierde op aensijenlijcke en avantagieuse conditien, so hebben haer Ed. Mo. mij seer ernstig versogt, ten eijnde ick het selve beroep op Utrecht voor dese reijse soude willen excuseren. Twelck als ick gedaen hadde, en vervolgens van haer Ed. Mo. versogt wierde een voorslagh te doen, waer bij ick de avantages van de Universiteit tot Utregt hijer in Frijsland soude menen te bekomen, en daer tegens seijde, dat ick aen de genereusiteit van de Heren Staten van Frijsland egenen regul wilde setten, maer dat ick soude afwagten, t'gene haer Ed. Mo. mij daer voor souden willen accorderen, en dat ick daer mede wilde gecontenteert zijn, so ben ick dijenthalven van wegens de Heren Staten seer sollemnelijck bedanckt geworden, en hebben haer Ed. Mo. mij daer neffens van selfs de eere gedaen van mijn tractament des jaers te vermeerderen ter somma van 400 guldens, waer mede ick in plaetse van elf hondert vijftigh guldens, die ick te

professor had already established a reputation with his first publications. We heard Grævius' judgment earlier: he was the only law professor who was not an ignoramus in letters.

From Utrecht to Leiden

But neither could Utrecht keep Noodt for long. He did attend the commemoration of the fiftieth anniversary of Utrecht university in March 1686,[18] but a few months later he was gone. That a man of his qualities eventually would end his career in Leiden was to be expected. And because he had an excellent supporter on the board of governors there, as we already know, the transfer was only a matter of time. Even so, when plans were made to win him over for Leiden, the governors proceeded very carefully.

On 8 February 1686 the governors and burgomasters of Leiden discussed the state of the law faculty and took the decision to appoint a fourth professor, in order to restore the faculty, once one of the most important, 'to its former splendour and reputation'.[19] The economic crisis ensuing from the French–Dutch war had affected Leiden no less than Nijmegen, Franeker, and Utrecht. Whereas before 1675 the faculty regularly had four professors and a lecturer, between 1675 and 1685 there were only three (without a lecturer from 1679), and occasionally two. With the nomination of Noodt in 1686 the number of four was reached again.

As far as quality was concerned, the third quarter of the seventeenth century was not a golden age for Leiden. Daniel Colonius (professor, 1648–72) does not seem to have published any legal work

voren gehad hebbe, voortaen des jaers sal hebben eene somma van sesteijnde half hondert guldens. Invoegen ick UED. derve in bedencken geven, of ick wel redenen hebbe om te changeren, ten waere dat mij conditien, die merckelijck beter waeren, op een seer fatsoenlijcke en eerlijcke maniere mogte gepraesenteert worden. Bovendien dat ick mene, dat ick met voorbehoud van mijn reputatie, die ick bij alle eerlijcke luijden geern soude houden, de Universiteijt van Frijsland so haest niet soude behoren te verlaten. Insonderheijt gelettet, dat ick voor omtrent ses weecken deselve hebbe toegeseijd, dat ick het beroep op Utregt, 't geen mij doenmaels gedefereert wierde, voor dese reijse soude declineren, en dat ten aansijen van de voorsz. provintie soude even veel zijn, of ick des onaengesijen naer Utregt, of naer Heijdelbergh quame te vertrecken.' Peter Noodt did a private sounding at the request of rector Fabricius of Heidelberg university. This Peter Noodt is a son of Gerard's father's half-brother, Gerard, who was born in Nijmegen in 1594 and married in Hamburg in 1617 to Salome Neijmans (Register; see Appendix 1). The Noodts really were a cosmopolitan family.

18. Kernkamp, 1936: 277.

19. Molhuysen iv: 42.

at all,[20] A. Beeckerts van Thienen (1654–69) only some occasional pieces,[21] S. Marchant (1658–70) nothing,[22] A. Rusius (1658–78) no more than his inaugural lecture.[23] G. C. Crusius (1669–76) has some merit for Roman law studies,[24] but mainly published didactic works,[25] and J. F. Böckelmann (1671–80)[26] likewise owes his reputation less to his scholarly work than to his compendium, which was still in use in law teaching at the beginning of the nineteenth century.[27] Only Antonius Matthæus III (1672–1710) and Johannes Vœt (1680–1713) have won enduring fame. Together with Noodt they indeed restored Leiden's name as one of the best law faculties on the continent.[28]

Though, once again, the unanimous choice was Noodt, they decided first to sound him out privately. Governor Van Beverningk, the experienced diplomat, took charge of this[29] and not without success, of course. He knew Noodt from the days of the peace-conference in Nijmegen, some ten years before. That the private approach remained a secret is beyond doubt. We have no trace of it from any other source. In the meantime Noodt will also have been busy preparing for his marriage, which took place on 22 April 1686 in the Hague. The official offer was made in the first days of July. On 2 July(?)[30] Noodt wrote to Van Eck:

Furthermore I cannot refrain from adding that yesterday I had the honour of being visited in the house of my mother-in-law[31] by Mr Van Beverninck,

20. Ahsmann–Feenstra, 1984: 81 f.
21. Ahsmann–Feenstra, 1984: 51 f.
22. Ahsmann–Feenstra, 1984: 159.
23. Ahsmann–Feenstra, 1984: nr. 553.
24. According to Lenel, 1927: 64 n. 6, he was the first to reconstruct correctly the edictal rubric 'de pactis et conventionibus'. See below, p. 257.
25. Ahsmann–Feenstra, 1984: 83 f.
26. Ahsmann–Feenstra, 1984: 55 f.
27. Feenstra and Waal, 1975: 36, with n. 151.
28. Feenstra and Waal, 1975: 35, say that Vœt dominated the law faculty during the last decades of the 17th century. I think this demands some qualification. Vœt certainly was the more popular teacher and a matchless compiler, but as scholars Noodt and Matthaeus III were his superiors by far. See the judgment by Kotzé, as cited by Roberts, 1933: 10. In the eighteenth century, economic conditions once more forced a reduction in the number of professors. Matthaeus III, who died in 1710, was not replaced, and for many years there were only three professors in the faculty.
29. Molhuysen iv: 42.
30. Noodt to Van Eck, Utrecht, July 1686, KB 135 D 19 zz, nr. 4. Noodt dated the letter 'desen Juli 1686 zijnde vrijdagavond met veel haest'. If he still used the Julian calendar, this might have been 2 July, if the Gregorian, 5 July.
31. The house stood on the eastside of the Fluwelen Burgwal. It was sold in 1722, see GA The Hague, Transportregister 1721–1730, nr. 376.

together with Mr Van Vesanevelt, burgomaster of Leiden, and Mr Burgersdijck as secretary of the governors of the university of the same town, and that in the name of the governors they offered me the chair of private and public civil law, on such honourable conditions that I found it appropriate to inform the gentlemen of Utrecht in the first place. For that purpose I have come here [that is, in Utrecht] today. I do not believe my message will please them very much, but the condition of my family and my affairs will demand that I do not allow myself to be kept here. In fact I have decided to tell this to the illustrious gentlemen at once, and at the same time, that the matter is open no longer, and that I have committed myself already.[32]

Evidently Noodt had no hesitation in accepting the nomination—which, in fact, he may have coveted for many years already—and the formal appointment was decided on 13 July. For the charge of private law he got 1,400 guilders, for public law 400,[33] together 1,800, that is, exactly what he had in Franeker three years before. Leiden did not pay an excessive sum to get its coryphaeus, though actually he was one of the best-paid professors. In his inaugural address in Utrecht Noodt had mentioned shrewdly how two nations (Friesland and Utrecht) had contended over him.[34] But naturally Holland, the most powerful nation of all, was to get away with the prize in the end.

In his letter of 13 August 1686,[35] J. Pesters from The Hague agreed with Van Eck that the academy of Leiden would be greatly adorned

32. As n. 30: '. . . Vorders kan ick mij niet wel dispenseren hier bij te voegen, dat ick gisteren hebbe de eere gehad, dat de Heer Beverninck met ende beneffens de Heer van Vesanevelt Burgem[eeste]r der stad Leiden en de Heer Burgersdijck als secretarius van de Heren Curatoren van de Universiteit der voorsz. stad mij aen het huis van mijn schoonmoeder hebben gegeven de visite en daer bij in name van welgemelte Heren Curatoren hebben geoffereert de professio juris civilis privati et publici op sodanen honorablen wijse, dat ick hebbe redenen gevonden omme de Heren van de regeringe der stadt Utrecht daer van kennisse te geven ten aller eersten, en ben ten dien einde op heden bereits alhier gearriveert. Ick gelove niet, dat mijn bootschap hier seer aengenaem wesen sal; maer de gelegentheit van mijn huis en van mijne affaires sal het vereischen, dat ick mij hier niet late ophouden; gelijck ick dan oock ben te rade geworden sulx aen haer Edele Grootachtb. aenstonts te verklaren, en met enen dat de saeck niet meer in zijn geheel is, en dat ick mij bereits geengageert hebbe.'

33. Molhuysen iv: 42. The formal letter of appointment is dated 31 Aug. 1686. Copy in UL Leiden, Arch. Sen. en Fac. I, 297; Documenta senatus 12, letter nr. 83.

34. *Opera* i: 616.

35. J. Pesters to Van Eck, The Hague, 13 Aug. 1686, UL Utrecht, MS 1000: 'Scholam Leydensem adventu Cl. Nootii maxime ornatu iri bene existimas . . . Qui causas indagare volunt, quae Cl. Notum hoc tempore ad suspiciendam illam provinciam quam oblatam saepius recusavit, impulerint, non aliam sibi fingere valent, quam suae mulieris ambitione, quae quanta possit, id tibi et doctorum auctoritate et experientia compertum esse puto.'

by the coming of Noodt. He also suggested that Noodt was asked by Leiden several times, but had turned down earlier offers. This is most unlikely, however. We know Noodt's name circulated in Leiden in September 1679 for the succession of Coeman,[36] and no doubt the same will have been the case in October 1681, after the death of Böckelmann, although then Huber was asked first. That Noodt himself was very interested in the vacancy left by Böckelmann appears from his letter to Braunius of 6 November 1681, in which he wrote: 'If you hear something from Leiden, or by a side wind, it would please me to be informed, because I do not hear much, in fact only general and loose speculations, without any detail. I do not believe much will be done before the return of Mr Van Beuningen,[37] that is, before his Excellency is sounded out.'[38] Noodt probably had hopes of being appointed himself, because he wrote rather sourly about the man who finally got the nomination: 'In Leiden at last someone named Vitri or Vitriarius from Geneva is appointed as law professor. But, as I hear, he is known to nobody. Time will show what miracles he will do.'[39] Neither in 1679 nor in 1681 is there a trace of a formal proposal to Noodt in our sources, so there will have been none. Pesters may have heard and misinterpreted something about the three proposals from Utrecht. And his contention that the ambition of Noodt's wife was behind his acceptance of the chair in Leiden may be summarily dismissed as empty gossip. Judging from what we know, it seems likely that Noodt had had his eye on Leiden for quite some time.

On 16 September 1686,[40] Noodt pronounced his inaugural address in Leiden. Neither about the ceremony, nor about the contents of the speech, do we have any information. When Noodt's son-in-law wrote his obituary,[41] he did not know the subject of this address, nor

36. See above, p. 34.
37. Koenraad van Beuningen (1622–93), *NNBW* vii: 118 ff.
38. Noodt to Braunius, Franeker, 6 Nov. 1681, UL Leiden, BPL 246: 'Indijen UEd. ijets hoort van Leijden, of van ter zijden konde horen, 't selve soude mij aengenaem zijn te verstaen; want ick hore daer van niet veel, immers niet, als generale en losse discoursen, sonder circumstantien. Ick gelove niet wel, datter veel sal gedaen worden voor de te rugge komst van de Heer van Beuningen, immers niet voor dat sijn Excell. dijen aengaende sal gesondeert zijn.'
39. Noodt to Braunius, Franeker, 18 Oct. 1682 (as n. 78): 'Tot Leiden is eijndelijck eenen Vitri, of Vitriarius van Geneve beroepen tot professor juris; maer die is, als ick hore, bij niemand bekend. Wat die voor miraculen doen sal, sal de tijd leren.'
40. Molhuysen iv: 40. Van den Ende did not have the date; Barbeyrac supplemented it from an announcement in the *Journal littéraire*, 17: 374.
41. ARA Tets van Goudriaan, inv. nr. 119.

was Barbeyrac able to trace it, in spite of all his efforts.[42] Yet there must have been some (written?) copies of the speech, because Grævius read it, and in a letter of 25 September eagerly asked Noodt, when it would appear in print: 'When will your speech appear? Or will we never see it? Please do not, I beseech you, deny yourself the praise and applause with which it is received by everybody, and us the pleasure that overwhelmed us when we read it.'[43] Noodt's reply, modest as usual, sounds like a cliché: 'You will not take ill that I did not publish my speech, which in fact was asked of me often by many, when you realize that a speech loses much of its charm when the diction fails. Furthermore, I have always disapproved of the opinion of those who think that each and every thing should be published.'[44] One wonders what the real reason was for leaving the speech unpublished. Remarkably enough, we do not even have the faintest hint at its subject. As we saw, the inaugural address in Franeker was not published immediately either, but it appeared in the *Opera omnia* in 1713. The Leiden speech did not. One can only guess why.

Five years after Noodt's inauguration in Leiden his portrait and that of his wife were painted by Willem van Mieris.[45] It was engraved by I. Tangena.[46] The portrait and the engraving show Noodt at his best: a friendly man without affectation, with a calm, open face and the shadow of a smile. Among the people he found in Leiden was his fellow-citizen from Nijmegen, Anton Schulting,[47] who in 1683 had taken his degree under Vœt and enrolled as advocate at the Court of Holland in the Hague,[48] but continued to live in Leiden as private

42. Barbeyrac, *Vita*, fol. 4v: 'At vero quoniam ipsius Orationis argumentum fuerit, ne nunc quidem mihi compertum est; quum illa non, ut moris est, typis descripta fuerit, nec ullum eius exemplum inter schedas defuncti repertum sit; frustra quoque quaeritur, qui haberet memoriam, aut alicunde audivisset, qua de re placuerit Nostro disserere in tanta celebritate.'
43. Grævius to Noodt, Utrecht, 25 Sept. 1686, ARA Tets van Goudriaan, inv. nr. 114: 'Oratio tua quando prodibit? Nunquamne visuri eam sumus? Noli quaeso te laude et applausu, quo excipietur ab omnibus, nos voluptate, qua perfunderemur illam legentes, defraudare'.
44. Noodt to Grævius, Leiden, 21 Nov. 1686, KB Kopenhagen: 'Quod orationem meam non publicavi, licet, ut id facerem a multis et saepe rogatus sim, non feres aegre, si cogitabis orationem multum gratiae amittere, cui actio deest; praeterea improbavi semper eorum rationem, qui quidvis edendum putant.'
45. Private collection. A photo in *Numaga* 2 (1955) 122 and 32 (1985) 75.
46. Personal collection. Noodt writes on 26 Mar. 1689 to Van Eck (UL Utrecht, MS 1000) to thank him for the verse he wrote on the portrait and promises to send a copy soon. There is no verse under the portrait.
47. *NNBW* i: 1462–4.
48. ARA Hof van Holland, inv. nr. 5943. Admitted 19 Oct. 1683.

scholar and tutor. He felt very attracted to Noodt, intellectually as well as personally, and was greatly influenced by him. Schulting, who had lost his father—Noodt's teacher in Nijmegen—in early youth, is said to have called Noodt his second father,[49] although Noodt was only twelve years his senior.

In Leiden, whose aula he called the *atrium libertatis batavae*,[50] Noodt studied and taught for nearly forty years. While publishing nothing during the years in Franeker and Utrecht, apart from the inaugural address in Utrecht, he brought out a series of works in the 1690s, among which are his best: *Probabilia* in four books, together with two books about jurisdiction and *imperium* and one on the *lex Aquilia* (1691, 1693); three books on interest and usury (1698); a discourse on the power of the sovereign (1699); and advice concerning the marriage of a mother's brother's widow (1699).[51]

3. Marriage and life in Leiden 1686–1725

Marriage

No doubt the most important change in Noodt's life during his stay in Utrecht was his marriage. On Monday, 22 April 1686 he married in The Hague[52]—at the rather advanced age of 38—Sara Maria van der Marck van Leur, then 27 years old.[53] Shortly before, on 5 April, bride and bridegroom appeared before Johannes Kervel, notary public in The Hague, together with Maria Pots, widow of Thomas van der Marck van Leur and mother of the bride, to sign the marriage-settlement.[54] In this they provided what was usual when the bride was of gentle birth and brought family property with her.

All community of property is ruled out. Inherited goods stay on the side where they come from. When one of the parties dies, leaving children behind, the inheritance devolves on the children, and the

49. *NNBW* i: 1463.
50. Address on freedom of religion (1706), *Opera* i: 635: '. . . ut fas sit Jurisconsulto, in atrio libertatis Batavae, agere causam generis humani . . .'.
51. Ahsmann–Feenstra, 1984: 176 ff., nrs. 423, 424, 431, 432, 436. On these works see below, Ch. 3.
52. The marriage was in the Scheveningse kerk. The notice of marriage was on 7 Apr. 1686, GA The Hague, DTB.
53. Born in The Hague, baptized 24 Nov. 1658 in the Grote kerk, GA The Hague DTB; died in Leiden.
54. ARA Tets van Goudriaan, inv. nr. 113.

other party gets nothing. For the upkeep of the household both parties bring in the income from their goods, and Noodt the income from his professorship besides. In case of divorce, the bride has the right to decide, after a proper period of deliberation, whether she will participate in gain and loss, or take back the goods she brought in. The bridegroom declares that, if he dies before her, she will have a *douaire* of 8,000 Carolus guilders. The bride wills him 4,000 guilders should she die first.

We do not know where and when Gerard and Sara met each other. J. Pesters from The Hague, whom we met before, has nothing to report but common gossip. On 2 April 1686 he wrote to Van Eck[55] that Noodt was preparing his marriage; rumour had it that he wanted the daughter of the lord of Leur, but that her mother, a widow, desired our professor.

The Van der Marck family presumably descended from a bastard of the well-known Lumey, Count Van der Marck.[56] The allodial high seigniory[57] of Leur near Nijmegen, in the country of Maas and Waal, which—though enclosed now by three motorways—still looks much the same as it must have done long ago, was bought by Thomas van der Marck,[58] canon of St John's in Utrecht[59] and later burgomaster of Schoonhoven, Sara Maria's father, on 29 March 1650.

It seems remarkable that this regent from Holland, who had no relations in Guelders, bought a seigniory there. Perhaps the main reason for the investment was that it allowed him to add 'Lord of Leur' to his name. During the period his family possessed Leur (1650–1748) they very much neglected it and seem hardly ever to have visited it.[60] Thomas van Leur died in Schoonhoven in 1676, ten years before Noodt married his daughter. As lord of Leur he was

55. J. Pesters to Van Eck, The Hague, 2 Apr. 1686, UL Utrecht, MS 1000: 'Cl. Noot jamdiu nuptias parat. Rumor est ipsum filiam Domini de Leur velle, sed matrem ejus viduam nostrum cupere professorem.'
56. Cf. Martens van Sevenhoven, 1977: 139.
57. A high seigniory has higher criminal jurisdiction, that is, the power to inflict capital and corporal punishment.
58. Member of the 'vroedschap' of Schoonhoven 1667, burgomaster 1673/4. Died 1676. His functions in Schoonhoven can hardly have been real. He seems to have lived mainly in The Hague. In 1666 he bought ⅔ of the concession of the pawnshop in Schoonhoven.
59. Curiously enough, in Utrecht the chapters, with their estate, survived the Reformation, and kept electing the clerical order in the States. Therefore, in the 17th and 18th centuries one finds lay regents with all kinds of ecclesiastical titles—and the concomitant powers and emoluments, of course.
60. Martens van Sevenhoven, 1977: 139.

succeeded by his son Nicolaas Thomas,[61] still a minor then, who also became burgomaster of Schoonhoven and canon of St John's, and furthermore deputy in the States of Holland and delegate in the Admiralty of Friesland. In 1700, a year after the death of Sara Maria, Noodt dedicated a book to him.[62] Nicolaas Thomas died unmarried and without leaving a testament, so the seigniory devolved on his mother Maria Pots, who donated it in 1713 to another of Sara Maria's brothers, Hendrik Adriaan,[63] canon of St Mary's in Utrecht. In 1704 Noodt dedicated a book to him also.[64] Hendrik Adriaan died in Haarlem in 1724, and left the seigniory to his son, whose widow was obliged to sell it in 1748.

Considering the fact that Noodt dedicated books to his brothers-in-law, we may assume that relations with his in-laws were fairly good. In respect to social status the Van der Marcks belonged to the patriciate of Holland, and stood a little higher than Noodt, the son of a Nijmegen bourgeois. In the marriage-settlement his wife is called 'honourable' (*Jonkvrouw*).[65] And as far as property is concerned, she also seems to be his superior.[66] Nevertheless, the famous professor will have been a desirable enough match.

We get an impression of her property from the closed mutual testament signed on 27 November 1693.[67] In it, both parties not only revoke all former wills,[68] but also the marriage-settlement of 1686. They appoint each other as universal heir. The survivor undertakes to bring up the children according to their station, and to give them, when they come of age, or marry with counsel and consent of the survivor, as much in goods or money, as he or she will deem fit, according to his own discretion. Furthermore they appoint each other as guardian over their children, with full and absolute powers regarding their education, the administration of their possessions,

61. Martens van Sevenhoven, 1977: 139. He was not born in Schoonhoven because citizenship was offered him on 16 Oct. 1673. He was burgomaster of Schoonhoven 1692–1703 and represented the city regularly in the Estates of Holland in the years 1706–11. He died in 1712.
62. Ahsmann–Feenstra, 1984: nr. 446.
63. Martens van Sevenhoven, 1977: 139.
64. Ahsmann–Feenstra, 1984: nr. 449.
65. ARA Tets van Goudriaan, inv. nr. 119.
66. The only feudal tenancy which Noodt had (together with his brother Johan), was the tithe of Eijckenhorst, which he inherited from his mother in 1680, see above, § 1 n. 41.
67. ARA Tets van Goudriaan, inv. nr. 115.
68. Mention is made of a will of Sara Maria from 1680.

and the appointment of further guardians on their death, excluding all jurisdiction or consent of magistrates or orphan's courts which, according to local or provincial customary law, might have authority in the matter.

Furthermore, Noodt's wife wills to her mother Maria Pots, if she dies before her husband and without leaving children, the following estates: her farms and lands in Piershil or Beijerland,[69] near the sluice in Lopik,[70] and in the Sterremeer;[71] furthermore, what she possesses in Zuiderkogge,[72] as well as her houses in Schoonhoven[73] and Hoorn.[74] Her other possessions—which are not specified—will go to Noodt. Evidently, Sara Maria had a considerable estate—on the face of it not a noble estate, but a collection of investments resulting from her father's successful enterprises.

From the legal point of view the mutual will is remarkable in several respects. The revocation of a marriage-settlement by mutual will—which could frustrate all intentions to provide that specific goods were 'kept in the family'—was not unusual, but still contested. Civil lawyers had discussed it for centuries.[75] In a case which happened to arise in Schoonhoven—the city where Sara Maria was born and her father and brother were burgomasters—the Court of Holland decided on 6 April 1487, and subsequently the grand Council of Malines on 5 September 1488, that such a repeal was

69. See v. d. Aa, Geogr. ix, 1846: 161 f. I was unable to ascertain in which of the six Piershilse polders Sara Maria's property was located.
70. Seigniory, formerly owned by the chapter of St Mary's in Utrecht (until 1846).
71. Or Starnmeer, polder in Kennemerland, south of the Schermer, embanked in 1643, see v. d. Aa, Geogr. x, 1847.
72. One of the four Drechterlandse koggen, polders in West Friesland, east of Hoorn. In it are the villages Schellinkhout, Venhuizen, and Wijdenes, see v. d. Aa, Geogr. xiii, 1851.
73. She seems to have had five houses in Schoonhoven, two adjacent ones in the Lange and Korte Wij(n)straat and three in the Lopikerstraat adjoining the property of Thomas van der Marck. The first two were sold by Gerard Noodt after his wife's death and made over on 23 and 27 June 1702. The other three, apparently given to his daughter as dowry, were sold shortly after her marriage by Jan van den Ende and made over on 27 June 1716. All five were sold to Pleun Willemse Rijerkerk (Rijderkerk). Rechterlijk Arch. Schoonhoven, inv. nr. 2366, fols. 72^{v}–74^{v}; inv. nr. 2367, fols. 73^{v}–74^{v}. I thank P. Muilwijk, Schoonhoven, for references.
74. I was unable to identify the house(s). The register of conveyances has a gap for the years 1684–1717. See B. M. de Jonge van Ellemeet, *Rijksarchieven in Noord-Holland: Inventaris der oud-rechterlijke en weeskamerarchieven*, The Hague, 1932, inv. nrs. 4526–68. Some soundings in notarial protocols of the period proved fruitless.
75. For older literature (postglossators, canonists) see Peckius, 1647: 489 f.

FIG. 1 Property of Sara Maria van der Marck van Leur according to the will of 1693, ARA Tets van Goudriaan, inv. nr. 115.

valid,[76] most likely on the ground often invoked in later cases, to wit, that one could not curtail one's freedom to will during one's lifetime, because 'testamenta hominum usque ad supremum vitae halitum ambulatoria sunt' (men's wills remain changeable until the last gasp of breath).[77] This opinion was defended by, among others, Everærts[78] and Peckius.[79] In Holland it prevailed until the codification period,[80] though it was challenged in court several times.[81] In Utrecht and other provinces, however, the opposite opinion prevailed: a marriage-settlement favouring a third party could not be

76. Kerckhoffs-de Hey, 1970: 108 ff.
77. Vœt, *ad Pand.* 23. 4. 62, and on wills in general, id. 28. 3. 3: '... quia ad extremum vitae halitum ambulatoria hominis voluntas est'.
78. Nic. Everaerts (1462–1531), *Responsa sive consilia*, cons. 119, 136, 138.
79. As n. 75.
80. Vœt, *ad Pand.* 23. 4. 62 f.; Rodenburg, 1653: 132.
81. Hollandsche Consultatiën ii, cons. 202, p. 393: cons. 293, p. 545; iii, cons. 188, p. 503 (opinion of Hugo Grotius, Rotterdam, 16 Apr. 1616); vi, cons. 76, p. 136; van den Berg i, 1781: cons. 23, p. 46, cons. 40, p. 76, iii, 1784: cons. 88, p. 195.

revoked by mutual will.[82] In the commissions preparing a national codification the matter was still a subject for ample discussion.[83]

Moreover, the mutual will of 1693 is an example of the exclusion of all jurisdiction of the local orphan's court. In the eighteenth century this became a standard clause.[84] Strangely enough, the validity of this clause never seems to have been contested in court, although the orphan's court was actually meant to protect children's interests, possibly even against surviving parents. Evidently we can see the hand of the law professor in the mutual will. Whether in the case of Gerard and his wife we can regard the revocation on the marriage-settlement as a sign of their 'extraordinary love and affection'—as was said in a case arising in Delft in 1609[85]—cannot be ascertained. But it is not improbable.

The Noodt family settled in Leiden in a house on the south-eastern corner of the Pieterskerkhof; Noodt himself lived there until his death in 1725.[86] From 1598 to 1658 it had housed the local pawnshop.[87] In 1670, at the division of an estate, the house devolved on Jacob Hackius. Noodt probably rented it at first. In 1693 the same Jacob Hackius is a witness of the deposition of the mutual will of Noodt and his wife.[88] Noodt bought the house from him on 7 May 1701 for 7,750 guilders in cash. It remained in the possession of his family until 1783, when his grandson Gerrit Abraham van den Ende sold it for 3,000 guilders. Apparently, the grave economic crisis affecting Leiden in the later eighteenth century greatly diminished the value of the house. In 1799 it was bought by the governors of

82. Radelant, 1637: dec. 84, num. 16 and 17; Rodenburg, 1653: 132; *Utrechtse consultatiën* i, cons. 60, p. 203, num. 1.
83. *Bronnen* ii, 1975: 28 f., 160 f. (draft Wierdsma, art. 86 f.), 329 (Wetboek Napoleon, art. 90), 350 (draft 1814, art. 127). The possibility of revocation, admitted in all these drafts, is excluded expressly in draft 1820, art. 383.
84. In The Hague—the only orphan's court that has been studied systematically—the clause appears in wills from the middle of the 17th century, but is not a standard clause until the 18th, see de Gou, 1943: 100 f., with further literature.
85. Hollandsche Consultatiën, cons. 293, p. 545.
86. Already in June 1687, at the burial of his first child, Noodt's address is 'beij de Pieterskerk'. The same address appears in the Naamwyser van de Ed. Achtb. Heeren Regenten der stad Leiden (Herenboekje), from 1709–1725 (seen in GA Leiden). See also Register Sevenhuysen (bonboek) fol. 174^{v}; Cohier familiegeld 28 May 1716; Verpondingen register 1716, fol. 161^{v}, nr. 323 (All GA Leiden). The tax on the house in 1716 was 36 guilders. I thank Mr Leverland of GA Leiden for his help in locating Noodt's house.
87. Register Sevenhuysen, fol. 174^{v} (GA Leiden). See Leverland and van Maanen, 1975.
88. See n. 67 on p. 68.

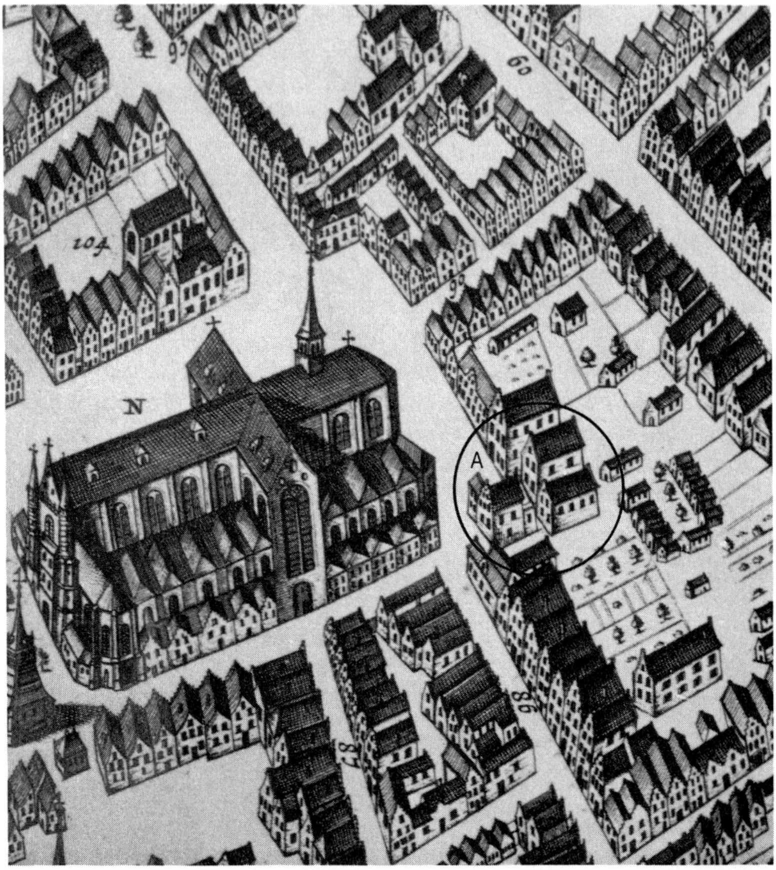

FIG. 2 Residence of Gerard Noodt on the Pieterskerkhof in Leiden, 1686–1725. Detail of map by Chr. Hagen, 1670.

Leiden university.[89] Until 1973 it housed the Walloon Library. Now it is an apartment house.

Noodt not only took part in university life, but also was an active member of the Reformed Church of Leiden. Like many of his colleagues (Vœt, Matthæus, Perizonius) he was an elder several times.[90] It may not be a coincidence that the last time he is mentioned

89. As n. 87.

90. In the Naamwyser (see n. 86) he is listed as such in the years 1690–2, 1695, 1700, 1701, 1704, 1705. Noodt seems to alternate with Vœt several times: 1693 Vœt, 1695 Noodt, 1697 Vœt, 1700 Noodt. In 1690 and 1705 both are elders.

as such is in 1705. After the rectorial address on freedom of religion, which cannot have pleased the theologians very much, he would not have been re-elected.

We do not know very much about Noodt's family life, apart from the moving testimony he gives after the death of his wife (see below). From his marriage with Sara Maria van der Marck five children were born,[91] but only one survived both parents. The others died within a few days or a year after birth. The will drawn up six years before Sara Maria's death still mentions two daughters, the twins Maria Gijsberta and Sara Hadriana,[92] who were born the previous year. Only Sara Hadriana remained alive.

Noodt's wife was not to live long. In the will of 1693 she is described as 'bodily in weak health'. Six years later, after a marriage of only thirteen years, she died at the age of 40, on 7 October 1699.[93] Before delivering she had frequent haemorrhages, which impaired her health to such extent that she died in childbirth.[94] Nothing is said about the child; it apparently did not survive the mother. Sara Maria was buried in the family grave in Dordrecht.[95] Her death fell on

91. On the basis of the register of baptism and burials in GA Leiden the following data can be established:

1. Hadriaan. Baptized Sunday, 8 June 1687 in the Hooglandse kerk, buried in the same week in the Pieterskerk.
2. Maria Gijsberta. Baptized Sunday, 26 Dec. 1680 in the Hooglandse kerk, died before 12 Sept. 1692. No notice concerning burial.
3. Sara Hadriana. Baptized Friday, 11 Aug. 1690 in the Pieterskerk, died before 12 Sept. 1692. No notice concerning burial.
4–5. Maria Gijsberta and Sara Hadriana. Baptized Friday, 12 Sept. 1692 in the Pieterskerk. Maria Gijsberta died after 26 Nov. 1693 (will) and, in any case, before 7 Oct. 1699 (death of Mrs Noodt). No notice concerning burial. Sara Hadriana was buried in Amsterdam, 20 Nov. 1759.

In the week of 17–24 Nov. 1691 a child of Noodt was buried in the Pieterskerk; this could be either the 2nd or 3rd child. Apparently the child with which Sara Maria was pregnant when she died (7 Oct. 1699) did not survive her; there are no notices concerning baptism or burial.

92. ARA Tets van Goudriaan, inv. nr. 115.
93. ARA Tets van Goudriaan, inv. nr. 115; Perizonius to Van Eck, Leiden, 8 Oct. 1699, UL Utrecht, MS 1000.
94. See the letter of Perizonius cited in the preceding note: 'Clarissimi Noodtii uxor heri in partu, vel eum praeveniens continuis sanguinis effluviis, et ita debilitata ante partum, animam efflavit, qua morte graviter affectus videtur maritus, neque id miror, quum illa morigera satis viro fuerit uxor.'
95. Noodt (as n. 1 on p. 74); GA Leiden, Buitenbegravingen, 8 Oct. 1699; Register Impost op het begraven le klasse 1695–1805, rechterlijk arch. inv. nr. 213. The tax was 30 guilders. GA Dordrecht, DTB 29: '1699 October 10, de huisvrouw van professor Noot'.

Noodt as a grievous blow—and that is no wonder, writes (the bachelor) Perizonius,[96] because she was a wife that was very obsequious to her husband. In fact, we know very little about her.

We get quite a different picture of her from a letter from J. Pesters to C. van Eck, concerning Noodt's appointment in Leiden, which I have cited before: 'Whoever wants to explore the causes that pressed Noodt to accept a nomination which he had refused several times before, can think of no other than the ambition of his wife. How much that can do is known to you, I trust, from the authority of learned men and experience.'[97] But we have already dismissed Pesters' idle gossip before. The few sources we have, speak about an obedient and dedicated wife, but naturally we must leave open how much of a stereotype this is. Maybe she knew how to *parendo imperare* (rule by obeying), as Noodt said the wife of his teacher Petrus de Greve did.[98] But all the same it seems exaggerated to ascribe the acceptance of the chair in Leiden to her ambition. Noodt had his own reasons for that, although no doubt the marriage may have been a reason to welcome an increase of income. He says as much himself in a letter to Van Eck that was cited before: 'The condition of my family and my affairs will demand that I do not allow myself to be kept here [i.e. in Utrecht].'[99]

Several times Noodt gave a very loving testimony about his deceased wife, and although there may be a lot of conventional images and erudition in all this, there is a personal tone as well. There are, by the way, not many professors who have expressed themselves in the same way in public. A week after his wife's death he wrote to his students, in a notification about the resumption of his lectures:[1] 'The unpropitious day of the seventh of this month has taken my beloved wife, Sara Maria van der Marck van Leur, an excellent

96. As n. 94.
97. See n. 35 on p. 63.
98. Oratio funebris, p. 14, col. 2 (Ahsmann–Feenstra, 1984: nr. 426).
99. See p. 62 f.
1. ARA Tets van Goudriaan, inv. nr. 116 (concept and fair copy): 'Abstulit mihi infausta dies quae fuit a.d. VII huius mensis, uxorem meam sanctissimam, Saram Mariam van der Marck van Leur, Foeminam egregiam, et castitate, prudentia, modestia, comitate, obsequio denique et fide, in suum Maritum, incomparabilem; cum qua sine querela vixi per tredecim annos, ei individua et suavissima omnis divinae et humanae rei societate conjunctus. Igitur illa mea carissima uxor qua quis meliorem non optet, fuit. Imo adhuc vivit, sed meliore sui parte, felixque Deo, et virtute sua, fruitur. Ego vero infelicissimus maritus quod ex ea mortale erat, ut voluit pietas et memoria humanae sortis, patrio intuli sepulchro; ac jacturam domus meae nimis intellego.'

woman, incomparable in chastity, prudence, modesty, and gentleness, as well as in obedience and faithfulness to her husband—with whom I have lived thirteen years without a quarrel, associated with her in the indivisible and most sweet union of all divine and human things.[2] In short, she, my dearest, has been a wife to me as nobody could wish a better one. In fact, she lives on with her better part, happily enjoying God and her own virtue. But I, most miserable husband, have buried what was mortal of her, as love and the memory of human fate demand, in her paternal grave. And I feel the loss of my family only too well.'

A similar, still more extensive memorial is printed three months later in the dedication of *Julius Paulus* to Sara's brother Nicolaas Thomas:[3] '. . . But what I have published before at various times, I have written in a more cheerful mind. For then my family stood unhurt, while my wife was still alive, that sweetest associate of my life and studies, your full sister Sara Maria van der Marck van Leur, a most beloved wife and splendidly equipped with all the virtues that befall this lovely sex. I am not a vain appraiser of my unhappiness; nor do I intend to magnify the causes of my grief. But I can hardly omit saying that, apart from the other gifts of mind through which she bloomed, she was incomparable in chastity, fidelity, truthfulness, modesty, gentleness, kindness; furthermore—which shows true love—she wanted nothing unless I wanted it, objected to nothing unless I objected to it.[4] As a result, one spirit, as it were, ruled both our bodies. But the more by her nature she surpassed all praise, the

2. D. 23. 2. 1, see Noodt, *Probabilia* ii. 9.

3. See p. 68. Fol. 3^r ff.: 'Sed ego quae ante hac edidi diversis temporibus, laetiore animo scripsi. Stabat enim integra domus mea, salva Conjuge mea, illa suavissima et vitae, et studiorum meorum, socia, sorore tua germana, Sara Maria van der Marck van Leur, foemina sanctissima, et cunctis virtutibus quae in amabilem hunc sexum cadunt ornatissima. Non sum ambitiosus infortunii mei aestimator; nec est mihi animus, intendere doloris causas. Silere tamen vix possum, eam praeter caeteras animi dotes, quibus effloruit, castitate, fide, verecundia, modestia, comitate, benevolentia, incomparabilem fuisse; denique, quae vera perhibentur amicitia, nihil, nisi quod ego vellem, voluisse, nihil, nisi quod ego nollem, noluisse; perinde, quasi uno spiritu utriusque corpus regetur. Sed quo longibus omnem animo superavit laudem, eo altius penetravit vulnus, quod eius morte, tam insperata, tam immatura, tam subita, pridem mihi vis divina inflixit: prorsus ut me jam nullius fortunae benignitate deinceps felicem effici posse existimarem. Ut tamen me levarem (quod suadebat ratio, et pietas quam unicae debebam Filiae, in qua, pro modo aetatis, apparet indoles virtutis, et materni ingenii simulacrum) praecipuum in adversis remedium, humanitatis studia, adhibui; quibus ut fallerem solitudinis meae infelices horas, hoc Opus, ut passae res sunt, conscripsi.'

4. See Noodt, *Probabilia* ii. 9.

deeper pierced the wound that an act of God inflicted on me not long ago through her death, so unsuspected, so untimely, so sudden—so deep that I believe no stroke of good fortune can ever make me happy again. But in order to relieve myself (which is impelled by reason, as well as by the love I owe to my daughter, in whom, in proportion to her age there appears a natural virtue and the image of her mother's character) I have turned to the best remedy in adversity, the study of letters (*studia humanitatis*). I have written, in order to forget the unhappy hours of my solitude, this book as circumstances permitted'.

More than a year after Sara Maria's death, on 30 January 1701, the will was opened and read by notary Kervel in The Hague, in presence of Gerard Noodt, her mother Maria Pots, and her brother Nicolaas Thomas, lord of Leur. Moreover, at the request of Noodt's mother-in-law, the reading was attended by two of her domestic servants.[5] An extract of the will, containing the provisions concerning guardianship and the exclusion of jurisdiction of the orphan's court, was presented by Noodt to the orphan's court in Leiden on 21 September 1701. Before the court he formally undertook guardianship.[6]

That the loss of his wife was a blow to Noodt can hardly be doubted. In fact, he never remarried, although he was only 52 when she died and still had a child of 7 to care for. But in all fairness it must be said that financially her untimely death did him no harm. Whereas under the marriage-settlement he would only have got 4,000 guilders, he now became, Sara Maria not dying childless, her universal heir, wth the sole duty to give his daughter, on her coming of age or marriage, in goods or money as much as he deemed fit. For his income this did not make a big difference, because the income from Sara Maria's property was already used for the maintenance of the household. But that he had become a man of property is borne out by the fact that, just three months after the opening of the will, he bought the house on the Pieterskerkhof, at what seems to be a fairly high price.[7]

5. The instrument recording the reading of the will, as well as its text, is in ARA Tets van Goudriaan, inv. nr. 115. An extract from 29 Mar. 1701 is in GA Leiden, Weeskamerarchief, inv. nr. 213; register van seclusiën Vol. L., fol. 246^v.
6. GA Leiden (as n. 5).
7. Noodt paid 7,750 guilders, GA Leiden, register Sevenhuysen, fol. 174^v. In 1657, 4,000 guilders were paid, while the greater was still terrain belonging to it, in 1783 3,000 guilders, and in 1799 3,500 guilders. Naturally, these prices must be regarded

Scholarly and academic pursuits

After the untimely death of his wife Noodt in all probability concentrated completely on his work. The little we know about his doings gives the impression of a rather unspectacular scholar's life. Apart from a vacation in Nijmegen or an occasional visit to The Hague or Rotterdam, we hear nothing about travels; and, naturally, congresses did not yet exist. Intellectual intercourse was mainly maintained by correspondence. Noodt taught, pulled his weight in the administration of the university, published regularly, wrote letters, and occasionally gave a legal opinion. Between 1699 and 1710 four new books were published: *Julius Paulus*, or concerning abandonment and killing of children by the ancients (1700);[8] *Diocletian and Maximian*, or concerning settlement and redemption of crimes (1704);[9] Observations in two books (1706);[10] Concerning the way bad faith in concluding contracts is punished (1709).[11] Besides, the work published before was re-edited under the title *Opera varia*,[12] the rectorial address on freedom of religion was published (1706),[13] as well as a second edition of that on the power of the sovereign (1705).[14] In the same period, translations in Dutch, French, and English of both rectorial addresses appeared.[15] According to Barbeyrac Noodt was very pleased with the French translation, which he personally corrected for the second impression.[16] Noodt also reviewed the Dutch translation personally. His fame grew steadily.

His reputation as an authority on the sources of Roman law is highlighted by the fact that his advice was sought on the project of a new edition of the Corpus Juris—an edition which, by the way, never came about. The ambition to bring out a new, critical, and annotated edition of this voluminous corpus of writings from Antiquity, which,

with circumspection. In the second half of the 18th century Leiden experienced a deep economic crisis, as a result of the decline of the cloth industry, and the prices of houses will have dropped accordingly.

8. Ahsmann–Feenstra, 1984: nr. 446.
9. Ahsmann–Feenstra, 1984: nr. 449.
10. Ahsmann–Feenstra, 1984: nr. 450.
11. Ahsmann–Feenstra, 1984: nr. 463.
12. Ahsmann–Feenstra, 1984: nr. 449a.
13. Ahsmann–Feenstra, 1984: nr. 451.
14. Ahsmann–Feenstra, 1984: nr. 437.
15. Ahsmann–Feenstra, 1984: nrs. 438, 439, 442, 444, 453, 454, 455, 456, 459, 460.
16. Barbeyrac, 1731: XIV.

in fact, formed the basis of all legal scholarship, belonged to the heritage of the elegant school. But the work was so demanding that only very few scholars completed it.

On 2 June 1705 Van Bijnkershoek wrote to Van Eck[17] that the Scottish scholar Alexander Cunningham[18] was negotiating seriously with editors in Amsterdam about the plan to bring out a new, annotated edition of the Corpus Iuris. To begin with, he hoped to edit the Digest in two octavo volumes, then the whole Corpus Iuris in two or three folio volumes. The Amsterdam editor, who evidently did not want to take chances with the vast enterprise, had instructed Cunningham to ask the opinions of Van Eck, Van Bijnkershoek, and Noodt. These are, in fact, the best experts living at that time in the Republic. Vœt was not asked, although he had at one time been Cunningham's teacher,[19] and was still friendly with him, because he

17. Van Bijnkershœk to Van Eck, The Hague, 10 Jan. 1705, UL Utrecht, MS 1000: 'Cunninghamus ille, quem nosti, jam serio agit cum Bibliopolis Amsterdammensibus, de nova Editione Corporis Juris; constituit primum solas Pandectus edere cum notis criticis, duobus voluminibus in 8, deinde universum Corpus tribus aut quatuor tomis in Folio cum observationibus quibuscunque. Bibliopolus Amsterdammensis de eo opere explorare jussit judicium tuum, Noodtii, meumque. Voetium adiri noluit, utpote cui in re critica nihil tribuit, quamvis eius quondam Praeceptor et etiamnum amicus sit. Laudavit quoque Voetius Tom. II. ad ff Cunninghami conjecturam quandam criticam ad 1. 7 ff de poenis [D 48. 19. 7. see Vœt, ad Pand. 48. 19. 2].'

18. On him, see Kelly, 1975: 29 f.; Feenstra and Waal, 1975: 86–8; Stolte, 1981: 14; Feenstra, 1986: 134 f. There is an earlier account of Cunningham's plans in a letter from Rob. Moray to Van Eck, Edinburgh, 23 Aug. 1689 (UL Utrecht, MS 1000). According to this letter, Cunningham was not yet planning an edn., but rather a systematic commentary (in the manner of Doneau's *Commentarii*), reordering the whole of civil law and solving all cruces and antinomies: 'nihil hic novi quod sciam molitur Minerva, praeter quam quod de Cuningamo quodam Scoto dicitur, quem aiunt commentarium in universum jus Romanum esse editurum in quo statuit, totam jurisprudentiam in meliorem ordinem redigere, quinetiam omnia juris aenigmata crucesque se clare et distincte explicaturum legesque contrarias explicaturum pollicetur. Quod certe si effecerit opus erit utile. Ipsum ego Cuninghamum non novi, sed non mediocris esse doctrinae fertur.'

19. From a grammatical point of view, it is not clear to whom the words 'Voetium adiri noluit . . .' refer, that is, to Cunningham or to the editor. But from the following sentence we can conclude that Cunningham is meant. Vœt's own words (*ad Pand.* 48. 19. 2) confirm van Bijnkershœk's statement. Vœt says that a conjecture was suggested to him by 'Clarissmus Cunninghamus, Scotus, auditor olim inter primos charus' (. . . whom once I cherished as one of my best students'). The question is: when did Cunningham attend Vœt's lectures? Not in 1686/7, when Cunningham accompanied Lord George Douglas on his grand tour. Vœt was already in Leiden by that time, and they chose Utrecht as first station on their tour. Their first message from there is of 13 July 1686, the last of 27 Mar. 1687. Naturally, it is possible that they made a trip to Leiden on that occasion, but this would hardly be enough to justify Vœt's words. Van Bijnkershœk says that Vœt

had contributed nothing in the field of textual criticism.[20] A few years later Cunningham was back in The Hague once more. On 6 September 1708 Van Bijnkershoek informed Van Eck that Cunningham, after travelling for some years[21] in Italy, Spain, and France, had returned to The Hague, where he hoped to prepare his edition for the press in a few months. But Van Bijnkershœk presumed that nothing would come of that,[22] and he was definitely right.

After Cunningham's plans were written off, Noodt's pupil Henrik Brenkman made preparations for his *iter italicum*.[23] Although Johannes Vœt was Brenkman's promoter, his work in legal philology, which won him European fame, was certainly more Noodt's field. We may regard him as Noodt's pupil.[24] He dedicated his first independent publication to Noodt.[25] But Brenkman's lifelong studies in the Digest did not produce the contemplated edition any more, for that matter, than the effort of Laurens Gronovius[26] or Alexander Cunningham. In 1720 Noodt and Schulting

was Cunningham's *praeceptor*, and anyway Cunningham was no longer a student by then. Most likely Cunningham studied with Vœt in Utrecht in his youth (between 1674 and 1680), as many of his compatriots did. That he does not figure in AS Utrecht is not decisive. This possibility would make the speculations of Kelly (1975: 33) about the reasons of the choice of Utrecht as the first stop of Lord George's grand tour superfluous. Perhaps Cunningham advised him to choose Utrecht because he already knew the city. See also Feenstra (1986: 134 ff.), who gives a slightly different translation of Vœt's words. I thank Feenstra for giving me part of Kelly's unpublished thesis for perusal.

20. See n. 28 on p. 62. And see Kotzé, as cited by Roberts, 1933: 10: '. . . nor can we count him as of equal weight as a civilian with Noodt, Schulting or Bijnkershœk'.
21. Van Bijnkershœk, in the letter cited below, n. 22, speaks of a quinquennium, but the period is, in fact, hardly more than three years.
22. Van Bijnkershœk to Van Eck, The Hague, 6 Sept. 1708, UL Utrecht, MS 1000: '. . . Novarum rerum hic nihil est nisi scire attinet, huc iterum appulisse illum Coningham, scotum, de quo nos nuper ad huc sermonem habuisse recordor. Per quinquennium abfuit in Italia, Hispania, Gallia, nunc aliquot menses hic morabitur et pollicetur, se diu cogitatum opus de nova editione Corporis Juris porro esse absoluturum, eique fini usum manuscripti Pandectarum et alia Bibliothecae meae instrumenta expetiit. Est tamen, cur credam, id opus numquam ad umbilicum deductum iri.' That Cunningham's plans were not realistic, indeed, appears from a letter of half a year later, in which van Bijnkershœk informs Van Eck that Cunningham will soon submit a specimen of his skill in textual criticism; van Bijnkershœk to Van Eck, The Hague, 21 Feb. 1709, UL Utrecht, MS 1000: 'Alexander Cunningham, quem novisti, promittit se brevi editurum specimen criticae suae.' Apparently this did not happen.
23. Stolte, 1981: 17 f.
24. Stolte, 1981: 10.
25. *De euremticis diatribe*, Leiden, 1706.
26. See Stolte, 1981: 18, 46.

were consulted about a project of the Leipzig editor Fritsch to make a new edition of the Corpus Juris of Gothofredus, on the basis of the edition of Van Leeuwen (1664), with additional tracts and notes.[27] Fritsch asked the advice of Dutch scholars through the Leiden printer Samuel Luchtmans. Van de Water drafted a scheme for the new edition, according to which it was to include the Index of Labittus, books of Agustìn, and Brenkman on proper names in the Digest, as well as material from the Fasti edited by Relandus. A learned scholar should collect all that was written to illustrate the text, in the form of short notes. All that Noodt and Schulting had to comment was that most of the notes of Anselmo[28] should be eliminated because they did not concern literature, and that they agreed with the inclusion of Labittus and Agustìn. Noodt offered to give a list of emendations discussed in his Commentary on the Digest up to Book 28. Later, Noodt's pupil Balthasar Branchu[29] was contracted by Fritsch (and paid nicely) to collect the harvest of the Dutch school,[30] but he died in 1725. The edition never appeared. An edition realizing—still, in fact, only partly—what the Dutch elegant school had in mind, did not appear until the end of the eighteenth century, and, significantly, not in Holland, but in Germany.[31] This foreshadows developments to come. By the beginning of the nineteenth century Dutch scholarship in Roman law has sunk back to insignificance and Germany takes the lead.

Noodt had a fair share in the administration of Leiden university.[32] He was rector in the year 1698–9, and once more in 1705–6, although, according to Perizonius, he had said several times that he did not desire the job, and many professors had been at the university for ten years or more without ever taking the rectorate.[33] With Perizonius

27. There is a bundle of notes on this project in the papers of van de Water, UL Leiden, BPL 191H. The edn. never appeared. In the same year a similar edn. was brought out by the Leipzig editor Gleditsch (Spangenberg, nr. 525).
28. On him Van den Bergh and Stolte, 1977: 239 n. 52.
29. See below, n. 68 on p. 105.
30. Gebauer, 1764: 56.
31. Gebauer–Spangenberg. On this edn., see Van den Bergh and Stolte, 1977: 241 f.
32. Noodt is dean of the law faculty in 1687, 1691, 1695, 1699, 1702, 1706, 1710, 1713, 1716, 1719, and 1722. See Acta facultatis juridici, vol. ii (1669–1745), UL Leiden, Arch. Senaat en Fac. inv. nr. 389.
33. Perizonius to Van Eck, Leiden, 21 Feb. 1705, UL Utrecht, MS 1000: 'Noodtius, licet ante sex annos rector fuerit, tamen denuo designatus est, licet saepe testatus fuerit, se id muneris neutiquam desiderare, et licet in iisdem partibus essent, qui duodecim et qui decimum jam annum in hac Academia agunt, nec unquam Rectoris munus gessint. Prensavit tamen Volderus pro eo Collegas, ut mecum et

and De Volder as his assessors, Noodt will practically get absolute power, Perizonius adds: 'What shall I say, it strikes me more and more that those who make a lot of noise and talk a lot about freedom, in fact are asking to be dominated, and maybe even harder than those who are dead and gone.' 8 February 1706, the day that Noodt resigned his second rectorate and spoke his address about freedom of religion, must have been a very emotional day for him, as we will see later. It soon brought him international fame.

Noodt certainly pulled his weight. Several times he was secretary of the senate; when he was reappointed as such in 1712, Perizonius testified that he had never once refused to do the job during the past nineteen years.[34] On 8 August 1712 Noodt, in his quality as secretary, delivered to the city council of Leiden the complaints of senate and students regarding the academic printer (appointed after the death of Abraham Elzevier) 'concerning the bad paper and letters, as well as the increase in the price of printing theses, which caused many students to take their degree in Utrecht and other neighbouring academies'.[35] The bugbear of masses of students migrating to Utrecht was used by Noodt once more on 17 December 1716, in the senate. It regarded another quarrel with the burgomasters of Leiden, concerning the fact that the decisions of the academic court were much too mild on students, much to the distress of Leiden shopkeepers. This time the bailiff had taken action against some students, in blatant violation of the *privilegium fori*.[36] Noodt urged that the numerous and rich English (in fact mainly Scottish) students in Leiden might very well take refuge in Utrecht, if academic jurisdiction was impaired.[37] Such an argument will always win, because the income of

cum Hottonio nominaretur. Ex nostra autem disciplina nominari jam nemo poterat nisi ego et Volderus, qui incassum nominari designantur, et apud nos regnum obtinet solus. Quid dicam? Magis magisque deprehendo illos qui clamant adeo et crepant libertatem, nihil aliud agere et quaerere, nisi ut dominentur, et iniquius ferme, quam priores. Sed haec omnia tibi solo dicta sunt.'

34. Perizonius to Van Eck, Leiden, 31 Jan. 1712, UL Utrecht, MS 1000: 'Secretarium nobis dare volunt iidem Praesides Deckerum, qui ante 4 annos id munus quoque gessit. Sed contra nitentibus aliis praeter illorum exspectationem, designabitur cras, ut mihi prorsus persuadeo, Noodtius, qui intra 19 annos id munus non abstinuit.'
35. Molhuysen iv: 259. Copies of other letters written by Noodt as secretary are in Documenta actionum 14, UL Leiden, Arch. Senaat en Fac., inv. nr. 299, nrs. 131, 132, 136, 137.
36. Apparently this concerned a civil case. In criminal matters two burgomasters of Leiden sat in the academic court.
37. Molhuysen iv: 284.

the professors is directly dependent of the number of their students. In principle, the university still is an enterprise operating in an open market, and traditionally students are regarded as critical consumers. But we happen to know that in this case Noodt's argument is just a hoax. In Utrecht there was no *forum privilegiatum* for academics at all!

In March 1709 Noodt and Boerhaave were instructed by the senate to arrange the burial and inspect the inheritance of Professor Burchard de Volder.[38] De Volder, Boerhaave's teacher, had died without family or known heirs.[39] Noodt also took part in the search for a successor to De Volder, who had been professor in philosophy and mathematics, and had won international fame because he was the first professor in Europe to give lectures in experimental physics with actual demonstrations (from 1675).[40] Noodt's efforts were directed—eventually in vain—at winning Johann Bernoulli (1667–1748),[41] the famous mathematician from Basle, for the chair in Leiden.

From 1695 to 1705 Bernoulli had been professor in Groningen, where he taught mathematics and 'philosophie experimentale'.[42] Then he had to return to Basle. He was married to Dorothea Falkner, who descended from a high-ranking local family and whose father had a prominent place in the city's government. According to Bernoulli's autobiography, it was his father-in-law who practically forced him to return to Basle, by threatening that he could no longer live without them.[43]

In August 1705 several concerted efforts were made to keep Bernoulli in the Republic. On the 18th he left Groningen and on his arrival in Amsterdam he learned that his elder and hardly less famous brother Jacob (1654–1705) had died in Basle. Some days later he travelled to Utrecht, which had made him an offer before.[44] He had a

38. Molhuysen iv: 238. Noodt and Bœrhaave are commissioned on 28 Mar. and report on 1 Apr., see also ibid., 178*. On 28 Mar. 1709 Noodt and Bœrhaave deliberate with Mr Willem van Swieten of the orphan's court on what is to be done with the inheritance. They decide that it will be sealed.
39. Molhuysen iv: 238, 178*.
40. De Pater, 1979: 5.
41. On him, see Wolf ii, 1859: 71–104. Wolf cites extensively from B.'s autobiography. And see *Hist.-biogr. Lexikon der Schweiz* ii, 1924: 193.
42. Wolf, 1859: 79. The governors of Groningen commissioned Bernoulli to establish an 'école d'experiences', the first to be established there.
43. Wolf, 1859: 80.
44. Kernkamp ii: 186 (27 Aug./12 Oct. 1703), 206 (31 Aug. 1705).

serious conversation with the first burgomaster, Dr Evert Sijpesteijn (1637–1710),[45] who made him a truly exceptional offer. Apart from the princely salary he would get, his wife was offered a considerable pension in case he died before her, payable even in Basle, if she preferred to return there.[46] Returning to the tavern after this conversation, he found a letter from De Volder inviting him to take over his Leiden chair. But the efforts were of no avail. Bernoulli was not master of his own destiny.[47] Back in Basle he got the chair of his deceased brother and was rewarded—and chained—with an additional salary and many honours.

On 21 May 1709, nearly two months after De Volder's death, Noodt wrote to Bernoulli to ask him, also on behalf of some unnamed friends (possibly colleagues and governors), whether he would be willing to succeed to De Volder.[48] Three specific questions are formulated:

1. Is he prepared to come if satisfactory conditions are offered?
2. Is he willing to teach all branches of philosophy and mathematics, publicly as well as privately? (In this respect special mention is made of mathematical physics,[49] the subject in which De Volder excelled, and of astronomy, for which there was a considerable collection of instruments in the astronomical tower.)
3. What salary does he want?

In the meantime Noodt apparently did not want to commit the university. Many candidates had been named. Some people were strongly in favour of Bernoulli, but others preferred someone else. Noodt urges Bernoulli not to make immoderate demands as regards salary. As a result of certain difficulties concerning the treasury, one cannot do very much. Noodt extols the attractions of Leiden, and the great number of students taking a degree in philosophy and mathematics. Stress is laid on the close relation with the department of medicine, headed by Boerhaave, 'amicus et collega meus'. Flattering

45. On him *NNBW* ii, 1201.
46. Wolf, 1859: 82; Bernoulli to Noodt, Basle, 4 Aug. 1709, UL Basle, MS L. I a 674, fol. 219^{r-v}. Written in Latin, the original is in Deutsche Staatsbibliothek Berlin-East. There is nothing about this in Kernkamp.
47. Wolf, 1859: 81.
48. Noodt to Bernoulli, Leiden, 21 May 1709, UL Basle, MS L I a 713, fols. 33–4.
49. Noodt writes 'Mataphysica', but this is a non-existing word according to Dr de Pater, Institute for the History of Sciences, University of Utrecht. Perhaps Noodt misread the abbreviation 'math.physica'. The error makes it clear that Noodt is not familiar with the subject.

Bernoulli, Noodt told him that he had often spoken about him with Boerhaave. Although Boerhaave does not know him personally, he has nothing but praise and esteem for his erudition.

The letter does not yet convey an official offer—as Bernoulli suggested later[50]—but only a private exploration.[51] Leiden followed the same tactic used in the case of Noodt himself. To begin with, the prospective candidate is sounded out by someone who knows him personally. By means of this, the university does not commit itself. Action will not be taken, Noodt wrote, as long as it is uncertain whether Bernoulli would not prefer his national academy to Leiden. There is a fear that another disappointment of expectations might do some harm to the dignity of the academy. Noodt and Bernoulli had met in 1698. In the spring of that year Bernoulli and his wife made a vacation trip from Groningen to Holland. In Amsterdam he visited Hartsœcker,[52] in Leiden De Volder, in The Hague Dierckens[53] and Hemsterhuis.[54] Apparently De Volder, being a bachelor and living alone,[55] was not in a position to put up Bernoulli and his wife properly, and so they were lodged with the Noodt family.[56] Back in Groningen Bernoulli wrote to Noodt to thank him for their hospitality.[57]

Bernoulli answered Noodt on 5 June 1709,[58] without giving a direct reply to Noodt's question. The message of De Volder's death has affected him. In a short time he has lost two friends, De Volder and Braunius.[59] He gives an extensive survey of all his problems, though, naturally, not mentioning his father-in-law directly. If he was alone, if he had no wife and children, if he had no property in

50. Wolf, 1859: 85.
51. Molhuysen has nothing about this.
52. See *Briefwechsel* i, 1955: n. 124, p. 433 n. 1. Hartsoecker made optical instruments, see Kernkamp ii: 165.
53. *Briefwechsel* i, 1955: nr. 124, p. 433 n. 1. It is not certain which member of the family Dierckens is meant, see Schuttevaer, 1982.
54. *Briefwechsel* i, 1955: nrs. 124 and 129. I cannot make out, who is meant. Probably a relative (the father?) of Tiberius Hemsterhuis (*NNBW* i: 1068) who studied in Groningen from 1698 under Bernoulli, Braunius, and Gousset.
55. See n. 39 on p. 82.
56. *Briefwechsel* i, 1955: nr. 124. There is an error in n. 1. Bernoulli did not stay with Noodt in Utrecht, but in Leiden, where Noodt lived from 1686.
57. *Briefwechsel* i, 1955: nr. 124.
58. Bernoulli to Noodt, Basle, 5 June 1709, UL Basle, MS L I a 674 fols. 217–18. Concept in Latin; the original letter is in Philadelphia.
59. See 93 on p. 21. Bernoulli and Braunius were both professors in Groningen during the years 1695–1705.

Basle, he would take the offer with both hands. But now he has an estate, the administration of which rests with him after the death of his father, and he has a wife, children, and a family there. Returning to Basle he has bought a house, which was done up at great cost. Twice already he has made a long and tiresome journey, first to the Netherlands, and then back. Both times he was forced to sell a great many goods, which he could not take with him, at a considerable loss. And now that he is back, and enjoying his rest, he would be obliged to travel once more. In fact, he asks Noodt's advice: What would you do under such circumstances? Up to now, he has not taken any decision. He has told nobody about it, not even his wife: 'I would not like to frighten her before that is necessary.'

The question regarding the desired salary is answered by asking another one. What can he expect? He does not want to dictate conditions himself,[60] but nevertheless he makes a hint that hardly can be misunderstood: he expects a salary of 2,000 guilders or more. In Groningen, he says, he got 1,500, which, considering the cost of living, would equal much more than 2,000 in any other region of the Republic. Now this seems a rather thin disguise indeed. One can hardly believe that the cost of living in Leiden would be 30 per cent more than in Groningen! Furthermore, Bernoulli points, without specifying however, to the offer made by Utrecht four years ago (that is, the widow's pension), suggesting that Noodt will know about it[61] (which indeed seems to have been the case). He turned down that offer then, but Noodt will understand that, under present conditions, he cannot afford to take any risk.

Apparently, such demands were far beyond what Leiden was prepared to offer, but Noodt did not give up at once. His letter of reply of 8 July 1709[62] opens with a counter-stroke. According to Noodt's 'friends', Bernoulli has not yet made it sufficiently clear what he intends to do with astronomy, for which there is an extensive and precious collection of instruments in Leiden. In fact, Bernoulli had not said a word about astronomy yet. As regards the disguised salary demands Noodt acts dumb. They have not been able to find out what Bernoulli wants, but they can easily understand that it is a

60. 'Absit enim a me ut eos ipse praescribam.'
61. 'Nosti etiam sine dubio, quas conditiones ab Ultrajectinis oblatos repudiaverim . . . quid si enim paulo post morerer, quid de vidua, quid de liberis meis fieret? Redirent-ne in patriam?'
62. Noodt to Bernoulli, Leiden, 18 July 1709, UL Basle, MS L I a 713 fols. 31–2.

great deal. As he wrote before, some people would prefer another candidate, and asking too much might easily be used as a pretext to exclude Bernoulli. It is always easier to prevent something than to promote it. If he wants the chair, he must be reasonable and take the opportunity, because there might never be another one. Bernoulli can only count on the salary of De Volder, or possibly a little less. The amount—1,855 guilders—is written out three times in Noodt's letter. No philosopher or mathematician before De Volder ever had as much.

What a lot of problems Bernoulli does have! Noodt wishes they did not exist. But he cannot solve them all, nor can the academy. The matter of the widow's pension has been considered, but in vain. Leiden university never gives anything like that, and so Bernoulli must not count on it. The same applies for his house and properties. Naturally travel expenses on behalf of the academy will be repaid.

Noodt's letter has a more general interest, because it enumerates all the earnings a professor eventually may expect:

1. Salary, for De Volder 1,800 guilders;
2. Toga money and compensation for the abolition of hunting rights, 55 guilders;
3. Freedom of duties on wine, cheese, soap, coffee, and tea;
4. Possibly the rectorate, 1,000 guilders or more, or the post of secretary of the senate, 600 to 700 guilders;
5. Graduation fees;
6. Private lectures: 80 to 100 students in philosophy that pay a dukaton (3 guilders) each, and 4 students in algebra that pay 100 imperials each.

Naturally, there is a possibility that Bernoulli might get a rise, if the academy flourishes and he is successful, but that remains uncertain and no promises can be made on that point.

In his letter of 4 August,[63] Bernoulli finally turned down the offer from Leiden. On these conditions he cannot come. Not that they are not honourable in themselves, but they do not seem a considerable improvement on his present wealth, not, at least, to such degree that he would be willing to undertake such a drastic migration for it, with all the disadvantages enumerated in the first letter. He regrets, in particular, that they can do nothing for his wife and children, if he

63. See n. 46 on p. 83.

were to die before them, which means that he would be in worse conditions than in Utrecht, that not only offered him a salary, hardly less than Leiden, but moreover a widow's pension, payable wherever she would like to go. If the offer from Utrecht could not keep him in the Republic, much less can that of Leiden get him to leave his fatherland once more, at the cost of many troubles and considerable losses. He is not impressed by the troubles of the Treasury of Leiden, but if they are real, they should come back later, when peace has been restored,[64] and appoint a lecturer as substitute in the meantime. From the whole of the correspondence we may conclude that Bernoulli found the proposal from Leiden very flattering—in his autobiography he mentions it extensively—but never seriously considered accepting it. And it seems doubtful whether Noodt ever did expect anything else.

Noodt intervened in favour of academic autonomy in 1714, when the governors were intending to appoint a theologian who was not on the select list of the senate.[65] 'So much for public liberty in this country,' Perizonius complains, 'so much are laws and advice valued.' But Noodt has taken up the matter with one of the governors and strongly protested.[66] In the academic senate Noodt several times spoke for student interests, mainly in matters of freedom from fiscal duties;[67] but, naturally, for a professor partly deriving his income from student fees this is not completely altruistic.

As might be expected, Noodt's correspondence regularly concerned recommendations of members of his family or friends for jobs or legal proceedings. In the Dutch regent system relations and recommendations were essential to get any job, from professor to roadman. For a professorship a reputation as a scholar was important, no doubt, but usually one would have little chance of getting the job without a promoter in the board of governors. When Cuper gave up his chair in Deventer, to become deputy in the States-General at The Hague, Noodt recommended Cœtier as his successor;[68] Cuper

64. Apparently Bernoulli hints at the war of the Spanish succession, 1701–14.
65. On 1 Nov. 1713 S. H. Van Til died and on 29 Aug. 1714 the governors appointed T. H. van de Honert as his successor; Molhuysen iv: 264 f. There is nothing in Molhuysen about the incident reported by Perizonius.
66. Perizonius to Van Eck, Leiden, 14 Feb. 1714, UL Utrecht, MS 1000: 'Haec est jam hisce in regionibus publica libertas. Ita hic valent leges et Resp[onsa?]. Vix tamen credo id perfecturos fuisse. Sed Noodtium adiit Crucius et haec interminatum est.'
67. 6 June 1695 (Molhuysen iv: 111); 17 Mar. 1707 (Molhuysen v: 227).
68. Noodt to Cuper, Franeker, 11 Feb. 1681, KB 72 G 20: '. . . so neme de vrijheijt van UEd. seer gedijenstig en ernstig te versoecken, indijen UEd. geen ander interest

adopted the recommendation and Cœtier was nominated on his advice.[69] And when Van Eck was appointed 'superarbiter' in an arbitration between Mr and Mrs Criex and Mr Van der Does, Noodt urged him 'that he will be so good as to take care that Mr and Mrs Criex shall not be prejudiced in their rights, if they have any. I am sure you will take care of that sufficiently of your own accord, out of love for the justice that must be observed between all men, but especially between people who are so closely related. But the friendship I have the honour of experiencing from you makes me believe that you will not take it ill from me, if I surmise that you will also take this serious recommendation of mine in due consideration. With your permission, I will rely on that, and if some opportunity presents itself, I will gladly reciprocate.'[70] Such an attempt at influencing a legal decision privately may seem not correct in our eyes. And

heeft, dat het UEd. belijeven mogt de goetheyt te hebben van de Heer Professor Coetier tot de selve professie gerecommandeert te houden. Mijn Heer, ick soude dese vrijheijt niet nemen, ten ware ick van sijn studien ten volsten verseeckert was, en dijenthalven in conscientie geloofde, dat hij veel bequaemheijt heeft om de stad van Deventer in desen dijenst te doen. Want ick doe dit puir uyt mijn eijgen selfs, en soude noijt willen oorsaeck geven door mijne recommandatie tot eenen ongeluckige electie van een professor. Maer ick hebbe van joncks af aen met den gem[elten] Hr. Coetier omgegaen en hem altijd niet alleen van een geluckig oordeel en treffelijcke maximen omtrent sijne studien, maer oock van veel neerstigheijt bevonden. Invoegen ick oock dickwils de eere gehad hebbe van fraeije dingen en geleerde gedagten bij hem te sijen, die mij seer wel behaegden. Behalven dat hij in sijne saecken te exprimeren facijel is, dat hij oock daerenboven heeft eenen goeden en vrindelijcken omganck, en daer door bequaem is om met studenten om te gaen. Dat hij oock tot Harderwijck al voor den oorlog eenigen tijd de professie met succes bedijent heeft en alnog eenige jonge borsten, als ick hore, tot Aernhem met gelijck succes in collegie institueert. Invoegen dat hij het ambagt niet eerst behoeft te leren, gelijck anderen, die eerste beginnen, doen op perijckul van de stad en verscheide jongeluijden; maer dat hij de professor genoegsaem sal mede brengen.'

69. Van Slee, 1916: 128.

70. Noodt to Van Eck, Leiden, 22 May 1697, UL Utrecht, MS 1000: '. . . dat het deselve believen mochte so goed te zijn, van te sorgen, so veel doenlijck dat de voorsz. heer en juffrouw Criex in haer recht, so sij in desen hebben mochten, niet mogen vernadeelt worden. Ick ben wel verseeckert, dat UEd. de selve sorge sal genoeghsaem van selfs draegen; ter liefde van de justitie welcke tusschen alle menschen, doch insonderheit tusschen so na geallieerde en verwante persoonen behoord geobserveert te worden. Maer de vriendschap die ick de eere hebbe, van met UEd. te houden, doet mij gelooven, dat de selve mij niet sal qualijck afnemen, als ick mij verbeelde, dat UEd. oock om dese mijne seer serieuse recommandatie alle billijcken reflexien nemen zal. Ick sal mij, met UEd. permissie, hier op verlaeten en bij gelijcke of andere gelegentheden geerne doen het reciproque.' A certain M. Criex from Utrecht took his degree with Noodt in Franeker, 19 Oct. 1680, see AP Franeker.

perhaps Noodt himself was not too easy about it either, considering the circumspection with which he formulates the request. Noodt recommended his pupil Henricus Cannegieter as conrector for the grammar school in Arnhem, a useful proposition. Cannegieter proved to be a success and in 1720 was appointed rector.[71]

Noodt thanked Joan Huydecoper for his—unfortunately vain—efforts to get his nephew appointed assay-master with the Netherlands East Indies Company (VOC) in the Indies.[72] Alas, the proposal was outvoted in the board of directors, but Noodt hopes that he can count on Huydecoper's attachment in the future, 'if in course of time something would come up, in which my nephew, who has a very honest and modest character and is qualified in several fields, might make himself useful to the Company. I would not dare to ask this grace of you, Sir, unless your well-known generosity in doing good to all honest people trying to get on in fair ways would suggest to me that you will not take ill, Sir, what freedom I take for my nephew, regarding whom nature demands that I do care as much as I would do for my own son.' Apparently, Noodt's nephew was more successful later in getting a job with the VOC. From a letter of Boerhaave to Sherard, dating from 15 December 1726, we learn that someone with that name is on his way to or from the East Indies.[73] On the other hand, Grævius asks Noodt to recommend a certain Grevius of Zwolle for an appointment in Nijmegen.[74]

71. Bots, 1975: 393; M. van Hoorn and D. van Drunen, in Bastiaanse, Bots, and Evers, 1985: 245.
72. Noodt to J. Huydecoper, Leiden, 21 Oct. 1700, RA Utrecht, Familiearchief Huydecoper, inv. nr. 385. I thank mr. A. Koenhein for this reference. '... so er met ter tijds iets mochte openkomen, waer in mijn Neef, die een seer eerlijck en modest naturel heeft, en voorts sich tot verscheide saecken heeft bequaem gemaeckt, de Compagnije soude konnen dienste doen. Ick soude deese gratie bij UWelEd. Gestr. niet derven versoecken, indien des selfs bij mij beproefde genereusiteit, van geern wel te doen aen eerlijcke luijden die sich door goede wegen soecken voort te setten, mij niet dede verbeelden, dat UWelEd. Gestr. mij niet soude misduijden dese vrijheit die ick neme voor mijn Neef, waer aen de natuire wil dat ick mij, als voor mijn soon, late gelegen zijn.'
73. Bœrhaave to Sherard, Leiden, 15 Dec. 1726, Lindeboom, 1962: 149: 'Mais ils auront des menaces de Meester Cornelis quand monsieur Noodt sera au cabo de buena esperanza.' I do not know to what event Bœrhaave refers. I thank Bernard Stolte for this reference.
74. Grævius to Noodt, Utrecht, 8 Oct. 1686, ARA Tets van Goudriaan, inv. nr. 114, 3.

Later years

Noodt's only daughter, Sara Hadriana, baptized 12 September 1692, married in 1713[75] Johan van den Ende, notary and advocate in Amsterdam and a son of the well-known and very rich advocate and Arminian Abraham van den Ende.[76] Presumably, Noodt had known father and son Van den Ende for many years. In 1699 the son enrolled as a law student in Leiden, so he was actually a student of Noodt's. In March 1706 Noodt and Bœrhaave were commissioned by the senate, as we saw before, to arrange the burial and inspect the inheritance of De Volder. At the inspection, Noodt is assisted by two advocates who were most likely his acquaintances, Van den Ende and Petrus de la Court.[77] The first will be Van den Ende, junior. Petrus de la Court, member of a well-known Leiden family, enrolled as a law student in Leiden in 1681 and in Utrecht in 1685, while Noodt was teaching there.[78] When Noodt's student Henrik Brenkman was arranging his Italian journey, Abraham van den Ende brought him into contact with Jean le Clerc,[79] professor at the Remonstrant seminary in Amsterdam, who gave him an introduction to Newton, the English ambassador at the Medici court in Florence.[80] It seems likely that Noodt, in his turn, introduced Brenkman to Van den Ende. On 20 February and 13 March 1711 Noodt confirmed legal opinions of father and son Van den Ende.[81]

75. The marriage-settlement is made on 7 June 1713 in the house of Gerard Noodt, before notary Paulus van Crombrugge, in the presence of Abraham van den Ende, Gerard Noodt, Maria Pots, and Hendrik Adriaan van der Marck van Leur, who all signed the additional protocol, in which the amounts of dowry and morning-gift are stated, see ARA Tets van Goudriaan, inv. nr. 85. The notice of marriage is done on 18 July 1713, see GA Leiden, Oud Rechterlijk Archief, inv. nr. 89, Kerkelijke ondertrouw, fol. 186. The marriage is taking place on 8 Aug. 1713, see the Bruiloftszang door L. Kramp, ARA Tets van Goudriaan, inv. nr. 86.
76. His fame as jurist is based primarily on two collections of legal opinions. As is noted on the title-page, the collection ed. by v. d. Kop, 1769–82, mainly consists of opinions by A. and J. van den Ende. Likewise 110 out of 174 opinions in Barels, 1780–1, are from his hand. There are also opinions by his son; cf. Roberts, 1942: 45. The record of his notarial practice in Amsterdam, 1666–1703, is in GA Amsterdam. Van den Ende is admitted as advocate by the Hof van Holland, 8 June 1682: 'Mr Abraham van den Ende Amstelod.-Bat.' ARA Hof van Holland, inv. nr. 5943 (Register advocaten etc.).
77. Molhuysen iv: 238.
78. AS Leiden: 30 Sept. 1681: Peter de la Court, Lugduno-Batavus, 20, J[ura]; AS Utrecht: 1685.
79. On him *NNBW* iv: 430.
80. Brenkman, 1722: 85; Stolte, 1981: 18.
81. Barels ii, 1781: nr. 63, p. 254; v. d. Kop ii, 1782: nr. 103, p. 512.

As we saw, Johan van den Ende studied law in Leiden, but not only there, apparently. He inscribed in Leiden in 1699, and again in 1715, both times *honoris ergo*, that is, without paying.[82] In 1715 he is noted as Dr, but as far as we know he did not take his degree in Leiden. According to Perizonius, he was not as successful in the profession of notary and advocate as his father, but the father gave him a dowry of at least 70,000 Carolus guilders.[83] In fact, the sum was 15,000 guilders, still a considerable amount. Van den Ende was also much older than his bride.[84]

In the letter just cited, Perizonius gives another interesting piece of information: Johan van den Ende will change from the Remonstrant to the Reformed religion in view of his marriage (*religionem mutabit*). The last we hear of Sara Hadriana van den Ende-Noodt, who went with her husband to Amsterdam, is a letter of condolence she wrote, on 27 February 1758, to Frans van Limborch, Advocate-Fiscal of the Domains in The Hague and a relative of the famous Remonstrant minister Ph. van Limborch.[85] She died in 1759, leaving

82. We do not know why he did not pay in 1699, because poverty cannot have been the reason. In 1715, of course, he was Noodt's son-in-law, and usually the family of professors was exempt from payment. Why van den Ende inscribed in 1715, being a Dr already and living in Amsterdam, is not clear either. Perhaps he could profit in some way from the tax freedoms. See AS Leiden: 758, 842.

83. Perizonius to Van Eck, Leiden, 15 June 1713, UL Utrecht, MS 1000: 'Filia ejus [sc. Noodtii] desponsata est filio van den Endii Amstelaedamensi et Arminiani, sed divitus valde. Filius notarium agit et Advocatum, sed infelicem; verum religionem mutabit, et a patre 70,000, immo amplius ne agunt, Carolinorum ad uxorem tuendam accipiet.' Although an Arminian, Abraham van den Ende did not have his son baptized in the Remonstrant, but in the Walloon church, where he was baptized himself. See GA Amsterdam, DTB. The dowry and morning-gift accorded Sara Adriana in the marriage-settlement amount to 15,000 guilders, see ARA Tets van Goudriaan, inv. nr. 85.

84. She is still 20 (see n. 91 on p. 73). He was baptized in the Walloon church in Amsterdam, 7 May 1679 (GA Amsterdam), so at his marriage he is 34. When enrolling in Leiden in 1699 he gives his age one year too old (21), in 1715 three years too young (33), see n. 82. He later added his mother's name to his own, calling himself Jan Ham van den Ende. For his admission as advocate at the Hof van Holland, see ARA Tets van Goudriaan, inv. nr. 84. He is admitted on 5 Sept. 1703. The record of his notarial practice, apparently continuing that of his father, 1704–22, is in GA Amsterdam. In the taxation of 1742 he figures as advocate, and is among the most well-to-do citizens of Amsterdam. He lives in a house (on the Keizersgracht near the Spiegelstraat), rented for 1,900 guilders a year, has four maid-servants, a carriage with four horses, a country-house (Treslong in Hillegom), capital shares above 2,000 guilders, and an income of 15,000 guilders a year; see Oldewelt, 1945: ward 57, no. 3899. He was buried in the Oude Kerk at Amsterdam, 2 Dec. 1747 (GA Amsterdam, DTB 1049, 75).

85. Amsterdam, 27 Feb. 1758, UL Amsterdam.

one son, who bore the names Gerrit Abraham after both grandfathers.[86]

In 1713 Noodt seems to have felt rather depressed and decided to stop writing.[87] As his last book he published his *Opera omnia*, which he presented, among others, to his old friend Gisbert Cuper. Cuper thanks him in a long letter,[88] somewhat ashamed because he had not answered Noodt's previous letter, dating from 1709. The printing privilege of the *Opera omnia*, which Noodt requested personally, dates back to 1710.[89] In the preface to the *Opera omnia* Noodt takes his leave from his readers:

> For myself, I do not know whether I will endeavour anything more. The age of 66 reminds me of the law of Nature, which puts an end not only to flowers and plants and other living things, but also to men—for some early, for some late, for all the same. How could I hope in good sense to be excepted from this? Therefore I have decided to do what people are accustomed to do, when they are about to go abroad. In time, they collect their vessels, and decide, when it still is possible, what has to become of their affairs and belongings.[90]

The works published before are revised for this edition, some slightly, some thoroughly. Some texts are added that had remained

86. She was buried in the Oude Kerk at Amsterdam, 20 Nov. 1759 (GA Amsterdam, DTB 1049, 118^{v}). Her son Gerard was baptized 21 Aug. 1718 in the Walloon church (GA Amsterdam, DTB 134, fol. 52). On 17 May 1770 two instruments were handed over to the magistrate of Leiden, one from the university, attesting that Noodt left his daughter Sara Adriana as sole heir, another from Amsterdam, dated 26 Feb. 1760 and attesting that Gerrit Abraham van den Ende is sole heir of Jan and Sara Adriana van den Ende. On 4 Feb. 1783 Noodt's former house on the Pieterskerkhof was sold for Gerrit Abraham van den Ende, for 3,000 guilders, to Angelique Maria Rucker, see GA Leiden, Register Sevenhuysen, fol. 174^{v}.
87. Noodt to Cuper, Leiden, Sept. 1713, KB 72 G 20, nr. 22: 'Also ben te raade geworden, te maecken een einde van schrijven, so hebbe geresolveert, alle mijne voor desen uitgegevene wercken, met eenige vermeerderinge, te laten herdrucken, en daer bij te doen het een en het andere 't welcke noch hadde gereet liggen.' See also the letters Leiden, 6 Mar. 1716, to Van Eck (UL Utrecht, MS 1000) and J. van de Water (KHA G 16–A 258).
88. Deventer, 20 Oct. 1713, KB 72 G 20, nr. 38.
89. Privilege, 25 Mar. 1710, ceded to Johannes van der Linden, jun., Leiden, 27 Apr. 1713. Printed in *Opera omnia*, 1713 (Ahsmann–Feenstra, 1984: nr. 464). According to Perizonius, the indices to this edn. were made by one Dukerus Haganus, by whom is meant, no doubt, Perizonius' pupil C. A. Duker, then vice-principal of the gymnasium in The Hague (*NNBW* iii: 306). Perizonius to Van Eck, Leiden, 13 July 1713, UL Utrecht, MS 1000: 'Indicem in Opera Noodtii confecit, quod certo scio, Dukerus Haganus, nec dubio quin mendas ille quoque annotaverit et collegerit.'
90. *Opera omnia*, Leiden, 1713, Ad lectorem, p. ii.

unpublished thus far: two books on usufruct, one book on agreements and transactions (*De pactis et transactionibus*, cf. D 2. 14 and C 2. 3), and the Franeker inaugural address on civil prudence.[91]

Considering the words of the preface just cited, it seems hardly surprising that in 1716, when another book by Noodt appeared,[92] they thought in Leipzig that it was a posthumous work.[93] The letters with which he sent the new book to Van Eck and Van de Water sound rather like an apology. To Van Eck he wrote: 'I had the intention to write no more, but apparently writing is a *suave delirium*; and it became true, as you prophesied, that I would not be able to remain true to my intention.'[94] And on the same day he wrote to Van de Water: 'You should not be surprised that I had the intention not to write any more, and now am beginning again. Because, apart from the fact that *ambulatoria hominis voluntas* [man's will is changeable], the reason why I have done so, is that, on the one hand, I feel better in my old age than I had hoped to be for some time, and, on the other hand, that I do not know how to fill my spare time any other way. Besides, it is not a bad pastime to make good studies palatable (as far as possible) for others.'[95]

Apparently, Noodt had been in low spirits for some time, maybe partly on account of the marriage of his only daughter. At the beginning of 1714 P. de Toullieu[96] wrote to Van Eck that he had

91. About these works see below, pp. 155, 252, and 255.
92. The first part of the commentary on the Pandects, Books 1–4, Ahsmann–Feenstra, 1984: nr. 475.
93. H. Post to Van Eck, Leipzig, 25 May 1716, UL Utrecht, MS 1000: 'Celeberrimi Noodii opus posthumum parum haec aestimant eruditi. Actorum Lipsiensium collectores quid de eo sentiant, magnopere scire desidero, cum sciam Waechtlero injuctum esse munus, ut de eo judicium ferret'.
94. For reference, see n. 87. 'Ick was van meninge, niet meer te schrijven, maer het schijnt, dat het zelve schrijven is een suave delirium; en het is waer geworden, dat UWeled. heeft geprophetееrt, dat ick in het voorsz. voorneemen niet wel en zoude konnen bestandig blijven.'
95. For reference, see n. 87. '. . . voorts believe UEd. zig niet te verwonderen, dat ben geweest van meninge, niet meer te schrijven, en egter dit nu weer beginne te doen. Want behalven dat is ambulatoria ominis voluntas [man's will is changeable], zo ben daer toe bewogen eensdeels, omdat mij (God zij gelooft) in desen mijnen ouderdom beter bevinde, als van mij voor eenigen tijd hebbe gehoopt gehad, andersdeels, omdat mijnen ledigen tijd niet wete anders te besteden; ook is het niet van het argste amuzement, goede studien (zo veel doenlijk) smakelijk te maken aan anderen.'
96. 1669–1734. On him, see Haubold, 1809: 196; Jugler ii, 1775: 211–19 and vi, 1780: 344 f. Not in *NNBW*. He was a pupil of Van Eck and Huber in Franeker and studied for one year in Leiden, where he will have met Noodt. He was professor in Lingen and in 1717 he was inaugurated in Groningen, together with Barbeyrac.

heard from Leiden that Noodt's health and fortitude were somewhat shaky.[97] But obviously he recovered quickly and in his loneliness had no other pastime than studying and writing. That he started a commentary on the Pandects—an ambitious project, more fitting a scholar in the prime of his life—will have something to do as well with the unexpected death of Johannes Vœt, at the beginning of September 1713, and only a few months after the appearance of the 'final' *Opera omnia*.[98] Most likely, Noodt would not have wanted to compete with his close colleague while he was still alive. Vœt's Commentary on the Pandects had a tremendous success. It was a very cleverly made and practically useful synthesis of Roman law as it applied in Holland. On its appearance, in 1698/1704, it was received very well, and in 1707 a second impression was already needed.[99] But Vœt's untimely death must have made a difference for Noodt. After all, a Commentary on the Digest was the usual *magnum opus* of the truly great Romanist. Vœt's commentary did not give an adequate picture of the state of humanist legal scholarship in the Dutch elegant school, for which purpose it had never been intended.[1] For all its qualities, Noodt's commentary never really could compete with that of Vœt, if only because it remained unfinished.

As we have already seen, Noodt's academic activities continued as usual during these years.[2] In the first place, he taught. We have the

97. De Toullieu to Van Eck, Lingen, 1 Mar. 1714, UL Utrecht, MS 1000: 'Litteras Lugduno-Bat. accepi e quibus animadverto . . . item nonnihil inclinare Cl. Noodtii vires et vegetum huius robur. Sic rursus devenietur ad te.'
98. Vœt died on 9 Sept., during a vacation in Utrecht. Noodt sent his *Opera omnia* to Cuper in the first days of Sept., before Vœt's death, but they had come out of the press at the beginning of June, see Perizonius to Van Eck, Leiden, 15 June 1713, UL Utrecht, MS 1000: 'Apud nos Noodtii opera omnia conjunctim in unum volumen formae, ut dicitur, Quarto jam prodierunt in publicum.'
99. Feenstra and Waal, 1975: 42; Ahsmann–Feenstra, 1984: nr. 1061.
1. According to the preface, Vœt had more practical objectives in mind. He tries to satisfy, among others, those 'quibus ingratum atque superfluum videri posset, difficiles Theoriae Romanae quaestiones discussisse, non ita quotidianum in foro usum praebentes, quibusque adeo sordet, quicquid de jure Quiritium tersum licet nitidumque, promitur'.
2. On 6 Dec. 1717 the senate asked Noodt to inspect the will of Thysius, in order to see if it contained any provisions in connection with the Bibliotheca Thysiana, Molhuysen iv: 292. On 2 Oct. 1722 Noodt informed the senate that the law faculty had granted the beneficium Boekelmanianum to Augustinus van Staveren, Molhuysen iv: 329. On 7 Feb. 1725 the seniors of the three faculties, Bœrhaave, Noodt, and a Marck were delegated by the senate to discuss in the Rijnlands Huis a nasty problem of precedence with the members of the States of Holland who were visiting Leiden for the celebration of the 150th anniversary of the university, Molhuysen iv: 367.

notes of his lectures on the Pandects from the years 1712,[3] 1713,[4] 1715/16,[5] and 1721.[6] As usual, Noodt gave his public lessons every day (vacations and days of festivities, inaugurations, graduations, and book auctions excluded) at 9 o'clock in the morning. From September 1721 (Noodt was 74 by that time!) they were even held an hour earlier, because the young Vitriarius, who was rector at that time, liked to lecture at 9 o'clock himself. Noodt had no objections.[7] The last *series lectionum* preserved which mentions Noodt dates from September 1724, hardly a year before his death.[8] Unfortunately, the series gives no information about the subjects Noodt read. From beginning to end the same formula is used: important subjects from public and private law.[9] It is not certain, for that matter, that the public lessons announced in the series were actually given. Later in the eighteenth century it often proved not to be the case.[10] Apart from the public lessons, Noodt privately read the Institutes,[11] and presumably the Pandects as well, most likely for

3. UL Gent, MS 280.
4. (Formerly?) Bibl. van Zyl, Cape Town, see Roberts, 1942: 226.
5. UL Leiden, BPL 696; Edinburgh, NLS MS 17810, fol. 19^r–58^v, notes of Lord Milton (Andrew Fletcher), starting Tuesday, 16 Sept. 1715, and not going beyond Book 1 of the Digest. On Lord Milton, see A. Murdoch, *The people above: politics and administration in mid-eighteenth century Scotland*. Edinburgh, 1980.
6. *Dictata Cel. G. Noodt ex ore eius excerpta in totas Pandectas* [by J. C. Rücker] PB Leeuwarden, MS Hof 10 [Voorda Collection]. 4 vols. On the penultimate leaf of vol. iv there is a note saying that the lectures ended on 10 July 1721.
7. Molhuysen iv: 324: '... nec Cl. Noodtius se intercedere.'; id. Appendix nr. 999, p. 160*.
8. Molhuysen iv: Appendix nr. 1011, p. 188*. In his letter to Barbeyrac of August 1724 Noodt wrote that his poor health had forced him to reduce his public as well as his private duties, Barbeyrac, 1731: LXXVI; id., *Vita*, fol. 7^v.
9. The first series preserved mentioning Noodt is of Feb. 1694, Molhuysen iv: Appendix 914, p. 45*; for the last, see n. 8. We only have more detailed information about the subjects Noodt taught in 1693. Then the Leiden professors delivered a report to the governors, dating from 9 Feb. 1693, see Molhuysen iv: 11. Noodt taught on the following titles: de patria potestate (C 8. 46/Inst. 1. 9); de accusationibus (D 48. 2/C 9. 2), quaestionibus (D 48. 18/C 9. 41) et poenis (C 48. 19/C 2. 3); de transactionibus (D 2. 15/C 2. 4); de his qui notantur infamia (D 3. 2); de procuratoribus et defensoribus (D 3. 3); de restitutione in integrum (D 4. 1). This is, indeed, a fair sample of interesting topics of private and public civil law: some law of persons, some criminal law, some procedural law, some contracts and delicts. See further on Noodt's lectures below, Ch. 3, § 5.
10. Kernkamp iii: 615 f.
11. The lecture notes on the Institutes, written in 1710 by R. W. de Bachman from Emmerich (UL Leiden, BPL 191x) have on the title-page: '... explicata in collegio domestico.'

students lodged with him in the first place. Vœt did the same.[12]

Noodt was secretary of the senate in 1712/13 and, as we saw, spoke for academic autonomy. When in the autumn of 1713 Vœt died, Noodt by coincidence was in an excellent position to get his fellow-townsman Anton Schulting appointed as a successor. Thoughts about his own impending retirement will have played a role in this as well. Perizonius reported the developments regularly to Van Eck, who at that moment was regarded as a possible candidate himself—at least by his friends.[13] It seems unlikely, however, that in 1713 Van Eck was seriously considered as successor to Vœt.[14] He was 51 already, and had for twenty years been professor in Utrecht. Apart from being a neo-Latin poet of some quality, he had a reputation as a scholar of Roman law and as teacher of some of the best jurists in the Republic (of Van Bijnkershœk above all),[15] but apart from a very successful textbook he did not have many publications to his name and in this respect must have disappointed expectations in Utrecht.[16]

On 16 September 1713, ten days after Vœt's death, Perizonius gave Van Eck his opinion about the succession. The governors would be wise if they had Vœt succeeded by Van Eck, Noodt by Schulting, and Vitriarius by his son.[17] But on 27 September he wrote that he expected Schulting to get Vœt's chair,[18] and on 9 October he

12. See Vœt, Elementa juris secundam ordinem Institutionum Justiniani in usum domesticae exercitationis digesta, Ahsmann–Feenstra, 1984: nr. 1094.
13. Not only Perizonius, but also De Toullieu frequently hinted at a possible nomination of Van Eck to Leiden (De Toullieu to Van Eck, Lingen, 1 Mar. 1714; Groningen, 8 June 1719, both UL Utrecht, MS 1000). Van Bijnkershœk intervened for Van Eck in Oct. 1713, in connection with the succession to Vœt, see below, p. 97
14. Molhuysen has nothing about this. Already on 11 Sept. the governors of Utrecht considered it probable that Van Eck would be appointed in Leiden as successor to Vœt and on 18 Sept. they decided to give him 1,800 guilders plus the title 'professor juris hodierni'. Van Eck promised not to take an offer from elsewhere. But in Leiden at that moment nothing had yet been decided. On 19 Sept. governors decided to ask the advice of the law faculty, which on 26 Sept. proposed Schulting (Molhuysen iv: 267). And already by then Perizonius was sure that Schulting would get the job (see at n. 19). Schulting's appointment was decided on 9 Oct. and he accepted on 24 Oct. Apparently Van Eck was never seriously considered as successor to Vœt. But neither did he inform his friends Perizonius and van Bijnkershœk about his promise to the governors of Utrecht.
15. See Haubold, 1809: 139 f.
16. Van den Bergh, 1986*b*: 44.
17. Leiden, 16 Sept. 1713, UL Utrecht, MS 1000: 'Te potissimum Voetio, ac Noodtio demum Schultingium, Vitriario demum Filium successorem dandum, si Curatores Academiae consultum velint.'
18. Leiden, 27 Sept. 1713, UL Utrecht, MS 1000: 'Nunc designatum iri credo

reported that this had indeed been decided.[19] He had his doubts whether the governors, by appointing Schulting, had taken due care of the academy, although he gladly acknowledged that he was a very learned man.[20] Schulting's nomination was not only strongly advocated by Noodt, who attended the meeting of the board of governors together with the rector, but also by burgomaster Crucius, whose sister was married to the Nijmegen alderman Van den Berg, Schulting's uncle,[21] as well as by some people from The Hague, among whom was the well-known counsel Erpecum.[22] Perizonius was certain that Van Bijnkershœk had written to the governors to recommend Van Eck. When his letter was read, Schulting's advocates kept silent and did not know how to gainsay it, but they did not change their opinion.[23]

In the first decades of the eighteenth century, with Noodt and

Schultingium, cujus causam agit non tantum Noodtius, qui cum Rectore Magnifico vocatus in concessum Curatorum studiosissime eum laudavit, sed et consul Crucius.'

19. Leiden, 9 Oct. 1713, UL Utrecht, MS 1000, see n. 23.
20. Letter as cited in n. 166: 'an Schultingium nunc creando consuluerunt Academia, valde dubio, licet doctissimum esse virum ultro et lubens agnoscam.' Hardly half a year later De Toullieu wrote to Van Eck (Lingen, 1 Mar. 1714, UL Utrecht, MS 1000) that the doubts of Perizonius were confirmed: 'Litteras Lugduno-Bat. accepi e quibus animadverto non fefellisse Cl. Perizonium opinionem suam de successu Cl. Schultingii intra spem futuro'. But naturally such assertions, which were rather meant as expressions of friendship to Van Eck, cannot be taken seriously.
21. Schulting's father was married to Catharina van den Berg (GA Nijmegen, OAN Doopboeken NH Kerk). Her father was a councillor and alderman, and her brother likewise. Catharina's signature is under a receipt for the payment she gets as widow of Johan Schulting (a quarter of his salary of f. 225), GA Nijmegen, Gymnasium, inv. nr. 449.
22. A pupil of Schulting's. Wilhelmus van Erpecum from Amsterdam enrolled in Franeker, 18 May 1693 (AS Franeker, 9168) and again in 1698 (id., 9805). He disputed *theses controversae* under *praeses* Schulting in Franeker, 14 Nov. and 23 Nov. 1696, see Schulting, 1738 (Ahsmann–Feenstra, 1984: nr. 623). He was made *doctor juris* by Schulting after an excellent disputation on 12 May 1699. AP Franeker, p. 72.
23. Letter as cited in n. 19: 'Decretum est hodie a Curatorius et Consulis vocare Schultingium, additis annuis mille sexcentorum Carolinorum. Ampliss. Rosenbomius, sed solus, Westenbergium designavit. Si de duobus vocandis retulisset ad Collegium, forsan uterque fuisset electus. Schultingium commendaverunt et foverunt, quam maxime, Ampliss. Crucius, cujus soror, ut nosti, fuit nupta van den Bergio Neomagensi scabino, avunculo Schultingii, tum Noodtius noster, cui ille est devotissimus, denique Hagenses aliquot, inque iis celebris causarum orator Erpecum . . . Quod Ampl. Binkershoukius de te huc vocando scribit certissima sunt. Num qui Schultingium faverunt, tum quieverunt, nec profecissent quidquam, sed diu aliter visum'.

Schulting in the chairs of the law faculty, humanistic legal scholarship was at its height in Leiden, but the most conspicuously humanistic lectures were given by Matthaeus III (died 1710). The lectures of Noodt and Schulting on the Institutes, explaining Roman institutions, inevitably contain an antiquarian element,[24] but Noodt's lectures on the Pandects were mainly dogmatic. He also discussed topical subjects like torture and referred to contemporary law occasionally. He partly taught something which we would call social philosophy today. And Schulting also read subjects—like 'contract'—in the manner established by Böckelmann.[25] From 1694 Matthæus in his public lessons on the Codex no longer followed the *ordo legum*, but gave a palingenetic treatment of the constitutions promulgated by successive later Roman emperors.[26]

In 1717 Noodt met Barbeyrac,[27] who had been appointed professor in Groningen. On Barbeyrac's arrival in Amsterdam Jean le Clerc organized a small welcome party which was attended by a smiling Noodt. On that occasion Noodt told Barbeyrac once more how pleased he was with the French translation of his rectorial addresses.[28] Barbeyrac, a refugee since the revocation of the Edict of Nantes (1685), and Noodt, who knew religious persecution from his family's history, were both advocates of toleration, and indeed must have been rather congenial. Later, it was Barbeyrac who did much to honour the memory of Noodt. In 1731 when presenting his life of Noodt to Van den Ende he wrote:

Je n'ai jamais perdu d'Ami, dont la perte m'ait été plus sensible, que celle de Monsieur Noodt, votre Beaupère, et je voudrois bien qu'il vécut encore, pour que je n'eusse pas eu occasion de faire son Eloge, dont il n'avoit pas besoin, etant connu et personellement, et par ses beaux ouvrages. Mais puis qu'il a plu Dieu de le retirer de ce Monde, je me suis fait un plaisir de témoigner publiquement la vénération que j'ai pour sa mémoire, et de lui

24. There are synoptic notes of the lectures on the Institutes by Noodt and Schulting, UL Leiden, BPL 695. See below, p. 282.
25. Molhuysen iv: 134* (Series Feb. 1714: 'actions'); 136* (Series Feb. 1615: 'contracts'). Schulting taught contracts until the end of the summer semester of 1720; see ibid., 154* (Series Feb. 1720).
26. Molhuysen iv: 45*, Series Feb. 1694: Justinian; 55*–63*, Series Sept. 1696–Sept. 1697: Arcadius and Honorius: 65*–80*, Series Feb. 1698–Feb. 1700: Gordianus; 93*–101*, Series Feb. 1703–Feb. 1704: Gallus, Volusianus, Valerianus, and Gallienus; 107*, Series Sept. 1706–Sept. 1709: Constantine; 122*, Series Feb. 1710: Constantine II, Constans, and Constantius.
27. Barbeyrac, 1731: xiv. They met in Amsterdam, see Meylan, 1937: 121.
28. Barbeyrac, 1731: xiv.

rendre justice sans aucune ombre de flatterie. En ne disant que la pure vérité, j'ai laissé parler mon cœur, et je n'ai rien écrit avec tant de plaisir et de faculté que cet Eloge historique.[29]

In June 1719 there were rumours, De Toullieu wrote to Van Eck,[30] that they intended to appoint a new law professor in Leiden. They said that Noodt was growing old (he was 72, in fact!) and it did not go very well with Schulting. Therefore, they considered adding an extra colleague, and in that case, De Toullieu thinks, they will come to Van Eck once more. But if the governors actually had plans to give Noodt an adjunct, they may not have had Van Eck in mind, but rather his pupil W. Best, who was professor in Harderwijk.[31] According to Haubold, Best was on the point of being appointed in Leiden in 1719, when he died.[32] But there is nothing of all this in our sources, and perhaps De Toullieu simply misunderstood some vague gossip. Actually, in 1719, not Noodt, but Vitriarius was ill, and in September his son was appointed in his place.[33] Noodt remained in office as before. In 1723, however, J. O. Westenberg from Franeker was appointed in Leiden, because, as the governors said, 'several law professors are very old and weak'.[34]

An important student who took his degree with Noodt in 1718 was D. G. Strube, who later made a career in the service of the king of Hanover and played a decisive role in the formation of the law faculty in the newly founded university of Göttingen, which was modelled on Dutch institutions.[35] Another German student was Bernhard Heinrich Reinold (1677–1726), who became professor in Duisburg and Frankfurt on the Oder and was a strong propagandist of the Dutch school in Germany.[36] A student who remained particu-

29. J. Barbeyrac to J. van den Ende, Groningen, 26 May 1731. ARA Tets van Goudriaan, inv. nr. 92.

30. De Toullieu to Van Eck, Groningen, 8 June 1719, UL Utrecht, MS 1000: 'Rumor est novum professorem juris Leidae creatum iri. Dicunt senescere Cl. Noodtium, nec ita feliciter succedere cum Cl. Schultingio, adeoque de collega ipsis adjugendo cogitari. Sic rursus ibitur ad te.'

31. 1683–1719; on him, see *NNBW* vii: 113. Barbeyrac and A. v. Haller speak rather critically about him, see Lindeboom, 1958: 96 f.

32. Haubold, 1809: 194. Nothing about this is found in Molhuysen, nor in *NNBW*.

33. Molhuysen iv: 307 (21 Oct. 1719).

34. See Feenstra, 1984: 57.

35. Not in Molhuysen iv. On Strube (1694–1776) see *Allg. deutsche Biogr.* 36, Leipzig, 1893: 635 f.

36. Reinold was born in 1677 in Olfen near Hamm, Westphalia. At the age of 17 he went to the newly founded university of Halle (1690) where he stayed only two years (1694–6) and did not take a degree. For several years he had various jobs,

larly grateful to Noodt's teaching was Pieter van der Schelling, who took his degree in 1721 in Leiden on a thesis concerning the *lex Rhodia de jactu*, dedicated to Van Alkemade and Noodt. In 1745 he dedicated his *Histori van het notarisschap . . . mitsgaders de Engelsche praktyk* to Noodt's son-in-law Van den Ende with a long poem, in which he recalls how Noodt stimulated his studies in law and history:[37]

mainly as private teacher or governor of students on academic tour, finally as teacher of princes at the court in Copenhagen, where he stayed three years. He enrolled in Leiden, 15 Aug. 1703 (AS Leiden), where he heard Noodt and Perizonius (and will have met Brenkman), but he took his degree in Utrecht with van Muyden, 1 Apr. 1705 (AP Utrecht). The thesis, discussing some differences of Roman and canon law—not quite an elegant subject—according to a trustworthy witness was hardly an hour's work and so lean that Van Eck, then dean of the faculty, laughed at it when he inspected it. Reinold was advocate in Bremen, professor in the gymnasium of Bremen (1709) and Herborn (1710), as well as in the universities of Duisburg (1712) and Frankfurt on the Oder (1714). In 1722 he was appointed member of the academy in Berlin. He suffered seriously from melancholia. In 1724 he got an offer from Groningen, but decided to stay in Frankfurt, where he died 22 May 1726. In law he was mainly an autodidact. His work, ed. by Jugler, primarily consists of critical observations in the humanist tradition. Among other things, he published a speech about the foundations of natural law (which influenced Wieling), another one about the inscriptions of the fragments in the Digest, a defence of the order of the *Edictum perpetuum*, and a *Programma de optima dicendi discendique juris Romani methodo*. He was in contact with Brenkman. Back from Italy, Brenkman sent him a facsimile transcription of a page from the Florentine manuscript of the Digest (Reinold, 1755: 726) and later he cited Reinold's opinion concerning the authority of the *Florentina*, from which it appears that Reinold (like Cujas and Noodt) did not regard F as flawless (Brenkman, 1722: 214, 217, 245, 461; cf. Stolte, 1981: 67, 69). Reinold's Duisburg inaugural address (9 June 1712) on the inscriptions of the fragments in the Digest and the Codex is also printed, with remarks by Wieling, in Wieling, 1727: 179f. Opposing Thomasius (one of his former teachers in Halle!), he contended that only Roman law, not German law, should be taught in universities, an opinion which hardly can have helped to make him popular. Apparently he was not a scholar of the first order and only taught at second-rate universities. But that may not be enough to explain the *damnatio memoriae* he experienced in the 19th century (he is not in the *Allgemeine Deutsche Biographie*!). Possibly his position has more to do with this. With the Historical School began a period in which the achievements of the Dutch school and its students were systematically slighted or ignored. His life by J. F. Jugler in the preface to Reinold, 1755, which is copied by Landsberg (Stintzing and Landsberg iii. 1, Text p. 165, Notes p. 110). Landsberg erroneously gives the name as Reinhold, and Schneppen (1960: 103, with reference to Stintzing and Landsberg!) as Reinhard. Landsberg (followed by Schneppen) says that he was professor in Königsberg, but this is a mistake. On him, see also Haubold, 1809: 156f.

37. Molhuysen iv: 281; P. v. d. Schelling, *Diatribe . . . de lege rhodia de jactu*. Leiden, 1721; id., *Histori van het notarisschap . . . mitsgaders de Engelsche praktijk*. Rotterdam, 1745. I thank Mr A. F. Gehlen, Maastricht, for these references.

Van Noodt, wiens raad, en vlyt, en naam
My porde, om in de Regtsgeleerdheid
(Daar hy, op wieken van de Faam
Gevœrd, en vry van Schoolverkeerdheid,
Gestaag aanhield) op d'eere-trap
Des Leeraars, lang verzuimd, te stygen,
En door Hem, in die Wetenschap
Myn Vorderaar, dat Regt te krijgen.
Ik hou dit Werk zelfs als een vrugt
Van zynen Raad, aan my gegeeven,
Die van der jeugd wierd door een zugt
Tot Regt, en Oudheen aangedreeven;
Maar, door verkeering met dat Ligt
Der Regtsgeleerdheid meer ontstoken,
Myn lust veranderde in een pligt
Op't woord van Noodt met klem gesproken:
'Uw weeten baat aan andren niet,
Ten zy zy ook uw weeten weeten . . .'

The last years of Noodt's life are clouded by an unusually sharp polemic with Cornelis van Bijnkershœk, which will be discussed later in greater detail.[38] In 1719, in his *Opuscula varii argumenti*, Van Bijnkershœk published a treatise on the right to kill, sell, or abandon children in ancient Rome.[39] In this he contested the thesis of Noodt, published in 1700 in his *Julius Paulus*, that until fairly late, and, in fact, still under the first Christian emperors, it was not punishable under Roman law to expose children. According to Noodt the prohibition dates only from 374. Seemingly, Van Bijnkershœk only touches on Noodt's thesis in passing, but, in fact, it was the purpose of the whole treatise. This is apparent from a letter Van Bijnkershœk wrote to Van Eck, directly after the appearance of the *Julius Paulus*.[40] Noodt, who had a reputation for peaceability, and as a rule did not enter in a public debate with his critics, rejoined in 1722 with a 'Friendly answer',[41] which, in fact, is rather sharply formulated in places. Apparently he was irritated, not least perhaps by the succinct suggestion of Van Bijnkershœk that Noodt's thesis was not original,

38. See below, p. 211 ff.
39. De jure occidendi, vendendi et exponendi liberos apus veteros Romanos. In: *Opuscula varii argumenti*. Leiden, 22 Mar. 1719.
40. Van Bijnkershœk to Van Eck, The Hague, 22 Mar. 1700, UL Utrecht, MS 1000. On this, see further below, p. 211 ff.
41. Ahsmann–Feenstra, 1984: nr. 477. Never before had Noodt reacted to criticism from van Bijnkershœk; see below, Ch. 4, at n. 90.

but was taken from Lipsius. Van Bijnkershœk, a man who rode the high horse, and did not easily admit to being wrong, retorted with 'Further considerations' (1723),[42] whose tone was much sharper still. Noodt commented on this rather scornfully in his Commentary on the Pandects,[43] which, extended now to Book 27, appeared in the middle of 1724, in the last edition of the *Opera omnia* that was to be edited by Noodt personally.[44] Van Bijnkershoek admitted later that he had some regrets about his sharp tone.[45] In fact, it can hardly be argued that the famous senior professor of Leiden, with whom he had seemed to be friends for so many years, was treated with all due respect. But, however that may be, the sharp dispute between the two most famous Dutch jurists of their time no doubt attracted the attention of the republic of letters, at home as well as abroad. We do not know whether their friendship—they had known each other personally at least since 1696,[46] and exchanged visits regularly[47]—survived the debate. But Noodt died within a year anyway.

Noodt had always been very strong and healthy.[48] Apart from the malaria he caught in Franeker at the end of 1680,[49] and which lasted about a year, we hear nothing about any illness. Neither do we know whether his shaky condition in 1713 had a medical cause.[50] Quite to the contrary, he is always described as robust, and having a healthy

42. *Curae secundae de jure occidendi et exponendi liberos apus veteres Romanos ad virum clarissimum Gerardum Noodt*. Leiden, 1723.
43. Book 25, tit. 3, *Opera* ii: 534.
44. See n. 63.
45. See Star Numan, 1869: 214 and see further, p. 216.
46. Van Bijnkershœk wrote to Van Eck, The Hague, 14 June 1696, UL Utrecht, MS 1000, that Noodt has visited him at home and studied his Digest manuscript: 'Clariss. Nootius nudius quartus me consuluit de isto manuscripto, et verba fecit de lectione quorundam l[egum] sub Tit. d. usuris, ad quem commentatus est. Dixit se brevi fortasse hunc commentarium daturum publico. An porro nonnullo requisiturus sit ex Manuscripto, quibus de in genere tantum loquutus est, ignoro.' The letter is ed. by van den Bergh, 1984: 282 f.
47. Van Bijnkershœk to Van Eck, The Hague, 14 Jan. 1701, UL Utrecht, MS 1000: '... Cl. Noodtium brevi editurum esse observationes juris; ita mihi ipsius narrabat ante triduum, cum hic me inviseret.'; van Bijnkershœk to Van Eck, The Hague, 3 Mar. 1705, ibid.: 'Cl. Noodtius mihi praelegit magnam partem Observationum criticarum ...'; Perizonius to Van Eck, Leiden, 1 Feb. 1710, UL Utrecht, MS 1000: 'Fuit nuperrime [Bijnkershœkius] cum uxore in hac urbe, et laute satis ab Noodtio nostro est acceptus ...'.
48. Obituary, ARA Tets van Goudriaan, inv. nr. 119. In Aug. 1724, when his health begins to fail him, Noodt himself writes to Barbeyrac: 'J'ai néanmoins de quoi remercier Dieu, qui me fait la grace d'être dans un age si avancé, sans maladie, sans douleur, c'est à dire sans avoir sujet de me plaindre.' Barbeyrac, 1731: LXXVI.
49. See above, p. 43.
50. See above, p. 93.

complexion. In 1705 Perizonius wrote that Noodt was in perfect condition, as his correspondent, Van Eck, would know for himself. The burgomaster of Arnhem Swæn, when passing through Leiden, had visited Noodt and on that occasion Noodt declared that the rumours circulating about his bad health were false. And, in fact, Swæn did find him in perfect health.[51]

But during the last three years of his life, Noodt was ailing.[52] His son-in-law attributed this to the fact that his powers were consumed by his extensive studies and the worries of his profession. But that does sound rather like a conventional image. Noodt's illness is not unusual for a man of advanced age—he is in his mid-seventies—and apparently had other causes. Noodt had fits of apoplexy.[53] In old age, these are usually caused by high blood-pressure, and, eventually, arteriosclerosis. We have no proof that Noodt had high blood-pressure, but on his second engraved portrait he really looks much too fat. And maybe the 'healthy complexion' had something to do with it too.

Three years before his death, his friend and colleague Hermannus Bœrhaave, the world-famous physician,[54] treated him. Noodt and he had known each other for many years.[55] In a letter to Cox Macro, dating from 1710, Bœrhaave called Noodt his 'best friend'.[56] Bœrhaave was writing to Macro to thank him for sending some treatise, possibly relating to freedom of religion.[57] He drew Macro's

51. Perizonius to Van Eck, Leiden, 25 July 1705, UL Utrecht, MS 1000: 'Nudius tertius per hanc urbem et vestram quoque, rediit Arnhemum Consul Swaenius cum Filio. Hagae fuerat et consederat inter Ordines qui vocantur Generales. Collocutus hic fuit cum nostro Noodtio, qui falsum ait, quod de eius sequiore valetudine spargitur, quum tamen valide valentem deprehenderit, quam te ipsum comperiat.'
52. Obituary, as n. 48.
53. Obituary, as n. 48; Barbeyrac, 1731: LXXVIII. The illness was well defined already in the 17th century. Noodt had also trouble with walking, which he had liked to do in the past, see Barbeyrac, 1731: LXXVI.
54. On him, see *NNBW* vi: 127–41; Lindeboom, 1968.
55. See above, p. 82 (1709).
56. Bœrhaave to Cox Macro, Leiden, 22 June 1710, Lindeboom, 1962: 18 (Latin text), 19–20 (English trans.): 'Nescio an videris quae de hac re scripsit Spinosa in ultimis capitibus tractatus theologici-politici, aut an tuos venerit ad oculos tractatus anonymi de jure Ecclesiasticorum. Etiam placuit mihi super hac re mirifice optimi mei amici Gerardi Noodt oratio de religione a magistratis Imperio jure gentium libera.'
57. Because Macro (1683–1767), an antiquarian and collector, did not publish anything during his lifetime, we do not know which treatise is meant. On Macro, see *Dict. Nat. Biography* 35, 1893: 283 f. Macro studied medicine in Leiden under Bœrhaave in 1703.

attention to three treatises which it is interesting to see mentioned in the same breath: Spinoza's *Tractatus theologico-politicus*,[58] the treatise *De jure Ecclesiasticorum*—published anonymously, but likewise ascribed to Spinoza[59]—and Noodt's rectorial address on freedom of religion, which, he says, has pleased him exceedingly. Bœrhaave, who gave up theological studies and the prospect of becoming a minister because he was suspected of Spinozism,[60] must have felt congenial with Noodt. Both shared the same liberal rational attitude. When Bœrhaave wrote to Macro he did not seem to know that in 1708 an English translation of Noodt's address, made by John Savage,[61] had been published in London.[62] Perhaps Noodt himself did not know this either.

About a year before his death Noodt prepared the final edition of the *Opera omnia* for the press. It appeared in September[63] 1724, in two folio volumes at Johannes van der Linden junior's in Leiden.[64] In the first volume there are two additional works,[65] and some of the older pieces are worked over once more. The Commentary on the Pandects—volume two—is completed as far as Book 27. However, the hope that he might finish it (books 28–50) proved groundless as a result of his poor health. He gave a vivid description of his condition in a letter to Barbeyrac of August 1724: he cannot walk long distances and does not sleep very well; the studies that once were his favourite pastime are now fatiguing.[66] In the preface of 1724 he made clear to his readers that he would not get beyond Book 27. Neither

58. Amsterdam, 1670.
59. Constans, L. A., *De jure ecclesiasticorum liber singularis.* Alethopoliapud Cajum Valerium Pennatum [Amsterdam], 1665. The authorship in uncertain, however. The book is also ascribed to Lodewÿk Meyer and Pieter de la Court. Nyhoff, 1914.
60. Lindeboom, 1968: 46 f.
61. 1673–1747. Savage travelled with James Cecil, 5th Earl of Salisbury, in Europe for eight years, 1698–1706, visiting most countries on the continent. See *Dict. Nat. Biogr.* 50, 1897: 340.
62. See Adams, Averly, and Robinson, 1982; Ahsmann–Feenstra, 1984: nr. 442. Copies are in University Library Cambridge, King's Inns Library Dublin, British Library, Bodleian Library Oxford.
63. De Toullieu wrote to Van Eck, Groningen, 23 Sept. 1724, UL Utrecht, MS 1000, that he had received a copy: 'Sic instituit Cl. Noodtius, at pro generositate sua mihi exemplar novae suae editionis curavit nomine suo offerri, sane nihil tale exspectavisti.'
64. Ahsmann–Feenstra, 1984: nr. 465.
65. Amica responsio to van Bijnkershœk (Ahsmann–Feenstra, 1984: nr. 477) and Responsum in causa matrimoniali (Ahsmann–Feenstra, 1984: nr. 432).
66. Barbeyrac, 1731: LXXVI f.; *Vita*, fols. 7 f.

his vigour of judgment nor his memory have left him, but now, nearing 80, he is overtaken by old age. The studies that once were his joy now fatigue him. De Toullieu, who had become professor in Groningen in the meantime, wrote to Van Eck[67] that the young scholar Balthasar Branchu,[68] who took his degree with Noodt in 1718 and had published two small volumes with observations,[69] was busy completing the commentary under Noodt's direction. But nothing would come of that. Branchu died even before Noodt, in March 1725.[70]

On Monday, 13 August 1725, when Noodt was staying in his son-in-law's country-house Treslong in Hillegom,[71] he was seized by the 'beginnings of a stroke', at 7.30 in the morning. In the afternoon, he was brought to Leiden by coach, a trip of some 15 km which he stood reasonably well. But the strokes came ever more frequently and this time not even a Bœrhaave could do anything about it. On Wednesday, 15 August 1725, Noodt died 'very devoutly and with much courage',[72] at the age of 77 years and 11 months.

The next day, the senate of the university decided that Schulting, or if he was indisposed, Vitrarius junior, would pronounce the obituary speech. As usual, the seniors of the senate were asked to pay a visit of condolence to the family. Noodt's family thanked them for their kind words, adding that Noodt had always spoken with great esteem of the rector and the senate, and that he hardly would have wanted an

67. De Toullieu to Van Eck (as n. 210): 'Dicunt isti rei, sub ipsius [sc. Noodtii] ductu, operam dare Eruditissimus Branchu. Fiat ita potius, quam nihil.'
68. He was born in The Hague. On him, see Adelung i, 1784; Haubold, 1809: 199. According to Gebauer he was asked and paid considerably by the Leipzig editor Thomas Fritsch to collect and edit in short notes the contributions of the Dutch elegant school for a new edn. of the Corpus Juris; see Gebauer, 1764: 56.
69. He took his degree on 7 Nov. 1718 on a thesis 'ad Julii Pauli J.C. fragmentum ex libro XXII Quaestionum' [= D 48. 10. 14], Molhuysen iv: 274*. He published *Observationes ad jus Romanum, Leibnitius contra Barbeyraccium vindicantes et disputationes duae ad Julium Paulum*. Leiden, 1721; *Observationum ad jus Romanum decas altera*. Leiden, 1723. On Branchu's interpretation of C 8. 40. 22, see Herberger, 1985.
70. De Toullieu to Van Eck, Groningen, 10 Apr. 1725, UL Utrecht, MS 1000. He was buried (the name being spelled mr Balthazar Brankhue) in the week of 10–17 Mar. 1725 in the Vrouwekerk in Leiden, GA Leiden, Reg. Begravingen. Roberts: 59 (on the authority of Holtzendorff) erroneously gives 1769 as the year of his death.
71. See v. d. Aa, Geogr. xi, 1848: 311. Gerrit Abraham van den Ende inherited the country-house.
72. Obituary, as n. 48. A. v. Haller notes in the diary of his voyage to Holland (1725–7): '. . . auch verstarbe kurz nach meiner Ankunft der bekannte Rechtsgelehrte Noodt'. Lindeboom, 1958: 37.

PETER NOODT, IN SYN LEVEN
GEMEENSMAN DER STADT NYMEGEN
GESTORVEN 21 MAY, EN BEGRAVEN
30 MAY 1680
GYSBERTA BIESEMAN DES SELFS
HUYS VROUW, GESTORVEN 16 IULY
EN BEGRAVEN 25 IULY 1680
GERARD NOODT, IN SYN LEVEN DER
BEIDEN REGTEN DOCTOR EN
PROFESSOR OP DE UNIVERSITEIT
TOT LEYDEN, ALDAER GESTORVEN
15 AUGUSTUS, EN HIER BEGRAVEN
22 AUGUSTUS 1725
N° 745

obituary speech, since he had forbidden one to be delivered at his funeral.[73] As far as we know no speech was held.

His body was transported to Rotterdam, and from there on a yacht to Nijmegen,[74] his father's city, which he had avoided ever since the revolts which took place there shortly after the beginning of the century. On 22 August,[75] he was buried in the grave of his parents in St Steven's, as he had promised his mother long ago.[76] His heirs respected his last wish, but, according to Roukens, not wholeheartedly. The burial, he says, was on the cheap.[77] The body was brought from the ship to the oilseller's shop, and from there it was carried to St Steven's in a simple procession, without any pomp (in order to cut costs), but in the presence of all decent citizens, the complete city government, and many of his pupils. The inscription, added to the tombstone, is most simple:[78]

GERARD NOODT, IN HIS LIFE
DOCTOR OF BOTH LAWS AND
PROFESSOR IN THE UNIVERSITY
OF LEYDEN, DIED THERE
AUGUST 15, AND BURIED HERE
AUGUST 22, 1725

73. Molhuysen v: 7. From a senate decision of 1 Mar. 1737 it appears that the family later donated Noodt's portrait to the university. The senate then ordered the making of uniform frames with inscriptions for various portraits, Molhuysen v: 166. The portrait still is in the senate room. See *Icones Leidenses*.
74. Obituary, as n. 48.
75. The obituary has 21 Aug., but the stone 22 Aug. The latter date is confirmed by the burial-book of St Steven's; cf. GA Nijmegen, RBS 1187.
76. Obituary, as n. 48; Register.
77. Roukens, 1767: 9.
78. GERARD NOODT, IN SYN LEVEN DER/BEIDEN REGTEN DOCTOR EN/PROFESSOR OP DE UNIVERSITEIT/TOT LEYDEN, ALDAER GESTORVEN/15 AUGUSTUS, EN ALHIER BEGRAVEN/22 AUGUSTUS 1725. Drawing in ARA Tets van Goudriaan, inv. nr. 121. There are many errors in the transcription of the text in this drawing; see the photograph.

FIG. 3 (on facing page) Tombstone of Gerard Noodt and his parents in the Church of St Steven, Nijmegen. Copyright: Jan van Teeffelen, Nijmegen.

3

Works

1. General intellectual background

The elegant tradition

If we want to put Noodt's work in context, we first must know something about the humanistic philological tradition to which it belongs, the so-called elegant school.[1] But this in turn asks for a perspective on the development of civil law since the Middle Ages. Therefore I begin with a rough sketch of this.

The basis of civil law, continental legal science, or *jus commune*, was laid in the Middle Ages. Like the two other higher studies of the medieval university—theology and medicine—it started from the study of a voluminous corpus of writings handed down from Antiquity and provided with authority.[2] For theology, that corpus naturally consisted primarily of the Bible, for medicine, of the corpus Hippocraticum and Galenus, for law, of the codification of Roman law promulgated by the emperor Justinian in the sixth century, later called the Corpus Juris Civilis.[3] This was studied according to generally accepted scientific methods,[4] not only for purely scientific reasons, but also with a view to its practical application, because the text had authority. Learning how to handle texts always implied the need for two skills: being able to read them, and knowing how to argue on the basis of them. In the dominant model of a science in the Middle Ages the authoritative text has a central place. Every thesis, every argument can only be accepted if it can prove its identity before the authoritative corpus, that is, if it is based on allegations.[5]

The importance of the text implied that due care should be taken in

1. See Wieacker, 1967: 166 ff.; Troje, 1977: 615 ff.; Van den Bergh, 1985*a*: 45 ff.
2. Van den Bergh, 1985*a*: 25 f.
3. See, on this codification, Schulz, 1963: 288 and *passim*. Medieval legal science in fact not only contained study of the Corpus Juris Civilis (that is, civil law) but also canon law and feudal law; for reasons of convenience I only discuss civil law here.
4. See Otte, 1971.
5. Van den Bergh, 1985*a*: 25 f.

the establishment of its reading. This was an essential part of the method. We live in a world dominated by the printed word (though for how much longer?). As a result, many things which once formed the core of the methodology of legal scholarship—textual criticism, knowledge of manuscripts and writings, philology—have now become marginal, at best the concern of specialists.

Always, interpretation of the text was preceded by establishing its *vera lectio*. This rule, already established in Antiquity,[6] implied comparing different available manuscripts as a standard procedure. Only where uniform texts were available for teaching purposes may this have been omitted. In the medieval programme for handling a text the reading of it was followed by discussion of parallel and opposing texts, the recounting of generally applicable arguments that could be drawn from the text (*generalia*, *notabilia*), and discussion of the legal case (*casus*). The programme itself is proof of the close link between knowledge and application of the text, a link determined by the fact that the text was regarded as having authority.

Jurists trained in this technique of handling texts soon proved to be useful in medieval society and politics, especially in the processes of state formation that were gaining momentum in the thirteenth century. Before long, we find jurists in ever growing numbers in royal and county administrations, city governments, boards, councils, and courts of every kind. As a result, the Corpus Juris was applied more and more in legal practice, wherever local law (laws, ordinances, custom) did not obtain.[7] The medieval method of handling texts had some special implications. Understanding the text did not necessarily mean to understand its historical sense. Medieval jurists misunderstood many texts, though the misunderstanding often proved fruitful for the development of legal science and practice.[8] The meaning of a great number of rather rare Latin words was guessed wrongly by the glossators, but often this was of little importance from a legal point of view. And because the text—any text—had authority, it could be used in ways which do not seem acceptable to us now. Often a text was used in the discussion of a subject which had absolutely nothing to do with its original context. The structure of legal science, moreover, meant that around the nucleus of the text grew an ever expanding body of glosses upon

6. Quintilian, *Inst. or.* 1. 4. 3: '. . . et enarrationem praecedit emendata lectio . . .'.
7. Van den Bergh, 1985*a*: 31 f.
8. For the concept of productive misunderstanding, see Hoetink, 1986: 31.

glosses and commentaries upon commentaries, which in the end no single person was able to master completely.

Against all this a new, critical, and philological movement arose, beginning in Italy in the fifteenth century, and forming an offshoot of humanism, which had its roots in thirteenth-century Italy.[9] That movement was inspired by enthusiasm for Antiquity, but apart from scholarly motives it also had political ones.[10]

The traditional higher studies at first strongly resisted this kind of modernism, which went, moreover, with much abuse of 'barbaric' jurists. And that resistance did not have purely scholarly motives either. With their technique of handling authoritative texts as expertise, jurists had risen to formidable social and political power and held influential positions everywhere in the government of the Church, of princes, and of cities. Humanistic philology therefore really may have been something of a challenge to the authority of jurists.

As a result of this resistance, humanism could only penetrate legal science very slowly and celebrated its first real triumphs in that field only in the first decades of the sixteenth century. And, even then, part of legal humanism, erudite as it was, had little or no relevance from a strictly legal point of view. But here a proviso is in place. Humanism never brought about a fundamental reorientation of legal science, but that had not been its intention. Traditional accounts of the battle between *bartolisti* and *culti* seem to distort the issue a bit. Humanism did not present a new paradigm for legal science. Law remained a science of texts of authority, the Corpus Juris kept its central position, and the purpose of its interpretation remained legal throughout. In fact, many emendations discussed by humanists were not critical problems concerning the constitution of the text but antinomies defined as such by the glossators. We will find this in Noodt's work too. Just as Osler[11] concluded for Budé, we can say that for Noodt 'there was no contradiction between interpreting the Digest in the light of the history, languages and literature of Antiquity, and in regarding it as a work of authority'.

What the humanists did achieve was a considerable extension of the scientific programme for handling classical legal texts. In order to understand a text, one must be aware of the *usus loquendi*, that is, linguistic usage, of the period in which the text was written, the

9. Osler, 1983: 29 f. 10. Troje, 1977: 616 f. 11. 1985: 211.

objects and institutions named in it, current philosophies of classical times. Besides, there are technicalities to consider which partly belong to the *arcana* of legal scholarship: the study of *inscriptiones* and *subscriptiones*, which in Justinian's codification are added to each text, the study of Greek phrases and texts in the Corpus Juris, the study of interpolations, that is, textual changes made by Justinian's compilers on his instructions.[12]

Naturally, each of these subjects had its experts, and not every lawyer was expected to master the complete programme. But he had to learn something about it in his legal training lest he stood tongue-tied in a legal debate. Even the most specialized research of *antiquitates* and *elegantiae* in principle had its legitimate place in the overall concept of a legal science in which all that might improve the understanding of a text might also lead to new or better applications, and thus might prove to be of some practical value.[13] In a science of authoritative books which unites understanding and application, the relation of theory and practice is not conceived in the same way as we understand it now. When, for instance, humanists discussed the meaning of 'colluctatio', 'pancratium', and 'pugiles exercere' in D 9. 2. 7. 4,[14] they were not doing anything new. The glossators had done the same and humanists only brought new evidence from classical sources to an old debate. Apart from that, they added a moral overtone: the purer ancient Roman law was known, the more humane the world would become. But that did not imply that they believed themselves able to improve on the glossators in every respect. Someone like Budé acknowledged this implicitly when he accepted the authority of the glossator Accursius as a jurist, but criticized him as a man of letters.[15] No doubt textual criticism could not help jeopardizing canonized text versions to some extent. So, it is true that in the work of humanistic jurists, lay some seeds of the 'historicization'[16] Roman law experienced in later ages. This was

12. See, for this programme in its final stage, Eckhard and Walch, 1802: Book I, chs. I–VII.
13. Troje, 1972*b*: 51. One might also put this negatively: nobody could be sure that any work on the text would never prove to be of any consequence in court.
14. See Van den Bergh and Stolte, 1977: 259.
15. Cited after Osler, 1983: 124: '. . . cujus ut iurisperiti auctoritatem sequi, non ut literatoris soleo'. Grotius moulded this into the elegant dictum that the glossators 'saepe optimi sint condendi juris auctores, etiam tunc cum conditi juris mali sunt interpretes' (*De jure belli ac pacis*, Prol. § 54). This anticipates the idea of 'produktives Missverstehen', on which see Hoetink, 1986: 31.
16. See Maffei, 1968: 176 and *passim*.

bound to weaken the close link between understanding and application; in the long run, legal scholars began to divide into academics and practicians. But even in the seventeenth century this was rather a difference of degree than of principle. Naturally, legal science never can be anything but a theoretico-practical compound.

Legal humanism had its triumphs mainly in France—for that reason it was called *mos gallicus*—in the first decades of the sixteenth century. It was also a success in terms of propaganda.[17] Many of the things that made Alciato and Budé famous are found in Italian humanists of the quattrocento whose names have been forgotten.[18] The university of Bourges was the centre of legal humanism for nearly half of the sixteenth century. Practically all the famous humanistic jurists taught there for a shorter or longer period, though not in perfect harmony, to put it mildly.[19] That scholarship and politics had something to do with each other is brought out by the fact that most French humanistic jurists were Huguenots. Bourges, by the way, was an important Huguenot stronghold during the civil war. This allegiance decided the fate of the French elegant school. Those who did escape the massacre of St Bartholomew's night 1572 fled the country. Brissonius was killed, Hotman and Doneau fled.[20] The young Republic, among other Protestant countries, took up the refugees, and the university of Leiden, founded in 1575, benefited greatly from it. The famous philologist Scaliger, as well as the jurist Doneau, taught there[21] and laid the basis for a long tradition in humanistic philology. Leiden is not a humanistic university, if one ever existed. The university could not cease to be first and foremost a training centre for officials—ministers, jurists, and doctors. This meant that in legal training, as well as in practice, the structure of civil law that had emerged in the Middle Ages remained dominant. One had to learn to find one's way in the books, to read texts and to argue on the basis of them, as before. But humanistic erudition was held in high esteem in Leiden,[22] as it was, in fact, by the merchant élite of the new state, and this implied a relative openness to new ideas. In the seventeenth century Leiden became the widely acknowledged centre of a new flourishing of legal humanism, the Dutch elegant school. It

17. Osler, 1983: 2.
18. Osler, 1983: 29 f.
19. Eyssell, 1860: 47 f., 71 f.
20. Eyssell, 1860: 96 ff.
21. On Scaliger, see *NNBW* v: 660 f.; on Doneau in Leiden, see Eyssell, 1860: 117 f., Feenstra and Waal, 1975: 16 f. Bibliography of Doneau in Ahsmann–Feenstra, 1984: nr. 105 ff.
22. See Schneppen, 1960: 116 f.

took over the lead in Roman legal scholarship from the French and had its heyday roughly between 1670 and 1730. But, until late in the eighteenth century, philological work was done in the Republic which drew the attention of all of learned Europe.[23]

A central position in the Dutch elegant school was taken by Gerard Noodt, with Henrik Brenkman as his most distinguished pupil. Among the others the first place was taken by Noodt's townsman Anton Schulting, who in a strict sense was not his pupil[24] but who seems to have been greatly influenced by him. Others were Cornelis van Eck with his three learned pupils—the famous Cornelis van Bijnkershœk and Professors Pierre de Toullieu and Willem Best—J. J. Wissenbach, U. Huber,[25] A. Wieling, H. Cannegieter, and H. J. Arntzenius. They all worked in close contact with philologists like Gronovius, Græevius, Perizonius, and Duker. In the eighteenth century there were also some distinguished Greek scholars who did some work in Byzantine law, like Reitz, Jensius, and Ruhnkenius.

The continuity between the French and Dutch schools can be demonstrated in ambitious research programmes as well as in minor subjects. Major topics that were on the programme of both schools—apart, of course, from emending the text of the Corpus Juris, and of the Digest in particular[26]—were the publication of critical and annotated editions,[27] the reconstruction of the praetorian edict,[28] the palingenesia of classical legal writings,[29] and the search for Justinianic interpolations.[30]

A minor question which is discussed time and again in the context of *auctoritas poetarum*[31] concerns the interpretation of Cicero, *De*

23. Apart from Leiden, Franeker was important and elegant jurists were also teaching in Utrecht and Groningen.
24. He studied in Leiden and took his degree there in 1683. Noodt only arrived in Leiden in 1686.
25. His position is somewhat ambiguous. In his Franeker inaugural address as law professor (1666) he seemed to adhere to the humanist school (cf. van der Vlugt, 1916: 8), but in his Dialogue (Huber 1688*a*; see above, p. 54 f.) he was rather more negative and rejected humanism's most characteristic scientific purpose, that is, criticism. The title of his *Digressiones justinianeae* (1688), however, says that the book contains 'varia et imprimis humaniora juris'.
26. Troje, 1977: 645 f.
27. Troje, 1977: 640 f.
28. Troje, 1977: 747. The idea of reconstructing the praetorian edict on the basis of the inscriptions and Ulpian's *Libri ad edictum* was voiced for the first time by Agustìn, see Otto i, 1733: col. 1457.
29. Troje, 1972*b*: 62 f.; Troje, 1977: 784; Stolte, 1981: 9 ff.
30. Palazzini Finetti, 1953.
31. Van den Bergh, 1974.

legibus ii. 23: does this text prove that the twelve tables were written in metrical form, or not? The question, brought up by Budé (1467–1540), and answered in the negative by the very learned Antonio Agustìn (1516–86), was still discussed by Van Bijnkershœk in 1716, Everard Otto in 1730, Gabinus de Wal in 1825.[32] Another example is the question: what is meant by *margaritas extricatas* in D 9. 2. 27. 30. From the gloss we learn that the term was already puzzling medieval jurists. The Spanish humanist Nebrija (1444–1522) proposed the meaning 'unstrung pearls',[33] but Budé was not satisfied and tried another explanation. Cujas (1522–90) gave still another one.[34] The philologists Casaubon (1559–1614) and Leunclavius (1533–93) had something to say on it as well, and Gerard Noodt tried to overcome the contradiction between Budé and Cujas in his monograph on the *lex Aquilia* (1691).[35] Finally, Brenkman (1681–1736) rolled up the whole debate in an extensive note on the text,[36] adding some erudition of his own; he demonstrated his knowledge of Italian by stating that such pearls are called *perle sciolte* in Italy.

From a legal point of view, such questions may indeed seem hardly relevant, and, in fact, later generations have often criticized the Dutch elegant school for being antiquarian and not sufficiently juristic.[37] But this verdict stands in the need of some qualification. Just as the French school obscured the achievements of preceding Italian humanists, the very influential German Historical School in the nineteenth century obscured those of the Dutch. This is not so much due to Von Savigny himself, though it is often said that his criticisms were immoderate.[38] It was especially Jhering's unsubstantiated 'la mort sans phrase', published in 1857 in the opening statement of his *Jahrbücher*,[39] which established an unfavourable opinion of the Dutch school that was widely accepted, mostly without independent research.

32. See Van den Bergh, 1964: 16, with n. 56.
33. Osler, 1983: 59 f., spec. 62.
34. *Obs. et emend.* 18. 37.
35. Cap. 15, *Opera* i: 161 f.
36. See van den Bergh and Stolte, 1977: 240, 280.
37. See e.g. van Apeldoorn 1937: 33; Kunst, 1969: 77; Söllner, 1969: 171. But see Troje, 1977: 617.
38. Stolte, 1981: 81.
39. Jhering, 1857: 22: 'Die gelehrtesten rechtshistorischen Untersuchungen früherer Zeiten, wie z.B. der ganzen holländischen Schule, haben das wahrhafte Verständnis des römischen Rechts—ich meine darunter nicht das rechtshistorische, sondern das juristische—um nichts gefördert, sie haben den juristischen Sinn der allein dieses Verständnis fähig ist, vielleich mehr unterdrückt und auf Abwege geleitet, als erweckt und angeregt.' See on this Van Oven, 1933: 54.

Apart from the fact that philological minutiae have a value of their own, seemingly abstruse antiquarian subjects on closer investigation may very well prove to have importance in practice. In this respect more has to be said on the question of textual criticism, especially because Noodt is often criticized on that count. This is a problem with a long history in legal humanism. In the Middle Ages something like a *textus receptus* had established itself in the form of the text adopted in Bologna and for that reason was called *littera bononiensis*. When humanists began to criticize this text the situation was not necessarily improved. Apart from Angelo Poliziano (1454–1494),[40] who seriously tried to identify manuscripts and made full collations, even where the text was evidently corrupt, most of the early humanists were still far removed from modern principles of text edition and textual criticism.[41] Humanists simply took as a starting-point some text—written or printed—which was currently in use, the *textus receptus* or *littera vulgata*,[42] and tried to emend it, as far as it seemed incomplete or corrupt, *codicum ope* or *ingenii ope*, that is, with the help of other, often arbitrarily chosen, manuscripts that one could lay one's hands on, or with the help of conjectures.[43] *Ingenium* not only included clever thinking, but also a preferably encyclopaedic knowledge of ancient literature.

There existed no method of making a systematic recension by comparing a great number of manuscripts, making a *stemma codicum*, or selecting one manuscript as archetype.[44] Usually scholars only emended those passages in the *textus receptus* which were corrupt or incomprehensible, the so-called *loci difficiliores*.[45] Some of these had troubled jurists from the days of the glossators, but there was no closed list of them.[46] Much depended on the *textus receptus* taken as the starting-point. Where this seemed unproblematic no questions were asked.

In the collections of *loci difficiliores* no systematic distinction was made as yet between textual problems (mutilated, rare, or

40. Grafton, 1983: 22 f.; Osler, 1983: 69–106.
41. Kenney, as cited by Osler, 1983: 1; for a critique of Kenney's account of the history of classical scholarship see Grafton, 1977.
42. On the meaning of these terms see Timpanaro, 1971: 13; Stolte, 1981: 73 f.
43. See Timpanaro, 1971: 1 f.
44. Osler, 1983: 198 f. For a history of textual criticism see Timpanaro, 1971; Reynolds and Wilson, 1974.
45. They were also named *loca difficiliora*, *loci difficillimi*, *cruces*, etc.
46. Brenkman's list of *loci difficillimi* is given by Stolte, 1981: App. 3, 104 f.

nonexistent words, lacking fragments in Greek, lacunae, ungrammatical sentences, etc.) and juristic, dogmatical ones (sentences legally incomprehensible or senseless, antinomies, etc.), although jurists naturally tended to be more susceptible to problems of the second kind. The lack of this distinction implied that one could not yet draw a line between constitution and interpretation of a text, which is one of the basic, if never fully attainable, postulates of modern philology.[47]

One specific peculiarity of humanistic philology, to our eyes, was that one used any manuscript one happened to lay one's hands on. Exact methods of identifying and dating manuscripts and of establishing their relative value in the pedigree of textual tradition were not yet available—even in the seventeenth century. This explains why, for instance, Noodt, Cunningham, and Brenkman as a matter of course consulted the Digest manuscript recently bought by Van Bijnkershœk.[48] A scholar could show his erudition and augment the authority of his emendations by referring to some manuscript. And the lustre of this was even greater when the manuscript was not generally accessible. Such a reference naturally flattered the owner as well. The manuscript one has in hand has always had a special attraction. We find a trace of this even with Mommsen, who counted his own Digest manuscript among the manuscripts he used for his edition.[49] Without doubting the venerability of this manuscript, which once belonged to the humanist Colladon (1508–94), we may well ask whether it really is so much more important than some of the hundreds of manuscripts he eliminated.

Only Noodt's pupil Brenkman, in his *Historia Pandectarum* (1722), gives precise descriptions of all the manuscripts he consulted: with such exactness, in fact, that nearly all of them can be identified even today.[50] He is also the first jurist who, applying the principles set out by Montfaucon, tried to date manuscripts to the age in which

47. Naturally, even now a sharp line cannot always be drawn, for instance when we have a *codex unicus*.

48. For Noodt and Cunningham, see Van Bijnkershœk to Van Eck, respectively The Hague, 15 Dec. 1696 and 6 Sept. 1708 (both UL Utrecht, MS 1000). For Brenkman, see Brenkman, 1722: 86, 259, 289; Star Numan, 1869: 353; Feenstra, 1971*a*: 214 n. 34. It is characteristic that the second manuscript Van Bijnkershœk bought, a fine but absolutely unimportant manuscript of the complete Digest from the 14th century (now UL Leiden, BPL 11D), was esteemed much higher than the Bijnkershœkianus I (now BPL 6C). Now the appreciation is completely reversed.

49. Codex C, Editio major, Praef. pp. xxxxvii, lxxxxv.

50. See Stolte, 1981: App. 4.

they were written.[51] But in some cases not even he could do better than use the old, vague indications 'antiquus', 'antiquissimus', 'recentior', or 'recentissimus'. And, apart from the famous Codex Florentinus, not even Brenkman made full collations of the many Digest manuscripts he saw. For all but the *Florentina* he inspected, in the traditional humanistic way, only a series of *loci difficiliores*. And this too was the advice Van Bijnkershœk had given him, citing the well-known Greek proverb quoted in D 1. 16. 6. 3: 'Not everything, not always, not from all.'[52]

As we saw, humanist editors often made emendations not on the basis of a manuscript reading but purely on conjecture.[53] Especially where proper names or very rare words were concerned, which can be easily mutilated in manuscript tradition, one simply searched ancient literature for some word that looked similar and was more or less in tune with the subject. Whether there really existed a Digest manuscript which could confirm such a reading, was a question that did not necessarily arise then. Nevertheless, emendations based purely on conjecture had much less authority than those for which an existing manuscript reading could be adduced.[54]

Jurists, for that matter, often showed an independent attitude towards manuscript tradition. After all, their aim never was pure, disinterested knowledge of Antiquity. There are hotly debated differences of opinion already among French humanist jurists, which are repeated about a century later in the Dutch elegant school. Cujas—who was regularly opposed by Doneau[55]—said that for him *ratio juris* often carried much more weight than any manuscript which can be easily corrupted.[56] The jurist, in other words, pretends

51. Stolte, 1981: 79.
52. Brenkman, 1722: 395.
53. See for Budé, Osler, 1983: 136, and for Cujas, Troje, 1971: 118.
54. Kenney, as cited by Osler, 1983: 162. An essential prerequisite for conjectural emendation was *necessitas emendandi*; 'arbitrary conjectures are the lowest form of pseudo-scholarship' (Grafton, 1983: 171). Cf. Huber, 1688*a*: 44: 'Nam si toleranda sine manusciptis est emendandi licentia, duntaxat tam evidens esse debet, ut minus facile refelli quam adstrui et approbari possit; quod de talibus, quae tuendis opinionibus, in quibus Interpretes discrepant, adhibentur, nullo modo licet adfirmare . . .'.
55. Eyssell, 1860: 90 and *passim*.
56. *Obs. et emend.* 1. 1: 'Sed plus ipse rationi juris tribuo quam ulli scripturae, qua quidem nulla res est, quae facilius depravari possit'. One usually does not cite, however, the rest of the sentence: 'nec tamen etiam scriptorum librorum auctoritate careo'. So here *ratio* and *scriptum* are not opposed, after all. Cujas adds that he always has laid great care on the collation of manuscripts and has collected a

to know by reason alone what Justinian should or would have written.[57] If the manuscript reads differently, this may be caused either by the carelessness of the compilers or by the slovenliness of scribes. So the reading in itself does not prove much. This is an attitude, by the way, which can be found in many Romanists even today.

This juristic attitude to sources is not to be regarded simply as a matter of arrogance. It has its roots in epistemological ideas which have strongly influenced modern European thought[58] and were instrumental in determining the province of legal science. In the terms of Aristotle, the knowledge of the jurist is not speculative but practical. This distinction is based on a presumed link between knowing and making or doing. The maker has special knowledge about the things he makes, knowledge 'from within' (archetypal), that is, knowledge about the purpose and composition of what is made. About the things we did not make (the world, the soul), we can only have speculative (ectypical) knowledge 'from the outside'. Practical knowledge is normative; the maker knows what result was envisaged, and therefore he can judge it.[59] This is roughly what Cujas must have meant when he put *ratio juris* higher than manuscript authority. The archetype of legal opinion is not some manuscript, however old and venerated, but *ratio juris*.[60] According to Leibniz legal science had a double principle: *ratio* and *scriptura*.[61] He did not

great number of them, in two of which he found the reading he suggested. In other cases the preference for *ratio* is more evident. See *Obs. et emend.* 3. 13: 'Et opinio haec mea nullis quidem, quos legerim, libris scriptis vel antiquis adiuvatur, juris tamen ratio ipsa per se sufficit . . .'. But here again *ratio* is confirmed by a source, that is, the *Paraphrasis* of Theophilus. The most explicit statement is in *Obs. et emend.* 15. 21: '. . . in eo perstare me copellit . . . et ratio ipsa, cui scriptum servire debet potius, quam scripto ratio; et longe maior culpa rationi evidentissimae, quam scripto inferentis vim. Si clames, vim adferri scripto, clamem, dum arcte vis tenere scriptum, vitiare te et corrumpere rationem; quod vitium certe illo longe deterius, aut hoc potius vitium.' I thank Douglas Osler for bringing the latter two passages to my attention.

57. Jurists were not exceptional in this, for that matter. At the beginning of the 18th century Richard Bentley said nearly the same as Cujas; see Timpanaro, 1971: 10. And, a century later, Moritz Haupt once said that he was prepared to read 'Constantinopolitanus' where a manuscript had a single 'o', See West, 1973: 53.

58. Schröder, 1979: 15 f.; Tully, 1980: 22.

59. Tully, 1980: 23.

60. Agustìn's deduction that all controversies were to be solved according to the reading of F (see Otto, 1733: col. 1431) is not conclusive and not accepted by all jurists. And Cujas' statement is less extreme if we also take into consideration the second part of the sentence, which usually is not cited, see n. 56.

61. Leibniz, 1974: II § 4; on Leibniz, see Otte, 1983.

say which should prevail when the two lead to opposing results, but of course this was most evident. Although he stated that the authority of the law was not subject to demonstration (*stat pro ratione voluntas*),[62] reason had the last word. If it seemed impossible to give the *scriptura* a reasonable sense, even the most conservative critic would choose to emend the text, not to abandon reason. Naturally, the implication of this was that the text of the Corpus Juris no longer had final authority in legal matters. But it took many years before this was fully realized.

Conjectures not based on manuscript authority are also found in Noodt's work and although in this respect he was no exception among his contemporaries, they will have been at least part of the reason for criticizing him as *criticus aliquando audacior* (at times a rather bold critic).[63] Noodt's work and the criticism levelled against it are part of a long tradition in legal humanism, and it is no coincidence that contemporaries label the Dutch elegant school as a branch of the *schola cujaciana*. Doneau criticized emendations in the same way, and partly in the same words as, for example, Huber criticized those of Noodt:[64] 'In the first place [I reject an emendation] which upsets, without any urgent need of emendation, a reading that is publicly received in all codices . . . And I know that in our time there are many who offend against this in no slight manner. But what would be certain in the books, and in all Antiquity, if we were allowed to change old and accepted readings as often as we like according to our interest and judgement?'

That Noodt regularly emended, *ingenii ope*, may be due partly also to the fact that at that time in the Republic there were hardly any very old manuscripts accessible.[65] And being a rather bold critic was

62. Leibniz, 1974: II § 4; Otte, 1983: 15.

63. The formula is from Haubold, 1809: 137. See already Perizonius to Van Eck, Leiden, 2 Apr. 1706 (UL Utrecht, MS 1000): 'Quod ad emendationem ejus attinet, audax et dura est, inserens quippe integram vocem decem litterarum, sine ullis eius vestigiis in manuscriptis. Ista ratione facile omnia possimus nostram ad sententiam redigere.' Huber (1688*a*: 44) also remarked that Noodt emended without manuscript authority. See also Gerretzen, 1940: 64 f., and see below, p. 306 ff.

64. 'Primum [emendationem rejicio] quod nulla necessitate emendationis cogente, lectionem publica fide omnium codicum receptam invertunt . . . in quo scio quam non parum multis hae aetate peccetur. Quid enim erit in libris et omni vetustate certi, si quoties visum est, pro commodo et arbitrio nostro, licebit vetres et receptas scripturas mutare?' (Comment. on D 45. 1. 34, cited after Eyssell, 1860: 90 n. 233).

65. Apart from the MS of Van Bijnkershœk (now UL Leiden, BPL 6C) there only was the one in Kampen and possibly the one in Roermond. Besides, according to

certainly not on a par with the *temeritas* of an editor like Haloander.[66] In many cases Noodt's emendations were moderate and, in the light of the humanistic tradition, his work seems even rather cautious. Several humanists—among them famous ones like Alciato, right at the beginning[67]—had the cheek to invent nonexistent 'very ancient manuscripts' to give their own conjectures a fictitious authority.[68] 'Nunquam vidit' (he never saw it) became almost a standard clause in humanistic criticism. But Noodt never did such a thing and it seems not without reason that his honesty is praised.

Perizonius regularly criticized Noodt's liking for emendations in his letters to Van Eck,[69] and some scholars see in Perizonius the beginning of a more modern philological attitude.[70] But his attitude does not differ very much, in fact, from that of Doneau a century earlier, and we should not believe that Perizonius really had anything like a better, more systematic, and scientific method of emending texts. His recipe, like that of many of his contemporaries, mainly consisted of greater circumspection and modesty. This is a recipe, for that matter, which is inspired partly by the proper interests of scholarship itself. Too great a boldness in textual criticism might well encourage complete scepticism with regard to the sources of our knowledge of the past.[71] Against this scepticism, which was labelled Pyrrhonism then, Perizonius himself directed an academic address.[72]

If nothing were certain any more in the old books, the position of the authority of jurists itself would become questionable. This

Brenkman (1722: 259), Noodt's brother-in-law H. A. van der Marck van Leur possessed a MS. See also Star Numan, 1869: 352. On the Bijnkershœkianus and the MS in Kampen, see Feenstra, 1971*a*: 214 f. That MSS were scarce in the Republic is said expressly by Van Bijnkershœk in a letter to Van Eck, 30 Oct. 1696 (UL Utrecht, MS 1000, ed. Van den Bergh, 1985: 277 f.): '. . . quia noveram, vel raro, vel nuspiam corpora manuscripta in hisce regionibus reperiri . . .'.

66. On *temeritas haloandrina* see Troje, 1971: 29; Van den Bergh and Stolte, 1977: 241 n. 60; Osler, 1983: 200 f.
67. Osler, 1983: 184 ff.
68. Osler, 1983: 71, 184 ff. For a similar suspicion concerning Le Caron see Grafton, 1983: 145.
69. See above, n. 63; p. 45; and below, Ch. 4, at n. 95.
70. Gerretzen, 1940; Meyer, 1971.
71. A well-known example of this scepticism is De la Mothe de Vayer's discourse, 'Du peu de certitude qu'il y a dans l'histoire', published in 1668.
72. 'De fide historiarum contra Pyrrhonismum', Leiden, 6 Feb. 1702. On this, see Smitskamp, 1953; Meyer, 1971: 143–7.

tended to limit the scope of critical debate in civil law. The debate, again, had a long pedigree, and it mainly concerned the Digest text. Very roughly speaking, the tradition of the Digest is divided in two. On the one hand, we have the famous, nicely written, and nearly complete manuscript from the sixth century, which since 1406 has been kept in Florence and whose reading therefore is called the *littera Florentina*. On the other hand, there is an enormous mass of manuscripts from the Middle Ages which are at least some five or six centuries younger.[73] These manuscripts are connected directly or (mostly) indirectly with legal education as it took form in Bologna and soon spread all over Europe. Because in Bologna there were institutions aiming at the production of uniform texts in adequate quantities for teaching purposes, the readings of these manuscripts often show considerable similarity. Therefore we are accustomed to speak about their reading as the *littera bononiensis*.[74] But this is, in fact, rather misleading, because there never really existed anything like one, established, uniform, generally accepted text. Already in the Middle Ages the Florentine manuscript was regarded as the oldest and the most venerable. But its authority, great as it might be, was never regarded as absolute. Moreover, the manuscript was no more accessible then than it is today.

Angelo Poliziano introduced a new attitude to the study of the Digest text. He was convinced that the *Florentina* was the archetype of all existing Digest manuscripts, a conviction for which undisputable proof was brought only half a century later by Torelli. Poliziano was the first to undertake, in the 1480s, a systematic collation of the *Florentina*, a work that remained unfinished because of his untimely death. Torelli's proof that all Digest manuscripts were dependent on the *Florentina* was published for the first time by the very learned Spanish bishop and diplomat Antonio Agustìn. After that it took another ten years before, through the Torelli edition (1553), the *littera Florentina* was completely available. But this did not end the debate over the Digest text, because it was clear enough that the *Florentina* had a number of lacunae which could be properly filled by manuscript readings from the Bolognese tradition. And, apart from this, it was difficult to deny that manuscripts from this tradition had better readings in many cases.

Agustìn's opinion was that one should stick to the *Florentina* in all

73. See Schulz, 1916, and recently Stolte, 1984*a*, with further literature.
74. See Schulz, 1916; Stolte, 1981: 65 ff.

circumstances.[75] But Cujas was not quite convinced of that,[76] and his attitude was followed by many scholars in the Dutch elegant school.[77] Noodt seems to have had the same attitude, although, as far as I know, he never expressed himself on the question in his published works.[78] The metaphor Agustìn used to prove his point is not without meaning: one should never desert the *Florentina* just as one should never desert the banner of the commander under whom one is campaigning. It is a matter of power, after all. For a science aiming at the production of valid arguments for the present from a corpus of texts handed down from Antiquity, doubt about the reading of the text itself was always dangerous. The problem presented itself more or less in the same way to jurists and theologians (medicine already began to change around 1600 from a science of texts to an empirical science). If there is no certainty about the true text, and one does not want to indulge in scepticism, there remain only two possible alternatives. Either one must allow anyone to accept the reading which conforms best to his own reason and interest—that is, to make his own text—or one should stick to the *textus receptus* in all circumstances, as Protestant theologians urged. But to enforce this, one would need a powerful central authority which could establish one authoritative reading, as the Roman Catholic Church did with the Bible. Because neither possibility was

75. 'A Florentina lectione, tamquam a signis ducis, sub cujus auspiciis militatur nusquam esse recedendum.'
76. According to Troje, 1971: 48 n. 137, he never gave a systematic exposition of his position, but I do not know whether this should have been expected; Doneau, Huber, Noodt, and Schulting were no more explicit on the subject. Anyway, there are clear statements like that in *Obs. et emend.* 2. 1: '. . . nec enim fidem habendam esse censeo his, qui ceteras omnes ex Florentinis dimanasse profitentur'. And see *Obs. et emend.* 2. 25. Cf. Troje, 1971: 115 f.; Brenkman, 1722: 240.
77. In Holland Cujas was followed by Van Eck (*Princ. jur. civ.* sub tit. D 1. 2 nr. 16.) and by Schulting (1720: 10; 1737: 208 n. 3 i.f.). And see already Schulting's letter to Van Eck, Leiden, 23 Apr. 1690 (UL Utrecht, MS 1000); 'Video itaque Taurellium Augustinum aliosque ita censere, omnes codices, qui hodie exstant, e Florentino derivatos; quod sane de plerisque verum esse non nego, sed an de omnibus idem judicandum? Id sane non sequitur ex illis quae hi adducunt; et longe aliud visum Cujacio, non minus idoneo in hac controversia judici . . .'. Noodt's pupil Brenkman, on the other hand, was a staunch advocate of the *Florentina* all his life, see Stolte, 1981.
78. The one very concise remark I found is in the introduction to his lectures on the Digest (BPL 575, fol. 14^v): 'Ergo hac in parte prodesse possunt variae lectiones, talis est una editio Accursii et florentina. Et putant quidam exemplar florentinum esse ipsius imperatoris Justiniani. Et hoc est optimum quoque, utpote quod habet inscriptiones, quod alia exemplaria non habent. Sed illud exemplar tamen quoque habet vitia.'

feasible in civil law, jurists could do no more than try to restrict critical debate to the unavoidable minimum. Thus, orthodox jurists in the seventeenth century accepted as an axiom, among others formulated by Huber,[79] that no emendation of the *Florentina* was allowed as long as the text could be given a reasonable legal sense without one. The only job left for textual criticism (that is, after the publication of the *Florentina*) is, according to Huber, to fight against sagacity in the search for errors in this manuscript. An enormous amount of sophistication has been spent, on the other hand, to give some acceptable legal sense to even the most obviously corrupt texts of the *Florentina*. According to Van Bijnkershœk there were two leading principles for any critic: *necessitas emendandi* and *modestia*.[80]

The attitude of orthodox jurists is comparable to that of orthodox theologians like Gisbert Vœt, who—for similar reasons—simply denied any corruption of the text of the Bible and propagated an extremely literal interpretation.[81] Vœt enumerated three restrictions to the right of interpretation:

1. that the temerarious desire for innovation not be dominant;
2. that the theologian not devote his entire work to such parerga;
3. that the common and established orthodoxy not be prejudiced under the pretext and name of sacred or Oriental philology.[82]

In legal literature one can find similar strictures, although, naturally, the Digest was not believed to be inspired by God like the Bible. Religious and juristic orthodoxy went together in jurists like Doneau and Huber.

Noodt, on the other hand, took a much more liberal or modernist position, as we will see presently. This does not mean, by the way, that he broke away from the traditions of his profession in any conceivable way. The Corpus Juris remained the focus of all his work and on the whole he was a rather moderate critic in most cases.[83] Any

79. '. . . nisi obstaret axioma: non esse recedendum in emendationes textus Florentini, quibus recta et juridica non desit interpretatio': Huber, 1700: 541; cf. Huber, 1690: P. II, L. I, c. I.

80. Stolte, 1981: 90. *Modestia* was also a prerequisite of criticism for Perizonius, see Meyer, 1971: 153.

81. McGahagan, 1976: 81. 82. McGahagan, 1976: 81.

83. Palazzini Finetti, 1953: 242, 333 f.; cf. Vriemoet, 1763: 590: 'Adhibuit modesto judicio suo artem criticam . . .'. Qualifications like *audacia* or *modestia* no doubt were stereotypes, which were based on criticism by colleagues, but as a rule not tested by thorough research.

opposition between Noodt and Huber concerning the relative value of *ratio* and *scriptum*, though possibly reinforced by current Cartesianism, was, in fact, a reprise of the debate between Cujas and Doneau.[84] Neither opponent dreamed of departing from traditional legal science.

With respect to the humanists it can easily be established that many of the problems they were tackling with new philological methods are, in fact, traditional *cruces* produced by medieval methods of interpretation, and not solvable with these in a satisfactory way.[85] The same can be said of Noodt. Often the starting-point for his observations is a traditional antinomy dating from the Middle Ages.[86] Anyone asking for a qualified *ratio* or *necessitas emendandi* may have misgivings about such emendations, but one should not make anachronistic demands on seventeenth-century scholars. Only where a fairly sharp line can be drawn between *recensio* and *emendatio*, between constitution and interpretation of the text (that is, not earlier than the nineteenth century),[87] can one dismiss in principle emendations which have dogmatic rather than critical reasons. But even now not every Romanist accepts such a rigorous principle as a matter of course. Apparently, *ratio juris* still has a role to play, not only in modern theories of legal interpretation[88]—where the text of the law has replaced manuscript authority—but even in legal history.[89]

Rationalism and natural law

As I have said, humanism is also a critical movement in other than the philological sense. The earliest humanistic legal writings already abound in abuse of jurists. Philological research was directed, sometimes expressly, at overthrowing established theories and interpretations. In humanism there is already something like a crisis of authority and tradition. Human reason is regarded as having its own

84. See above, at n. 64.
85. For examples from Alciato see Osler, 1983: 190, 192.
86. See below, p. 143.
87. For the orthodox principle see e.g. Schulz, 1916: 15, 17. And, for a general survey, see Timpanaro, 1971.
88. The belief in *ratio juris* was expressed emphatically by Jhering, 1857, see n. 39: only the 'juristischen Sinn' is able to attain 'das wahrhafte Verständnis des römischen Rechts'. See also Scholten, 1934: 59 ff.
89. See e.g. Ankum, 1983: 171 f.

value.[90] But, as we have seen, for legal science this did not imply a complete change. Humanism regarded Antiquity—and Rome above all—as the absolute model to be followed in every respect. So the Corpus Juris, handed down from Roman Antiquity, lost nothing of its authority. Better knowledge of historical and literary data might result in better translation of difficult or rare words, reconstruction of Greek fragments, more adequate insights in Roman institutions. Sometimes it might even overthrow an interpretation which had a tradition behind it dating back to the glossators. But all this did not affect the authority of the text as such.[91] Naturally, textual criticism of humanistic philologues could not help ending the relative certainty of traditionally established readings,[92] but the effect of this should not be exaggerated in retrospect. Certainty had never been absolute; all through the Middle Ages the Digest remained a 'living text'. In this respect there is, as I said earlier, no fundamental divide between medieval and humanistic legal scholarship.

All this began to change in the first half of the seventeenth century, when the rising tide of rationalism challenged authority and tradition, denied the validity of medieval methods of arguing, and put human reason in a central place. Descartes spoke critically of the 'sciences of books, or at least those whose reasonings are only probable and which have no demonstrations'.[93] What he meant by the sciences of books is clear enough; they are primarily the higher studies of the Middle Ages, law and theology in particular. The idea of deducing legal propositions not from the Digest or Codex, but from axioms, in the same way as was done in mathematics, was not entirely new,[94] but now it was given a concrete and extremely

90. See, on *ratio* in Cujas, Troje, 1971: 118 f. and see n. 56.
91. See Piano Mortari, 1978: 7.
92. Van den Bergh and Stolte, 1977: 228.
93. '... sciences des livres, ou du moins celles dont les raisons ne sont que probables, et qui n'ont aucunes démonstrations ...': Descartes, 1953: 133. Naturally this statement of Descartes was nothing new. Galenus was the first to demand expressly that all sciences follow the same method as geometry (Schüling, 1969: 11). In the Middle Ages it was held that 'methodus demonstrativus nobilior est non demonstrativo' (Herberger, 1981: 208). The criticism that jurists knew nothing of demonstrations had already been voiced about the end of the 15th century by Nicoletto Vernias (Herberger, 1981: 11 f.).
94. Cf. already Duaren (1509–59): 'causae et fontes ... elementa juris et fundamenta maximarum disputationum sicut in geometria punctum, linea, superficies'. Cited after Piano Mortari, 1978: 399. And see Herberger, 1981: 260 f. Valentin Forster (1613) proposed to reduce law to 'regulae generales', which then could be ordered 'more geometrico', Herberger, 1981: 248.

popular form by the new natural law, for which Hugo Grotius laid the basis—although his *De jure belli ac pacis* (1625) was, in fact, far from presenting a strictly axiomatic–deductive system of law. It promised, however, to produce a scientific system of law that complied with the dominant ideals of a science and became the prevailing social philosophy of the age. Grotius incorporated on the one hand the formal methods of reasoning of scholasticism,[95] on the other hand the erudition of humanism. According to Grotius, testimonies of poets, writers, and philosophers from Antiquity, if sufficiently unanimous, could prove the truth of some legal proposition, or at least adorn the discourse,[96] which in the rhetorical tradition was a value in itself.

Rationalism, in the form of Cartesianism, had an immense influence on intellectual life in the Republic, roughly between 1640 and 1680.[97] Nowhere else, leaving France aside, did Cartesian ideas have such an impact, or were so bitterly fought.[98] Noodt's years of apprenticeship (1662–9) roughly coincide with the period in which the battle between adherents and opponents of Descartes is at its height.[99] One of Noodt's first university teachers was Theodoor Craanen, a convinced and militant Cartesian.[1] In the two and a half years that Noodt studied mathematics and philosophy under him, he must have been introduced directly to the new philosophy. Among Noodt's friends and acquaintances were Cartesians like Braunius and Cyprianus Regneri ab Oosterga.

Descartes showed a different attitude towards Antiquity. In fact, we find in him all the elements that will characterize the position of the moderns in the well-known 'querelle des anciens et modernes', which takes place later in the seventeenth century.[2] The authority of

95. See, on the sources of Grotius in general, Feenstra, 1972, 1974, 1978, all with further literature, and, for further studies on Grotius, the bibliography in *Satura Feenstra*, Fribourg, 1985. The system of *De jure belli ac pacis* shows the same mixture of deduction and disputation (*quaestio*) as scholasticism; see Schüling, 1969: 29. Grotius himself calls the discussion of the question of just war a disputation: 'in hac disputatione quaerimus . . .' (I. 1. 2. 3).
96. Prolegomena, §§ 40, 47.
97. Gerretzen, 1940; Thijssen-Schoute, 1954; McGahagan, 1976.
98. F. Sassen, introduction to Thijssen-Schoute, 1954.
99. See Thijssen-Schoute, 1954; McGahagan, 1976.
1. On him, see Sassen, 1962: 114; McGahagan, 1976: 334.
2. Gerretzen, 1940: 7 f. Needless to say, Descartes was not the only one who was critical of Antiquity. In Germany one finds similar ideas in e.g. Christian Thomasius. For French influences on Thomasius, see Lieberwirth, 1984: 63 f., and especially on Descartes' influence, p. 67.

Antiquity is challenged directly. Cyprianus Regneri ab Oosterga published as a young man a treatise with the provocative title 'On the injustice of some Roman laws'.[3] For his attempt to apply Cartesian logic to law[4] he was sharply criticized.[5] The attack on authority and tradition was bound to hit traditional civil law at its heart. Roman law itself was henceforth measured by reason, and natural law set up as a new fundamental legal doctrine beside it.[6] The emancipation of public law was soon to follow.

Regneri ab Oosterga's programme was more critical than would be acceptable even to a 'modernist' like Noodt, and therefore it could have no success. His *Censura*[7] intended literally to censor *all* sources of civil law in the same way, on the basis of *mores Belgicae* and general Christian custom. His censorship comprised three elements: *confirmare*, *illustrare*, and *refutare*. This is the programme for an extremely radical *usus modernus*, which was heavily criticized, e.g. by the German jurist Haberkorn.[8] No wonder that it did not appeal to the more orthodox Huber.[9] Regneri ab Oosterga, moreover, was not a very erudite jurist. Noodt, who is a generation younger, takes rather an intermediate position. On the one hand, he is more of a traditional civil law jurist than Regneri ab Oosterga, on the other, he is more liberal and rationalist in his interpretations than Huber.

Cartesianism, of course, could never have been accepted wholesale in a field of science like civil law, where a corpus of books handed down from Antiquity took the central place, and authority and tradition had an important role to play. Descartes himself, for that matter, did not believe that his method could be applied in law or theology. Was not the relative stability of the text of the Corpus Juris itself due to tradition alone? Had not the critical work of humanists, in the eyes of many, made matters problematic enough already?[10] Was not the binding force of the Corpus Juris, from a strictly legal point of view, based on nothing but custom?[11]

'Erubescimus si sine lege loquimur' (We are ashamed when we have to talk without the law—that is, without a fragment from the

3. Regneri ab Oosterga, 1640.
4. Regneri ab Oosterga, 1638.
5. By Saxe; see Jugler i, 1773: 331 f., de Wal, 1825: 194.
6. See Coing, 1970: 36.
7. For bibliographical references, see Roberts and Dekkers.
8. See Jugler ii, 1775: 336.
9. See above, p. 58 f.
10. See Van den Bergh and Stolte, 1977: 228 f.
11. See Wieacker, 1967: 206.

Corpus Juris), Bartolus had said.[12] But what could replace the Corpus Juris to relieve jurists of their shame? Natural law by itself certainly never could, although later in the eighteenth century some jurists claimed that it should take the place of Roman law as subsidiary law.[13] It would have been impossible to dispense with authority and tradition without abolishing legal science itself, and so deprive jurists of their expertise. Therefore, most jurists—and not only they—were eclectics, and only took from Cartesianism what seemed useful. In fact, it is nearly impossible to label any one scholar straightforwardly as a Cartesian.

Now it cannot be our task to ascertain which elements of Cartesianism were taken over by whom in civil law; the matter awaits further research.[14] But it is important to understand the general intellectual climate in which Gerard Noodt lived. Without labelling him a Cartesian we may conclude, I think, that rationalistic tendencies are stronger in his work than in that of many of his contemporaries. In his younger years, when criticizing Tribonian, he did not fail to add obligingly that he did not do this out of *novandi libido* (lust for novelty).[15] But even then he was not prepared to accept the reproach that he had too little respect for the majesty of Roman law: 'I foresee in my mind that there will be people who are dissatisfied with all I have written in this chapter, because they think the majesty of civil wisdom [i.e. Roman law] is not revered enough by someone who dares to think that sometimes something human has failed Tribonian or someone of the prudentes, [even if he does so] not out of hate against them, or out of lust for innovation, but for manifest reason and the study of truth, to which all good men must be directed. I wish that those keep to their own affairs, and, if the gods permit, scrupulously defend the errors of the old (*veteres*). I for my part will take care not to deliver a most beautiful art easily to superstition, or to be the cause that the Corpus Juris is enervated and falls down, because I am making it a laughing stock by trivial and

12. Bartolus super Auth. (on Nov. 18. 5. 1). I used the ed. of Lyon, 1557. The expression must, in fact, be much older than Bartolus.
13. See, on Van der Marck and his pupils, Jansen, 1987*b*.
14. Neither Thijssen-Schoute, 1954, nor McGahagan, 1976, discussed the position of jurists in any detail. For Huber, see Veen, 1976: 183. Naturally, in the ferment of early Enlightenment thought Descartes was certainly not the only important thinker. We will meet the names of Locke, Bayle, and Spinoza later.
15. *Prob.* 1. 9. 7, *Opera* i: 23. In fact, criticism of Tribonian had a long standing in humanism, and already Budé criticized him for being dormant.

stupid evasions, and that the minds of the young, who are rising to great things, shall be seized with chicanery as with a pestilent torpor.'[16]

But again it would be a mistake to attribute Noodt's critical attitude towards Tribonian solely to the influence of Cartesian rationalism. In fact, it has a long and direct pedigree in the elegant tradition. Noodt's words, as just cited, must have reminded informed contemporary readers of a notorious debate from some decades previously. As we know, Justinian himself ordered the compilers to adapt fragments from classical jurists to contemporary conditions,[17] and the early legal humanists already noted various texts where Tribonian actually seemed to have done this. But the theme was given a much more critical turn by François Hotman,[18] who began to criticize sharply Tribonian, and eventually even Justinian's codification itself, with a stream of the invectives to which humanists seemed to be addicted. This kind of 'Tribonian-scourging', which was continued by Hotman's pupil Vulteius, was put into a more sophisticated scientific form and introduced into the Republic by Vulteius' pupil Antonius Matthæus I, whose nephew and very devoted pupil Johann Jacob Wissenbach—in medieval terms the *dominus domini* of Noodt[19]—published in 1633 his very controversial *Emblemata Triboniani*, for the greater part a compilation of allegations of interpolations by Hotman, Cujas, and others. This small book caused no small stir in the world of learning (and actually made Wissenbach's career). Van Bijnkershoek even contemplated for some

16. *Prob.* 1. 9. 7 (text according to the first edn., Leiden, 1674; the *Opera* text has slight differences): 'Praesagit mihi mens mea, fore, quibus ea passim, quae scripsi hoc capite, sint displicitura, quia existimant non satis comiter coli majestatem civilis sapientiae, si quis vel in Tribonianum, vel prudentum aliquem cecidisse interdum humani quidpiam autumet, non tam odio ductus eorum aut novandi libidine, quam ratione manifesta et studio veritatis, ad quam omnes bonos collimare fas, jusque est. Sed hi, velim, res suas sibi habeant, et si diis placet, tueantur sancte errores veterum. Ego vero ei rei curabo, ne facile superstitioni donem artem pulcherrimam, neve levibus, atque inanibus effugiis ludibria quaedam excitando efficiam, ut corpus juris enervetur, et cadat, animique juvenum ad magna surgentes calumnia, velut pestilenti sydere, afflentur.' Huber (1700: 407) copies these 'very beautiful' words, but thinks he can justify Ulpian in this case 'sine superstitione adversus errata veterum'.
17. C. Deo auctore, 7 = C 1. 17. 1. 7.
18. I follow the excellent and still very readable short account by Heineccius, Praef. in Wissenbach, 1736: pp. iii–xxvi. There were humanists before Hotman who criticized Justinian and Tribonian, see Palazzini Finetti, 1953: 43 f., but most of them were not jurists. On Hotman, see also Baron, 1888; Van Kan, 1922.
19. In Franeker Wissenbach was the teacher of Noodt's teacher, Petrus de Greve.

time writing a whole book against it, but later dropped the idea. The anti-Wissenbach was written later by Johannes Wybo, a pupil of Van Eck.[20]

The fundamental issue was clear enough in the days of Hotman. Many wondered how a jurisprudent could be so imprudent as to try to cut down his own vineyard, to abolish the art he was teaching himself.[21] Apparently Noodt was referring succinctly to this debate, and had learned something from it as well. Far from trying to abolish the art, he believed that it was exactly slavish adherence to the 'errors of the old', not criticism, that would lead to its abolition. This is an argument that has been used in debates between conservatives and innovators, orthodox and modernists of all times. Reasonable as it may have sounded, it would not convince someone like Van Bijnkershœk. For him Noodt was perhaps anyway tainted with the heresy of the Tribonian-scourgers (*Tribonianimastigiae*). This may help to explain the sharpness of their later debate.

In his Utrecht inaugural address of 1684 Noodt clearly endorsed the modernist position. He spoke about the enormous recent advances of the sciences, which greatly surpassed the knowledge of Antiquity, and wondered why the science of society was lagging behind—a question puzzling many of us even today. Later in life he expressed the 'modern' standpoint in an album inscription written for Johannes Ihring and dated 14 August 1720:[22] 'Useless would be the tedious toil in studies, if it was not allowed to find something better than the people who are past and gone.' But when Noodt said that it is 'allowed' to find something better, he may still have had in mind the strictures against novelties by the theologians Gomarus, Gisbert Vœt, and others.[23] His open, critical attitude towards Antiquity, his acceptance of natural law, his robust rationalism make Noodt a true representative of early—mainly academic—Enlightenment. In this respect, his two famous rectorial addresses do not stand isolated from the rest of his scholarly work. Moreover, he laid much

20. J. Wybo, *Tribonianus ab emblematibus Wissenbachii liberatus*. Utrecht, 1729; other edn. Halle, 1736.
21. Heineccius, in Wissenbach, 1736: p. xii. The same metaphor is used by Bavius Voorda against van der Marck: 'quasi vero vel propria vineta caedere', see Voorda, 1762: 19 f.
22. 'frustra foret in studiis longior labor, si non liceret reperire meliora praeteritis'; KB 74 H 47, fol. 80.
23. See p. 123, and McGahagan, 1976: 38.

stress on the historical development of Roman law.[24] Roman law, he used to say, did not fall from heaven one day like a shower, but developed gradually.[25] In this respect Noodt stands out among his contemporaries and anticipates the Historical School. His work, moreover, proves that students of natural law were not altogether ahistorical.[26]

Evidently, for Noodt Antiquity no longer was the model of perfection. He admired the Corpus Juris, but despised the Romans for their bellicosity.[27] He acknowledged the advances made by the sciences in modern times.[28] He proposed to give natural law a place in the law curriculum beside Roman law,[29] and actually practised this himself.[30] He frequently stressed the historical relativity of traditional prescriptions. Biblical prohibitions of taking interest were written for the Hebrew state, not for all mankind,[31] and Christ's exhortion to 'lend without hoping for anything in return' (Luke 6: 35) should not be taken literally, but as a hyperbole. Similar arguments are used in the question of the prohibited degrees in marriage. Biblical prohibitions are Hebrew law, not natural law.[32]

From some of the subjects just mentioned, we can already see to what extent the debates between orthodox and modernists, between Voetians and Cartesians, influenced Noodt's choice of subjects. Led by Gisbert Vœt, whose ideas were closely related to those of the English puritans,[33] orthodox ministers fought all worldly tendencies that the commercial success of the young Republic had brought with it. When they stressed biblical prohibitions to take interest they

24. Haubold, 1809: 137, calls him a 'progressuum juris Romani diligens observator'. See also J. de Wal, 1852: 72 f.
25. See e.g. *Opera* i: 614 and below, p. 310.
26. Cf. van den Bergh, 1979: 30 ff.
27. Inaugural address, Franeker, see *Opera* i: 611.
28. Inaugural address, Utrecht, see *Opera* i: 617.
29. See below, p. 155 ff. At that time there were no chairs for natural law in any law faculty. Around the turn of the century in the Republic several professors gave private lectures on natural law, but formal chairs were only instituted in the middle of the 18th century (the first in Utrecht, 1746). Pufendorf's specially created chairs in Heidelberg (1660) and Lund (1667) were not in the law faculties. In fact, the appointment in Heidelberg met with opposition from the university, see Wieacker, 1967: 306.
30. From Leiden we have lecture notes of his (private) *Collegium Grotianum* of 1708, UL Leiden, BPL 191. It is a lemmatic comment on *De jure belli ac pacis*.
31. *Opera* i: 194, and see below, p. 184 f.
32. *Opera* i: 647, and see below, p. 287.
33. McGahagan, 1976: 28.

touched the central nerve of commercial capitalism.[34] In the context of their literal interpretation of the Bible they also wanted to extend the prohibited degrees of marriage in the Republic to in-law relations.[35] The considerable degree of religious toleration which was maintained in the Republic—and which the regents primarily may have seen as a condition for successful commerce—was regarded by the orthodox as the subordination of religious principles to commercial interest.[36] On all these points—interest, prohibited degrees, and toleration—Noodt, speaking as a jurist, brought his massive erudition to the side of 'true freedom', which, in fact, may hardly be surprising, considering the fact that he was a scion of a merchant family in 'Arminian' Nijmegen.

The combined critical potential of humanistic philology and natural law rationalism provided him with the instruments to do so effectively. What Noodt's method could achieve can be seen in his *Julius Paulus* (1700), which was published between the two famous rectorial addresses. This book, which seemingly concerns a purely antiquarian subject, is in fact a piece of history-debunking with an actual interest that did not escape his contemporaries. According to Noodt, the sources of Roman law prove that until the second half of the fourth century—that is, mind you, well into the reigns of the first Christian emperors—the killing and abandoning of children was not punishable under Roman law. This implies that classical jurists cannot be regarded as a model of humanity in every respect and that Christendom did not (as had generally been assumed) put an end to the repugnant practices of the ancients immedately. Though the classical jurist Julius Paulus speaks against it in the Digest, his words are not binding rules (*regulae*), but moral admonitions (*præcepta*). In one stroke this thesis posits the historical relativity of moral rules and 'unchanging' Christian principles, and denies that every text from the Corpus Juris is to be regarded as legally binding. These are very alarming thoughts indeed, especially for a judge like Van Bijnkershœk, who, by the way, kept his disquiet to himself for nearly twenty years and came out with his critique on the *Julius Paulus* only in 1719.[37]

34. McGahagan, 1976: 50 f. *Usurae*, for that matter, had long been a cherished subject of humanistic jurists; see Troje, 1977: 711 f.
35. See below, p. 285.
36. McGahagan, 1976: 90.
37. See below, p. 211 ff.

Methodus Noodtiana

We have an account of Noodt's method dating from some half-century after his death and written by two law professors, both at home in the elegant tradition. I think this account can best be discussed here, as a kind of excursus, although it may seem to duplicate some things that have been said in the preceding paragraphs.

In a memorandum dated 19 June 1773[38] the governors of Groningen university wrote to the law faculty that in their opinion too little time was spent on the history of law (*historia juris*) and that it was too much when both professors taught the Institutes as well as the Pandects. Would it be possible to alternate these courses and teach, apart from more history of law, subjects like *jus feudale* or *jus canonicum* instead? As might have been expected, the answer of the law faculty, then consisting of L. C. Schroeder (1724–1801)[39] and J. Cannegieter (1731–1804),[40] both having a commission to teach *jus civile*, was in the negative:

History of law is integrated in the courses of the Pandects wherever it seems useful. If one taught it as a separate subject for more than two hours one would not have students. In most universities there are two professors for *jus civile*, even more so because usually the teaching methods of the various professors differ in no mean way. One will occupy himself mainly with the explanation of Roman law from the point of view of modern law (*ex iure novo*), illustrating the various cases it contains with examples and interpreting the controversies of ancient law, all, as one usually says, according to the method of Bachoff (*methodo Bachoviana*). Another will prefer the *jurisprudentia elegantior*, as it is called usually, or the method of Noodt (*methodus Noodtiana*), adding criticism, the explanation of the more notable and obscure laws, historical development (*successus juris*), and national law (*jus patrium*).[41]

Naturally, we should not take this account, which does not seem to be more than an occasional argument, too seriously. But, roughly speaking, it gives a fair impression of the two schools in jurisprudence that had existed for two ages but which, in fact, had already been on the wane for some time. The first answers more or less to the partly bartolistic programme of the *usus modernus pandectarum*:[42]

38. Jonckbloet, 1864: 288.
39. v. d. Aa vi, 1852: 160; Boeles, in Jonckbloet, 1864: 83 f.
40. v. d. Aa ii, 1852: 35; Boeles, in Jonckbloet, 1863: 94 f.
41. Jonckbloet, 1864: 289.
42. See Söllner, 1977: 501 f.

1. Explanation of Roman law *ex iure novo*: that is, not antiquarian or overly dogmatic, but with a view to contemporary economic and social conditions, national law, and legal practice.
2. Treating *casus* with examples. *Casus*[43] have been a didactic device since the Middle Ages.
3. Explanation of *controversiae juris antiqui*: that is, of antinomies in the Corpus Juris. This again is a subject that has been prominent in legal training since the days of the glossators.

That this teaching programme bears the name *methodus Bachoviana* may come as a surprise. R. Bachoff von Echt (1575–1634)[44] published a commentary on Books 1–4 of the Digest,[45] which could hardly be called epoch-making, though it certainly was a step in the gradual development from explanation according to the *ordo legum*[46] to systematic exposition according to subjects. Bachoff begins with a summary of the contents of each book or title, which is followed by exegesis of the most important texts. But the name *methodus Bachoviana* may rather be explicable by the fact that his dogmatic commentary on the Institutes was very successful, especially in Holland where it was closely followed by Vinnius (1588–1633),[47] whose commentary on the Institutes had a very wide circulation. And certainly Bachoff was no friend of humanists.

The name of *methodus Noodtiana* for the other current in legal studies naturally highlights Noodt's fame in the late eighteenth century, but it can hardly be regarded as being very specific. *Methodus Cujaciana* might have done as well. The elements enumerated here are:

1. *Ars critica*: that is, textual criticism. About this enough has been said in the preceding paragraphs.
2. Explanation of the most notable and obscure laws, that is, *loci difficiliores*. The problematic texts meant here may be partly the same as the *controversiae* enumerated under the *methodus Bachoviana*, partly other ones. But the treatment is different. *Controversiae* are in principle harmonized by the methods developed by the glossators, *loca difficiliora* are tackled with philological methods (textual criti-

43. Coing, 1973: 213 f.
44. Stintzing and Landsberg iii. 1, 1898: 683 f.
45. Stintzing and Landsberg iii. 1, 1898: 685.
46. That is, the order in which the fragments appear in the various parts of the Corpus Juris.
47. See Feenstra and Waal, 1975: 28 f., n. 104.

cism, emendation, lexical and grammatical data, historical criticism).[48]

3. *Successus juris* or legal development. This concerns not only what we would call now external history of Roman law, but also legal development. This element would be the most appropriate to justfy the name *methodus Noodtiana*, because, as we saw earlier, Noodt was regarded as an expert in this.[49]

4. *Jus patrium*: national or indigenous law. This element comes as something like an afterthought and one may seriously doubt whether it is characteristic of Noodt's method. His published books are all concerned with classical Roman law and only in his lectures does he refer sometimes to *jus hodiernum* or *jus patrium*. But, on the whole, *jus patrium* may well be placed in the account of the elegant tradition. In fact, it was the French humanistic jurists who published the first editions of important sources of Germanic law, such as the *leges barbarorum* and the *capitularia*.[50]

Naturally, it is quite another matter whether the two professors in Groningen were really representatives of the two different schools. Most likely they were not. For the teaching of the Institutes both used the *Elementa* of Heineccius,[51] and Cannegieter used Böckelmann's *Compendium*[52] besides. For external history of Roman law both used J. A. Bach's very successful *Historia jurisprudentiae Romanae*.[53] For the Pandects Cannegieter followed Westenberg[54] while Schroeder treated *loci difficiliores*. Cannegieter's work clearly belongs to the elegant tradition,[55] whereas Schroeder had studied in Marburg under Hombergk zu Vach,[56] a distinguished scholar in the same tradition. So perhaps the governors of Groningen university were right after all in thinking that the two professors greatly duplicated each other's teaching.

48. *Cruces* and *controversiae* are juxtaposed, apparently for the same reason, in a letter of Rob. Moray to Van Eck, Edinburgh, 23 Aug. 1689, UL Utrecht, MS 1000.
49. See p. 131.
50. Troje, 1977: 667 f., 709 f.
51. *Elementa juris civilis secundum ordinem Institutionum*, Amsterdam, 1725, and many other impressions. On Heineccius, see *NNBW* i: 1105. For the data about the teaching of Cannegieter and Schroeder, see Boeles in Jonckbloet, 1864: 83, 94.
52. Ahsmann–Feenstra, 1984: nr. 32 ff.
53. Leipzig, 1754, and several other edns., see Roberts, 1942: 42.
54. On him, see Feenstra, 1984.
55. For his works, see Dekkers: 32. He ed. the *Tituli ex corpore Ulpiani* and the *Collatio*, and published observations on *loca difficiliora*. He was not quite as learned as his elder brother H. Cannegieter (1723–1804, see *NNBW* x: 169).
56. See Jugler i, 1773: 341 f.

2. Years of growth—writings 1668–91

Disputatio juridica de adquirenda, retinenda et amittenda possessione[57]

It was a long-established practice in university training to defend two or more *disputationes* during the course of one's studies.[58] A *disputatio*, consisting of a series of theses on one subject, was meant to be a practical exercise in disputing, which was part of any intellectual training and, of course, was regarded by jurists as of the essence of their trade.[59] But, in fact, it seems to have been a rather formal affair through which one showed oneself able to argue and make citations in the prescribed manner. If the thesis concerned some right or institution, the subject could be treated according to one or other of the well-established dogmatic schemes: What is it? How do we acquire it? How can it be maintained? How do we lose it? For each subject there was a standard range of antinomies and questions to be treated.[60] In the seventeenth century, disputations as a rule seem to have been written by the professor, and the student's task was only to defend them. Many professors published collections of disputations in their own name: Wissenbach,[61] Huber,[62] and De Greve.[63] Several monographs (e.g. Huber's *De jure civitatis*) were first published as a series of disputations.[64] A system often used in the Republic was the *disputationes anniversariae*, a series of disputations spanning an academic year and following the *ordo legum* of the Institutes or the Digest.

The professor presided over the debate and intervened when the student did not stand his ground. Disputes done for training were not held in public, but disputations *pro gradu* could be, with differing degrees of solemnity and costs. As still can happen today, sometimes

57. Ahsmann–Feenstra, 1984: nr. 420.
58. Horn, 1893; Simon van der Aa, 1914; Schüling, 1969: 78 f.; Feenstra, 1985*a*, 1985*b*; Ahsmann, 1986: 8 f.; Roelevink, 1986: 117 f.
59. Huber, 1688*a*: 54.
60. Canoy-Olthoff, 1983: 19 f.
61. *Exercitationum ad 50 Pandectarum libros*. Franeker, 1653–8. There are several later edns. There are also collections of disputations on the Institutes and on the title *De diversis regulis juris*, see Roberts, 1942: 339.
62. *Eunomia romana*, published posthumously by his son Zacharias in Franeker, 1700.
63. See Dekkers; Hermesdorf, 1970*a*, *b*, 1971.
64. Cf. Feenstra, 1985*b*.

a student became the victim of quarrelsome professors. The conflicts in which Huber was involved broke out over a thesis,[65] and the same can be said for many of the debates between Cartesians and Voetians.[66]

Noodt defended his second *disputatio*—the first was written by Petrus de Greve[67]—on 27 June 1668[68] and although with this he concluded his legal training in Nijmegen, it was not a disputation *pro gradu*,[69] because Noodt did not take his degree there. Nevertheless, it was defended in public, as the title-page says. Noodt was an exceptionally good student and the young university will have welcomed the occasion for a public show. As we saw, in his autobiography he proudly states that he wrote the second disputation himself and that De Greve presided over it in complete silence, without adding a word of his own.[70] Noodt's authorship—he signs the dedication as 'auctor'[71]—is confirmed by internal evidence. Apart from very frequent laudatory citations of his teacher De Greve ('acutissimus', 'celeberrimus', 'excellentissimus', 'consultissimus', 'subtilissimus'), the thesis has a number of citations from classical authors quite uncommon in this kind of literature:[72] Tacitus, Ovid, Plautus, Seneca, Gellius, Suetonius, Virgil, Servius. Noodt makes his allegiance to the elegant tradition clear from his very first publication.

The disputation contains twenty-one theses which treat the subject according to the scheme just mentioned. Possession is defined legally as the holding of something belonging to someone else with the intention of holding it for oneself (I). It is divided into civil and natural possession—which is not the same as detention as jurists sometimes assume erroneously (II). It is acquired *corpore et animo*, and the various questions regarding the quality of *corpus* and *animus*

65. See above, p. 55 f.
66. See McGahagan, 1976, *passim*.
67. Ahsmann–Feenstra, 1984: nr. 419, defended 8 Apr. 1668.
68. Julian calendar.
69. Disputations and dissertations (there was no sharp distinction between them) were either *exercitii gratia* or *pro gradu*, see Canoy-Olthoff, 1983: 16; Feenstra, 1985*a*.
70. See above, p. 23.
71. Not as 'auctor et respondens', as is said by Canoy-Olthoff, 1983: 26.
72. Canoy-Olthoff, 1983: 26. There are other striking differences from the other disputation, defended by Noodt but written by De Greve. As against eight citations from classical authors De Greve has only one. On the other hand De Greve has five citations from the Basilica, Noodt none. As regards *doctores* (jurists) Noodt has sixteen names cited 70 times, De Greve sixty-one, cited 125 times.

are treated successively (III–XIII). How can possession be maintained (XIV–XV)? What are its effects (XVI–XVIII)? How is it proved (XIX)? How is it lost (XX)? Finally, the question is discussed whether possession is a matter of fact or of law (XXI). According to Noodt it is both. As far as its nature is concerned it is a matter of fact, but, because of the qualities and effects the law has attached to it, it is a matter of law as well.[73] The thesis that possession is at once fact and law was made famous by Von Savigny in his epoch-making monograph on possession (1803) and then became an issue in debates on the origin of property.[74] Von Savigny presents it as an established fact and refers for proof to the thesis of the Dutch jurist A. J. Cuper.[75] It is rather remarkable that the young Noodt had already reached the same conclusion in 1668.

In the whole disputation there is only one reference to contemporary law ('hodie'), but among the abundantly cited authors there are *practici* (Bachov, Schneidewin, Fachineus) as well as humanists (Cujas, Duaren). Naturally, we should not expect great originality in such a disputation[76]—that would rather have been regarded as reprehensible. The student only had to show that he was master of the subject as it had taken shape in the tradition of *jus commune*, and that he was able to discuss it in the approved manner. From a technical point of view, however, the quality of Noodt's disputation is very high.

Probabilia juris civilis

In 1674, at the age of 27, Noodt published his first major publication, *Probabilia juris civilis*, Book I.[77] The book was dedicated to four Nijmegen magistrates, among whom is Arnold Cœrman, the man on whose advice he had turned to the study of law.[78] It was issued in

73. Noodt cites as proof D 41. 2. 49. 1 ('. . . possessio non tantum corporis, sed et iuris est') and D 47. 4. 1. 15 ('. . . possessionem . . . quae facti est et animi').
74. F. C. von Savigny, *Das Recht des Besitzes*, Giessen, 1803 (I used the 6th edn., 1837), p. 30. And see Kelley, 1984: 130ff.
75. *Observationes selectae de natura possesionis*. Leiden, 1789. On A. J. Cuper (1765–1831), see *NNBW* i: 660–1. Von Savigny (as n. 18): 30: 'So ist also Besitz (in dem oben bestimmten Sinne) Factum und Recht zugleich. Die vielen Verhändlungen anzuführen, welche man bey Schriftstellern über diese Frage findet, wäre so unnutz, als ihre Lectüre unbelehrend ist. Cuperus hat die sache in Ganzen richtig und gründlich dargestellt, auch hat sich seitdem kein Zweifel hierüber gezeigt.'
76. Cf. Horn, 1893: 4.
77. Ahsmann–Feenstra, 1984: nr. 421. The dedication is dated 1 July 1674.
78. See above, Ch. 2, § 1, at n. 80.

Leiden by the printer Felix Lopez de Haro.[79] The quality of the printing, or rather correction, seems to have been rather poor. Perhaps the book was made in a hurry, and Noodt, then living in Nijmegen, may not have had an opportunity to proof-read. Apart from an error in page-numbering (64 is followed by 69) there are many errors which are not nearly completely corrected in the list of errata. Some errors must have been corrected after publication in the copies the editor had in stock. Page 37/38 is pasted in; it is a new page to correct a haplography on p. 38.[80] Likewise for pages 85/100 a new quire is pasted in. And there remained a major uncorrected haplography in the quotation of D 41. 1. 7. 5–6 on p. 2.[81] The book seems to have been fairly well received. As we saw before, ambassador Van Beverningk was very pleased with it, and it made also a big impression on Wächtler.[82]

The book contains thirteen essays on various problems of civil law which conform to the model of the humanistic *observatio*,[83] a type of literature not determined by forms of teaching—as were all medieval types of literature—but by the course of individual study and research. As usual, the essays are not arranged according to the *ordo legum* or any systematic order. Sometimes in one *observatio* several connected problems are treated.[84] The authors whose work Noodt discusses most frequently belong to the same school: Budé, Cujas, Govea, Connannus, Duaren, Hotman, Pithou, Antoine Faure, Haloander, Reyvært, and several others.[85] Evidently Noodt inscribes himself in the elegant tradition, the *mos gallicus*. There are only some slight peculiarities. In some chapters[86] the argument develops into a discussion of problems of natural law. This is no true innovation of Noodt's. As we saw before, Grotius had already combined formal methods of reasoning with humanistic erudition in the construction of natural law theory, and this partly continued rationalistic tendencies already present in humanism. That the young Noodt was influenced by Grotius' *De jure belli ac pacis* was noted already by Wächtler.[87]

79. See Lopez de Haro, 1985.
80. The pasted-in page is in the copies in East Berlin, Staatsbibliothek, Gb 11701; Basle, UL, Mio X. 4; Edinburgh, Advocates Library, A 67. 3. The original page is in Edinburgh, Advocates Library, A 68. 3.
81. From *flumen* (Mo ii: 488: 35) to *flumen* (Mo ii: 488: 37).
82. See the preface in Wächtler, 1680.
83. Troje, 1970: 35; 1977: 671 f.; Grafton, 1983: 17 f.
84. e.g. *Prob.* 1. 2; 1. 13.
85. For an overview of the humanist school, see Troje, 1977: 677 f.
86. *Prob.* 1. 5; 1. 7; 1. 8; 3. 1; 3. 2.
87. Wächtler, 1733: 209.

If we remember Descartes' critical attitude towards the sciences of books 'dont les raisons ne sont que probables',[88] it may come a bit as a surprise that Noodt, whom we believe to be influenced by the new philosophy, chose *Probabilia* as the title of his first book. From what he says to explain it to his readers, we may conclude that, apart from the modesty of a young scholar, a clear appreciation of the relativity of historical knowledge inspired it. 'I often disagree with other expositors,' he admits, 'but everywhere I give full respect, even to the feeble. Which respect is lacking in many, who loudly reproach even the great names and in my opinion rather seek to win glory by doing injury to others than to further plain truth. I do not put such a high prize on fame and will not protest if they will do to me what I have done to others. If some greater expert, driven by an equal observance to mankind, will kindly show that I am erring, I will not be guilty of resisting reason: my intention is to give plausible opinions, not decrees, not to determine what is ambiguous, but only to explain what seems plausible to me.'[89] That the title may indeed be taken as testimony of methodological consciousness is suggested by the fact that in the words just cited Noodt refers to Cicero's discussion of scientific method in the *Academica priora*, opposing *probabilia* and *dereta* exactly in the same way as does Cicero.[90] The idea that it is impossible to attain certainty beyond what is probable naturally belongs to the tradition of scepticism and goes back to Carneades.[91] That the same applies to Roman law and legal science in general was also defended by Noodt's younger contemporary, Christian Thomasius. It was labelled *scepticismus juridicus*.[92]

88. See above, § 1, at n. 93.
89. Noodt, 1674: *Praef. ad lectorem*: 'Nam etsi a reliquis interpretibus haud infrequenter dissentiam, ubique tamen sarta tecta manet infirmarum quoque personarum reverentia, quae adeo plerisque deest, ut etiam maximis nominibus faciant convitium, atque, ut mihi videtur, magis ex aliorum injuria gloria captent, quam ingenuae veritati studeant. At mihi fama vilius constat, nec recuso, quo minus idem jus sit alteri in meo, quod mihi in alieno sumpsi. Sed et si peritior quisquam, communi ductus humanitatis officio, erranti comiter monstret viam, non committam, ut rationi relucter: Probabiles quippe edere institui opiniones, non dare decreta, nec definire, quae sunt ambigua, sed quid mihi videatur verisimilius, enarrare.' Huber (1688*a*: 44) turns this statement against Noodt to prove that his emendations do not have the required *necessitas emendandi*: 'Id tamen existimo, emendationes ejus esse plerasque non necessarias atque ita comparatas, ut ab aliis, sicut ipse fatetur in praefatione sua, refelli non nequeant.'
90. *Academica priora*, ii: 109–10; cf. Herberger, 1981: 57. Noodt's words 'nec definire, quae sunt ambigua' seem to correspond with Cicero's 'in incertis enim nihil est probabile'.
91. See Popkin, 1967: 449 ff.
92. Herberger, 1981: 322 f.

Five years after Book I, in 1679, a new edition of the *Probabilia* is brought out, now in three books.[93] As far as Book I is concerned, it is not a new edition. The pages of the first edition are reissued with a new title-page and dedication; only the index is reset.[94] This time the book is dedicated to Hieronymus van Beverningk. Apart from the general title-page (*Probabilium juris civilis libri tres ad Hieronymum Beverningium* . . .) Books II and III have a separate title-page and pagination. Apparently those already in possession of Book I could buy them separately.[95] Books II and III each have twelve chapters. Finally, in the edition of 1691,[96] a fourth book is added, again containing twelve chapters.[97] The book remains dedicated to Van Beverningk, who actually died at the end of 1690, but his name has disappeared from the title-page. As far as the text is concerned, even this edition is not the final one. Noodt refined its text in successive editions (1705, 1713, 1724).[98]

Reviewing all four books of *Probabilia* we may call them typically humanistic, especially in respect of the methods Noodt used and the way in which he argued. Several times the meaning of words is

93. Ahsmann–Feenstra, 1984: nr. 422.
94. In the copy in Edinburgh, Advocates Library, A 68. 3, Book I is even without the corrections in pages 37/8 and 85/100; see above, p. 139.
95. UL, Basle, Mio X 4, and Edinburgh, Advocates Library, A 68. 3, consist of the reissue of Book I with Books II and III (in Edinburgh as separate volumes), but Edinburgh, Advocates Library, A 67. 3 consists of Book I in the 1674 edn. with Books II and III in one volume. All books in Edinburgh are from the library of Lord George Douglas. One of them has been bound only recently.
96. Ahsmann–Feenstra, 1984: nr. 423.
97. Two of these are rejoinders to criticisms on earlier chapters. *Prob.* 4. 3 discusses once more the emendation proposed in *Prob.* 1. 4, and *Prob.* 4. 8 answers Huber's criticism, voiced already in the dialogue of 1684 (Huber, 1688*a*: 44 f.) and elaborated later in the Digressiones.
98. *Opera varia*, 1705; *Opera omnia*, 1713, 1724 (Ahsmann–Feenstra, 1984: nrs. 425, 464, 465). I have made random collations of *Prob.* 1 in the various edns. From this it appears that the text was worked over substantially in 1691 and 1724. The 1705 edn. has only slight changes, apart from the addition of an inscription in *Prob.* 1. 2. Apparently, the edn. of Leiden: F. Haaring, 1693, is only a title edn. The publisher Felix Lopez de Haro made his last edns. in 1693 and died in 1694; see Lopez de Haro, 1985: 12. From random collations made in the 1691 and 1693 edns. it appears that the printing of the text of both is identical; only the preliminary pages (title, dedication, *elenchus capitum*, corrigenda) are reset. Noodt himself did not count 1693 as an independent edn. until the end of his life. In the *Opera varia* of 1705 the edn. of the *Probabilia* is counted as the 3rd (1679, 1691, 1705), that of *De jurisdictione* and *Ad legem Aquiliam* as the 2nd (1691, 1705). Consequently, the *Opera omnia* of 1713 give their edns. as the 4th and 3rd respectively. But the edns. in the *Opera omnia* of 1724 are counted as the 6th and 5th respectively.

discussed, with an impressive show of lexical knowledge.[99] In many cases Noodt argues on the basis of inscriptions and other palingenetic data, making use of the Index of Labittus.[1] Sometimes the Basilica are adduced as proof.[2] The numerous cases where he argues on the basis of presumed false solution of *notæ* or sigla by some scribe[3] deserve special attention and will be discussed below. In some cases Noodt discusses logical arguments.[4] As is usual in this type of literature, Noodt not only proposes emendations of his own but also refutes those of others, e.g. A. Faure,[5] Cujas, Govea and Scipio Gentilis,[6] Raevardus,[7] Corasius and Baro,[8] and Elbertus Leoninus.[9]

This is all very much the ordinary stuff of humanistic legal literature. In a letter to Noodt to thank him for sending a copy of the 1691 edition, Cuper nicely sums up what in his opinion is the task of a law professor: 'To inquire into the concealed meanings of the ancients, to seek arguments from ancient monuments and from the most distinguished authors, with which you prove your own opinion and ruin that of others, that is, in my opinion, really acting like a jurist and a law professor.'[10] A new element, and a sign of Noodt's growing historical consciousness may be that he tried to distinguish, in a text from Paul *ad Sabinum* (D 33. 2. 1), the parts written by Sabinus from those which contain Paul's comment.[11] As far as the contents are concerned, and especially with regard to Noodt's own proposals for emendation, there are some particularities to note. I found, in fact, only three observations concerning problems that may be called typically humanistic, because they were never discussed by medieval

99. e.g. *Prob.* 1. 4: 'praetor'; 1. 7–8: 'communis–publicus'; 1. 9: 'mores maiorum'.
1. e.g. *Prob.* 1. 3 and 1. 9. In 1674 a new edn. of the *Index legum* of Labittus was brought out by van Gelder in Leiden, see Camus-Dupin ii, 1832: 569. A copy is in the Max Planck Institut für Rechtsgeschichte in Frankfurt.
2. e.g. *Prob.* 1. 10.
3. *Prob.* 1. 13; 2. 4, 2. 5, 2. 10; 3. 3, 3. 5; 4. 4.
4. e.g. *Prob.* 1. 3: invalidity of the *argumentum a contrario*; 1. 5: invalidity of the *argumentum ab inclusione unius ad exclusionem alterius.*
5. e.g. *Prob.* 1. 6; 2. 7.
6. e.g. *Prob.* 1. 6; 2. 6.
7. *Prob.* 2. 12.
8. *Prob.* 1. 2.
9. *Prob.* 2. 4.
10. Cuper to Noodt, The Hague, 16 Dec. 1690 (Draft, KB 72 G 20, 33): 'Inquirere in abstrusos veterum jurisconsultorum sensus, ex monumentis etiam antiquis, et auctoribus optimae notae argumenta petere, quibus sententiam tuam firmes, aliorum destruas, hoc mea sententia est vere jurisconsultum et professorem agere . . .'. See, for similar expressions of earlier humanists, Grafton, 1983: 18.
11. *Prob.* 2. 3.

jurists. In *Probabilia* 1. 6 Noodt argues an emendation on the ground that the praetor (unlike the *præfectus vigilum*) had no police power. In *Probabilia* 2. 5 the relative competence of the *præfectus urbis* and the *præfectus vigilum* is discussed. In *Probabilia* 3. 3 the question of how many types of *exsilium* there were is discussed; this discussion, concerning D 48. 19. 16, was initiated by Budé. Two other observations may be called humanistic in a wider sense: *Probabilia* 1. 13 discusses the condemnation of tutors; *Probabilia* 2. 1 treats an aspect of the problem of jurisdiction which will be treated more fully some years later in *De jurisdictione et imperio*. Against these five observations with a 'humanistic' subject there are no less than fifteen—that is, about one third of the whole—in which the starting-point for Noodt's essay is an antinomy already noted in the Accursian gloss.[12]

In the great majority of these cases[13] Noodt tries to solve the medieval antinomy by emendation. By definition, in all these instances the problem is not caused by some corruption of the text, but by a contradiction (or a presumed one) of a legal or dogmatic nature. No wonder that only for a minority of these emendations is there actually a manuscript reading to confirm it. There are only three for which this proves to be the case, but regarding two of these Noodt himself was not aware of the fact. The 'non sicut si' conjectured by Noodt in D 7. 1. 15. 4 (Mo i: 221: 13) is actually found in one

12. This particularity was already noted by Huber, 1688*a*: 4. The observations are:

Probabilia	*Text*	*Gloss*
1. 1	D 41. 1. 7. 5–6	sed vix est
1. 2	D 8. 1. 15	non potest
1. 3	D 8. 3. 6	ususfructus
1. 4	D 13. 7. 13. 1	ut in commodato
1. 10	D 9. 3. 5. 4	actione
2. 6	D 41. 2. 3. 3	naturalis possessio
2. 7	Inst. 2. 1. 35	cultura
		cura
3. 4	C 7. 32. 9	improbe
3. 5	C 9. 41. 1	principis
		praescriptionis invidia
3. 8	D 7. 9. 5. 3	licet per omnia
3. 9	D 3. 5. 6. 3	actionem
4. 2	C 4. 54. 6	conveniat
4. 4	D 12. 4. 16	proclivior
4. 6	D 22. 2. 7	usurae
4. 12	D 17. 6. 4–5	non intererat

13. *Prob.* 1. 2 being the exception. Here Noodt is not emending but tries to solve the crux by interpretation.

manuscript.[14] But apparently Noodt was not aware of the much older and more elegant conjecture to read 'non sic, ut', which Mommsen adopted in the *editio major*.[15] Noodt's transposition of 'tamen' in D 7. 8. 10 pr. (Mo i: 244: 3) was endorsed by Mommsen because it seems to be confirmed by the Basilica. And, finally, Noodt's suggestion to delete a 'non' in D 17. 1. 6. 4 (Mo i: 480: 27)[16] finds some support from the fact that some medieval manuscripts have this reading.[17] But only in the last case did Noodt know of the existence of a variant reading through the Accursian gloss.

The other eleven emendations discussed here are emendations *ope ingenii*, that is, not founded on manuscript authority. Now this in itself is no reason to dismiss them out of hand. As we saw, in Noodt's day such emendations were perfectly acceptable and even today most Romanists would not feel qualms about them. A more conservative critic like Van Bijnkershœk made them as well and Huber only demanded strict proof of their necessity. So, when they were criticizing Noodt, the issue was not the validity of such emendations *per se*, but the appropriate degree of modesty and conservatism in textual criticism. But, even while making allowance for this, we cannot deny that Noodt made some conjectures which seem to justify his reputation as a *criticus aliquando audacior*. For instance, his suggestion to read in D 9. 2. 5 pr. (Mo i: 278: 20) not 'Cornelia' but 'Aquilia'[18] seems rather ill founded. In this case not only F and the vulgates have this reading, but apart from the Digest the text is transmitted independently in the same form in Collatio 8. 3. 3. So if ever the manuscript tradition is beyond reasonable doubt, it is here. Therefore, to Noodt nothing was left but to suggest that Ulpian made an error himself, writing in a hurry. Adducing observations of Plautus, Gellius, and Suetonius that people under pressure often make mistakes in their writing, elegant as it may be, is not enough to corroborate the conjecture. Some of Noodt's contemporaries, indeed, would not have rejected this as an inadmissible *ad hoc*

14. *Prob.* 1. 4. MS Ottob. lat. 1605, Vatican City, Biblioteca Apostolica Vaticana, see Gebauer–Spangenberg, n. 58 *a.h.l.* (a note of Brenkman) and Stolte, 1981: 110.
15. loc. cit.; this reading is found in MSS Trevis. and Bijnkershœk I (now Leiden, BPL 6C), in some vulgate edns. (?), as well as in the edns. of Blaublomme (1523) and A Porta I (1547), see Gebauer–Spangenberg n. 58 *a.h.l.*
16. *Prob.* 4. 12.
17. See Mommsen, *editio major a.h.l.*
18. *Prob.* 1. 9. The emendation is criticized by Schulting, Huber, and Van de Water; see Van den Bergh and Stolte, 1977: 256 and Gebauer–Spangenberg n. 23 *a.h.l.* (Brenkman).

hypothesis, but rather because they regarded it as disrespectful to suppose that the *veteres* had made an error. The result, naturally, is the same.

Other examples of rather doubtful emendations are in D 41. 2. 3. 3 (Mo ii: 504: 11),[19] where Noodt suppresses another 'non' although F and the Bolognese manuscripts have the same reading, in D 7. 9. 5.3 (Mo i: 248: 31),[20] where Noodt adds two letters, and in D 22. 2. 7 (Mo i: 644: 8),[21] where seven letters are added, all without a trace in any manuscript. There is one case to which Brenkman gave special attention during his *iter italicum*, apparently because Noodt and Van Bijnkershœk disagreed on it. In the case treated in D 9. 3. 5. 4 (Mo i: 295: 10),[22] Noodt remarked (as had, in fact, been done in the gloss *actione*) that there was no place for the *actio legis Aquiliae* here, but only for an appropriate *actio in factum*. Therefore Noodt suggested reading 'in factum' instead of 'Aquilia', supposing, once more, an error of Ulpian. This was indeed a rather bold emendation. Van Bijnkershœk emphatically defended the reading of F.[23] Brenkman inspected seven manuscripts, none of which differed from F. In only one manuscript, above the word 'actione', the word 'utilis' was written in a different hand.

A special set of cases is formed by those texts in which Noodt does not dispute the reading of the Florentine manuscript itself, but suggests that the reading is the result of false solution of sigla or abbreviations by some copyist[24] (either a scribe of Ulpian's original, one from the post-classical era, or one of the Florentine manuscript itself). Apparently Noodt took special pride in these emendations, judging by the fact that in later editions (from 1691) he added as a motto to the *Probabilia* Justinian's prohibition of the use of sigla and 'compendious riddles' in the writing of the Digest.[25] Earlier

19. *Prob.* 2. 6.
20. *Prob.* 3. 8: 'usumfructum⟨ve⟩'.
21. *Prob.* 4. 6: 'in quibusdam contractibus etiam ⟨ex pacto⟩ usurae debentur', see Gebauer–Spangenberg n. 40 *a.h.l.*
22. *Prob.* 1. 10, Gebauer–Spangenberg n. 37 *a.h.l.* (Brenkman, with addition of Gebauer). Frier's suggestion (1980: 140 n. 192) that 'scholarship on this very interesting passage is virtually nonexistent' seems an exaggeration.
23. *Observationes* 1. 13.
24. *Prob.* 1. 13 (D 50. 16. 42); 2. 4 (D 7. 1. 15. 4); 2. 5 (D 12. 4. 15); 2. 10 (D 49. 16. 4. 13); 3. 3 (D 48. 22. 5); 3. 5 (C 9. 41. 1); 4. 4 (D 12. 4. 16).
25. C deo auctore 13: 'Ne autem per scripturam aliqua fiat in posterum dubitatio, iubemus non per siglorum captiones et compendiosa aenigmata, quae multas per se et per suum vitium antinomias induxerunt, conscribi . . .'.

humanists, among them Budé and Cujas,[26] had taken an interest in these sigla, but Noodt seems to have been the first to use them systematically for the purpose of emending classical texts. That it was a conspicuous feature in his work is confirmed by the fact that Huber, when attacking Noodt (without mentioning his name), defines the discussion of 'signorum et notarum ænigmata' three times over as characteristic of a despicable kind of textual criticism.[27] Noodt argues mainly on the basis of the *notæ* of Valerius Probus, but also of similar collections.[28] He tried his hand at this for the first time in the final chapter of Book I, where *notæ* of Paulus Diaconus were used.[29] Apparently for Noodt this was something new, and the possibilities may have been suggested to him by his friend Cuper. With his letter of 5 May 1678 Noodt sent him two observations, intended for Book II, in which emendations were proposed on the basis of sigla.[30] In these *notæ* of Probus were used.

From the point of view of modern scientific methodology we might say that such hypotheses concerning errors of scribes of the *Florentina* are mostly inadmissible, because hardly ever can we conceive a way of falsifying them.[31] But scholars of past ages, without formulating it this way, seem no less reluctant to accept such

26. *Obs.* 4. 31. The emendation in D 40. 9. 8 ('fideicommissum' is the result of false solution of the sigla 'F. C.', which according to Probus can also mean 'fraudandi creditoris') is endorsed by Mommsen (Mo ii: 471: 11).
27. Huber 1688*a*: 8, 32, 47. And see Van Bijnkershœk, *Opera* i: 9.
28. Apart from Probus, Noodt cites the notes of Magno, as well as Paulus Diaconus. The notes of Magno were published together with the Codex Theodosianus and other pre-justinianic sources by Cujas, Lyons, 1566 and by F. Pithou, Paris, 1586. I do not know which edn. Noodt used, possibly Putschius's edn. (Hanover, 1605) of the *grammatici latini* (containing the notes of Probus, Magno, and Paulus Diaconus) which Schulting (1720: 7) also recommended to his students. It was the authoritative edn. of the period. On these *notæ* see Bilabel, s.v. 'siglae', *RE* 2nd ser. iv. 2 (1923) 2279–315; Weinberger s.v. Kurzschrift, *RE* xxii (1922) 2218–31; Gärtner, Kleine Pauly (1979) v: 180–2. Modern edns. are based on that of Mommsen in Keil, *Gramm. lat.* iv, Leipzig, 1864; e.g. *FIRA* ii, 1940: 453 ff.; Girard and Senn, 1967: 8 ff.; and see Teitler, 1983: 199 f.
29. *Prob.* 1. 13. 1.
30. Noodt to Cuper, Nijmegen, 25 May 1678 (KB 72 G 20): 'Alterum probabilium meorum librum brevi edere institui, in eo praeter caetera emendationes ex siglis, notisque aliquot. Ex his exemplum ad te unum, atque alterum mitto, rogans serio de istis ut arbitrii me tui certiorem facias. Qualecunque id fuerit, mihi gratum, acceptumque erit. Daturum enim secundum religionem animi tui censeo, et ut censeam victus munere tuo sum. Studium enim in eo mei, affectumque tuum praebuisti, vim simul judicii doctrinaeque tuae.' The observations were printed as *Prob.* 2. 4 and 2. 5.
31. For a similar, more recent example, see Van den Bergh and Stolte, 1977: 248 n. 88. For a recent example of a sound argument based on sigla see Stolte, 1984: 152 f.

conjectures, based on hypothetical errors of hypothetically stupid scribes that went unnoticed by hypothetically negligent correctors. Possible it certainly is, but is it really probable as a common supposition? Even less likely are most of the conjectures Noodt based on so-called *geminationes*. We will come to them presently.

In the *Probabilia* we already find another typical aspect of Noodt's work to which some of his contemporaries took exception, viz. his critical attitude towards Antiquity, and towards Tribonian and classical jurists in particular. As we saw before, he anticipated being criticized for this.[32] Now, when he was claiming that Tribonian or Ulpian were only human, it was for minor errors, supposedly made in haste, or while acting under a misapprehension (*Probabilia* 1. 9). With Scævola it was another matter. Noodt claimed that in a case concerning the actions to which the creditors of an inheritance were entitled, Scævola gave a false opinion (recorded in D 2. 15. 14), against established law as well as against his own better knowledge (as recorded in D 2. 15. 3), to do a friend a favour.[33] The antinomy, to be sure, had already been noted by the glossators,[34] who had tried to solve it in their own subtle ways. But Noodt's explanation was unheard of. For contemporary readers it really must have smacked too much of the scepticism of a Montaigne (a judge himself, by the way), who told of a judge who, when finding in his books a topic that was highly controversial among jurists, noted in the margin: 'question pour l'amy'.[35]

Huber was among the many jurists who took exception to this conjecture. 'It must be said,' he wrote 'that this kind of criticism is absolutely new and very invidious . . . Not that we believe jurists are less punished in the underworld than any other class of humans, or that we would affirm they always have been immaculate priests of Themis. But this is too paradoxical, that they should have put their dishonesty in books, and that the wretched men were not even able to follow the proverb "if it cannot be done chastely, then at least cautiously".[36] After discussing the texts, Huber concludes by

32. *Prob.* 1. 9. 7, see above, p. 128 f. Criticizing Tribonian was nothing new, of course, in the humanist tradition. Budé had already done this in his *Annotationes ad Pandectas*.
33. *Prob.* 2. 2: 'Atque haec quo magis considero, eo magis censeo, Scaevolam non ex animi sui sententia respondisse, sed ut amico rem gratum acceptumque faceret, a jure certo, quam oporteret, recessisse longius.'
34. Gloss *pro parte hereditatis a.h.l.*
35. *Essais* 2. 12 (*Œuvres*, Pléiade, p. 566).
36. Huber, 1700: 123 f.: 'Fatendum est, hoc genus censurae esse valde novum et invidiosum. Non quod Jurisconsultos minus ac alios homini ordines, suos pati

turning against Noodt his own 'excellent digression' about not wanting to be the cause that the Corpus Juris was made a laughing-stock. But Noodt found all this not worth refuting and maintained his conjecture even after reconsideration many years later.[37]

Needless to say, modern philologists would not accept such conjectures, but there is more that seems rather doubtful now. In order to make plausible his most famous and most contested emendation, the change of 'ut' to 'at' in D 13. 7. 13. 1 (Mo i: 409: 22),[38] in the first impression of the *Probabilia*,[39] he pointed to the likeness of the 'Gotticae litterae' a and u. Now we cannot be too sure what Noodt meant by 'gothic letters'. In the humanist tradition the term had no precise historic meaning and could indicate all kinds of script not either classical or humanist.[40] And, indeed, several medieval scripts can have an open a resembling u.[41] So mistaking one letter for the other was something of a standard example of scribal error, and Noodt will have come across this while studying classics. But, as a matter of fact, all this seems of little relevance to the transmission of the Digest text. In Roman book script, and particularly in the Florentine manuscript (from which all medieval manuscripts descend), both letters cannot be as easily confounded. In later editions of the *Probabilia* Noodt suppressed the reference to gothic script, but maintained the argument of the likeness of the two letters. It is not very convincing, though—at least to our eyes—to suggest the likeness of letters without indicating which script is meant.

More problematic still is the subject of *geminationes*. Several of Noodt's conjectures were based on them.[42] He believed, as in fact most contemporary legal scholars did,[43] that ancient scribes used to

manes putemus, aut eos semper intemerato Themidis sacerdotio fungi adseverimus, sed quod nimis paradoxum sit, eos dedecora sua in libris contulisse, nec illud nimis tritum "si non caste saltem caute" servare scrivisse miseros.' See already the dialogue of 1684 (Huber, 1688*a*: 47). Best (1745: 85) also criticizes the conjecture as 'novam atque inauditam' and 'odiosam'. He aptly remarked that in fact Noodt did not solve the antinomy. Wächtler is also very critical about this, nor is de Toullieu convinced.

37. In *De pactis* (1713), ch. XXII (*Opera* i: 546).
38. See below, p. 154 and 312.
39. Noodt, 1674: 56.
40. See Rizzo, 1984: 115 f.
41. e.g. the Visigothic script in which *inter alia* the *Collatio Mosaicarum et Romanarum legum* was written (Grafton, 1983: 123), or the Carolingian minuscle (West, 1973: 24; Reynolds and Wilson, 1974: Plate XIII).
42. *Prob.* 2. 4; 3. 4. Other examples in *Observationes* 2. 16 (*Opera* i: 336 f.) and in *De pactis* 3 in fin. (*Opera* i: 494). On *geminationes* see Van den Bergh, 1985*b*.
43. See Best, 1745: 20 ff.

indicate the gemination of letter, syllables, or even whole words, by using capitals. If a copyist had to write 'et etiam' he could abbreviate this as 'ETiam'. Likewise, 'SIcut' would mean 'sicut si'.[44] Noodt states peremptorily that this system was used in Antiquity: 'It is certain that the ancients, when letters had to be geminated, used capitals, but only once. Furthermore it is certain that by this manner of writing often the order, not only of letters, but even of syllables was obscured.'[45] Later he went still further, assuming that scribes could even indicate gemination of whole words by writing them in capital letters.[46]

Naturally Noodt was not the first to believe this. His authority was Elbertus Leoninus,[47] but others had discussed the matter long before him.[48] The whole idea, however, was totally mistaken, and it seems one of those ironies of history that it was Torelli, the man who gave the world the first complete edition of the Florentine manuscript, who introduced the concept of *geminatio*, which was to become a pest of textual criticism of legal sources. Gemination with capitals was his invention (he was very specific on this point)[49] and was meant to serve a special purpose in his Digest edition, which appeared in 1553. He wanted to give an absolutely truthful type-facsimile of the Florentine manuscript. But naturally, as every manuscript, this one had its flaws too. The scribes often made orthographic errors (e.g. writing a V for a B) and omissions. Now, to warn his readers that some reading of F was faulty or not good Latin,

44. *Prob.* 2. 4.
45. *Opera* i: 41: 'Constat enim Veteres, ubi geminandae essent literae, usos majusculos esse, sed semel; etiam constat in eo scribendi genere saepe inversum fuisse ordinem non literarum tantum, sed syllabarum quoque.'
46. *Observationes* 2. 16, *Opera* i: 337. Therefore, Best's claim that he was the first to suggest this (Best, 1745: 22) seems unfounded.
47. *Opera* i: 41.
48. See Pithou, 1656: 186 f. and *passim*. From Jac. Gothofredus (*Animadv. jur. civ.* c. 9) are the following examples concerning D 12. 4. 16: oportet (Mo i: 459: 16), Gotho: opoRtEt = oporteret; dationes pro aliis quibus (Mo i: 459: 16–17), Gotho: dationes PRO aliis quibus = dationes pro aliis pro quibus. This is the reading of the Bolognese text, which Gothofredus explains by gemination. Even as excellent a classicist as Joseph Scaliger believed that gemination with capitals was used in Antiquity, but already Casaubon knew better, see Grafton, 1983: 311 n. 38. Van Oven (1953: 284) even believed that taurellian asterisks were in the *Florentina* itself.
49. *Lectoribus*, § 9: '. . . scietis non temere, sed dedita opera positas . . .'. See also Brenkman, 1722: 359 ff.; van den Bergh and Stolte, 1977: 240. Agustìn had suggested putting all such orthographic remarks in footnotes, see his letter to Torelli, Bologna, 20 Oct. 1543; Flores Selles, 1980: 174.

Torelli used capitals.[50] When we see 'CornelI' we know that 'Cornelii' is the correct form. 'ScriBsit' must be read as 'scripsit', 'inquiD' as 'inquit', 'sENTia' as 'sententia', 'necESSEt' as 'necesse esset', etc. Torelli's system, however, was not very exact. In some cases (e.g. 'sENTia') the capitals indicated that the scribe wrote the word in this form, but the ordinary corrector rectified it. In others it indicated correction by a later hand, in still others Torelli's own emendation.[51]

To make things worse many scholars assumed (apparently Torelli's *lectoribus* was as scarcely read as Mommsen's *Præfatio*) that this system of using capitals came from Antiquity,[52] and at once misunderstood it as a system of abbreviation. Now this is quite unlikely in itself. Systematic use of capitals is, in fact, fairly modern. It is true that sigla were written in capitals or a double i could be written as a long I (quite conspicuously in the epigraphic texts in which Noodt took such an interest), but that is a different matter. Admittedly, even modern editors are occasionally willing to suppose abbreviation without any outward sign in the manuscript;[53] a case in point is the suggestion, endorsed by Mommsen, to read in D 1. 2. 1 (Mo i: 3: 15) 'prius' as 'Populi Romani ius'. But most of Noodt's emendations on the basis of presumed gemination can be dismissed out of hand now.

Before indulging in a rather dim view of Noodt's achievement as a philologist, however, it is only fair to say that none of the very learned jurists who were his contemporaries were any better. Van Bijnkershœk[54] as well as Schulting[55] accepted *geminatio* and none of Noodt's critics rebuked him for the use he made of it. The chimera was, in fact, to live on for more than a century. Willem Best recommended it in 1707[56] as the most excellent device for emending texts. His book was reprinted without substantial criticism on this point in Germany in 1745, and in 1809 Haubold still believed that

50. The idea of geminatio with capitals may have been suggested to Torelli by epigraphic material, where one often finds a long I for double i, e.g. CornelI = Cornelii.
51. Examples in Van den Bergh, 1985*b*: 528.
52. See n. 50. There is, in fact, no proof of the use of gemination with capitals in Antiquity and the few places adduced by Neuhaus in Best (1745) do not prove what they were meant to do.
53. This was also accepted in the 17th century, see Jean le Clerc's *Ars critica* (5th imp. Amsterdam, 1730), ii. 165.
54. *Observationes* (*Opera* i: 8).
55. He proposes an emendation by gemination in D 12. 6. 41: SIne tutoris auctoritate = si sine tutoris auctoritate. See Schulting, 1720: h.t. § 18, and Schulting, 1738: Decad. XLIV, § 9.
56. Best, 1745: 20 ff.

Best's account of the art of textual criticism of legal sources was commendable, although Best was not as good in exercising the art himself.[57]

The only grave error, Best says, made by practically all older authors (which was Noodt's error as well), was to assume that in the Florentine manuscript geminations were indicated by capitals. This is not the case; Torelli said specifically that he added them himself, and if this is not proof enough, Best adds, the very learned Cunningham has affirmed the same, and he learned it in his turn from Laurens Grononvius, who carefully studied the Florentine manuscript himself.[58] But the idea of *geminatio* itself, as introduced by Torelli, is an excellent one. That the restrictions inherent in Torelli's system were ignored by Best is clear enough. In most cases Torelli used gemination to emend words whose reading in F was unequivocal but made no good Latin ('necesset', 'casibusa', 'sentia', 'locommuni'). Among the odd thirty examples enumerated by Best there are only three where the words have good Latin form but make no sense in the context.[59] Now, even if it seemed acceptable to generalize from these few cases, it is one thing to assume that sometimes a scribe made an error by missing one of two identical letters or syllables,[60] but quite another to accept that this was used deliberately as a system of abbreviation, a system, moreover, without any outward sign to warn the unwary reader.[61]

But, once accepted without restriction, the idea really seemed to open endless possibilities for further development. Geminations soon became something like pure metaphysics (Best uses the qualifications 'arcanum' and 'mysterium'). They were not observable from any outward mark and could only be deduced from the order of

57. Haubold, 1809: 194: '. . . in constituendis artis criticae, qua libro juris civilis spectat, regulis magis laudandus, quam in ipsa arte exercenda'.

58. Best, 1745: 21. He erroneously speaks of Jacob Gronovius; it was, in fact, his son Laurens who collated the *Florentina*, see Stolte, 1981: 18, 46.

59. D 47. 10. 18. 4 (Mo ii: 781: 35): transferre personae putationem > transferre *per* personae putationem—Mommsen has a different emendation; D 49. 15. 12. 3 (Mo ii: 888: 7) ut redierit > ut redierit, *erit*—Mommsen accepts a different reading of the text; D 50. 16. 208 (Mo ii: 952: 2): non singulares > non singulares *res*—Mommsen endorses a different, older emendation.

60. This is what Pithou (1656: 61, 186, 187) suggests; it is also accepted by Mommsen, see e.g. D 39. 1. 3. 1 (Mo ii: 375: 22): locommuni > loco *co*mmuni; D 30. 4 (Mo ii: 1: 14–15): estultius > est *st*ultius. This is all the more likely because F has no spacing between words. See in general West, 1973: 24; Reynolds and Wilson, 1974: 204 f.

61. Best, 1745: 20.

letters and words. Everybody could do it, like making a crossword-puzzle, provided he was an accomplished expert in Roman law. Moreover—and here Best's enthusiasm leads him into a *petitio principii*—they give a criterion by which to judge the quality of critical work: when it is absolutely uncertain whether the scribe had gemination in mind, that critic deserves belief who clarifies the text with only the help of a gemination.[62] The main reason Best gives for his belief in geminations testifies to a nearly magical belief in the text itself: the critic who explains the text by gemination adds nothing new of his own invention to it.[63]

Best is surprised that the useful art of gemination is practically unknown to writers on textual criticism.[64] Possibilities really are unbounded. Not only letters, but even whole words, and why not periods, can be added on the sole supposition of an intention of the scribe. Furthermore, Best adds a series of 'quasi-geminations': in every m, n, or u, an i is hidden; in every m an n, etc. From a single m you can make 'm in', 'in m', or 'm, n'; from a single n 'ni'; from 'sub' 'si sub'. So it is really no problem to read 'immature' where your text has 'mature'. And because it was an established fact that t and d are often confused, out of 'illud' you can make 'illud ut', etc.

If Best was surprised that most experts on textual criticism ignored geminations, we certainly are not. Needless to say, the system is absolutely arbitrary. It is, in fact, rather surprising that Best, who clearly saw the arbitrariness of the use of *notæ*, did not notice it in this case. Let me give only one example. From a simple 'necesse' you might make (apart from 'nec esse') 'necesse esse', 'ne necesse', 'necesse, ne', 'nec necesse esse', 'ne necesse, se', 'necesse nec esse', 'nece, necesse esse', or whatever would be appropriate to make the text in question read what you think it must read. But naturally we must not judge the achievements of legal philology of two centuries ago by present-day standards. Modern philology may have its *arcana* as well, and at least a few emendations by gemination have survived (e.g. D 30. 4, Mo ii: 1: 14–15: est *st*ultius).

To strike a balance we may conclude that Noodt really is an outstanding jurist and interpreter. He sees legal problems and can formulate them with exquisite clearness. As an example, one should

62. Best, 1745: 27.
63. Best, 1745: 27.
64. Best, 1745: 27. They actually are ignored in Jean le Clerc's *Ars critica*, Amsterdam, 1697, the standard work on textual criticism in its day.

read his explanation of D 41. 1. 55, the well-known text of Proculus concerning the question of whether the wild boar becomes the property of the hunter who set the snare as soon as it is stuck.[65] This is a text, for that matter, which even present-day teachers cherish, wherever Roman law is still taught.[66] Noodt explains the text with perfect clarity and develops an original theory of natural limitations to possession. If his essay is not totally convincing as a piece of historical scholarship[67] and not all his emendations are acceptable, there remains a lot that is worth considering.

By 1674, in the first book of his *Probabilia*,[68] Noodt had published his most famous conjecture, which later was heavily attacked for originality as well as validity. The problem is this. In D 13. 6. 5. 2–3 Ulpian sketches the outline of a theory of liabilities in various contracts, using *utilitas* as a criterion:

Nunc videndum est, quid veniat in commodati actione, utrum dolus an et culpa an vero et omne periculum. et quidem in contractibus interdum dolum solum, interdum et culpam præstamus: dolum in deposito: nam quia nulla utilitas eius versatur apud quem deponitur, merito dolus præstatur solus: nisi forte et merces accessit (tunc enim, ut est et constitutum, etiam culpa exhibetur) aut si hoc ab initio convenit, ut et culpam et periculum praestet is penes quem deponitur. sed ubi utriusque utilitas vertitur, ut in empto, ut in locato, ut in dote, ut in pignore, ut in societate, et dolus et culpa præstatur. Commodatum autem plerumque solam utilitatem continet eius cui commodatur, et ideo verior est Quinti Mucii sententia existimantis et culpam præstandam et diligentiam et, si forte res aestimata data sit, omne periculum præstandum ab eo, qui aestimationem se præstaturum recipit.[69]

65. *Prob.* 2. 6 (*Opera* i: 44). See, on Noodt's discussion of this text, Donahue, 1985: 617 ff.
66. Hausmaninger, 1980: 30.
67. So Donahue, 1985: 619.
68. *Prob.* 1. 4. Later, in reaction to criticisms put forward by Wächtler and others, he discussed the matter once more in *Prob.* 4. 3.
69. 'Now we must see what is to be in an action concerning a loan, whether evil intent, or also negligence, or even every risk. And indeed in contracts we sometimes are liable for evil intent alone, sometimes also for negligence. For evil intent in a deposit, because, as this has no utility for the depositary, he rightly is liable for dolus only, unless maybe a reward is added (for in that case one is also liable for negligence, as is ruled also in an imperial constitution), or when it was agreed from the beginning that the depositary would be liable also for negligence and risk. But when the utility of both parties is concerned, as in sale or hire, dowry, suretyship, or partnership, one is liable both for evil intent and for negligence. A loan, however, is usually only in the interest of the borrower, and therefore the opinion of Quintus Mucius is the most plausible, that he is liable for negligence and diligence. And if perhaps a thing of estimated value is given, he who has undertaken to give the amount estimated is liable for every risk.'

So, according to this text, the borrower is liable for *dolus*, *culpa*, and *diligentia* (*custodia*), because usually the contract of *commodatum* is made in his interest. But in D 13. 7. 13. 1 Ulpian seems to say precisely the opposite:

Venit autem in hac actione [i.e. actio pigneraticia?] et dolus et culpa, ut in commodato: venit et custodia: vis maior non venit.[70]

Here it is said that in *commodatum* the borrower is liable only for *dolus* and *culpa*. The contradiction was noted already in the Accursian gloss,[71] and many scholars had tried their hand at it. Noodt suggested removing the contradiction by the change of only one letter and a slight shift of punctuation:

Venit autem in hac actione et dolus et culpa. At in commodato venit et custodia. Vis maior non venit.

Now, even Noodt's fiercest opponents could not deny that this emendation really was a model of elegance.[72] Later, Noodt proved not to have been the first to come across the idea, and it seems doubtful whether he really solved the problem. But we will discuss this later.[73]

Perhaps even better is the emendation proposed in D 7. 8. 10 pr.[74] The text reads as follows:

Si habitatio legetur, an perinde sit atque si usus, quæritur. et effectu quidem idem pæne esse legatum usus et habitationis et Papinianus consensit libro octavo decimo quaestionum. denique donare non poterit, sed eas personas recipiet, quas et usuarius; ad heredem tamen nec ipsa transit nec non utendo amittitur nec capitis deminutione.[75]

70. 'In this action both evil intent and negligence are considered, as in a loan; the duty to guard is also considered, but not circumstances beyond one's control.' On this text see Van den Bergh, 1982*a*: 606 ff. with further literature.
71. Gloss *ut in commodato* ad D 13. 7. 13. 1.
72. See Huber, 1700: 541: 'hanc emendationem . . . suppeditat elegantem et modestam, quae ingenio et probabilitate sua, sicut laudem, ita plenum quoque adsensum mereretur, nisi . . .'. The change of only one letter was regarded as the *nec plus ultra* of conjecture already by 16th-century humanist philologists like Vettori and Faerno, see Grafton, 1983: 56, 66.
73. See below, Ch. 4, at n. 44.
74. *Probabilia* 3. 7.
75. 'If a bequest was made of a servitude of dwelling, the question arises whether this is the same as if use is bequeathed. And indeed Papinian agrees in book eighteen of his *Quaestiones* that the effect of both legacies is practically the same; generally [dwelling] cannot be donated, but embraces the same persons as is the case with the user; it does not descend to an heir, however, and it is not lost by non-use, nor by loss of civil rights.'

The text summarizes the differences and similarities of the servitudes of *usus* and *habitatio*. As it stands, it seems to suggest that the servitude of *usus* does not end by the death of the legatee, which is evidently false. Noodt solves the problem by a simple transposition of 'tamen':

. . . ad heredem nec ipsa transit; nec tamen non utendo amittitur, nec capitis deminutione.

This solution is endorsed by Mommsen[76] because it gets support from the translation by Stephanos in the Basilica.[77] Now this really confirms that Noodt was an *interpres primarius* of the Corpus Juris. Stephanos, law professor in Berytus in the time of Justinian or shortly after,[78] was a most distinguished expert, who made a very close translation of the Digest.

De civili prudentia

The inaugural address Noodt gave in Franeker on 16 October 1679, but which was published for the first time only in the *Opera omnia* of 1713,[79] is an excellent statement of Noodt's position as a legal scholar in the ongoing discussion of his day. To explain its meaning we must begin by saying something about the concept of *civilis prudentia* itself.

Whereas the expression *civilis sapientia* is used once in the Digest as a synonym for the jurist's knowledge of civil law,[80] the term *civilis prudentia* is not found in any legal source, and in fact only once in all the remains of ancient literature.[81] It seems to have the meaning of political or administrative proficiency. A certain Lauricius is praised as a *homo civilis prudentiae* because he managed to bring the Isaurians to order more by threats than by harsh measures.[82]

Such a *hapax legomenon* is a boon for humanists who want to show

76. Mo i: 244: 3, with n. 1 and the note at line 3: '. . . unde commendatur transpositio particulae *tamen* quam proposuit Noodtius . . .'.
77. As we have seen, Noodt himself was not aware of this.
78. See Scheltema, 1970: 4, 24 f. and *passim*; Van der Wal and Lokin, 1985: 41.
79. In the index it is announced as 'hactenus inedita', so Dekkers: 124 is wrong in giving an edn. of Franeker, 1679. See also, p. 41 with n. 15; cf. Ahsmann–Feenstra, 1984: nr. 427.
80. D. 50. 13. 1. 5: '. . . est quidem res sanctissima civilis sapientia . . .'.
81. Amm. Marc. 19. 13. 12; cf. *Thes. L.L.* III Fasc. VI, 1214, 7.
82. '. . . Lauricius missus est rector, homo civilis prudentiae qui minis potius quam acerbitate pleraque correxit'.

the breadth of their erudition. And in general, moreover, *prudentia* was valued higher than *sapientia*, as Budé said.[83] It is a theoretico-practical compound, comprising not only knowledge but also practical skills. The term *civilis prudentia* was introduced, or at least made popular, by Hermann Conring as a synonym for *politica*,[84] in the context of a polemic with jurists. As such, the term remained in use, although not frequently, well into the second half of the eighteenth century.[85] A rather late example is the inaugural address of H. C. Cras (1739–1820) about the *civilis prudentia* of promoting commerce (1771).[86]

Since the Middle Ages jurists—with their skill in handling legal texts—had been the technical experts of state formation. Many had made brilliant careers and attained advancement in the service of kings and princes. But the bureaucratic apparatus of the absolutist state, rising since the sixteenth century, demanded more than the traditional skills of a jurist. Mercantilist policy, expanding in the seventeenth century, needed knowledge of economics, finance, statistics, state history, diplomatics, et cetera.[87]

In the sixteenth century the relation of law and politics appears to be a growing problem and in the seventeenth the discussion is very lively.[88] Conring follows Joachim Hopper (1523–76), who in a book that appeared posthumously[89] defended the thesis that there is a *vera jurisprudentia* which has a much greater scope than the traditional one. The theme is already discussed in the theses Conring defended in Leiden in 1629[90] (where he used the term *moralis prudentia*), and it engaged him all his life.[91]

83. Cited by Piano Mortari, 1978: 327, 355 f.
84. Conring, 1730: iii: 277: 'vox prudentiae civilis idem quid notat ac vox politices'. And see a letter of Conring, 1730: vi: 570: 'De civili prudentia. Habeo jam tum affectum methodum prudentiae deliberativae, verum etsi ante me nemo, quod scio, tale quid vel tentaverit . . .'. And see Veen, 1976: 119, 150f.
85. For literature, see Lipenius ii, 1757: 226; iii, 1775: 404; iv, 1789: 340. In later additional vols. (1817, 1823), it is no longer an entry.
86. *Oratio de civili prudentia in promovenda mercatura*. Amsterdam, 1771.
87. In the 18th century in Germany these so-called 'Kamerialwissenschaften' were often taught in special schools (e.g. Kameralschule Kaiserslautern), which competed with traditional law faculties.
88. See Veen, 1976: 117 ff. and *passim*.
89. *Seduardus sive de vera jurisprudentia* (1590): re-ed. Conring, Brunswick, 1656.
90. *Theses variae de morali prudentia*, Conring, 1730: iv: 335 f.
91. *Disputatio de natura ac optimis auctoribus civilis prudentiae*, 1639, Conring, 1730: iii: 2; *Theses miscell. de civili prudentia*, 1650, Conring, 1730: iii: 277; *De civili prudentia liber unus*, 1662, Conring, 1730: iii: 280 f. Propolitica, 1663.

Already in the Leiden theses *politica* is put above *jurisprudentia* as a more comprehensive as well as a more fundamental science. To the jurists the knowledge of positive law is allotted as the proper field, and here for the first time we find something like a formulation of legal positivism—by a non-jurist. Every science has its own *principia* (principles, presuppositions, axioms). For jurists existing positive laws take that place. 'Therefore the jurist is ashamed to speak without the law, like the philosopher without principles taken from nature; and he does not discuss whether the law is correctly and usefully made. For him it is enough that it is as it is written. No science examines the truth of its own principles, but it supposes them'.[92] From this follows a clear conclusion as to the relation between the student of politics and the jurist: 'Illius est declarare, quid justum sit, hujus vero, quis justus'.[93] *Jurisprudentia* is, in other words, no more than the *pars judicialis* of Aristotelian *politica*.[94] Later Conring puts even more stress on the relative insignificance of *jurisprudentia*. It is the least important part of *civilis prudentia*; *politica* is much more important.[95] Roman law especially is Conring's target. In *De origine juris Germanici* (1643) he proved that the story of the formal promulgation of the Roman Corpus Juris in the Holy Roman Empire was a myth. It may be that the qualities of Roman law are widely acknowledged, but that does not make it binding law. It makes quite a difference whether something is appreciated positively, or must be obliged as law. The fact that there are sensible rules in Roman law does not oblige to its application. Every nation is free to act less sensibly. And if there are rules of natural law recorded in the Corpus Juris they have no extra authority *because* they are in it.[96]

In his address Noodt takes a clear position in this debate. As the rules of rhetoric demand, he begins by conceding something to his opponent. He agrees that there is nothing more sublime than *civilis prudentia* and that it—as Conring had maintained against Tabor[97]—contains much more than Roman law alone.[98] After this, Noodt

92. 'Erubescit ergo jurisconsultus sine lege loqui, ut Philosophus sine principiis ex natura petitis; nec disputat, an lex recte vel utiliter lata sit, sed sufficit ipsi, quod ita sit scripta: nulla enim disciplina principiorum suorum veritatem quaerit, sed supponit.'
93. The one must explain who is just, the other what is right.
94. Cf. Veen, 1976: 118.
95. *De civili prudentia*, § 16, Conring, 1730: iii: 293 f.
96. Conring, 1730: iv: 194.
97. Cf. Conring, 1730: iii: 2.
98. *Opera* i: 609: '. . . nec, ut putet aliquis, haeret inter solemnia fori, civilesque leges populi Romani'.

takes a long detour to reach his goal. Reason teaches us that all mankind has one purpose, a friendly, quiet, and happy life. But how can such a society be realized without law? Then Noodt paints man's original position: sad and precarious loneliness. This painting of a situation where man is a wolf to man does not necessarily prove the influence of Hobbes, although his work certainly was much discussed in the Republic. Antiquity knew two visions of the original position, one of a golden age, another of a world where men lived as wild beasts in loneliness and without any knowledge of general interest, law, or morality. The classical description of the second vision is that of Lucretius,[99] and Noodt evidently follows him. Only by law can primitive man gradually and with much effort be brought under the yoke of the *civilis conjunctio*, that is, society, which is the basis of all human happiness. Take law away and then tell me: where is freedom, property, inheritance, contract, good faith, and the binding force of obligations?[1]

From a lengthy discussion of natural law it follows that there are matters with regard to which it is indifferent, and here *jus civile* comes in. From this comes the institution of judges, kinds of property, contracts, obligations, guardianships, donations, and testaments. So far so good. But if, as was said, a single right reason determines the one true purpose of men and societies all over the world, how then can it be explained that so many different and conflicting laws are in force in various times and places?

Like Conring[2] Noodt rejects the solution of Grotius, who defined *jus gentium* as the law of the more civilized peoples. All peoples have the same goal—the *societas vitae civilis*—and all laws are aiming at this, but along different roads. One people prefers this, another that, according to what each thinks the most advantageous. Here Noodt adds an historical reflection: what once obtained is gradually changed, because it is found to be in error, or new opportunities arise. What once was good and honest becomes bad through change of circumstances. With changes of time and place the ways and means leading to the common utility vary. Although Noodt opposes Conring, he has learned at least one thing from him: historical consciousness.

After this introduction Noodt turns to science: which science can teach us what is favourable or harmful for the common good? And

99. *De rer. nat.* v: 925–1010.
1. *Opera* i: 610.
2. 1730: iv: 622.

then he makes a sharp turn towards Roman law. The Romans must be despised because of their many wars of conquest, says Noodt, making another concession to Conring,[3] but they have always held the *civilis prudentia* in reverence and their *jus civile* is very much worth studying.

Next Noodt extensively discusses the various criticisms of Roman law, or perhaps rather of civil law jurists, which had been voiced, among many others, also by Conring—who is not named. Roman jurisprudence is said to be cold and empty, to applaud futilities, to exalt a mediocre science, far removed from wisdom and genius, which depends less on judgment than on memory. It troubles over syllables, tortures itself about single letters, is mostly concerned with chicanery of words, often considering rainwater, streams, gutters, the collecting of nuts: that is, with trifles.[4] It seldomly engages in important affairs and is least of all concerned with the high matters of the state. This old and frequent reproach paints the jurist as no better than a manual worker.[5]

One may say that jurisprudence is concerned with trifles, Noodt replies, but if one wants to obtain a quiet and orderly society, one cannot afford to overlook anything. It is rather to be praised in jurisprudence that in pursuing great things it does not disregard minor ones. After this, Noodt unfolds the whole programme of Roman law studies, with special stress on humanistic philology—which Conring regarded as superfluous[6]—as well as on the importance of historical consciousness: Roman law was not made in one day or by one brain; it is the product of a long evolution.[7] In any case Noodt rejects simple practical legal training, 'simplex et ad usum spectans doceri'. The last argument for legal science is again historical: Noodt speaks about the riches which explain why Roman jurisprudence after so many ages is applied in courts and studied in academies all over the world. Legal science now consists partly of Roman law, partly of natural law.

One might object that Noodt's argument cannot have convinced

3. Noodt, *Opera* i: 611: '. . . Cujus quamquam scelus per bella ampliandi imperii, neglecta humani generis societate, detestor . . .'; cf. Conring, 1730: iv: 622: 'Quantumvis autem Romani ad illum modum se habuerunt, non tamen omnia eorum bella fuerunt justa. Allecti sunt saepius magnitudine praedae.'
4. Cf. Conring, 1730: iii: 293.
5. *Opera* i: 612.
6. *De civili prudentia*, Conring, 1730: iii: 292.
7. *Opera* i: 614.

anybody who was not prepared to be convinced—which the majority of his audience still will have been. The address resembles Von Savigny's famous pamphlet, *Vom Beruf unsrer Zeit fur Gesetzgebung und Rechtswissenschaft* (1814), in that it turns from general reflections on the original position (of mankind as the rational ultimate unity, for Noodt; of the nation as the organic ultimate whole, for Von Savigny) towards Roman civil law rather forcibly. Nor was Noodt the first to oppose Conring's ideas.[8] Nevertheless, one cannot deny the rhetorical quality of the address. The subject is topical and of crucial importance for the profession: Noodt's treatment of it is pleasantly robust. He plunges straight in at the deep end, does not omit any of the usual reproaches of Roman law, and gives them a fair airing. He shows that he is familiar with ongoing debates and that he knows his classical authors, without indulging in scholarly pedantry. The theme is especially apt for an inaugural address, because it is directly relevant to law teaching. If the place of Roman law is duly vindicated, on the basis of Noodt's argument natural law can be given its place in the law curriculum as well. All in all, Noodt manages to do what jurists have done with so many attacks on their profession at an earlier or later date: simply absorb them. *Civilis prudentia*, meant to present an alternative for the dominant position of *juris prudentia*, became just one of its titles in the end. So we may assume that the words of praise Noodt received after the ceremony were not mere courtesy.

Finally I would like to stress two elements in this address in particular. Anybody still presuming that jurists under the spell of natural law were profoundly ahistorical should read Noodt's address. He acknowledges an unchanging, eternal law, revealing itself to human reason, but that only contains a small part of all law. For all the rest of law, history is a dominant factor. So much at least has Noodt learned from Conring. Law grows with the habits, opportunities, and difficulties of the state—not by legislation but by inner forces, as von Savigny would say later—and it does not always remain the same. As the wind changes the aspect of clouds, so the fortunes of public and private affairs often change the law. In order to understand the fate and development of any single law one must carefully study the periods of its promulgation, change, and abolition. Noodt also stresses the historical development of legal science.

8. See e.g. D. J. F. Graswinckel, *De jure majestatis*, The Hague, 1642; a reply to Conring's attack on Grotius in *De finibus imperii*.

Secondly, it seems worth noting how Noodt, following Cicero,[9] stresses the relation between law and freedom. He formulates elegantly one of the underlying principles of bourgeois legality: 'But this is no servitude of men, but of the law . . . And this is true and complete freedom. There is no other. That citizen is free who, safe under the rule of law, has nothing to fear. He can do anything he wishes, beyond wishing to do what the laws forbid.'[10]

De causis corruptae jurisprudentiae

Noodt's inaugural address in Utrecht, read on 12 February 1684, and appearing in print the same year,[11] is directly relevant once more to the job he is taking up. It discusses the causes of the corruption of legal science—a rather traditional theme for inaugural addresses and academic treatises[12]—and traces these back to legal education.

The exordium is a subtle mixture of *captatio benevolentiae* and boasting. Noodt opens with the confession that he is afraid and nervous. Yet it is not for the first time that he is addressing a public audience. Nor can he say that he did not expect such a concourse of distinguished and learned men. But the people of Friesland and Utrecht have battled over him; the Utrechters have tried to get him three times over and have appointed him by unanimous vote of all concerned. So he is afraid to disappoint them. Then he puts the question he intends to treat before his audience: why were former times enlightened by the names of so many excellent jurists, while our days are dark and ignoble and illuminated only by the light and glory of a few? Hardly anything praiseworthy is accomplished by legal science, and Roman law, which was once held in great esteem by scholar and political leader alike because of its excellent equity and manifold wisdom, now mainly seems to present useless subtlety,

9. *Pro cluent*. 53: 146; cf. Van den Bergh, 1982*b*: 28.
10. *Opera* i: 611: 'Non enim est haec hominum servitus sed legis . . . At haec vera libertas est et solida. Alia non est. Videlicet liber est civis qui legum imperio securus, nihil metuit. Idem potest facere omne quod vult: ultro nolens, facere quod legibus facere prohibetur.'
11. Utrecht: F. Halma; Ahsmann–Feenstra, 1984: nr. 428. This edn. has the title *De caussis* . . . with double s. But the *Opera omnia*, from the 1st edn. in 1713, has the title as given here. This edn. has laudatory verses of C. Vitringa, J. Schotanus, J. Perizonius, and C. Van Eck.
12. See e.g. the address of M. Tydeman (Harderwijk, 1787) who gives further literature in n. *c*, pp. 5 ff. See Lipenius i, under the entry 'jurisprudentia corrupta'.

which is far removed not only from learning and elegance, but also from common practice and life.[13]

But civil law itself, which has been applied in courts and taught in academies in all nations for so many centuries, cannot be the cause of this. The art of law is not fickle or subtly trifling. It has its origin and meaning in the human need to join together with others. The law is, so to speak, the mind of society; the main grace of law is reason, and *civilis sapientia*[14] is the light of reason itself. Nor is it likely that the nature of things decays, or that human abilities melt away and become unfit to learn and maintain the art by which the bond of human society is tied. How could one believe that seriously, now that we see new and enormous advances in the other sciences every day? To take only one example: was there ever a time when the research into the secrets of nature reached such real, not only pretended perfection? If medicine, astronomy, mechanics, and mathematics have progressed far beyond what diligent and learned Antiquity could aspire to, why should we believe that only the science of society is so unhappy that nature, while being enough for the others, seems to be malicious and dispensable for her?[15]

The ancients could obtain their excellence in civil law only by elaborate and assiduous study. Their art not only demanded the memorizing, but also the understanding of the laws; it embraced not only rough first principles but the whole range of knowledge. Apart from knowing how human society came about and what rules were good and bad according to its nature, it touched on geometry, dialectics, letters, Latin, public and private customs, and many other things. Pure knowledge, moreover, was not enough. In order to be prepared for action the art was to be completed by practical training, aiming at the formation of understanding and the power of judgment.

So was Cato maior, so Sextus Pompeius, who directed his outstanding wit to excellent knowledge of civil law and perfect mastery of geometric and stoic philosophy, so Labeo, Salvius Julianus, Papinian, Ulpian. But *civilis prudentia* has lost its high status long ago and here we come to the main reason for the corruption of legal science. By the name of jurist we no longer designate the man who knows all divine and human matters, who is

13. *Opera* i: 616.
14. Noodt apparently uses the wrong term here; one would rather expect *civilis prudentia*.
15. *Opera* i: 617.

able and useful in conducting private and public affairs, but any advocate who hopes to gain from his dark and mean science not honour, but a nice fee before anything else.[16] Those who are accustomed to this, could they afford to see jurisprudence as anything but a vile and unfree kind of work? Could they understand its gradual historical development? Would they fill their minds with the study of humanity, the wisdom of natural law, and the law of nations, before hearing the laws of the Roman people? Would they make an effort to understand the customs of Rome and master the vocabulary and syntax of the Latin language? Would they train themselves to be able to judge jurisprudence itself, so that they could discuss truth not only with learned and unlearned interpreters, but with the architects of the law (i.e. the compilers) themselves? They do not. And so they come to the art without due preparation. They think they are very learned and happy when they hardly understand the short compendium of the art, have memorized definitions, distinctions, and solemn formulae of actions, have reduced the extensive art to strait schedules and a few stupid questions.[17]

They mix up everything and despise all careful historical interpretations as below the dignity of jurists and rather belonging to the trifles of grammarians and philosophers. Even more so, they consider it ridiculous that some deficient script demands careful study of manuscripts and editions, that by lucky guesses dislocations and corruptions are healed, that the corruption of texts by the false solution of abbreviations is conjectured, that punctuation is restored, that glosses are thrown out, that lacunae are supplied with the help of other texts, etc. Here Noodt sums up the whole programme of humanistic legal philology, as exercised by himself.[18]

There are many teachers of law, however, who by laziness, ignorance, or the hope of gain and a big audience spell out fables. They corrupt ignorant youth against the intentions of their parents and the interests of the state. If students do not get proper teaching and are not gradually brought up to the excellent and the sublime, nor trained in true and honest labour, they waste the age that is appropriate and intended for study in luxury and leisure, and later will have

16. *Opera* i: 619. This is a conventional argument. Roman jurists were not paid, while modern lawyers are. So still Schorer, 1777.

17. *Opera* i: 619. Noodt's stress on the importance of the humanistic method is echoed by Van Bijnkershœk in the preface of his *Obs. jur. rom.*

18. *Opera* i: 619.

neither the inclination nor the opportunity to inquire into what they have never heard, read, or learned. And so they will bring to their advanced age no other asset than stupidity and remorse.[19]

It is especially against the newly introduced use of compendia—of which his Utrecht colleagues Van der Muijden and Van de Poll were champions!—that Noodt's attack is directed. It is often said that the old and royal road is steep and rough, long, dark, and heavy. The vulgar and compendiary road, on the contrary, is flat and direct, easy for everyone, and not insuperable even for the slow and senseless. Its shortness conforms to the frailty of the human condition, which urges us to study quickly in order to gather fruits. The more students waste time and effort by laziness of inclination and intellect, the more studies must be plain and simple and lead rapidly and surely to legal science.

But all this is wrong. Can we believe that nature has treated mankind so badly that it has given no brains to so many men of good birth? It is true that men differ from each other as regards fortune, riches, birth, and honours. But, asks Noodt, using an argument of Descartes,[20] what is distributed more equally than good brains? Nobody thinks himself a fool. Do we not see even in small children sparks of the divine spirit and an outburst of effort? If these are extinguished gradually, must we blame culture or nature for that? Certainly not nature.

There will be some, of course, who are shipwrecked. But it is no reason to abandon good reasoning that not all can learn it, however hard they try. Sometimes agriculture does not bring the contemplated harvest and often a storm frustrates the hope of the seafarer. But that is no reason to neglect the fields or the study of maritime matters. Moreover, the study of law in the old way may not be as difficult as it seems from afar, if it is directed in the right way and proceeds in the proper historical perspective.

The ambiguity of words is deceptive. What is called speed is in fact delay and what bears the name of compendium is a loss to wisdom. Noodt's criticism is not unqualified, though. Naturally, an introduction to the first elements of law cannot dispense with a compendium of the Institutes.[21] But the study of Pandects and Codex must be

19. *Opera* i: 619 f.
20. *Discours de la méthode*, première partie (Descartes, 1953: 126): 'Le bon sens est la chose du monde la mieux partagée.'
21. *Opera* i: 621.

done in the sound, traditional way. Noodt ends his allocution to the students with the word of the dying Septimius Severus: *laboremus*, let us exert ourselves.

The Utrecht inaugural address is a nice and well-ordered piece of rhetoric, in which Noodt expresses his views on law and legal training with his usual vigour. He clearly sees the realities of university life in his day. Since the sixteenth century, universities had increasingly become aristocratic institutions,[22] where members of the nobility had special privileges, and dancing, fencing, and sports were taken more seriously than studies by the majority of students. Noodt's ideal is legal humanism. His examples of great jurisprudence in classical times are Labeo, Salvius Julianus, Pomponius, Papinian, Ulpian, and Paul; in modern times Alciato, Budé, Duaren, Hotman, Doneau, Giphanius, Gothofredus, and, above all, Cujas.[23] But it is not just legal philology that is his central concern. A broad humanistic training in law, letters, history, and philosophy—not aiming at pure knowledge but at the formation of insight and judgment—is the most appropriate one for the future leaders of the Republic. Luxury and leisure in youth make for remorse in old age and are harmful to the Republic. Noodt is not an odd antiquary lost in an idealized past. He clearly takes sides with the 'moderns' when he boasts that the natural sciences and mathematics in recent times have made progress far beyond the hope of Antiquity.[24] And he seems to have a Rousseauish view of human culture (anachronistically speaking) when stating that new-born children have excellent qualities which are gradually extinguished by culture.[25]

As a whole, the address is a self-conscious expression of the humanistic ideal of bourgeois culture in the Dutch Republic, from a jurist's point-of-view. But naturally Noodt's expectations were not very realistic, and his sharp attack on the compendiary method, introduced into Holland by Böckelmann,[26] was no doubt controversial. It provoked an even sharper reply by Ulrik Huber, who published his 'De ratione juris docendi et discendi diatribe per modum dialogi' only a few months after the address.[27] It is presented as a dialogue between Böckelmann, Crusius, and Huber, but the

22. De Ridder-Symoens, 1985; Frijhoff, 1981: 64 ff. and *passim*.
23. *Opera* i: 621.
24. *Opera* i: 617.
25. *Opera* i: 620.
26. See Feenstra, 1985*a*.
27. The address was published in Feb. 1684; the 1st edn. of the dialogue appeared in Sept. See Perizonius to Rijcke, 19 Sept. 1684, UL Leiden, BPL 337; cf. above, p. 54 f.

disguise is very thin indeed. That the dialogue was directed against Noodt's address is clear from a letter by Perizonius,[28] and confirmed by internal evidence. Passages from the address are cited literally,[29] and even its title appears when an address 'De causis corruptae jurisprudentiae' is ascribed to Crusius,[30] which he in fact never gave.[31] Huber only adds a word-play of his own invention: a *compendium* is said to be nothing but a *dispendium*.[32] To philosophize about the happy disposition of the human mind (which, as we saw, Noodt actually did), says Huber through the mouth of Böckelmann,[33] without directing eyes and mind to that which is essential, is nothing but 'splendide nugari', to talk splendid nonsense. Huber does not stop at the defence of the *methodus compendiaria*, but launches a sharp attack on each and every person who takes his pride in humanistic philology. To teach this is sane stupidity, to teach it before students have got an overview, in the form of paratitla, of the whole of the law, 'superat omnem stultitiam'.[34] By the way, Noodt never proposed this. Noodt's *Probabilia* are criticized as well, and here again it is clear that Huber, while purporting to address Crusius, is in fact citing from the preface of Noodt's book: 'But I am of the opinion that his emendations are often not necessary, and proved in such a way that they can be confuted by others, as he says himself in his preface.'[35] That certainly was playing foul with Noodt's words, but Noodt never published a direct reply to any of this.

De jurisdictione et imperio libri duo

After the publication of the *Probabilia* in three books (1679), it was twelve years before Noodt brought out another book. Neither in Franeker nor in Utrecht did he publish anything apart from the Utrecht inaugural address. We do not know whether his new teaching obligations, the fever he caught in Franeker (1680–81), or married life (after 1686) were responsible for this. Anyway, between 1668 and 1691 Noodt published no more than five books, that is, about one every five years. His most prolific period starts with the publication of one of his best, *De foenore et usuris*, in 1698, a year

28. See n. 169.
29. Huber, 1688*a*: 8, 11, 34.
30. Huber, 1688*a*: 7.
31. Cf. Ahsmann–Feenstra, 1984.
32. Huber, 1688*a*: 6 e.a.
33. Huber, 1688*a*: 30.
34. Huber, 1688*a*: 32.
35. Huber, 1688*a*: 41; cf. Noodt, *Prob.*, 1: Praefatio.

before his wife died. From that year to 1710 there is practically one publication each year, among them seven major works, that is, one every two years. During the last part of his life the number of publications drops again to an average of one every four years.

In the last months of 1690[36] Noodt published with Felix Lopez in Leiden in one volume, together with four books of *Probabilia*, two monographs: *De jurisdictione et imperio libri duo* and *Ad legem Aquiliam liber singularis*.[37] The three parts each have independent pagination. The same three titles are reissued in one volume two years later,[38] now by F. Haaring, who remained Noodt's publisher until 1706. This is only a title-edition.[39] The same three titles finally appear together once more in 1705, now under the title *Opera varia*.[40]

The two books nicely reflect the two parts of Noodt's teaching assignment in Leiden: the *lex Aquilia* belongs to private law, *jurisdictio* and *imperium* to public law. With the work on *jurisdictio* and *imperium* Noodt took up a central issue of the humanist tradition, on which much ink had been spilt already.[41] Questions of Roman public law had been on the research programme of humanists from the very beginning.[42] But, in fact, interest in the subject is much older than that. The glossators, whose work developed in the middle of the Italian political arena of the twelfth century and who had close links with various emperors of the Holy Roman Empire, took an interest in *imperium*. The *lex imperium* (D 2. 1. 3), with Ulpian's obscure distinction and definition of *merum* and *mixtum imperium*, was hotly debated by the glossators,[43] and with it was connected a well-known pun. The Emperor Henry VI in 1191 asked the jurists, Lotharius and Azo, who had the *merum imperium*. Lotharius said: only the emperor. But Azo claimed—more truthfully, in fact—that all high rulers had it. The emperor then rewarded Lotharius for his

36. On the title-page is the year 1691, but from a letter to Cuper, thanking Noodt for sending the book, it can be established that it appeared towards the end of 1690; Cuper to Noodt, The Hague, 16 Dec. 1690 (KB 72 G 20, 33). It seems to have been usual for printers to put the date of the next year on the title-page from October. Noodt had finished *De jurisdictione et imperio* not long before. On 26 Mar. 1689, he wrote to Van Eck (UL Utrecht, MS 1000): '. . . nijn tractaet de jurisdictione et imperio, 't geene ick nu vaerdigh hebbe, en misschijn in het korte zal uitgeven'.

37. Ahsmann–Feenstra, 1984: nr. 423. *De jurisdictione et imperio* is dedicated to Noodt's one time promoter Willem van Haren, governor of Franeker university. *Ad legem Aquiliam* is dedicated to J. Borre van Amerongen.

38. Ahsmann–Feenstra, 1984: nr. 424. On this edn. see above, p. 141 with n. 98.

39. See above, n. 98 on p. 141.

40. Ahsmann–Feenstra, 1984: nr. 425.

41. See Troje, 1977: 706 f.

42. See Maffei, 1968: 95 ff.

43. See the gloss *a.h.l.* and Gilmore, 1941: 15 f.

answer by giving him his horse. Azo, who got nothing, wryly remarked (if we try to save something of the pun by rhyming): 'Because of my answer, which was fair, I missed the mare, but that was not fair.'[44]

The question of *jurisdictio* and *imperium* was the subject of a ferocious battle of words between the humanistic jurists Baro and Duaren, both then professors in Bourges. In 1545 Govea published a commentary on D 2. 1. 3 and a little later Duaren treated the same subject. Baron criticized both in his lectures. Govea and Duaren then both published a rejoinder, that of the latter containing an excessive amount of abuse, even for a humanist. Unavoidably, the students took sides and Duaren left Bourges for Paris until Baron's death in 1550.[45] Other humanistic jurists tried their hand at D 2. 1. 3 as well, among them Cujas,[46] A. Faure, Scipio Gentilis, and others.[47] In the Republic the issue seems to have been revived by Wissenbach.[48] Discussion in the Dutch elegant school was not accompanied by the same amount of abuse, though. Noodt had touched on the subject of Roman public law already in two observations of his *Probabilia*;[49] he lectured on subjects of Roman public law all his life. Huber opposed Noodt's interpretation of D 2. 1. 3,[50] and Schulting, Wieling, and others touched on the matter as well.

Noodt's book fits perfectly with the type of the humanistic monograph[51] which is a series of observations on connected subjects, put in a more or less systematic order. Noodt really tried to treat the subject systematically, and judging from the index it would seem that he succeeded in this to a considerable extent. Book I opens with the question what jurisdiction is (I), which is followed by a discussion of the relation of *jurisdictio* and *imperium* (II–III), *imperium merum* and *mixtum* (IV–VI), *praetor* and *judex* (VII–IX), *decretum* (X), *consilium* (XI–XII), *judicis datio* (XIII), and *litis contestatio* (XV). Book II discusses the various aspects of the mandate of *jurisdictio* or *imperium* (I–XI) and prorogation (XII–XV).

But this seemingly systematic order is a bit misleading. The treatment of *litis contestatio* (1. 15), for instance, is far from complete.

44. F. C. Von Savigny, *Geschichte des römischen Rechts im Mittelalter*, iv, 2nd imp., 1850 (anastatic repr., Bad Homburg 1961): 180ff: 'amisi equum, quia dixi aequum, quod non fuit aequum'.
45. Eyssell, 1860: 47 ff.; Vogt, 1971: 16 f.
46. *Obs. et emend.* 21. 30.
47. Troje, 1977: 701.
48. Wissenbach, 1736.
49. *Prob.* 1. 6 and 2. 5.
50. Huber, 1700: 84 ff.
51. Troje, 1977: 689.

In fact, it is no more than an *observatio* in which one text is emended. Moreover, the development of the argument leads to fairly wide digressions, as, for instance, in 1. 14, where one text on *dolus malus* (D 4. 3. 7 pr.) is discussed and emended. In fact, development of the argument seems to be the main link, not only between the chapters of a monograph, but also between various books. Some questions touched upon in the *Probabilia* lead to *De jurisdictione et imperio*, and, in its turn, the discussion of D 4. 3. 7 pr. (1. 14) will be the starting-point for a separate monograph, *De forma emendandi doli mali*, appearing in 1709.[52]

An overview of similarities with and differences from the *Probabilia* may give us an impression of Noodt's development since 1679.[53] As before, Noodt likes to argue emendations on presumed false solution of *notæ* and sigla by inept copyists, who 'make an error out of ignorance or haste, but anyway rather imprudently than unwontedly'.[54] Of the seven emendations defended in this monograph, three are argued this way.[55] Enough has been said already on the hypothetical character of such emendations. There is only one for which textual tradition at least seemed to give some reason for doubt.[56] There are others which, again, will seem rather audacious to more conservative textual critics. In four cases, words or lines which seem out of place from a dogmatic point of view are expunged as glossemes by some interpreter.[57] In D 4. 3. 7 pr. a line of no less than twelve words is deleted in this way,[58] in spite of the acknowledged fact that the Basilica seemed to confirm the generally accepted reading. In D 38. 15. 2. 1–2 four words are expunged in passing ('ut hoc obiter addam'), without much of an explanation.[59]

52. Ahsmann–Feenstra, 1984: nr. 463; see p. 244 ff.
53. Naturally, the *Probabilia* were revised for the 1691 edn. as well, but this mainly seems to have been a matter of smoothing the Latin and adding a reply to critics.
54. *Opera* i: 126: '. . . ut, cum legendum esset modis istis, librarius illum ex principium ejusdem capitis, aut imperitia aut festinatione lapsus, utique magis imprudenter quam insolite, repeteret'.
55. 1. 7 (C 3. 3. 2); 1. 15 (C 8. 40. 10); 2. 7 (D 40. 2. 17. 1), *Opera* i: 110, 115, 126. The emendation of C 8. 40. 10 was proposed in *Prob.* 2. 1, *Opera* i: 34 ff.
56. C 3. 3. 2; Noodt refers to the notes in the edn. of Russardus (1560), *Opera* i: 101.
57. D 38. 15. 2. 1–2 [vel . . . exposcit], Mo ii: 363: 36–7; D 4. 3. 7 pr. (see n. 56); D 50. 16. 42 [sed more civitatis], Mo ii: 937: 6; C 3. 13. 4 [post litem contestatam]. Noodt's emendation of D 38. 15. 2. 1–2 is noted by Wlassak, *RE* 4: 212 f., s.v. *cognitio* and by Solazzi, 1928: 18.
58. *Opera* i: 113 [aut nullam . . . circumscriptus est], Mo i: 120: 29–30. Lenel, *Pal.* ii: 466 cites Noodt's emendation but has doubts: 'Haud scio an hoc comma . . . potius interpretis cuiusdam quam Ulpiani sit.'
59. *Opera* i: 106 [vel . . . exposcit], Mo ii: 363: 36–7.

There is one marked difference from the *Probabilia*: while some sources and authors from Antiquity do not seem to be cited less, and possibly rather more, modern authors are only seldomly cited. Neither the Accursian gloss nor Cujas or A. Faure, to name only a few who were cited regularly in the *Probabilia*, are mentioned in the present monograph. The only names that appear are those of Giphanius, Connannus, and Gothofredus, Connannus being the only one whose opinion is refuted.[60] Apparently the Leiden professor, whose reputation seems to have been established well enough in the meantime, feels no need to prove the extent of his reading or to score by criticizing others. Thus he builds up a reputation for peacefulness and avoidance of literary quarrels. Honesty is another quality he seems keen on demonstrating. There is an interesting passage in 2. 13, which seems worth quoting in full, although in part it may be no more than a formula. Noodt proposes to expunge from C 3. 13. 4 the words 'post litem contestatam' because they make the provision of that constitution senseless. After giving his reasons he continues:

This I had written almost in this manner and laid aside for further deliberation, when later, while doing something else, I happened to stumble on Codex Theodosianus 2. 1. 6, at which I found a conjecture of Jacob Gothofredus[61] which was not far from this one of mine. Let me say frankly what happened: as soon as I saw it, it annoyed me that what I thought I was the first to have observed was already anticipated by him. But when considering the matter further I soon began to laugh at this ambition of mine, and I was pleased, because that which I noted as a conjecture in my notebook was confirmed by the opinion of this learned and celebrated man and, may I add, by the authority of the sentence of the said constitution.[62]

60. *Opera* i: 112. In the *Probabilia* opinions of eight authors were refuted.
61. *Codex Theodosianus cum perpetuis commentariis Jacobi Gothofredi*, 6 vols. Leipzig, 1736–45. i: 95. Gothofredus also thought that the words 'post litem contestatam' were interpolated.
62. *Opera* i: 131: 'haec fere ita scripseram, et ad ulteriorem deposueram deliberationem, cum deinde aliud agens, forte incidi in 1. Cod. Theod. de jurisdictione; ad quam comperi conjecturam V. Cl. Jacobi Gothofredi, ab hac meam non abhorrentem. Dicam autem quod res est, ingenue: simul videbam eam, pigebat me, quod me primum animadvertisse existimabam, id ab illo jam occupatam esse. At re ulterius perpensa, ipse mox coepi hanc meam ridere ambitionem, gavisusque sum, quod ex suspicione in adversariis meis animadvertam, id judicio viri eruditi ac praeclari, addam, et auctoritate similis sententiae d. 1. 6 confirmatum videre.' Noodt had already presented the same reflection as a consolation to Van Eck in his letter of 26 Mar. 1689 (UL Utrecht, MS 1000). Noodt endorsed a conjecture of Van Eck, but remarked that it was already proposed by Cujas: '. . . so mene dat UEd. redenen

Naturally, this honesty is a little ambiguous. While stressing that he had found the conjecture independently, he points out that he is only human, but has no intention of adorning himself with borrowed plumes. And, at the same time, he mobilizes the authority of Gothofredus and the Codex Theodosianus for his own glory.

Noodt's *De jurisdictione et imperio* is one more instance of the continuity of the elegant tradition in France and the Netherlands. In this tradition it is an important, though perhaps not epoch-making book, which confirms Noodt's reputation as an excellent interpreter and a rather bold critic. The legal problems are analysed in concise form. What strikes us is the down-to-earth manner in which jurisdiction is defined in the opening sentences. Jurisdiction is made up of *jus* and *dicere*, and *jus dicere* is defined, making use of the words of Paul in D 1. 1. 11, as pronouncing what is deemed useful by all or many in the state. And because it is evident that a public declaration of what is useful can only be made after (judicial) inquiry, and would have no effect unless backed by the power to compel, by nature jurisdiction includes *pronunciatio*, *cognitio*, and *executio*.[63]

In this book Noodt for the first time used a new instrument for the interpretation of classical legal texts, viz. epigraphic material from ancient monuments. The inscription we now find in Book I of the *Probabilia* (1. 2) was added only in the 1705 edition. Although Gabrieli seems to suggest that it was Noodt who introduced research of epigraphic material as a source for the study of Roman law,[64] this is not exactly true. Alciato and Cujas had both used inscriptions

heeft omme sigh te verblijden, dat hij de avantage heeft van met so eenen voortreffelijcken man gekomen te zijn in de selve gedachten, sonder van den selven juist in desen geweten te hebben. Ick hebbe dickwils gelijcke rescontres gehad, en sal oprechtelijck bekennen, dat het mij dan wel gebeurt is, dat het mij in het eerste geweldigh speet, dat ick bij iemand onvoorsiens vont, 't geene ick andersins selfs geconjectureert hadde, en dat ick de saecke een wenig meer geconsidereert hebbende, niet alleenig begon te lacchen bij mij selfs met dese mijne ambitie, maer oock daerenboven mij begon te verheugen, dat ick mijne speculatien sach besteed te zijn door het oordeel van braeve en bereits verstorve luijden, insonderheit om dat ick geloofde, dat ick daer door te meerder redenen vonde om op mijne verdere of andere gedachten insgelijx staet te maecken; waer van ick oock mene vermaen te doen in mijn tractaet de jurisdictione et imperio . . .'. The argument is partly a conventional one. Scaliger wrote (as a rather poor excuse) that he was pleased he had divined something which Galen himself had noticed, see Grafton, 1983: 183.

63. *Opera* i: 93.
64. 1968: 327: 'Recò allo studio delle fonte in particolare contributi con quello epigrafico.'

(Alciato may really have been the first jurist to do so),[65] and the Italian humanist M. A. Galvani discussed some inscriptions in his book on usufruct,[66] which was actually studied by Noodt.[67] But none of them gave useful references (Cujas, for example, refers to 'lapides Capitolini' or 'antiquae inscriptiones').[68] Noodt at least was a good scholar. He not only gave references but really may have been the first systematically to consult printed collections of inscriptions to see what they had to offer the student of Roman law. It is not a wild guess to suppose that his learned Nijmegen friends Smetius junior and Cuper were instrumental in arousing his interest. Already in 1679 Noodt had discussed with Cuper the question of when Caracalla got the title Augustus and whether Septimius Severus ever used the name Antoninus. In his lengthy reply Cuper adduced, *inter alia*, a score of inscriptions from Gruter's collection.[69]

In retrospect one may doubt whether this was all that important from a legal point of view. Only in a minority of the cases treated has the inscription really the strength of an argument.[70] In most cases their use seems hardly more than illustrative. But within the research programme of humanistic legal philology as a whole the study of epigraphic material certainly was a valuable development. In *De foenore et usuris* (1698) fifteen inscriptions are cited, the highest number in all of Noodt's published works. *De jurisdictione et imperio* has six inscriptions, *Ad legem Aquiliam* and *De usufructu* (first published in 1713) five each. Later, citations drop to insignificant numbers. In *Julius Paulus* (1700), *Diocletianus et Maximianus* (1704),

65. See e.g. Alciato, *In tres posteriores Codicis Iustiniani Annotationes*, Argentinae, J. Schottus 1515, pp. 3, 8, 12, 23; *Praetermissa*, 1518, Book I, i.v. mancipes, militia, nummus; *Dispunctiones*, Lugduni, S. Gryphius, 2. 27, 3. 1, 3. 4, 4. 1; Cujas, *Obs. et emend.* 2. 21, 3. 4, 10. 37, 13. 36. I thank Douglas Osler for references.
66. Marcus Aurelius Galvani, *De usufructu dissertationes variae*. Padua, 1650. Later imps.: Geneva, 1676, Tübingen, 1788. See (in Tübingen edn.) pp. 71, 125, 259, 268, 366, 369, 370, 374, 376, 378, 418. Galvani was born in Ferrara, where his father, a famous collector of antiques, was professor. He became professor himself in Pisa and Padua and died in 1659.
67. Cf. *Opera* i: 448, 463.
68. Of course, Alciato and Cujas could not have done better. The first useful collection of Latin inscriptions was made by the Fleming Martin Smetius and published posthumously, Leiden: Lipsius, 1588. Calderini (1974: 9) confuses this Smetius with the Smetii from Nijmegen, the famous collectors of Roman antiquities. Noodt mostly used the collection of Janus Gruter (1560–1627) published in 1603. He also cited the collection of Reinesius, *Syntagma inscriptionum antiquarum*, Leipzig and Frankfurt, 1682.
69. Cuper to Noodt, Deventer, 1 Nov [1679], KB 72 G. 20, fols. 27–32.
70. e.g. in *De foenore et usuris* 2. 1, *Opera* i: 205 f.

and *De forma emendandi doli mali* (1709), no inscriptions are cited; in the *Observationes* (1706) only one. But naturally not every subject was equally suited to the finding of relevant epigraphic material. The great majority of inscriptions (29 out of 37) come from Gruter's *Corpus inscriptionum*, but most inscriptions in *De jurisdictione et imperio* are from the collection of Reinesius, which appeared in 1682.

For the rest, we can hardly expect truly original theses in the treatment of a subject that had been discussed so intensely for so many ages by so many distinguished jurists. In his interpretation of D 2. 1. 3, and especially with the thesis that *jurisdictio* and *imperium* are synonyms, Noodt leans on Cujas (which Huber does not fail to note),[71] and several of his other interpretations can be traced back to the Accursian gloss. After all, the number of possible explanations of Ulpian's abstruse definitions is not unlimited. If Noodt's opinions are not all his own (and he never claims that they are), this does not mean that they are second-rate. The study of Roman law has always been a work of many, and truly new insights are rare. From a modern point of view, the only thing lacking in Noodt's treatise might seem to be that he does not discuss older literature on the subject at any length and that, consequently, the book does not give us the slightest impression of the history of its treatment from the Middle Ages. But that, I think, would hardly have been conceivable as a reproach in the seventeenth century, when the literary history of legal science had yet to be invented.[72] And informed contemporary readers will have found many more anonymous citations than we are able to discern now. Science forgets much as it develops, and even historians cannot retrieve everything.

Ad legem Aquiliam liber singularis

The second monograph published in 1690 with the four books of *Probabilia* concerns the *lex Aquilia*. This is a plebiscite, presumably dating from 286 BC,[73] which made actionable all losses from the

71. Cujas, *Obs. et emend.* 21. 30; Huber, 1700: 84. Noodt also cites Wissenbach and Scipio Gentilis.
72. The first preliminaries for such a history were the lectures on *historia literaria* of Roman law which J. C. Rücker, pupil and successor of Anton Schulting in Leiden, began to give in the 1740s. Lecture notes of these are in great numbers in UL Leiden. Only a very small part of this was published, see Ahsmann–Feenstra, 1984: nr. 552. H. W. Tydeman had plans to edit the lecture notes, but nothing came of it.
73. On this, see Kaser, 1971: 161 f., 619 f.

killing of slaves or cattle, or damage to property by someone else's fault. Since the reception of Roman law in the Middle Ages the *actio legis Aquiliae* became the general action for compensation of extra-contractual damage, and texts from the relevant titles of the Corpus Juris (e.g. concerning unlawfulness, fault, causation, reasons for excluding liability) formed the basis for the general principles of modern criminal law.[74]

Noodt's book on the *lex Aquilia* is an excellent example of a humanistic monograph, very elegant as well as terse and lucid from the legal point of view.[75] For humanists the Digest title *ad legem Aquiliam* (D 9. 2) never seems to have been as favourite a subject as *jurisdictio* and *imperium*. Not that it did not have a lot to offer to humanistic philologists: geographical data (52.2) and scenes from daily streetlife in ancient Rome (11 pr.), texts on various games (7.4; 45.3), a text on the making of a diatret-glass (27. 29), various *hapax legomena* (in 27. 30, 29. 2, 29. 4, 52. 1). Naturally such niceties attracted attention from the very beginning of the humanist movement,[76] and some emendations were proposed very early on, e.g. by Bartolini (*c.*1495).[77] Cujas also contributed some famous emendations.[78] But, as far as I know, no humanistic monograph on the *lex Aquilia* was published before that of Noodt.[79] The reason for this may be that it was a rather technical legal subject, without the political relevance that was so prominent in *jurisdictio* and *imperium*, *usurae*, or the *lex regia*. The *lex Aquilia* is, as Noodt says, for the protection of public discipline, but through private civil actions.

Naturally, the *lex Aquilia* was dealt with in the law curriculum and in commentaries on the relevant titles of the Institutes (4. 3), the Digest (9.2), or the Codex (3. 35). Consequently, it was the subject of

74. Kaufmann, 1958.
75. See e.g. Z. Huber, 1703: 87: '. . . observavit Cl. Noodtius elegantissimo et tersissimo tractatu ad legem Aquiliam'.
76. For the discussion of 'dolor' in D 9. 2. 52. 1, see Van den Bergh and Stolte, 1977: 246 f., and Brenkman's note, ibid.: 300 f.
77. 'forn⟨a⟩carius' in D 9. 2. 27. 9, which emendation was published later by Budé in his own name; see Osler, 1983: II, II, 15.
78. e.g. 'e⟨r⟩um' in D 9. 2. 23. 3 (Mo i: 282: 21), see Cujas, *Obs. et emend.* 27. 11; Van den Bergh and Stolte, 1977: 270; Noodt, *Opera* i: 158 and 345.
79. François Baudoin treated the law in a monograph on a series of Roman laws: *F. Balduini Comm. ad leges Voconiam, Falcidiam, Juliam, Papiam Poppaeam, Rhodiam, Aquiliam*. Basle, 1559. Chifletus seems to have been the first to discuss the (unknown) contents of chapter 2 of the *lex Aquilia*.

disputations and dissertations as well.[80] It seems to have become a favourite subject for dissertations—quite understandably—in Leiden during the professorate of Noodt. Lipenius, who is not nearly complete, counts seven Leiden dissertations on the *lex* between 1691 and 1719, that is, an average of one every four years.[81]

In the preface, expounding the importance of the subject, Noodt strikes a rather unusual note. The *lex Aquilia*, he says, aimed at the protection of property of the *plebs* and the lower classes against the injustice of their equals, but particularly against the noble and powerful 'to whom the plebs is exposed day and night, in the city and in the countryside, in the crowd and in solitude, on land and sea, as long as those can hope to go unpunished because of their dignity from riches or birth, while the others have difficulty in defending themselves because of their obscure and weak position'.[82] Such an insight, apparently inferred from the fact that the *lex Aquilia* was a plebiscite, testifies to the growth of Noodt's historical consciousness, and, whether it has some foundation or not, it is characteristic of the way the study of Roman law developed in the nineteenth century that we do not discuss it today: the Pandectists simply erased it from the agenda as one of those things that had nothing to do with the 'wahrhafte Verständnis' of Roman law and could only taint the apolitical sanctity of positivistic legal science. This picture of the high and the mighty mercilessly preying on the lower classes may well have appealed to contemporary republican readers, as an image of their own society as seen by a bourgeois. But, Noodt adds, the *lex Aquilia* does not only help the *plebs*: it keeps peace and safety for wellnigh all citizens. In a variation of a phrase of Cicero,[83] the *lex Aquilia* is called the drag-net not only of all baseness but even of the least fault. The limit of this law is not the 'narrow innocence' which (according to Seneca)[84] is usually the rule of law, but virtue and wisdom.[85] This explanation points to what may have been an

80. Lipenius, whose bibliography is by no means exhaustive, counts some 31 titles between 1591 and 1751.
81. As I said in the introduction, I have not done any systematic research concerning dissertations defended under Noodt. This is a subject for further research.
82. 'iniuria . . . saepe nobiliorum, potentumve, quibus plebs in die et nocte, in urbe et ruri, in celebritate et solitudine, terra marique, hoc magis obnoxa est, quo magis illis a dignitate, opibus, aut natalibus, spes impunitatis, isti ab obscura et tenui conditione difficilior vindicta est' (*Opera* i: 137).
83. *De nat. deor.* 3. 30. 74: 'everriculum malitiarum omnium'.
84. *De ira* 2. 28. 2: 'quam angusta innocentia est, ad legem bonum esse'.
85. *Opera* i: 137.

important reason for Noodt to treat the *lex Aquilia*: the duty to compensate damages done to others is one of the axioms of natural law.[86]

Noodt's exposition of the *lex Aquilia* is very systematic and, in fact, does not seem to differ greatly from what one would find in a good modern textbook of Roman law.[87] After treatment of the origin of the *lex Aquilia* (I), the contents of its first chapter are discussed (II): it is concerned with the killing of slaves or cattle, but later the killing of free people was brought under it as well. Then the meaning of *iniuria occidere* is discussed at length (III–IV). After this, follow various topics affecting the scope of the law: *levis castigatio* (VI), *culpa* and *casus* (VII), *imperitia* (VIII), the difference between *occidere* and *mortis causam præbere* (IX). Next the question is discussed, against whom the *actio legis Aquiliae* may be brought (X). In this context various connected problems are explored: the reasons for excluding liability (*furiosus*, *impubes*), causation, and the position of the heir. After that, the other side is discussed: who can bring the action (XI)? Finally, the question of what may be obtained by the action is treated (XII).

As Friedrich August Wolf once said, with respect to interpolations, to find the real thing you must have the nose; those who always have a cold will find nothing.[88] There are topics which perfectly enable us to judge scholars from the past in this respect, and one of them is the question of the content of chapter 2 of the *lex Aquilia*. After the find of Gaius' Institutes in the Verona palimpsest (1816), *all* conjectures made by scholars in the past, even by the most distinguished, proved to be wrong. But Noodt was not taken in; he really had mastered the *ars nesciendi*. Because we know nothing about the abrogated second chapter of the *lex Aquilia* it is useless to speculate about its contents (XIII).[89] The third chapter, concerning unlawful damage to property, is treated in the same way as the first: What is the text of the law (XIV)? What is the meaning of *urere*, *frangere*, and *rumpere* (XV)? What are the necessary qualifications

86. Grotius, *De jure belli ac pacis*, Prol. § 8.
87. See e.g. Kaser, 1971; Nicholas, 1962.
88. Schulz, 1916: 40.
89. Gaius iii: 215 was as yet unknown. Unlike Noodt, Vœt (*Comm. ad Pand.* 9. 2. 5) and Van Bijnkershœk (*Obs. jur. rom.* 1. 13) speculated on the contents; like many others, both proved to be wrong. Apparently, here Noodt is the more practical jurist through being a better historian. That Noodt mastered the *ars nesciendi* was also noted by his biographer Barbeyrac.

(*corpore corpori datum*, XVIII; *injuria*, XIX)? Against whom and by whom can the action be brought (XX)? What can be obtained by it (XXI)? This scheme is interrupted only for discussion of some emendations (V, XVI) and a special case (XVII). Apparently, not even the finding of the Institutes of Gaius in Verona in 1816 has changed much in our knowledge of the *actio legis Aquiliae* (chapter 2 of the law is totally unrelated to 1 and 3). The most striking difference from modern textbooks, apart from some minor changes in the order of treatment of the various aspects, may well be that relevant literary texts from Antiquity are hardly cited in them any more. This, again, is the effect of the 'Historical' school and Pandectism.

In this treatise Noodt moderately indulges in the idiosyncrasies of humanistic philology (Huber found nothing in it to criticize). Other authors are criticized only a few times, and no more than six rather modest emendations are discussed, which mainly concern real textual, not merely dogmatical problems.[90] Of these six emendations, three are of Noodt's own invention, but none of them was acceptable to Mommsen, mainly because the Greeks concur with the reading of the *Florentina*. And Brenkman regarded only Noodt's emendation of D 9. 2. 41 pr. worth considering, judging from his system of annotation: it is the only one recorded in a note with an arabic figure.[91]

This monograph gives us some impression of the way in which

90. D 9. 2. 2 pr. (Mo i: 277: 36) 'quadrupedem⟨ve⟩ pecudem', emendation proposed by Hotman, endorsed by Noodt but rejected by Van Bijnkershœk; see Van den Bergh and Stolte, 1977: 254 n. 2.

D 9. 2. 5 pr. (Mo i: 278: 20) 'ergo et ⟨Aquilia⟩ tenebitur', emendation proposed by Noodt but rejected by Schulting, Huber, and van de Water, see Van den Bergh and Stolte, 1977: 256 n. 6. Noodt had discussed this emendation in *Probabilia* 1. 9 and returned to it in *Observationes* 1. 5.

D 9. 2. 13. 3 (Mo i: 281: 12) 'si ⟨modo⟩ post mortem', emendation proposed by Haloander and supported by Noodt but rejected by Mommsen because F and the Basilica concur, see Van den Bergh and Stolte, 1977: 266 n. 2.

D 92. 23. 3 (Mo i: 282: 21) 'posse e⟨r⟩um Aquilia agere', emendation proposed by Cujas and endorsed by Noodt and Mommsen. Noodt returned to this in *Observationes* 2. 25; see Van den Bergh and Stolte, 1977: 270 n. 3.

D 9. 2. 41 pr. (Mo i: 290: 12) 'est ⟨furti⟩ et injuriarum', emendation proposed by Noodt but rejected by Mommsen because F and the Greeks concur; see Van den Bergh and Stolte, 1977: 259 n. 2.

D 9. 2. 45. 4 (Mo i: 291: 2) 'possent, ⟨damnum⟩ dederint', emendation proposed by Noodt but not noted by Brenkman. Mommsen has a different emendation.

Apart from emendations in the Digest, Noodt proposed two in the Collatio and one in Seneca.

91. See n. 90.

Noodt combined Roman law and natural law. Discussion of the limits of legitimate self-defence (*vim vi repellere licet*) gives occasion for some natural law speculation.[92] The discussion of legal problems passes easily into moral statements. As an example I quote Noodt's discussion of the famous (though presumably academic) case that was treated by several classical jurists: suppose one man inflicts a deadly wound on a slave, but another man actually kills him.[93] According to the opinion of Julian, as recorded in D 9. 2. 51 pr., the *actio legis Aquiliae* can be brought against both men. But, Noodt claims, the opinion of Julian is neither in conformity with reason, nor with practice. According to Celsus, Marcellus, and Ulpian, the first man is only liable for wounding, the second for killing the slave (D 9. 2. 11. 3). And, what is more, from D 9. 2. 15. 1 one may conclude that on another occasion Julian himself concurred in this opinion. This brings Noodt to a discussion of whether a change of opinion is commendable or reprehensible. Classical jurists often defended contradictory opinions, and the Emperor Justinian speaks frankly of two contradictory opinions of a jurist as excellent as Papinian (C 6. 2. 22. 3a). 'Seneca preferred frankness just as much as we do, because he wrote:[94] "It is no fickleness to give up an acknowledged and exposed error. We should say frankly: I had a different opinion, I was mistaken. It is a perseverance of insolent stupidity to say: what I have said once, whatever it is, must remain fixed and firm." Thus the ancients, those venerable and strict men, acknowledged with the same frankness their own errors as well as those of others. And it would not be insolent, or unworthy of Julian, to indicate and at once praise in him a change of mind equal to his greatness of character.' One is reminded of Walt Whitman's beautiful answer, when accused of having changed his mind: 'I contain multitudes.' A new direction in legal scholarship, typical of the era of Enlightenment (and not a very commendable one—on this point Jhering and I would concur), is becoming as evident here as anywhere else. Natural law is a kind of social philosophy and education seems to become the main purpose of the law professor. Needless to say, the glossators did not fail to notice the contradiction between D 9. 2. 11. 3 and 51 pr.,[95] but they solved it in their own way: although both texts speak of a deadly wound, there is no contradiction, because in the one case it was certain that the slave would die from the first wound, in the other not.

92. *Opera* i: 141 f.
93. D 9. 2. 11. 3 and 51; *Opera* i: 154 f.
94. *De benef.* 38.
95. Gloss *teneri* on D 9. 2. 51 pr.

This solution no doubt would not win an award for elegance, but at least it has the merit of being soundly legal.

To give an impression of the quality of Noodt's monograph I rather take as an example another subject, which he treats with all the riches of his humanist erudition: the case of the immature olives. There is a marked antinomy—and again one, to be sure, that had not escaped the glossators—between D 9. 2. 27. 25 and D 33. 2. 42. According to the first text, the cropping of immature olives makes one liable to the owner of the olive trees under the *lex Aquilia*. But the second text, which concerns usufruct, discusses the problem in a more general perspective and with different results: fruits are what are useful to man; therefore one should not look to natural maturity, but to the moment at which it is most expedient for the owner or tenant to pick them. Consequently, because immature olives yield more than they will do when cropped maturely, it is certain that immature olives count among fruits.

So here is the problem: how can the cropping of immature olives be detrimental if they yield more than mature ones? There can be no liability under the *lex Aquilia* when there is no loss. The most drastic example classical jurists gave to explain this is the case where a young slave is castrated and as a result becomes more valuable as a singer or a eunuch (D 9. 2. 27. 28). The solution of the gloss[96] is hardly convincing: immature olives are said to yield more, because they produce a bigger quantity of liquid, but the quality is less healthy and good; therefore, there is liability under the *lex Aquilia*. Apparently, the glossator stuck to his books and had no practical knowledge of the production of olive oil, which must have been practised in Italy in his day in much the same way as in Antiquity. Naturally Noodt, who lived in the cold north and never once left his country, did not have any such knowledge either, but he knew the agricultural tracts from Antiquity, and there was the answer. The best oil, the *olio vergine*, was pressed, as in fact it still is today, from olives which had not yet fully matured. According to Columella, its price was twice as high as that of oil pressed earlier or later. 'Immature' is an ambiguous word. The Romans used to distinguish various degrees of maturity, from still nearly raw to overripe, each yielding a different quality of oil. Although virgin oil is the best, the owner may have reasons for choosing the harvest time that best suits him. The outsider harvesting

96. Gloss *Aquilia tenebitur* on D 9. 2. 27. 25 and gloss *plus reditus habet* on D 33. 2. 42.

immature olives is trespassing on the owner's property rights. The owner is the ruler of his own goods,[97] and he is free even to abuse them. That is the reason why he may bring the *actio legis Aquiliae* when someone else has cropped his immature olives.

Naturally, this solution implies that for Noodt the basis of the action is not damage done to an object, diminishing its objective value, but the subjective *interesse* or *utilitas* of the owner. Although neither Noodt, nor Brenkman, who praised it abundantly,[98] said as much, it is evident that this solution is perfectly in line with the *usus modernus* of the *actio legis Aquiliae*, which had introduced this extension of the scope of the action in the sixteenth century.[99] This time, the jurist wins over the humanist.

On this point, something more has to be said, because it seems there is a wide gap between Noodt's stated intentions and what he actually does. In the preface he said that the utility of the *lex Aquilia* was a special reason to study it.[1] But Kaufmann concluded that Noodt's monograph describes the *actio legis Aquiliae* as if in the seventeenth century it was still virtually the same as in ancient Rome. In Noodt's book we find no trace of the *usus modernus*,[2] as it had developed in legal practice, and consequently the book does not seem to have had any influence on legal reality.[3]

True as this may be, I think some qualification is needed here. We would seriously misconstrue Noodt's intentions if we concluded from his stress on the public utility of the *lex Aquilia* that he meant to describe the action under that law as it functioned in seventeenth-century legal practice. The relevance of humanistic philology to everyday life lies elsewhere. For a humanist, Antiquity is the example of all that is human. And in the natural law thinking of the era of Enlightenment this idea is linked with a new didactic purpose. A precise, scientific description of a legal institution from ancient Rome is of practical value first of all because it may help to elevate present-day practice to higher standards of humanity. Therefore, in a country

97. Noodt here paraphrases C 4. 35. 21, a text which from the Middle Ages was used frequently as a description of property rights.
98. See Van den Bergh and Stolte, 1977: 278 f., note tt.
99. See Kaufmann, 1958: 46 ff. Earlier, Noodt denied, against many other scholars, that *intercepta utilitas* could be a cause for bringing an *actio legis Aquiliae* (*Opera* i: 138), so he is not wholly consistent on this issue.
1. '. . . ut quam publice utilis est Aquilia, tam cognoscendi voluptate jocunda sit'. *Opera* i: 137.
2. Apparently the one just mentioned is overlooked by Kaufmann.
3. Kaufmann, 1958: 124.

where rules of public office have not yet fully developed, and where in several cases bailiffs are known to have exceeded their powers,[4] it is undoubtedly of great practical importance when Noodt observes, for instance, that, according to the Corpus Juris, lower magistrates do not have the right to castigate free people.[5]

3. Years of achievement—writings 1698–1709

De fœnore et usuris libri tres

After the 1691 publication it took seven years before Noodt published a new book. But they were not years of idleness. The monograph on interest and usury, which appeared in the middle of 1698,[6] is one of his best.[7] It is dedicated to the well-known Amsterdam burgomaster Nicolaas Witsen (1641–1717),[8] a man who certainly knew the ins and outs of commercial capitalism. Evidently, the book was long in the making. Already five years before, in 1693, copies of a draft were circulated *ad amicos*. Perizonius received one and wrote to Van Eck expecting that he would get one as well.[9] By then Noodt must have been working on it for some years. And in December 1696 he consulted a text from the Digest title *de usuris* in the manuscript that van Bijnkershœk had bought shortly before.[10] On that occasion, Noodt announced that perhaps he would publish the book very soon. So it seems that Noodt took every care to prepare it as best as he could, and this may be an indication of the importance he attached to it. Van Bijnkershœk, incidentally, was apparently not among the friends who received an advance copy.

Usury was an extremely popular subject among humanists.[11] In the Middle Ages, taking interest fell under a papal prohibition, and therefore the glossators took little interest in the classical texts; one of

4. See below, p. 217 ff.
5. *Opera* i: 145, with reference to D 40. 9. 17. 1.
6. Ahsmann–Feenstra, 1984: nr. 431. The dedication is dated 7 May 1698.
7. Jugler ii, 1775: 374, with further references.
8. *NNBW* iv: 1473–9. Witsen also corresponded with Noodt's friend Cuper. I do not know when and where Noodt and Witsen got to know each other.
9. Perizonius to Van Eck, Leiden, 4 July 1693 (UL Utrecht, MS 1000): 'Apud nos Clariss. Noodt mihi ad Amicos librum suum de foenore et usuris, quem quin tibi etiam brevi sit missurus nullus dubito.'
10. Van Bijnkershœk to Van Eck, The Hague, 15 Dec. 1696 (UL Utrecht, MS 1000). For the text, see Van den Bergh, 1984: 282 ff.
11. Troje, 1972*a*: 25 ff.; 1972*b*: 59; 1977: 711 ff.

these even remained without an apparatus of glosses, which is rather exceptional. As a result they grossly misunderstood them; so they assumed that 'centesimae usurae' was an interest rate of 100 per cent, a usurious rate which made the papal prohibition only the more understandable. In the sixteenth century, literature on *usurae* was immense. At first, philological problems were discussed (the rates meant by *centesimae*, *semisses*, *trientes*, etc.), but later various legal, economic, and social issues were discussed, the papal interdiction being the central concern. In 1524 in Paris there appeared what seems to have been the first monograph on the subject.[12] Papal legislation, which was based on the Bible, became ever more in conflict with the rising tide of commercial capitalism. Nevertheless, orthodox Catholics and even Protestants upheld the prohibition, though usually admitting a series of more or less ingenious devices to restrict it, or even to escape it altogether. Others, among whom in the seventeenth century Gerard Noodt has a prominent place,[13] rejected the prohibition forthwith. The question remained under discussion well into the eighteenth century, when Pope Benedict XIV (1740–58) urged the interdiction once more.[14] Among the famous jurists who defended it was Noodt's senior contemporary Jean Domat (1625–96), a Jansenist.[15] Usury was also one of the favourite topics of the Vœtians[16] in their fierce battle against worldly tendencies in the Republic.

Therefore, it hardly needs to be explained why Noodt, the scion of a Nijmegen merchant family and a professed humanistic jurist, took up the subject. As we have seen, it is only one of a series of topics on which he opposed the opinion of contemporary orthodox theologians. And anyway it is clear enough where Noodt's sympathies lie. In the first half of the seventeenth century, a sharp literary debate on interest took place in the university of Leiden, between the pro-

12. Troje, 1972*a*: 133 n. 19; 1977: 711.
13. Troje (1977: 712 f.) does not mention Noodt's monograph and on the other hand seems to overrate the importance of that of Salmasius.
14. Encyclical letter, *Vix pervenit*, 1 Nov. 1745, Gasparri i: 939 f.
15. Noodt cites his (then still anonymous) *Loix civiles dans leur ordre naturel*, i (1689), see *Opera* i: 184.
16. McGahagan, 1976: 9 and *passim*. In 1646 the professors of theology of Utrecht published an opinion condemning pawnshops and arguing that the Church should not allow pawnbrokers to communicate (*Res judicata*, Utrecht, 1646). The *classis* of Leiden published against this a *gravamen* defending the opposite opinion (*Res judicanda, gravamen en advys van de classis van Leyden*. Leiden: Verbiest, 1658).

fessors Maestertius[17] and Salmasius.[18] The young Cyprianus Regneri ab Oosterga, the Cartesian, took part in the debate and criticized Salmasius, the conservative, who *inter alia* defended the absolute right of princes.[19] Likewise, Noodt criticizes Salmasius throughout his book and, moreover, uses unusually sharp words.[20] Salmasius had tried to emend and explain the text 'with such unhappy results that it is no use either to cite or to refute his opinion'.[21] Elsewhere he is called ignorant.[22] No doubt Perizonius will have liked this. Perhaps the vindication of the honour of jurists (who back in the fifteenth century had been criticized for their ignorance in this matter by Ermolao Barbaro),[23] against philologists as well as theologians, was an additional reason for the Leiden law professor to write this book.

In it no trace is left of an exegetic treatment of the Digest title *de usuris* according to the *ordo legum*. Nor is it a loose collection of connected observations. Treatment is strictly systematic and the book may be, in fact, one of the earliest systematic legal monographs. In Book I, after discussion of the terminology, the question of the justification for taking interest is treated exhaustively. Book II is concerned with interest rates: what the maximum rate is, which rates do exist, etc. Book III discusses in what manner an obligation to pay interest may come into existence and by which facts it is abolished. So here we have a perfect example of the scheme which is used in all modern codifications to describe any legal institution: definition—content—origin—end.[24] It is interesting to see how Noodt gradually came to grips with the problem of systematic exposition. *De jurisdictione et imperio* is still a collection of connected observations, put in a largely ephemeral systematic order; *Ad legem Aquiliam* is a major step forward, although there still are a few observations which break

17. On him, see Feenstra, 1982*a*.
18. 1588–1653. French philologist, professor in Leiden.
19. See Meyer, 1971: 22.
20. *Opera* i: 207, 210, 218, 245.
21. 'Tentavit quoque hanc legem Salmasius . . . et corrigere et illustrare, sed successu tam infelici, ut nihil opus sit, ejus sententiam hic aut attulisse aut refutasse.' *Opera* i: 218.
22. *Opera* i: 245.
23. See Troje, 1972*a*: 131.
24. Most elements of the scheme are found in D 1. 3. 41 (Ulp. 2 *Inst.*): 'Totum autem ius consistit aut in adquirendo aut in conservando, aut in minuendo; aut enim agitur quemadmodum quid cujusque fiat, aut quemadmodum quis rem vel jus suum conservet, aut quomodo alienet aut omittat.'

the order of treatment; finally, in *De fœnore et usuris* a perfectly systematic treatment is realized.

The monograph shows the full measure of Noodt's outstanding scholarship. He has complete command of the relevant literature. Even Ermolao Barbaro, the first scholar to establish the correct meaning of *usurae centesimae*, is cited. For the seventeenth century, this seems rather unusual, because, as has been said before, the French school, and in this case Budé's *De asse* in particular, had greatly obscured the contributions of earlier Italian humanists. Noodt discusses every one of the traditional arguments. His argument is always clear and acute. If you make a profit by using my money, why should you not pay for it? If you rent my house or land you pay for it as well.[25] Naturally, one must love and care for others as much as for oneself, but that goes for you as well as for me. And when you are enriching yourself by using my money, you certainly do not fulfil the law of humanity any more than I do when I practise usury.[26] The traditional arguments against the analogy of taking interest and hiring are refuted one by one.

Taking interest is not an invention of nature, but nor is it forbidden by it. It is an institution of *jus gentium*, like servitude and property.[27] And nobody would condemn cities because they are not an invention of nature. If there is abuse of interest, this does not vitiate its use: it is not the interest that is to be blamed for its abuse, but the avaricious man who abuses it. If all that is abused sometimes should be forbidden, you should forbid water, fire, wine, and food as well.

The biblical prohibition to take interest is Hebrew civil law, not *jus gentium*.[28] Even if God himself prohibited the Jews to take interest, he only prohibited it to them. This appears from the Bible itself, because God did not prohibit the Jews to take interest from foreigners.[29] And there is a plausible historical reason why the Jews were forbidden to take interest from each other. The Hebrew state

25. This argument had already been discussed and, naturally, rejected by Thomas Aquinas, *ST* 2a 2ae 78. 1.
26. *Opera* i: 186.
27. *Opera* i: 192. This is what Thomas Aquinas held, see Hallebeek, 1986: 91.
28. The division of Mosaic law into a part which only binds Jews and another one which is *jus gentium* is traditional. It is found e.g. in Hotman's *Antitribonian*, see Baron, 1888: xviii. Noodt will have learned it from Grotius's *De jure belli ac pacis* 1. 1. 16. But Grotius did not apply the distinction to the prohibition of interest, which he regarded as divine law binding Hebrews and Christians alike.
29. *Opera* i: 193, referring to Deut. 23: 19–20, 15: 6, and 28: 44. Noodt is aware that Lev. 25: 35–6 has a different rule.

was not yet established then or was still very young and weak. So there was reason to eliminatc possible sources of internal discord. Likewise, Christ's instruction, 'Lend without hoping for anything in return' (Luke 6: 34, Matt. 5: 42), must not be taken literally but hyperbolically. Taken literally, it would abolish not only interest but also selling, hire, and barter, which were all well-established institutions under the Old Testament. Christ said himself (Matt. 5: 17) that he did not come to change one iota of the law, and therefore this cannot have been his intention. What Christ urged was the same as Seneca stressed: there is more to humanity than the narrow innocence of being good according to the law.[30]

It is interesting to compare Noodt's attitude with that of Grotius on this point. Grotius[31] followed scholastic tradition to the letter. He accepted that the divine interdiction to take interest bound Christians as well as Hebrews, because divine law goes above all other kinds of law. But, at the same time, Grotius would not have been a Dutchman if he had not accepted all scholastic subterfuges invented to evade the interdiction to the point of practically annulling it: yes, it is forbidden to take interest, but it is a totally different contract to stipulate compensation for the fact that you must do without your money for a long time, or for the fact that you cannot make profits with it yourself, or for costs, or for the risk that the sum may be lost. For Noodt, on the other hand, the biblical prohibition is not *jus gentium*, and scholastic subtleties to evade papal strictures are just bad law: 'it is a worthless interpretation of the law to uphold the words of the pope and at the same time circumvent their meaning and intention'.[32] And, in fact, you may be worse off with all the subtleties of canon law, because in civil law there is a maximum rate of interest, which could easily be exceeded in a contract for *id quod interest* (as accepted in canon law). So while you intend to curb greed, you may in fact be encouraging it.[33]

Noodt's book shows the characteristic mixture of natural law and Roman law. In the discussion of the admissibility of taking interest, the focus is on *jus gentium*, but for all technical matters (rates of interest, interest on delayed payments, legal maxima, compound interest, procedure) discussion concentrates on the interpretation of

30. *Opera* i: 201; Seneca, *De ira* 2. 28.2; Cicero, *De off.* 2. 18.
31. *De jure belli ac pacis* 2. 12. 21. 3.
32. *Opera* i: 202.
33. *Opera* i: 202.

the sources of Roman law. Here Noodt can show all his skills as a Romanist, as well as his massive erudition. Only very few emendations are proposed.[34] In these, he uses the techniques we have already met; one gemination is suggested, and once Noodt argues on the evidence of the *notæ* of Probus. His emendation of D 46. 3. 72 is endorsed in substance, with some change in form, by Mommsen.

Noodt gives special attention to the historical development of the Roman law of interest. Republican law was changed during the early principate, and there were other changes in the second century AD; finally, Justinian determined legitimate rates of interest anew, and gave a series of other relevant provisions. An emendation of Faure is rejected because it is superfluous if sufficient notice is taken of historical development. Evidently, Noodt has gained self-confidence as a legal historian; in older literature he criticizes a general 'ignorantia historiae usurarum'.[35]

Another interesting feature is that Noodt recapitulates the arguments put forward by the moneylenders themselves:

> But when I take interest for the use of my money, I do not take anything but a compensation for its use. So when I take interest, I am not unjust, because I do not take what is yours, but what is mine. For I take a price for the use that I have conceded to you. But if you would like to use my money for your profit, and allow me no profit for that use in exchange, you would be unjust, because you would not let the law be the same for you and me. This is what the moneylenders urge, and rightly so.[36]

As we will see presently, Noodt knew some moneylenders personally from Nijmegen (that his house in Leiden once accommodated the local pawnshop is a pure coincidence, of which he may not have been conscious). He may have been the first jurist to discuss the arguments of men of the trade and thus introduced a 'sociological' argument in a debate which till then had centred exclusively on the

34. Noodt suggests that a *geminatio* must be read in an inscription published by Gruter (*Opera* i: 206). He endorses a conjecture of Cujas on D 17. 1. 10. 3 (*Opera* i: 213). He suggests interpolation of C 4. 65. 17 (*Opera* i: 214; see Palazzini Finetti, 1953, and *Index Int. Codex*, 1969: 89). He discusses emendation of D 22. 1. 4. 1 (*Opera* i: 217) and suggests a conjecture in D 12. 1. 40, using *notæ* of Probus (*Opera* i: 239). He suggests emendation of D 46. 3. 72 (*Opera* i: 259); this emendation is treated more fully in *Observationes* 1. 16, *Opera* i: 314 f.); it is endorsed by Mommsen, see Mo ii: 712: 33.
35. *Opera* i: 259; with his stress on the importance of historical development Noodt follows in the footsteps of Cujas (See Troje, 1972*b*: 59 f.), but the idea gets a much greater scope here.
36. *Opera* i: 186.

correct interpretation of authoritative texts from the Bible and the Corpus Juris, in principle ignoring the opinions of the participants in the respective social field. Indeed, Molina and Lessius had already discussed the arguments of the merchants in matters of interest, sometimes rejecting and sometimes accepting them,[37] but they were theologians concerned with morals.

A sharp attack on Noodt's monograph was made posthumously in 1729 by Christoph Raab from Duisburg university.[38] Raab was born around 1682 in Kalkar, studied letters and philosophy in Leiden,[39] and theology in Duisburg. After a short term as a minister in Cologne, in 1709 he was appointed as extraordinary professor in Duisburg, but only in 1723 did his appointment as ordinary professor follow. In 1729 he was rector for the second time. For some time he seems to have been suspended on a suspicion concerning his orthodoxy. He died in 1748.

Now, if there were doubts about his orthodoxy, there certainly cannot have been in the case of his opinion on the taking of oaths. Or was it precisely to allay suspicions that he defended a most rigorous opinion there? However that may be, Raab held that Christ's admonition not to take oaths (Matt. 5: 34, Jacob 5: 12) should be taken as literally as possible. Oaths should be avoided, unless absolutely necessary. Now this was a position which was totally at odds with everyday practice, in which the taking of oaths no doubt was even more frequent than it is nowadays. Justus Henning Böhmer, professor in Halle and writer of the standard work, *Jus ecclesiasticum protestantium usum hodiernum* (1720), thought that Christ's word should not be taken literally and did not, in fact, prohibit the taking of oaths. After discussing a series of arguments to that effect, he finally proposed the argument that Gerard Noodt used in a practically identical case, that is, the question whether Christ's word 'Lend without hoping for anything in return' must be taken so literally as to forbid not only the taking of interest, but even reclaiming the principal.[40]

With this Noodt's monograph came directly under attack, but apparently Raab did not feel too easy about it. In the years that he

37. See Weber, 1959: 153 f., 182, and *passim*. I thank Gerhard Otte for the reference.
38. Raab, 1729.
39. AS Leiden, 14 Sept. 1699: 'Cristophorus Raap Calcaria-Clivensis, 17 P et L'.
40. Tom. 1, lib. ii, tit. 24, § 19. 4th imp. Halle, 1738, p. 1276: 'Ad dissolvendum hoc dubium meditationem Gerardi Noodt, vir clarissimi . . . facio meam.'

studied in Leiden (1699–1703), Noodt was at the zenith of his fame, and Raab attended his private lectures with profit several times.[41] So Raab begins by acknowledging that Noodt argues effectively ('non inepte').[42] Several times he expresses his respect for his former Leiden teacher. Noodt is sharp-witted and erudite, and he has many merits besides. Moreover, he is not an avaricious man himself[43]—apparently, the sum he charged Raab for his private lectures had been reasonable. Noodt would have done better to refrain from writing a book on interest and usury in a nation which in these bad times is prone enough already to indulge in what is against the principles of the reformed religion.[44] Raab then supposes that Noodt was brought to his position by his ancestors, who were honourable, no doubt, but who (as Raab had been told by dependable people and is an established fact) for a series of years rented the local pawnshop in Nijmegen from the magistrates and earned their money in this way.[45] This remark, which we might seriously misconstrue if we took it as an early example of the sociology of science, is taken up as a grave insult in Nijmegen. The young Roukens indignantly opposes it.[46] How can one think that the patriciate of Nijmegen would occupy itself with something as infamous as a pawnshop? If the calumniator had studied public records carefully, he would have found no Noodt, Canis, Biesman, or Das as lessee of the pawnshop. No, the 'rabid Raab'[47] does not deserve any credence.

Roukens is probably right. I found, in fact, no member of the families named by Roukens as lessor of the pawnshop.[48] But that is not the whole story. For half a century the pawnshop was leased, in effect, to a member of the Nijmegen patriciate who was, moreover, an acquaintance of the Noodts: Willem Water(s), father and son. Here are, no doubt, the *fœneratores* whose arguments Noodt recapitulated.

41. Raab, 1729: suppl., p. 159: '. . . quem et ego olim Leidae privatim docentem cum fructu aliquoties audivi'.
42. Raab, 1729: suppl., p. 155.
43. Raab, 1729: suppl., p. 160: '. . . virum alias haud avarum'.
44. Raab, 1729: suppl., p. 160: '. . . potuisset is libro de Foenore et usuris, in Natione per se ad eam hisce cooruptis temporibus contra principia reformatae religionis . . . exercendam prona, scribendo supersedere'.
45. Raab, 1729: suppl., p. 160.
46. Roukens, 1767: 5.
47. Roukens, 1767: 6: 'hoc rabioso Rabio'.
48. I thank the personnel of the Nijmegen municipal archives for their help in my research of this point.

On 10 June 1627, the concession of the pawnshop was leased for ten years to Willem Water, who formally acted as attorney for the children of the late pawnbroker Philip Darmel.[49] This he claimed to do many years later still, but in fact he seems to have run the pawnshop himself. Water must have been born around 1605. On 9 September 1623, he enrolled as law student in Franeker.[50] Two years later he appears to have the licenciate and seeks admission to the Nijmegen bar.[51] In 1636 the concession of the pawnshop is renewed for twelve years,[52] although the city council had decided earlier, in view of the poor financial situation of the city, to let it by public auction to the highest bidder.[53] The council's policy always wavered between seeing the pawnshop as a milch cow or as a benevolent institution for the poor. The conditions of the new lease were substantial: a lump sum of 3,000 guilders and yearly 75 guilders for the poor, to be divided in equal portions over the hospital, the orphanage, and the poorhouse. In 1649 the concession is renewed once more, for sixteen years this time, and conditions are made more onerous. By that time, the Darmel children must have been well in their thirties! The lump sum is cut in half, but the yearly payment increased to 500 guilders, of which 75 guilders were for the poor.[54] In the meantime, Mr Willem Water, sen. had become a prominent man. From 1649 to 1662 he was member of the city council ('raadsvriend'), from 1663 till his death in 1670 alderman; he had several other offices, including those of governor of the university and the grammar school.[55] Apparently, he was among the city's intellectuals. In 1667 he wrote a laudatory verse in a book of the Nijmegen law professor Petrus de Greve,[56] which he signed as member of the city council ('senator') and alderman ('scabinus').

In September 1664, half a year before the third term of his lease

49. GA Nijmegen, OAN RS, 6 June 1627. Before then he had rented the bank provisionally for one year, see RS, 13 Apr. 1626 and 14 Mar. 1627.
50. AS Franeker, nr. 2055.
51. GA Nijmegen, OAN RS, 2 Nov. 1625.
52. GA Nijmegen, OAN RS, 3 Aug. 1636.
53. GA Nijmegen, OAN RS, 12 June 1635.
54. GA Nijmegen, OAN RS, 25 June 1649.
55. *Het stadhuis van Nijmegen* (Nijmegen, 1982): 181. On Jan. 1670, after his death, his official functions were reallotted by the city council. They were: governor of the university, governor of the grammar school, artillery-master, chief provisor to the council, provisor of the lepers, and captain of the Broerstraat.
56. P. de Greve, *Dissertationes ad Institutionum imperialium loca difficiliora*. Nijmegen, 1668. The verse is a duodecastichon. The signature reads: 'Wilh. Water JCTus, Reip. Neomag. Senat. et Scabin.'

expired, the council appointed delegates to deliberate with Mr Willem Water (an alderman himself, mind you) about the ways and means to exploit the pawnshop 'with the greatest profit to the city and the least harm to the poor'. In any case, the interest rate of 22 per cent must be reduced to 12 or 13 per cent.[57] Apparently, no agreement was reached. On 23 December 1664 the council decided to advertise that the bank would be leased by public auction to the highest bidder 'at the going out of the burning candle'.[58] As far as advertising was concerned, no half measures were planned. The auction was to be announced in the newspapers, as well as by posters, in the provinces of Brabant, Guelders, Holland, and Utrecht. If the auction had no success, the bank would be administered by delegates from the council and a cashier.[59] An extensive code of regulations for the bank was drafted and passed by the council in January 1665.

But, after this, nothing more is heard of the matter and it seems likely that Willem Water, sen. in fact kept the concession until his death in 1670.[60] Only a few years later a new pawnmaster was appointed. By then Willem Water, jun. had climbed to much more respectable offices. He was born in 1627,[61] the year in which his father leased the bank for the first time. In 1644 he enrolled as law student in Leiden.[62] I found no trace of his professional occupation in Nijmegen after his return from Leiden, *c.*1649. It seems likely that he worked with his father in the bank. It took him many years to make a political career. In 1671 he was nominated administrator of the orphanage of the poor, the same function as Noodt's father held in the citizen's children's orphanage. On 12 May 1674 he accepted a post as a member of the provisional city government instituted by William III,[63] which suggests he was a bit of an opportunist. Nijmegen regarded the autocratic measures of William as unlawful, and, as we saw, Noodt's father protested formally. Anyway, Willem Water became a member of the council and alderman.[64] But an incident in 1677 proved that he was not yet fully aware of what

57. GA Nijmegen, OAN RS, 28 Sept. 1664.
58. On this custom, see De Cock, 1897: 29; Wohlhaupter, 1937; Beyerman, 1959.
59. GA Nijmegen, OAN RS, 23 Dec. 1664.
60. Buried 16 Jan. 1670, GA Nijmegen, OAN Register St Steven 27.
61. Baptized 5 Oct. 1627, GA Nijmegen RBS 1164.
62. AS Leiden, 13 Sept. 1644: 'Wilhelmus Water Neomago-Gelrus 22 J.' At that time he was, in fact, not 22 but still 16. Apparently, he gave an older age, as usual, to avoid being pressed to enrol in the *artes* faculty first.
63. Maris, 1984: 124.
64. *Het stadhuis* (as n. 55): 181.

befitted a man in his position. In January of that year he accepted an appointment as clerk to the city court, but when the city council protested that one could not be member of the council and city clerk at the same time, he gave up the second office immediately.[65] In 1678 he was made librarian and in 1685 he finally reached the top as burgomaster and—like Peter Noodt—auditor of the city.[66] After doing his turn as burgomaster for two years he was alderman again from 1687–9. He died in 1690 at the age of 62.[67]

So it is true, after all, that the father of a member of the Nijmegen city patriciate (and perhaps that member itself) exercised the sordid trade of a pawnbroker, although he was not, as far as I know, a relative of the Noodts. But there is no doubt that Noodt knew both Waters well enough. In 1662–3, when Noodt as best pupil spoke the valedictory address at the grammar school, Water, sen. was one of its governors. In 1677 Noodt, Water, jun., and J. Verstegen gave a legal opinion to the Noble Court of Elst, concerning an important estate.[68] And in a letter Noodt wrote to his father from Franeker on 19 October 1679, he asked him to give his greetings to 'de Heer Waters'.[69] So we may conclude that the gossip reported by 'rabiate Raab', though not exact, was not too far from the truth either.

De jure summi imperii et lege regia

The echo which Noodt's first rectorial address, delivered in the aula of Leiden on 9 February 1699,[70] received among a wide audience, cannot be explained by the novelty of the subject or the originality of Noodt's ideas. The theory of sovereignty had been under discussion for many years and Noodt's position, though fairly radical in the eyes of some of his contemporaries, was deeply rooted in the tradition of political theory in the Republic, which from its inception was preoccupied with the justification of the Dutch revolt, but which, through the work of De la Court, Spinoza, Van der Muelen, and Huber, had reached a very high theoretical level by the end of the

65. GA Nijmegen, OAN RS, 7 Mar. 1677.
66. GA Nijmegen, OAN RS, 7 Feb. 1678; 2 Jan. 1685.
67. Buried at St Steven's, 13 May 1690, GA Nijmegen OAN, Rek. Stevenskerk, 33.
68. Van den Berg iii, 1784; nr. 135, pp. 339–46.
69. ARA Tets van Goudriaan, inv. nr. 105.
70. Ahsmann–Feenstra, 1984: nr. 436. Noodt's address does not figure in Kossmann, 1960.

century.[71] In the Republic Hobbes's absolutistic ideas had been contested long before.[72] Ideas similar to those of Locke had been developed independently[73] and a new synthesis of political theory was forged by Huber.[74] If it is true that political theory in the Republic in the seventeenth century in a way prefigured the development of theory in the Enlightenment and revolutionary France,[75] we may add that it may have been, among other things, Noodt's address, through its French translation by Barbeyrac, that summarized some of the Dutch achievements in political theory and made them known in Europe outside the small academic circles that read learned Latin treatises.

What made Noodt's address remarkable, moreover, were its style and the occasion. His argument, based on natural law and humanistic legal philology, was as clear, well-reasoned, and vigorous as ever. It was expressed in strong and unambiguous terms, and in the sublime Latin that matched the subject. That the rector of prestigious Leiden university expressed such opinions *ex cathedra* at that time was truly notable. As a journalist wrote in the *Journal littéraire* of 1714: 'La conjoncture du tems dans laquelle M. Noodt prononça ce Discours, fait bien voir son amour pour la verité. Ce fut pendant la vie de Guillaume III Roi d'Angleterre, qui a été tout puissant dans ce païs. Un pareil Discours ne pouvait guère manquer de déplaire à ce Prince, mais malgré tout cela M. Noodt ne voulut pas cacher ni déguiser ses véritables sentimens.'[76]

Naturally the journalist only speculated about the feelings of William III, but there is no doubt that Noodt's address must have displeased absolutists in every quarter and would have been regarded as anathema in the France of Louis XIV. Barbeyrac criticizes some journalists who treated Noodt's address as a seditious pamphlet and himself as no more than a pamphleteer, a *faiseur de discours*.[77] Noodt's stance is quite different indeed from that of Locke, who lived under the same king. He kept the authorship of the *Two treatises* a secret, even to his best friend, until after his death.[78]

From the Middle Ages, two ideas about the origin of sovereign

71. Kossmann, 1960.
72. Kossmann, 1960: 24 and *passim*.
73. Kossmann, 1960: 71 ff.
74. Kossmann, 1960: 82 ff.; Veen, 1967.
75. Kossmann, 1960: 59. And see Leeb, 1973.
76. *Journal littéraire*, 1714, 4: 1, art. iv. 62–97. I thank the much regretted Anneke Canoy-Olthoff for this reference.
77. Barbeyrac, 1731: 39 n. 1.
78. Clapp, 1967: 489.

power were defended: in the words of Ullmann,[79] the descending and the ascending theory of power. The first held that power was given to princes and magistrates by God. This was, for instance, the official doctrine in France. Naturally, the principle was elaborated in various ways. One consequence drawn by many was that if the king did wrong only God could punish him. According to the ascending theory, power was given to the ruler by the people. Arguing from this principle, scholars could reach widely different doctrines. Was the giving of power a revocable mandate or a definite transfer? Was power given unconditionally or under the terms of a social contract or constitution? Did the people give up its power completely and forever, or did it keep some power to itself? Did it have the right of rebellion in case the ruler became a tyrant? And specifically: who were the people?

In the Republic most scholars accepted in principle that power came from the people.[80] This was in line with the official state ideology, expressed *inter alia* in the *Placcæt van Verlatinge* of 1581, with which the States-General formally renounced their allegiance to Philip II. The king had been accepted under certain conditions and, as he had constantly violated them, the people was no longer bound to obey him.[81] Naturally, the notion of the people in this context was misleading. In fact, it was not the people, but only the body that had a share in political power, that is, the estates, that played a role.

The basis of sovereign power was under discussion in the humanistic intellectual circles to which Noodt belonged. In 1689 Ulrik Huber and Jacob Perizonius, both then professors in Franeker, had a sharp debate on the issue. Perizonius, Noodt's friend, argued that government power rested on mandate; Huber held that it was transferred by the people once and for all, was absolute and indivisible, and could never be taken back.[82] In the same context—it was a humanistic debate and the example of Antiquity still took a central position—the Roman *lex de imperio* or—as it was usually called—*lex regia* was discussed; that is, the law by which the Roman people invested the *princeps* with his *imperium*.

The story of the debate on the *lex regia* is long and complicated.[83] The Roman republic saw the institution of the *lex de imperio*, a law

79. Ullmann, 1975: 30f. and *passim*, with further literature.
80. Cf. Kossmann, 1960: *passim*; Veen, 1985*a*: 322.
81. Veen, 1982.
82. Veen, 1985*a*: 322.
83. See Morel, 1970; Veen, 1985*a*.

by which the consuls chosen in the meeting of the people were formally invested with *imperium*. In the first century of our era, the Roman *princeps* began to use this old legal formula for a new purpose. Augustus had accumulated his various powers over a period of many years, but later his successors received the same powers on succession in one law, the *lex de imperio*. This law formed an ideological legitimization of the new phenomenon of monocratic power; Ulpian (D 1. 4. 1. pr.) expressly refers to it as the foundation of the legislative power of the *princeps*. At some time this must have been a serious, if mainly formal, constitutional problem.[84] Naturally, in the time-honoured list of public acts of institutions which could set the law, the *constitutio principis* had no place. So the traditional canon must have been adapted to the growing dominance of imperial legislation somewhere in the first or second century.[85] It is not certain at what date this *lex de imperio* got the name *lex regia*, the term used by Ulpian and Justinian[86] and therefore the term received in the Middle Ages.

The glossators naturally knew the *lex regia* from the Corpus Juris, but as they mostly were defenders of absolute imperial power—to which they owed part of their success—they gave little attention to it.[87] Placentinus taught that the Roman people transferred all the power they had had in the republic once and for all to the emperor and held nothing back.[88] But, in the middle of the fourteenth century, discussion was revived when in Rome a bronze tablet was found which—according to the dominant but still contested opinion of scholars—contained a fragment of the *lex de imperio* given to the Emperor Vespasian (69–79) at his inauguration.[89] The tablet immediately became an issue in contemporary political debate. The tablet was fixed on the wall in the basilica of S. John Lateran (where it remained until 1576) and surrounded by paintings showing how the Roman senate invested Vespasian with the *imperium*. The learned Roman leader of the people, Cola di Rienzo (1313–54), who was in power, organized a meeting in the basilica. After the text of the fragment was read and the powers of Vespasian enumerated, Cola di Rienzo's speech reached its climax: 'Now you see, my Lords, so mighty was the Roman people that the emperor received his power

84. Traces of the debate in Gai. 1. 5 and C 1. 14. 12.
85. Kaser, 1978: 107.
61. D 1. 4. 1 pr.; Inst. 1. 2. 6.
87. See the gloss on D 1. 4. 1 pr.
88. The text in Van den Bergh, 1982*b*: 63.
89. *FIRA* i: 154f.

from it.'[90] So Cola di Rienzo founded the sovereignty of the Roman people on the tablet.

Discussions about the interpretation of the tablet ranged very wide indeed. There were mainly two theories that were defended, and both of them were related to the political attitudes of the scholars in question. And, naturally, both theories were elaborated in various ways, with the result that a great variety of doctrines developed. One branch of theory held that the Roman people yielded its power once and for all, and without retaining anything for itself—*donner et retenir ne vaut*. This was what seemed acceptable to at least some of the defenders of absolute monarchy. In fact, it reduced the *lex regia* to a purely historical phenomenon, marking the transition from the republic to the principate in ancient Rome.

The other theory was much more controversial. If you read the tablet carefully, Noodt contended, you will see that the people did not give the emperor unqualified sovereign power, but rather a series of precisely defined items. And if the emperor received *imperium* under certain conditions, it could be taken back when the emperor, by violating the conditions of his acceptance, became a tyrant. Here the notion of the *lex regia* merged with the medieval institution of the 'joyeuse entrée', which was often regarded as a kind of contract between prince and subjects.[91] This was a dangerous theory. It postulated sovereignty of the people, if not as the normal condition—one could hardly think of a state without a prince—then at least in the extreme case of tyranny. This complex of ideas actually played a role in the justification of the rebellion of the Netherlands and became part of the Republic's state ideology. Echoes of it are found as late as 1796 in the indictment against William V, the prince who, according to the patriots, had committed high treason and by this fact had liberated his subjects from their allegiance to him.[92]

In France, however, discussion of the *lex regia* was not allowed at all. The king had his power from God, not from the people. In the sixteenth century an advocate pleading before the Parlement de Paris dared to suggest that the king had received his power from the people

90. Von Beseler, 1929: 159 f.
91. Reibstein, 1972.
92. See B. Voorda and J. Valckenaer, *Rechtsgeleerd advis in de zaak van den gewezen stadhouder, en over deszelfs schrijven aan de gouverneurs van de Oost- en West-Indische bezittingen van den staat*. Ingeleverd ter vergadering der provisionele representanten op den 7 January 1796; met wederleggende aanteekeningen van een Hollansch Rechtsgeleerden [Tollius], 1796: 218 f.

through the *lex regia*. The 'gens du roy' immediately protested fiercely and it cost the poor man his job. In 1590 the advocate-general Severin spoke 'la mort sans phrase' over the detested theory: France is not governed by the ancient *lex regia* of the Romans, but by other customs. It is by God and succession, not by vote or election, that the king reigns.[93] Naturally, scholars tried in various ways to reconcile the *lex regia* with absolute kingship, but that is not relevant to our purpose. I only want to stress that Barbeyrac, who translated Noodt's address into French and thus made it famous all over Europe, was a refugee from the absolutist France of Louis XIV.

In the Republic, the *lex regia* was much discussed, together with the theory of sovereignty, in the second half of the seventeenth century. In 1661 Martin Schoock published a pamphlet in which he denied the historical existence of the *lex regia*.[94] Schoock was a learned, but rather controversial pamphleteer, who began as a follower of Gisbert Vœt and therefore opposed Cartesians, Catholics, Remonstrants, and Socinians.[95] In 1643 he published a book in his name, which Vœt later admitted he had written himself. Ulrik Huber wrote an extensive refutation of Schoock.[96] Because Huber was mainly interested in the general theory of the state, he did not give an accurate picture of the historical development of the *lex regia* in Antiquity. For him it was still, as for Placentinus, the historical act which marked the transfer of power from the Roman people to the *princeps*. Already in 1671, however, the famous Leiden classicist J. F. Gronovius, in a rectorial address, gave a much better historical account of the gradual accumulation over a long period of various powers by Augustus. Only his successors had these powers summarized in one law at their inauguration, and even then some of them refused to take some titles. Because Gronovius died at the end of 1671, the address was only published seven years later.[97] Noodt followed the views of Gronovius concerning the history of the *lex regia* in Antiquity in his own address.[98]

No doubt for Noodt personal experiences from his youth in Nijmegen mixed with his scholarly interests. When in 1672 William III came to power, the eastern provinces of the Republic were in for some very disconcerting experiences. Utrecht, Overijssel, and Guelders, 'liberated' after the retreat of the French in 1674, were

93. Morel, 1970: 552.
94. Cf. Veen, 1985*a*: 323 f.
95. Cf. Kossmann, 1960: 27.
96. Veen, 1985*a*: 323 f.
97. Cf. Barbeyrac, 1731: 232 n. 1.
98. *Opera* i: 629.

treated rather like occupied territories. It took some time before Holland was prepared to accept them again as members of the Union. The full powers the States-General gave to William on 20 April 1674, to arrange government in the three provinces, were used by him to establish absolute rule there. In Guelders he even made a bid for the monarchical position.[99] The detested 'Regeringsreglement' imposed by William in 1675 put an end to republican freedom and city democracy in Nijmegen as well. Magistrates were no longer to be elected, but nominated by the prince. As we have seen, Noodt's father, speaker of the 'gemeenslieden' in Nijmegen, fiercely protested against the new ordinance. Several of William's creatures soon sought to institute a tyrannical government.[1] Noodt may very well have been thinking of them when he said 'There are so very few who stand for the people, whereas the most under the figure of the prince plead for the tyrant'.[2] In the eastern provinces the oppressive character of aristocratic absolutism, which perhaps was a bit more theoretical in Huber's Friesland,[3] was a bitter reality and the people had no chance to safeguard themselves against it by demanding a constitution. From 1675 half of the bourgeoisie (the 'gemeente') was simply excluded from any political influence and the chances for its families to be admitted amongst the *optimates* in a regular way were very lean indeed. When in 1702, after William's death and only three years after Noodt's address, the 'gemeente' demanded to be restored to its political rights, the aristocrats flatly refused and the result was a bloody rebellion, the proper beginning of the century which was to end with the great revolution.[4] In this context it may be interesting to note that in the closing sentence of his rectorial address on the *lex regia* Noodt refers to the fact that the new rector of Leiden was appointed by royal letters as well.[5]

In liberal intellectual circles all over Europe, confronted as they were by growing absolutism, Noodt's traditionally republican address, marking the revival of the concept of sovereignty of the people which was forbidden in France and largely forgotten in Dutch

99. Rogier, 1954: 197; Wertheim-Gijse Weenink, 1975: 229.
1. Rogier, 1954: 197.
2. *Opera* i: 623. 'Adeo rari sunt qui pro populo stent, cum plerique, sub Principis persona agant tyranni causam.'
3. Cf. Kossmann, 1960: 102.
4. See above, Ch. 2, § 1, at n. 55.
5. *Opera* i: 633: '. . . Regias enim exspectatis literas, quibus in proximum annum mihi successor, Magnificus Academiae Rector, dabitur'.

political theory during the first half of the century,[6] made a fairly radical impression. If Locke's second treatise (with which Noodt's speech shares several arguments as well as some theoretical flaws) can be regarded as one of the documents preparing the ground for modern democratic government, Noodt's speech deserves a place in its own right beside it. As we will see, its influence actually reached to the revolutionary period at the end of the eighteenth century. It did not draw as immediate and widespread attention, however, as the address on freedom of religion in 1706. Although a second impression appeared in 1705,[7] Noodt's international fame seems to take off only with the appearance of the French translation of both addresses by Barbeyrac in 1707,[8] which was followed by the first English translation by John Savage (after Barbeyrac) in 1708.[9] Both addresses were reprinted several times, but the first Dutch translation of the address on freedom of religion appeared immediately in 1706,[10] that of the other address only ten years later.[11] This translation had only one impression, that of the other address six. Not counting the various editions of the *Opera omnia*, the address on freedom of religion had fifteen editions,[12] that on sovereignty ten.[13]

I have already referred to John Locke several times, and not without reason. There are obvious parallels between the first part of Noodt's address and Locke's second treatise, which appeared in 1690. Their natural law reasoning concerning the origin of sovereignty roughly runs along the same lines. Both accept the modern, individualistic concept of natural law, in which individual self-preservation is the supreme commandment of God to men.[14] Both defend, following Grotius and against Spinoza,[15] that the natural state of freedom for all men is not a state of licence.[16] Both

6. Kossmann, 1960: 23.
7. Ahsmann–Feenstra, 1984: nr. 437.
8. Ahsmann–Feenstra, 1984: nr. 438.
9. Ahsmann–Feenstra, 1984: nr. 442.
10. Ahsmann–Feenstra, 1984: nr. 453. Repr. in 1707, 1716, 1719, 1734, and 1774, see Ahsmann–Feenstra, 1984: nrs. 454–8.
11. Ahsmann–Feenstra, 1984: nr. 444.
12. Two in Latin (1706, 1708), six in Dutch (1706, 1707, 1716, 1719, 1737, 1774), three in French (1707, 1714, 1731), two in English (1708, 1781), and two in German (1724, 1728). See Ahsmann–Feenstra, 1984.
13. Two in Latin (1699, 1706), two in Dutch (1716, 1784), four in French (1707, 1714, 1731, 1775), and two in English (1708, 1781). See Ahsmann–Feenstra, 1984.
14. Noodt, *Opera* i: 626: 'An quis ambigit hanc esse naturae legem, ut quisque quod ei utile est, sequatur, ac quod noxium est, evitet; ea vero lege quam Dei providentia ad humani generis salutem jussit, nemo se solvere debet . . .'; cf. Kossmann, 1960: 72.
15. Kossmann, 1960: 57.
16. Noodt, *Opera* i: 624; Locke, Essay 6 (60).

conclude that power is given to the prince by the people, both assume a social contract, and both accept the right of rebellion.

Naturally, there are differences too. Partly they result from the different scope of each work. Noodt had no intention of elaborating a political theory, but only wanted to discuss the concept of sovereignty as a jurist involved in humanism and natural law. Therefore, many topics dealt with by Locke are not found in Noodt's address. But there are also material differences. Noodt is evidence of the advances made by Dutch political theory in the seventeenth century. Social contract is not the only form in which the people can give power to the prince. It can also give up its sovereignty without making any condition or constitution, and it may even deliver itself in slavery to a victor.[17] Not that this makes a difference to Noodt: in all cases, natural law limits the rights of the ruler. So the people have, in effect, inalienable rights. But varieties of transfer of power from people to prince are not discussed by Locke. Neither is the *lex regia*, which seems more of a continental humanistic topic.

It seems improbable that Locke influenced Noodt directly. It must be remarked, in the first place, that the *Two Treatises* were published in English, a language which Noodt (and Barbeyrac, for that matter) most likely did not read. When preparing the address on the freedom of religion, six years later, Noodt could make use of Locke's *Epistola de tolerantia*, published in Holland in 1689 and 1705, and Barbeyrac has pointed out some parallels there.[18] But the *Two Treatises*, published anonymously moreover, seem to have been still unknown to Barbeyrac in 1731.[19] Although by 1691 a French translation of the treatises had appeared anonymously in Amsterdam,[20] Locke's influence on political theory in France seems mainly to have expanded in the second half of the following century.[21] In so far as they use similar arguments, Locke and Noodt will have drawn on the same sources. In the Republic, Van der Muelen seems to have developed independently a theory almost identical with Locke's; it

17. On these various modes in Huber's theory, see Kossmann, 1960: 90 f.
18. See below, p. 227.
19. In the 1731 edn. of the French translation in which Barbeyrac published the life of Noodt and made additions to his notes, no reference to Locke is found yet.
20. *Du gouvernement civil, ou l'on traitte de l'origine, des fondemens, de la nature du pouvoir et des fins des sociétez politiques*, translation. Amsterdam: A. Wolfgang, 1691. Announced in the *Bibliothèque universelle et historique*, May, 1691. See Bots *et al.*, 1981: 243.
21. Olivier-Martin, 1948: 659.

actually appeared a year before the *Two Treatises*.[22] Noodt and Locke had some friends in common among the Amsterdam Remonstrants, but naturally this does not imply that they knew each other. In Locke's correspondence only one reference to Noodt is found. On 29 August 1700 Benjamin Furly wrote from Rotterdam that Noodt had paid him a visit that same day and had asked him to give his compliments and a copy of *De imperio* to Locke.[23] This suggests that Noodt only heard about Locke after the publication of his own address, perhaps from someone like Jean le Clerc.

Noodt's address, which has as its telling motto Tacitus' saying (*Hist.* 1. 1) about the rare happiness of the times in which one can think what one wishes and say what one thinks,[24] is a nice sample of his main research interests. The first half,[25] concerning the legal theory of sovereignty, is devoted to natural law speculations; in the second half,[26] which concerns the *lex regia*, humanistic legal philology takes a central place. Noodt tries to capture his audience immediately, abruptly opening with a discussion of the differences between prince and tyrant. Noodt is amazed that great and brilliant men have attributed the same rights of sovereignty to both, although they are more different than anything else. One rules with the consent of his subjects, the other against their will; one has his eye on the common interest, the other only on his own; one is godlike, the other is like a huge and cruel monster coming from his lair, only causing terror, flight, and destruction.

The power of the prince is determined by the law, not by his fancy. And yet many claim that it is of the essence of sovereignty that the prince is not bound by law (*princeps legibus solutus*), to such extent even that if the prince follows his own interest instead of that of his subjects, they can do nothing about it, except deserve the glory of obedience and suffering, with only God to punish him. They say that it is better for subjects to suffer from the crimes of the prince than for the prince to be corrected by his subjects, to prevent them being

22. Kossmann, 1960: 71 f. If, however, Laslett's thesis that Locke wrote the 2nd treatise between 1679 and 1681 is correct, the date of publication is not decisive; cf. Clapp, 1967: 498.
23. Locke, 1982: no. 2761, pp. 126–7.
24. Tacitus became very popular with anti-machiavellist political theorists in the 16th century, when Lipsius did important work on him, and he was much read in the 17th century too; see Stolleis, 1980: 12 f.
25. *Opera* i: 624–8. See the marginal notes of Barbeyrac on his translation, Amsterdam 1731.
26. *Opera* i: 628–33.

destroyed. To Noodt this doctrine is utterly repugnant. It deforms the *imperium*, intended for the peace and welfare of mankind, into its ruin.

It is an error to think that luxury, greed, violence, cruelty, perfidy, and all the other vices that licence breeds are qualities of majesty. The greatest majesty of all is God's, and he rules in accordance with the laws he has set himself. Why, then, should it be different for a prince? Why not demand that he who is said to represent God on earth follow God's example and let himself be led by reason? Sovereignty is not instituted by God, but if it was, it would be blasphemy to assume that God entitled the prince to commit crimes. Yet princes did not descend from heaven, they were chosen by men. Natural reason brought men together and made them establish the rules and powers without which society could not exist. To explain this Noodt gives the traditional picture of the origin of society. In nature all men were free and equal. All are endowed with the same instinct of self-preservation and therefore all have the same right to everything nature has made available for that purpose. But the natural right of everybody to seek anything that is useful was not licence to commit crimes. Nature gave man reason as a superior gift.

It was by natural drives that man sought the society of his fellows: sexual attraction, the tedium of loneliness, the hope of advantages, the consideration of his fragile state as a single man. But, in the long run, experience taught that if each man continued to act according to his natural freedom and by his own judgment, there would never be peace and quiet. This consideration made some men unite and form a state. And because it was impossible for all men to come together at any moment to regulate affairs, they chose a person of known trustworthiness and skill to judge cases, and finally they surrendered their natural power to him.

The conclusion from this is that princes were not instituted by nature. Men, made by nature the judges of their own interest, chose leaders by their own will and convention. We cannot assume that men were such fools as to choose squanderers of the common weal for princes, or freely agreed to be driven, milked, shaved, murdered, skinned, and devoured like cattle. Neither reason nor natural law allows this. Magistrates only have the power they need to maintain that public society without which nobody could be free and safe. If they go beyond that they no longer act as magistrates or princes.

It makes no difference whether the prince was instituted under the terms of a contract or not. The law of nature which obliges man to seek his own interest prohibits his self-destruction. So if the prince ruins the people, he can never do this by its consent and lawfully. Even if the people surrenders, it does so in what it sees as its best interest in the situation. The law of nature is that everybody seeks what is useful and avoids what is harmful, and from that law, which God's providence has given for the preservation of the human race, nobody must release himself, nor could he if he wished. If a people has given itself in servitude, there is no rule between master and servant. Both have the same natural right to judge and vindicate their own interest. The master may try to kill them, but they have the right to fly or fight back and kill the master. Property is not an absolute right either. The reason for things to be divided was common welfare, not squandering. Even civil law has taken measures against dissipation. And even the right of life and death given by Roman law with respect to slaves and sons was not intended for their destruction, but for their correction.

The second part Noodt opens with the discussion of yet another objection: the prince is said to be free of the laws by authority of civil law itself, on account of Ulpian's famous saying *princeps legibus solutus est* (D 1. 3. 31). Noodt begins by making it clear that for him Antiquity no longer has absolute authority: 'I would expect reason, not authority. In discussing matters of sovereignty it is not the law of one minor society that concerns us, but only the law of that greater one which spans the whole earth'.[27] If, nevertheless, one would like to discuss civil law, Noodt is prepared to do so.

You say that the prince is not bound by the laws. But by what laws, civil as well as natural? Ulpian makes no distinction. So is the prince not bound by universal and eternal natural law? Yes he is, but the prince is bound by natural law only unto God, not unto his subjects. So had Nero nothing to fear from the law when he poisoned Brittanicus? But that cannot be true, and it is not. From other texts of the same Ulpian (D 43. 8. 2. 10; D 5. 2. 8. 5) as well as from constitutions (C 6. 50. 4; C 6. 23. 3) it is clear that the *princeps* is bound by natural as well as civil law.

Yet Ulpian writes, you say, that the *princeps* is not bound by the laws? But by force of what law? By force of the *lex regia*, you say

27. *Opera* i: 628: 'Ego vero non auctoritatem, sed rationem exspectabam. Cum enim de jure Imperii disputamus, non lex huius minoris civitatis quaestioni est, sed illum majoris quae cum sole finis metitur.'

(here Noodt directly opposes Huber), by which the Roman people transferred all its rights and powers to Augustus? But Augustus was never given *imperium* by a *lex regia*.[28] As Johannes Gronovius has proved, he accumulated his powers over a long period. No doubt Augustus was freed from some laws, but not from all. The fragment of the *lex de imperio Vespasiani*[29] proves that this is the truth. It says literally that Vespasian is free from the laws from which his predecessors were freed and bound to those to which they were bound.

To this is added a palingenetic argument, which Cujas had proposed. In D 1. 3. 31 Ulpian does not speak of the laws in general but only, as the inscription of the fragment proves, of the *leges Julia et Papia Poppæa*. The plural *legibus* does not have to mean all or many laws. Latin usage, which is so important for the study of Roman law, proves that the word may often refer just to a single law. But even if the Roman people gave the *princeps* the power to alter the law, it did this with a reason and not as a licence for its own ruin. This again is proved by the very words of the *lex de imperio Vespasiani*: The *princeps* is given the power to do what he thinks fit 'for the good of the republic and for the dignity of divine and human, public and private matters'.[30] The people never allowed the *princeps* to do everything with unbounded licence, nor did it give him immoderate and boundless powers. The *lex regia* can indeed be compared with the mandate of *libera administratio* to a procurator under private law.

Noodt does not deny that many emperors did the most terrible things. But they were monsters, not men. They did not act on the authority of the *lex regia* and were regarded as tyrants. And the senate treated them as such, when it declared Nero a public enemy, ordered the memory of Domitian to be erased, and the body of Commodus to be dragged along by a hook and thrown in the Tiber.

Finally, Noodt discusses arguments of a more pragmatic nature. Away with a doctrine, they say, which violates the regard for *imperium* and loosens the bonds of human society. It is true that where there are men, there are vices, and especially in courts. And even if there were not, ordinary people would remain suspicious.

28. Here Noodt seems directly to contradict Huber; cf. Veen, 1985*b*.

29. Noodt, *Opera* i: 630, says that it is in the basilica of St John Lateran, but in 1576 by order of Gregory XIII it had been transferred to the Capitoline museum, see *FIRA* i: 154.

30. Noodt, *Opera* i: 631; cf. *FIRA* i: 156: 'utique quaecunque ex usu rei publicae majestate[que] divinarum huma[na]rum publicarum privatarumque rerum esse censebit, ei agere facere ius potestasque sit . . .'.

Even good plans can come to a bad end and often people judge intentions from results. Moreover, what seems virtue to one is vice to another. If the height of *imperium* depended on the fickleness of ordinary people, this would make any government miserable and uncertain. But would one prefer instead that the people could not depose even the worst of princes? This is contrary to natural reason and to the experience of most peoples. One may call it a dangerous doctrine, weakening the position of magistrates, which are necessary for human life. But what has a good prince to fear, a prince who takes care of general peace, who justly and courageously defends the goods, the lives, and the freedom of his citizens, who does not hold scholars in suspicion but furthers their efforts? Certainly one must not depose a prince lightly, but when it comes to the worst the people has the right as well as the duty to put the tyrant down. It is not by birth or country that we distinguish the citizen from the enemy. If I am treated wrongly, it makes no difference whether it is by the enemy, a highwayman, or my sovereign. The injustice is the same in each case. If the people is forced to defend itself against cruelty and injustice, it is not responsible for the ensuing civil war. The Emperor Marcus Antonius himself acknowledged this when he said that all emperors who were killed were responsible for this themselves. Hardly ever was a good prince killed.

As usual, Noodt does not give references—apart from the one to Gronovius—but it is evident that at various points he was following earlier French humanists. Apparently he shared with them the general view that the prince was the mandatary of the people. Nor did Noodt name his 'absolutist' opponents, but we can be fairly certain that the late Ulrik Huber was prominent among them. Most 'absolutist' theses rejected by Noodt—the unhistorical interpretation of the *lex regia*, the idea that the Roman people conferred all its sovereignty on Augustus unconditionally and irrevocably, the thesis that the prince is free to do injustice, that only God may punish the king, that the people must suffer every wrong—are found in Huber's work.[31] If, for the historical account of the development of the *lex regia*, Noodt duly acknowledged his debt to Gronovius, there is one point for which he largely deserves the credit, and in which he shows himself far superior to Huber as a legal historian. It seems that Noodt was the first scholar in his age actually to read closely the inscription

31. See Veen, 1985*a*; 1985*b*.

of the *lex de imperio Vespasiani*. If Huber had done so, how could he have ignored the express provision that Vespasian was bound to the laws his predecessors were bound to, a passage absolutely irreconcilable with his theory?

If, as Barbeyrac maintained, Noodt's address was a fine piece of scholarship and not a seditious pamphlet, it was certainly a good specimen of the explosive mixture that humanistic philology and natural law theory could brew. Its influence actually reached to the revolutionary days at the end of the eighteenth century.[32] The great jurists of the preceding age were still authorities then, and just as the patriots criticized the 'absolutist' Huber as a furtherer of tyranny,[33] so Noodt was extolled as the champion of the sovereignty of the people. In 1784, at the high point of the patriot revolt which was to founder only three years later, a new Dutch translation of Noodt's address was published.[34] On the verso of the title-page, the anonymous translator put a quotation from the constitution of Pennsylvania and his lengthy preface sets the address in its correct perspective. Although Price and Priestley[35] have defended the natural rights of mankind on the most fair grounds, they are not yet generally accepted. There are jurists who try to wrest sovereignty from the Dutch people, who further unrest, who bow to one servant of the state, who try to undermine the constitution and to fetter the Dutch people in the chains of despotism. There are even professors proposing theses which make the foundations of the Dutch commonwealth shudder and which, if accepted, would make the servant rule over its master and turn the people into slaves.

Therefore, there is every reason to expound the doctrine of sovereignty of the people. For that reason, the translator wants to present Noodt's address once more. It does not contain despicable theses or mean sophistries. The free citizens will find proof here of their inviolable sovereignty; they will see that all regents and even the

32. See Leeb, 1973: 39, 72, 136, 171, 208.
33. Kossmann, 1960: 100.
34. Ahsmann–Feenstra, 1984: nr. 445. The translator used the 1714 edn. of Barbeyrac's translation (Ahsmann–Feenstra, 1984: nr. 439); see his preface, p. x.
35. Works by Price and Priestley were translated by the famous Dutch patriot Joan Derk van der Capellen tot den Pol, and in ideas and terminology the translator's preface is very close indeed to Van der Capellen's *Aan het volk van Nederland* (1781). But Van der Capellen cannot be identical with the translator because the first died in June 1784, while the last fact mentioned in the preface is the final deposition of Brunswick-Wolffenbüttel by the States of Holland (the annulment of the Act of Advisorship), 18 Aug. 1784.

despotic monocrat receive their power from the people; they will learn that the people does not have to tolerate crying maltreatment, even if it has transferred sovereignty without any terms of contract.

The anonymous translator even stresses the timeliness of Noodt's address for his own days. It shows how laudable it was that the citizens of Utrecht demanded that a regent whom they detested be excluded from the council hall.[36] It will make them praise the sovereign of Holland now that he has dismissed from that province the Duke of Wolffenbüttel.[37] It will teach, finally, that no regent is above the law and that if the hereditary stadholder violates the laws of the union, the terms of his nomination, and natural law, if he tries to subvert the constitution with the help of foreign nations, mercenaries, and the army, the citizens are fully entitled, with the assent of God himself, to fight him, depose him, and even punish him. And this was what actually happened, if only in 1795 and with help of the French revolutionary armies.

We do not know who the translator was. Most likely he was a jurist, and he betrays his provenance from the eastern provinces of the Republic[38]—from which so many patriots came—by one word in his translation. In the discussion of the various powers of Augustus,[39] 'consul' is translated as usual as 'burgomaster', but 'tribunicia potestas' is translated by a word that is at home only in Overijssel and Guelders: 'magt van Gemeensman'.[40] With this word a circle is closed. The *Regeringsreglement* of 1675, against which Noodt's father Peter, 'gemeensman' in Nijmegen, had protested, barred part of the citizens from political influence and thus became one of the foments of discontent, which exploded for the first time in 1702 and finally issued in the broad stream of patriotic revolt and revolution. The same period marks the shift of focus from democracy in the city to democracy in the state.

36. This refers to the Orangist R. M. van Goens, who was forced to give up his place in the Utrecht city council in June 1783; cf. Schama, 1977: 85.
37. This refers to the decision of the States of Holland to declare the Act of Advisorship null and void, 18 Aug. 1784; Brunswick left the Republic in October, see Blok iii, 192: 607.
38. He could have belonged to the patriot circle in Deventer around Van der Capellen tot den Pol, see ORG 1984, and see n. 35.
39. *Opera* i: 629; Noodt, 1784: 80.
40. 'Gemeensman' was the term for representatives of the 'gemeente', e.g. in Deventer and Nijmegen. From 1674 the 'gemeente' was excluded from political influence on the city government, which was monopolized by the regent families.

Julius Paulus sive de partus expositione et nece apud veteres

The importance of studying carefully the historical development of Roman law, which was stressed in *De foenore et usuris*, is even more prominent in the book that appeared two years later: *Julius Paulus*, or concerning the exposition and killing of children among the ancients.[41] And, likewise, the distance from orthodox Christian positions is widening. As the subject seems purely 'antiquarian', it may come as a surprise to modern readers that the book was so controversial. Barbeyrac regarded the subject as not very important and towards the end of the eighteenth century the debate on infanticide in Antiquity was regularly cited by champions of codification as a standard example of the uselessness of Roman law.[42] Yet the book went through three impressions and was attacked more sharply than any other, and by no less a scholar than Cornelis van Bijnkershœk. This is another indication that the relevance of scientific research was judged by differing criteria then as now.

The central issue of the book was at what moment in history exposing and killing new-born children was prohibited.[43] It was undisputed, at least since the days of the first humanists, that ancient Greeks and Romans, like numerous other primitive tribes, did not regard it as a crime to expose or kill new-born children which were deformed or which one could not afford to feed properly. According to Philo Judæus it was widely believed that a child was hardly a human being before it began to be fed. As far as the paterfamilias was concerned, this was only an aspect of his right over life and death, the *ius vitæ necisque*,[44] but mothers could also expose their new-born children with impunity. From the Middle Ages it had been generally accepted that the Christians had immediately put an end to this despicable custom. The writings of the fathers contained numerous eloquent denunciations of the pagan habit; they condemned contraception as well as abortion in all circumstances.[45] The glossators did

41. Ahsmann–Feenstra, 1984: nrs. 446–8.
42. Barbeyrac, *Vita*; Noodt, *Opera* i: 7^{v}; Pilato de Tassulo ii, 1774: 127; Schorer, 1777: 4–6, 41; van der Vlugt, 1916: 12. Another example of the unhappy effect of *ars critica* on legal practice, and another debate between Van Bijnkershœk and Noodt concerned D 10. 4. 3 pr.; see below, Ch. 4, at n. 98.
43. *Opera* i: 567.
44. Kaser, 1971: 60 f.
45. The Aristotelian distinction between *foetus inanimatus* and *animatus* (for the male foetus 40 days after conception, for the female 80 days) was received in civil as well as in canon law (C 32, q. 2, c. 8; Gregorius XIV, cons. *Sedes Apostolica*, 31 May

not notice anything different in the Corpus Juris. They assumed that in all cases of abortion or killing of children, the *lex Cornelia de sicariis et veneficiis* (81 BC) applied.[46] The early humanists, who knew their classical authors well enough, did not depart from established opinion. As distinguished scholars as Cujas, Rævardus, and Giphanius, while sensing some problem, never challenged it. It was the classicist Justus Lipsius who first suggested that the exposing and killing of new-born children might only have been made a crime in the fourth century, in the reign of the Emperors Valentinianus, Valens, and Gratianus. Noodt undertook to prove this hypothesis, which Lipsius had only formulated in a casual way, in due form and with all the wealth of his erudition. It was a thesis with far-reaching implications.

The first part of the book is strictly chronological. After discussing the attitude of the Greeks, Noodt treats the regulations of Romulus and of the Twelve Tables, which limited the right to kill new-born children without completely prohibiting it. Later these rules fell in desuetude, and neither during the republic nor under the principate, or under the rule of Diocletian and his immediate successors, was the killing of children a criminal offence. Constantine, the first Christian emperor, did not punish parents who had exposed their children, but ordered the children to be fed and taken care of (C. Th. 11. 27. 1), and allowed parents in extreme poverty to sell their children, stipulating only that they could not reclaim them later, unless they repaid expenses incurred for feeding and education (C 4. 43. 2). It was in 374 that the Emperors Valentinianus, Valens, and Gratianus ruled that everyone should feed his own children and that the exposing and killing of them was a capital crime (C 8. 51. 2 and C 9. 16. 7). There is, to be sure, a famous text of the classical jurist Julius Paulus, who lived in the second century (D 25. 3. 4), saying that not only does he who suffocates an infant seem to kill it, but also he who throws it away, refuses to feed it, or exposes it in a public place, leaving it to the mercy of others. But from this text we cannot conclude that exposing was already a crime in classical times.

Noodt tries to explain this text away by two methods. First, he

1591, Gasparri i, 1933: 330; the distinction was only abandoned with the constitution *Apostolicae sedis* of Pius IX, 12 Oct. 1869, Gasparri iii, 19: 24, see Roberti, 1968: 88), but the killing of a *foetus inanimatus*, though not homicide punishable by death, none the less was a crime, see Reiffenstuel vi, 335.

46. Gloss 'perfocat' on D 25. 3. 4.

contests the validity of the *argumentum a consequentia* with a series of examples from literary as well as legal sources. Often we may not hold true what logically seems to be implied in the word of an author; e.g. D 27. 10. 4 speaks of the unequal *potestas* of both parents, whereas it is evident that only the father, not the mother has *potestas* over a child in the legal sense.[47] Secondly—and this is an interesting and dangerous theory—one must distinguish between *decreta* and *praecepta*, between *jus civitatis* and *jurisprudentia* or *civilis sapientia*.[48] The art of law comprises theory and practice or, as Noodt puts it, *scientia* as well as *actio*; therefore law, like (Aristotelian) philosophy, contains *decreta* which appeal to *scientia*, and *praecepta* which guide actions. *Decreta* may be true or false, *praecepta* only state what is a desirable course of action.[49] The most famous text in the class of *praecepta* naturally is the maxim from Ulpian's *Regulae* which is recorded in D 1. 1. 10. 1: 'Juris praecepta sunt haec: honeste vivere, alterum non lædere, suum cuique tribuere.'[50] Paul's words in D 25. 3. 4 belong to the same class. They do not state positive law of classical times but give an admonition towards justice.

This leads Noodt to an interesting discussion of the function of laws. Ulpian's *præceptum* is compared with the words of Modestinus in D 1. 3. 7: 'The power of the law is to command, to forbid, to permit, and to punish.' The law has to command or to forbid, not to recommend or dispute.[51] Its aim is not to pursue wisdom, but to protect human society from stupid and wicked people. But Modestinus rightly says that the law also permits. It must permit a lot because it cannot contain everything, and it is meant for imperfect people. If it is written on a model of perfect wisdom and does not allow for the imperfections of the age or the frailty that is common to all mankind, the law will become vain or unjust. But this implies that the man who wants to be good and just must not have before his eyes the tables of the law, but primarily the union of human society. If the

47. *Opera* i: 577. Solazzi suggested that the words 'etsi . . . potestas' were interpolated, see *Index int. a.h.l.*
48. *Opera* i: 582 f.
49. Noodt thus adapts the Aristotelian distinction between theoretical and practical syllogisms, see Mulder, 1984: 192 f.
50. 'The maxims of the law are these: to live honestly, not to damage another man, to give everyone his due.' Modern Romanists often regard only the *suum cuique tribuere* as essential, the rest as Stoic ornamentation; on the text, see Diesselhorst, 1983; Van den Bergh, 1986*c*: 265.
51. In the same context Noodt also cites the well-known passage from Seneca, *Epist.* 94: 'Jubeat, non disputet, etc.'

laws serve that union, they must be followed; if not, we should serve not the law but society. In this context Noodt cites once more Seneca's saying[52] about the narrow innocence of being good according to the law.

This discussion foreshadows theories of legislation of the codification era, though there is as yet no trace here of the aspirations of the law-givers of enlightened absolutism, for whom the law was no less an educational project than a code. Likewise, it touches on the question of the relation between legal rules and principles, which has troubled legal positivism and recently was the subject of a debate between Hart and Dworkin.[53] It is quite clear that Noodt's theory, for all its moral gravity, implies that positive law has no more than relative value and can be put aside in the name of the union of human society, which in effect makes for great judicial freedom. It is to this idea that Van Bijnkershœk particularly took exception. And the relativity of positive law becomes all the more conspicuous through Noodt's stress on historical development.

Nobody can be so ignorant of human affairs as to assume that they have remained the same in all ages and places. Noodt has always been convinced that the art of civil law did not fall from heaven one moment like a shower, or spring up overnight like mushrooms. It has grown slowly by experience of utility, nor has it remained unchanged over the ages. It has varied with changes in human needs, gravity, resources, softness, roughness, learning, religion, war, and peace. Therefore we must restore everything to its own age.[54] Here, in 1700, we already find all the elements (except climate) of the research programme of a history of legislation that was to be achieved only half a century later in Montesquieu's *l'Esprit des loix* (1748). When the *Julius Paulus* was published Montesquieu was barely two years old and Gibbon still unborn.

Noodt also formulates in pristine form the idea of legal evolution:[55] sometimes it happens, when human habits grow milder, that a principle which thus far belonged to the *praecepta juris* is transformed into a rule and gets the compulsive force it did not have before.[56] This is what happened with the rules concerning the

52. *De ira* 2. 28.8, see above, at n. 30 on p. 185, and p. 175.
53. See Dworkin, 1977: ch. II and III.
54. *Opera* i: 567. The same idea is already expressed succinctly in the Utrecht inaugural address (1684), *Opera* i: 620; cf. van der Vlugt, 1916: 19. Noodt's historical argument is echoed by Saxe, 1787: 23.
55. On the history of this idea, see Stein, 1980.
56. *Opera* i: 584.

exposing and killing of new-born children in the fourth century, but it can be illustrated by several other examples, such as the law concerning abortion, fideicommissa, and the *beneficium excussionis* in suretyship.

In retrospect, it is hardly surprising that the whole complex of Noodt's ideas was rejected by Van Bijnkershœk, whose sensitivity may have been increased by the fact that he was a former student of theology and an orthodox Christian, and later became a judge in the Hoge Raad. Van Bijnkershœk saw very clearly the arbitrariness of a jurisdiction basing itself solely on principles of natural law.[57] He published his refutation of Noodt's book only in 1719,[58] but his correspondence with Van Eck proves that the shock was immediate and strong. On 22 March 1700 he writes:[59] 'You ask me whether I have seen Noodt's *Julius Paulus* forsooth? I have seen it (he sent it to me as he usually does with his works), read it, and damned it, as the famous Apostate said. But I am not free to say this. I will be forced nevertheless to refute the whole of this book by refuting an interpolation they consider to have been made in D 28. 1. 11.'[60] Curiously enough, Noodt neither discussed this text, nor the interpolation suggested by earlier humanists. The inaccuracy of Van Bijnkershœk's reading is another proof of his anger; Noodt is identified automatically with the Tribonian-scourgers.

'I have seen it, read it, and damned it': these are grave words. Noodt's conclusion, that until the second half of the fourth century the exposing or killing of children was no crime, implied that all classical jurists—those models of human perfection—had condoned this dire custom and that the first Christian emperors did not put an end to it. Van Bijnkershœk believed that this was not consistent with

57. See the preface to his *Obs. jur. rom.* (1710), Van Bijnkershœk i, 1767: 6.

58. *Opusculum de jure occidendi, vendendi et exponendi liberos apud veteres Romanos*, in id., *Opuscula varii argumenti*. Leiden, 1719. See Star Numan, 1869: 453 and 476.

59. Van Bijnkershœk to Van Eck, The Hague, 22 Mar. 1700 (UL Utrecht, MS 1000): 'Rogas an viderim Noodtii Julius Paulus scilicet? Vidi equidem (misit enim ad me, ut solet sua), et legi, et damnavi, inquiebat Apostata ille, sed hoc mihi dicere non licet. Cogar tamen libri illius summam refutare ad emblema, quod statuunt in fin. 1. 11 ff. de lib. et post.'

60. This concerns the words 'nec obstat, quod licet eos exheredare, quod [quos] et occidere licebat'. Several humanists had suggested that for 'licebat' must be read 'licet' and this was endorsed by Wissenbach, 1736: 81. And see Van Bijnkershœk i, 1767: 353. On the text see also Mommsen, 1899: 618 n. 4; Ferrini, 1899: 380 ff.; Bonfante, *Corso* i, 1963: 112.

the dignity of the Roman people, but Noodt retorted[61] that this question was not a matter of feeling or of law, but of fact: 'I will not take my arguments from what is good or just or honourable, or, on the other hand, from what is wicked or absurd. I have experienced that all such arguments, whenever they concern social life, either of human beings or of societies, are fallacious and therefore of no value to prove facts. I think that such proof can only be taken where, given the human condition, it can be found safest: that is, in witnesses and stories from the time that things happened.'[62] Here Noodt formulates, with all desirable clearness, the principles of modern historical research. 'Everybody knows that a later situation depends upon an earlier one,' he says, 'unless some innovation intervened. A mutation, which is a matter of fact, must be proved. A simple negation, however emphatic, is no proof.'[63] If Van Bijnkershœk believes that the custom of killing and exposing children is below the dignity of the Roman people, what about the ancient Greeks? It is a fact that the laws and customs of peoples are not universally nor always guided by what is honourable and good. Nor is the opinion about what is useful or noxious, just or unjust, honourable or wicked, the same in all times and places.[64]

But the Greeks do not bother Van Bijnkershœk; it is the authority of the Roman Corpus Juris that is at stake. Even though the dictum of Seneca which inspired Noodt may claim authority from D 50. 17. 144 pr.—saying that not all that is allowed is honest[65]—and Noodt's idea that the Corpus Juris not only contains binding rules, but also moral precepts, was not absolutely new in itself,[66] it directly seemed to endanger the legal authority of Justinian's codification in a period when the foundation of its binding force became an issue of serious dispute.[67] 'Consequently, if you now refer this part of Paul's book, and another time that of another jurist whom Tribonian included in the Digest to the moral precepts, I am afraid that the authority of the law is overturned to a monstrous degree, and that what Justinian wanted to be the law is being regarded as the speech of some rhetor or

61. In his *Amica responsio*, 1722, Ahsmann–Feenstra, 1984: nr. 477, *Opera* i: 591 f.
62. *Opera* i: 591. 63. *Opera* i: 596. 64. *Opera* i: 602.
65. 'Non omne quod licet honestum est.'
66. The idea that the Corpus Juris not only contains positive rules but also advice is found already in the gloss 'virtus' on D 1. 3. 7. Noodt discusses this text in ch. 10 of the *Julius Paulus*, but apparently does not know the gloss. His authorities are classical authors, not jurists.
67. See Luig, 1977*a*.

philosopher.'[68] In a historical perspective Van Bijnkershœk's misgivings do not seem totally unrealistic. Later in the eighteenth century, when the inadequacy of the Corpus Juris as legislation was criticized ever more strongly, one of the major complaints was that in it positive law was mixed up with all sorts of definitions, logical and metaphysical truths, rules of natural equity, and principles of Stoic philosophy.[69]

That Noodt's ideas had a real impact can be seen in a disputation which is found in manuscript among Noodt's papers, and which may have been defended under his presidency in 1706.[70] Here it is said straightforwardly: 'Because nothing in this world, however excellent, is perfect in every respect, it is no wonder that even our *jus civile* has defects, and that it contains several laws which can by no means escape the reproach of being unjust.'[71] And as a first example the author points quite judiciously to C 1. 5. 4 (AD 407), which threatens severe penalties against heretics. In a Protestant nation one could hardly take exception to this example. The theme of the injustice of some Roman laws, for that matter, was not new in Leiden; it had been debated between Maestertius and Cyprianus Regneri ab Oosterga half a century before.[72]

The question of who was right in this debate which attracted the attention of the learned world all over Europe[73] can be put on different levels. There is no doubt that both contenders were past masters in their art and formulated the issue with excellent clearness, though not with the courteousness one might expect among close friends. That numerous laws from the Corpus Juris had fallen in desuetude was common stock in the *usus modernus*, but a book like Groenewegen's *De legibus abrogatis* (1649) never challenged the

68. Van Bijnkershœk i, 1767: 359.
69. See Jansen, 1987*b*: 286 and *passim*.
70. ARA Tets van Goudriaan, inv. nr. 122. Florens de Lange of Gouda took his degree in Leiden, 9 Apr. 1706, with a thesis on the *Lex Julia majestatis*, see Molhuysen, *Bronnen* iv, *242. The identification is not absolutely certain, however. The fact that the MS (not in Noodt's hand) is found in Noodt's papers might just as well indicate that he did *not* accept the thesis. The same ideas as voiced in the *Julius Paulus* are found in the introductory lectures on the Pandects that Noodt gave in Leiden; see below, p. 278 f.
71. 'Cum nihil, licet videatur optimum, in hoc mundo ab omni re parte perfectum, non igitur mirum est quod jus nostrum civile . . . suis quoque laboret vitiis, et in eo varias occurrant leges, quae injustitiae notam effugere minime possunt.'
72. See Feenstra, 1982*a*: 305 ff.
73. Some data are given by Star Numan, 1869: 214–19 and 478–9. In 1770 a thesis about the debate was defended in Leiden, see Van Neck, 1770.

authoritative framework of civil law, while Noodt's book seemed to do just that. The authority of a text from the Corpus Juris is no longer given; each one can be put to the test of historical and rational criticism. This is a new step in the gradual 'historicization'[74] which began with humanism and was reinforced by natural law theory.

As for the tone of the debate, however, Van Bijnkershœk is probably more to be blamed than Noodt. He certainly was a man with a very high opinion of himself, who did not easily admit to be wrong.[75] Noodt, the dignified Leiden professor with a sound international reputation, who was nearly thirty years older and considered him his close friend, had certainly more than one reason to be annoyed. It was definitely unfriendly to suggest—and to repeat about five times—that Noodt had done no more than copy a theory of Lipsius 'who was more an expert in letters than in law'.[76] This was an exaggeration, and moreover Noodt had straightforwardly acknowledged his debt to Lipsius, which Van Bijnkershœk failed to mention. He should have known Noodt well enough, though, to realize that he was not a man to adorn himself with borrowed plumes. But maybe we should not overrate the word 'friendship'. In his *Curae secundae* (1723) Van Bijnkershœk reproached Noodt for having kept 'more silent than a fish'[77] during the three years in which he was preparing his *Amica responsio*. But that reproach is hardly convincing now that we know that Van Bijnkershœk himself kept his misgivings about Noodt's *Julius Paulus* to himself for nineteen years, during which both men were friends and visited each other regularly.

There may be other, hidden reasons for a growing estrangement between the two men. In 1710, in the preface to his *Observationes juris romani*, Van Bijnkershœk had launched a sharp and notorious attack on young lawyers and judges, who knew nothing of Roman law any more and believed they could do anything with equity. They replaced the authority of the law with their own subjective, arbitrary *jurisprudentia cerebrina*. He blamed the law faculties for this lamentable situation: one would think that these people had not learned to follow Roman law, but rather to conspire against it.[78] In Leiden this

74. The term is coined by Maffei, 1968: 176 and *passim*.
75. See Star Numan, 1869: 219 n. 4. The text is from a loose leaf in MS BPL 1073 (UL Leiden), lecture notes by Rücker. This MS was intended for publication by H. W. Tydeman.
76. Van Bijnkershœk i, 1767: 359.
77. Van Bijnkershœk i, 1767: 372: '. . . pisce magis obmutuisti'.
78. Van Bijnkershœk i, 1767: 6.

could hardly be seen as anything but a direct attack (by a man who had once hoped for an academic career himself) on the faculty, as well as on Noodt personally. Noodt had pleaded for the integration of natural law in the law curriculum in his Franeker inaugural address back in 1679. He actually put much natural law in his books as well as in his lectures and in Leiden he gave private lectures on Grotius' *De jure belli ac pacis*.[79]

And this was not all. While pleading for the usefulness of the *ars critica*, Van Bijnkershœk distinguished in the same preface between good and bad criticism. Among the examples of stupid criticism he also enumerated, as his teacher Huber had done, 'quas libet notas fingere',[80] that is, to argue for emendation on the basis of presumed false solution of (fictitious) abbreviations by some scribe. Now this could point to nobody but Noodt. Perizonius was certain that Noodt felt unhappy about Van Bijnkershœk's *Observationes* and he was quite surprised that he never said a word about it, even though he received Van Bijnkershœk and his wife at his home.[81]

A few years before the appearance of Van Bijnkershœk's *De jure occidendi* (1719), rumours began to circulate in the Republic about the fact that Noodt's most famous emendation[82] had been proposed long before by someone else. The suggestion was that Noodt was guilty of plagiarism. The source of these rumours, which sooner or later must have been reported to Noodt, was not hard to trace; it was the young Abraham Wieling,[83] a correspondent and protégé of Van Bijnkershœk. Now the senator himself all but accused Noodt of plagiarizing Lipsius. This began to look like a campaign to harm Noodt's scholarly reputation and asked for a sharp response. Even a peace-loving man cannot keep his peace in all circumstances. And apparently the reply had some success, if only temporarily. The allegation of plagiarism was published by Wieling only six years after Noodt's death,[84] and although Barbeyrac rebutted the calumny, some of it has stuck until the present day.[85]

In the preface to the *Curae secundae* (1723) Van Bijnkershœk

79. UL Leiden, BPL 191, see below, p. 282.
80. Van Bijnkershœk i, 1767: 9; cf. Huber, 1688*a*, see above, p. 146.
81. Perizonius to Van Eck, Leiden, 15 Dec. 1709 and 1 Feb. 1710 (UL Utrecht, MS 1000).
82. The change of 'ut' to 'at' in D 13. 7. 13. 1; see below, p. 314 f.
83. For further details, see below, Ch. 4, at nn. 113 f.
84. Wieling, 1758: 177.
85. See *NNBW* ii: 1000.

added insult to injury by saying that, in fact, he had intended to attack a thesis of Lipsius 'which you merely dressed up a little',[86] and that thus far he had abstained for reasons of friendship from treating subjects which Noodt had emended 'against the will and to the anger of Themis'.[87] These words were about the worst insult one could throw at a jurist. If the tone of Noodt's *Amica responsio* is sometimes sharp and in general rather condescending, Van Bijnkershœk's *Curae secundae* really are a poor show of disputatiousness. Later, he confessed to Heineccius—who subscribed to Noodt's thesis—that he had gone a little too far.[88] Noodt replied to Van Bijnkershœk's objections, still rather condescending, in the second part of his Commentary on the Pandects (1724). The debate could have ended already, but it pleased the senator to attack Noodt once more with a book called *Curae secundae*, 'I was obliged to read it.' Noodt continues,

> But I read it cursorily, not finding it deserving an extensive study, much less requiting the author, who only gives a confused repetition of his earlier book. For the rest there is nothing new except sophistries, abuse, and insults which are no good for the question. Whether this befits a learned and honourable man, he must see for himself. I do not envy someone seeking idle and useless things the unbounded freedom to amuse and satisfy himself. For myself I am safe against abuse and I would rather keep in mind as an example to follow this word of Pythagoras: divine providence has given men two most beautiful gifts, to embrace the truth and to do good to others.[89]

But this too is partly literary convention. As it seems, Noodt bore no malice; he sent Van Bijnkershœk the new edition of his *Opera omnia* as usual, with a courteous note.[90]

As far as the historical question itself is concerned, Noodt is undoubtedly Van Bijnkershœk's superior.[91] He formulates excellently the principle of *interpretatio duplex* in its modern meaning: 'Anyone who is only a little learned knows that fragments of the Pandects must, in order to be understood correctly, be considered in two ways, on the one hand according to the intention of their ancient

86. Van Bijnkershœk i, 1767: 371: '. . . sententia Lipsii, a te nonnihil interpolatam'.
87. Van Bijnkershœk i, 1767: 371: '. . . invita et irata Themide'.
88. Star Numan, 1869: 214.
89. *Opera* ii: 534.
90. Star Numan, 1869: 215.
91. Cf. Haubold, 1809: 143, who says that Van Bijnkershœk is '. . . historiae jurisprudentiae minus gnarus'.

authors, on the other according to the purpose of Justinian.'[92] Modern Romanistic research has justified Noodt, although his name is nowhere mentioned: the right to kill, expose, or sell children was only abolished in the fourth century.[93] And the words of Paul in D 25. 3. 4? They can only date from the same century and must be regarded as interpolated![94] One can hardly say that this solution is much more elegant than that of Noodt. If it leaves the legal quality of the Corpus Juris intact—Justinian's compilers no doubt meant it to be a legal rule—this happens at a moment when there is no longer a good reason to do so. Hardly anywhere in the world is the Corpus Juris as such still a binding code of law. Nevertheless, only very recently have some Romanists endeavoured to suggest that perhaps the Roman concept of legal validity was quite different from ours.[95] Under the sway of the *mos geometricus* we have interiorized since the seventeenth century a binary concept of validity: a rule is either binding or it is not. But there is ample evidence that Roman jurists knew many shades of legal validity, from strictly obligatory to merely desirable. Maybe Noodt's *Julius Paulus* might get a new actuality in this context. After all, he was an *interpres primarius* of Roman law. And if the boasting about two millenniums of civil law scholarship is to be more than cheap ideology, it is high time to study its history in greater detail.

Diocletianus et Maximianus sive de transactione et pactione criminum

Four years after the *Julius Paulus* Noodt published a new book, which was rather different in focus. It conformed to the type of a humanistic monograph, though being perfectly systematic: 'Diocletianus and Maximianus, or concerning the transaction and bargaining over crimes' (1704).[96] Noodt's stated purpose was to help free the existing legal system of one of its most conspicuous imperfec-

92. *Opera* i: 604. For the modern notion of *interpretatio duplex* see Dernburg i, 1902: 78; Riccobono, 1947; Feenstra, 1953; Betti, 1954: 132; 1955: 936, 947 f.
93. Mayer-Maly, 1979: 214. Heineccius and Gebauer had already sided with Noodt, see Star Numan, 1869: 214.
94. Bonfante, *Corso* i, 1963: 112: 'certamente interpolata'; Kaser, 1975: 204 n. 17; Mayer-Maly, 1979: 214. See also *Index int. a.h.l.*
95. Cf. Van den Bergh, 1986*c*: 68.
96. Ahsmann–Feenstra, 1984: nr. 449. The book was dedicated to Hendrik Adriaan van der Marck van Leur, brother of Noodt's deceased wife. It had no preface.

tions, to 'make the law more conform to the light of reason'.[97] The thesis is formulated in all clearness at the outset: according to the law of the Pandects and Codex a bargain over any crime, whether capital or other, is neither valid nor admissible. Only the suspect of a crime punishable by death may be pardoned, if he tries to save his life by making a payment.

Noodt's words are no exaggeration. The history of the transaction of crimes in the low countries is a continuing story of abuse of power and corruption.[98] Bailiffs in particular had a bad reputation. The bailiff (*baljuw*) was a public servant (the office was created in the twelfth century) who exercised tasks of administration and jurisdiction in the service of a sovereign lord. He was at once head of the police and chief prosecutor in his district. Therefore, he had practically unlimited discretionary powers in the prosecution of crimes.[99] These included the freedom to bargain with a suspect even before bringing a formal accusation—although formally this was forbidden. Such transactions were mostly beyond control of the court. In many cases, especially in rural districts, the bailiff had the right to propose persons for court membership, which meant that they were dependent on him rather than vice versa.

But not only the bailiff could bargain. After the suspect was brought to court and a formal accusation was made, the court still could decide at any time not to proceed further if a suitable sum was paid. Eventually, this could frustrate the suspect's hope of a fair trial. When, for instance, the court was convinced of his guilt but doubted the possibility of getting sufficient proof for a formal condemnation, it could demand, or rather extort, a payment to end proceedings, which went by the rather euphemistic names of 'compensation' or 'submission'. Because prisons were very unhealthy and criminal trials a bad risk even for the innocent, suspects were easily persuaded or, if necessary, bullied into a transaction.

Accounts of such corruption are recorded from the fourteenth century until the very end of the Republic in the eighteenth. It was not even necessary for a crime to be committed; accusations could be framed just as easily. A woman who died after a long illness was

97. *Opera* i: 271.
98. See Van den Bergh, 1857; 's Jacob, 1936: 6 ff.; Van der Poel, 1942: 99 ff.; Van Rompaey, 1961; Hovy, 1980; Van de Vrugt, 1982: 50 f. I thank Mrs Van de Vrugt for references. For other abuses of office by bailiffs, see e.g. Van Putte, 1978 and Smits-Veld, 1983.
99. Van den Bergh, 1857: 236.

accused of having committed suicide. Thus the heirs were pressed to pay a considerable sum from her estate to the bailiff, if only to avoid a trial which could ruin the honour of the family.[1] Accusations of adultery were a favourite source of income because people of rank had every reason to avoid scandal, even if they were perfectly innocent. Sometimes prostitutes were pressed to co-operate with the bailiff for that purpose.[2] Catholics paid large annual sums to safeguard themselves against raids on their clandestine churches.[3]

One of the more notable cases happened in The Hague in 1674, and Noodt may well have heard of this. The bailiff van Banchem already had a bad reputation for other reasons. He had taken part in the assassination of the De Witt brothers and was rewarded with the office. An old Jewish jeweller from Amsterdam who was staying in The Hague was invited by someone to visit a countess who would be interested in buying diamonds, and to bring some stones for inspection. Shortly after he had entered the house—negotiations had barely started—the bailiff burst into the room accusing the jeweller of an attempt at fornication. The poor man was arrested and the diamonds taken from him. After maltreatment and severe threats, the bailiff let him go on the condition that he would leave the diamonds and keep his mouth shut. Later it appeared that the bailiff, the 'countess', and the man who had invited the jeweller were all part of a conspiracy to rob him.[4]

Naturally such corruption did not remain unnoticed and in fact some bailiffs were prosecuted and punished. The Hof van Holland, which was competent in cases of abuse of office, made a real effort to maintain the rule of law. But on the whole it was unable to put an end to the evil practice. Nor could the law-giver. The *Criminele Ordonnantiën* of 1570 absolutely prohibited transaction over crimes, but this was never effective.[5] Neither laws nor prohibitions could stop abuse, because it was, in fact, a structural problem. Bailiffs bought their office at a high price, often combined with an annual payment, and it was understood that they were to make an income and pay their debt from fines and confiscations. They usually leased the office to a deputy who had to make a living from it as well. The combination

1. Van Rompaey, 1961: 57.
2. Van den Bergh, 1857: 246; Hovy, 1980: 418.
3. Van den Bergh, 1857: 248.
4. Van den Bergh, 1857: 256.
5. Hovy, 1980: 415. Several other legislative measures were taken earlier and later with little success.

of wide discretion, lack of effective control, and pressure to pay their debt of office often proved too strong for honesty. Moreover, the borderline between legal transactions and illegal extortions was far from unambiguous. In legal literature, different opinions were defended on nearly every point of the law. And, as we saw, the courts themselves regarded it as perfectly legal to persuade suspects with all kinds of threats to buy off prosecution.[6]

As far as civil law was concerned, the legal basis of the power to transact was found in a constitution of the Emperors Diocletian and Maximian of AD 293 (C 2. 4. 18), which seemed to say that it was not forbidden to bargain over a capital crime, except adultery, but that transaction of other crimes was not allowed, except for *crimen falsi*. Noodt set out to demolish this basis thoroughly by proving that the constitution said nothing of the sort. With this, he flew in the face of *communis opinio*, which had been authoritatively stated only very recently by his *collega proximus* Johannes Vœt.[7] Noodt's interest in the matter is seen in his *Ad legem Aquiliam* (1691), where he says that according to the Corpus Juris lower magistrates do not have the right to harass free people. Apart from the many notorious stories of extortion, his family history may have provided him with a personal reason for writing this book. When in 1619 his maternal grandmother Willemken van Wanrade was arrested for having organized a prohibited Remonstrant religious meeting in her house, the case was settled—after arrest, several interrogations, and serious threats of imprisonment—by the payment, or rather extortion, of a considerable sum.[8] Legally, this must have been a 'submission', for as far as we know criminal proceedings in due form never took place.

Noodt's book thus seems to illustrate the political relevance of humanistic scholarship, which is often overlooked. He does not write fierce pamphlets against the abuse, demanding immediate reform, but sets out to prove patiently, with all desirable philological acuity, that the legal or historical foundation of the power in question is nonexistent and the power itself therefore a corruption. This was exactly what Valla had done with regard to the *donatio Constantini*. According to D 2. 14. 7. 14 and D 2. 14. 27. 4, transactions concerning

6. Hovy, 1980: 413 f.
7. *Comm. ad Pand.* (first published 1698) 2. 15. 18–19. In an addendum to vol. ii of his commentary (Ahsmann–Feenstra, 1984: nr. 1059), which appeared only a few months after the *Diocletianus et Maximianus*, Vœt published an extensive refutation of Noodt's main thesis concerning C 2. 4.18.
8. See Janssen, 1983: 70 ff. For further details, see below, p. 229 ff.

public affairs are invalid, and therefore there can be no bargaining over public crimes. A pact contracted by someone who has no power to transact does not have an appropriate cause, but rather an illicit one, especially when it is done for money, because it is a manifest corruption.[9] It is not transaction, but extortion.[10]

Naturally, Noodt's book is not original in every respect. C 2. 4. 18 had been under discussion ever since the days of the glossators, in theory as well as in legal practice,[11] and not without reason. The various meanings of *crimen capitale* are already discussed in the gloss,[12] and likewise the distinction defended by Noodt, but rejected by Bartolus, Baldus, and Jason, viz. that the accused was allowed to transact to avoid a death sentence, but the accuser was liable under the *senatusconsultum Turpillianum*.[13] Another question was how to explain the words 'capital crimes, except adultery', because we know that adultery was not a capital crime in the days of Diocletian and Maximian. This leads Noodt to an historical excursus, comparable to that in the *Julius Paulus*, concerning the question of when adultery was made a capital crime. Noodt concludes that this can only have been the case under the reign of Constantine, and that therefore the words 'excepto adulterio' in C 2. 4. 18 are interpolated. This had already been suggested by Cujas and several others.[14]

Noodt's knowledge of the history of the sources of Roman law allows him to bring a totally new element to the discussion of C 2. 4. 18, which leads to a completely different interpretation of that text and which—not without reason—is given pride of place in the second chapter, where the discussion actually begins.[15] From the inscription of C 2. 4. 18 we learn that it was addressed to a private person named Valens,[16] this means that it is not a constitution but a rescript, that is, the answer to a letter from a private person putting a question of law before the emperor. This is essential for a correct interpretation of the text. Such an answer may be given by a letter of reply or by

9. *Opera* i: 275, see also 280.
10. *Opera* i: 286.
11. See e.g. the gloss 'prohibitum' *a.h.l.*
12. Gloss 'capitali' *a.h.l.*
13. Gloss 'prohibitum' *a.h.l.*: 'Scilicet accusato, sed accusanti est prohibitum.'; Noodt, *Opera* i: 279. The opinions of the glossators were by no means unanimous, for that matter.
14. Faber, Van Giffen, Schifordeger, Wissenbach, see *Index int. Cod. a.h.l.*
15. *Opera* i: 272.
16. In the now current edn. of Krüger, the name of the addressee is Valentinianus; this is also the reading of the Haloander edn., see Gebauer–Spangenberg *a.h.l.*

subscription. Although Ulpian states emphatically that there is no difference in legal authority between constitution and rescript (D 1. 4. 1. 1), the two are contrasted in C 2. 42. 3, and from D 48. 18. 1. 19 we learn that a rescript can be repealed by a subsequent constitution. A constitution rules generally and directly and thus may make new law, a rescript cannot. In a rescript the emperor only answers the question laid before him and merely states what is established law on that point. Naturally, it has legal authority, because it is the emperor who speaks, but a rescript cannot be interpreted in the same way as a constitution. When interpreting constitutions one may use arguments *a contrario* and *a consequentia*, because the emperor does not have a special case in mind but the common good. With regard to a rescript, however, such arguments are often invalid and even dangerous. What the rescript does not say is not necessarily excluded, because it only means to give an answer to what was asked in the *libellum*. And because the emperor only has the intention to declare what is the established law, we must interpret his words in the light of what we know the law to be from other sources. Therefore, the words 'transigere vel pascisci . . . non prohibitum est' cannot be taken to mean that a transaction over public crimes is valid, because from other sources, e.g. D 2. 14. 7. 14 and 27. 4, we know that it never was. So the words must mean something totally different: he who bargains over a capital crime is not punished.[17] The text says nothing about the validity of the transaction itself because that was not asked and did not need to be: it was and is invalid in any case, whether contracted over capital crimes or any other. And even the rule as given in the rescript has only a restricted sense in the light of other sources: the suspect is pardoned for reasons of humanity; it is only natural to try to save one's neck and therefore the *benignitas* of the emperor excepted him. But the accuser does not escape chastisement.

It cannot be denied that this interpretation, though partly speculative,[18] is much more satisfactory from a logical point of view. In the

17. *Opera* i: 279.
18. This point is stressed by Vœt (*Comm. ad Pand.* 2. 15. 19): how do we know that Valens is a private person and not a magistrate? Vœt, *Comm. ad Pand.* 2. 15. 19: 'Sed Valentem illum reum fuisse accusatum, non accusatorem, non magistratum, qui Principem de jure consulere potuit, subsumi facilius quam probari posse confido; cum nullum ejus indicium ex lege appareat, neque sine aliqua probationis specie tale quid pro basi atque fundamento explicationis substerni queat.' Noodt's interpretation is indeed no more than probable. In the inscriptions of many constitutions the quality of the addressee is mentioned, but the fact that it fails in the present one can hardly be regarded as conclusive evidence that Valen(tinianu)s

traditional interpretation it is hard to explain why bargaining over capital crimes should be allowed, but not over lesser ones. Noodt once more shows the full range of his legal and historical scholarship, and he is quite aware of the aim and the wider implications of his new interpretation of C 2. 4. 18: 'Let us help the law, by driving out an obscurity that is exceedingly dangerous for it.'[19] 'When I teach against the architects of our law [i.e. the compilers], although with proper modesty, I might possibly seem rather bold. But even here I am excused from temerity by a zeal for the truth which is regarded as praiseworthy by everybody, except by those who are disgusted with their own as well as with the common good.'[20] In using historical knowledge to show that 'it ain't necessarily so' and thus trying to help free society from a source of oppression, the book is in the best tradition of the humanistic movement. Here we do not have an odd antiquary, but a jurist in his own right with full consciousness of his social responsibilities.

Naturally, the new theory concerning the interpretation of rescripts could be criticized and will have been regarded with suspicion by orthodox jurists, though it was not quite as dangerous as the theory exposed in the *Julius Paulus*. And it was rather naïve—as, in fact, was most humanistic scholarship—as regards the possibility of changing society through intellectual work. Noodt's proof that transactions over crimes were illegal under the Corpus Juris could no more stop abuses than could prosecutions and legislation. A century later, during preparations for his criminal code of 1809—the first criminal code actually to obtain force of law in the Netherlands, if only for two years—King Louis Napoléon ruled an absolute prohibition of transactions once more,[21] but it had just as little enduring success. Innumerable transactions—plea bargains—are made every day now, for instance concerning tax law and traffic offences, and the judicial system would simply grind to a halt if they were to be ruled out. But to speak out against abuses in the legal system which are taken for granted by most jurists, even if it is unsuccessful, remains an act worth remembering. It may not be the least difference between

was a private person. On the other hand, Vœt seriously misrepresents Noodt's argument. Noodt said nowhere than Valen(tinianu)s was an accused, only that he was a private person. Even today there seems to exist no comprehensive study on the names of addressees of imperial constitutions. See, in general, Volterra, 1971.

19. *Opera* i: 279.
20. *Opera* i: 293.
21. *Précis*, 1810: 14; see Van Binsbergen, 1949: 25.

legal technicians (*legulei*) and jurists, that the latter feel responsible for the quality of their legal system.

De religione ab imperio jure gentium libera

On 8 February[22] 1706, at the end of his second term as *rector magnificus* of Leiden university, Noodt delivered the address on freedom of religion[23] which instantly caught the attention of all Europe and proved his most enduring title to fame. Jean le Clerc immediately published an extract of the address in French.[24] Enthusiastic reviews with a synopsis also appeared in Jacques Bernard's *Nouvelles de la république des lettres*,[25] as well as in the *Bœkzaal der geleerde werelt*.[26] A Dutch translation appeared the same year,[27] translations into French and English within two years.[28] Two German translations appeared in 1724 and 1728,[29] and a translation into Swedish was even made, but it remained unpublished.[30] Many editions of the Latin text and the translations appeared. In one Dutch collection, which appeared in 1734 and was reprinted in 1774,[31] it was put side by side *inter alia* with Locke's letter on toleration.

Toleration was a much discussed topic in Noodt's day, as it had been for many years.[32] Especially in the Dutch Republic, which sheltered many refugees from France and elsewhere, discussion was so lively in the last decades of the seventeenth century that in 1687 Jean le Clerc declared—presumably with some exaggeration—that people scarcely spoke of anything else.[33] It was also in Holland that Locke, prompted by the Remonstrant theologian Philip van Limborch[34]—whom we will meet again presently—wrote his *Epistola de*

22. Barbeyrac, 1731: 119, marginal note, gives the date as 6 Feb., misreading the Latin date 'VI Id. Febr.'
23. Ahsmann–Feenstra, 1984: nr. 451.
24. *Bibliothèque choisie* xi: 253.
25. May 1706; Amsterdam: Desbordes, 1706: 582–7.
26. April/May 1706; Amsterdam: Halma, 1706: 350–62.
27. Ahsmann–Feenstra, 1984: nr. 453.
28. Ahsmann–Feenstra, 1984: nrs. 438, 442.
29. Ahsmann–Feenstra, 1984: nrs. 461, 462.
30. Transl. by Joh. Edemark: Tal om samvetsfrihet, huvuledes den i naturen och menniskors lag är grundad. MS, UL Uppsala, 35pp.
31. Ahsmann–Feenstra, 1984: nrs. 457, 458.
32. For a short overview, see Den Tex, 1926: 35 f.; Klibansky, 1968: p. x; Cranston, 1967: 143 f.
33. Klibansky, 1968: p. xiv.
34. Klibansky, 1968: pp. viii f.

tolerantia towards the end of 1685 and that Bayle and Spinoza, who made important contributions to the theory of toleration,[35] lived.

If around the turn of the century people in several parts of Europe began to have enough of dragonnades and stakes,[36] the battle over freedom of religion had by no means been won. Noodt's address remained controversial enough, especially in Catholic countries. The pirated editions of his *Opera omnia* which appeared in Cologne (1732, 1763, 1784)[37] left it out without any notice to the reader; the subtitle 'Four Speeches' was simply changed to 'Three Speeches'. The edition of the *Opera omnia* appearing in Naples in 1786[38] contained the address, but added a lengthy note by the censor, the Reverend J. F. Confortius (1743–99),[39] refuting its main thesis.[40] Perhaps Confortius later changed his opinion. He took part in the 1798 revolution, was a minister of the republic, and consequently was decapitated after the restoration the following year. Confortius erroneously called Noodt a member of the *factio Arminianorum*.[41]

35. On Bayle, see Labrousse, 1985; on Spinoza, Den Tex, 1926: 95 f.
36. Den Tex, 1926: 81.
37. Ahsmann–Feenstra, 1984: nrs. 469, 470, 471.
38. Ahsmann–Feenstra, 1984: nr. 472.
39. Gian Francesco Conforti (1743–99), a priest, was theologian, jurist, and professor of sacred and profane history at the university of Naples. As a royalist and anti-curialist he advocated a purely spiritual Church without secular power. In his *Antigrotius* (1780) he combated Grotius' opinion (*De imperio summarum potestatum circa sacra*, 1647) that public religious practice (as opposed to private conviction) was a political matter and could be ruled by the government. Conforti defended that 'Christiana pietas ab omni imperio libera est', but he opposed toleration and held that Christian governments had a duty to prosecute heretics. In his *castigatio* of Noodt (*Opera omnia* (Naples, 1786): ii: 408–12), however, he takes a different position. Noodt has restricted the powers of government too much and he who, following Noodt, would make the powers of the sovereign dependent on consensus of the subjects, promotes anarchy (ibid., p. 411). Governments have always had powers in religious matters (ibid., p. 412). In the 1780s Conforti became 'revisore dei libri esteri' for the kingdom of Naples and Sicily, and in that capacity banned books by Voltaire, Mably, Rousseau, Raynal, Mirabeau, and Bayle. His position as royalist and anti-curialist became precarious when, influenced by the French Revolution, King Ferdinand IV and Pope Pius VI made an agreement. He was arrested in 1796 and two years later came out of prison as a republican. He was Minister of the Interior in the republic and after the restoration was executed on 7 Dec. 1799. On him, see P. Villani, in *Dizionario biografico degli italiani*, vol. 27, Rome: Istituto della Enciclopedia Italiana, 1982: 793–802.
40. See e.g. *Opera omnia* (Naples, 1786): ii: 411: 'Deinceps autem illud ipsum rejiciendum est, quod Noodtius in perexiguum et angustum locum summam Imperii potestatem conclusit.' See on this *castigatio* also the *imprimatur*, *Opera omnia* (Naples, 1786): i.
41. *Opera omnia* (Naples, 1786): ii: 408.

If the theme is not new, Noodt's address is still of special interest for several reasons. In the first place, he does not plead—as most of his contemporaries did—for toleration, that is, indulgence in teachings which the government may very well detest and has every legal right to prosecute, even if it is unable to do so effectively—which had been one of the main arguments for toleration for many ages.[42] Noodt's thesis is the absolute freedom of religion from all interference by the government: the prince has no rights over his citizens in matters of religion. Perizonius, who attended the academic session and reported about it to Van Eck the same day, understood it as such, as is proved by his synopsis: '... demonstrating that everybody must be allowed freedom of religion, in which the prince has no right'.[43] And although Noodt may have thought only of private freedom of conscience, some of the terms he used were such that they could easily be extended to public religion as well,[44] or even to intellectual freedom in general. This is an important difference. As Mirabeau said, some ninety years later, tolerance is a virtue, whereas freedom is a right.[45] From a modern point of view, the difference may seem to have lost much of its meaning, because we have learned that declared rights may be just as precarious as tolerance,[46] but for the eighteenth century the distinction was essential and in fact one of the issues of the great Revolution.

So Noodt's position among his contemporaries seems to be fairly radical once more. I am not competent to make a detailed analysis and comparison of the many treatises on freedom of religion that appeared in the period, but if we look for Noodt's predecessors we may possibly find more in Bayle[47] or Spinoza than in Locke. As we

42. Den Tex, 1926; cf. Noodt, below, p. 236.
43. Perizonius to Van Eck, Leiden, 8 Feb. 1706, UL Utrecht, MS 1000: '... disserentem de libertate religionis cuique relinquenda, in quam princeps nullum habet jus'.
44. So it was understood by Confortius, *Opera omnia* (Naples, 1786): ii: 408: 'Hoc sibi edisserendum suscepti, religionem sive publicam sive privatam ab omni imperio esse liberam ...'.
45. Cf. Den Tex, 1926: 30.
46. Den Tex, 1926: 31.
47. There are references to Bayle's *Comentaire philosophique* (1686–8, see Labrousse, 1985: 33 f.) in Barbeyrac's notes, see Barbeyrac, 1731: 120 n. 1; 148 n. 1; 153 n. 2; 180 n. 1; 182 nn. 1 and 2; 198 n. 1; 201 n. 2; 214 n. 1; and 219 n. 2. In most cases Barbeyrac indicates parallel arguments in Bayle and Noodt. Likewise, Confortius turns arguments, used by the critics of the 'atheist' Bayle, against Noodt. Naturally this does not prove that Noodt was actually influenced by Bayle. In the literature on toleration, series of commonplace arguments were generally used. On the other hand, Bayle was a staunch defender of absolutism (see Labrousse, 1985: 75 f.), which Noodt strongly opposed in *De jure summi imperii*.

saw before, Bœrhaave put Noodt and Spinoza side by side.[48] The difference between Noodt and Locke is exactly that between rights and toleration, and has important consequences. Locke excepted some groups from toleration, e.g. Roman Catholics and atheists.[49] When however, as Noodt stated, the prince has no right at all over religion, there can be no exceptions to freedom. The only restriction Noodt accepted was that the government may punish a group which, under the guise of religion, propagates false testimony, deceit, murder, theft, rape, and adultery.[50] The peace and order of civil society was the main concern of both Locke and Noodt, and on this point they reached similar results, but by very different routes.

I do not deny any possible influence of Locke on Noodt. In fact, it is most likely that the latter knew the *Epistola de tolerantia*, of which a second impression—in fact a title-edition—with Locke's name was published in 1705 in Amsterdam.[51] The famous Amsterdam Remonstrant Abraham van den Ende was Noodt's friend—his son later married Noodt's daughter—and through him he had contact with Jean le Clerc as well as Philip van Limborch. Van den Ende put Noodt's pupil Brenkman in touch with le Clerc in 1709 when he needed an introduction to get access to the Digest manuscript in Florence.[52] Van Limborch received Noodt's address 'through our common friend Van den Ende'[53] and wrote an enthusiastic reply. So Noodt certainly was familiar with the milieu where the publication of Locke's letter was prepared. In his notes to the French translation of Noodt's address Barbeyrac gives nine references to Locke's *Epistola*[54] but these do not suffice to establish the exact relationship between the two works. Some references are very vague and others concern age-old commonplaces in the literature on toleration, which Noodt could have picked up anywhere. We cannot even exclude the possibility that Noodt took some ideas (e.g. the thesis that violence is ineffective to influence the will) directly from Tertullian and Lactan-

48. See p. 104.
49. Cf. Den Tex, 1926: 79; Gough, 1968: 40ᵛ.
50. *Opera* i: 636.
51. Klibansky, 1968: p. xxxvi.
52. Stolte, 1981: 18.
53. Ph. van Limborch to Gerard Noodt, Amsterdam, 6 Apr. 1706, UL Amsterdam, 6 III D. 17 fols. 108–9. (autograph draft): 'Dissertationem tuam . . . a communi nostro amico D. van den Ende accepi.'
54. Barbeyrac, 1731: 146 n. 1; 149 n. 1; 153 n. 2; 170 n. 1; 171 n. 2; 174 n. 1; 198 n. 1; 204 n. 1; 215 n. 2. Unfortunately, it is difficult to check these references because the edn. of Klibansky does not give the page numbers of the original edn.

tius, in whose works he was very well read. As is the case with the address on sovereignty, the common ideas of Locke and Noodt concerning the original position, the beginning of society, the social contract, et cetera, may be traced to a common source (Grotius, Pufendorf) rather than be regarded as proof of influence of one upon the other. Until more detailed studies are made, the question of influences cannot be decided definitely.

Apart from being rather radical, Noodt's address is important because it is the work of a jurist. The debate on toleration was mostly dominated by philosophers and theologians and therefore had more impact on public opinion than on state practice. Romanists moreover could not deny—as Confortius does not fail to note[55]—that the later Roman emperors frequently decided questions concerning the Christian religion and were apparently regarded as fully entitled to do so. State authority in matters of religion was often justified by absolutists by reference to Constantine or Justinian. This may have been the main reason why Noodt founded his theory of the freedom of religion completely on *jus gentium* and cited only one legal text.[56] With this Noodt made a major contribution to the development of a legal theory of human rights.

Finally it is important that Noodt spoke as *rector magnificus* of Leiden university. He was fully aware of the significance of the occasion: explaining the choice of subject, he said that 'it must be the duty of a jurist, in the hall of Batavian freedom,[57] to plead the case of all mankind, and on the basis of inviolable natural law and *jus gentium* to speak for the freedom of that greater Republic which is united by the society of God and men and is not bounded by mountain or river or wide spaces, but only by the ocean and the path of the sun'.[58] The importance of the occasion is stressed also by Philip van Limborch in his letter to Noodt: 'I congratulate the country that, in its most famous academy, in the presence of theologians, the cause of the freedom of conscience which is common to all its residents was

55. *Opera omnia* (Naples, 1789): ii: 412.
56. *C.Th. de malef. et math.* 9: *Opera* i: 644.
57. That is, the aula of Leiden. Leiden university was erected by William of Orange after the city had withstood the Spanish siege. The term 'atrium libertatis' itself was of classical origin, see e.g. Cic. *Mil.* 22. 59; Liv. 25. 7; 45. 15; Tac. *Hist.* 1. 31.
58. *Opera* i: 634: 'Ut fas sit Jurisconsulto, in atrio libertatis Batavae agere causam generis humani, et ex sanctissimo Naturae ac Gentium Jure loqui pro libertate reipublicae illius majoris quae Dei et hominum societate conjungitur, nec fere monte aut flumine aut exiguis spatiis, sed demum oceano et solis via terminatur.'

defended by the rector magnificus with such candour and such weight of arguments'.[59]

In this case it again seems likely that experiences of his family in Nijmegen played a role in the formation of Noodt's ideas. The government which in 1618 was appointed by Prince Maurice immediately started a fierce campaign against the Remonstrants.[60] Its zeal was such that in the winter of 1631/2 Prince Frederik Hendrik had to ask it to act a bit more correctly towards its citizens.[61] As we have seen, Peter and Jacob Noodt went into exile. Noodt's maternal grandmother Willemken van Wanrade, a militant old lady, was a victim of persecution and wrote her experiences down for her children and grandchildren in a moving document which is preserved in the city archives of Nijmegen.[62] Young Gerard Noodt will have read it or at least heard about the episode.

After Willemken had attended, on 24 October 1619,[63] Remonstrant service in the neighbourhood of Kleve she was summoned to the city hall and interrogated for the first time. She got a fine of 25 guilders. Some years later the situation became more serious. On 6 March 1622 at about 9 o'clock in the evening, burgomaster Kelffken appeared with his men at her door, prompted by the rumour that a service was being held in her house. Kelffken gave orders to draw a cordon around the house, 'as if it concerned a brothel' and tried to get entry by banging and shouting for two hours. When no answer came he sent for the city smith in order to force the door. After having tried in vain to enter through a cellar they succeeded via the attic-window of a neighbouring house. The house was searched from top to bottom but nothing was found. Willemken was alone at home. Asked by Kelffken why she had not opened up, she said 'that in the evening she held her house closed to rabble', and that the conduct of the city magistrate was worse than that of the Duke of Alva. After a sharp altercation Kelffken went away.

On 8 March Willemken was summoned to the city hall. When

59. Van Limborch to Noodt, Amsterdam, 6 Apr. 1707; UL Amsterdam, III D 17, fol. 108: 'Gratulor patriae, quod in academia illius celeberrima, in auditorio theologico, causa libertatis conscientiarum, omnibus illius incolis communis, tanta cum *parrèsia* tantoque argumentorum pondere, a rectore magnifico sit defensa'.
60. Janssen, 1983: 68 f.
61. Poelhekke, 1978: 182.
62. GA Nijmegen, Arch. familie Biesman, inv. nr. 12.
63. I follow Janssen, 1983: 70–2.

asked which minister had preached in her house she replied 'that she would follow her Saviour Christ and all martyrs and give no answer on such a question'. The burgomaster then said that if she persisted, she would be obliged to take an oath of innocence. She replied that she had no duty to do that and accused the gentlemen of applying constraint of conscience. When the burgomaster denied this, because everybody was free to live in his house without organizing religious services, Willemken replied that everybody must be free to do what God commands and refrain from what God forbids. Then she gave the burgomaster an extensive account on two examples from the prophet Daniel which proved that one must obey God rather than the king: the three boys in the oven and Daniel in the lion's den. But the burgomaster did not let her finish and asked again which minister had preached in her house. After repeatedly refusing to answer Willemken was condemned to pay within eight days two fines of 25 and 200 guilders, or to take the oath.

For a few weeks she was left alone and she thought that Easter had made the magistrate see the error of its ways, but he had only let it pass to avoid a riot of the 'gemeente'. On 27 April she was summoned to the city hall again and Kelffken asked why she had not paid her fines. Willemken replied that she owed nothing to the gentlemen, 'and as far as the ordinance is concerned, they may take that with them on the day of the Lord and answer for it to the judgement of God, who will judge rightly the wrong they do to me'. Kelffken then pronounced the verdict of the government: she was to be kept in custody until she had paid. In vain she claimed her citizen's right to be released on bail.[64] Together with another woman she was put in custody.

After hearing nothing for eight days she wrote a sharp letter to the city council. Like the apostle Paul, who invoked his Roman citizenship when he was threatened with flogging (Acts 22: 25), she invoked hers: 'I am a citizen's daughter, a widow, and I appeal to my civil right to be bailed out and to get a trial'. She reminded the council of the fact that the father of Kelffken, when he was imprisoned 'in the city of papists', was allowed the right to be released on bail and to stand trial. Why not her too? 'You do not want to be worse than the Jews and heathens were with regard to Paul and the papists with regard to your father?' But no reaction came, and on 9 May she wrote again.

64. On this right, see Moorman van Kappen, 1983: 76f.

On 15 May she was brought before the council at last and given the choice of paying the fines or taking the oath. If she refused she would be put in prison for a month. The prospect of being imprisoned 'among whores and thieves in foul smell' frightened her, but Kelffken was adamant. Willemken reacted terribly when they tried to drag her to prison. Screaming, she clung to the doorbolt of the city hall, but the scene did not help and finally Willemken gave in. She sent someone to her friends to get the money. Kelffken demanded that the money be brought before sunset, and although this was done she still had to stay in prison that night.

On the morning of 16 May she was admonished by Kelffken. She must refrain 'from calling the gentlemen tyrants' and from saying that they had not given her a fair trial. He threatened her with corporal punishment and banishment if she had a service in her house again. But Willemken had recovered herself and replied with unabated fierceness: 'You have the money now. May God grant that it is taken from you as you took it from me. But I will leave revenge to God, who will judge you at some time. And there will be no appeal from that'. Like all the defenceless Willemken only could summon the gentlemen before God's judgment-seat; popular belief had it that judges who were summoned in that way certainly would come to grief.[65]

As we have seen, Noodt's father was not as firm as Willemken. Between 1642 and 1644 he returned to the Reformed Church,[66] no doubt in order to be eligible for political office in the city. But the fact of such constraint itself will have been regarded as humiliating, and in fact the conversion cannot have been more than external. If Gerard Noodt himself was regarded as an 'Arminian',[67] he may have inherited some of it from his father. As Noodt stresses in his address, the mind cannot be forced by coercion.

Considering the background just sketched, it is understandable that the address concerning freedom of religion had a very special meaning for Noodt. Here, on this famous rostrum, fully conscious of his authority as rector of Leiden university, he spoke for freedom of religion and gave a voice to his ancestors who had suffered from persecution:

I know, dear listeners, that I enter a road which is full of envy, hate, and slander, when I say to those whom it concerns that free people are suppressed

65. Hardung, 1934; Sinninghe, 1944: 207; Holzapfel and Erler, 1973: 424.
66. See above, p. 13. 67. See above, p. 225.

by such a misplaced bondage. But it is a good thing to do, because I hope you will welcome it when I succeed in treating such a great and grave subject, which is as dangerous for the great as for the small, with the grace of God and the help of our ancestors—those very strong people—our ancestors who have spared neither their blood nor their riches to exterminate the shame of their time and to ban from free minds a bondage which is as unlawful as it is despicable and unworthy and who are admired by all good and wise people all over the world.[68]

Legend has it that Noodt, totally against his habit, grew very pale at the commencement of the address and trembled over his whole body.[69] Perizonius, who was present, does not confirm this, but he says that Noodt spoke with a truly grave and husky voice. Furthermore he remarked that two or three times Noodt took the text in his hand, which he did without hesitation or shame, and as it were intentionally, as if he could not see with his eyes the text which was spread out before him (and printed in large letters) in the usual way. There were also some silences, not long but conspicuous enough. Perizonius regarded all this as incompatible with decorum.[70] Whether they were signs of Noodt's nervousness we can only guess.

Noodt may well have been thinking of his grandmother when he stressed that coercion in matters of religion has no effect: 'Believe me, there is no place here for pride and harshness and the will is not formed by prison, flogging, torture, beating, and violence'.[71] Like Willemken, Noodt stressed that everybody should be free to do what God commanded, and refrain from what he forbade. And the following extract from Noodt's address sounds like a posthumous reply to the gentlemen of Nijmegen who forbade Willemken to call them tyrants:

68. *Opera* i: 635. 69. Roukens, 1769: 6.

70. Perizonius to Van Eck, Leiden, 6 Feb. 1706; UL Utrecht, MS 1000: 'Nos hodie audivimus Noodtium, publice disserentem de Libertate religionis cuique relinquenda, in quam Princeps nullum habeat jus. An Theologis omnibus satisfecerit, incertus sum, quum ex lege naturae omnia repetierit, certe non usus sit principiis Theologicis. Disserebat autem austera prorsus et fusca voce. Sed et plus vicies vel tricies chartam in manus sumebat, ut deficientem memoriam juvaret. Quod tamen sine haesitatione aut rubore faciebat, et quasi consulto, quum ita consisteret, ut oculis suis scripturam chartae ante se, ut solet, depositae, perspicere non posset. Neque tamen satis decorum erat, pro tam frequenti concione toties chartam ad oculos admovere, et aliquoties non sine intervallo silentii, non longi quidem, sed quod satis animadverti posset, quaerere sapientia verba. Stylus ipsius erat, qui solet, argutiis et acutis veterum dictis ornatus, et ad locutionem Senecae aliquantulum formatus.'

71. *Opera* i: 637.

I am of the opinion, esteemed audience, that the prince is entitled to have great and dominant authority in civil affairs, but that he is not above others in matters of religion, as if he could give a rule to religion and sanction it by punishment of transgressors. This is the right of the divine, that is, some one else's authority. The prince can do no good here and not even escape the reproach of tyranny.[72]

Another reason for Noodt's anxiety will have been that—as Van Limborch remarked[73]—he had several orthodox theologians in his audience, who definitely cannot have been pleased by the address. Perizonius also hints at this: 'I am not sure whether he will have satisfied the theologians, because he deduced everything from natural law and certainly is not familiar with the principles of theology'.[74] For Van Limborch Noodt had even put the theologians in default. After praising Noodt exuberantly he continues:

It should be the task of theologians to carry the light before others with such a laudable intention. But they, pretending that cruel zeal for the glory of God, tend, in fact, to increase separations. If they really feel what they pretend, you may rightly speak against them that word of our Lord: 'You do not know of what spirit you are; the Son of Man did not come to ruin souls, but to save them!' I thank God that he gave you such courage that you were not afraid to deter your audience in that academic ceremony from such a pernicious error, which destroys love, the soul of the Christian religion, and the least fallible sign by which our Lord wants to recognize his disciples.[75]

Presumably in Noodt's audience there was one theologian with regard to whom he had a special ground for anxiety.[76] That was

72. *Opera* i: 638.

73. See n. 59.

74. Perizonius to Van Eck (as n. 70): 'An theologis omnibus satisfecerit, incertus sum, quum ex lege naturae omnia reperietur, certe non usus sit principiis theologicis.'

75. Van Limborch to Noodt (as n. 59): 'Theologorum fuerat, in tam laudabili instituto facem aliis praelucere. Verum illi zelum pro gloria divina praetexentes crudele illud, vere, secas ingeminare solent, quibus, si vere quod praetexent sentiunt, merito salvatoris illud opponas: nescitis cujus spiritus sitis: Filius hominis non venit anima perdere, sed salvare. Deo gratias ago qui tibi hanc mentem dedit, ut in solemnitate illa academica a tam pernicioso errore, qui charitatem, religionis Christianae animam, signumque minime fallax unde discipulos suos agnosci vult Servator, perimit, auditores tuos deterrere veritus'.

76. When Noodt gave the address the theological faculty had four professors. Apart from Johannes a Marck, they were H. Witsius (professor in Leiden 1698–1707, see *NNBW* iii: 1445), S. van Til (professor in Leiden 1702–13, see *NNBW* x: 1027), and F. Fabricius (professor in Leiden 1705–38, see *NNBW* iii: 380). Witsius was a pupil of Vœt and initially a staunch propagandist of his puritan ideas. But in later life he ceased to be a party man. In 1706 he was 70. Van Til was a Coccejan, Fabricius a moderate Coccejan.

Johannes a Marck,[77] professor in Leiden since 1689, but before that in Groningen, where he was the fierce opponent of Noodt's old friend Braunius.[78] Already in 1675, when he and Noodt were still in Nijmegen, Braunius had defended Dutch toleration against a foreign attack.[79] His expertise in Hebrew was the main reason for his nomination to Groningen, where he became one of the teachers of the great Hemsterhuis.[80] Being regarded as a Coccejan in theology and a Cartesian in philosophy, he soon came under the suspicion of heterodoxy. Therefore the governors appointed as his colleague—and even as head of the faculty—the staunchly orthodox Johannes a Marck, who soon began a sharp controversy with his *collega proximus*. So a Marck could very well stand as a model for the cantankerous theologians whom Van Limborch criticized. During the first years of the debate between Braunius and his orthodox opponent Noodt must have followed it at close quarters, because he lived in Franeker and corresponded regularly with Braunius, his old friend from Nijmegen. From one letter we may conclude that Noodt gave him legal advice (perhaps on a conflict with the governors).[81]

Noodt presents the theme straightaway and argues in his usual, direct, and robust manner: he intends to combat the opinion of those who believe that man is entitled to order or forbid others to follow a certain religion and to fight indolence with wars and jurisdiction. Such an opinion does not proceed from reason or zeal for God or men, but from greed, ambition, and lust for power.[82]

Religion is given to each of us by God's grace; it only depends on his inspiration. For the rest, it is free and beyond every sovereign authority. Nobody can be received into a religious community against his will and unknowingly. According to human law, nobody can be forced by weapons or law to enter, to stay, or to accept everything the community believes.[83] In everything that concerns the well-being of the body, in matters of sale and hire, in the arrangement of individual and social life, man decides for himself

77. (1656–1731), *NNBW* ix: 648.
78. *NNBW* vi: 191.
79. Braunius, 1675; see also *NNBW* vi: 190.
80. Gerretzen, 1940: 5.
81. Noodt to Braunius, Franeker, 27 Apr. 1681, UL Leiden, PL 246 (not an autograph): 'Seer gaern zoude ick uw Ed dienst doen, omtrent het opstellen van de bewuste Duplyck, maer mijn swakheid, die ick van de voorgaende siekte behouden heb, en die nu noch daer by comt, overmits weer ingestort ben, maeckt mij 't selve t'enemael onmogelijk.'
82. *Opera* i: 634.
83. *Opera* i: 635.

whether he wants to farm, to seek riches in commerce on land and sea, or rather to devote himself to letters and philosophy. In all these matters he is left to himself, why not, then, in matters of religion also?

If one wants to force men to accept a religion, one not only fights men, but God himself. If God had wished to do so, it would have been quite easy for his omnipotence to give all men one religious conviction, just as he gave everybody the same feeling of good and bad, hunger and thirst, cold and heat. Here Noodt, following Grotius, uses the analogy of moral convictions and arithmetic. 'Just as not even God could make that two and two be not four', wrote Grotius, 'he could not make that that which is intrinsically wrong would not be wrong.'[84] Noodt turns this into an argument for freedom of religion. Are we not certain that God could have done with regard to his service what he did with regard to numbers? Here he has given all men the same notion of truth, which is the glory of that beautiful and indispensable art. All sciences need rules to attain certainty, but there is one which stands supreme. In all places, in all times, with all peoples—Dutch, English, Germans, Italians, Spanish, French, Africans, Indians, Scythians, and Americans—it applies without respect of status, fortune, or belief that, if we go down to the fingers, three and two are five. And that truth cannot be subverted by any argument, whether inspired by hatred, superstition, greed, ambition, or whatever passion. But God in his wisdom wanted something else with regard to numbers than with regard to religion. Therefore it is immense foolishness or arrogance when a man arrogates to himself what is God's alone.[85]

After this Noodt gives his argument based on natural law. After a sketch of the original position—which we already know from his address on sovereignty—he concludes that in that position man has no right to decide about God and his service and force the recalcitrant by violence. How, then, could the prince claim such a right of judgment and punishment over his subjects? Society is formed by a contract of individuals and these could not give the prince what they did not have themselves. Certainly, the prince needs powers to maintain society. But because his sovereignty is intended for the good of society, that which leads elsewhere is outside his powers. *Imperium* is not invented to curb freedom, but to manage it for the common good. As liberals would say in later ages, Noodt stipulates

84. *De jure belli ac pacis* 1. 1. 10. 5.
85. *Opera* i: 636.

that the state is no moralist. It is not the task of princes to enlighten the minds by instruction, to mellow the fierce and stubborn springs of passion by wisdom, nor to lead bad morals by advice and discussion to virtue. This remains the care and glory of the *eruditum otium*.[86]

After this Noodt discusses one by one all the arguments brought forward for the thesis that religion should be subject to the *imperium* of man. Noodt naturally accepts the traditional thesis that all religions are equivalent,[87] or at least that the superiority of one above the other cannot be proved. All over the world there are various denominations of Christians, not to speak of Jews, Heathens, and Mohammadans; this debate cannot be decided by reason or natural law alone.[88] Here we find various themes which Noodt had treated in other works. If the infidel does injustice to God, man must leave revenge to him. With what right would man revenge an injustice that is not done to him?

And then there is the argument that one can help a man bound for eternal damnation by torture or death, even against his will. Does not one prevent the mad man from throwing himself in a river or chasm? Cannot everybody appeal in the name of someone who is sentenced to death, even if the convict submits to the judgment? Does not the doctor do many painful things in the interest of our health? But that argument does not obtain. Cruelty always remains cruelty.[89] Violence, moreover, has no effect on the mind. What if a tyrant wanted to force me to believe that three and two are eight? He might threaten me with all his bloody arts, but when I count my fingers nobody can convince me that three and two are more than five. Threats are useless. I can cheat, I can lie, I can say what pain forces out of me, but I cannot believe what my intellect denies. It is the same with religion. Likewise Noodt refutes the thesis that the law must make man virtuous. Here one confuses the task of law with that of religion. The law does not demand that people do good; it is satisfied when they do no harm to others. The law has only regard for actions, it does not prescribe virtuousness, but only conduct that is useful for society. If it forbids vices it does not demand that we hate them, but only penalizes actions that are harmful for society. The law can regard as a good citizen someone who is a bad man in other respects.

The argument that religious meetings are often the source of

86. *Opera* i: 638.
87. Cf. Van Dooren, 1983–4: 49. Klibansky, 1968.
88. *Opera* i: 639.
89. *Opera* i: 640.

conspiracies and breaches of the law is likewise rejected. Here one can follow the example of the Roman senate who punished the excesses of the Bacchanalia but did not forbid the actual religious rites. Nether is the fact that a religion is new a reason to prohibit it, or otherwise one should accept that Nero was right when he prohibited the new Christian religion. Many questions which are hotly debated in religion are no concern of the state and lose all interest after some time. How much did the people fight over the sabbath? And who still believes that the question of the antipodes, which was discussed by Lactantius and his contemporaries, is relevant for religion? Who thinks that it is important from a religious point of view whether the sun moves or the earth? Opinions change with the times. According to canon law, taking interest is a crime and there are still people among us who would prefer such a strict rule. But in our state another opinion prevails and everybody is convinced that taking interest is as acceptable as hire.[90]

It is not the task of the law-giver to punish everything that is disagreeable to God. In Rome abortion was not punished for many centuries, although people detested it. The despicable habit of killing or abandoning new-born children was not a crime with the Greeks, nor with the Romans, not even under the Christian Emperor Constantine.[91] And the fact that Mosaic law punished superstition is no argument either. What obtains for Israel does not necessarily obtain for us.[92] Israel was a theocratic state. Every state has its own situation and it is impossible that the law applying in one state should be binding for all men, in all places, and at all times, just as there is not one medicine for all illnesses. Many of the Mosaic laws do not apply in our republic; they forbade interest, but allowed polygamy and divorce. In religion, Noodt concludes, only the rule of God applies, not that of men.

Noodt's address must have made a deep impression.[93] It seems

90. Cf. Noodt's *De foenore et usuris*, above, p. 181 ff.
91. Cf. Noodt's *Julius Paulus*, above, p. 207 ff.
92. The argument was used by Noodt in *De foenore et usuris* (above, p. 181 ff.) as well as in his advice concerning a marriage (below, 6, p. 284 ff.).
93. See the very extensive *Vorrede* of the German transl., Frankfurt and Leipzig, 1724 (Ahsmann–Feenstra, 1984: nr. 461): 'Est ist des berühmten Gerhardi Noodts gelehrte Rede von der Gewisssens-Freyheit von sehr vielen vernünftigen Leuthen in Europa so wohl aufgenommen worden, dass die unterschiedliche in Lateinischer, Holländischer, Englischer und Französicher Sprache heraus gekommene Editiones derselben in kurtzer Zeit alle auffgegangen und die Exemplaria angefangen rar zu werden.'

likely that the orthodox ministers of Leiden, who cannot but have disliked it, took measures against him. After 1706 he was never again a member of the elders and deacons of the Reformed Church, as he had regularly been before. But in the history of the Enlightenment the address has its indelible place. One of its particular qualities is the completeness with which a great number of arguments in favour of discretion of the government in matters of religion is discussed and refuted.[94] As an example of legal argumentation on the basis of natural law, it is a masterpiece, candid, acute, and without verbosity or ambiguity. But as a piece of rhetoric it is also very fine and effective. Although not all Noodt's arguments are new and some of them could easily be criticized, the address remains an important station on the road to complete freedom of religion.

Observationum libri duo

For Noodt 1706 was a year of success. Only a month after the spectacular address on freedom of religion his Observations appeared,[95] a work that by its title alone refers to the great tradition of humanistic legal scholarship. In the same year, his address on sovereignty and the *lex regia* was reprinted and a Dutch translation and excerpts in French of his address on freedom of religion published. The *Observationes* were in preparation for quite a while. In January 1701 he had announced their imminent appearance to Van Bijnkershœk,[96] and in June of the following year Van Bijnkershœk and Noodt discussed an emendation by Noodt to D 14. 2. 9 (*Observationes* 1. 13), a text on which Van Bijnkershœk was planning to publish a study himself. They agreed that the one who was first to publish would mention the other's study;[97] Van

94. See the *Vorrede* (as n. 93).
95. Ahsmann–Feenstra, 1984: nr. 450. Perizonius to Van Eck, Leiden, 12 Mar. 1706 (UL Utrecht, MS 1000): 'Noodtii nostri Observationes te jam accepisse credo.'
96. Van Bijnkershœk to Van Eck, 14 Jan. 1701 (UL Utrecht, MS 1000): '. . . Cl. Noodtium brevi editurum esse Observationes juris: ita mihi ipsius narrabat ante triduum, cum hic me inviseret'.
97. Van Bijnkershœk to Van Eck, The Hague, 2 June 1702 (UL Utrecht, MS 1000): 'Proxima hebdomade Libellus meus typis incipit describi. Clar. Noodt inter *Observationes juris*, quae edet, caput singulare destinavit *legi 9 ff. de lege Rhodi. de jactu*, ut mihi non ita pridem me inviserens, significavit. Habet ille conjecturam criticam de *tè Italia*, quam eo tempore mecum communicabat. Ego quum inter eas, quas dabo ad d.l. eandem ei monstrassem in adversariis meis, ita inter nos convenit, ut qui prior prodeat, de alio moniturus sit.'

Bijnkershœk, who eventually was the first, did so,[98] and Noodt mentioned their conversation of 1702 likewise in his Observations.[99] At that moment they still seem very friendly. In March 1705 Noodt announced to Van Bijnkershœk that he hoped to publish a single book of Observations that autumn,[1] and in January 1706 the book is actually in the press.[2] It has two books, one with eighteen observations, the other with twenty-seven, in which some thirty-one emendations in total are proposed, not all of his own invention, of course. Of these, only three were later endorsed by Mommsen.[3]

The general characteristics of Noodt's work as found in his *Probabilia* are confirmed by the Observations. He is an acute jurist who has full command of all the philological methods of his time. To prove some point of Latin idiom or to support some emendation parallel texts from classical authors of every kind are cited abundantly. That he has excellent knowledge of Latin is proved, *inter alia*, by his observation that 'ceterum' not only means 'for the rest', but also 'otherwise' (= *alioquin*).[4] He does not seem to be an expert, on the other hand, in medieval Roman law. He ignores the difference between Accursius and his son Franciscus Accursii[5] and elsewhere ascribes to the Accursian gloss what in fact belongs to the much younger *casus*.[6] But on such points most of his contemporaries would hardly do better.

Noodt clearly reflects the attitudes of his day and class in the reinterpretation of D 7. 1. 28.[7] In this text Pomponius says that one can will the usufruct of gold and silver coins that one was accustomed to use as gems. This is an irregular case, because normally one can only use or have fruits from money by spending it, and therefore, if money is willed, we usually have *quasi-ususfructus*: the usufructuary becomes owner of the money under the duty to repay an equivalent amount at the end of usufruct.[8] The gloss explained the text by suggesting that it concerned coins worn as a necklace. This suggestion was

98. C. van Bijnkershœk, *Ad L. Axioosis IX de lege Rhodia de jactu liber singularis, et De Dominio maris Dissertatio*. The Hague, 1703: ch. IV in fine; see Star Numan, 1869: 208.
99. *Opera* i: 312.
1. Van Bijnkershœk to Van Eck, The Hague, 3 Mar. 1705 (UL Utrecht, MS 1000).
2. Van Bijnkershœk to Van Eck, The Hague, 18 Jan. 1706 (UL Utrecht, MS 1000).
3. D 33. 2. 43 (*Obs*. 2. 12; Mo ii: 114: 16) 'et⟨si rerum⟩ quod'; D 42. 1. 53 (*Obs*. 1. 8; Mo ii: 542: 16) 'appellatur ⟨ternisve [Noodt: tribusve]⟩ litteris'; D 46. 3. 72 (*Obs*. 1. 16; Mo ii: 712: 33).
4. *Obs*. 2. 14.
5. *Obs*. 2. 14.
6. *Obs*. 1. 10.
7. *Obs*. 1. 5.
8. Kaser, 1971: 306.

endorsed, and dressed up with humanistic learning, by Donellus and Connannus. Noodt suggests a different solution: maybe Pomponius had a coin collection in mind. The *usus* of such a collection consists in the delight resulting from assiduous collecting, as well as from contemplation and display. Therefore such a collection can be given in usufruct. In the seventeenth century, coin-collecting was a favourite pastime of learned men and in many auction catalogues one finds lists of coins auctioned with the library.

Arguments which Noodt uses frequently are the false solution of sigla or *notæ*,[9] *geminatio*,[10] palingenetic data deduced from *inscriptiones*,[11] and transposition of words.[12] On one occasion epigraphic material is adduced,[13] and historical development is stressed again.[14] The surprising results reached with the principle of *geminatio* in its further development can be illustrated nicely by *Observationes* 2. 17, though Noodt here uses the technique in exactly the same way as e.g. Jacob Gothofredus.[15] If you need some letters to form a missing word, you may take them anywhere you can find them. The opening sentence of D 16. 2. 60 reads:

Socium, qui in eo, quod ex societate lucri faceret, reddendo moram adhibuit, cum ea pecunia ipse usus sit, usuras quoque eum praestare Labeo ait.[16]

Cujas[17] concluded that an 'aut' must have fallen out, because a few lines below it is said expressly 'si aut usus ea pecunia non sit, aut moram non fecerit'.[18] Noodt suggests that the 'aut' is concealed in 'adhibuit'. Supposing that the manuscript had 'AdhibUiT' and the scribe overlooked the capitals, we may reconstruct 'adhibuit *aut* cum ea'. Another possibility would be to assume that the original had 'adhibuit, cVm Ea'; then you would get 'adhibuit, cum*ve* ea'. In *Observationes* 2. 16 Noodt proposes a whole series of emendations by gemination, among which is the doubling of a whole word in D 3. 3. 35.[19]

As was the case in the *Probabilia*, only a minority of cases treated

9. *Obs.* 1. 16; 2. 3; 2. 22; 2. 25.
10. *Obs.* 1. 18; 2. 16; 2. 17.
11. *Obs.* 1. 7; 2. 5; 2. 11; 2. 27.
12. *Obs.* 1. 8; 1. 18.
13. *Obs.* 2. 27.
14. *Obs.* 2. 23.
15. *Animadv. jur. civ.*, c. 9.
16. 'The partner who is in arrears in rendering the profit he made from the partnership, because he used the money himself, must also pay interest, says Labeo.'
17. *Obs. et emend.* 13. 15.
18. 'if he has not used the money or is not in arrears'.
19. (Mo i: 90: 20): '. . . liberti *patronus*. Patronus libertum . . .'.

are not dogmatical, but real textual problems,[20] and many of the problems in question were antinomies already discussed in the gloss.[21] In *Observationes* 2. 23 Noodt even defends Accursius' interpretation of C 5. 14. 4 against the criticism of Muretus, because if we pay due attention to the historical development of Roman law—of which naturally neither Accursius nor Muretus was aware—Accursius seems to be right. The legitimation of children by subsequent marriage was introduced only by Constantine (307–37), so someone in the era of Gordianus (240) could hardly have dreamt of it: 'Your very bright erudition does not permit you to ignore, Muretus, that someone who wants to interpret old laws must always pay attention to the history of the science of law, which did not fall from heaven one day like a shower, but has grown gradually through the custom of men and the opportunity of the ages.'[22] Here it is very clear, by the way, that history of legal science for Noodt was not an antiquarian hobby but an instrument for correct legal interpretation; Noodt, the jurist, had no problem in siding with Accursius. Another scholar who is attacked, as in *De foenore et usuris*, is Salmasius. This leads to a rather uncommon stress on the difference in expertise between jurist and classicist: 'I am rather surprised that such an absurd opinion is approved by someone who is no fool; unless we must forgive someone who professes not to be a jurist for ignoring legal reason. But for this we may reproach him: why does he engage in civil law, of which he is no expert at all?'[23]

Apparently Noodt had learned something from his critics concerning the correct attitude of a critic: 'I will not change anything rashly,'[24] he says, and elsewhere he duly confesses his modesty with respect to the classical jurists: 'It is not consistent with my modesty to assume that if there is some fault here, it is Gaius' fault. For who would believe that such a man was so ignorant of the law in which he was engaged that he would not know that you cannot pledge the property of someone else?'[25] In many cases Noodt's emendations are really quite modest, but there are some cases which confirm his reputation as a bold critic. Several times, while suggesting the erasure of a sentence,[26] or the addition of words,[27] he acknowledges bluntly

20. e.g. *Obs.* 1. 18; 2. 10; 2. 12.

21. e.g. *Obs.* 1. 7; 1. 8; 1. 9; 1. 12; 2. 1; 2. 12; 2. 27.

22. *Opera* i: 344.

23. *Opera* i: 330. Later, Van Bijnkershœk, when criticizing Noodt's *Julius Paulus*, stressed that Lipsius was no jurist. See above, p. 214.

24. *Opera* i: 301.

25. *Opera* i: 303.

26. *Obs.* 1. 9.

27. *Obs.* 2. 6; 2. 9; 2. 10; 2. 22.

that this goes against the whole of the manuscript tradition, including the *Florentina* and the Basilica.[28] Although he follows the example of Cujas in putting *ratio juris* above text tradition, we cannot deny that there is some truth in the judgment of later generations that levity in conjecturing 'ist das leidige Erbteil der Noodt'schen Schule'.[29] In D 7. 1. 13. 5 (Ulp. 18 *ad Sab.*), a text concerning the question of what a usufructuary can do with the goods in his possession, Noodt[30] cuts out a sentence of no less than twenty-four words ('et si forte . . . deicere potuit') against the authority of F and the Basilica, because he simply cannot believe that Ulpian would allow the usufructuary to cut down vineyards or orchards if a mine of some kind would promise better returns. That the Basilica have these words, says Noodt, only proves that the addition to Ulpian's text was made before Justinian's time. Naturally, this does not follow. A reading appearing in F and the Basilica could very well originate with Justinian's compilers. Noodt's expertise in the history of legal science evidently does not extend to Byzantine law. Noodt defended this emendation again in his monograph on usufruct (1713). It is not very convincing, though, and is rejected by modern Romanists.[31] The only interesting point here is that Noodt contemplates the idea of early post-classical changes in Ulpian's text (that is, changes made before Justinian's time), an idea explored systematically only centuries later.[32]

Noodt's colleague and friend Perizonius had voiced his misgivings about his lust for emendation in a letter to Van Eck, written shortly after receiving the *Observationes*. 'Many things' he wrote 'which he solicits with his emendations can be explained in a regular way, if I am not very much mistaken.'[33] And in his next letter, after reconsidering Noodt's discussion of D 12. 4. 16,[34] he wrote about the emendation, which was proposed earlier in the *Probabilia* (1691): 'As far as his

28. *Obs.* 1. 9; 2. 6; 2. 10. Examples of rather bold emendations are the expunction of 24 words in D 7. 1. 13. 5 (*Obs.* 1. 9; Mo i: 220: 19 f.); the replacement of 'in factum actione' by 'hac actione' in D 20. 1. 11. 1 (*Obs.* 2. 9; Mo i: 583: 8); the replacement of 'in usu' by 'iuris' in D 33. 10. 9. 2 (*Obs.* 2. 10; Mo i: 141: 17), and the expunction of 'legata' in PS 3. 6. 31 (*Obs.* 2. 22).
29. W. Noodt, 1921: 44.
30. *Obs.* 1. 9.
31. Vangerow, i, 1856: 736, regards the period as genuine.
32. See Wieacker, 1960.
33. Perizonius to Van Eck, Leiden, 12 Mar. 1706 (UL Utrecht, MS 1000): 'Multa certe, quae ille suis sollicitat emendationibus, recte, ni valde fallor, exponi queunt.'
34. *Prob.* 4. 4 and *Obs.* 1. 17.

emendation is concerned, it is bold and rough, because he inserts a whole word of ten letters without so much as a trace in the manuscripts. In this way we can easily edit any text according to our own opinion.'[35]

Naturally not all observations have practical importance for lawyers. An example is the discussion of D 14. 2. 9, a fragment in Greek from the jurist Volusius Mæcianus.[36] The text says that someone who shipwrecked in Italy was despoiled by tax gatherers in the Cyclades. How could this happen? Many humanists, among them such prominent scholars as Hugo Grotius and Jacob Gothofredus, proposed a score of solutions. Given the plausibility of a slip of the pen of some scribe writing a geographical name with which he was unfamiliar, you simply have to look for a name that seems more plausible. Gothofredus suggested reading 'Ikaria', the name of an island in the eastern part of the Ægean. Van Bijnkershœk and Perizonius both contributed material from ancient sources to support this conjecture which, in fact, has obtained till our day.[37] But Noodt suggested on the basis of texts of Livy and Pliny the reading 'Æthalia' instead, being the name of an island between Samos and Lesbos. If it proves that Noodt is very well read in Latin literature, it seems difficult to argue that this conjecture is any better than that of Gothofredus. Both islands are in the eastern Ægean and not quite among the Cyclades, so neither of the proposed conjectures really solves the problem. And anyway it is not for jurists, in our opinion, to decide such a question. But we cannot invoke the glossators as the more practical jurists here. They did not fail to discuss the question and gave a solution which testifies to their lack of interest in ancient geography: the Cyclades are Italian islands![38] So for the glossators this was not an antiquarian question. In fact, they discussed much odder questions. This was not where the difference between glossators and humanists lay.

We should not regard the example just given as representative of the whole of the *Observationes*, for that matter. If they confirm Noodt's reputation as a very learned man and a rather bold critic at

35. Perizonius to Van Eck, Leiden, 2 Apr. 1706 (UL Utrecht, MS 1000): 'Quod ad emendationem ejus attinet, audax et dura est, inserens quippe integram vocem decem litterarum, sine ullis vestigiis in manuscriptis. Ista ratione facile omnia possumus nostram ad sententiam redigere.'
36. *Obs.* 1. 13.
37. See Mo i: 421: 28.
38. Gloss 'Cyclades' *a.h.l.* '. . . Insulae sunt Italiae . . .'.

times, they also show him as one of the best Roman law scholars of his day. Several of his interpretations remain worth considering and, after all, a score of three emendations endorsed by Mommsen is not bad at all, considering the fact that he expunged the greater part of the critical effort of Roman law scholars between the thirteenth and the nineteenth century.

De forma emendandi doli mali in contrahendis negotiis admissi apud veteres

In April 1709[39] Noodt published a monograph, that, from a Romanist's point of view, as well as for its place in the development of an important civil law doctrine, may be one of his most interesting ones: 'On the manner of amending deceit in the formation of contracts among the ancients.'[40] It concerns the problem discussed in modern Romanistic literature under the catchword *dolus in contrahendo* (a term Noodt does not yet know).[41] According to Brutti, Noodt's was the first modern treatment of the subject.[42] It is also 'modern' for the clear consciousness of historical development and discontinuity which it demonstrates, perhaps too modern for the taste of most of Noodt's contemporaries.

The book took long to appear. It was announced with its full title at the end of Book I, chapter XIV, of *De jurisdictione et imperio* (1691), where the central text D 4. 3. 7 pr. was discussed for the first time.[43] Or did it just lie in store for many years? This is suggested by the fact that, from a systematic point of view, it seems less well organized than some books that were published earlier, e.g. *De foenore et usuris*.[44] Perhaps in his younger years he did not feel confident enough to publish a thesis on a vital doctrine of civil law which, as he

39. Noodt announced the book to Perizonius in Feb., see Perizonius to Van Eck, Leiden, 18 Feb. 1709; see also Van Bijnkershœk to Van Eck, The Hague, 21 Feb. 1709 (both in UL Utrecht, MS 1000). Noodt sent it to Cuper and to an unknown person with letters dated 17 Apr. 1709 (KB 72 G 20) and 21 Apr. 1709 (Centr. Bur. Genealogie, The Hague, doss. Noodt).
40. Ahsmann–Feenstra, 1984: nr. 463.
41. See Stein, 1958; Kaser, 1971: 487f. n. 32. The term *culpa in contrahendo* was created by Jhering (1861: 7); cf. Medicus, 1986.
42. Brutti, 1973: 82.
43. *Opera* i: 114.
44. As in *De jurisdictione et imperio* there are fairly wide digressions, e.g. chs. 6, 11, and 16. Noodt acknowledges this in the opening sentence of ch. 13: 'Sed ut diverticulo revertar . . .'.

knew well enough,[45] flew in the face of the long-established *communis opinio*; an opinion, moreover, which his *collega proximus* Johannes Vœt had enunciated authoritatively only a few years before in volume i of his commentary on the Pandects (1698).[46]

The law concerning deceit in the formation of contracts, as established by the Accursian gloss,[47] elaborated by the postglossators,[48] and generally accepted until Noodt's monograph, hinged on two distinctions. First, we must distinguish between contracts *stricti juris* and *bonae fidei*. A contract *stricti juris* made by deceit is valid in civil law, but may be invalidated by praetorian remedies: the *actio* and *exceptio doli*. As far as contracts *bonae fidei* are concerned, we must distinguish whether the deceit has actually caused the other party to enter the contract (*dolus contractui causam dans*), or merely concerns secondary conditions (*dolus in contractum incidens*). In the first case the contract is null and void *ipso jure*, in the second case it can be contested either with the relevant contractual action (e.g. the *actio empti* in a case of sale) or with an *exceptio doli*.

Noodt's main intention is to dispute the validity of the second distinction; this has no basis in the Corpus Juris nor in any other source from Antiquity.[49] Moreover, it makes no sense; if it really had a good justification, it should obtain in contracts *stricti juris* as well.[50] And finally it is at odds with well-established principles of Roman law, e.g. that in *bonae fidei* actions the *exceptio doli* is superfluous, because the words 'ex fide bona' in the formula enable the judge to consider *dolus* without an express authorization to do so.[51]

The introductory chapters are concerned with preliminary matters: *dolus* as *vox media* (I)[52] and the definition of *dolus* in the sources (II). The central thesis is expounded in chapter III. Noodt is quite

45. *Opera* i: 356, see below.
46. *Comm. ad Pand.* 4. 3. 3 f.; and see Zoesius, *Comm. ad Dig.* (1675): 138.
47. Gloss 'si in hoc ipso' on D 4. 3. 7 pr.; see also gloss 'aut fraudandi' on D 17. 2. 3. 3; gloss 'venderet' on D 19. 1. 13. 4; gloss 'bonae fidei sunt' on Inst. 4. 6. 28. And see Van Oven, 1953: 273; Stein, 1958: 89 f.
48. Baldus *a.h.l.*; Bartolus, Angelus Aretinus, and Jason on Inst. 4. 6. 28.
49. Fransen's interpretation of Noodt's book and its intention (Fransen, 1946: 278 f.) is erroneous.
50. This is a very strong argument against the 'innere Berechtigung' of the distinction, as far as classical and medieval Roman law are concerned, but it lost its point when in the German *usus modernus* the difference between contracts *stricti juris* and *bonae fidei* was eliminated, and henceforth the distinction in effect applied to all contracts.
51. *Opera* i: 356 f.
52. On this, see Carcaterra, 1970; Wacke, 1977: 221.

aware that an attack on a generally accepted doctrine of civil law is controversial, and therefore he begins with a rather elaborate *captatio benevolentiae*:

But as far as I am concerned this sentence, although accepted by unanimous vote, cannot be proved and retained in the republic of letters without violating the care of civil law. I fear, however, that it will seem plain boldness for a single man of moderate cleverness and little erudition to abrogate a doctrine supported by the judgment and assurance of so many illustrious men for many ages. But my modesty was overcome by the noble plan to free jurisprudence from an error which is no less dangerous than disgraceful.[53]

Chapter IV discusses the distinction of contracts *stricti juris* and *bonae fidei* which, according to Noodt (and many others), does not belong to natural law but to the subtleties of the Roman forum. Gaius Aquilius Gallus was the first to propose the *actio* and *exceptio doli* in the praetorian edict. Chapters V and VI discuss matters concerning *dolus* in contracts *stricti juris*. Chapters VII to XIII discuss various aspects of *dolus in contrahendo* in contracts *bonae fidei*. The contract is null and void, the deceived had no use for an *exceptio doli*, but he can sue the deceiver with the relevant contractual action, even if the contract itself is null.[54] He can even bring an action 'quantum intersit deceptum non esse'[55] in spite of the absence of any contract. Chapter XIV discusses and emends D 4. 3. 7 pr., the *sedes* of the disputed doctrine. Chapter XV treats the meaning of 'resolvi', 'rescindi', and similar terms and the final chapter discusses the effects of *metus*.[56]

Building on developments in natural law theory since Grotius, Noodt defines *dolus* dogmatically as an impairment of the freedom of judgment, which is an absolute precondition of human society. Without that freedom you could not suppose a binding social contract. The point is discussed in the context of the distinction of *dolus bonus* and *dolus malus* (I). The difference between the two is in the purpose that is served. By the law of human society (which truth as well as all other virtues must serve) dissimulation is no vice and may be *dolus bonus* when truth would ruin a man. The same applies when someone protects himself or another by dissimulation against a person who is not guided by the laws of reason on account of

53. *Opera* i: 356.
54. The same is accepted by Wacke, 1977: 239, who adduces D 18. 1. 62. 1, exactly the same text as adduced by Noodt, *Opera* i: 372.
55. 'For as much as he has an interest not to be deceived'.
56. On *metus* see now Hartkamp, 1971.

madness, anger, or drunkenness. Reason never condemns devotion to human society, and what promotes this community is good. Men owe each other the truth because they are bound together by natural reason as if by a tacit law and form some society of law 'which cannot exist unless everybody has complete and unimpaired freedom to judge and decide about his own interest according to his own free will'.[57] Man must not seek truth for the sake of truth, but because respect for truth furthers the common weal, which can hardly be expected when truth is neglected. Here the notion of *dolus* is linked directly to a fundamental precondition of the social contract, and natural law and Roman law are combined in the usual way: natural law takes care of principles, Roman law of all technical questions.

From a technical point of view, Noodt's treatment shows the usual acuteness and erudition. Only very few and rather moderate emendations are suggested, and once he argues, convincingly, on the basis of the *Notæ* of Probus.[58] The only major expunction he proposes is in D 4. 3. 7 pr. This emendation was discussed in *De jurisdictione et imperio* (1691),[59] and is defended here with still greater elaboration. The text reads as follows:

Ulp. Lib. undecimo ad edictum. Et eleganter Pomponius haec verba 'si alia actio non sit' sic excipit, quasi res alio modo ei ad quem ea res pertinet salva esse not poterit. nec videtur huic sententiae adversari, quod Julianus libro quarto scribit, si minor annis viginti quinque consilio servi circumscriptus eum vendidit cum peculio emptorque eum manumisit, dandam in manumissum de dolo actionem (hoc enim sic accipimus carere dolo emptorem, ut ex empto teneri non possit) aut nullam esse venditionem, si in hoc ipso ut venderet circumscriptus est. et quod minor proponitur, non inducit in integrum restitutionem; nam adversus manumissum nulla in integrum restitutio potest locum habere.[60]

57. *Opera* i: 353 f.; cf. Brutti, 1973: 84.
58. Chapter VII, *Opera* i: 362.
59. Book I, Chapter 14, *Opera* i: 113 f.
60. 'And Pomponius elegantly explains the words "if there is no other action" in this way, that the interest of the one whom it concerns cannot be saved in another way. And this opinion does not seem to be contradicted by the fact that Julian writes in the fourth book that if someone younger than 25, misled by the advice of his slave, sells him with his peculium, and the buyer lets him free, an *actio de dolo* must be given to the one manumitted (for we suppose that the emptor caused no deceit for which he could be sued *ex empto*), or the sale is null and void when he is misled precisely to sell. And the fact that he is described as a minor is no reason to give an *in integrum restitutio*, because against a person manumitted an *in integrum restitutio* cannot take place.'

Evidently the text is not without serious textual problems. The passage 'hoc enim . . . possit' (Mo i: 120: 28–9) is only put in brackets by modern editors in order to save an appearance of logic for the text as a whole. Moreover, we should read 'ex vendito' instead of 'ex empto', as was noted already in the Accursian gloss.[61] And the word 'aut' (Mo i: 120: 29) is problematic. According to Torelli it is not in F, was added by an ancient hand, but was not necessary for the reading of the text.[62] Brenkman believed that it was a more recent addition,[63] but Mommsen (or rather those who did the collation for him) ascribed it to the ordinary corrector of F.[64] Van Bijnkershœk informed Noodt that the 'aut' stood in his own manuscript,[65] as well as in a score of *editiones vulgares*, which gives Noodt the opportunity for an elaborate laudation of the senator.[66]

But the main difficulty with the text was, and still is, in the words 'aut nullam . . . circumscriptus est', which have never been explained in a satisfactory way.[67] As it stands, the text says that deceit *of a third party* (the slave) would make a sale null. This is contrary to all we know about classical Roman law and could only have been written by someone believing in the doctrine that error is a defect of the will vitiating consensus regardless of the question of who its author was. Noodt suggests that the passage is a glosseme, the addition of some inept interpreter of Roman law. He elaborately expounds the reasons for this suspicion and even gives a reason why the glosseme could have slipped into the text. Nevertheless, he does not claim that his emendation is more than probable,[68] and he is well aware that the passage itself is found in the whole of the manuscript tradition, including the Basilica. With this expunction the distinction of *dolus*

61. Gloss 'ex empto' *a.h.l.*; cf. Noodt, *Opera* i: 378. This is the only point discussed by Wacke (1977: 237 n. 229), who rightly suggests, for that matter, that this is a slip of minor importance.
62. This is indicated by putting the word between asterisks: *aut*. Van Oven (1953: 284) erroneously believed these asterisks stood in F itself.
63. See Gebauer–Spangenberg, *a.h.l.* n. 35.
64. F^1 = 'Scriptura primaria a correctore ordinario mutata.'
65. This is the MS Brenkman called Bynk. I (now Leiden, BPL 6C). This gives us a *terminus post quem* for the finalizing of *De forma emendandi doli mali*. Van Bijnkershœk acquired the MS on 4 Oct. 1696, see Van den Bergh, 1984.
66. *Opera* i: 378. Perhaps Van Bijnkershœk felt uneasy about this conspicuous laudation in the context of one of Noodt's bold emendations, and therefore felt obliged to disassociate himself publicly from Noodt's critical work a year later in the preface to his *Observationes juris romani*.
67. So Sprenger, 1898: 364 and Wacke, 1977: 241, whose own explanation is not convincing either. See Van Oven, 1953: 282 f.; Stein 1958: 89.
68. *Opera* i: 378, see also *Opera* i: 113 f.

causam dans and *incidens*, which for many reasons could not be classical Roman law anyway, loses its sole basis in the text of the Corpus Juris, the text, in fact, for the explanation of which it was invented by the glossators in the first place. Naturally the expunction of no less than twelve words, though getting some support from the problematic state of the introduced word 'aut',[69] was regarded as rather bold criticism by more orthodox philologists and jurists. Perizonius wrote about it to Van Eck in fairly sharp words: 'For a long time I have judged the textual criticism of our friend in many cases as rather rough. With regard to l. 7 [D 4. 3. 7 pr.] he says himself wantonly that the word "aut" is found in manuscripts as well as in all old editions and yet he wants to expunge the whole clause or the whole sentence. But this is burning and cutting.'[70] The same criticism, with exactly the same motivation, is repeated by scholars until the end of the nineteenth century.[71] In retrospect, however, there is much to say in favour of Noodt's emendation, if we realize that it is, properly speaking, not an emendation, not textual criticism, but very acute historical criticism. The difference between textual and historical criticism was not yet fully understood in Noodt's day, however, and his sense of historical consciousness was rather uncommon. Or, as Haubold put it, he was guided 'von einem, damals noch seltenen, richtigen Geschmacke'.[72] It seems that, after all, he is justified by the better part of modern Roman law scholarship.

We do not know what actually motivated Noodt's rejection of the classicity of the distinction of *dolus causam dans* and *incidens*. Maybe he was inspired partly by Grotius, who rejected (for natural law) the various distinctions concerning *dolus* 'which come from Roman law, either civil or praetorian, and some of which are not quite true and accurate'.[73] To vindicate Roman law from the false imputation of a defective doctrine would be reason enough to write a book, but it

69. This is stressed by Brenkman; see Gebauer–Spangenberg *a.h.l.* n. 35.
70. Perizonius to Van Eck, Leiden, 13 May 1709 (UL Utrecht, MS 1000): 'Crisin Nostri jamdudum in plerisque duriorem judicavi. Ipse in l. 7 fatetur ultro etiam particulam *aut* in manuscriptis et in omnibus antiquis editionibus reperiri, et tamen totum Comma vel sententiam totam vult deleri. Hoc vero est urere et secare.' From Perizonius' words we may assume that Van Eck had criticized Noodt's conjecture as well. It was rejected likewise by Huber, 1700: 179 (who refers, of course, to *De jurisdictione et imperio* 1. 14); Schulting and Smallenburg, *Notae ad Digesta* (1804–35), *a.h.l.*; Hagemeister, 1720; Nettelbladt, 1744. See Brutti, 1973: 88.
71. See e.g. Glück, 1867: 115 f.; Sprenger, 1898: 364.
72. Haubold, 1812: 307. See further Van den Bergh, 1985*b*.
73. *De jure belli ac pacis* 2. 11. 6. 1.

does not explain Noodt's claim that the doctrine is dangerous as well as disgraceful. This is all the more conspicuous because various scholars (ancient as well as modern) have claimed that the distinction conforms with reason or logic.[74]

But perhaps Noodt's position is the more realistic one. In the scholar's den the distinction may seem just and logical, but in practice it causes serious problems of proof and may work as no more than an invitation to chicanery, if not a licence for judicial arbitrariness. In many cases the result wholly depends on what the pretendedly deceived party declares, or the judge construes, to have been his intention. As Noodt remarked very aptly, the price—which is the standard example of an incidental consideration—may very well be the exact reason why a contract was made.[75]

Established law is slow to die, however. As Noodt himself would no doubt have expected, his attack on a doctrine deeply entrenched in the civil law tradition did not win an immediate victory, although it did not fail to appeal to many scholars.[76] In Germany young Daniel Nettelbladt (1719–1791) defended the traditional doctrine in 1744,[77] and so did Hellfeld (1764), Glück (1790), and Thibaut (1803).[78] In France it was maintained throughout, e.g. by Pothier[79] and Domat.[80] Consequently, it was codified both in the *Preussische Allgemeine Landrecht* (1794)[81] and in the *Code civil* (1804).[82]

But scientific development in the Pandectist School shows a different picture. Von Savigny no longer heeded the medieval distinction of *dolus causam dans* and *incidens*,[83] and Puchta eliminated it

74. Thibaut i, 1834: 11; Sprenger, 1898: 362 f.; Wacke, 1977: 241.
75. See *Opera* i: 458; for some telling examples from German legal practice, see Sprenger, 1898: 367 ff.
76. See Thibaut ii, 1834: § 451 n. *g*, p. 11; Van Oven (1953: 290) speaks about a 'succès espéré' without substantiating the supposition. From Noodt's own words we can infer that he did not expect immediate success.
77. See J. H. Reuter, *De doli incidenti et causam danti in contractibus effectu*. Halle: J. C. Hendel, 1744. D. Nettelbladt was *praeses* of this disputation and therefore it is assumed that he wrote it, though this is not certain. But see also D. Nettelbladt, *Systema elementare universae jurisprudentiae*, Halle: Renger, 1749; cf. Brutti, 1973: 89.
78. Hellfeld i, 1806: § 295; Glück, 1867: 115 f.; Thibaut ii, 1834: 11.
79. *Traité des obligations*, num. 31.
80. *Loix civiles* 1. 18.
81. I. 5 §§ 349, 358–9.
82. Art. 1116. See also *Wetboek Napoleon voor het Koningrijk Holland* (1809): art. 1029; *Burgerlijk Wetboek* (1838): art. 1364. For further data on codifications influenced by the *Code civil*, see Wacke, 1977: 243 with n. 260.
83. *System* iii, 1840: 98 f. and *Beilage* viii: 326–473; cf. Van Oven, 1953: 291. This

completely from the discussion of error.[84] In the dogmatic system, emphasis moves from deceit of one of the contracting parties (as an impediment to consensus) to error of the other (as a defect of the will). This shift seems to take its origin with Grotius.[85] Likewise, the idea that deceit made contracts *bonae fidei* null and void *ipso jure* is abandoned.[86] Windscheid mentions both theories as doctrines from the past.[87] In modern textbooks of Roman law they have no place, although discussion has not stopped altogether.[88]

So, materially, Noodt was justified by the better part of modern Roman law scholarship, though most German Pandectists disdained citing him. Nobody has doubted ever since that the distinction of *dolus causam dans* and *incidens* is a medieval doctrine. In 1953 Van Oven duly vindicated Noodt's merits as the first to expunge the glosseme 'aut . . . circumscriptus est' from D 4. 3. 7 pr.[89] He is even more audacious himself and expunges twice as much, that is, the whole passage 'hoc enim . . . circumscriptus est'. The first part is a marginal gloss which slipped into the text, the second a Byzantine gloss written—as Noodt had argued—by an inept interpreter of

might seem to need some qualification. Von Savigny apparently follows Grotius (see n. 73) and, like him, seems to retain the notion of *causam dare* when he writes (p. 112): 'Gegenwärtig fassen wir den Irrtum bloss in der Beziehung auf, da er als Beweggrund zu einer Willenserklärung erscheint.' But this concerns error, not *dolus*, and neither D 4. 3. 7. pr. nor the medieval distinction is discussed in Von Savigny's very extensive treatise.

84. *Pandekten-Lehrbuch* (1838 and later): § 57; *Cursus der Institutionen* (1847 and later): ii: § 209.
85. See *De jure belli ac pacis* 2. 11. 6. 1 and 2. It seems, however, that Grotius retained the essence of the medieval distinction when distinguishing between *error in quo fundata est promissio* and incidental error. The term 'causam dans' is actually used with regard to *dolus*, *vis*, and *metus* in *De jure belli ac pacis* 2. 17. 17. Cf. Fransen, 1946; Diesselhorst, 1959: 82 ff.; Feenstra, 1971*b*: 99.
86. Neustetel, 1818; Puchta, 1877: 86; Von Savigny, *System* iii, 355; Vangerow, 1856: 293 ff. And see ALR 1. 5 §§ 349 f.; *Code civil*, art. 1117. It is interesting to note that for Von Savigny the interests of trade motivate the rejection of nullity: 'In dieser regelmässigen Unwirksamkeit des Irrtums liegt sogar die einzige Rettung des Verkehrs gegen gränzenlose Unsicherheit und Willkür.'
87. Windscheid i, 1891: § 78 n. 5; Vangerow (1856: 293) calls the distinction of *dolus causam dans* and *incidens* 'die früher herrschende Lehre'; Dernburg (i, 1902: § 104) likewise ignores the medieval distinction, but this seems to revive in the last decades of the 19th century; see Sprenger, 1898: 359 and 373 f.
88. The medieval doctrine is rejected by Van Oven, 1953: 278; Stein, 1958: 89; Casavola, 1968: 148. It is not mentioned in Kaser's handbook. Recently Wacke (1977: 240) argued—not quite convincingly—that the distinction between *dolus causam dans* and *incidens* is 'materially' classical law.
89. Van Oven, 1953: 288; see also Brutti, 1973: 82 ff.

Roman law. Naturally this was not the final word.[90] Positions defended, contested, and abandoned long ago are frequently defended anew (often without adequate knowledge of their history), only to be abandoned again in the next generation, *et sic in infinitum*. This is what sometimes gives one qualms about Roman law as an intellectual and scientific pursuit. But Noodt's reputation as an *interpres primarius* of classical Roman law stands as firm as ever.

4. Years of maturity—Writings 1713–1724

De usufructu libri duo

The first edition of the *Opera omnia*, which appeared in Leiden in 1713,[91] contained as a new item[92] a treatise on usufruct in two volumes. The book must have been written roughly between 1711 and 1713,[93] in a period that Noodt was not at his best. Not that his humanistic erudition shows any flaws. In describing the rights and duties of the usufructuary classical jurists went into minute details and used a great number of technical and uncommon terms which invited explanation and learned comment. What is a statue or image? What are *nomismata*, *metalla*, *specularia*? What is meant by *exercere feras*, *solarium*, *refugium*, *meritorium*, *coenaculum*, *carrucas*, *librarius*? What kinds of plastering (*tectoria*) and flooring (*pavimenta*) did the Romans know? Here Noodt shows an impressive parade of learning. He cites every possible author from Antiquity, including mathematicians, astronomers, gromatici, medical authors, architects, and fathers of the Church. He is able even to criticize the distinguished Casaubon for citing Ambrosius wrongly![94] But one can have too much of a good thing. One begins to wonder what is the use of all this, even while realizing that there did not yet exist at that time something like the *Realencyclopädie*. In most cases philological explanation and legal interpretation are treated successively, and

90. For Wacke's thesis see n. 67 on p. 248. He is followed by MacCormack, 1983: 524, but neither gives an adequate discussion of the critical problems of D 4. 3. 7 pr.

91. Ahsmann–Feenstra, 1984: nr. 473.
92. The index says 'ante numquam editi'.
93. Noodt cites frequently C. A. Duker's *Opuscula varia de latinitate jurisconsultorum veterum*, which appeared in Leiden in 1711. On Duker, note 89 on p. 92.
94. *Opera* i: 416.

mutually they seem to have little or no relevance. This is where the humanistic ideal of a complete reconstruction of Antiquity reaches the bounds of credibility.

Moreover, in nearly all of his emendations and explanations Noodt is repeating himself, and often he copies practically literally—with or without reference—parts from earlier works like the *Probabilia*,[95] *Ad legem Aquiliam*,[96] and the *Observationes*.[97] Evidently Noodt intended to bring together in this monograph and in that on *Pacta* (see below) the main results of his legal and philological work, but he even repeats himself within *De usufructu*.[98]

As a systematic monograph on usufruct the book nevertheless has its merits, and in view of that purpose even some of the repetitions just mentioned may be justified. Systematization of civil law was one of the tasks of legal scholarship. The system of treatment is perfect.[99] Book I is devoted to the definition of usufruct and the rights and duties of the usufructuary. What is usufruct? (I–II) What is its nature (III)? What kind of things can be objects of usufruct (IV)? What rights does the usufructuary have with regard to a fundus (V–VI), its chattels (VII), and its implements (VIII)? What about the usufruct of a house (X–XIV)? What about servitudes (XV)? What about the usufruct of slaves (XVI) and cattle (XVII)? What about the *cautio usufructuaria* (XVIII–XIX) and quasi-usufruct (XX–XXII)? Book II discusses the way in which usufruct can be established, the causes by which it ends, and the remedies by which it can be maintained: establishment by legacy (I), by *pactiones et stipulationes* (II), by verdict of a judge (III), by statutory provision (IV); expiration (V) by death (VI) or *capitis deminutio* (VII) of the usufructuary, by *non usus* (VIII–IX), by *in iure cessio* and *consolidatio* (X), and by change or destruction of the object (XI). Chapters XII–XIII discuss some other details of expiration,

95. On D 7. 1. 15. 4 and D 8. 6. 11 (*Prob.* 2. 4) *Opera* i: 40 and 440; on D 33. 2. 1 (*Prob.* 2. 3) *Opera* i: 38 and 441; on D 41. 1. 30. 3 and D 41. 1. 7. 5–6 (*Prob.* 1. 1) *Opera* i: 2 and 470.
96. D 7. 1. 48. 1 versus D 9. 2. 27. 25 (*Ad legem Aquiliam* 17) *Opera* i: 163 and 401.
97. D 7. 1. 28 (*Obs.* 1. 5) *Opera* i: 301 and 398; D 7. 1. 13. 5 (*Obs.* 1. 9) *Opera* i: 306 and 403; D 7. 1. 62 (*Obs.* 1. 10) *Opera* i: 308, 387, and 401; D 7. 1. 61 (*Obs.* 1. 12) *Opera* i: 311 and 418; D 7. 1. 14 (*Obs.* 2. 16) *Opera* i: 404 and 420; D 7. 1. 15. 4 and D 8. 6. 11 (*Obs.* 2. 16) *Opera* i: 336, 440, and 462; D 33. 2. 43 (*Obs.* 2. 12) *Opera* i: 332 and 443.
98. An emendation of D 7. 1. 14 is treated on pp. 404 and 420, two emendations in D 7. 1. 7. 2 on pp. 412 and 420, an emendation of D 8. 6. 11 on pp. 440 and 462.
99. The progress in systematization is evident if we compare Noodt's monograph with that of M. A. Galvani (Pisa, 1650), which is some sixty years older. That book evidently grew out of a series of disputations and still bears the traces of it.

chapter XIV the *actio negatoria*, chapter XV the *vindicatio servitutis*, chapter XVI the interdicts *unde vi* and *uti possidetis*.

As in all his printed works, Noodt only discusses classical and post-classical Roman law, without the slightest hint at later developments in the civil law tradition, apart from some commonplace criticism of the glossators. But nevertheless it is evident that he is heir to that tradition. As in earlier works, the problems demanding interpretation or emendation are often those defined by the Accursian gloss. This is the case with the last sentence of D 7. 1. 13. 5, which says that an usufructuary might cut down vines, orchards, and olive trees if a pit of some kind promised greater returns. As we saw before, Noodt cuts out no less than twenty-four words, a rough intervention.[1] Other problems already discussed in the gloss are D 7. 1. 13. 7, saying that the usufructuary may make a new window,[2] or the antinomy between D 7. 1. 61 and 7. 6. 1.1, concerning the question whether the usufructuary may make a new gutter in a wall or may complete an unfinished building.[3] The contrast in treatment of this problem with that of D 7. 1. 13. 5 could hardly be greater. In both cases the solution of the gloss is rejected, but in 13. 5 the problem is solved, in the words of Perizonius, by burning and cutting, here by imaginative legal interpretation.

As far as the philological apparatus is concerned, we find the usual instruments. Some inscriptions are cited,[4] some palingenetic arguments[5] and geminations[6] used. But not everything is humanistic philology. Several times not only the problem, but also the solution of the glossators is endorsed. For D 7. 1. 9.1 Noodt follows the reading of the Vulgate as against F and the Basilica.[7] In the antinomy between D 7. 1. 15. 7/16 and D 7. 6. 2, concerning the question of whether an owner can impose a servitude on the estate during the term of the usufruct, Noodt follows the solution of the gloss.[8] Inst. 2. 4. 3 says that a usufruct perishes 'non utendo per modum et tempus'. Usually this is understood to mean that the usufruct ends if it is not used in accordance with the conditions set by general convention (use as a *bonus pater familias*) or by the testator in question, or not within the set term. Noodt suggests that 'per modum et tempus' is a

1. *Opera* i: 404. Defended earlier in *Obs.* 1. 9; *Opera* i: 306.
2. *Opera* i: 517.
3. *Opera* i: 311, 418.
4. *Opera* i: 397, 402, 420, 424.
5. *Opera* i: 389, 427.
6. *Opera* i: 404, 412, 420, 440, 462.
7. Reading 'lapides' instead of 'apes' (Mo i: 217: 27): *Opera* i: 402.
8. Gloss 'servitutes' on D 7. 6. 2 in fine; cf. *Opera* i: 423.

hendiadys and refers to the term of *non usus* set by the Emperor Julian (C 3. 33. 16. 1), that is, ten or twenty years.[9] This interpretation was suggested in the Accursian gloss,[10] but Noodt does not seem to be aware of this.

Of earlier works on usufruct Noodt only cites one or two, but on the other hand he extensively cites and praises nearly all his Dutch friends and co-workers in the field of humanistic legal philology: Gisbert Cuper,[11] Anton Schulting,[12] Henrik Brenkman,[13] C. A. Duker,[14] Willem Best,[15] and Cornelis van Bijnkershœk.[16] This is a fair sample of the Dutch elegant school in the first decades of the eighteenth century.

Some of Noodt's suggestions, though perhaps not of the greatest importance, have proved worthwhile. The interpunction of D 41. 1. 49 and D 41. 1. 23. 3 he suggested is accepted by Mommsen.[17] And an interesting suggestion is that Inst. 2. 1. 37 may have been taken from Gai. 2 *Res. cott.* (D 22. 1. 28).[18] This is accepted as certain now,[19] but even though the likeness of both passages is only too obvious, the relation between Justinian's Institutes and Gaius could only be ascertained after the Verona palimpsest was found in 1814. Even if this book may not be as inspired and innovative as some of Noodt's earlier work, it certainly confirms his reputation as a Romanist and jurist.

Ad edictum praetoris de pactis et transactionibus liber singularis

The *Opera omnia* of 1713 contain yet another monograph that was being published for the first time:[20] 'A single book on the praetorian edict concerning pacts and transactions.' This book was, like several others, long in the making. In January 1701 Noodt announced in a personal conversation to Van Bijnkershœk that he would soon publish his Observations (which actually appeared in 1706), which would be followed by a commentary on pacts that could be expected

9. *Opera* i: 462.
10. Gloss 'per modum et tempus' on Inst. 2. 4. 3.
11. *Opera* i: 398.
12. *Opera* i: 405.
13. *Opera* i: 408.
14. *Opera* i: 418.
15. *Opera* i: 423.
16. *Opera* i: 449.
17. Cf. *Opera* i: 425, Mo ii: 498: 36; *Opera* i: 428, Mo ii: 494: 3.
18. *Opera* i: 429.
19. Cf. Mo i: 639: 41 and Krüger's edn. of the Institutes *a.h.l.*
20. In the index it is announced as 'nunc primum editus'.

to appear in the same year.[21] But judging from the books cited he worked on his text until 1710.[22] We do not know why publication was postponed for so many years. The book itself hardly seems controversial and the fact that he rejects an emendation by Van Bijnkershœk in D 2. 14. 7. 12[23] cannot be a sufficient reason. More controversial is chapter XXII, in which a thesis is maintained which was defended for the first time in Book II of the *Probabilia* (1679) and for which Noodt was severely criticized, viz. that the jurist Scaevola gave an opinion (as recorded in D 2. 15. 14) against his better knowledge of the law, to please a friend.[24] As we saw, Huber considered it odious, and many others criticized it. Reconsidering the thesis after more than thirty years, in the light of all that was brought against it, Noodt still sees no other possible explanation: 'I know that for some years many scholars, aroused by this observation of mine as if by a war trumpet, have run to the defence of Scaevola with various arguments. But I cannot remember that anyone has adduced anything that could acquit Scaevola, at least if we stick to the problem on which Scaevola's advice was asked.'[25]

The order of treatment is as systematic as usual. Chapter I discusses the origin of the edictal clause as an elaboration of rules set by the twelve tables; here Noodt once more stresses the importance of historical explanation for correct understanding. Then follow the way in which *pacta* can be concluded (II), the scope of *pacta conventa* (III–IV), the proof of consensus (V), the content and purpose of the edict (VI), the distinction of *pacta publica* and *privata*, and of *pacta privata* in *pacta legitima* and *pacta juris gentium* (VII–IX), *nuda pacta* (X), *pacta adjecta* (XI–XII), *pacta legitima* in the Justinianic sense (XIII), *donationes* (XIV), unjust and unlawful pacts (XV–XIX), and finally questions concerning the persons who may conclude *pacta* and the benefits and losses that may result from them (XX–XXVII).

The edictal title *de pactis et transactionibus* was under discussion

21. Van Bijnkershœk to Van Eck, The Hague, 14 Jan. 1701 (UL Utrecht, MS 1000): '. . . de re litteraria nihil fere mihi nunciatum memini quod tu nescias, nisi forte Cl. Noodtium brevi editurum esse *Observationes juris*. Ita mihi ipsius narrabat ante triduum cum hic me inviseret. Observationes illae praecedent commentarium de pactis, quem parat, et hoc etiam anno exspectari jubet.'
22. He cites Van Bijnkershœk's *Observationes juris romani*, which appeared in 1710, but not Duker's *Opuscula varia de latinitate veterum* (Leiden, 1711), although these contain a relevant passage of Valla concerning *pascisci* and *pactum*.
23. *Opera* i: 507, see below.
24. See above, p. 147.
25. *Opera* i: 549.

among French as well as Dutch humanists long before Noodt, and it still is today. According to Lenel, the Leiden professor G. C. Crusius (1644–76) was the first to reconstruct correctly its rubric (*de pactis et conventionibus*).[26] But there are scholars, among them Schulz,[27] who believe that the true wording of the rubric was *de pactis conventis*. And the distinction between *pacta publica* and *privata*, divided further into *legitima* and *juris gentium* (D 2. 14. 5–7), still seems to await a satisfactory explanation.[28]

As the title of the book indicates, Noodt concentrates on the correct interpretation of the edictal clause concerning pacts, as it is recorded in D 2. 14. 7. 7.[29] With its stress on the wording and interpretation of the praetorian edict, the book anticipates Noodt's commentary on the Digest, which began to appear in 1716 and was regarded as a major step forward in the reconstruction of the *Edictum perpetuum*.[30]

Noodt points out that although the wording of the edictal clause is very general—and therefore its application expanded greatly later—originally pacts belonged to the preliminaries of procedure; the edict only had the *pactum de non petendo* in view.[31] From the numbering of books in the *Libri ad edictum* of Ulpian and Paul—from which in fact the bulk of fragments were taken—we can conclude that the order of titles in the Digest departed from that of the edict, in which the titles *de edendo* and *de pactis et conventionibus* preceded *de in jus vocando*.[32] Another apt observation is that there was no separate edictal title *de transactionibus*, because no edictal words are cited in the Digest title with the same rubric (D 2. 15). Similar palingenetic arguments are used frequently in this book and are very characteristic of it.[33] The humanistic *elegantiae* which take up nearly half of the monograph on usufruct are rather scarce here. The focus is on careful legal interpretation of the praetorian edict and this is a new development in Noodt's scientific work. Only one inscription is discussed.[34] As far as emendations are concerned, hardly anything new is found. Some geminations are discussed,[35] and sometimes the possibility of

26. Lenel, 1927: 64.
27. Cf. Lenel, 1927: 64 n. 6; Schulz, 1963: 149; 1969: 470; Soubie, 1960: 41, 152.
28. Kaser, 1971: 527 n. 44.
29. See also Lenel, 1927: 65.
30. See below, p. 266 ff.
31. *Opera* i: 483 f. So still Schulz, 1969: 470.
32. *Opera* i: 484. Cf. Lenel, 1927: 59 f.
33. e.g. *Opera* i: 491, 498, 514, 515, 519, 535.
34. *Opera* i: 548.
35. *Opera* i: 494 (D 12. 6. 65. 1); 497 (D 36. 1. 80. 16 and D 2. 15. 12).

false solution of sigla is considered as ground for emendation,[36] but nearly all emendations were published before in the *Probabilia*,[37] *De foenore et usuris*,[38] *Julius Paulus*,[39] and the Observations.[40] And the few minor emendations that are new unfortunately confirm Noodt's reputation for emending rather loosely. In D 2. 14. 5 he adds an 'aut' without manuscript evidence or anything like an explanation,[41] and in D 50. 17. 27 he wants to read 'nec si, cum' although all manuscripts have 'nisi tunc cum'.[42]

It is interesting to note citation habits of the time. When Noodt proposes a simple emendation of one letter in C 8. 42. 6 (factum > pactum)[43] he adds a laudatory phrase on Cornelis van Bijnkershœk, who had suggested a similar emendation in C 2. 18. 22.[44] But when he rejects an emendation in D 2. 14. 7. 12 as superfluous,[45] he does not mention that it was proposed by the same Van Bijnkershœk.[46]

As we noted before, Noodt's work, though avowedly purely humanistic, has strong links with the civil law tradition. Many problems treated here were defined as such in the gloss: the meaning of *pacta legitima* in D 2. 14. 5–6,[47] the division of *pacta privata* into *pacta legitima* and *pacta juris gentium*,[48] the difference between 'contra legem' and 'in fraudem legis',[49] the antinomy between D 2. 15. 13. 1 and D 36. 1. 80. 16 concerning transaction about a fideicommissum,[50] that between D 2. 15. 6 and C 1. 4. 19 concerning the question whether you can transact over a will before you have seen its text,[51] and that between D 2. 15. 9 and D 45. 1. 22. 6 concerning transaction over an estate.[52]

36. *Opera* i: 499 ('per pacem' in D 2. 14. 5); 523 (D 20. 6. 5); 529 (D 2. 14. 7. 11).
37. On D 22. 2. 7 (*Prob.* 4. 4, *Opera* i: 76 and 520); C 8. 13. 23 (*Prob.* 2. 8, *Opera* i: 48 and 521); D 20. 6. 5 (*Prob.* 2. 8 and 4. 10, *Opera* i: 49, 83, 522); D 20. 6. 7. 2 (*Prob.* 4. 11, *Opera* i: 84, 524).
38. D 22. 2. 7 (*De foen.* 3. 3, *Opera* i: 238).
39. D 2. 15. 6 (*Opera* i: 578–9).
40. C 8. 42. 6 (*Obs.* 2. 24, *Opera* i: 344 and 492); D 12. 6. 65. 1 (*Obs.* 2. 16, *Opera* i: 336 and 494); C 5. 14. 4 (*Obs.* 2. 23, *Opera* i: 343 and 552).
41. '. . . fit per pacem ⟨aut⟩ quotiens . . .' (Mo i: 63: 9). *Opera* i: 500.
42. *Opera* i: 537; cf. Mo ii: 958: 33 f.
43. *Opera* i: 492. The emendation had already been proposed in *Obs.* 2. 24, *Opera* i: 344 f.
44. *Obs. jur. rom.* 1. 7.
45. *Opera* i: 504.
46. *Lib. sing. ad lex lecta* (1697), c. 5.
47. *Opera* i: 500; gloss 'legitima' on D 2. 14. 6.
48. *Opera* i: 498; gloss 'publica' on D 2. 14. 5.
49. *Opera* i: 529; gloss 'adversus leges' on D 2. 14. 7. 7.
50. *Opera* i: 497; gloss 'debere' on D 2. 15. 3. 1.
51. *Opera* i: 535; gloss 'transigi' on D 2. 15. 6.
52. *Opera* i: 495; gloss 'non summovetur' on D 2. 15. 9.

Noodt not only repeats emendations that have already been defended. He defends Accursius against Muretus and, as we saw before, he also reconsiders his attack on Scaevola (because the text in question is from the Digest title *de transactionibus*). Likewise, he repeats the thesis defended in *Diocletianus et Maximianus* (1704) that bargaining over public crimes is forbidden and must be regarded as corruption and extortion.[53]

Reconsideration leads to a different conclusion in one case only. In *Probabilia* 2. 8 (1679) and 4. 10 (1691) Noodt defended a rather incisive expunction in D 20. 6. 5. pr.[54] But now he offers, as an alternative for the scrupulous, a way of retaining the relevant words. We may be dealing with a figure of speech: if the words are referred not to the sentence directly preceding but to the one before that, they make sense. 'It is not, I confess, a laudable way of writing to put together what you have to say without any order. But such confusion is not infrequent with the ancients. They were only human, like us, often accurate, but sometimes less so.'[55] After referring to a place where he made a similar observation[56]—this form of construction was called *synchisis*[57]—Noodt adds 'I had this text ready for edition for some time already when I learned from a private letter sent to me by the learned jurist Willem Best that a similar idea occurred to him recently . . . As this pleased me, I regarded it as in keeping with the society of studies to make a no less honourable than friendly note of it.'[58] The alternative Noodt had to offer, however, can hardly have seemed attractive to the true believers. The text may be saved as it stands, but only at the price of accepting that the ancients were only human and sometimes sloppy in composition! In any case *ratio vincit, vetustas cessit*.

A nice illustration of the vicissitudes of text tradition is offered by D 3. 3. 58 (Paul 71 *ad ed.*). In the Mommsen edition the text reads as follows:

> Procurator, cui generaliter libera administratio rerum commissa est, potest exigere, novare, aliud pro alio permutare.[59]

53. *Opera* i: 531 f.; cf. p. 217 ff.
54. He suggested cutting the words 'cum forte alius hypothecam possidebit' (Mo i: 598: 8–9), see *Opera* i: 49, 83.
55. *Opera* i: 523.
56. *Obs.* 2. 26 on D 48. 19. 27. 1, *Opera* i: 345.
57. Cf. Vossius, *Inst. or.* 4. 1 in fine; Alciatus, *Parerg.* 10. 11; see *Opera* i: 346 and 523.
58. *Opera* i: 523.
59. 'The procurator to whom the free administration of an estate is committed, can

In the Florentine manuscript the word 'novare' is lacking, but in this case unquestionably the Bolognese version is the better one. It is confirmed not only by the Basilica, but materially by D 46. 2. 20. 1 (Paul 72 *ad ed.*), which expressly says that a *procurator omnium bonorum* can effect a novation. The word 'novare' is in our text in many medieval manuscripts,[60] as well as in early printed editions such as the Venice edition of 1488.[61] But under the influence of the humanistic belief in the supreme authority of the *Florentina* text tradition became unstable in the sixteenth century. Haloander (1529) leaves the word out of the text, but notes in the margin that other editions have it. The edition of Hugo a Porta (Lyons, 1549) does exactly the opposite: 'novare' is in the text but a marginal note says that it is lacking in other editions. Gothofredus (1583) decides the matter for many ages: 'novare' is out and will stay out until the second half of the nineteenth century. The editions of Gebauer–Spangenberg (1776) and Kriegel–Herrmann (13th impression 1870!) relegate it to the footnotes as a Vulgate reading. Noodt defends the reading with 'novare' on account of the Basilica and D 46. 2. 20. 1,[62] but it is only with Mommsen's edition (1870) that 'novare' is finally back in the text again. In his *editio major* Mommsen refers only to the Basilica. No mention is made of the medieval manuscripts—including Mommsen's Codex V[63]—that have the verb.[64] But the omission is corrected in the *editio stereotypa*. Here 'novare' is ascribed to codex S, the hypothetical *codex secundus* which supposedly was used together with the Florentine manuscript by the makers of the Bolognese version, and which is regarded as the source of a score of readings in the *Bononiensis* that give a genuinely better text than the *Florentina*.

Among other things we can learn from this text why Noodt was regarded as belonging to the *schola cujaciana*. Although in his printed books he never expressed himself directly on the matter, we may safely conclude from a case like this that he, like Cujas, did not accept Agustìn's axioma that the Florentine manuscript should prevail on all

exact payment, substitute a new obligation for an existing one, change one thing for another.'

60. Brenkman counted nine MSS, among them Cod. Vat. I (Mommsen's Codex V).
61. Repr. anastatically, Turin, 1969.
62. *Opera* i: 557.
63. See n. 60.
64. See Gebauer–Spangenberg *a.h.l.* n. 73. Brenkman even called this the *(lectio) communis*.

occasions. Naturally it must be added that the still undisturbed trust in *ratio* made the question of the genuine text less critical than it may seem to us now. Noodt chooses freely and without methodological principle what he believes to be the best text. Sometimes he prefers Haloander's text above the reading of the Florentine manuscript,[65] sometimes he opts for the Bolognese version,[66] sometimes for the *Florentina*. With this goes what we would regard as arbitrariness in the argumentation of emendations. An 'elegantissima conjectura' of A. Faure concerning C 2. 4. 2 is rejected because all manuscripts have the word in question and the Greeks likewise: 'Therefore nor will I recede from the constant reading.'[67] But in D 20. 6. 7. 2 an incisive expunction is defended against the authority of all known manuscripts: 'Even if all manuscripts have these words, what do they have to do with the question treated here?'[68] But such arbitrariness is not characteristic of Noodt. What is characteristic may be his candour. Others give very principled statements of method and yet do just the same in practice. This may be a consequence of the primacy of *ratio juris*, although even today scholars often seem to forget their solemn declarations of method as soon as they get to work. In retrospect, however, one understands easily why a science of law based on reason alone was doomed to meet a grave crisis when its certainty proved illusory. No wonder that not a few Romanists are reluctant to accept this even now.

De pactis et transactionibus is one of Noodt's better books. As a monograph on pacts it leaves little to be desired, and modern Romanists will find much in it that remains worth considering. As an interpreter of Roman law Noodt is in excellent shape here. As a rather curious postscript I add that this monograph was cited as late as 1914 in a judgment of the court of Hertogenbosch.[69] A shopkeeper was in arrears with the payment of rent. The lessor, making use of his legal privilege (tacit lien of *invecta et illata*) attached all the goods in the shop. The shopkeeper, and a third party claiming to be the owner of the goods, opposed the attachment. Art. 1186, par. 1 in fine of the *Burgerlijk Wetboek* expressly says that the lessor can take goods present on the premises irrespective of ownership, but the question

65. On D 2. 14. 17. 3 and D 2. 14. 22, *Opera* i: 494 f.
66. On D 3. 3. 58, see above.
67. *Opera* i: 491.
68. Noodt cuts the words 'ne sit res obligata' (Mo i: 598: 31), *Opera* i: 524.
69. Arrondissementsrechtbank 's-Hertogenbosch, 11 Dec. 1914, NJ 1915, p. 72; W 9735.

was raised whether *invecta et illata* included a shop's stock on hand. The court, going back on Pothier, gave an affirmative reply. Vœt and Noodt are cited as authorities for old Dutch law (Vœt, in fact, with more justification than Noodt, because the latter does not precisely discuss the question of the shop's stock). The judgment was criticized in the new *Tijdschrift voor rechtsgeschiedenis* (Legal History Review) by a legal historian,[70] who claimed that there is no proof that in this case our civil law goes back to Roman law and authors like Vœt and Noodt. This led to an interesting discussion concerning the authority of history in legal interpretation. No doubt the court did not have a correct picture of the history of the lessor's privilege. Meijers gave a far better sketch of it later,[71] against which Scholten maintained (in another question concerning the same article) that even the most perfect historical knowledge could not decide matters of legal interpretation.[72] At which Hoetink remarked that the difference between historical interpretation and legal history as postulated by Scholten could not be maintained in the light of recent developments in the philosophy of knowledge.[73] But this debate, erudite as it was, need not detain us here. Suffice it to note that Gerard Noodt could still be cited as a legal authority in court, more than three quarters of a century after the Dutch civil code had come in force.

Commentarius ad Digesta seu Pandectas

In March 1716,[74] three years after the publication of his *Opera omnia* and the announcement to his readers that he doubted whether he could ever undertake anything more because the age of 66 prompted him to contemplate life's end,[75] Noodt published the first part of what was the greatest enterprise of all in civil law: a Commentary on the Pandects.[76] No wonder that in Leipzig they thought this was a

70. Van Kuyk, 1920–1: 5; cf. Hoetink, 1949: 8, now in trans. in Hoetink, 1986: 139.
71. *Weekblad voor privaatrecht, notarisambt en registratie*, 1939: nos. 3619–21; *Verzamelde privaatrechtelijke opstellen* ii, 1955: 152 ff.
72. The disagreement between Meijers (who sided with the Hoge Raad) and Scholten concerned the question whether the lessor should be in good faith as to the ownership of the *invecta et illata*, see Meijers, l.c. and Scholten in Asser and Scholten ii (8th imp. 1945): 384 ff.
73. Hoetink, 1986: 141 ff.
74. Noodt presented the book with letters of 9 Mar. 1716 to Johan van de Water (KHA, G. 16–A. 258) and Cornelis van Eck (UL Utrecht, MS 1000).
75. *Opera omnia*, Leiden, 1713: ad lectorem.
76. Ahsmann–Feenstra, 1984: nr. 475. I have seen the copy in UL Amsterdam.

posthumous work; but they were wrong not to think much of it.[77] Noodt evidently had overcome the *abaissement vital* of the years around 1713 and was in full intellectual vigour. He wrote the commentary on the first four books of the Digest in seven months, all in his spare time and without detracting from his office.[78] From this information, and allowing some months for printing, we may infer that Noodt began his commentary in the spring of 1715, in his 68th year.

In the preface he goes to some length to explain the obvious contradiction.

> Although many men, excellent in dignity and scholarship, and my friends, I believe, have often requested me urgently to compose a commentary on the Pandects according to my own insights, I could never bring myself to do so, because it is an affair of great scope and labour, which demands abundant erudition, a judgment adequate for the subject matter, the fullest knowledge of all that is contained in the fifty books. So you may wonder why I undertake what was asked of me in the flower of my life, now that I have very nearly completed it, after I had decided to put an end to writing. But no doubt because I am used to serious labour from my youth I did not long persist in spending my old age, which I enjoy, thank God, happily and without its inconveniences, in idle leisure, a kind of rest.[79]

This confession of a workaholic is not wholly convincing and, as I said earlier, I suspect that there is another reason for beginning a commentary on the Digest at that age: the quite unexpected death, in September 1713, of his colleague Johannes Vœt, whose very successful Commentary on the Pandects dominated the market completely, as it continued to do for a long time afterwards. The difference in content and scope of both commentaries could hardly be expressed more clearly than in their respective prefaces. They are model expressions of the programme of the *usus modernus* and the elegant school respectively. Both are concerned with law, legal training, and their impact on society. Vœt expresses the aspiration of the *usus modernus* towards a legal science led by practical purposes, Noodt's preface sounds like a swan-song of the humanistic belief that better philology makes for purer Roman law and unadulterated Roman law is the best for all human society.

Vœt intends to combine Roman and contemporary law, theory

77. H. Post to C. van Eck, Leipzig, 25 May 1719, see n. 93 on p. 93.
78. Praefatio, *Opera* ii: fol. 1^{v}.
79. *Opera* ii: fol. 1^{v}.

and practice, rules and principles with *usus fori*. He will try to explain the law, clarify controversies, reconcile contradicting laws. Antiquities he will only touch with the tips of his fingers and for the rest he will refer to those who have studied them, so that anybody who is tired by the grave precepts of law and the difficult and embarrassing controversies of legal practice, and who wants to relax in the lovelier pastures of the *humaniora*, may promenade there to his liking.

Noodt's purpose is totally different. The fragments of the old jurists are not all from one time, nor from one sect, nor one of a kind. Besides, they are not put in systematic order, sometimes displaced, often abridged, moreover mutilated and interpolated, often obscure and complicated. Therefore they must be studied carefully, taking into account history and legal development (*progressus juris*), Latin idiom and usage, the information offered by *inscriptiones*, the constants and variations of manuscripts and editions, and, finally, careful and necessary emendation and punctuation. His constant care will be to reconstruct and interpret the *Edictum perpetuum*. For the rest he refers to his two inaugural addresses *De civili prudentia* (Franeker, 1679) and *De causis corruptae jurisprudentiae* (Utrecht, 1684), which he wants to be read as a preface to his Commentary on the Pandects. This accounts for his scientific and educational purposes regarding the study of Roman law.

If we usually consider Vœt, the spokesman of the *usus modernus*, as a more modern jurist and Noodt as a traditional humanist clinging to a great but dying tradition, the labels must be changed if we look at them from a slightly different angle. Vœt, though not ignorant of the achievements of humanism, is in fact still more of a traditional Bartolist, and even as far as systematic treatment is concerned, he takes no account of the advances made by Donellus and by contemporaries like Domat. Noodt's preface could still be subscribed to by every modern Romanist as a statement of scientific programme. All the elements of modern Romanist studies (which, under the influence of German domination, are believed to begin around 1900) are already there: history, legal development, palingenesia, interpolations, etc. But naturally Vœt's programme was better tuned to the needs of training jurists whose scientific expertise in most cases was no more than instrumental to their social position of power.

Noodt did not want to take more time in writing his commentary, although the whole could have been riper, and he could have made use of Anton Schulting's *Jurisprudentia vetus ante-justinianea* (which appeared in 1717), as well as of the variant readings brought back by Henrik Brenkman from his new collation of the *Florentina* and other manuscripts, which the learned world ardently awaited (and which never appeared).[80] But delay might have proved fatal because of his advanced age.

What about the result? It is not for him to judge it, but without boasting he may say that he has, if not explained many things more clearly and completely than before, exposed many things that were recently found or discovered and as yet unknown.

> But most of all I have taken pains to ensure that Jurisprudence, which is regarded by many as not very delightful, but rather as sad and austere and on the whole, as it is, as no more than idle and empty subtlety, can be read henceforth as a beautiful and elegant history of the civil affairs of public as well as private concern of the Roman people, which is in no way alien to natural reason and the cult of wisdom but, quite to the contrary, is most appropriate to rule communal life—without which the human race cannot exist—through laws and rules in accordance with the variety of affairs, times, customs, and opportunities.

In 1724, in the second edition of his *Opera omnia*, the commentary extends to the end of Book 27 of the Digest. So he completed, on average, nearly three books of the Digest per annum. As he explains in the preface, he had plans to complete the commentary as far as Book 50 (which would, at this rate, have taken him another eight years), but he overestimated his capacities. Thank God, he is pleased to have more strength than many of his age, and he cannot complain of the vigour of his judgment or the reliability of his memory, capacities advantageous and necessary for the job. But this proved not to be enough. His old age, as he nears 80, tells him that he will not get beyond Book 27. He must give up, now that the studies are tiring him which once were his delight. The reader will accept him ceasing to write because he has done enough; perhaps others will take over.[81]

Though written at a very advanced age, Noodt's commentary has none of the weaknesses of an *Alterswerk*.[82] As one critic wrote, its only disadvantage was that it remained unfinished. With regard to every relevant Digest title Noodt discusses its place in the succession

80. Brenkman travelled through Italy and France 1709–13, see Stolte, 1981: 17f.
81. *Opera* ii: fol. I.
82. The author of the piece in the *Miscellaneae observationes* of July–August 1733 (J. van de Water, see below, p. 295) judges differently, l.c., p. 112.

of titles and the question whether this reflects the order of the edict.[83] Next comes the question whether there was a separate edictal clause for the subject. If this seems to have been the case, its wording is reconstructed from extant sources and all its elements are explained *kata podas*, much in the same way as classical jurists did ('deinde ait praetor . . .'). Naturally, in all this Noodt amply cites from relevant non-legal literature as well. In addition he gives, particularly for titles which are of central concern for civil law (e.g. *de contrahenda emptione*, D 18. 1), a full systematic treatment of all relevant legal aspects of the contract.

It is hard to say what exactly Noodt's contribution to the reconstruction of the praetorian edict was. There is no recent systematic study of the history of legal scholarship in this field.[84] Needless to say, in many cases Lenel gives a different reconstruction of an edictal clause than Noodt, but that is hardly decisive. Lenel only very exceptionally cites literature from before Rudorff, his direct predecessor in edictal reconstruction. Just as Mommsen eliminated the bulk of the critical effort of humanism with regard to the constitution of the Digest text, so did Lenel with the attempts at reconstruction of the edict. Only very exceptionally are we allowed a glance at past scholarship. With regard to the edict *de calumniatoribus* (3. 6), Lenel[85] denies, against Ranchinus, Westenberg, Heineccius, and Karlowa, that the words 'si quis despectus esse dicetur' belonged to the wording of the edict. The fact that Noodt had also denied this[86] is not worth mentioning. In one other case Lenel rejects a reconstruction defended by Ranchinus, Noodt, and others as untenable,[87] and that is all. We cannot say without further detailed study in what sense these isolated instances might be representative. For the time being we can do no more than rely on the informed opinion of a specialist who studied the history of scholarship in this field long ago.

The very able Haubold has a very high opinion of Noodt's work. In view of his own plans to make a new effort at the reconstruction of the *Edictum perpetuum* he published in 1797 a detailed study of the

83. e.g. D 2. 13 *de edendo*: in the Digest this title and *de in jus vocando* come after *de jurisdictione*, whilst we may conclude with certainty from the palingenesia that in the edict they preceded that title.
84. The only fairly recent study is Kipp, *RE* v, 1905: 1946.
85. 1927: 106.
86. *Opera* ii: 102.
87. 1927: 60 n. 2.

historia literaria of similar efforts in the past.[88] After evaluating the work of Eginhard Baro, Ranchin, Hubert van Giffen, Jacob Gothofredus, and others, this is what he has to say about Noodt:

More important progress in the study of the Edict was made at the beginning of this century by the efforts of the excellent Noodt. His comprehensive humanistic erudition and profound insight into the spirit of the legislation, led by the right intuition, which was still scarce then, has no doubt contributed much to this branch of our studies as well. Therefore it is a true loss to our science that his Commentary on the Pandects, in which his main purpose was the reconstruction of the Edict, only contains the first twenty-seven books, although we know from some earlier publications by his hearers that he has reconstructed the whole of the Edict in his lectures.[89] Though Noodt's merits regarding the reconstruction of the Edict are generally acknowledged, I do, I believe, nothing superfluous when I draw my readers' attention on some qualities of this learned work. One will find that in Noodt's Commentary not only is every paragraph of the Edict documented with the most appropriate evidence, but also most of the evidence is rigorously verified. Therefore this work, which is indispensable anyway, is at the same time a very helpful guide for similar critical efforts. But Noodt was not content with the separation of genuine and spurious materials, especially the words of commenting jurists from the wording of the edict itself. He also shows with his usual sagacity how the classical jurists treated the matters covered by the Edict and modified them by their interpretation. Therefore Noodt's Pandect-system contains many very instructive hints, that have an undeniable influence on the reconstruction of the Edict as a whole, for instance the observation that the praetor never mentioned the *actiones contrarias*.[90]

I do not think much has to be added to this authoritative judgment by Haubold. The only remarkable fact is that Kipp, who in his article in the *Realencyclopädie* (1905)[91] gives no literature but Haubold's

88. Haubold, 1812: 285 ff. (1st edn., 1797). It is very characteristic that Lenel does not say a word about this.
89. Haubold refers here to J. van der Waeyen, *Diss. de aedilitio Edicto* (Leiden, 1720): 16 and to Wieling in the preface to the *Fragmenta Edicti Perpetui* (Franeker, 1753). See also Stintzing and Landsberg, iii. 1: Notes, p. 109, which refers to the work of Westenberg (whom Noodt, according to oral tradition, as reported to Haubold by Uhl, even accused of plagiarizing him) and to B. H. Reinold, another hearer of Noodt's (on him, see above, p. 99). He says that the method of reconstructing the edictal clause and then commenting on it in the way classical jurists used to do was typical of Noodt's teaching. But I have found no lecture notes which reflect this method. See below, p. 281 f. Reinold (1755:730) refers to the first part of Noodt's Commentary on the Pandects.
90. Haubold, 1812: 307–9.
91. Vo. *edictum perpetuum*, *RE* v: 1946.

article from which I just cited, does not mention Noodt at all. This may be symptomatic of the underestimation of the Dutch school. In order to show how much even modern 'neo-humanistic' studies of Roman law remain within a positivistic framework and fall behind the humanistic achievement of someone like Noodt, I need to add only one example. One of the texts which has taken a central place in discussions about the relation of law and custom since the days of the glossators[92] is C 8. 52(53). 2:

> Consuetudinis ususque longaevi non vilis auctoritas est, verum non usque adeo sui valitura momento, ut aut rationem vincat aut legem.[93]

The language of the constitution is problematic and especially the meaning of the word 'ratio' has been discussed endlessly: is it reason, public interest, legal principle, natural law, equity?[94] Noodt[95] is, as far as I know, the first to suggest that the emperor may have had a very special case in mind here: 'consuetudo' might very well mean religious custom, more precisely Roman pagan ritual. We know that Constantine—who issued the constitution in question—made Christianity the official religion of the empire, and we also know from Lactantius that Christians tried hard to obtain from the emperor the abolition of Roman pagan rituals, so perhaps the constitution was concerned with this question, which would make quite a difference to its interpretation. I do not deny that the suggestion is rash and speculative, but nevertheless it opens up very interesting perspectives, and it seems simply astounding that so much progress has been made in historical studies and yet no modern study concerning law and custom—including my own—ever contemplated that possibility.

It would go far beyond the scope of this review to give a detailed discussion of the whole of Noodt's Commentary on the Digest, which contains 590 pages in folio. As far as method is concerned—nicely summarized, as we saw, in the preface of 1716—the book shows no further developments from earlier work, and as regards its special qualities enough has been said already. The work with which in 1724 Noodt concluded half a century of publications in Roman

92. Van den Bergh, 1986*d*, *passim*.
93. 'Custom and ancient use have no mean authority, but their weight is not such that it would subdue reason or law.'
94. Cf. Brie, 1899: 31; Van den Bergh, 1986*d*: 71.
95. *Opera* ii: 15.

law no doubt confirms his reputation as one of the great Romanists of his day—and perhaps of all time.

5. Lectures

Law teaching

Law teaching in the seventeenth century took three forms: public lectures (*lectiones*), private lectures (*collegia*), and disputations (*disputationes*).[96] Public lectures were held every day during the academic year, except on feast days and other days excepted by the senate. They were rather unpopular and for the eighteenth century one cannot be sure that lectures announced in the printed *series lectionum* were actually given.[97] But they were formally abolished only in 1815 in the first statute on universities. Private lectures—*collegia domestica*—were more attractive for several reasons. They were not given in a cold university hall, but in a heated room in the professor's house. There was more freedom in the choice of subject and teaching was more attuned to student demands. New subjects like natural law and *jus publicum* were often treated in private lectures before they became part of the official curriculum. Students paid a fee of 30 or 40 guilders a year for private lectures. Professors mostly lived in big houses, where they could have a lecture room; they often also lodged students. In some cities there were professor's houses owned by the university, but as we have seen Noodt bought his own house in Leiden.

The level of lectures no doubt varied considerably. Professors often used a standard textbook, on which simple lemmatic explanations were given; Böckelmann's *Compendium*[98] and the *Principia* of Van Eck[99] and of Westenberg[1] remained in use well into the nineteenth century. Disputing was regarded as an essential element of legal training. Training disputations were held every week, usually

96. There is no sharp distinction between *collegia* and *disputationes*. A *collegium* can be a class devoted to lecturing, disputing, or a combination of both. A *collegium disputatorium* can be either a class where training disputations were held or an association of students which regularly met for the training of disputing (cf. the Dutch word 'dispuut' for a small student association).
97. Kernkamp iii: 615 f.
98. Ahsmann–Feenstra, 1984: nr. 32 f.
99. Van den Bergh, 1986*b*: 41, 47.
1. Ahsmann–Feenstra, 1984: nr. 1139; Feenstra, 1984.

on Saturday, and each student would act as *defendens* two or three times during his period of study. Disputations were written in most cases by the professor. He often published afterwards in his own name a coherent series of disputations, e.g. on the Digest or on some special subject (*disputationes anniversariae*), with or without mention of the names of individual *defendentes*. Often such a series of disputations formed the basis of a monograph, e.g. Huber's *De jure civitatis*.[2] Different from the *disputatio exercitii gratia* was the *disputatio pro gradu* which formed part of the examination for a doctor's degree.[3] It was held in the senate room or publicly in the aula. During the eighteenth century students usually wrote the thesis themselves. Public promotion was rather expensive and therefore did not occur frequently.

Noodt gave public as well as private lectures and we still have several manuscripts of lecture notes, which will be discussed below. Only from Leiden do we have a significant number of printed *series lectionum* for the period, but, as I said above, they do not give detailed information about the subjects Noodt taught; from beginning to end the announcement reads: 'important subjects of public and private law'.[4] As far as can be concluded from extant manuscripts of lecture notes, Noodt gave private lectures on the Institutes and on Grotius' *De jure belli ac pacis*. From Franeker he wrote to his father that he also gave private lectures on the Digest;[5] he will have done the same in Utrecht and Leiden. I have not done systematic research concerning the disputations defended under Noodt's presidency,[6] but as far as we know he never published a series of disputations in his own name, as among others his teacher Petrus de Greve had done.[7] Noodt's teaching was different from the ordinary in the following respects. He wrote his own lectures and, except for the private lectures on Grotius, he never used a textbook. None of his monographs seem to have grown out of series of disputations, but to have been conceived as such.

2. Feenstra, 1985*b*: 296.
3. See above, n. 58 on p. 136.
4. 'publici privatique juris illustres materias'. Cf. n. 9 on p. 95.
5. Noodt to father, Franeker, 25 Oct. 1679, ARA Tets van Goudriaan, inv. nr. 105: '. . . En hebbe in het Collegie over de Instituta al in de twintig studenten, en over de Pandecten acht.'
6. A few in Nijmegen, 18 in Franeker, 9 in Utrecht, and during the thirty-nine years in Leiden presumably much more than 200.
7. See p. 22.

Curriculum reform

In the second half of the seventeenth century there are changes in the law curriculum which signify a departure from the traditional teaching of Institutes, Pandects, and Codex. Antonius Thysius (1565–1640), who was professor of theology and poetics in Leiden, from 1639 also taught *ius publicum*.[8] In 1667 Beeckerts van Thienen got an assignment for *jus publicum* in the Leiden law faculty, and in February 1669 he actually announced lectures on it,[9] but he already died shortly afterwards. His successor Böckelmann introduced something new: methodical treatment of a special subject (i.e. *actiones*) through all parts of the Corpus Juris.[10] From September 1671 he also taught *jus publicum*.[11] In 1681—the year that Böckelmann died—Vœt announced lectures on obligations, according to the method introduced by Böckelmann.[12] In the same year natural law appeared in the series;[13] Böckelmann's successor, P. R. Vitriarius, also taught natural law from 1682. Noodt had an assignment for private and public law and taught natural law privately. Between 1690 and 1710 humanistic ideas have a growing impact on the law curriculum in Leiden under the influence of Noodt and Antonius Matthaeus III. In 1696 the latter begins a series of lectures, continued until his death in 1710, in which the constitutions of successive later Roman emperors are treated chronologically and palingenetically.[14]

In 1692 the law faculty of Leiden played an important role in a drive for the reform of teaching in the grammar school as well as in the university. The theme of the decay of studies was not new. Already in 1670 governors and burgomasters of Leiden concluded that too many students entered the higher faculties too soon and without sufficient mastery of Latin, with the result that they were unable to express themselves correctly.[15] The senate, asked for advice, naturally laid the blame totally on the grammar schools, who

8. Cf. Ahsmann–Feenstra, 1984: 241.
9. Molhuysen iii: 237*.
10. Molhuysen iii: 235*: 'ius actionum ex Pandectis omnique alia parte juris repetitum justa methodo dicebit'.
11. Molhuysen iii: 237*.
12. Molhuysen iii: 269*: 'materiam obligationum ex omnibus iuris civilis partibus explicabit.'
13. Announced by Böckelmann, see Molhuysen iii: 269*.
14. Molhuysen iv: 45*–122*.
15. Molhuysen iii: 240.

sent their pupils prematurely to the university.[16] The governors decided to bring the matter to the attention of the States of Holland, the only competent body in this matter, but nothing happened after that.[17]

In 1692 action went much further, but finally did not result in reform either. It seems likely that Noodt played an important part in the action, as far as the law faculty was concerned. The ideas about the law curriculum and its adequate preparation in grammar schools proposed by the Leiden law faculty show many similarities with Noodt's Utrecht inaugural address.[18]

In April 1692 Mr Van Halewijn alerted governors and burgomasters to the decay of legal studies 'which is progressing every day'. Because young men from the most distinguished families pursued that study and went on to get the most distinguished jobs, the danger for the Republic was evident as well as imminent. It was decided that the law faculty should be asked for advice.[19] The law professors gave their opinion orally on 18 June and were then asked to put it in writing.[20] Their opinion, signed by Antonius Matthaeus III, Johannes Vœt, P. R. Vitriarius, and Gerard Noodt was dated 1 July; it was discussed by governors and burgomasters on 9 July.[21]

The law professors[22] saw four causes for the decay of studies. In the first place, parents gave their children much too licentious and luxurious an education, with the result that they developed no appetite for learning, because they thought that studies were only important for those who had to make a living by them later. Secondly, boys were promoted prematurely from grammar school and without adequate knowledge of Latin. Thirdly, they went directly to the higher faculties, bypassing the arts faculty and a training in Greek, which is indispensible for law students on account of the *Novellae*, the fragments of Modestinus in the Digest, and various constitutions of Justinian. In the fourth place, students, wanting to leave the academy as quickly as possible, only looked for professors who promised to promote them as soon and as easily as possible. There were even professors who boasted that they could make an advocate in a year.

16. Complaints about grammar schools were of long standing, see e.g. Rademaker, 1967: 166 f.
17. Molhuysen iii: 247.
18. See above, p. 161 ff.
19. Molhuysen iv: 103 f.
20. Molhuysen iv: 104.
21. Molhuysen iv: 105.
22. Molhuysen iv: 32* f.

Measures for redress followed from the causes indicated. Grammar schools should be forbidden to graduate students without mastery of Latin and some training in Greek. Secondly, law teaching by people who were not professors should be forbidden and, as Justinian had done, the government should forbid law teaching, with the penalty of a considerable fine, in all cities except three. Thirdly, it would not be bad to prescribe the minimal duration of law studies in such a way that professors could not make this illusory. Naturally, some rule should be made with regard to law students from other universities who came to Leiden to take a degree.

The governors and burgomasters decided on 9 July that Van Halewijn should take up the matter with grand pensionary Heinsius and, as a result of this, it was decided on 1 November that Leiden's representatives should bring the matter as soon as possible before the States of Holland.[23] The States decided on 18 November to refer the matter to the governors and burgomasters of Leiden and ask them to draft a regulation.[24] The draft, with a lengthy explanatory memorandum, both written by Van Halewijn, was drawn up on 20 December,[25] and discussed in a joint meeting of governors and burgomasters and the senate on 28 December.[26]

The explanatory memorandum reflects several ideas expounded in Noodt's inaugural address in Utrecht, but naturally not all of these ideas were original to Noodt. One cannot study law without knowledge of classics. One must know the history of the Roman republic and monarchy, the various forms of legislation, the magistracies, and the forms of procedure. In the dark ages the common opinion of doctors took the place of truth. One did not know whether a Roman law could be applied in present conditions or was only meant for a special occasion. Apart from Latin and Greek, ancient mathematics and philosophy must be studied as well. In modern philosophy sound reason is taken as the basis with rejection of all authority and therefore people think that ancient philosophy no longer has any use, but that is a mistake. In the law faculty students are content with the reading of compendia, which offer the first principles and general grounds of the law, without further study of serious books. Although students get a degree in both laws they usually do not know anything of canon law. Nor have they heard anything of feudal

23. Molhuysen iv: 105, 107.
24. Molhuysen iv: 107 and 33*. Res. St. Holland, 18 Nov. 1692.
25. Molhuysen iv: 108 and 34* f.
26. Molhuysen iv: 99 and 109.

law and related matters.[27] Governors and burgomasters did not rely blindly, however, on the advice of the law professors. They asked them to report about the subjects they were teaching. On 9 February 1693 the professors sent in their reply.[28]

The States of Holland received the draft on 6 February 1693, but action soon slowed to a halt and apparently no final resolution was taken.[29] The provision that no law degree would be given in Leiden unless the student had passed two examinations, one in law and court practice (including canon law and feudal law) and one in Roman history, rhetoric, and philosophy, made it practically impossible for students from other universities to take a degree in Leiden without studying there. In December 1692 the senate of Utrecht got wind of Leiden's plans. It was afraid that jurists with degrees from other universities than Leiden might be barred from public office in Holland.[30]

On 7 February 1693 the senate decided to ask the burgomasters of Utrecht to do something about the proposal, which by then was on the agenda of the States of Holland, but only a week later it got hold of a copy of the draft-regulation.[31] On 27 March the burgomasters asked the senate if there was anything to add to the considerations formulated against the plans of a restoration of studies in Leiden in 1670; the senate believed that no addition was needed.[32] Prompted by the burgomasters, the States of Utrecht then sent a fierce protest to those of Holland, dated 29 March 1693,[33] and that was the end of the matter.

Lectures on the Digest

The manuscript BPL 575, acquired by Leiden University Library in 1861,[34] is the most important. It is in Noodt's handwriting and

27. It might seem remarkable that (apart from court practice) contemporary law (*jus hodiernum*, *jus patrium*) does not figure among the gaps in legal training lamented by the law faculty, but that subject belonged to the teaching assignment of Johannes Vœt, one of the participants in the action.
28. Molhuysen iv: 111.
29. I thank Mr A. C. Koenhein for his research in the archives of the States of Holland, ARA The Hague. He found nothing in the incoming correspondence of the States, nor in the archive of Heinsius.
30. Kernkamp ii: 123; Kernkamp, 1936: 285–7.
31. Kernkamp ii: 125.
32. Kernkamp ii: 127.
33. Date according to the Julian calendar. Text of the letter in Kernkamp ii: 133–7; Res. St. Holl., 9 Apr. 1693.
34. It is bound in 2 vols. On the front page it has the inscription 'Ex bibl. L. C. Luzac

contains an explanation of the whole Digest in two volumes. For a manuscript of lecture notes it is unusually densely written, without columns, with very small margins,[35] and on both sides of the leaf. The handwriting, though undoubtedly Noodt's own, is rather small as well. The manuscript is interleaved with paper from a different mill (Amsterdam) and bound in leather. Apparently it was Noodt's private copy from which he gave his lectures. The manuscript bears no date.

In a preface Noodt discusses the name and composition of the Digest. After explaining the name and discussing various abbreviations of it, Noodt explains why the work was divided into fifty books and seven parts and how in the Middle Ages this division into seven parts was replaced by a division into three parts: *Digestum vetus*, *Infortiatum*, *Digestum novum*. For the term 'infortiatum' there is no explanation, according to Noodt. After explaining how the books are divided into titles, the titles into fragments, and the fragments into paragraphs, the order of subjects in the Digest is discussed. The order which was followed in the composition of the Digest was that of the *edictum perpetuum*, with some exceptions. The fragments were taken from the books of the ancient jurists. Noodt explains how this was done, what the inscriptions mean, and what interpolations are. Here he points to the independent transmissions of several texts in the *Mosaicarum et Romanorum legum collatio*, which makes it possible to get an exact picture of the changes made in the text by Tribonian. Further, Noodt explains Justinian's orders to write the text of the Digest out in full, without the use of sigla and *notæ*, and the prohibition against commentaries, except *paratitla*.

The effect of the beautiful work of the compilers and its importance can be proved by one argument. The fact that it contains rules which are necessary for the conservation of human society is demonstrated not so much by the fact that it necessarily obtained in Justinian's time in the whole of the Roman empire, as that nowadays, when there are so many kingdoms and republics who can make their own laws, the Digest and the whole Corpus Juris is used all over

dono dedit vidua S. L. du Rieu 1861.' It seems likely that the MS was already in the possession of Elie Luzac (L. C.'s father). There is an item 'Noodt, Dictata ad Pandectas' in the auction catalogue of his books (Leiden, 1799; Bibliotheek Vereeniging, NV 671, no. 93). I have studied the MS personally, but in this section I also use transcriptions made by Mr J. J. Brinkhof, formerly my assistant in Nijmegen.

35. Left and right 16 mm, above and below 12 mm.

Europe, not out of necessity, but voluntarily. The reason is that modern law-givers hardly could improve on this excellent book.

Justinian's boasts are not true in every respect, however. The claim that the work contains no antinomies and no errors is certainly unfounded. There are glaring antinomies like that between D 2. 15. 12 and D 2. 15. 3. Not all thirty-six jurists from whose books the fragments were taken were of the same opinion. Moreover, they did not live at the same time, but in different ages. Furthermore, Tribonian did not do the work alone and his many assistants were not all of the same opinion. This is all the more evident if we consider the short time of only three years in which the work was done. Therefore, the intention that there would be no antinomies was not realized. We must not accept easily, however, that there is an antinomy, because the context of laws often makes a big difference. To avoid an antinomy one must first understand the meaning of the Latin phrase and, secondly, know the structure of the Roman republic and its old customs. Furthermore, one must realize that the Digest only contains fragments from the jurists. Often something which is said casually in one text is treated extensively in another. In that case, the passing remark must give way. Likewise, a general rule cannot stand against a specific definition. For this reason, jurists say that it is a poor doctor who cites a general rule when a decision can be given in exact terms.

Furthermore, it must be observed that the law did not fall from heaven one day, but was introduced, corrected, and changed during many ages, according to the needs of the Roman state. This was first a republic, then a principate. In the old days morals were severe because of the poverty of the period, but later the state became rich and powerful and then bad morals and luxury grew. What first was laudable became despised later. We must also consider legal development. In one place there is one rule of law, while in another a different custom is followed. The jurists lived in different times and under different emperors, and if we realize this we can understand that a rule which did not exist under one emperor became accepted law later. So texts can contradict each other and both be perfectly true. If this is not sufficient to solve the problem we must consider interpolations of Tribonian. Furthermore, we must pay attention to inscriptions, because often a text which seems to be a general law by itself proves to be meant for a special case, if we look at the inscription and compare the text with other texts from the same book. So, if we look at the inscription of D 2. 15. 6, we will see that the jurist never meant what he seems to say there. There we must use the Index of Labittus[36] and to understand the lives of the jurists Bertrandus is good.[37]

If all this does not suffice to solve our problem we must try criticism, which is the replacement of one letter, which makes no sense, by another one. Interpreters complain that all jurisprudence is corrupted in that way, which is uncertain and full of dangers. But they are not justified in saying this, for criticism is an element of interpretation. Interpreters say that criticism must not be made unless there is an extreme necessity. But nobody will do such a thing without need, and on the other hand we should not assume that the classical jurist was stupid and did not know what he said or wrote. Their books have been frequently transcribed without adequate correction. So the Emperor Theodosius himself confirmed the many books of jurists, but he said that someone should take care to obtain accurate copies and then these would have authority.[38] In this matter we may use various readings, like the text of Accursius and the *Florentina*. And some think that the *Florentina* is Justinian's own copy. It is also excellent because it has inscriptions, which other manuscripts do not have. But even the *Florentina* has defects. Other editions are those of Haloander,[39] Vintimille,[40] Charondas,[41] and Russardus.[42] Furthermore, we can emend texts by punctuation because the ancients did not use any. Editors have introduced punctuation with perfect justification, but they have often erred. Therefore, punctuation is arbitrary, so if you can make an emendation with the help of this it is good and valid. It should be noted that

36. Jac. Labittus, *Index legum omnium quae in Pandectis continentur* . . ., Paris, 1557. There are several later edns., among them a Leiden edition of 1674, and one with a preface by N. H. Gundling, Frankfurt and Leipzig, 1724 (these two edns. are mixed up by Camus-Dupin). The Index of Labittus is also in Wieling, 1727.
37. Joannes Bertrandus (1527–94) was *praeses* of the *parlement* of Toulouse. His *Bioi nomikoon sive de jurisperitis libri duo* were published posthumously in Toulouse, 1617. They were reprinted in Leiden, 1675, and Halle, 1718, see Lipenius ii: 452. Noodt does not mention W. de Groot's *De vitis Jurisconsultorum*, Leiden, 1690. This might be used as a weak *terminus ante quem* to date Noodt's manuscript. In the Commentary on the Digest (1716) Noodt says that W. de Groot's book is 'in the hands of everybody' (1. 2, *Opera* ii: 11).
38. Noodt refers to C. Th. 1. 4. 3 in the Mommsen edn. In older edns. this is 1. 4. 1.
39. Gregorii Haloander, Neurenberg, 1529 (Spangenberg, nr. 143a).
40. Jacobi Vintimilii, Paris, 1548 (Spangenberg, nr. 195a).
41. Ludovici Charondae, Antwerp, 1575 (Spangenberg, nr. 289a).
42. Ludovici Russardi, Lyons, 1561 (Spangenberg, nr. 240a).

Noodt, when describing the advantages of the *Florentina* over other manuscripts, does not mention the *Graeca*.

The explanation of the Digest naturally often takes a lemma as a starting-point, but sometimes discussions go beyond the text. The first title of the Digest, *De justitia et jure*, gives ample opportunity to discuss some general doctrines which are dear to Noodt. Justice is a condition of the mind, not an act. So a just man does not cease to be so by an unjust act, because it is human to err. Digest 1. 1. 10 speaks of *jus suum*, that is, the power and dignity given to someone by public law, not unconditionally, but without violation of common utility: 'non autem simpliciter, sed salva communi utilitate'.[43] This formula is very dear to Noodt, we find it in all his lectures, also in those on the Institutes and on Grotius. It is explained by a well-known example, which has been used before, with slight variation of circumstances, by Cicero and e.g. Thomas Aquinas. If Titius deposits his sword with me while being sane, but later asks for it back when he is drunk and wants to hurt somebody, I must not give it back to him, because that would be unjust. I have a duty to give it back, but not immediately, only when the other has come to his senses again. Other examples are in D 16. 3. 31 pr. and 1, according to which money deposited by someone who is later exiled and whose effects are confiscated, must not be given back to the person in question but to the fisc, and the spoils deposited by the robber must be given back to the owner if he comes to claim them.

With regard to the *tria juris praecepta: honeste vivere, alterum non laedere, jus suum cuique tribuere*, Noodt explains—as we already know—that these are not rules of law properly speaking, but exhortations to justice. His discussion of the concept of *jus gentium* shows that—anachronistically speaking—Noodt was a culture relativist.[44] *Jus gentium* is, says Ulpian,[45] the law that human nations use. It is also defined as that which natural reason defines for all nations; so it is, like natural law, 'dictamen rectae rationis', the dictate of right reason. Some scholars add that *jus gentium* is not what all nations accept, but only the more civilized ones. But that is an imperfect definition, because then immediately the question arises which nations are the more civilized. Every nation finds itself and its

43. Vol. i: fol. 15^{v}.
44. The concept of cultural relativism is connected with the work of F. Boas and his pupils, see Kluckhohn, 1964: 160 f.
45. D 1. 1. 1. 4.

customs best, as is proved by the well-known example from Hieronymus,[46] which comes, in fact, from Herodotus.[47] (Here we find Noodt once more in the company of the sceptic Montaigne, who used the same example several times.)[48] The king of Persia received deputations from different people in his kingdom who had very different habits with regard to the care of their dead. First there came a group that used to bury its dead. The king said that he had heard that they buried their dead, but he would prefer them to eat them. The deputation answered that it would do anything to please the king, but they could never bring themselves to the cruelty of devouring their own parents. Then the king spoke to the other delegation and asked why they would not rather bury their dead than eat them. But they protested that they did not know a better place to bury their dead than in their own body. So it is not easy to decide which nations are civilized. All nations have only one purpose, the conservation of mankind, but they seek it by different ways.[49]

As for the explanation of the Digest itself I restrict myself, for reasons of space, to one example only, the title *De contrahenda emptione*, D 18. 1.[50] Noodt does not explain, as a medieval professor would have done, all the fragments in that title, but gives—in very simple Latin and in strict didactic form—a systematic exposition of the Roman law of sale (in fact, under this title he treats the titles 1 to 5 of Book 18 of the Digest).[51] *Emptio venditio* is a contract *juris gentium* and *bonae fidei*, based on *consensus* concerning certain goods and a certain price. All these elements are treated successively in a systematic fashion. Why is a sale *juris gentium* and what is the meaning of *bona fides*? Nothing but consensus concerning the price and goods is needed. The price must consist in *pecunia numerata* and be fixed, or at least be determinable (such as when it is left to a third party to fix it). The goods must exist at the time the sale is contracted,

46. Vol. i: fol. 16^r.

47. iii: 38. According to this version, the Persian King Darius asked some Greeks on what condition they would be prepared to eat their father's dead body and then asked some Indians (Calliatae) whether they would agree to burn their father's dead body. Both refused indignantly, and this proves, concludes Herodotus, that every people regards its own customs as the best. It is remarkable, and significant for Noodt's scant knowledge of Greek, that he cites Hieronymus and does not seem to know the story from Herodotus.

48. *Essais*, I. xxiii and II. xii; Montaigne, 1967: 115, 565.

49. Vol. i: fol. 16^v.

50. Vol. i: fol. 168^r–174^r.

51. Fo. 174^r. The explanation of title 1 is followed by that of title 6 'nam titulus secundus tertus quartus et quintus sub hoc titulo primo sunt explicati.'

except in the case of *emptio spei*. Furthermore, they must be *in commercio*, although it is possible to buy a *res religiosa* 'per consequentiam', for example, when it forms part of a *fundus*. One cannot buy one's own goods and there are other specific prohibitions, e.g. the sale of children or the export of certain contraband goods. For the rest, the goods can be *res mobiles* and *immobiles*, *res corporales* as well as *incorporales*, such as servitudes and rents. Special cases which demand a detailed discussion are the sale of an inheritance and the sale of claims. Finally there are three effects of the contract to consider. In the first place, one cannot recede from the contract once it is perfect, except in the case of an *in diem addictio* or *lex commissoria*. Secondly, from the moment the contract is perfect, *periculum* and *commodum* of the goods sold pass to the buyer. And thirdly, there is the question of what actions are born from the contract.

The whole treatment is strictly dogmatic and only very few humanistic topics are discussed.[52] Noodt refers several times to his published books, but only once to another author, namely Vinnius.[53] There is only one reference to a rule of Roman law—the restriction of cessions in C 4. 35. 22—which is not received in Dutch law.[54] But in this respect our title may not be wholly representative. The general principles of the Roman law of sale were received practically unrestricted. There is one other peculiarity to note. In citing texts from the Corpus Juris Noodt not only gives the words of the rubric, as usual, but also the numbers of book and title, in the way that this is done in the early nineteenth century: '1 1 D de addictione in diem lib. 18. Tit. 2'. Apparently Noodt does this as a service to his students—he never did it in his published works—and it indicates that the medieval habit of citing the rubric and memorizing texts in this way is coming to an end.

To illustrate how Noodt treats a contemporary problem in his lectures we may take his discussion of torture in the context of D 48. 18 (*de quaestionibus*).[55] Torture is a weak and dangerous kind of proof. Some people who cannot endure pain confess all kind of things for fear of punishment, while others can bear anything, as is said in D 48. 18. 1. 23. Now the question is whether torture can be acceptable. It must be noted that in all Europe, except in England and Aragon, torture is used. But wrongly, because it is against natural law. It was not known in Mosaic law, nor against free men in Rome when the

52 e.g. vol. i: fol. 171^r, 172^r.
53. Vol. i: fol. 171^v.
54. Vol. i: fol. 172^r.
55. Vol. ii: fol. 190.

republic was still free. It was in use with regard to slaves and later, when the form of the constitution was changed, its use extended among the Romans. In Greece torture was used against slaves as well as free men under kings and tyrants. Now, if we ask for the reason why torture is not acceptable, it is that it is a weak kind of proof. Many can bear pain, many cannot. It can also depend on the torturer, who can treat someone more lightly or more severely. Furthermore, it should be noted that torture is meant to establish the truth, that is, to find out whether a punishment should be imposed or not. Now, often torture is a greater punishment than that which is imposed on the culprit after his confession. Therefore, it is unjust. There is yet another reason: a man is forced by torment to betray himself, for if he confesses, he must die, if not, he is tortured. Anyway, whatever the outcome, he must be harmful to himself. Therefore it is better that a man should be condemned after being found guilty through witnesses, and absolved if not. For it is better to absolve a bad person than to punish an innocent one.[56]

There is one more point to be noted. These lectures on the Digest, of which we do not know the date of composition (the last work cited is *De forma emendandi doli mali*, 1709),[57] nor whether they were meant for public or private lectures, show no similarity with Noodt's Commentary on the Digest, of which the first part was published in 1716. While the reconstruction of the praetorian edict is the key to the commentary, in these lectures only occasionally is the wording of the edict discussed. As we know, Noodt must have lectured on the reconstruction of the edict before publishing his commentary.[58] So Noodt must have given other lectures on the Digest than those contained in BPL 575. This fact is also brought out by other manuscripts. While we have several manuscripts of lecture notes conforming to the Leiden autograph,[59] there is also another type of

56. Naturally, there were earlier scholars who opposed torture, e.g. Antonius Matthæus II, in *De criminibus* (1661). But Matthæus still found torture acceptable in two cases, that is, in the case of *crimen laesae majestatis*, and in order to trace accessories, if it concerned a heinous crime and was evident that the culprit could not have perpetrated it on his own; see Van de Vrugt, 1982: 38. With Noodt I found no such restrictions, but naturally in his lectures he did not give an exhaustive treatment of the subject. Thomasius wrote a *Dissertatio de tortura e foris Christianis proscribenda* (1705); see R. Lieberwirth, 1960.

57. Vol. i: fol. 173ʳ.

58. So Haubold, 1812: 309, who refers to the dissertation of J. van der Waeyen, *De aeditilitio edicto*, Leiden, 1720.

59. UL Gent, Hs 280 (written by J. C. Mathiassen, Leiden, 1712); GA Nijmegen, 11 C

lecture, of which the notes completed in 1721 by the later Leiden professor J. C. Rücker give the best example.[60] They do not contain the introductory tracts and give a lemmatic explanation of the most important fragments of each title. There are other manuscripts of the same type extant and a similar manuscript was published in 1842 by Huguenin,[61] who purported to publish the remainder of Noodt's commentary on the Digest, but did nothing of the sort.

Lectures on the Institutes

Notes from lectures on the Institutes of Justinian are still extant in Leiden,[62] Ghent,[63] Edinburgh,[64] and Amsterdam.[65] Dated manuscripts are from 1686 (Edinburgh) and 1710 (Leiden, BPL 191x). The lectures on the Institutes were given privately, 'in collegio domestico'.[66] In content, especially, the introductory part shows considerable similarities with the lectures on the Digest. Once more, Noodt stresses that justice demands that everyone be given his due 'salva communi utilitate' and again this is illustrated by the story of the man who deposited his sword and asked for it back after he had gone mad. For the rest, the comment on the Institutes is mainly simple and lemmatic. A special type of note occurs in BPL 695. Notes from lectures on the Institutes by Noodt and Schulting are written down synoptically, with Schulting on the recto and Noodt on the verso pages. One wonders why a student should attend the private lectures of two professors whose lectures to a great extent ran along

2 (undated, incomplete). In the MS Leiden BPL 191y (4 vols.), written by H. de Beaufort (who enrolled at Leiden, 30 Apr. 1705, AS Leiden 785) edictal clauses are discussed with some regularity, though not always.

60. PB Friesland, Leeuwarden, Voorda-collection HS Hof 10; 4 vols. In vol. 4 on the penultimate page: 'Finis d. 10 Jul. 1721'. On the verso pages are notes from lectures by Schulting and Westenberg.
61. Ahsmann–Feenstra, 1984: nr. 476.
62. BPL 191*x*. 2 vols. (written by R. W. de Bachman from Emmerich, 1710); BPL 695 (synoptic notes of Noodt and Schulting, without date or owner's entry but dating from after 1713); BPL 2322. 2 vols. (without date or owner's entry. At the end, a list of *Definitiones et divisiones*).
63. MS 281. 1 vol., complete. (see de Saint-Genois, 1849–52, p. 204, no. 214, from the library of Lammens).
64. National library Adv. MS 28. 4. 9 (i–iv). 4 vols., complete, dated 1686; owner's entries 'J. Campbell' and 'Alex Leslie his book'.
65. Univ. of Amsterdam, Law Institute, room prof. Ankum (B202), 1 vol., incomplete, no date or owner's entry.
66. See BPL 191*x*, vol. ii.

the same lines. But perhaps he copied one set from a fellow student. As might be expected, 'antiquarian' explanations of Roman institutions play a considerable part in these lectures.

Collegium Grotianum

The University Library of Leiden preserves a manuscript made by H. Gockinga in 1708 of private lectures by Noodt on Grotius' *De jure belli ac pacis*.[67] As we have seen, Noodt pleaded for the inclusion of natural law in the law curriculum in his Franeker inaugural address of 1679, but if he gave lectures on that subject in Franeker and Utrecht we have no proof of it. The lectures give a simple lemmatic explanation, which is sometimes critical and often stresses Noodt's relativistic attitude. Let me give a few examples. Grotius regards marriage with parents of every degree as forbidden by natural law,[68] but according to Noodt he failed to prove that thesis. Neither the argument that a man marrying his mother cannot give her due respect nor the argument that decency forbids marriage with one's daughter is conclusive. Decency is not a product of nature but of education and constitution and there are several peoples with good morals, like the Persians, who show no horror for such marriages. Grotius believes that all Christians accept the rule but that is not the same as proving that it conforms to natural reason.[69] Grotius says that people who are totally destitute of reason can have no property but doubts whether there exist peoples who are totally insane,[70] but Noodt has no doubt: what we call good is called bad by others and vice versa. In the next paragraph Noodt criticizes Aristotle for saying that people who are mad are by nature slaves. King Carlos II of Spain was evidently mad, but he was not a slave, nor can one say the same of a people.

6. Legal advice

It seems that the giving of legal advice—often in the form of the draft of a judgment—was not as institutionalized in the Republic as it was in Germany, where every law faculty had its own 'Spruchkollegium'. German advice-giving was based on the institution of 'Aktenversendung',[71] which was introduced in the sixteenth century; courts

67. BPL 191.
68. *De jure belli ac pacis* 2. 5. 12. 2.
69. BPL 191, fol. 73^{v}.
70. *De jure belli ac pacis* 2. 22. 10. 1.
71. *HRG* i: 84–87.

did not decide the case themselves but sent the file to a 'Spruchkollegium' and afterwards communicated its opinion to the parties. Although 'Aktenversendung' was introduced in Overijssel and Guelders, it was not a general practice in the Republic. Dutch professors, moreover, were generally better paid than their German colleagues and therefore less obliged to look for extra earnings. The frequent complaints heard in Germany about professors who were so busy making extra income that they neglected their teaching obligation are not known from the Republic. But naturally state control of professors was less strict in the Republic than in the German absolutist 'Fürstenstaat'.[72]

Noodt was not very active in giving legal advice. I have found not more than twenty opinions bearing his signature, and fourteen of these are no more than simple confirmations of opinions given by others. In most cases Noodt signed as member of the law faculty of Nijmegen, Franeker, or Leiden.[73] Only three times did Noodt sign a confirmation alone; two of them concerned advice of J. and A. van den Ende. Only two opinions deserve closer attention.

Advice concerning a case of marriage

The only opinion Noodt gave alone and therefore the only one of which his authorship is certain dates from 17 February 1696. It concerned the question whether the government could give dispensation to marry the widow of one's maternal uncle. The opinion had several editions in Dutch,[74] as well as in a Latin translation by the Groningen professor A. A. Pagenstecher.[75] According to Pagenstecher it drew much assent and was not only transcribed but also translated in other languages.[76] It was published for the first time in 1700 in volume iii of the *Utrechtse consultatiën*, together with a letter from Pagenstecher to Noodt.[77] From a letter of Pagenstecher to Van Eck it appears that the latter was responsible for the publication.[78]

72. See e.g. Burmeister, 1974.
73. On the opinions of the Leiden law faculty see also Fischer, 1961.
74. Ahsmann–Feenstra, 1984: nrs. 432–4A.
75. Ahsmann–Feenstra, 1984: nr. 435.
76. Pagenstecher to Noodt, Groningen, 14 Sept. 1669, in *Utrechtse Consultatiën* iii: 596.
77. *Utrechtse consultatiën* iii: nr. 141, pp. 589–95.
78. A. A. Pagenstecher to C. van Eck, Groningen, 8 June 1700 (UL Utrecht, MS 1000): 'Gratias tibi ago, Nobilissime vir, pro amicitiae isto officio quo negotium meum gessisti in edendis istis meis ad Cl. Noodtium litteris.'

Noodt himself must have been instrumental in this, but he did not include the advice in his *Opera omnia*, apparently because he did not regard it as part of his scholarly work. It was Barbeyrac who put it in the 1735 edition.[79] Apparently, Noodt's advice on the matter had been asked ten years before through the intermediary of Græviius, but we do not have that advice.[80]

Questions concerning marriage with in-laws were much discussed in the Republic in the seventeenth century.[81] Orthodox theologians postulated that the prohibitions of Leviticus 18 did apply in the Republic, as was indeed the custom in some provinces. But most jurists were opposed, if only for reasons of precedent[82] and on the practical political consideration that marriage prohibitions must not be extended without necessity. For example, on 25 September 1695 the theological faculty of Utrecht university ruled that someone was not allowed to marry the widow of his grandfather's brother.[83] One member of the law faculty (Johan van Muyden) concurred, but the faculty as such (L. van de Poll and C. van Eck) advised to the contrary.[84] The letter of 10 November 1686 in which Græviius introduced to Noodt a man from Deventer who wanted his legal advice on a similar matter nicely sums up the situation:

The bearer of this letter, a friend from Deventer with the kindred of whom I once was very intimate, wants your advice and asks urgently for an opinion on the marriage he has contracted, but which some magistrates as well as some theologians regard as forbidden by divine law. But others deny this and are of the opinion that such a marriage is forbidden neither in divine nor in Roman law. The man asks you to declare sincerely what is your opinion, and, if that is your conviction, to pronounce in his favour and to procure, if possible—and I believe it is—the opinion of some theologians, for instance Wittichius and Lemonon. Regard whatever study or work you do for this excellent man as devoted to me.[85]

79. *Opera* i: 645–8.
80. See the letter of Græviius to Noodt, Utrecht, 10 Nov. 1686, ARA Tets van Goudriaan, inv. nr. 114. It is possible, of course, that Noodt's opinion of 1686 (supposing he gave one) is identical with that dated 17 Feb. 1696. Noodt may have publicly issued the advice only ten years after he actually gave it.
81. See e.g. *Utrechtse consultatiën* iii: nrs. 9 and 12; Van der Kop, ii: nrs. 19–22.
82. A series of precedents from Guelders is cited in Van der Kop, ii: nr. 22, pp. 77f.; among which is a decision concerning one Roelof Noodt, dating from 1637.
83. *Utrechtse consultatiën* iii: nr. 9, pp. 48–73. For a similar case decided by the theological faculty of Leiden, see Eekhof, 1921: 79f.
84. Ibid., pp. 57–73.
85. (As n. 80): 'Qui has tibi feret, amicus Daventriensis, cujus cognatis utor olim familiarissime, habet de quo te consulat, tuumque efflagitat responsum de

The case on which Noodt advised was this: A, aged 40, wanted to marry B, aged 42 and widow of C, the brother of A's mother. According to the provincial custom the marriage was forbidden. The question arose whether the government could give dispensation. There can be no dispensation, Noodt begins, from rules of natural law or *jus gentium*, but, according to the common opinion of jurists, prohibitions of marriage are not natural but civil law. The son of Edward III married, with papal dispensation, the widow of his great-uncle and Philip II even married his sister's daughter. Furthermore, Noodt cites a series of cases in which the States of Utrecht and Guelders had given dispensation. After this come the main arguments.

That the prohibition of incest is not natural law is proved by the Bible itself, because God wanted the whole of the human race to begin with marriages between the sons and daughters of Adam and Eve. Vinnius, invoking theologians, answered that it happened out of necessity and with the tacit dispensation of God, but that nevertheless incest was against nature. But that argument of Vinnius, though backed by the authority of Augustine, is not valid. For God there was absolutely no necessity to create only Adam and Eve. He had it in his power to create four or six or more men and women instead of just one man and one woman. Therefore, it was God himself who decided that marriages between collaterals or even between brother and sister were not prohibited by natural law.

That such marriages are not prohibited in *jus gentium* is proved by the fact that many highly cultured peoples practised them—the Egyptians, Athenians, and Spartans. And in Rome the marriage between an uncle and his brother's daughter was allowed. Similar practices are known from the Bible, e.g. Sarah, Abraham's wife, was the daughter of his father but not of his mother, Jacob had the two sisters Lea and Rachel as wife and Amram, the father of Moses and Aaron, was married to his father's sister.

If it is true, as Vinnius says, that people have an aversion for such marriages this is not a matter of nature but of education. The

matrimonio, quod contractus est, sed quod nonnulli magistratus, et nonnulli Theologi improbant tanquam lege divina vetitum. Alii vero hoc inficiantur, et nec lege divina nec Romana vetitum esse tale connubium censent. Quid tibi placeat, ut ex animi tui sententia pronuncies, et, si tuus animus fert, secundum se pronuncies, non nullusque Theologorum, si fieri potest, et credo posse, Wittichii nimirum et Lemonii decreta ei conficias rogat. Quicquid studii operaeque in virum optimum conferes, in me collatum existimabo.'

prohibitions which Moses gave in Leviticus 18: 12–14, Noodt says, citing Grotius,[86] are not moral precepts and generally binding, but only positive Hebrew civil law. This is not only clear from the fact that the marriages of Jacob and Amram were in direct contravention of these prohibitions. Moses' law contradicts itself because Leviticus 18: 16 forbids the taking of a brother's wife while Deuteronomy 25: 5 orders a man to take his brother's widow as wife. This proves that such prohibitions are not immutable rules of morals and natural law, but civil law which can be changed according to needs and circumstances.

Noodt's advice goes to the heart of the matter and it is characteristic for the robust and acute juristic argument with which authority from the Bible is dissected. His main argument[87] is the thesis, taken from Grotius, that Mosaic marriage prohibitions are Hebrew civil law and therefore do not bind Christians in general. Two years later, in *De foenore et usuris*, Noodt was to extend this argument to the Mosaic prohibition to take interest, which Grotius himself had accepted as still binding on all Christians. This is a nice example of how arguments from natural law could help to curb the authority of the Bible and orthodox theologians.

Advice to Vittorio Amedeo II

When in 1714, after the peace of Utrecht, Vittorio Amedeo II regained his kingdom of Savoy (now enlarged with Sicily) from France, one of his first aims was to remedy the very confused state of the law by making a systematic compilation of all the laws promulgated by his predecessors.[88] In the course of preparations a major conflict arose among the jurists involved, mainly concerning the regulation of fideicommissa, a problem that concerned many lawgivers in the eighteenth and nineteenth centuries. In order to solve the problem, a series of eight questions was formulated and sent for advice to a number of learned jurists in Italy and to the professors in Leiden. Schulting, Noodt, and Vitriarius, constituting the law faculty of Leiden,[89] signed their reply on 1 December 1717. It had its influence on the codification,[90] but remained unpublished until

86. *De jure belli ac pacis* 1. 1. 16.
87. Cf. Pagenstecher to Noodt (as n. 76).
88. See Viora, 1927: 3 f.; Hoetink, 1928: 345–6.
89. See the text of the advice, Viora, 1927: 35.
90. Viora, 1927: 47 f.

Viora unearthed it in the archives in Turin. Before publishing it, he asked J. C. Naber of Utrecht university to find out whether or not it had already been published and Naber confirmed, 'after careful research in Dutch libraries',[91] that this was not the case. Nevertheless, the advice was not, as Hœtink claimed,[92] completely unknown. C. A. den Tex cited from it in 1839.[93]

The fact that the jurists in Turin, apart from asking a number of Italian jurists, only sought advice in the Republic, is solid proof of the great international reputation Dutch legal scholarship had at that time. The intermediary was Guiseppe Osorio,[94] a bright young man whom Vittorio Amedeo brought with him as *garde de corps* from Sicily and to whom he gave an opportunity to complete his education by a *peregrinatio academica* to Holland. He stayed there from 1717 to 1719, studied law in Utrecht under Vitriarius junior and also went to Leiden (where he may have heard Noodt).[95] In 1719 he was appointed ambassador in The Hague and later he made a great career as a diplomat and minister in the service of Savoy. It may seem somewhat surprising that Vitriarius junior, to whom Osorio presented the questionnaire, did not put it before his own faculty in Utrecht, but passed it on to his father in Leiden, but it will not have been doubted that the most famous Dutch jurists of the day lived there.

Of the eight questions five concerned the legislation of fideicommissa and they clearly show the intention of the legislator to restrict that institution as far as possible.[96] Other questions concerned the number of witnesses required for an oral military testament and the exclusion of members of religious orders from all succession (aiming at reduction of the volume of goods in mortmain). The eighth question resuscitated the age-old idea of the so-called 'Law of citation' promulgated by the Emperors Theodosius II and Valentinianus III in 426:[97] would it be a useful remedy for the confused state of the law to limit the number of doctors that could be cited and fix that number by drawing up a list of named authorities?

The replies from Leiden conform to what we already know to be Noodt's ideas. Rules concerning testaments are not natural but civil law and therefore the legislator is free to make any provision he likes

91. Viora, 1927: 3 n. 92. Hoetink, 1928: 345. 93. Den Tex, 1839: 6.
94. (1697–1763) *Enciclopedia italiana* (Trecani), app. i, 1938: 909 f.
95. Viora, 1927: 10 f. There is no inscription in AS Leiden.
96. Viora, 1927: 18. 97. Schulz, 1963: 282.

as long as he respects certain principles of fairness. Restrictions on fideicommissa should not be made retroactive; when a fideicommissum is made effective by the death of the testator it should not be used to provide for the urgent needs of its possessor, nor should it be made liable for regimental debts. The reply to the last question is quite understandably in the negative. One can no more expect doctors to agree to serious restrictions of doctoral authority than foxes to accept a prohibition to take hens. The Leiden professors stated that such a rule might withhold from the parties what they think necessary to win their case. It would be dangerous to make a list of authors, because then one would often find no decision in the authors included, while one could find such a decision in others. It should be the task of the judge to curb evidently superfluous allegations and teach the advocates not to make abuse of them. Although, on the whole, the advice seems to fit Noodt's way of arguing, neither from internal evidence nor from the order of subscriptions can we conclude anything concerning its authorship.

Other legal opinions

In order to be complete I give a list of opinions and confirmations signed by Noodt. As I said before, nothing can be said of Noodt's authorship of any of these. We may only assume that he did agree, or at least did not find it worthwhile to oppose the theses of the respective opinions.

1670 July 10, Nijmegen.
Opinion by P. de Greve and Gerard Noodt in a criminal case. Someone who is summoned three times and is still absent cannot be regarded as guilty.[98]

1677 July 2, Nijmegen.
Opinion (draft-decision) by G. Noodt, W. Water, and J. Verstegen in a case of succession. Invalidity of fictitious transactions to evade the prohibition of a *donatio mortis causa*. Decision pronounced by the Adelijke Gericht des Ampts Overbetuwe.[99]

1682 December 3, Franeker.
Confirmation by S. Schelkens, U. Huber, and Gerard Noodt of an

98. Barels, 1778: 4–7.

99. Van den Berg iii: 339–46.

opinion in a case of succession. The *portio legitima* of the mother of a son who died in the Indies is one third of his inheritance.[1]

1693 November 10, Leiden.
Confirmation by J. Vœt and G. Noodt of an opinion concerning the interpretation of a marriage-settlement.[2]

1701 January 5, Leiden.
Opinion by J. Vœt and G. Noodt in a criminal case concerning slander. The Court of Culemborg took over the opinion verbatim in its judgment of 20 January 1701.[3]

1701 May 19, Leiden.
Confirmation by A. Matthaeus III, J. Vœt, P. R. Vitriarius, and G. Noodt (that is, the complete law faculty of Leiden) of an opinion concerning witnesses to a testament.[4]

1704 June 14, Leiden.
Confirmation by J. Vœt, P. R. Vitrarius, and G. Noodt of an opinion concerning Isaac Hurgronje, burgomaster of Vlissingen. Unpublished.[5]

1707 March 30, Leiden.
Confirmation by J. Vœt and G. Noodt of an opinion in a criminal case concerning the question whether an officer who fails to prosecute is punishable.[6]

1709 June 3, Leiden.
Confirmation by G. Noodt of an opinion concerning a criminal case.[7]

1709 November 16, Leiden.
Confirmation by G. Noodt and J. Vœt of an opinion concerning a case of voluntary subjection to jurisdiction.[8]

1711 January 16, Leiden.
Confirmation by J. Vœt and G. Noodt of an opinion concerning the legal hypothec of children on the inheritance of their mother.[9]

1. Van den Berg iii: 373.
2. *Utrechtse Consultatiën* iii: 507.
3. Stolte, 1979: 421–7.
4. *Vervolg op de Hollandsche Consultatiën* ii: 40.
5. KB 72 D 37/10.
6. Barels, 1778: 340; Van der Kop i: 504 f.
7. Van der Kop i: 195.
8. Van der Kop i: 54.
9. *Vervolg op de Hollandsche Consultatiën* ii: 90.

1711 February 20, Amsterdam.
Confirmation by G. Noodt of an advice by J. and A. van den Ende concerning personal liability of the director of a company for damages resulting from bankruptcy of his contracting party.[10]

1711 March 13, Leiden.
Confirmation by G. Noodt of an advice by J. and A. van den Ende concerning the *portio legitima* of a mother.[11]

1711 June 21, Leiden.
Confirmation by J. Vœt, G. Noodt, and P. R. Vitrarius of an opinion concerning the duty of extradition.[12]

1711 October 7, Leiden.
Confirmation by J. Vœt, P. R. Vitrarius, and G. Noodt of an opinion by A. van den Ende and others concerning the reclamation of ships of the Dutch East Indies Company taken by the enemy and recaptured by the English.[13]

1719 September 27, Leiden.
Confirmation by P. R. Vitriarius, G. Noodt, and A. Schulting of an advice concerning the responsibility of a merchant for the contents of a closed letter he transported.[14]

1725 February 13, Leiden.
Opinion of J. O. Westenberg, G. Noodt, A. Schulting, and J. J. Vitriarius in a case of poisoning by a girl aged 11.[15]

10. Barels ii, 1781: 254.
11. Van der Kop ii: 517.
12. Van der Kop ii: 537f.
13. Barels i, 1780: 276.
14. Barels ii, 1781: 364.
15. Barels, 1778: 330f.

4

Noodt and his Critics

During his lifetime Noodt was highly esteemed, as a lover of freedom as well as one of the best legal scholars of the world famous Dutch school. Several of his works received very favourable reviews.[1] Among those who praised Noodt are such eminent scholars as Heineccius[2] and even Augustin Leyser,[3] who generally did not think much of the Dutch. And if we must be suspicious of the praise Huber voiced when he was about to attack one of Noodt's emendations, we may still note that according to him 'in these days in our art nobody has written more neatly and learnedly'.[4] The very able Haubold summarizes opinion authoritatively in 1809:[5] Noodt has excellent knowledge of all kinds of literature, apart from post-Justinianic law, which is proved sufficiently by the light he throws everywhere on philosophers and the best ancient writers. He is an 'interpres primarius', an explainer of Roman law of the first order, a careful observer of the historical development of Roman law, who also has contributed much to the reconstruction of the praetorian edict. His style is concise but elegant and he shows genius as well as judgment. Noodt is praised, moreover, for some qualities that are exceptional in literary scholars of every age: he is not quarrelsome and he does not shrink from saying openly that he does not know something.[6] He plainly stated that it was useless to speculate about the contents of chapter 2 of the *lex Aquilia*,[7] because nothing was known about it (before the discovery of Gaius' Institutes in the Verona manuscript in

1. *De foenore et usuris* (1698) was reviewed in *Supplem. actor. eruditor.* iii: 234 f. and in Neocorus and Sikens, *Bibl. nov.* ii: 644–53. The *Observationes* (1706) were reviewed in *Acta erud.* 1707: 239 f. For *De religione* (1706), see above, p. 224.
2. *Ad tit. D. de pignorat. action.* § 129.
3. *Meditationes ad Pandectas*, specim. 153.
4. Huber, 1700: 179, 'quo nemo tersius et doctius his diebus in arte nostra scribit . . .'.
5. Haubold, 1809: 136 f.
6. Barbeyrac, 1731: LXXXIII; Arntzenius, 1788: 49 f.; Jugler vi, 1780: 370.
7. See above, p. 176.

1816), and this is what he wrote in his Commentary on the Pandects at title 13. 3 (*De condictione triticaria*): 'I will give no explanation of this title: I am not used to teaching others what I do not understand myself'.[8] After careful study of all proposed interpretations he had found none that was convincing.

But naturally Noodt did not escape criticism. It was not just that his ideas about freedom of religion were bound to displease orthodox theologians,[9] that believers in absolutism loathed his theory of sovereignty,[10] or that people frowned at his mild scepticism. To prove your own opinion and destroy those of others was, as Cuper summed it up nicely,[11] the essence of any run-of-the-mill literary scholarship. Even the anonymous author who took up Noodt's defence after his death[12] rejected some of his emendations and proposed what he considered as better ones. Because he gave a well-balanced judgment, it seems worthwhile to take a closer look at his article.

A few years after Noodt's death there was a remarkable output of critical studies. In 1731 Abraham Wieling[13] published what amounted to an allegation of plagiarism and Barbeyrac brought out his life of Noodt, in which he specifically undertook to refute that allegation.[14] In 1732 the Leipzig *Acta eruditorum* published posthumously Christfried Wächtler's notes on Book IV of Noodt's *Probabilia*[15] and in 1733 C. H. Trotz published in Utrecht a collection of Wächtler's critical essays.[16] Fame always has a bandwagon-effect. One of Wächtler's main titles to fame was his sustained criticism of Noodt's works, beginning in 1680 and continuing in the *Acta* eruditorum after Noodt's death. And Niellius, whom we will meet later, had been practically forgotten when he made a name posthumously because someone found out that Noodt's most famous emendation had been suggested by him long before.

In 1733 an anonymous friend of Noodt's published in the *Miscellaneae observationes in auctores veteres et recentiores*[17] a critique of Wächtler's posthumous notes. Barbeyrac had not much to say about Wächtler in 1731 and even after Trotz had edited a collection of *Waechtleriana*, that is, in the Latin version of his life of Noodt

8. *Opera* ii: 305.
9. See above, p. 233 f.
10. Barbeyrac, 1731: XXXXI.
11. See above, p. 142.
12. See below, at n. 22.
13. Wieling, 1731.
14. Barbeyrac, 1731: LXXXV–LXXXVIII.
15. Nov. 1732.
16. Wächtler, 1733.
17. Amsterdam, 1733: iii. 1, July–Aug., 110–30; iii. 2, Sept.–Oct., 271–301.

appearing in the *Opera omnia* edition of 1735, Barbeyrac still made nothing of the sustained criticism by Wächtler.[18] For this he was severely criticized in the *Acta eruditorum*[19] as well as by C. H. Trotz, who in 1738 published an *Apologia pro Waechtlero*.[20] It is small wonder that Barbeyrac could not make much of Wächtler, whom Noodt had not condescended to mention by name anywhere in his works. As I said before, Barbeyrac was not much of a Romanist and would hardly have been able to discuss technical questions of interpretation and criticism adequately.

The anonymous author in the *Miscellaneae observationes* at least was a specialist. The question is, who was he? He is a jurist from Utrecht and he says of himself that once *litterae humaniores* and elegant jurisprudence were his delight, but that his career prevented him from devoting himself completely to them. But now he regarded it as his duty to honour, defend, and protect one through whom he made progress. That was the only reason why he took up arms again and tested his old forces.[21] I think that there is one Utrecht jurist who fits this description perfectly: Joannes van de Water.[22] He was born in 1689, enrolled as law student in Leiden in 1709, and the following year went to Utrecht where he took his degree in October 1710,[23] under Van Eck. He dedicated his thesis to his teachers: Noodt, Van Muyden, Van Eck, and Burman. He became clerk-substitute, advocate, and finally senator in the Court of Utrecht. He was not only a pupil of Noodt—whom he called the most excellent furtherer of elegant legal scholarship—from their correspondence it is clear that later they were also friends. In his younger years humanistic legal philology was indeed his delight; he published *Observationes* (1713) and the Institutes in the edition by Cujas with the commentary of Janus a Costa (1714).[24] He presented a copy of the last book to Noodt,[25] and asked for Noodt's comments on the idea of improving the Index of Labittus and making a similar palingenetic index of the Codex. Noodt discouraged the idea; he had not ventured to encourage a reprint of Labittus himself, because he was growing old and he was the only one in the academy who still used it; there were, moreover, only a few lovers of such books.[26] In 1716 Noodt

18. Jugler vi, 1780: 373.
19. 1736: 250.
20. In H. Hugo, 1738.
21. *Misc. obs.* iii. 1: 110.
22. *NNBW* iv: 1441.
23. Van de Water, 1710.
24. Dekkers, 1951: 187.
25. Noodt thanks him in a letter of Oct. 1714, BPL 885.
26. Noodt to Van de Water, Leiden, July 1714, UL Amsterdam, 16. Cf. II. 2.

presented Van de Water with a copy of the first part of his Commentary on the Pandects.[27] In 1720 Van de Water made a scheme for a new edition of the Gothofredus edition of the Corpus Juris which was planned by the Leipzig editor Fritsch.[28] But in his thirties he gradually turned away from humanistic studies,[29] and found his life's work in a different field as editor of the *Groot Placaatbœk* of Utrecht (1729–33), for which the printing contract was signed in 1724. In the preface to this work (1729) he even joined the growing choir of scholars lamenting that university students had to spend many years of their youth studying the Greek and Roman constitutions, without learning anything about the public law of the Republic. With this he must have seemed to have gone over to the camp of the enemies of Roman law.[30] That may explain why nobody ever seems to have suspected him of writing a defence of Noodt.

Van de Water begins with the observation that scholars who are famous during their lifetime are often much attacked after death (Cujas is a case in point); fame perishes quickly. It may be objected that only after death can we make a final assessment of someone's merits, but often critics do not seem to be inspired by zeal for the truth, but by ambition, jealousy, and hate. This also was Noodt's fate. Van de Water is not so partial that he approves of everything. He knows that Noodt did not show the same diligence everywhere. Especially the Commentary on the Pandects show signs of decreasing vigour. The author would have preferred Noodt not to have published his *Amica responsio* to Van Bijnkershœk, although he does not like the latter's *Curae secundae* any better. But as far as it went, the debate was adequately done. Van Bijnkershœk was one of the very few who could judge Noodt's work, and as in the High Court so also among the erudite Van Bijnkershœk wanted to act as judge, not as dictator. The unhappy quarrel, however, became a sign for attack on the part of all kinds of second-rate scholars. The author will not name those who, desiring to obtain a chair, did not shrink from false

27. Noodt to Van de Water, Leiden, 9 Mar. 1716, KHA G 16–A 258.
28. There is a bundle of papers on this project in the collection of notes by Van de Water, UL Leiden, BPL 191 H. Van de Water not only advised Fritsch, but also Gebauer, who after Branchu's death was asked by Fritsch to edit the planned edn., see Gebauer, 1764: 55 f., where a long letter of Van de Water to Gebauer is printed (58–63).
29. From his *adversaria* (Leiden BPL 191 H) it is clear that he kept reading and taking notes.
30. See Jansen, 1987*b*: 151.

adulation to win the favour of the powerful.[31] When he meets junior advocates in The Hague or Utrecht it appears that they understand nothing of Noodt's vigorous work, but they know well how to cut it up with fictitious incriminations. In academies it has gone so far that stolid youngsters, whose ultimate aim in studies is to learn the first principles of the law with the help of compendia and the like, do not hesitate to discuss conjectures and emendations with singular confidence.[32]

The first to criticize Noodt was the Dresden advocate Wächtler, but his heirs would have been wise if they had suppressed the notes to Book IV of the *Probabilia* which were published posthumously in the *Acta eruditorum*.[33] After this Van de Water gives a detailed discussion, chapter by chapter, of the criticisms brought against Book IV. Wächtler is, by the way, not his only opponent. Chapters 4 and 5, concerning D 12. 4. 16, were not criticized by Wächtler but by Huber, so in that case he is Van de Water's target.[34]

According to Van de Water, there are some scholars who make a point of disagreeing with Noodt: Wächtler, Huber, Vœt, and some recent ones whom he passes over in silence.[35] I think that Vœt does not belong here; although his opinions differed frequently from those of Noodt—he is rather a representative of the *usus modernus*—as far as I know he only once published a critique, albeit a very extensive one, of a thesis by Noodt.[36] I believe there is something more to be said about the others. And also about Van Bijnkershœk, who had criticized Noodt long before his attack on the *Julius Paulus*. It is not true, as some biographers have said, that Noodt never reacted to his critics. Book IV of the *Probabilia* (1691) contains extensive rebuttals to criticisms by Wächtler as well as Huber,[37] and his reply to Van Bijnkershœk in 1722 was really rather sharp.[38] But what we may say, and what is remarkable enough in his age, is that Noodt was not disputatious and frequently preferred to ignore the attacks by

31. This may be a hint at Van Bijnkershœk's protégé A. Wieling, see below, p. 314.
32. *Misc. obs.* 1733: 111–12.
33. *Misc. obs.* 1733: 113.
34. *Misc. obs.* 1733: 126f.
35. *Misc. obs.* 1733: 123. The last may be again a reference to Wieling.
36. It concerns the interpretation of C 2. 4. 18. Vœt published this first in an addendum to the second volume of his Commentary on the Pandects (1704) and inserted in later in *Comm. ad Pand.* 2. 15. 19. See above, n. 18 on p. 222. Noodt is not named as opponent, but it is evident that he is the target.
37. *Prob.* 4. 3, *resp.* 4. 7.
38. Cf. the judgment of Van de Water, *Misc. obs.* 1733: 112.

others. So he never replied to the criticism in Huber's Dialogue (1684) and *Eunomia romana* (1700), or in Van Bijnkershœk's *Observationes juris romani* (1710). Most likely, neither Huber nor Van Bijnkershœk, nor Perizonius for that matter, would have done the same.

Christfried Wächtler

Christfried Wächtler[39] was only five years younger than Noodt. He was born 18 November 1652 in Grimma, studied at the gymnasium in Meissen, and in 1668 entered Leipzig university, where he studied philosophy, letters, and theology. His only legal subject were private lectures on Grotius' *De jure belli ac pacis* by Jacob Thomasius, the father of Christian. In 1670 he took a BA and after another year of study he became trainee in the office of an advocate in Dresden. In 1674 he returned to Leipzig to study law, which he finished a year later. After a short period as secretary to a diplomat he returned to Dresden as a minister's secretary. In 1680 he fled the plague and went to Wittenberg, where in the same year he took his law degree on a thesis *De gradibus culparum*. Some years later he finally settled in Dresden and practised as advocate until 1703. According to his biographer he lacked neither the talents nor the relations to get a professorship, but he preferred the quiet life as advocate and later as 'Privatgelehrter'. He died on 5 September 1732. He was a very erudite man who wrote on theological as well as legal subjects, but mainly in reaction to the work of others. He was very active as reviewer and correspondent for the Leipzig *Acta eruditorum*, where, apart from other books, he treated many books of the Dutch school. Besides Noodt he reviewed the work of Best, Brenkman, Van Bijnkershœk, Otto, Schulting, and Van de Water.[40]

When preparing his thesis in Wittenberg he stumbled on Book I of Noodt's *Probabilia* (1674),[41] which made quite an impression on him and inspired study as well as comment.[42] The next semester he happened to find Books II and III of the *Probabilia* (1679) and he was

39. Trotz, in Wächtler, 1733; Jugler v, 1779: 153–69; *Allg. deutsche Biographie* 40, 1892: 442 f.; Stintzing and Landsberg iii. 1, 1898: 168.
40. For a list, see Jugler, 1779: 163 ff.
41. I follow the account in the preface to Wächtler's *Notæ ad Noodt*, Wächtler, 1733: 193.
42. Chr. Wächtler, 1680. There is a copy in the National Library of Scotland, Edinburgh.

'delighted with this new and excellent crop of our epoch'. Now he published a book with comment on all three books of the *Probabilia*.[43] Apparently he felt the need of some *captatio benevolentiae*: he believes that he deserves a prize, not reproach. One thing he proposes to do is to supply relevant passages from the Basilica, for which he relied on his friend W. Lyser.

Wächtler's thesis on the degrees of liability was provoked especially by Noodt's famous emendation of D 13. 7. 13. 1.[44] As we saw, this text says that borrower and pledgee are only liable when the thing they keep perishes or is damaged intentionally or through negligence, whereas D 6. 5. 2–3 and D 13. 6. 18 pr. say that the borrower is liable not only for intention and negligence, but also for *custodia*.[45] Noodt tried to solve the contradiction, which had been noted in the gloss, by the change of one letter and the shift of a comma. His proposal seemed so simple and elegant that it was applauded by many.[46] Even Huber could not deny that it was elegant and modest and deserved applause for its cleverness and probability.[47] But Wächtler was not convinced. He pointedly remarked that Noodt, by solving one contradiction, created another one. Though the antinomy concerning the liability of a borrower was eliminated, in its place arose one concerning that of the pledgee. If we read the text as Noodt suggests, it says that the pledgee is only liable for *dolus* and *culpa*. But from Inst. 3. 14. 4 and C 8. 13. 19 it seems to follow that he is liable for *custodia* as well. Noodt gave a lengthy reply to this in Book IV of the *Probabilia* (1691),[48] a trifle superior and not mentioning Wächtler's name: 'This is clear to everybody, but it is not clear to the man who wrote notes on my *Probabilia*'.[49] Trotz later accused Noodt of depreciating Wächtler,[50] which may be a bit exaggerated. Noodt's remark does not seem to go beyond what is normal in literary debates and not citing the name of an opponent was quite usual. It is rather more strange that the editors of the *Acta eruditorum*, when reviewing the third impression of the *Probabilia*

43. Chr. Wächtler, 1681. Advocates Library Edinburgh.
44. *Prob.* 1. 4 (later discussed again in *Prob.* 4. 3). See above, p. 153 f.
45. See Van den Bergh, 1982, with further literature.
46. e.g. Crusius, Heineccius, Thomasius, and Eckhard; cf. also Wächtler, 1733: 202.
47. Huber, 1700: 541.
48. *Prob.* 4. 3, *Opera* i: 71 f.
49. *Opera* i: 72: 'Haec cuique liquent; non liquent illi qui ad Probabilia mea notas scripsit.'
50. Trotz, in Wächtler, 1733: xxxviii.

(1691) and noting Noodt's replies to Wächtler's notes, did not mention his name, though they must have known it perfectly well.[51] But anyway Noodt's reply was well argued, though it did not decide the matter. The extent of liability of the pledgee has remained in dispute till this day.[52]

On the whole, Wächtler certainly knew what he was talking about. He did not, like Huber, believe that the *littera Florentina* had absolute authority,[53] he brought relevant texts from the Basilica to the discussion,[54] and he praised Noodt where he thought it was deserved. Recognizing Noodt's quality as historian of Roman law, he remarked e.g. that nowhere was the chronology of the praetorship of C. Aquilius Gallus discussed more carefully and that Noodt deserved praise for this.[55] On the other hand, he did not greatly appreciate Noodt's lavish use of non-legal authors from Antiquity, and against Noodt's innovations in critical method he often brought no more than the usual conservative objections. It is better to explain a text than to emend it.[56] With regard to Noodt's suggestion that Scaevola might have given an advice to please a friend he acknowledged that often opinions are given sordidly and for favours. This is not only a vice of modern times. With regard to opinions given *ex auctoritate principis*, however, this is a dangerous theory. What should be thought of all the other opinions recorded in the Digest?[57] Concerning the use of *notæ* Wächtler did not doubt that old manuscripts abounded with that kind of riddle. But after Justinian has forbidden the use of *notæ* in transcriptions of his Digest, it is imprudent to accuse scribes of extraordinary sluggishness which could be easily noted. Once we accept the argument of false solution of *notæ* by some scribe we may use it elsewhere too, and soon wherever we like. Thus the whole manuscript could be put in doubt.[58]

Now this kind of argument does not hold much water. The introduction of a new instrument of textual criticism naturally does not imply the proposition to discard *necessitas emendandi* and judgment in its application. Acceptance of Wächtler's criticism would mean that in philology no innovation of method would ever

51. Trotz, in Wächtler, 1733: XXXVII.
52. Cf. Van den Bergh, 1982*a*: 605 f., with literature.
53. Wächtler, 1733: 296: 'harum enim exemplar non est absolute authenticum'.
54. e.g. on D 9. 3. 5. 4 (*Prob.* 1. 10), and on D 50. 16. 42 (*Prob.* 1. 13); Wächtler, 1733: 218, 222.
55. Wächtler, 1733: 459.
56. Wächtler, 1733: 207.
57. Wächtler, 1733: 228.
58. Wächtler, 1733: 297 f.

be admissible. By this I do not mean that Noodt's use of *notæ* is always correct, but only that it should be criticized with more adequate arguments such as Van Bijnkershœk used.

Trotz gives a full list of *Waechtleriana* in the *Acta eruditorum*, for which he relied on A. F. Rivinus in Leipzig. But the list is not as accurate as he assumed. The reviews, or rather summaries, of *De forma emendandi doli mali* (1709) and of Branchu's *Observationes* (1722) are evidently not Wächtler's,[59] and this is likely for the notice of *Diocletianus et Maximianus* (1704).[60] The review of the first part of Noodt's Commentary on the Pandects (1716)[61] will be his, because from a letter from Post to Van Eck we know that Wächtler was asked to do it.[62] It is, on the whole, not unfavourable and closes with the following remark: 'The first part of the Pandects was completed in seven months and we pray God that the rest will appear soon, and without the intervention of death, in good order. They also deserve the abundant erudition of Mr Noodt, his judgment matching the subject-matter, his very extensive reading, and his profound thinking.'[63]

Ulrik Huber

As noted before, Huber, though making contributions to the *humaniora juris* himself, did not favour one of the main activities of the elegant school, that is, criticism, and in general had widely differing attitudes from Noodt. Although their legal analysis of texts was roughly similar, Huber was not an expert in ancient history and had little regard for textual criticism. The only task left for legal scholarship was, in his opinion, to fight the inclination to find errors in and suggest emendations to the *littera Florentina*. He adhered to Agustìn's axiom that one should stick to that manuscript's reading in all circumstances. Only when it was absolutely impossible to give the text some correct legal meaning might one consider emendation. By itself this no doubt was a sound principle. In effect it especially curbed the humanistic tendency to apply the apparatus of textual

59. To the review in *Acta erud.* 1709: 411–13 is added an extract from a letter from Wächtler to Mencke. At the end of the review in *Acta erud.* 1722: 248–57 a review by Wächtler is announced.
60. *Acta erud.* 1704: 227–31.
61. *Acta erud.* 1717: 193–204.
62. H. Post to C. van Eck, Leipzig, 25 May 1716 (UL Utrecht, MS 1000).
63. *Acta erud.* 1717: 203.

criticism to the solution of antinomies and other dogmatic puzzles which had nothing to do with real textual problems. In a legal system based on books of authority Noodt's more free style of emendation, with an undefined *ratio juris* as the final test, certainly had questionable aspects. On the other hand, one might doubt whether Huber fully realized the extent of real textual problems in the *Florentina*.

Huber's criticism of Noodt shows peculiar variations. In his dialogue *De ratione juris docendi et discendi* of 1684 he launched a sharp attack not only on Noodt's Utrecht inaugural address, but also on his *Probabilia* and on critical studies in general. In the preface he professed to have some doubt whether to publish it: what is written with passion often pleases less when finished. But finally he had decided not to suppress the edition. Noodt saw the main cause of the decline of legal studies in the use of compendia, by which the wide-ranging art of law was reduced to strait schedules and often inept questions, and the whole apparatus of humanist philology was regarded as troublesome and stupid diligence.[64] Justinian's Institutes themselves are the example of a compendium. To speculate about the qualities of the human intellect without looking at reality is nothing but *splendide nugari*. The quality of teaching in grammar schools is lamentable. New students know nothing of elegant letters, history, Greek, Latin, and philosophy. Huber especially stresses—touching a weak spot indeed—that Noodt said nothing about the knowledge of Greek, as if that language were no more important to the study of law than Swedish or Lappic.[65] If students do not even have adequate preparatory training, it would be plain stupidity to despise a compendium, but to teach them the riddles of sigla and *notæ*, the emendation of misplaced punctuation, the distinction of glosses and variant readings, the repair of dislocations and corruptions, et cetera.[66] But to teach that before the student has an overview of the whole of the law surpasses all stupidity.[67]

All this is put in the mouth of Böckelmann. Now Huber speaks for himself. He agrees with the indignation of Crusius against those who only want to speed up studies and would teach nothing but compendia. But instead of repeating that debate he will rather begin with an overview of the history of law teaching. Already in the law schools of the later Roman empire only part of the subject-matter was taught extensively, the rest condensed. Moreover, Huber opposes those

64. Huber, 1688*a*: 8.
65. Huber, 1688*a*: 30.
66. Huber, 1688*a*: 32.
67. Huber, 1688*a*: 32.

who claim that the art of law is contaminated and violated when attention is paid to contemporary law. The law must always be adapted to the use of its time. After an overview of medieval law teaching Huber comes to the *culti*. Huber distinguishes three different schools, two who connect the study of law and letters and a third one with other aims. The first school restricts itself to Roman law and does not wish to do anything but to explain and mend the Corpus Juris; to this group belong Cujas, Duaren, and Doneau. The second group mixes the study of ancient law with that of contemporary law and practice; excellent representatives of this group are Zasius, Alciatus, and Viglius. The third group does not so much study law, that is the art of the good and equitable, as the antiquities and philological problems contained in the Corpus Juris; to these belong Antonio Agustìn, Budé, and Raevardus.[68.]

Then Huber criticizes the search for interpolations and emendations. What Noodt called the ancient *via regia* is indeed the military way of cutting knots with the sword.[69] Certainly, critical studies are the summit of legal scholarship, but nothing is worse than rashness and extravagance of criticism. Bad criticism corrupts the laws and weakens the whole body of the law. To teach the art of emendation before the ends and ways of the whole art of law are taught in a methodical way is useless and against the principles of good teaching. This is what gave rise to the old proverb that only those who understand nothing of the law dedicate themselves to its emendation.[70]

The dialogue was dressed up as one between Böckelmann and Crusius, two Leiden professors who were both dead, and Noodt's name was nowhere mentioned. So only insiders could see through the disguise. Perizonius, however, had no doubts about its true intention:

> Our Huber has written a dialogue between himself, Böckelmann, and Crusius, in which he by means of Crusius attacks Noodt and, while assailing him, shows himself very unfair to all who exercise criticism and teach letters. Yet I urge you to see and read it. Because I do not doubt that it will be for sale in your town. The title is *About the method of teaching and learning the law*.[71]

68. Huber, 1688*a*: 41. 69. Huber, 1688*a*: 41. 70. Huber, 1688*a*: 42.
71. Perizonius to Rijcke, Franeker, 19 Sept. 1784, BPL 337: 'Huberus noster scripsit dialogum inter ipsum et Bokelmannum ac Crusium, in quo per latus Crusii petit Notum, et dum in eum incurrit, plus satis iniquum se probat omnibus qui Crisin

Noodt will have read the dialogue, but preferred to ignore it.

In the second impression of his *Digressiones justinianeae*, which appeared in 1688 and to which the dialogue was annexed with some changes in title and text, Huber still kept up appearances. In a passage which must have been written before 1686, because Noodt is called professor of Utrecht, the tone is still most courteous.[72] Huber calls him his close friend. Noodt has written a most elegant comment on D 48. 22. 5.[73] Huber will simply present his dissenting opinion, giving reasons (trying to explain the text *without* changing anything in the reading of the *Florentina*), so that the reader can decide for himself. And he hopes that the reader will appreciate that such differences of opinion among friends are the most innocent thing in the world.

In the *Praelectiones*,[74] the tone gets less friendly. Huber rejects an interpretation of D 48. 8. 1. 3 defended by Noodt,[75] without mentioning his name, saying that those who defend this opinion 'are a great way off from the way of reason and Themis'. Noodt published his opinion only in 1691, together with an extensive reply to Huber, but, as he says in the reply,[76] he had expounded his opinion already in public lectures some years before, probably in Franeker. How much the words of Huber, as just cited, had annoyed Noodt appears from the fact that he cites them at the beginning of his reply as well as at the end: 'I have explained my opinion and that of the most learned Huber; it remains for you to judge whose opinion is the furthest from the way of reason and Themis, mine or his.'

Huber certainly was not the man to leave it at that. Apparently he made a systematic study of the 1691 edition of the *Probabilia*, *De jurisdictione*, and *Ad legem Aquiliam*, and he came up with no less than ten emendations he regarded as objectionable. In his *Eunomia romana*, a series of disputations *exercitii gratia* published posthumously in 1700 but written between 1692 and 1694, these were discussed thoroughly.[77] It seems that this time discussion of emendations was not contrary to the correct method of law teaching. Eight

aliquando exercent, et humaniora profitentur. Enim suadeo videas et perlustres. Nam apud vos venire nullus dubito. Titulus est *De ratione juris docendi et discendi*.'

72. Huber, 1688*b*: 551 f. 73. *Prob*. 3. 3. 74. Huber, 1690: 677.
75. *Prob*. 4. 7. Noodt's reply to Huber is in 4. 8. 76. *Opera* i: 80.
77. Huber, 1700: 67 (D 1. 8. 2; *Prob*. 1. 8); 84 (D 2. 1. 3; *De jurisd*. 1. 2); 123 (D 2. 15. 14; *Prob*. 2. 2); 179 (D 4. 3. 7. pr.; *De jurisd*. 1. 14); 354 (D 7. 8. 10 pr.; *Prob*. 3. 7); 358 (D 7. 9. 5. 3; *Prob*. 3. 8); 406 (D 9. 2. 5. pr.; *Prob*. 1. 9); 420 (D 9. 3. 5. 4; *Prob*. 1. 13); 519 (D 12. 4. 16; *Prob*. 4. 4); 541 (D 13. 7. 13. 1; *Prob*. 1. 4).

cases were from the *Probabilia*, and two from *De jurisdictione*; in *Ad legem Aquiliam* evidently not much could be found. Huber does not omit traditional laudatory phrases in describing his opponent, whose name is not mentioned, but in most cases he rejects his opinion. The sharpest criticism was of Noodt's explanation of D 2. 15. 14,[78] in which he had suggested that the classical jurist Scaevola had given an advice in violation of the law to favour a friend, indeed not one of Noodt's most orthodox pieces of scholarship and one to which many others also took exception.[79] For the rest, Huber repeated time and again that Noodt's proposals went against textual tradition, that he did not demonstrate *necessitas emendandi*, that one should stick to the *littera Florentina* in all circumstances but the most extreme.

In September 1693 Cornelis van Eck, who had just changed a chair in Franeker for one in Utrecht, sent Noodt copies of the disputations '*pro eunomia romana*' that were directed against him. Noodt replied that he considered them 'very cold and not worth refuting'.[80] A year later Huber died.

Cornelis van Bijnkershœk

The debate on the *Julius Paulus* opened by Van Bijnkershœk in 1719, nineteen years after publication of the book, was not the first time he criticized Noodt. He may, in fact, as a student have been inculcated with a critical attitude towards Noodt's work by Huber, who was among his teachers in Franeker. In 1693 he defended under Huber two disputations *pro eunomia romana* and made a big impression in the event.[81] On the other hand, he did not have to learn a critical attitude from anybody. Later he criticized his former teachers as freely as anybody.[82]

In his book on the *lex Rhodia* (1702) he rejected, not without reason, all conjectures to replace the word 'Italia' in D 14. 2. 9.[83] Noodt was among those who had suggested such a conjecture. 'All manuscripts have that word and there are many ways in which it can

78. *Prob.* 2. 2.
79. e.g. Wächtler, Van Bijnkershœk, Van de Water, Best, and De Toullieu.
80. Noodt to Van Eck, Leiden, 3 Oct. 1693, UL Utrecht, MS 1000; for the text see above, p. 56. In Dutch 'cold' may mean 'unimportant' (een koud kunstje) as well as 'far from the subject'.
81. Star Numan, 1869: 39, 43 f.
82. Star Numan, 1869: 46 f.
83. See above, p. 243.

be explained correctly. Critics would do better to refrain from such attempts, if the *recepta lectio* has a good sense, unless they want to expose their most noble art to derision.'[84]

In the first four books of his *Observationes juris romani* (1710) Van Bijnkershœk disputed several of Noodt's emendations,[85] and in the preface he made some strictures on bad criticism,[86] particularly rejecting the use of *notæ* and sigla. This was a specific feature of Noodt; in Huber's dialogue it was even named four times. Like Perizonius[87] Van Bijnkershœk criticized rather sharply Noodt's proposal to emend D 12. 4. 16. In the text Celsus doubts whether the promise of a slave against money is a sale, while dogmatically there does not seem a reason for doubt. Noodt suggested adding a word on the hypothesis that the text was corrupted by the false solution of *notæ* by some scribe. Van Bijnkershœk rebutted: 'Among the *notæ* of the ancients I find none which might justify this conjecture. But to invent such notes, as he and others are accustomed to do, is not permitted in our profession'.[88] Leaving aside the question whether the argument from false solution of *notæ* is plausible in itself, Van Bijnkershœk urged that one should only use *notæ* when there is manuscript authority that they were actually used in Antiquity. No doubt this is a sound principle. But the most caustic censure is anonymous as usual. Touching on Noodt's suggestion that in D 2. 15. 14 Scaevola gave an incorrect advice to favour a friend, Van Bijnkershœk wrote that he shuddered referring to it.[89]

Such strictures did not go beyond accepted habits of scholarly dispute, however. One might well expect that in principle Van Bijnkershœk, the judge, would be a more conservative critic than Noodt, the academic, but there was no fundamental difference of method involved. Defending your own conjectures and destroying those of others was the stock-in-trade of scholarship. That may explain why Noodt, apparently somewhat to the surprise of

84. *Opera* ii: 105.
85. *Opera* i: 50 f. (D 47. 2. 56. 1; *Prob.* 2. 5); 96 (D 2. 15. 14; *Prob.* 2. 2)i; 206 f. (D 12. 4. 16; *Obs.* 1. 17). *Obs.* 2. 8: 5. 8; 6. 24, 8. 14.
86. See above, p. 215.
87. See below, p. 309.
88. *Opera* i: 207. Van Bijnkershœk's criticism is undoubtedly correct. In the lists of *notæ* in Putschius, 1605 (then the authoritative edn.), there is no evidence for the abbreviation 'PP', nor for Noodt's contention (*Prob.* 2. 5) that 'PV' could either mean *praefectus urbis* or *praefectus vigilum*. Probus, Magno, and Paulus Diaconus give distinctly different abbreviations for both terms.
89. *Opera* i: 96.

Perizonius (who was certain that Noodt regarded Van Bijnkershœk's strictures as less appropriate and did not recommend the *Observationes* to his students), did not react in any way and even gave a friendly reception to Van Bijnkershœk and his wife in his home in Leiden shortly after publication of the *Observationes*.[90] But then Perizonius seems to have been much more touchy on the point of scholarly honour than Noodt.

It was only after the sharp attack of 1719 that Noodt could no longer play dumb. The repeated reproach that Noodt had merely dressed up a little a thesis of Lipsius was a triple insult. First, it was a gross exaggeration, secondly, Noodt had acknowledged his debt to Lipsius fairly enough, and, thirdly, Van Bijnkershœk indirectly put Noodt's qualifications as a jurist in doubt. This was too much, even for a peace-loving man. Here lay the seed of the injury that was done to Noodt's reputation posthumously. That Van Bijnkershœk is at least partly responsible for this can hardly be doubted.

'*Criticus aliquando audacior*'

Although many of Noodt's emendations are modest and well argued, and a few even were accepted by Mommsen, most of his biographers agree that sometimes his conjectures were rather bold.[91] Here again it was Haubold who passed the authoritative judgment: 'Sometimes, however, he was a rather bold critic'.[92] Unfortunately, some later authors who summarized this judgment without independent research seriously distorted and exaggerated it.[93] This is not to deny that, at times, Noodt's emendations were indeed bold. We have noted several times how he suggested interventions that are incisive and go against the whole of the textual tradition, including the Basilica.[94] A small but particularly striking example may be the proposal to replace, for dogmatic reasons, the word 'Cornelia' by

90. Perizonius to Van Eck, Leiden, 15 Dec. 1709 and 1 Feb. 1710, UL Utrecht, MS 1000.
91. Jugler, 1780: 371; Stintzing and Landsberg, 1898: 165; W. Noodt, 1921: 44; *NNBW* ii: 1000.
92. Haubold, 1809: 157.
93. Landsberg (cited by W. Noodt, 1921: 44) speaks (in a passage concerning Westenberg) of 'weitgehende Leichtfertigkeit in Konjekturen, das leidige Erbteil der Noodt'schen Schule'; Goudsmit i, 1866: 11 n. 1 says that Noodt was 'vermetel in zijne beweringen en gewaagd in zijn gissingen' (reckless in his contentions and bold in his conjectures). The first part of this statement is totally unfounded.
94. See above, pp. 144, 169, 177, and 241 f.

'Aquilia' in D 9. 2. 5. Here, not only do F and the vulgates concur, but the text is transmitted independently in identical form by the Collatio.

Criticism of Noodt's work in this respect had been voiced by several of his contemporaries. As we saw before, Perizonius wrote rather critically to Van Eck about Noodt's lust for emendations after the publication of the *Observationes*. Many texts which Noodt disturbs with his emendations can be explained, Perizonius thought, in a correct way. He apparently regarded them as unnecessary. And when Noodt inserted a word of ten letters without any trace in the manuscript tradition, Perizonius remarked: in this way we can easily restore everything according to our own opinion. With regard to another incisive emendation, he used a traditional verdict: this is burning and cutting.[95] Huber even rejected Noodt's most famous emendation (in D 13. 7. 13. 1), because it violated the axiom that one should not depart from the reading of F as long as a correct legal interpretation of the text seems possible.[96] The text must be maintained as long as possible. *Necessitas emendandi* is an absolute, though not very precisely defined, prerequisite, but even then the most far-fetched explanation is preferable to the most modest emendation. That is, for orthodox scholars. Needless to say, scholars had different opinions on the matter and the terms of their debate were for the greater part clichés of long standing. Noodt, who is criticized for audacious emendations, frequently rejected the emendations of others as unnecessary. With regard to principles of criticism there was broad agreement. One should not emend a text without strict necessity. When emending one should be as modest as possible; the change of only one letter or a comma is the ideal. Conjectures are admissible but emendations for which there is manuscript authority in the form of some variant reading have greater authority. With regard to conjectures Huber formulates a criterion which quite interestingly reminds us of the Popperian preference of falsification to verification: an emendation without manuscript authority is admissible, but must be so evident that it is less easy to refute it than to affirm it.[97]

As far as Noodt and Van Bijnkershœk were concerned it was not always the former who was the more bold critic. To illustrate the importance of criticism in the preface of his *Observationes juris*

95. Perizonius to Van Eck, Leiden, 10 Feb. and 2 Apr. 1706, UL Utrecht, MS 1000.
96. Huber, 1700: 541.
97. Huber, 1688*a*: 44.

romani Van Bijnkershœk told of a case he had to decide as judge.[98] Sempronius and Maevius had a quarrel about some movable thing which was in the possession of the latter. Sempronius instituted an *actio ad exhibendum*, demanding that Maevius should bring forth the thing in question so that Sempronius could make out whether it was his property. Maevius replied that Sempronius first should describe it, invoking D 10. 4. 3. pr.:

In hac actione actor omnia nosse debet et dicere argumenta rei de qua agitur.[99]

Sempronius refused to do so and Van Bijnkershœk won over his colleagues in the High Court to his side by the suggestion that one should read 'discere' instead of 'dicere'. Later he found that there actually is a manuscript reading—that is, if we can believe Haloander—which has this form.[1] This reading completely overturns the meaning of the text: the actor must know and *be told* all the features of the thing. This is a bad reading, however. Brenkman inspected in vain seven manuscripts (among them both Bijnkershœkiani!).[2] He found *dicere* everywhere and remarked that the Basilica unequivocally confirm this reading. Noodt rejected Van Bijnkershœk's suggestion and defended the reading of the *Florentina* this time.[3]

With regard to the emendation of legal texts we have some special problems which do not seem to present themselves in the same way for literary texts. Legal texts call for dogmatic interpretation, with practical application as the final purpose. Since the days of the glossators, continental jurists have had to cope with antinomies in the Corpus Juris. The glossators tried to solve them by distinctions, but in the humanist tradition scholars frequently have applied the instrument of textual criticism to antinomies. Here one easily crosses the

98. *Opera* i: 8. On this case, see also Van de Spiegel, 1777: 35 f.
99. 'In this action the actor must know and tell all the features of the thing in question.'
1. Van Bijnkershœk refers to the edn. of the brothers Senneton, Lyons, 1549 (Spangenberg, 198a), but this goes back on Haloander, who noted the reading in the margin. It seems that Van Bijnkershœk believed he read it in his own MS (now BPL 6 C), but wrongly. For further literature see Noodt, *Opera* ii: 244.
2. Now BPL 6 C and 11 D. See Gebauer–Spangenberg *a.h.l.* Gebauer could only identify six MSS because he did not find the Bijnkershœkianus II in Brenkman's papers, see Stolte, 1981: 50. See also Van de Spiegel, 1777: 36; Anon., *Zekere gedachten*, 1778: 33.
3. *Opera* ii: 244.

borderline between *lectio* and *emendatio*. It is particularly difficult to prove *necessitas emendandi* in cases where the text poses a dogmatic problem. It is quite possible that jurists had different opinions and with some fantasy one can always construe a case in which the antinomy seems to disappear.

A case in point is D 12. 4. 16.[4] I gave you money in order that you gave me Stichus. Celsus poses the question whether this contract is analogous to a sale or only gives rise to a *condictio*. Since the days of the glossators this question has puzzled jurists. Is not the exchange of goods against money a sale in any case? Noodt tried to solve the problem by an emendation, assuming the false solution of *notæ* by some scribe: Celsus spoke about the exchange of a slave for foreign money. Perizonius thought that the emendation was audacious and did not solve the problem. How could Celsus regard the exchange of a slave against non-current coins as a sale? Huber also regarded the emendation as superfluous. Here the problem is indeed purely dogmatical. The text as such is unproblematic as regards manuscript tradition as well as Latin. One can easily invent a score of cases in which there is reason to doubt whether the promise in question is a sale. Perizonius tried his hand at one. Say I am captured by enemies and am in need of money to pay a ransom. I ask you to give it to me and you promise to do so on the condition that I give you my slave Stichus. Is this a sale? There seems reason to doubt it, especially when the amount of the ransom is disproportionate to the value of the slave. Therefore there is no *necessitas emendandi* concerning Celsus' text. From a legal point of view Perizonius' solution seems questionable. Would not the promise of a slave under these circumstances be regarded as a promise under duress and therefore not binding? If so, Celsus could never have asked whether this is a sale. But, in the first place, the purpose of our interpretation is of crucial importance here. If we want to eliminate an antinomy while saving the appearance of the authoritative text, Perizonius' suggestion may seem acceptable, but inventing facts for an *ad hoc* hypothesis without the slightest trace in the text itself would be regarded as objectionable by most modern scholars. So jurists and historians from the past and present may be at cross-purposes in several respects, and evidently there remains room for different opinions. Strict proof of *necessitas emendandi* only seems possible when the text is evidently corrupt or

4. Noodt, *Opera* i: 73, 75, 315; Perizonius to Van Eck, Leiden, 2 Apr. 1706, UL Utrecht, MS 1000; Huber, 1700: 519 f.

not good Latin. With regard to dogmatic problems it is indeed hard to prove.

There is another point to be considered. During the seventeenth century there is a general growth of historical consciousness and the foundations of modern scientific history are laid. In the 'Querelle des anciens et modernes' and the debate about historical knowledge, relativism, and scepticism ('historical Pyrrhonism'), fundamental issues were discussed. Mabillon laid the foundations of diplomatics, De Montfaucon of Greek paleography. Conring revolutionized the history of German law and together with others laid the foundations for the constitutional history of the Holy Roman Empire. Vico created an evolutionary history of civilizations. Noodt's work is part of this development. The growth of his historical consciousness can be followed in his work. Already in his Franeker inaugural address of 1679 he stressed that the study of civil law was not born on one day, nor was it the invention of one brain or the result of one occasion. It grew gradually, by virtue of customs, favourable conditions, and adversities of the state, and changed according to its fate. Therefore its study demands careful observation of the period in which a rule was issued, changed, or abrogated.[5] In the Utrecht inaugural address of 1684 he unequivocally sided with the 'moderns': the progress recently made by the natural sciences and mathematics must be the model for the science of society.[6] By 1700 he had found more expressive metaphors: Roman law did not fall from heaven one day like a shower, nor did it spring up overnight like a fairy circle. Civil law has grown slowly through experience of utility. It has varied with changes in human needs, gravity, resources, softness, roughness, learning, religion, war, and peace. Even the idea of legal evolution is formulated here.[7] In 1722 Noodt phrased the principle of *interpretatio multiplex*, as modern legal historians understand it, as well as the basic maxim of modern historical research: proof of facts, not sentiment, is what counts.[8] Apparently Noodt's contemporaries did not fully understand or accept his position and, as I said before, the

5. *Opera* i: 614. Noodt's words are echoed by F. Saxe, 1787, and exemplified in the thesis of J. J. G. Schadd (Harderwijk, 1802), see Veen, 1985*c*: 253.
6. *Opera* i: 617. These words confirm the thesis of Faber (1982: 29 f.) that modern historical sciences (especially the so-called auxiliary sciences like paleography, diplomatics, chronology, sphragistics, etc.) began to develop in the 17th century under the influence of the successes of the natural sciences.
7. *Opera* i: 567.
8. *Opera* i: 604; cf. Feenstra, 1953.

free expression of historical consciousness was bound to put the legal authority of the Corpus Juris in jeopardy even more than humanistic textual criticism did. This was the real issue of Van Bijnkershœk's attack on Noodt.[9].

Seen as textual criticism, some of Noodt's emendations, which are incisive and go against the whole of the manuscript tradition, are rather bold indeed. But in several cases modern Romanist scholarship has reached the same conclusion as Noodt (often without mentioning his name). From an historical point of view Noodt sometimes proves to be right after all.[10] In some cases this even proves to be true for his textual criticism proper. Noodt's emendation of D 7. 8. 10. pr. was regarded as 'almost useless' by Wächtler, but endorsed by Mommsen because the translation of Stephanus seems to confirm it.[11] As an historian of Roman law Noodt surpassed both Huber and Van Bijnkershœk.[12] His contemporaries did not yet realize the implications of the distinction between textual and historical criticism. In the humanistic tradition both were encompassed by the verbs *emendare* and *corrigere*.[13].

So, if it remains true that at times Noodt was a rather bold critic, this judgment cannot obtain now for as many cases as was thought around 1700. Finally, two more remarks need to be made. In the first place we should keep in mind that Noodt's most contested conjectures were mainly published—seven out of ten or so—in his early works, that is in Books I (1674), II, and III (1679) of the *Probabilia*. Though he never withdrew any of them later, in his best works of a riper age his criticism usually is rather more moderate. Secondly, we should remember that the Dutch school in general followed Cujas, for whom also, in the last analysis, *ratio juris* was more important than manuscript authority. It would be unfair to blame Noodt alone for this. And although *ratio juris* remains undefined throughout, for lawyers it still makes more sense than for philologists. Law never was a pure science and it never will be.

9. See above, p. 211 ff.
10. For an example see Van den Bergh, 1986*b*.
11. *Prob.* 3. 7; Wächtler, 1733: 319; see above, p. 155.
12. See Haubold's judgment of the latter (1809: 143). For Huber, see above, p. 196.
13. Cf. Rizzo, 1984: 243.

Noodt's 'plagiarisms'

The emendation of D 13. 7. 13. 1, Noodt's most famous conjecture, published in his first major publication in 1674 when he was only 27 years old, posthumously became his most disputed one, and the suggestion that jealousy played a role in this[14] does not seem wholly improbable. In itself that kind of accusation was commonplace in the humanistic tradition. Noodt shared the fate of being accused posthumously of literary theft with his model Cujas, and with Duaren and Willem Best.[15]

Around 1716 it became known in the Republic that the same conjecture as suggested by Noodt (the change of 'ut' to 'at', not the shift of punctuation)[16] was proposed about eighty years earlier by the German jurist Niellius. This fact was used to concoct an accusation of plagiarism,[17] which was published only after Noodt's death and mainly gained credibility by the fact that it was supported by Van Bijnkershœk. Although contemporaries like Barbeyrac, Van de Water, and Arntzenius[18] contested the accusation on good grounds, part of the stain has stuck till our day: *fama necat virum*.[19] The question is whether the accusation is justified.

Barbeyrac's main defence was to point out how easily some detail hidden in a book, even a book which we frequently have at hand, can escape our attention. As an example from Noodt's own work he points to an emendation of D 45. 1. 101, proposed by Crusius and endorsed by Noodt. The text reads as follows.

Modestinus lib. 4 de praescriptionibus. Puberes sine curatoribus suis possunt ex stipulatu obligari.[20]

As already noted in the gloss, this seemed to contradict other texts.[21] Noodt learned from Crusius that the antinomy could be solved by

14. See Van de Water, *Misc. obs.* 1733: 111.
15. For Cujas, see Spangenberg, 1822: 58 f.; for Duaren, Vogt, 1971: 49 n. 8; and, for Willem Best, the rather unlikely story in Jugler i, 1773: 437 f.
16. See above, p. 154.
17. Jugler vi, 1780: 370.
18. Barbeyrac, 1731: LXXXV f.; Van de Water, *Misc. obs.* 1733: 110 f.; Arntzenius, 1788.
19. Cf. *NNBW* ii: 1000.
20. 'Young persons can commit themselves by stipulation without assistance of their tutors.'
21. For modern Romanists there is no antinomy. They accept that consensus of the curator was not necessary to make the contract valid in classical times, but was made obligatory by Diocletian, see Kaser i, 1971: 370.

reading 'obligare': the pupil cannot be bound himself but he can bind others. In the first impression of Book I of the *Probabilia* (1674) Noodt exuberantly praised his friend Crusius and endorsed the emendation.[22] Many years later he learned from Vœt[23] that Simon van Leeuwen had suggested this emendation in his famous edition of 1663.[24] Neither Noodt nor Crusius saw this note and that is hardly surprising. They would never seek a conjecture in Van Leeuwen's notes, because they knew only too well that his scholarship in this field was not much esteemed;[25] or, as Spangenberg put it bluntly: 'Van Leeuwens eigene Anmerkungen sind erbärmlich'.[26] But there is more to be said on the matter.

It seems most likely that during Noodt's lifetime virtually nobody in the Republic had heard of the German jurist Johann Niellius (1571–97), who died at the age of 26 in Marburg. In 1716 rumours circulated in the Republic about someone who found an emendation before Noodt, but his name was unknown to all but very few scholars. Nicolas Arnoldi of Harlingen asked Van Eck most politely whether he could give him the name.[27] Even in Germany Niellius was known but in a very restricted circle. The only reason Jugler wrote a biography of this 'fast verloschenen Namen'[28] was that in the first decades of the eighteenth century it became known in the Republic as the name of an author who invented a conjecture long before Noodt.

Likewise, the little book, published in Marburg in 1594,[29] in which the conjecture was suggested rather casually, presumably was unknown in the Republic. The book was of strictly local circulation,[30] although it had five impressions (1594, 1597, 1606, 1615, 1629, all in Marburg) and it was a typical school-book. Niellius wrote a series of disputations for his students in Marburg, and apparently these remained in use as such for some decades after his death. But not even Wächtler in Dresden, Noodt's persistent critic, knew the

22. Noodt, 1674: 56 ff. Noodt eliminated the passage in the *Opera omnia* of 1713, but the emendation is mentioned in *De pactis et transactionibus* 20, which was published in the same volume for the first time. *Opera* i: 543.
23. *Comm. ad Pand.* I, 4. 4. 52.
24. Naturally this does not decide the question of authorship.
25. Barbeyrac, 1731: LXXXVIII; *Vita*, 9ᵛ.
26. Spangenberg, 1817: 894.
27. N. Arnoldi to C. van Eck, Harlingen, 4 July 1716, UL Utrecht, MS 1000, fol. 2ʳ.
28. Jugler ii, 1775: 98.
29. Niellius, 1597: 47 (disp. III § ult., *Coroll. sub* K).
30. Naturally, it became a collector's item after 1731. There is e.g. a copy in the Fürst zu Bentheimsche Bibliothek at Burgsteinfurt. I thank Robert Feenstra for this information.

book, or else he would not have missed the chance to score a point against him.[31]

The conjecture of the obscure Marburg lecturer was indeed extremely well hidden. The title of the little book which contained it was 'Disputed points of feudal law elucidated in eleven disputations'. Apart from the fact that Noodt himself never made a penetrating study of feudal law,[32] nobody would look in a school-book with that title for a conjecture concerning a Digest text, which belonged rather in a treatise on civil law.[33] The conjecture was, moreover, tucked away in a *corollarium*, a kind of extended footnote, to the third disputation.

How, then, could anybody but an initiate from Marburg have found the conjecture? This is not difficult to establish. Van Bijnkershœk was not the first to publish it.[34] He learned it from Abraham Wieling, his protégé, who became professor in Franeker in 1727 and in Utrecht in 1739, both times at his recommendation.[35] Wieling came from the same region as Niellius, the first being born in Hamm, the second in Wesel. So both were Westphalians. Wieling studied first in Marburg and feudal law was one of his subjects; in 1739 it was part of his commission in Utrecht. Between 1714 and 1719 he studied in Duisburg, where Everard Otto, another Westphalian from Hamm, was then professor. It is exactly in that period, in 1716, that we first hear of the rumour that Noodt's famous emendation was found by someone else before. Everard Otto, who had many contacts in the Republic and in 1720 became professor in Utrecht (where he was nicknamed 'the dictator'),[36] will have been the intermediary. It may have been in the same period, or shortly afterwards, that Wieling's association with Van Bijnkershœk began. Wieling published his scoop in 1731,[37] two years before Van

31. Cf. Barbeyrac, *Vita* 9^r.
32. Cf. Barbeyrac; Haubold (1809: 157) says likewise that Noodt was not an expert in medieval Roman law.
33. Jugler ii, 1775: 101.
34. He published it in 1733 in *Obs. jur. rom.* 6. 15; see also his note from the Brenkman papers, in the Gebauer–Spangenberg edn. at D 13. 7. 13. 1, n. 65. The note is re-edited by Van Warmelo, 1979: 230, who made an error in the transcription. Instead of 'Dispos.', one should read 'Disput.'
35. *NNBW*: v. d. Aa vii: 58. The author of the *Misc. obs.* seems to refer to this, see above, p. 295 f.
36. Stolte, 1981: 26.
37. Wieling, 1758. I used the edn. of Amsterdam: G. Mulder, 1758. I have not seen a copy of the Franeker edn. of 1731, but it is mentioned in most bibliographies and it

Bijnkershœk and six years after Noodt's death. It was also Wieling who made more of it than the pure coincidence that in all likelihood it was.

Wieling's attack on Noodt was indirect, but it had a double effect, because he not only criticized the emendation but also raised suspicions about Noodt's originality. Wieling regarded the emendation for which Noodt was praised abundantly by so many and even by Thomasius and Huber as superfluous. Niellius has proposed an unnecessary emendation for which there is no manuscript authority and which infuriates Themis, the goddess of law ('. . . invitis libris et irata veterum Themide . . .'). Quite surprisingly Noodt has appropriated that emendation ('suam facere') and it is incomprehensible why so many have praised him for it.[38] The words 'irata Themide' are especially interesting. Van Bijnkershœk had used them in 1722 against Noodt in his critique of the *Julius Paulus*, and they were exactly the words to which many took exception then and later. That Wieling's attack had an impact is clear from the fact that it prompted an answer from Barbeyrac in his life of Noodt, as well as from Van de Water in the *Miscellaneae observationes*. The degree of their contempt can be measured by the fact that neither cited Wieling by name.

The accusation of plagiarism, improbable already on account of the facts just mentioned, is even less likely because we know that Noodt had no inclination to claim the authorship of things that were not his own and openly acknowledged it when occasionally he had written something without knowing that it had been suggested already by someone else.[39] In 1691 Noodt published a proposal to explain a problematic text;[40] many years later he learned that his countryman Hubert van Giffen (Giphanius) had suggested it long before. In his Commentary on the Pandects[41] he acknowledged this freely:

Sic mihi sedit a multis annis. Ac nuper lubenter vidi, his similia jam

seems evident that Barbeyrac (1731) as well as Van de Water (1733) are reacting to Wieling's accusation of plagiarism (even though they do not mention his name), so I think the existence of the edn. is beyond doubt. Perhaps it was only a very limited or provisional edn. *ad amicos*. In that case Van Bijnkershœk's really was the first formal publication on the matter. See also Wieling's *Lectiones juris civilis*, Amsterdam, 1736.

38. Wieling, 1758: 177.

39. See above, p. 170.

40. *De jurisd.* 2. 13.

41. Book 21, title ii, published in 1724, *Opera* ii: 470; cf. Arntzenius, 1788: 48; *Acta erud.* Suppl. x: 96.

intercedisse suo tempore Huberto Gifanio, Viro Erudito et Claro, ad h[unc] t[itulum] C[odicis] quod dissimulare nolui.[42]

The accusation of plagiarism is all the more questionable if one realizes that it was published a few years after the famous *contentio litteraria* between Van Bijnkershœk and Noodt and after the death of the second. It was Van Bijnkershœk who began to cast doubts on Noodt's originality in his critique of the *Julius Paulus*. This attack could be refuted by Noodt personally, but a few years after his death the protégé came to the help of his master to accomplish a posthumous 'Charactermord'. Some of the stain remained even after the rebuttals of Barbeyrac and Van de Water. It proved fertile soil for Goudsmit's never substantiated accusation that Noodt freely plundered Donellus.[43]

Wieling's edition of a work of Chassanaeus from 1731, of which only a small number of copies was printed, circulated among a restricted group of scholars. And anyway Wieling had not a great name as a scholar. But with Van Bijnkershœk, President of the High Court, it was a different matter. Although he did not repeat Wieling's words and only said that Niellius found the emendation before Noodt, his relation with Wieling was known well enough and, as Van de Water in the *Miscellaneae observationes* suggests, by his prestigious position he may well have influenced young jurists who knew nothing of the matter but wanted to make themselves popular in high places.

I cannot refrain from hearing an undertone in the debate that seems worth noting, although I cannot deny that my suspicion is partly speculative. During the first decades of the eighteenth century continental legal scholarship was still dominated largely by the Dutch school, but by the second half of the century Germany was getting ahead. The university of Göttingen (1737) became a transfer station for Dutch elegant scholarship and the cradle of the 'second humanism'. Marburg, Giessen, and Leipzig became important centres too. Men like Hugo, Haubold, and Biener went beyond the achievements of the Dutch school and re-established the connection with classical philology, which was about to make new advances.[44]

42. 'I have been convinced of this for many years. But recently I saw to my pleasure that a similar idea concerning this text occurred in his time to Hubert Giphanius, a learned and esteemed man, which I do not want to conceal.'

43. See below, p. 318.

44. Wieacker, 1967: 366.

The Dutch school sank back into insignificance, together with the decline of the Republic which had once played a leading role in the European concert. During the next century, from Savigny to Mommsen, German scholarship was to reign supreme in the field of Roman law. For the growing self-confidence of German Romanists in the last decades of the eighteenth century, it cannot have been unimportant to know that the most famous conjecture of the leader of the Dutch school had been suggested eighty years before by a German scholar. Thus, after two centuries, Niellius got much more than his deserts.

As far as the case itself is concerned we can remark finally that accusations of plagiarism, which are endemic in the humanist philological tradition, often tend to be exaggerated. Anybody who is a little at home in the history of textual criticism must realize that for some *cruces* which puzzled the glossators there are only two or three solutions, which over the ages are invented, contested, and rejected over and over again.[45] Therefore, it seems rather unlikely that Niellius himself was the first to invent our conjecture. Duker pointed out that in his own manuscript copy of the Digest 'at in commodato' was noted in the margin 'more than hundred years ago'[46] and it is indeed improbable that no glossator or humanist would ever have considered the change of 'ut' to 'at'. Confusion of these words was regarded as one of the most common scribal errors in old manuscripts, especially because in some medieval scripts a and u looked very much alike. The argument is used, among others, by Scaliger, Burman, Perizonius, and Van Bijnkershœk.[47]

Naturally the value of such a conjecture is always open to dispute and by themselves such disputes are not very important. The real issue in the background always was the authority of the *littera Florentina* and, consequently, of the Digest itself. That is the gist of Huber's comment: Noodt's conjecture is elegant and modest and would deserve praise and applause from everybody for its cleverness and probability, if it did not clash with the axiom that no emendation of the Florentine text is admissible if a correct and legal interpretation is available.[48] But Noodt, following in the footsteps of Cujas, had a

45. Some examples in Van den Bergh and Stolte, 1977: 245 f.
46. See Gebauer–Spangenberg, *a.h.l.* n. 65, from the Brenkman papers. The whereabouts of the MS in question is unknown.
47. For Scaliger, see Grafton, 1983: 123; Burman on Grat. *Cynec.* vs. 68; Perizonius on Val. Max. 4. 3, extemp. num. 3; Van Bijnkershœk, *Obs. jur. rom.* 6. 15 in fine.
48. Huber, 1700: 541.

different attitude: no manuscript, however revered, could surpass *ratio juris*.

As I said before, a regrettable effect of Wieling's attack was that it created some a priori plausibility for other accusations in later ages, and particularly for Goudsmit's accusation that Noodt made extensive use of Donellus' commentaries. This is a curious affair. Joel Emmanuel Goudsmit (1813–82)[49] was born in Leiden, studied there, and in 1838 was appointed professor of Roman law in his *alma mater*. He died in Leiden too. He was a staunch adherent of the German Pandectist School and wrote in its tradition his *Pandecten-systeem* (2 vols., 1866–80), which was translated into several languages. It is an extremely systematic–dogmatic treatise of the general principles of Roman private law which, curiously enough, appeared in a period when the Pandectist School in Germany itself was already on the wane. Around 1860 Jhering made his conversion from 'Begriff' to 'Interesse' and in 1880 the work on the German civil code was well under way and Romanist scholarship turned toward new horizons.

Under German influence, Goudsmit's judgment of the Romanist scholarship of preceding ages, and especially of the Dutch school, was completely dominated by the overriding verdicts of the Historical School and of Jhering in particular. The well-known judgment the latter passed on Romanist historical scholarship in general and on the Dutch school in particular, published in the opening statement of his *Jahrbücher* (1857),[50] was copied out by Goudsmit with only minor restrictions.[51] Now Jhering, who was concerned with the development of abstract legal dogmatics, and who played off Savigny the systematist against Savigny the legal historian as well as against the whole of the elegant tradition ('durch das römische Recht über das römische Recht hinaus'),[52] never did any independent historical research on the work of the Dutch elegant school, and even less so Goudsmit. What the last has to say of Noodt[53] was simply copied—with some exaggeration added—from Haubold,[54] as can be seen from the following collation:

. . . par ingenii ac judicii vis . . . criticus tamen aliquando audacior.	. . . geleerd en scherpzinnig, was hij echter vermetel in zijn beweringen en gewaagd in zijn gissingen.

49. *NNBW* vi: 610.
50. Jhering, 1857: 1–52, esp. p. 22. On this, see Van den Bergh, 1986e.
51. Goudsmit i, 1866: 10.
52. Jhering, 1857: 52.
53. Goudsmit i, 1866: 11.
54. Haubold, 1809: 157.

Noodt's Commentary on the Pandects, says Goudsmit, copying Haubold once more, is important mainly for the reconstruction of the edict.[55]

When writing about Donellus, Goudsmit says that 'his excellent commentaries were esteemed only in later ages [that is, by builders of dogmatic systems like Savigny and the Pandectists], although in earlier ones many (e.g. our Noodt) had no scruple to copy many pages literally from him'.[56] The footnote to this passage does not provide the expected corroboration and Goudsmit never published anything like it elsewhere. Neither Eyssell[57] nor Savigny,[58] to whom Goudsmit refers, have a word on Noodt or his copying of pages from Donellus. Quite to the contrary. Eyssell rightly stresses that the leading scholars in Holland, following the method of Cujas, gave analytic explanations of texts with the help of history and philology, neglecting dogmatic studies. In their work they stuck to the *ordo legum* of the Corpus Juris and did not apply Donellus' dogmatic system.[59]

The fundamental difference in the expositions of Roman law by Noodt and Donellus can be established in Leiden at first sight, so to speak, if we compare the lecture notes of both which are kept in the University Library.[60] Donellus' treatment is strictly systematic and dogmatic, beginning with such items as: what is law?—the place and divisions of Roman law—change and abolition of laws—interpretation and explanation of laws. Noodt follows the *ordo legum* and gives under each title an analytical treatment, in fairly systematic order, of the respective doctrine, elucidated, if necessary, with the help of philology and history.[61] So, in all likelihood, Goudsmit simply made a slip and should have referred in parentheses to another Leiden professor, that is, to Vinnius, whose dependence on Donellus—his *dominus domini*—is a well-established fact and indeed is noted by Eyssell.[62]

We may add that nowhere in seventeenth- or eighteenth-century literature on Noodt have we found the slightest trace of an allegation that he copied pages from Donellus. Neither does the very well-

55. Goudsmit i, 1866: 11; cf. Haubold's judgment, above, p. 266f. and p. 292.
56. Goudsmit i, 1866: 7; and see Nelissen, 1880: 170; *NNBW* ii: 1000.
57. Eyssell, 1860.
58. Goudsmit refers to *System* vi: § 221.
59. Eyssell, 1860: 324.
60. Donellus: BPL 40 B I–II; Noodt: BPL 575.
61. Compare the judgment, concerning a special case, of Donahue, 1985: 620 n. 45.
62. Eyssell, 1860: 323; cf. Spangenberg, 1822: 66.

informed Haubold mention it. This is a remarkable fact, because if Noodt really had done something like that, it could hardly have escaped his most qualified and eager critics, such as Huber, Wächtler, Wieling, or Van Bijnkershœk. Naturally, I have no intention of denying that Noodt borrowed ideas from others, such as, to name only a few, Accursius, Bartolus, Cujas, Grotius, or Van Bijnkershœk. But that is what scholars have done in all ages, sometimes with, sometimes without due acknowledgments. Scholarship was never a one-man job but rather the result of accumulated efforts of many generations. But that is something quite different from plagiarism. Wächtler seems to strike the right balance. He noted that Noodt was influenced by Grotius' *De jure belli ac pacis* and that sometimes he proposed readings that proved to be found in the Greeks, but he wanted to keep himself very far from any explicit suspicion of literary theft.[63]

63. Wächtler, 1733: 209.

5

Conclusion: Noodt, the Man and the Scholar

Jean Barbeyrac wrote a fine description of his personal friend. He claimed that he told the plain truth and exaggerated nothing.[1] Allowing for a lot of stereotypes and although after Freud and the rest we have grown too sceptical to take all this for granted, it still seems worthwhile to cite him at length:

Noodt was well-built, had a fine figure, and a robust complexion. During all his life, except for the last years, he enjoyed a vigorous health, which matched his keen intellect. He had happy features, an appearance that mixed cheerfulness, candour, and kindness. He had an agreeable and easy conversation, a natural grace without pose or affectation.

He had a solid piety, enlightened, peaceful, and free of all superstition, ostentation, and hypocrisy. His honesty and integrity were well-tried. Without envy, bitterness, and rancour, he made himself esteemed and loved by all who knew him, and he had no enemies who dared to show themselves.[2] He was a good friend, helpful to everybody, who believed that he was born to do services to mankind as much as he could. As a lover of peace in the highest degree he took every care to avoid any occasion for fights and disputes. There were very lively ones in the Academies where he lived, but he never mixed in them and managed to keep good relations with every party. He particularly avoided literary disputes,[3] for which reasons would not have been lacking him if he had had the appetite to engage in them. And when he felt obliged to defend himself against those who attacked him he did it with honesty and all possible moderation. Only Mr Van Bijnkershœk has complained that he did not mitigate his expressions; and on that account the esteemed president believed he was entitled to rejoin with a rather violent

1. 1731: XC.
2. This may be a reference to the fact that Wieling published his attack on Noodt, which incited Barbeyrac to write a life of Noodt, only six years after his death, see above, p. 312 ff.
3. Barbeyrac, 1731: LXXXI, cites Noodt's own words from a letter: 'Non habeo dicere, me eruditas huiusmodi lites nunquam amasse: scis me evitasse eas semper.' See also Noodt's preface to the *Opera* edn. of 1713: 'Absit modo contumelia, a qua ipse abstinui diligentissime, indecoram arbitratus famam ab alterius imminutione petitam.'

FIG. 4 Portrait of Gerard Noodt of unknown date, designed and engraved by A. van der Laan (born *c.* 1690). It seems to have been used for the first time in the *Opera omnia* edition of 1735 (Ahsmann–Feenstra, 1984: nr. 466) and is found in successive Leiden editions. (From the 1767 edition in the Instituut voor Rechtsgeschiedenis, Utrecht.)

charge. In one word, Mr Noodt had such a happy disposition and he had developed it so well by study—which often produces a contrary effect—that he has always retained an interior and exterior calm which was favourable for himself as well as commodious to others with whom he had to do. I call as witnesses those who still live; I am sure they will say more than I because they knew him longer.

Never was a man less stubborn in his opinions, or less cross when he saw that others did not join them. When a law student or a candidate gave him a disputation he had written to examine and he found theses in it which opposed ideas that he held himself or shared with others, far from taking it ill or getting cross he indicated to the author what he might have forgotten and what could be favourable for the position he took.

He did not take the liberty, as is done often enough, to use all kinds of arguments, good or bad, to explain the laws or reconcile them at any price. If, after having consulted the best authorities and after having supplied what lacked them, he found no satisfactory answer, he did not take a decision but honestly acknowledged his ignorance. There is even a whole title of the Digest he did not explain on that account. It is not my custom, he said there, to teach others what I do not know myself. I perfectly know all interpretations suggested by the commentators, but weighing everything I am surprised that they are contented, although nobody has as yet proposed anything probable and therefore we know neither the nature, nor the purpose, nor even the name of that civil action. On that occasion he showed in a few words the disadvantage of presenting as known what is not. When, on the other hand, following the rules of criticism he was convinced of the content and scope of a law, or even found something in it that was contrary to equity or to other laws that were as clear, he did not trouble to do violence to its terms by forced attenuation or precarious conciliation. This is not my business, he used to say then, but that of the ancient jurists or the compilers or the emperor. I only act and must act as interpreter.

He used his time well. He sought a solid knowledge; he liked to go deep in the matter and devoted everything to the studies which were the main object of his affection. Therefore he did not pride himself on extensive reading, which spreads and consequently weakens attention and often leaves no more than superficial and poorly digested ideas. He did not read all kinds of books, good or bad, or those that practically do no more than repeat common knowledge. He restricted himself to the best and those he investigated thoroughly. The original works of Roman law and the authors from Antiquity, those were what he studied day and night, with which he nourished himself, where he found the material for so many beautiful works he published. In order to convince oneself one only has to give some attention to his style, which for that reason demands readers that are somewhat versed in the reading of ancient authors, especially those who liked to express themselves briefly. That taste for brevity came in part from his philosophical talent, which made him seek exactness and precision and kept him from all superfluity.[4]

Benjamin Furly described Noodt to John Locke in 1700 much more shortly, but essentially in the same vein: 'This day the professor Noodt of Leyden honoured me with a visit and understanding that my son was bound for England, and like to see you, desired his service might be presented to you. He is a hearty man and a lover of liberty'.[5] The word 'hearty' exactly covers the range of meaning conveyed by Barbeyrac's description: vigorous, healthy, cheerful, sociable.

If it would not evoke the wrong kind of association, we might call Noodt the prototype of a bourgeois intellectual. His provenance was undoubtedly bourgeois in the original sense. His father, a goldsmith, came from an old mercantile family and his mother, though belonging to the city patriciate, had a similar background. Her uncle Lambert was a merchant sailor, the first citizen from Nijmegen to sail round the world. It was this background which inspired Noodt's attack on prohibitions of interest as well as his plea for civil freedom and toleration. But Noodt was nothing like the nervous, conspiring, nail-biting kind of bourgeois intellectual we often find in caricature. All his portraits show a calm, contented, open face with the shadow of a smile, a man without pose, a humanist living in a world where beauty, reason, and law were not yet empty words. Noodt actually resented the revolutionary upheavals in Nijmegen between 1702 and 1708 and apparently disliked violence. He is said to have kept studying while the French besieged Nijmegen and opposed the plan to pay homage to the French king in his quarters before the city, saying that Mars and the Muses have nothing in common.

Though we may regard Roukens' anecdotes with some circumspection, his picture cannot have been too wide of the mark. We know at least from Noodt's own words that he disliked literary quarrels and tried to avoid them as much as he could. In this one respect he did not follow the example of Cujas, who was second to none of his opponents in the use of gross invective. It is not true that Noodt never replied to criticism, but the only really sharp reply was to Van Bijnkershœk in 1722. Perizonius, however, seems to doubt whether Noodt's silence really was a sign of wisdom or had other motives. In 1704, only a few months after Noodt's *Diocletianus et*

4. Barbeyrac, 1731: LXXX–LXXXV. 5. Locke, 1982: 127.

Maximianus, Vœt published part two of his Commentary on the Pandects; in an addendum he extensively criticized the new interpretation of C 2. 4. 18 Noodt had given in his book.[6] Perizonius reported to Van Eck: 'In any case I wrote as openly against the opinion of Gronovius not a tenth of what is written here against the opinion of Noodt, who however because of his usual wisdom, or what, to be sure, is interpreted as such, no doubt will consign it to oblivion by silence.'[7] We have seen from what he wrote about Huber in a letter to Van Eck that in private Noodt indeed could be very sharp.[8] But he was not disputatious and, as far as we know, he never moved in political circles, let alone in the shady world of journalists, printers, agents, and pamphleteers. As Barbeyrac stressed, Noodt was not a *faiseur de discours*. He stood aloof from all that.

It may be that Noodt really meant it when he wrote that his proposals were only probable and that he would gladly accept it if others showed him to be wrong. On the other hand, it may also be that he did not have a high opinion of his critics. He found the comments in Huber's *Eunomia romana* 'cold and not worth refuting' and, three times, in Utrecht in 1685,[9] and in Leiden in 1702 and 1713,[10] he wrote in an album inscription for a student as motto: 'Ne te quaesiveris extra'. The words from Persius[11] mean: do not seek outside yourself. Assuming that Noodt meant to imply the context of Persius' satire, this might shed some light on his opinion of academic life. What Persius meant can be summed up in a few words: in matters

6. J. Vœt, *Comm. ad Pand.*, Pars posterior. Leiden: Joh. Verbessel, 1704 (Ahsmann–Feenstra, 1984: nr. 1059). Noodt's book appeared in Jan. 1704 (see Perizonius to Van Eck, Leiden, 16 Jan. 1704, UL Utrecht, MS 1000), Vœt's in May. The Addenda are on four unnumbered pages after p. 1208; the criticism of Noodt is on fols. 2^v and 3^r. For Noodt's interpretation of C 2. 4. 18, see above, p. 220.
7. J. Perizonius to C. van Eck, Leiden, 28 May 1704, UL Utrecht, MS 1000: 'Certe Ego ad Aelianum ne decima quidem parte tam palam scripsi contra Gronovii sententiam, quam haec scripta sunt contra Noodtii sententiam, qui tamen pro solita sibi sapientia, quam scilicet ita interpretatur, silentio rem obliterabit haud dubie.'
8. Noodt to Van Eck, Leiden, 3 Oct. 1693, UL Utrecht, S 1000; see above, p. 56.
9. Page in the album of Engelbert ab Engelen, Utrecht, 30 Apr. 1685, UL Leiden, MS Pap. 21, fol. 58^r.
10. Page in the album of Arnold Kersenboom, Leiden, 1 Apr. 1702, KB 133 M 50, p. 120; leaf from the album of an unknown person, Leiden, 14 July 1713, Berlin, Staatsbibl. Preuss. Kulturbesitz, Sammlung Darmstädter, 2 h 1671 G. Noodt.
11. *Sat.* 1. 7. I thank Dr Heesakkers, Instituut voor Neofilologie en Neolatijn, Amsterdam, for the reference.

of literary judgment look to nobody outside yourself, because in Rome everybody is an ass! This opinion, by the way, fits a Cartesian frame of mind very well.

There are, indeed, in Noodt's profile, traits that justify calling him a bourgeois intellectual: his rationalism, his critical attitude towards those in power, his mild scepticism, his cultural relativism. Though sharing the humanist ideal of restoring the ancient world, he was never a blind admirer of Antiquity. He took the side of the 'moderns', loathed Roman imperialism, and was prepared to accept that classical jurists were only human and could make errors of composition or even eventually give an incorrect legal advice to favour a friend, just as their modern counterparts might do.

If Noodt was a religious man and a member of the Reformed Church all his life, he certainly was on the liberal side and openly sympathized with Arminians. Abraham van den Ende was his friend and his son Jan became Noodt's son-in-law. Noodt knew Jean le Clerc and his address on freedom of religion, abundantly praised by Philip van Limborch, was much read in Remonstrant circles in Amsterdam.[12] As Perizonius said, it hardly could have satisfied orthodox theologians. In his advice on marriage with an in-law Noodt likewise opposed their opinion.

As a scholar, Noodt was, I think, in the first place a jurist. He was very well read in Latin literature. Apparently he did not know much Greek, but in this respect he was no exception in his age. The renaissance of Greek studies in the Republic began a generation later with Tiberius Hemsterhuis. As far as his knowledge of Latin literature was concerned Noodt left contemporary legal scholars far behind in some respects, such as his acquaintance with the works of fathers of the Church such as Lactantius, Tertullian, Augustine, and Ambrose. Already in Franeker they were among the books he had on loan from the provincial library. He wrote good Latin, terse and clear and often expressive. According to Perizonius, his prose was modelled on the style of Seneca.

Noodt knew Roman history and institutions very well and, as an expert in the historical development of Roman law, he hardly had an equal among his contemporaries. We could follow the growth of

12. Three edns. of the Dutch translation (Ahsmann–Feenstra, 1984: nrs. 455, 456, 457) appeared in Amsterdam (1716, 1719, 1734) and two of them are found in the library of the Remonstrant church, now UL Amsterdam. A fourth was edited by the Remonstrant A. A. van der Meersch in 1774 (Ahsmann–Feenstra, 1984: nr. 458).

historical consciousness in his successive works, from the Franeker inaugural address of 1679 to the reply to Van Bijnkershœk in 1722, where the principle of *interpretatio multiplex* was formulated. Continuing the research tradition of Cujas he made real progress in seeing the classical jurists whose fragments are included in the Digest as historical persons, differing in age, background, and ideas. This was not self-evident. In 1640 Hahn still defended, and in Noodt's time Huber maintained, that there was no need for chronological study of Digest fragments, because Justinian had given all fragments, irrespective of their age, legal authority by promulgation in one moment.[13] Without formulating the idea of *Textstufen*, Noodt recognized the various transformations the texts of classical jurists could have experienced in classical, early post-classical, Justinianic, and medieval times. In his last work, the Commentary on the Digest, Noodt made substantial progress in the reconstruction of the praetorian edict. He mastered the whole apparatus of textual criticism available in his day and even introduced some innovations in the criticism of legal texts, that is, the systematic use of epigraphic material and of abbreviations. If Noodt's contemporaries did not appreciate such innovations very much and in retrospect the results do not always seem impressive, it certainly was important to explore the possibilities.

But, in spite of all this, I would hesitate to call Noodt a philologist. I do realize that jurists and classicists, both concerned with the constitution and explanation of texts from Antiquity, still were very close in those days and that Grævius called Noodt the only law professor well trained in letters. In fact, emendations and conjectures fill a great part of his work. But, even so, his primary aim was not to restore and explain classical texts for their own sake. Noodt never edited a classical text and in fact he does not seem to have owned a manuscript of the Corpus Juris. He inspected Van Bijnkershœk's manuscript of the *Digestum Vetus* (now BPL 6 C) on at least one occasion and so we must conclude that he was able to read it (naturally he was only interested in the text, not in the gloss), but mostly he used current editions like that of Russardus. We have seen that he often suggested emendations for which there was no

13. Heinrich Hahn, *Oratio de usu chronologiae ac historiarum in jure privato* (Helmstedt, 3 Sept. 1640). In: Wieling, 1727: Pars posterior, 127. Huber, 1687, I: II. i. 10 in fine (p. 106): 'Nam totus Pandectarum contextus est continuus et Justiniani proprius . . .' (with reference to C 1. 17. 2. 19); cf. Van der Vlugt, 1916: 10.

manuscript authority. But such conjectures were generally regarded as admissible, though of less value than those corroborated by a manuscript reading. Noodt does not seem to have been an expert in paleography, but we should keep in mind that modern methods of identifying and dating legal manuscripts were not available in his day. This began only with Brenkman in the next generation.

As for Cujas, acute legal analysis and interpretation of texts was Noodt's main concern and this was essentially a lawyer's job. Philology stood in the service of legal interpretation. In the last analysis, *ratio juris* might even be more important than any manuscript reading, however revered. And for Noodt *ratio juris* was the legal side of that human reason which in the era of Enlightenment was to become the ultimate norm. As Mencke nicely summed it up,[14] in all his works Noodt always tried to make civil law proceed a little more purely towards the light of reason. Here *ratio juris* already took on a progressive tenor. It was at the basis of Noodt's arguments against prohibition of interest, bargaining over crimes, absolutist government, religious repression, torture, et cetera.

To put Noodt's work in the right perspective, a general remark should be added. It is true that in the seventeenth century scholars did distinguish between the elegant school and *usus modernus*, but modern accounts of the history of European legal science tend to exaggerate the difference. It is a distortion to put glossators, Bartolists, *usus modernus*, and Pandectists as true lawyers on one side, the elegant jurists from the French and Dutch schools as mere antiquarians on the other. Jhering's well-known verdict on elegant jurisprudence and the Dutch school in particular[15] is too easily taken for granted.

Although humanist invective against medieval stupidity is known well enough and humanists made a real effort to reform law studies and curb the fatal, overwhelming flood of comments upon comments, their purpose—their paradigm so to speak—was not totally different from that of medieval jurists. Law as a science of authoritative texts was the same for both. Humanists did not address totally new questions. In many cases the same *hapax legomena* and *cruces* had been under discussion since the days of the first glossators, and the humanists, for all their better knowledge of ancient sources, institutions, and ideas, often did no more than bring new evidence to age-old debates. In the sixteenth century, most elegant jurists were

14. *Acta erud.* 1704: 227.

15. See above, p. 114, n. 39.

Bartolists in their legal practice and even Noodt frequently adheres to the opinion of an Accursius or Baldus. Many *loca difficiliora* which humanists tried to solve with the art of criticism were in fact antinomies which the glossators had established and tried to harmonize away. We have seen this frequently in Noodt's work too. This was, in fact, a real weak spot of humanistic scholarship. Addressing questions that were not real textual problems with methods of textual criticism, they often applied a good instrument to the wrong job and tended to mix up constitution and interpretation of the text. But naturally the separation was only made into a methodological postulate in the nineteenth century, and even then it was never fully realized.

The humanists shared with their medieval predecessors an unbroken belief in the Corpus Juris as binding law (though perhaps not in every word) and in the scholar's task to further its application by emending, analysing, and explaining it correctly. This humanistic attitude is still very clear when Noodt tries to prove that the distinction between *dolus causam dans* and *incidens* is not classical Roman law. By ridding the classical text of the gloss of an inept post-classical interpreter he hopes to rid legal practice of a doctrine that is inadequate and can only breed chicanery and injustice. This is not the work of an historian, let alone of an antiquary, but of a lawyer. That Noodt's hope proved idle in the end does not make it altogether irrelevant.

We may say in retrospect that criticism and historical consciousness could only help to weaken the authority of Roman law, which was soon to wane under the influence of the emerging nation state, the empire of reason, and the call for codification. But it is easy to be wise after the event. For Noodt, humanism had not reached its limit and his purpose, to make civil law conform more to human reason, was not a departure from its aims. Quite to the contrary; some of its political ideas seemed only to be reinforced by the rising tide of Enlightenment.

If we cannot call Noodt a philologist, he is even less a philosopher. Here again we must qualify our statement. As we saw, Barbeyrac praised Noodt's philosophical talent and Wächtler called him a profound thinker. That was not without reason. His education by the Cartesian Theodoor Craanen must have had a lasting influence. Noodt certainly had a sharp wit. His analysis is always acute and he made a habit of stressing the invalidity of traditional arguments such as the *argumentum a contrario*, *a consequentia*, and *ab inclusione unius ad exclusionem alterius*. He often used complicated logical arguments with great ease and apparent effect. In this respect, *De foenore et usuris* still stands out as the model of a well-reasoned treatise. Moreover, Noodt profoundly studied and all his life taught natural law.[16] In the first book of the *Probabilia* (1674) he shows a familiarity with Grotius' *De jure belli ac pacis* and in 1679 in Franeker he pleaded for the inclusion of natural law in the law curriculum, an idea which was only formally realized half a century later. Whenever Noodt discusses principles, for instance in the addresses on sovereignty and on freedom of religion, but also in other treatises, he argues from the original position of mankind, with the duty of self-preservation as the first commandment. This is the same kind of argument as we find in Grotius, Hobbes, Locke, Spinoza, and all the others, and Noodt fully masters it. Natural law really was a kind of social philosophy and he taught it as such to his students. Apart from Cicero, Noodt was strongly influenced by the ethical tracts of Seneca, who seems to have been one of his favourite authors.

But, nevertheless, we could not call Noodt a philosopher. He never developed any philosophical argument at any length, never made his own system of natural law, and in fact seems to have been rather eclectic, like Cicero, for instance. He frequently combines natural law and Roman law—the first for principles, the second for technicalities—without taking the trouble to make a systematic whole of them in a theory of the sources of law.

It may add some depth to Noodt's portrait if we compare him with his only slightly younger contemporary Christian Thomasius (1655–1728).[17] There are many striking similarities between them. Both were 'moderns', innovative spirits, believing in reason. Neither of them ever travelled abroad.[18] Neither blindly adored Antiquity and both advocated *scepticismus juridicus*, holding that in Roman law no certainty beyond the probable could be attained. Both introduced several new elements into legal doctrine. Apart from being natural law students, both were prominent legal historians, and in this field Thomasius' influence in Germany has been more important and lasting than that of Noodt, whose qualities as a historian of Roman

16. On Noodt as student of natural law, see also Moerkerk van Steel, 1856: 155 f.
17. On him, see e.g. Schubart-Fikentscher, 1977; Luig, 1977*b*; Hammerstein, 1972. For the intellectual background of Thomasius, see also Lieberwirth, 1984.
18. See C. Thomasius, *Juristische Händel*, Leipzig, 1720: Preface. I thank Prof. Rolf Lieberwirth for a personal communication on this point.

law have been greatly obscured by the German Historical School. Both were interested in matters of legal education. Both made important contributions to the human rights movement of the Enlightenment, Noodt advocating sovereignty of the people and religious freedom, Thomasius fighting witch-prosecution. Both made rather provocative deductions from natural law as regards marriage law, Thomasius arguing that the prohibition of bigamy, Noodt that prohibited grades and the ban on incest were not rules of natural law. Both opposed theologians on such issues and many others.

The differences, on the other hand, are hardly less evident. Thomasius' literary tastes seem to have been much more urbane than those of Noodt. He was very well read in contemporary French philosophy and literature and even edited a literary review for several years. As far as we know, Noodt mainly concentrated on classical literature and primary sources. There are no traces of his having read widely in fashionable contemporary literature. In this respect it may be of some relevance that Thomasius was born in a family of distinguished academics in Leipzig, the place of one of the oldest and most prestigious universities in Germany, while Noodt was the first academic from a merchant family in a relatively small town, which did not have very much to offer in terms of intellectual climate. On the whole, Thomasius was much more combative, much more critical of the Roman law tradition, much more of a self-conscious modernizer. Thomasius reduced Roman law in theory to the same marginal position as customary law and gave natural law and German law the first place. Noodt discussed contemporary Dutch law marginally in his lectures, but never in his monographs. All his life Noodt taught Roman public law on the basis of the Corpus Juris and natural law, whilst Thomasius was one of the founders of the new discipline of *jus publicum romano-germanicum*. He advocated substantial changes in legal education. Noodt actually did introduce a private course on natural law (*collegium Grotianum*), but fiercely opposed one of the most conspicuous innovations in the curriculum of his day, that is, the compendiary method. In Thomasius' work philosophy and dogmatic argumentation are more dominant and interest in legal philology practically absent. If, for both Noodt and Thomasius, reason and authority were contending principles of legal reasoning, for the latter the scales turned definitely in favour of reason. Noodt always sought to combine natural law reasoning for principles with the authority of the Corpus Juris for technicalities. He may also have been a better historian of classical Roman law than Thomasius, who, for instance, would never have dreamt of a reconstruction of the praetorian edict.

Noodt was a lawyer, indeed one of the few great legal scholars the Dutch republic has known and one of the greatest in Europe. It is interesting to confront Jhering's sweeping verdict of the uselessness from, a legal point of view, of the whole Dutch elegant school with the opinion of Viora, who sees a great difference in juristic personality between Noodt and Schulting.[19] The first was, according to him, a dogmatist and among the Dutch jurists the one who kept most to the old Italian system of treatment of the legal disciplines. The second, however, inclined to the *culti* and therefore to the French school. From a historical point of view there is much to say in favour of Viora's opinion. During the whole of the eighteenth century Noodt's work is discussed by lawyers in a dogmatic context, for example by Pothier, and this still is the case, in the first decades of the nineteenth century, with Merlin or Savigny himself.

We have seen how Noodt gradually came to grips with the systematic treatment of a subject. The *Probabilia* (1674–9) are an unsystematic collection of observations and *De jurisdictione et imperio* (1691) is a typically humanistic monograph, treating a series of loosely related topics in a rather ephemeral order. In *Ad legem Aquiliam*, published likewise in 1691, the systematic treatment is much better though there are still exceptions. *De foenore et usuris* (1698) is a mature systematic treatise. The same system is found in his later monographs and in his lectures. Comparing Noodt's work with that of his contemporaries another feature catches the eye: all his monographs are designed as such and not, as often used to be the case for others, ephemerically integrated collections of disputations. Therefore Noodt's work is of crucial importance for the development of the modern systematic legal monograph. Likewise, his lectures, with the exception of those on Grotius' *De jure belli ac pacis*, were not a lemmatic comment on some standard textbook, like Böckelmann's *Compendium* or Van Eck's or Westenberg's *Principia*. They are his own composition, following the order of titles of the Digest, but for the rest very systematic and clear, written in simple

19. Viora, 1927: 12 f. I have the impression that in general Italian scholars still know more about, and have a more balanced judgment of, the Dutch school than their German counterparts, although I gladly make an exception for Franz Wieacker.

Latin and without pedantry. There is something typically Dutch in all this. Just as the Republic maintained the framework of medieval sovereignty, the Dutch school upheld the ancient *ordo legum*; but within the old framework grew something new, a modern nation state and systematic legal science. This explains why the new was accepted so easily when in the revolutionary upheavals at the end of the eighteenth century the old fence finally collapsed.

No doubt what Noodt produced was mainly 'Professorenrecht', but in this respect he did not differ greatly from the Pandectists of the nineteenth century. In his published works Noodt always tried to treat ancient Roman law as purely as possible—which was generally regarded as a scholarly virtue in his day—and only in his lectures did he discuss questions of contemporary law. He was not among the great authorities of legal practice. He is scarcely cited by the High Court[20] and Roberts did not count him among the leading authorities of South African law.[21] But, naturally, use in legal practice was never the final test of legal scholarship, or else formularies and collections of decisions would be at the top.

Within a system of learned law, the law professor has his own place and his own responsibility. Noodt gave this an extra dimension. As Luther said, the lawyer who is no more than a lawyer is a poor thing. Noodt was a great legal scholar, with wit and imagination, but something more than that. He was a lover of freedom, and what is still more, he had the courage to speak up for it. In the aula of Leiden university, the *atrium libertatis Batavae*, he pleaded the cause of mankind from the same rostrum from which, in the same tradition, in 1941 Cleveringa protested against the dismissal of Jewish professors, *hæc libertatis ergo*. Noodt helped to shape the idea of law as a moral and critical force, a force in which, even after centuries of rather disconcerting experiences, we have not completely lost our faith today. Even though there are scientific doubts about the truth of the story, we have reason to remember Papinian, who had to die because he refused to condone fratricide on the ground that it was the emperor who did it. But then we should also remember Noodt. If law has its martyrs, then also its confessors.

20. Van Apeldoorn, 1937: 7, 33; in Pauw's *Observationes tumultuariae novae* Noodt is only cited twice (i, 1964: no. 400, p. 293; iii, 1972: no. 1196, p. 54). In the first case Noodt's opinion is rejected, in the second it is followed.

21. Roberts, 14 f.

APPENDIX 1. NOODT'S PEDIGREE FROM HIS OWN PAPERS

(ARA Coll. J. H. G. van Tets van Goudriaan, inv. nr. 101), with additions. b = born; d = died; BA = baptized; MA = married; BUR = buried. * = died very young.

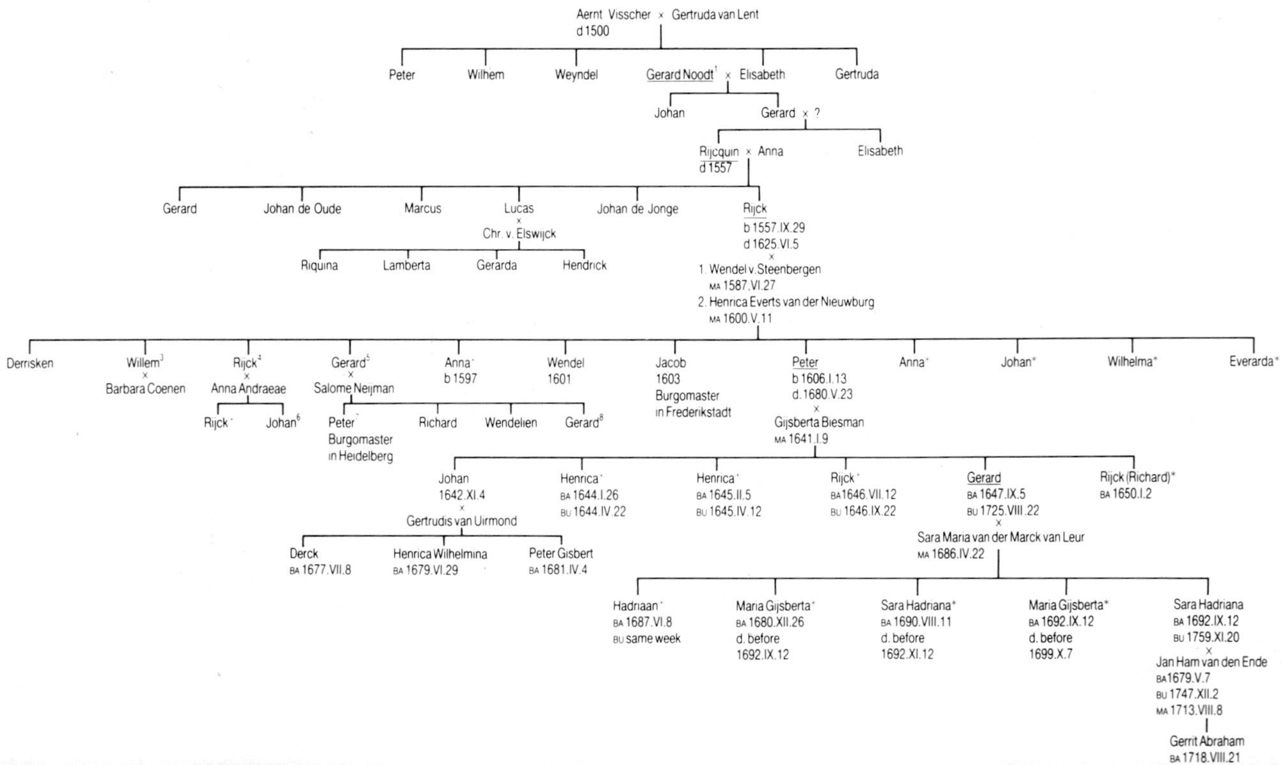

NOTES:

1. Bought a house on the corner of the Grotestraat and the Platenmakersstraat in Nijmegen in 1542. The house was sold in 1578.
2. Born 1588. Died 1665 in Culemborg. Unmarried.
3. Born 1590. Rich merchant in Warsaw. The one to whom Jacob and Peter Noodt went in 1622. Died at the age of 72 or 73.
4. Born 1592. In the service of the king of Sweden, commander of Minden in Westphalia. Died 1646 Feb. 24.
5. Born 1594. Married in Hamburg.
6. Commander of a regiment of Lüneburg and governor in Wolffenbüttel. Fought in many battles, e.g. in Hungary in a battle near Pecs against the Turks. Was killed in action against the French in the Elzas, together with his two sons, who had studied law and letters and were captains in his regiment. On hearing the news of their death his daughter Anna died too.
7. Born 1618.I.2. He was the one who sent to Noodt the offer of a professorship in Heidelberg. Married three times: 1. Catharina van Doorne, 1646.IX.21; six children, all dead in 1680. 2. Anna Margaretha Cator, 1657.VII.28; nine children. 3. Constantia de Volbergen, 1675.VII.21; no children.
8. Married in Hamburg 1657.II.15 to Sara van Loe. Had two daughters.

APPENDIX 2. NOODT'S CORRESPONDENTS

I. Letters from Noodt

To anonymous:

Leiden, 1709 April 21. Centraal Bureau Genealogie, Dossier Noodt.

To Johann Bernoulli:

Leiden, 1709 May 21. University Library Basle, L I a 713 fols. 31 f.
Leiden, 1709 July 15. University Library Basle, L I a 713 fols. 33 f.

To Johannes Braunius:

Franeker, 1681 February 18. University Library Amsterdam, 16 Cf. 1.
Franeker, 1681 April 27 (not autograph). University Library Leiden, BPL 246.
Franeker, 1681 November 6. University Library Leiden, BPL 246.
Franeker, 1682 October 18. RA Gelderland, Arnhem, Coll. van den Steen, van Ommeren en Wayenstein 94. Photocopy in University Library Leiden, BPL 1961.

To Gisbert Cuper:

Nijmegen, 1678 May 25. Koninklijke Bibliotheek, 72 G 20 fol. 6.
Nijmegen, 1679 August 9. Koninklijke Bibliotheek, 72 G 20 fols. 8–11.
Nijmegen, 1679 August 31. Koninklijke Bibliotheek, 72 G 20 fols. 12–13.
Nijmegen, 1681 February 11. Koninklijke Bibliotheek, 72 G 20 fols. 14–15.
Leiden, 1690 January 29. Koninklijke Bibliotheek, 72 G 20 fol. 16.
Leiden, 1709 April 17. Koninklijke Bibliotheek, 72 G 20 fol. 18.
Leiden, 1709 July 28. Koninklijke Bibliotheek, 72 G 20 fol. 20.
Leiden, 1713 September. Koninklijke Bibliotheek, 72 G 20 fol. 22.

To Cornelis van Eck:

Utrecht, 1686 July. Koninklijke Bibliotheek, 135 D 19 ZZ nr. 14.
Leiden, 1689 March 26. University Library Utrecht, MS 1000.
Leiden, 1693 October 3. University Library Utrecht, MS 1000.
Leiden, 1697 May 22. University Library Utrecht, MS 1000.
Leiden, 1716 March 9. University Library Utrecht, MS 1000.

To Johann Georg Grævius:

Leiden, 1686 November 21. Royal Library, Copenhagen.
Leiden, 1701 September 12. Royal Library, Copenhagen.

To Joan Huydecoper:

Leiden, 1700 October 21. RA Utrecht, Familiearchief Huydecoper, inv. nr. 385.

To Nicolaas Theodorus van der Marck van Leur:
Leiden, 1700 January 13. University Library Amsterdam, R 74.

To Marcus Meibom:
Nijmegen, 1678 December 14. Forschungsbibliothek Gotha Chart. A 413.

To Peter Noodt, the father:
Franeker, 1679 October 5 [date incorrect; must be Oct. 2]. ARA Coll. J. G. H. van Tets van Goudriaan, inv. nr. 105.
Franeker, [1679] October 9/19. ARA Coll. J. G. H. van Tets van Goudriaan, inv. nr. 105.
Franeker, 1679 October 25. ARA Coll. J. G. H. van Tets van Goudriaan, inv. nr. 105.
Franeker, 1679 December 8. ARA Coll. J. G. H. van Tets van Goudriaan, inv. nr. 105.
Leeuwarden, 1680 March 9. ARA Coll. J. G. H. van Tets van Goudriaan, inv. nr. 105.
Franeker, 1680 March 15. ARA Coll. J. G. H. van Tets van Goudriaan, inv. nr. 105.
Franeker, 1680 April 2. ARA Coll. J. G. H. van Tets van Goudriaan, inv. nr. 105.

To Peter Noodt, Heidelberg:
Franeker, 1680 May 1. ARA Coll. J. G. C. van Tets van Goudriaan, inv. nr. 111.

To Johan van de Water:
Leiden, 1714 July. University Library Amsterdam, 16 Cf. 2.
Leiden, 1714 October. University Library Leiden, BPL 885.
Leiden, 1716 March 9. Koninklijk Huisarchief, G16–A258.

II. Letters to Noodt

From Johann Bernoulli:
Groningen, 1698 June 27 (draft). University Library Basle, L I a 674, fol. 216. Printed in: Briefwechsel von Johann Bernouilli, edited by the Naturforschenden Gesellschaft in Basle, Basle, 1955: i: 432.
Basle, 1709 June 5 (draft; original in Philadelphia) University Library Basle, L I a 674, fols. 217–18.
Basle, 1709 August 4 (draft; original in Staatsbibliothek, Berlin). University Library Basle, L I a 674 fols. 219 f.

From Gisbert Cuper:
Deventer, 1679 July 31 (draft). Koninklijke Bibliotheek, 72 G 20, fol. 24^v.
Deventer, [1679] September 5 (draft). Koninklijke Bibliotheek, 72 G 20.
Deventer, [1679] November 1 (draft). Koninklijke Bibliotheek, 72 G 20, fols. 27^r–32^v.

The Hague, 1690 December 16 (draft). Koninklijke Bibliotheek, 72 G 20, fol. 33.

Deventer, 1708 January 11 (draft). Koninklijke Bibliotheek, 72 G 20, fols. 34^r–35^v.

Deventer, 1709 May 26 (draft). Koninklijke Bibliotheek, 72 G 20, fols. 36^r–37^v.

Deventer, 1713 October 20 (draft). Koninklijke Bibliotheek, 72 G 30, fols. 38^r–41^r.

From Carolus Andreas Duker:

[no place] 1719 June (draft). University Library Amsterdam, E 35.

From Johann Georg Græevius:

Utrecht, 1686 September 25. ARA Coll. J. G. H. van Tets van Goudriaan, inv. nr. 114.

Utrecht, 1686 November 10. ARA Coll. J. G. H. van Tets van Goudriaan, inv. nr. 114.

Utrecht, 1687 October 18. ARA Coll. J. G. H. van Tets van Goudriaan, inv. nr. 114.

From Jacob Gronovius:

[Leiden, October 1699] ARA Coll. J. G. H. van Tets van Goudriaan, inv. nr. 117.

From Henricus Kannegieter:

[No place or date; draft?] Provinciale Bibliotheek Leeuwarden, MS 1152, I, no. 19.

From Philippus van Limborch:

Amsterdam, 1706 April 6 [draft]. University Library Amsterdam, III D 17 108.

From Peter Noodt, the father:

Nijmegen, 1679 October 30. ARA Coll. J. G. H. van Tets van Goudriaan, inv. nr. 110.

Nijmegen, 1680 March 20. ARA Coll. J. G. H. van Tets van Goudriaan, inv. nr. 110.

From the Gedeputeerde Staten van Friesland:

Leeuwarden, 1683 February 27. ARA Coll. J. G. H. van Tets van Goudriaan, inv. nr. 112.

From O. Vitringa:

Franeker, 1704 November 5. ARA Coll. J. G. H. van Tets van Goudriaan, inv. nr. 118.

APPENDIX 3. LIST OF ARCHIVE MATERIALS

NB: For the letters see also Appendix 2.

Algemeen Rijksarchief, The Hague
Collectie Mr J. G. H. van Tets van Goudriaan.
Inv. nr.

84. Admission of Johan van den Ende as advocate on the Hof van Holland, 1703.
85. Marriage contract of Johan van den Ende and Sara Adriana Noodt, 1713.
86. Poem for the marriage of Johan van den Ende and Sara Maria Noodt by L. Kramp, 1713.
87. Certificate of baptism of Sara Adriana Noodt, 1692.
88. Poems for the silver wedding of Johan van den Ende and Sara Adriana Noodt, 1738.
89. Declaration of the secretary of the senate of Leiden University that Sara Adriana is the only surviving child of Gerard Noodt, 1725.
92. Letter of Jean Barbeyrac to Johan van den Ende, 1731.
95. Marriage contract of Gerrit Abraham van den Ende and Wilhelma van Dijk, 1749.
96. Mutual will of Gerrit Abraham van den Ende and Wilhelma van Dijk, 1750.
100. Inventory of pieces concerning the family Noodt made by Mr J. G. H. van Tets van Goudriaan.
101. Register van het geslagt van Noodt (autograph of Gerard Noodt). Genealogical, biographical, and autobiographical notes, *c.*1680.
102. Testimonies by burgomasters, aldermen, and council of Nijmegen concerning Jacob and Peter Noodt, 1626 and 1627.
103. Marriage contract of Peter Noodt and Gijsbertjen Biesman, 1641.
104. Instrument concerning separation of property in some graves in the Church of St Steven between Peter Noodt and Lucas Bonedt, 1671.
105. Letters of Gerard Noodt to his parents, 1679–80.
106. List of investitures of members of the Biesman family with tithe in the Eyckhorst in Wychen.
107. Register van het geslacht van de Bijesmans en eenige andere daer aen verwante familien (autograph of Gerard Noodt). Genealogical and biographical notes.
108. Doctor's diploma of Gerard Noodt, Franeker, 1669 June 9.

109. Appointment of Gerard Noodt as ordinary professor in Franeker; Leeuwarden, 1679 September 4.
110. Letters of Peter Noodt to his son, 1679–80.
111. Letter of Gerard Noodt to his nephew Peter Noodt, burgomaster in Heidelberg (draft), 1680.
112. Letter of the Provincial Executive of Friesland to Gerard Noodt, concerning a raise in salary, 1683.
113. Marriage contract of Gerard Noodt and Sara Maria van der Marck, 1686.
114. Letters of J. G. Grævius to Gerard Noodt, 1686–7.
115. Mutual will of Gerard Noodt and Sara Maria van der Marck van Leur, 1693, with protocol of its opening, 1701.
116. Announcement of Gerard Noodt to his students concerning the resumption of his lectures after the death of his wife (draft and original), 1699.
117. Letter of condolence of Jacob Gronovius to Gerard Noodt on occasion of the death of his wife, without date (1699).
118. Letter of O. Vitringa, 1704.
119. Obituary of Gerard Noodt; Dutch text written by Johan van den Ende, French translation by Jean Barbeyrac.
120. Th. Roukens, Oratio scholastica in laudem Gerhardi Noodt, etc. Nijmegen 1767.
121. Drawing of the tombstone of Peter Noodt, Gijsberta Biesman, and Gerard Noodt in the Church of St Steven, Nijmegen.
122. Disputation on C 9. 8. 5. 1.
123. Disputation on C 5. 47. 1 and D 18. 1. 4.

Collectie Hof van Holland

Inv. nr.

5943 Register advocaten, etc.

Rijksarchief in Gelderland, Arnhem

Archief Hof Gelre en Zutphen.

Inv. nr.

1176 Appoinctement-boeck 1667–1671.
1177 Appoinctement-boeck 1671–1676.
1178 Appoinctement-boeck 1676–1678.
1179 Appoinctement-boeck 1678–1680.
1201 Appoinctementen 1666–1679.
1202 Supplicatiën.

Coll. van den Steen, van Ommeren en Wayenstein.

Inv. nr.

94. Letter of Gerard Noodt to Johannes Braunius.

Rijksarchief in Friesland, Leeuwarden

Archieen van de universiteit te Franeker.
Inv. nr.
18. Diarium academiae 1664–1683.
19. Diarium academiae 1683–1717.

Gemeentearchief Amsterdam

PA 76 (de Graeff) inv. nr. 243. Doctor's diploma for Johan de Graeff, dated Leiden 1699 Febr. 15 and signed by Gerard Noodt as rector. Copy ibid. inv. nr. 399.
PA 195 (Bicker) inv. nr. 93. Declaration by Gerard Noodt that Joh. Bernardus Bicker has attended his lectures in Leiden (autograph).

Gemeentearchief Den Haag

Registers of baptisms and marriages.
Notarieel archief.
Inv. nr.
673. Instrument in which W. Crayvanger lays down that Gerard Noodt and Joh. Emants must be appointed executors of his will and tutors of his children. 1696 March 30.

Gemeentearchief Leiden

Registers of baptisms and burials.
Register Sevenhuijsen (bonboek), fol. 174^{v}.
Verpondingenregister 1716, p. 161^{v}: no. 323.
Cohier Familiegeld, 1716 May 28, p. 64.
Rechterlijk archief, inv. nr. 213, Register Impost op het begraven le klasse 1695–1805.
Weeskamerarchief, Register van seclusiën Vol. L. p. 246^{v} (1701).

Gemeentearchief Nijmegen

Registers of baptism and burials.
Raadsignaten 1627–1679.
Justitieel schepenprotocol 1669–1679.
Crimineel schepenprotocol 1669–1679.

Archief Gymnasium.
Inv. nr.
449. Receipts of payment of salary.
451. Arrangement concerning backpay of the widow of Petrus de Greve and the professors Teyler and Noodt (incomplete), 1684 (?).

Archief Biesman.

Inv. nr.

12. Historije van 't geene Willemken suster is wederfaren. Account of the arrest of Willemken van Wanrade.
13. Idem (copy).
18. Mutual will of Johan van Brienen and Gijsberta Biesman.
19. Instrument of annuity for Gijsbertje Biesman and Peter Noodt, 1642 Febr. 17.
56. Will of Gijsberta Biesman, 1670 July 30.

11 C 2 Dictata in Pandectas pars quarta (incomplete).

Gemeentearchief Schoonhoven

Register of conveyances inv. nr. 2366, fols. 72^v–74^r; 2367, fols. 73^v–75^v.

Koninklijke Bibliotheek, The Hague

72 D 37, 10	Confirmation of a legal advice by J. Vœt, P. R. Vitriarius and G. Noodt, Leiden, 1704 June 14.
72 G 20	Letters to and from G. Cuper.
133 M 50 p. 120	Page in the album of Arnold Kersenboom, Leiden, 1702 April 1.
74 H 47 p. 80	Page in the album of J. Ihring, Leiden, 1720 Aug. 14.

Universiteitsbibliotheek Leiden

ARCHIEF SENAAT EN FACULTEITEN

Inv. nr.

299 Documenta actorum.

389 Actorum facultatis juridici, Vol. II, 1669–1745.

MS BPL

40B	Notes of Digest lectures by Donellus, once owned (and perhaps made) by his pupil Gerardus Tuningius.
191b	[Noodt] Collegium Grotianum seu explicatio et interpretatio Grotii de jure belli ac pacis. H. Gockinga.
191	[Noodt] Dictata ad IV libros Institutionum, 1710. Scripsit R. W. de Bachman, Embrica-clivensis.
191h	Adversaria of J. van de Water.
191l	Index of notes taken by J. van de Water from ancient and modern authors, 1703.
191k	Dictata Antonii Matthaei in quatuor libros Institutionum imperialium.
191u	[Noodt] Excerpta ex dictatis in Pandectis seu Digestos (incomplete).

191y [Noodt] Notæ ad Digestorum seu Pandectarum libros L scripsit H. de Beaufort. 4 vols.
575 [Noodt] Explicatio Pandectarum seu Digestorum. 2 vols. (autograph).
648–663 Various volumes of notes of the lectures of J. C. Rücker on the literary history of Roman law.
695 Ger. Noodt et A. Schultingh, Dictata in Institutiones synoptice scripta Schultingii verba adversa pagina aversa Noodtii scripta sum.
696 [Noodt] Dictata ad Pandectas 1715–1716.
1072–1073 Notes of lectures of J. C. Rücker on the literary history of Roman law.
2322 Dictata ad Institutiones. 2 vols.
Page from an album.

Universiteitsbibliotheek Amsterdam

Juridisch Instituut kamer B 202. G. Noodt, Dictata ad Instituta (incomplete).

Universiteitsbibliotheek Utrecht

MS
1000 Letters to Cornelis van Eck. 3 Portfolios.
1095 Collection of manuscripts and adversaria of A. Coerman.

Universiteitsbibliotheek Gent

MS
280 Gerard Noodt, Dictata ad Pandectas. Written by J. C. Mathiassen, 1712.
281 Gerard Noodt, Dictata ad Instituta.

Provinciale Bibliotheek, Leeuwarden

MS
Hof 10 [Voorda collection] Dictata . . . Gerardi Noodt ex ore eius excepta in totas Pandectas. 4 vols. (completed 1721 July 10).

Staatsbibliothek Preussischer Kulturbesitz, Berlin

Sammlung Darmstädter 2 H 1671 Page from an album, Leiden, 1713 July 14.

National Library of Scotland, Edinburgh

Adv. Ms. 28. 4. 9 Lecture notes on the Institutes. 4 vols. Leiden 1686.
MS 17810 fols. 19^r–58^v Lecture notes on book I of the Digest.

BIBLIOGRAPHY

This is not an exhaustive list. Some works which are cited only once are found with their full title in the notes.

ADAMS, J. N., AVERLEY, G., and ROBINSON, F. J. G. (1982). *A bibliography of eighteenth century legal literature: a subject and author catalogue of law treatises and all law related literature held in the main legal collections in England*. Newcastle upon Tyne: Avero Publications.

ADELUNG, J. C. (1784–1897). *Fortsetzung und Ergänzungen zu C. G. Jöchers Allgemeines Gelehrten-Lexicon worin die Schriftsteller aller Stände nach ihren vornehmsten Lebensumständen und Schriften beschrieben werden*, 7 vols., Leipzig. Repr. (1960–1). Hildesheim: Olms. 1960–1.

AHSMANN, M. (1986). De juridische faculteit te Franeker 1585–1635: een studie over de professoren en hun onderwijs met lijsten van verdedigde disputaties. *The Legal History Review* 54: 3–72.

Album scholasticum Leiden. (1941): *Album scholasticum academiae Lugduno-Batavae 1575–1940*, samengesteld door C. A. Siegenbeek van Heukelo-Lamme and O. C. D. Idenburg-Siegenbeek van Heukelom. Leiden: Brill.

ANKUM, J. A. (1983). Quanti ea res erit in diebus xxx proximis dans le troisième chapitre de la lex Aquilia: un fantaisisme florentin. *Mélanges Jacques Ellul*. Paris: 171–83.

ANON. (1778). *Zekere gedachten over het zamenstel onzer hedendaagsche rechtsgeleerdheid met gepaste vrijmoedigheid beoordeelt*. The Hague.

APELDOORN, L. J. VAN (1937). Theorie en practijk van de rechtsbronnen in Holland in den tijd van Cornelis van Bynkershoek (1673–1743). *Tydskrif vir hedendaagse Romeins-Hollandse reg.* 1: 4–33.

ARNTZENIUS, H. I. (1788). *Oratio de optima iuris Romani antecessoris forma in Gerardo Noodtio, Noviomago, spectata*. Utrecht: van Paddenburg.

ARNTZENIUS, J. O. (1802). *Oratio de meritis Gelrorum in jurisprudentiam*. Harderwijk: Tyhoff.

——(1807). *See* Van Hasselt, 1807.

BAKHUIS, J. W. F. and IDENBURG, P. J. (eds.), (1920–1). Advies van de juridische faculteit betreffende de bevoegdheid van de Collegien ter Admiraliteit in commune delicten, 1782. *Militair rechterlijk tijdschrift* 16: 35–51.

BARBEYRAC, J. (1731). *Recueil de discours sur diverses matières importantes*, 2 vols. Amsterdam: Humbert.

BARELS, J. M. (1778). *Crimineele advysen, door verscheide voornaeme*

Nederlandsche rechtsgeleerden over gewichtige gevallen. Amsterdam: Gartman.

Barels, J. M. (1780–1) *Advysen over den koophandel en zeevaert: Mitsgaders verscheidene turbes, memorien, resolutien, missives, enz. enz. daer toe behoorende*, 2 vols. Amsterdam: H. Gartman.

Barnouw, P. J. (1963). *Philippus van Limborch*. Den Haag: Mouton.

Baron, J. (1888). Franz Hotmann's Antitribonian: Ein Beitrag zu den Codificationsbestrebungen vom XVI. bis zum XVIII. Jahrhundert. (Separate pr. from a Festschrift for the univ. of Bonn) Berne.

Bastiaanse, R., Bots, H., and Evers, M. (1985). *'Tot meesten nut ende dienst van de jeught': En onderzoek naar zeventien Gelderse Latijnse scholen, ca 1580–1815*. Gelderse Historische Reeks, 16. Zutphen: Walburg Press.

Begheijn, P. J. (1981). Bezoekers te Nijmegen in het laatste kwart van de zeventiende eeuw. *Numaga* 28: 108–18.

Berg, I. van den (1781–4). *Nederlands Advysboek, inhoudende verscheidene consultatien en advysen van voorname regtsgeleerden in Nederland*, 4 vols., 2nd imp. Kampen: de Chalmot.

Bergh, G. C. J. J. van den (1964). *Themis en de muzen: De functie van de gebonden vormen in het recht*. Haarlem: Tjeenk Willink.

——(1972). Een Nijmeegs dispuut over de privilegia scholarium. *Numaga* 19: 18–22.

——(1974). Auctoritas poetarum: The fortunes of a legal argument. In: A. Watson (ed.), *Daube Noster: Essays in legal history for David Daube*. Edinburgh and London: Scottish Academic Press: 27–37.

——(1979). Natural law and history of law: A note on Immink. In: J. E. Spruit (ed.), *Maior viginti quinque annis: Essays in commemoration of the sixth lustrum of the Institute for legal history of the University of Utrecht*. Assen: van Gorcum: 30–44.

——(1982*a*). Custodia and furtum pignoris. In: *Studi in onore di Cesare Sanfilippo*. Milan: Giuffrè: 603–14.

——(1982*b*). *Wet en gewoonte: Historische grondslagen van een dogmatisch geding*. Rechthistorische cahiers, 5. Deventer: Kluwer.

——(1984). Two letters of Cornelis van Bijnkershœk (1673–1743) concerning his acquisition of a manuscript of the Digestum Vetus (now UL Leiden, BPL 6C) and a new source for the study of Johan de Witt. *Lias* 11: 277–86.

——(1985*a*). *Geleerd recht: Een geschiedenis van de Europese rechtswetenschap in vogelvlucht* 2nd imp. Deventer: Kluwer.

——(1985*b*). Geminatio taurelliana: A note on humanistic philology and legal scholarship. In: *Satura Roberto Feenstra oblata*. Fribourg: Editions universitaires: 523–32.

——(1986*a*). Inleiding. In: G. C. J. J. van den Bergh, J. E. Spruit, and M. van de Vrugt (eds.), *Rechtsgeleerd Utrecht: Levensschetsen van elf* *hoogleraren uit driehonderdvijftig jaar Faculteit der Rechtsgeleerdheid in Utrecht*. Zutphen: Walburg Press and Stichtse Historische Reeks: 9–20.

BERGH, G. C. J. J. VAN DEN (1986*b*). Cornelis van Eck 1662–1732: Een dichter-jurist. In: G. C. J. J. van den Bergh, J. E. Spruit, and M. van de Vrugt (eds.), *Rechtsgeleerd Utrecht: Levensschetsen van elf hoogleraren uit driehonderdvijftig jaar Faculteit der Rechtsgeleerdheid in Utrecht*. Zutphen: Walburg Press and Stichtse Historische Reeks: 37–54.

—— (1986*c*). Jedem das Seine. In: J. B. J. M. ten Berge, G. J. H. van Hoof, A. Ph. Jaspers, and A. H. J. Swart (eds.), *Recht als norm en als aspiratie*. Nijmegen: Ars Aequi libri: 258–65.

—— (1986*d*). The concept of folk law in historical context: A brief outline. In: K. von Benda-Beckmann and F. Strijbosch (eds.), *Anthropology of law in the Netherlands: Essays on legal pluralism*. Verhand. Kon. Inst. Taal- Land- en Volkenkunde, 116. Dordrecht: Foris: 67–89.

—— (1986*e*). Geschichtsbewusstsein im 17. Jahrhundert: Die Verdunkelung der rechtshistorischen Leistungen der eleganten Schule durch die Historische Schule. *Akten des 26. Deutschen Rechtshistorikertages Frankfurt am Main 22–6 September 1986*. Frankfurt: Klostermann, 1987: 527–39.

—— and STOLTE, B. H. (1977). The unfinished Digest edition of Henrik Brenkman (1681–1736): A pilot-survey and edition of Digest 9. 2 ad legem Aquiliam. *The Legal History Review* 45: 227–305.

BERGH, L. P. C. (1857). De baljuwen. In: R. C. Bakhuizen van den Brink, L. Ph. C. van den Bergh, and J. K. J. de Jonge (eds.), *Het Nederlandsche Rijksarchief: Verzameling van onuitgegeven oorkonden en bescheiden voor de geschiedenis des vaderlands*. The Hague: Nijhoff i: 235–303.

BESELER, G. VON (1929). *Juristische Miniaturen*. Leipzig: Noske.

BEST, G. (1745). *Ratio emendandi leges Pandectarum Florentinarum auctoritate: accedunt orationes auctoris duae*, 2nd imp., ed. J. W. Neuhaus. Leipzig: Schoenermarck.

BETTI, E. (1954). Zur Grundlegung einer allgemeinen Auslegungslehre. In: *Festschrift für Ernst Rabel*, ii. *Geschichte der antiken Rechte und allgemeine Rechtslehre*, ed. W. Kunkel and H. J. Wolf. Tübingen: Mohr: 79–168.

—— (1955). *Teoria generale della interpretazione*, 2 vols. Milan: Giuffrè.

BEYERMAN, J. J. (1959). Een verpachting 'bij bernender kaersse' in 1537. *WPNR* 90 (1959): no. 44610.

BIJNKERSHOEK, C. VAN (1719). *De jure occidendi, vendendi et exponendi liberos apud veteres Romanos*. Leiden: J. van der Linden.

—— (1723). *Curae secundae de jure occidendi et exponendi liberos apud veteres Romanos ad virum clarissimum Gerardum Noodt*. Leiden: J. van der Linden.

—— (1767). *Opera omnia*, 2 vols. Leiden: S. and J. Luchtmans.

BIJNKERSHOEK, C. VAN (1926–62). *Observationes tumultuariae*, 4 vols., ed. E. M. Meijers, A. S. de Blécourt *et al.* Haarlem: Tjeenk Willink.

——(1978). Notæ selectae ad Pandectarum libr. XII Tit. 1–XXXV Tit. 2, ed. P. van Warmelo. *Acta juridica 1978* (Essays in Honour of Ben Beinart, vol. iii): 225–77.

BILDERDIJK, W. (1806). *Observationes et emendationes liber unus*. Brunswick.

——(1819–20). *Observationes et emendationes*, 2nd edn. with liber alter. Leiden.

——(1829). *Epistolae de Collatione legum Mosaicarum et Romanarum nec non specimen emendationis edicti imperatorum Diocletiani et Maximiani contra Manichaeos*. 2nd edn. Rotterdam: Smit.

BINSBERGEN, W. C. VAN (1949). *Algemeen karakter van het Crimineel Wetboek voor het Koningrijk Holland*. Utrecht: de Vroede.

BLOK, P. J. (1923–6). *Geschiedenis van het Nederlandsche volk*, 4 vols., 3rd imp. Leiden: Sijthoff.

BOELES, W. B. S. (1864). Levenschetsen der Groninger Hoogleeraren. In: Jonckbloet, 1864.

——(1878–89). *Frieslands Hoogeschool en het Rijks Atheneum te Franeker*, 3 vols. (i, ii. 1, ii. 2). Leeuwarden: Kuipers. [Noodt: vii. 1: 279–84].

BONFANTE, P. (1963). *Corso di diritto romano*, i. *Diritto di famiglia*. Revised edn. Milan: Giuffrè.

BOOM, J. VAN DEN and DRIESSEN, A. (1983). *Voorlopige lijst van studenten van de Kwartierlijke Academie te Nijmegen 1655–1679*. Nijmegen: Gerard Noodt Instituut.

Bronnen: *Bronnen van de Nederlandse codificatie sinds 1798*, 3 vols. to date. i. *Stukken van algemene aard: de gedrukte ontwerpen van 1804 en hun voorgeschiedenis*, collected by H. Aa, ed. J. Th. de Smidt and A. H. Huussen. Werken OVR derde reeks, nr. 22. Utrecht: Kemink, 1968; ii. *Huwelijks- en huwelijksgoederenrecht tot 1820*, ed. A. H. Huussen. Werken OVR derde reeks, nr. 22. Bussum: Kemink, 1975; iii. *Personen- en familierecht 1798–1820*, ed. H. C. Gall; *Rechtspersonen 1798–1820*, ed. F. M. Huussen-de Groot. Werken Stichting OVR, nr. 6. Zutphen: Walburg Press, 1981.

BRUTTI, M. (1973). *La problematica del dolo processuale nell'esperienza romana*. Milan: Giuffrè.

BUDER, C. G. (1756). *Bibliotheca juris selecta*, 8th imp. Jena: Cuno.

BURMAN, C. (1738). *Trajectum eruditum*. Utrecht.

BURMAN, P. (1727). *Sylloges epistolarum a viris illustribus scriptarum*, 5 vols. Leiden: Luchtmans.

BURMEISTER, K. H. (1974). *Das Studium der Rechte im Zeitalter des Humanismus im deutschen Rechtsbereich*. Wiesbaden: Pressler.

BOTS, H. (1975). Cultuurgeschiedenis: het intellectuele leven in Gelderland gedurende de 16e, 17e en 18e eeuw. In: J. J. Poelhekke, G. J. Mentink,

W. Jappe Alberts, and H. K. Roessingh (eds.), *Geschiedenis van Gelderland 1492–1795*. Zutphen: Walburg Press. ii: 385–428.

BOTS, H. (1978). Het Kabinet Smetius, een illustere Nijmeegse beziens-waardigheid, ook tijdens het vredescongres. *Numaga* 25: 170–84.

—— *et al.* (1981). *De 'Bibliothèque universelle et historique' (1686–1693): Een periodiek als trefpunt van geleerd Europa*. Studies van het Instituut voor intellectuele betrekkingen tussen de Westeuropese landen in de zeventiende eeuw, 7. Amsterdam: APA Holland University Press.

BRAUNIUS, J. (1675). *La Véritable Religion des Hollandois, avec une apologie pour la religion des Estats généraux des Provinces Unies, contre le libelle diffamatoire de Stoupe qui a pour titre 'la Religion des Hollandois'* [together with] *Le Conseil d'extorsion, ou la volerie des François exercée en la ville de Nimègue par le commissaire Methelet et ses suppots*. Amsterdam: A. Wolfgank.

BRENKMAN, H. (1722). *Historia Pandectarum seu fatum exemplaris Florentini, accedit gemina dissertatio de Amalphi*. Utrecht: W. van de Water.

BRIE, S. (1899). *Die Lehre vom Gewohnheitsrecht: Eine historisch-dogmatische Untersuchung*, i. *Geschichtliche Grundlegung (bis zum Ausgang des Mittelalters)*. Wrocław: Marcus.

Briefwechsel (1955): *Der Briefwechsel von Johann Bernoulli, herausgegeben von der Naturforschenden Gesellschaft in Basel*, i. Basel: Birkhäuser.

BRINKHOF, J. J. (1972). Enkele opmerkingen over de geldigheid van de aan de kwartierlijke academie behaalde doctorsgraad in de rechten. *Numaga* 19: 14–17.

BRINKHOFF, J. M. G. M. (1969). In en om de Stevenskerk. *Numaga* 16: 211–45.

—— (1978). Naschrift. *Numaga* 25: 182.

CALDERINI, A. (1974). *Epigrafia*. Turin: Società editrice internazionale.

CAMUS-DUPIN (1832). *Profession d'avocat*, i. *Recueil de pièces concernant l'exercice de cette profession*. ii. *Bibliothèque choisie des livres de droit qu'il est plus utile d'acquérir et de connaitre*. 5th edn. Paris.

CANNEGIETER, J. (1770). *Oratio de Romanorum jurisconsultorum excellentia et sanctitate*. Groningen: H. Spandaw.

CANOY-OLTHOFF, A. M. M. (1983). Een onderzoek naar de inhoud van een aantal zeventiende en achttiende eeuwse dissertaties over vruchtgebruik. In: G. van Dievoet and G. Macours (eds.), *Justicie ende gerechticheyt: Handelingen van het zevende Belgisch-Nederlands rechtshistorisch colloquium*. Acta Falconis, 83/3. Antwerp: Kluwer: 15–33.

CARCATERRA, A. (1970). *Dolus bonus/dolus malus: esegesi di D 4.3.1.2–3*. Naples: Jovene.

CASAVOLA, F. (1968). Dolus. *Novissimo digesto italiano*. iv: 148.

Catalogus (1983): *Nijmeegs zilver 1400–1900: Catalogi van het kunstbezit van de gemeente Nijmegen nr. 5*.

CLAPP, J. G. (1967). John Locke. In: P. Edwards (ed.), *The encyclopedia of philosophy*. New York and London: Macmillan. iii: 487–503.

CLERC, J. LE (1697). [Joannis Clerici] *Ars critica, in qua ad studia linguarum Latinae, Graecae et Hebraicae via munitur*, 2 vols., 5th imp. Amsterdam: Janssonio-Waesbergios, 1730.

COCK, A. DE (1897). Spreekwoorden en zegswijzen afkomstig van oude gebruiken en volkszeden. *Volkskunde* 10 (1897–8).

COING, H. (1970). Die juristischen Fakultäten der Aufklärungszeit: Geschichte einer Studienreform. *Jahrbuch der Akademie der Wissenschaften in Göttingen*. Göttingen: Vandenhoeck & Ruprecht: 34–55.

——(ed.) (1973). *Handbuch der Quellen und Literatur der neueren europäischen Privatrechtsgeschichte*, i. *Mittelalter (1100–1500): Die gelehrten Rechte und die Gesetzgebung*. Munich: Beck.

——(ed.) (1976). *Handbuch der Quellen und Literatur der neueren europäischen Privatrechtsgeschichte*, ii. *Neuere Zeit (1500–1800): Das Zeitalter des Gemeinen Rechts*, Part 2. *Gesetzgebung und Rechtsprechung*. Munich: Beck.

——(ed.) (1977). *Handbuch der Quellen und Literatur der neueren europäischen Privatrechtsgeschichte*, ii. *Neuere Zeit (1500–1800): Das Zeitalter des Gemeinen Rechts*, Part 1. *Wissenschaft*. Munich: Beck.

——(1985). *Europäisches Privatrecht*, i. *Älteres Gemeines recht (1500 bis 1800)*. Munich: Beck.

CONRING, H. (1730). *Opera*, 7 vols., ed. with commentary by J. W. Göbel (1970). Aalen: Scientia. Anastatic repr. of the edn. of Brunswick, 1730.

CRANSTON, M. (1967). Toleration. In: P. Edwards (ed.) *The Encyclopedia of philosophy*. New York and London: Macmillan. vii: 143–6.

CUIACUS, J. (1737). *Observationum et emendationum libr. XXVIII . . .* Praefationem de Cujacii adversariis et obtrectatoribus praemisit J. G. Heineccius. Halle: Impensis Orphanotrophaei.

DERNBURG, H. (1902). *Pandekten*, 3 vols. 7th imp. Berlin: H. W. Müller.

DESCARTES, R. (1953). *Œuvres et lettres*, ed. André Bridoux. Bibliothèque de la Pléiade. Paris: Gallimard.

DIESSELHORST, M. (1959). *Die Lehre des Hugo Grotius vom Versprechen*. Forschungen zur neueren Privatrechtsgeschichte. Cologne and Graz: Böhlau.

——(1983). Die Gerechtgkeitsdefinition Ulpians in D 1. 1. 10 pr. und die praecepta juris nach D 1. 1. 10. 1 sowie ihre Rezeption bei Leipniz und Kant. In: *Römisches Recht in der europäischen Tradition: Symposion aus Anlass des 75. Geburtstages von Franz Wieacker*. Ebelsbach: Gremer: 185–211.

DIEVOET, G. VAN (1980). De ontwikkeling van de rechtswetenschappen. *AGN* 7: 311–20.

DIONISOTTI, C. (1971). Filologia umanistica e testi giuridici fra quattro e cinquecento. In: *La critica del testo: Atti del secondo congresso inter-*

nazionale della Società italiana di storia del dirrito. Florence: Olschki. i. 189–204.

Donahue, C. (1985). Noodt, Titius and the natural law school, the occupation of wild animals and the intersection of property and tort. In: *Satura Roberto Feenstra oblata*. Fribourg: Editions universitaires: 609–29.

Dooren, W. van (1983–4). De godsdienstdialoog: Discussies over grondslag en verscheidenheid van godsdiensten. *Wijsgerig perspectief op maatschappij en wetenschap* 24: 45–51.

Duker, C. A. (1711). *Opuscula varia de latinitate jurisconsultorum veterum*. Leiden: J. van der Linden.

Dworkin, R. M. (1977). *Taking rights seriously*. Cambridge, Mass.: Harvard Univ. Press.

Eck, C. van (1688). *Vindiciae juris academici, decreto et auctoritate senatus Academiae Franequeranae scriptae et vulgatae contra . . . Ulrici Huberi enarrationem Authenticae 'Habita, Cod. 'ne filius pro patre' etc. conveniatur*. Franeker: Gyselaar.

Eckhard, C. H. and Walch, C. F. (1802). *C. H. Eckhardi Hermeneutica juris* recensuit perpetuisque notis illustravit C. F. Walch; editio nova auctior et emendatior curante C. W. Walch. Leipzig: Weidmann.

Eekhof, A. (1921). *De theologische faculteit te Leiden in de 17e eeuw*. Utrecht: Ruys.

Evers, G. A., Gras, E. J., Keyman, J. M., and Reynvaan, M. J. (1937). *Lijst van gedrukte geschriften over de Rijksuniversiteit te Utrecht: Proeve eener bibliographie 1636–1936*. Utrecht: Oosthoek.

Eyssell, A. P. T. (1860). *Doneau, sa vie et ses œvres*. Dijon: Decailly and Lamarche.

Faber, K.-G. (1982). *Theorie der Geschichtswissenschaft*. Munich: Beck.

Feenstra, R. (1953). *Interpretatio multiplex: Een beschouwing over de zgn. crisis van het Romeinse recht*. Zwolle: Tjeenk Willink.

——(1971*a*). Quelques remarques sur le texte de la Glose d'Accurse sur le Digeste vieux. In: *La critica del testo: Atti del secondo congresso internazionale della Società italiana di storia del diritto*. Florence: Olschki: 205–25; also in: R. Feenstra, *Fata iuris romani*: Études d'histoire du droit. Leiden: Univ. Press, 1974: 194–214.

——(1971*b*). De oorsprong van Hugo de Groot's leer over de dwaling. In: *Met eerbiedigende werking, opstellen L. J. Hijmans van den Bergh*. Deventer: Kluwer: 87–101.

——(1972). L'Influence de la scolastique espagnole sur Grotius en droit privé: Quelques expériences dans les questions de fond et de forme, concernant notamment les doctrines de l'erreur et l'enrichissement sans cause. In: R. Feenstra, *Fata iuris romani*. Leiden: Univ. Press: 1974, 338–63.

——(1974). Impossibilitas and Clausula rebus sic stantibus: Some aspects of frustration of contract in continental legal history up to Grotius (1974).

In: R. Feenstra, *Fata iuris romani*. Leiden: Presse universitaire de Leyde, 1974: 364–91.

FEENSTRA, R. 1978). Der Eigentumsbegriff bei Hugo Grotius im Licht einiger mittelalterlicher und spätscholastischer Quellen. In: *Festschrift für Franz Wieacker zum 70. Geburtstag*. Göttingen: Vandenhoeck & Ruprecht: 209–34.

——(1982*a*). Jacobus Maestertius (1610–1658): Zijn juridisch onderwijs in Leiden en het Leuvense disputatiesysteem van Gerardus Corselius. *Legal History Review* 50: 297–335.

——(1982*b*). Real rights and their classification in the 17th century: The role of Heinrich Hahn and Gerhard Feltmann. *The Juridical Review*: 106–20.

——(1984). Ein später Vertreter der niederländischen Schule: Johann Ortwin Westenberg (1667–1737). In: *Festschrift Heinz Hübner zum 70. Geburtstag am 7. November 1984*. Berlin and New York: de Gruyter: 47–62.

——(1985*a*). Johann Friedrich Böckelmann (1632–1681): Een markant Leids hoogleraar in de rechten. In: *Bestuurders en geleerden*, essays for J. J. Woltjer. Amsterdam and Dieren: De Bataafsche Leeuw: 137–50.

——(1985*b*). De Franeker juridische faculteit in nationaal en internationaal perspectief: Inleidende beschouwingen gevolgd door een studie over juridische onderwijsliteratuur sinds het midden van de zeventiende eeuw. In: G. Th. Jensma, F. R. H. Smit, and F. Westra (eds.), *Universiteit te Franeker: Bijdragen tot de geschiedenis van de Friese hogeschool*. Leeuwarden: Fryske Akademy: 289–304.

——(1985*c*). Een terugblik op de dissertatie als element in de juridische opleiding. *Ars aequi* 34: pp. xviii–xx.

——(1986). Scottish–Dutch legal relations in the seventeenth and eighteenth centuries. In: T. C. Smouth (ed.), *Scotland and Europe 1200–1850*. Edinburgh: 128–42.

——and WAAL, C. J. D. (1975). *Seventeenth-century Leyden law professors and their influence on the development of the civil law: A study of Bronchorst, Vinnius and Vœt*. Amsterdam and Oxford: North-Holland Publishing Company.

FERRINI, C. (1899). *Diritto penale romano*. Milan: Hoepli.

FISCHER, H. F. W. D. (1961). De adviezen van de Leidse professoren, in het bijzonder tijdens het professoraat van Everardus Bronchorst (1587–1627). *Legal History Review* 29: 463–83.

FLORES SELLES, C. (ed.) (1980). *Epistolario de Antonio Agustin*. Acta salamanticensia filosofia y letras, 115. Salamanca: Univ. Press.

FRANSEN, G. (1946). *Le Dol dans la conclusion des actes juridiques: Évolution des doctrines et système du code canonique*. Gembloux: Duculot.

FRIER, B. W. (1980). *Landlords and tenants in imperial Rome*. Princeton: Univ. Press.

FRIJHOFF, W. T. M. (1981). *La Société néerlandaise et ses gradués, 1575–1814: une recherche sérielle sur le statut des intellectuels à partir des registres universitaires*. Amsterdam: APA Holland Univ. Press.

GABRIELI, F. P. (1968). Gerard Noodt. In: *Novissimo digesto italiano*. Turin: Utet. xi: 327.

GALVANI, M. A. (1650). *De usufructu dissertationes variae*. Padua. (I used the Tübingen edn. of 1788.)

GASPARRI, P. (ed.) (1933–62). *Codicis iuris canonici fontes*, 9 vols. Rome: Typis polyglottis vaticanis.

GEBAUER, G. C. (1764). *Narratio de Henrico Brenkmanno, de manuscriptis brenkmannianis, de suis in Corpore Juris Civilis conatibus et laboribus: accedunt Mantissa de libro longe rarissimo bibliothecæ Antonii Augustini et vita Henrici Newtoni*. Göttingen: Vid. Vandenhoeck.

Gelders zilver (1955). Gemeentemuseum Arnhem 1955 (= Werken Gelre no. 28). Arnhem: Vereniging Gelre.

GENDEREN, J. VAN (1953). *Herman Witsius*. The Hague: Guido de Bres.

GERRETZEN, J. G. (1940). *Schola hemsterhusiana: De herleving der Grieksche studiën aan de Nederlandsche universiteiten in de achttiende eeuw van Perizonius tot en met Valckenaer*. Nijmegen and Utrecht: Dekker & van de Vegt.

GEURTS, P. A. M. and JANSSEN, A. E. M. (1975). Gelderland van 1566–1609. In: J. J. Poelhekke, G. J. Mentink, W. Jappe Alberts, and H. K. Roessingh (eds.), *Geschiedenis van Gelderland 1492–1795*. Zutphen: Walburg Press. ii. 97–131.

GILMORE, M. P. (1941). *Argument from Roman law in political thought 1200–1600*. [1941] Reissue New York: Russell & Russell, 1967.

GIRARD, P. F. and SENN, F. (1967). *Textes de droit romain*, i. 7th edn. by a group of Romanists. Paris: Dalloz.

GLÜCK, C. F. (1867). *Ausführliche Erläuterung der Pandecten nach Hellfeld: Ein Commentar*, iv. 3rd imp. Erlangen: Palm & Enke.

GOU, L. DE (1943). *De weeskamer van 's-Gravenhage*. The Hague: Trio.

GOUDSMIT, J. E. (1866–80). *Pandecten-systeem*, i. *Algemeen deel*; ii. *Verbintenissen, algemene leer*. Leiden: Hazenberg.

GOUGH, J. W. (1968). Introduction. In: Locke, 1968.

GRAADT JONCKERS, R. H. (1869). Een kloeke Geldersche vrouw. *Geldersche Volksalmanak*: 168.

GRAFTON, A. (1977). Review of E. J. Kenney, *The classical text* (1974). *Journal of Roman Studies* 67: 171–6.

——(1983). *Joseph Scaliger: A study in the history of classical scholarship*, i. *Textual Criticism and exegesis*. Oxford: Clarendon.

GRONOVIUS, J. (1712). *Honoraria dissertatio de lege regia, habita die et loco solito quum magnifici rectoris insignia denuo deposuit*. Leiden: Luchtmans.

HAGEMEISTER, J. A. (1720). *Dissertatio juridica inauguralis de dominio ex contracto doloso non translato*. Halle: C. Henckel.

HALL, J. VAN (1824). *Oratio de meritis Belgarum in excolendo historico juris Romani studio*. Amsterdam: Stadsdrukkerij.

HALLEBEEK, J. (1986). *Quia natura nichil privatum: Aspecten van de eigendomsvraag in het werk van Thomas van Aquino (1225–1274)*. Nijmegen: Gerard Noodt Instituut.

HAMMERSTEIN, N. (1972). *Jus und Historie: Ein Beitrag zur Geschichte des historischen Denkens an deutschen Universitäten im späten 17. und 18. Jahrhundert*. Göttingen: Vandenhoeck & Ruprecht.

HARDUNG, S. (1934). *Die Vorladung vor Gottes Gericht: Ein Beitrag zur rechtlichen und religiösen Volkskunde*. Bühl-Baden: Konkordia a.g.

HARTKAMP, A. S. (1971). *Der Zwang im römischen Privatrecht*. Amsterdam: Hakkert.

HASSELT, G. VAN (1807). J. A(rntzenius), Considerabilen toeloop voor de H. School van Franequer, onder G. Noodt (Edition of a letter from Noodt to Braunius, Franeker, 18 Oct. 1682) In: G. van Hasselt, *Geldersch Maandwerk*. i: 351–3.

HAUBOLD, C. G. (1809). *Institutiones juris Romani litterariae*. Leipzig: Hinrichs.

——(1812). Ueber die Versuche, das prätorische Edict herzustellen. *Hugo's Civilistisches Magazin*, 3rd imp. Berlin: Mylius. ii. 285–326 (1st imp., 1797).

HAUSMANINGER, H. (ed.) (1980). *Casebook zum römischen Sachenrecht*, 4th imp. Vienna: Manzsche Verlags- und Universitätsbuchhandlung.

HAZARD, P. (1973). *The European Mind 1680–1715*, trans. J. Lewis May. Harmondsworth: Penguin.

HELLFELD, J. A. (1806). *Iurisprudentia forensis secundum Pandectarum ordinem*, i. New edn. Jena: Croeker.

HERBERGER, M. (1981). *Dogmatik: Zur Geschichte von Begriff und Methode in Medizin und Jurisprudenz*. Jus commune Sonderhefte, 12. Frankfurt: Klostermann.

——(1985). Hanc methodum a mathematicarum scientiarum studiosis mutuari possumus: Balthasar Branchu und die logikorientierte Interpretation von Codex 8. 40. 22. *Jus commune* 13: 107–23.

HERMESDORF, B. H. D. (1970*a*). Petrus de Greve: Naar aanleiding van het eerste lesrooster (1656) van de kwartierlijke universiteit te Nijmegen. *Numaga* 17: 4–8.

——(1970*b*). Een vluchtige blik in de Kwartierlijke Akademie van Nijmegen. *Numaga* 17: 108–13.

——(1971*a*). Rumoer in de Nijmeegse Kwartierlijke Akademie. *Numaga* 18: 24–8.

——(1971*b*). Casus-colleges in de kwartierlijke academie van Nijmegen. In: *Uit het recht*, ed. P. J. Verdam. Deventer: Kluwer: 161–73.

Hoetink, H. R. (1928). Een onuitgegeven advies van Noodt, Schulting en Vitriarius. *Weekblad voor privaatrecht notarisambt en registratie* 59, no. 3046, pp. 345–6.

——(1949). *Historische rechtsbeschouwing*. Rectorial address (English trans. in Hoetink, 1986). Amsterdam.

——(1986). *Opera selecta*, ed. J. A. Ankum and G. C. J. J. van den Bergh. Zutphen: Terra.

Holzapfel, O. and Erler, A. (1973). Josaphat. *HRG* 2: 424–6.

Hooft, J. A. M. van 't (1978). Nijmegen en de vredesonderhandelingen 1675–1679. *Numaga* 25: 113–36.

Horn, E. (1894). *Die Disputationen und Promotionen an den deutschen Universitäten vornehmlich seit dem 16. Jh.* Centralblatt für Bibliothekswesen, 11. Leipzig.

Hovy, L. (1980). Schikking in strafzaken in Holland tijdens de Republiek. *Nederlands archievenblad* 84: 413–29.

Huber, U. (1682). *Auspicia domestica exercitationum, quibus otium, quod Illustres frisiae ordines ei apud Academiam suam fecerunt, occupare constituit. Accedunt amoeniora quaedam alia.* Franeker: J. Gyselaar.

——(1687). *Praelectiones juris civilis pars prior, quae est secundum Institutiones Justinianaeas* . . . Franeker: J. Gyselaar, H. Amama, and Z. Taedama.

——(1688*a*). *De ratione juris docendi et discendi diatribe per modum dialogi* (1st imp. Franeker, 1684). Ed. with his *Digressiones justinianeae in partes duas, quarum altera nova, distinctae, quibus varia et imprimis humaniora juris continentur; insertus est de jure in re et ad rem, quod dicitur, tractatus et adjecta De ratione* . . . Franeker: J. Gyselaar, H. Amama, and Z. Taedama (with separate pagination of the dialogue).

——(1688*b*). *Digressiones justinianeae in partes duas, quarum altera nova, distinctae, quibus varia et imprimis humaniora juris continentur* . . . Franeker: J. Gyselaar, H. Amama, and Z. Taedama.

——(1690). *Praelectiones juris Romani pars III. Quae est ad Libros unum et triginta posteriores Pandectarum.* Franeker: H. Amama and Z. Taedama.

——(1700). *Eunomia romana sive censura censurae juris justinianaei.* Franeker: L. Strick.

——(1978). *Oratio [III] qua disseritur quamobrem jus publicum olim in academia nostra professione publica non sit honoratum*, tr. by F. Akkerman, T. J. Veen, and A. G. Westenbrink; notes by T. J. Veen. Zwolle: Tjeenk Willink.

Huber, Z. (1703). *Dissertationes juridicae et philologicae* . . . Franeker: H. Amama, A. Jelneri, and B. Wybranda.

Hugo, G. (1830). *Lehrbuch der Geschichte des römischen rechts seit Justinian oder der meist civilistischen gelehrten Geschichte.* 3rd imp. Berlin: Mylius.

HUGO, H. (1738). *De prima scribendi origine et universa rei literariae antiquitate; cui notas, opusculum de Scribis, Apologiam pro Waechtlero, praefationem et indices adjecit C. H. Trotz*. Utrecht: H. Besseling.

Icones Leidenses (1973): *De portretverzameling van de Rijksuniversiteit te Leiden*, samengesteld in opdracht van de Stichting Historische commissie voor de Leidse universiteit. Leiden: Rijksuniversiteit.

Index int. E. Levy and E. Rabel (eds.), *Index interpolationum quae in Iustiniani Digestis inesse dicuntur*. Weimar: Böhlaus Nachf, 1929–35.

Index int. Cod. G. Broggini (ed.), *Index interpolationum quae in Iustiniani Codice inesse dicuntur*. Weimar: Böhlaus Nachf, 1969.

S'JACOB, P. (1936). *Geschiedenis, theorie en practijk van artikel 74 Wetboek van Strafrecht*. The Hague: Nijhoff.

JANSEN, C. J. H. (1987*a*). Over de 18e eeuwse docenten natuurrecht aan Nederlandse universiteiten en door hen gebruikte leerboeken. *Legal History Review* 55: 103–15.

—— (1987*b*). *Natuurrecht of Romeins recht: Een studie over leven en werk van F. A. van der Marck (1719–1800) in het licht van de opvattingen van zijn tijd*. Leiden: Brill.

JANSSEN, A. E. M. (1983). Remonstrantse remotie in Nijmegen (1622–1623). *Numaga* 30: 68–75.

JENNISKENS, A. H. (1973). *Magistraat te Nijmegen 1619–1648* (Nijmeegse studiën, 2). Nijmegen: Gemeentearchief.

JHERING, R. (1857). Unsere Aufgabe. *Jahrbücher für die Dogmatik des heutigen römischen und deutschen Privatrechts* 1: 1–52.

—— (1861). Culpa in contrahendo oder Schadensersatz bei nichtiger oder nicht zur Perfektion gelangten Verträgen. *Jahrbücher für die Dogmatik des heutigen römischen und deutschen Privatrechts* 4: 1–112.

JOCHER, C. G. (1750–1). *Allgemeines Gelehrten-Lexicon*, 4 vols. Leipzig. Repr. Hildesheim: Olms, 1960.

JONCKBLOET, W. J. A. (1864). *Gedenkboek der Hoogeschool te Groningen ter gelegenheid van haar vijfde halve eeuwfeest op last van den Akademischen Senaat uitgegeven*. Groningen: Wolters.

JUGLER, J. F. (1773–80). *Beyträge zur juristischen Biographie oder genauere litterärische und critische Nachrichten von dem Leben und den Schriften verstorbener Rechtsgelehrten auch Staatsmänner, welche sich in Europa berühmt gemacht haben*, 6 vols.; i. Leipzig: J. S. Heinsius, 1773; ii. ibid., 1775; iii. Leipzig: P. G. Kummer, 1777; iv. ibid., 1778; v. ibid., 1779; vi. ibid., 1780.

KAN, J. VAN (1922). François Hotman en de codificatiepolitiek van zijn tijd. *Tijdschrift voor rechtsgeschiedenis* 3: 1–11.

KARSTKAREL, P. and TERPSTRA, R. (1985). Van Jeruzalem tot het Fries Athene: Het kruisherenklooster en de academiegebouwen te Franeker. In: G. Th. Jensma, F. R. H. Smit, and F. Westra (eds.), *Universiteit te*

Franeker 1585–1811: Bijdragen tot de geschiedenis van de Friese hogeschool. Leeuwarden: Fryske Akademy: 206–22.

KASER, M. (1971). *Das römische Privatrecht*. 1: *Das altrömische, das vorklassische und klassische Recht*. 2nd imp. Munich: Beck.

——(1975). *Das römische Privatrecht*. 2: *Die nachklassischen Entwicklungen*. 2nd imp. Munich: Beck.

——(1978). Zur Problematik der römischen Rechtsquellenlehre. In: *Festschrift für Werner Flume*. Cologne: Schmidt: 101.

KAUFMANN, H. (1958). *Rezeption und usus modernus der actio legis Aquiliae*. Forschungen zur neueren Privatrechtsgeschichte. Cologne: Böhlau.

KELLEY, D. R. (1984). *Historians and the law in postrevolutionary France*. Princeton: Univ. Press.

KELLY, W. A. (1975). The library of Lord George Douglas. MA thesis, Univ. of Strathclyde.

KENNEY, E. J. (1974). *The classical text: Aspects of editing in the age of the printed book* (Sather classical lectures, 44). Berkeley, Los Angeles, and London: Univ. California Press.

KERCKHOFFS-DE HEY, A. J. M. (1970). Een Gorkumse erfeniskwestie. *Holland* 2, nr. 4/5: 108–17.

KERNKAMP, G. W. (1936). *De Utrechtsche Academie 1636–1815. De Utrechtsche Universiteit 1636–1936*, i. Utrecht: Oosthoek.

KLIBANSKY, R. (1968). Preface. In: Locke, 1968.

KLUCKHOHN, C. (1964). Cultural relativity. In: J. Gould and W. L. Kolb (eds.), *A dictionary of the social sciences*. London: Tavistock: 160–2.

KOLMAN, R. J. (1952). *De reductie van Nijmegen (1591), voor- en naspel*. Groningen: Wolters.

KOP, C. VAN DER (1769–82). *Nieuw Nederlandsch Advys-boek, dienende tot een vervolg op het Nederlands Advys-boek van mr. Isaac van den Berg*, 2 vols. The Hague: H. Backhuysen.

KOSSMANN, E. H. (1960). *Politieke theorie in het zeventiende-eeuwse Nederland*. Verhand. Kon. Ned. Akademie van Wetenschappen, Afd. Letterk. NR 67, no 2. Amsterdam, North-Holland Uitg. Mij.

KUNST, A. J. M. (1969). *Historische ontwikkeling van het recht*, i, 2nd imp Zwolle: Tjeenk Willink.

KUYK, J. VAN. (1920–1). Historische wetsuitlegging. *Legal History Review* 2: 1–41.

LABROUSSE, E. (1985). *Bayle*. Trans. by Denys Potts. Oxford: Univ. Press.

LAMZWEERDE, M. A. VAN (1776). *Consultatien advysen ende advertissementen van rechten*. Arnhem: W. Troost. (The Voorreden gives a survey of famous jurists from Guelders.)

LANGE, H. (1980). Vom Adel des Doctor. In: K. Luig and D. Liebs (eds.), *Das Profil des Juristen in der europäischen Tradition: Symposion aus Anlass des 70. Geburtstages von Franz Wieacker*. Ebelsbach: Gremer: 279–94.

LEEB, I. L. (1973). *The ideological origins of the Batavian revolution: History and politics in the Dutch Republic 1747–1800.* The Hague: Nijhoff.

LEIBNIZ, G. W. (1974). *Nova methodus discendae docendaeque iurisprudentiae*, with an introduction by Gustav Hartmann. Glashütten im Taunus: Verlag Detlev Auvermann.

LENEL, O. (1927). *Das edictum perpetuum: Ein Versuch zu seiner Wiederherstellung*, 3rd imp. Leipzig: Tauchnitz. Repr. Aalen: Scientia, 1956.

LEVERLAND, B. N. and MAANEN, R. C. J. VAN (1975). *De Leidse leenbank: Drie eeuwen spanning tussen winst en weldadigheid.* Leiden: Gemeentelijke Archiefdienst.

LIEBERWIRTH, R. (ed.) (1960). *Christian Thomasius, über die Folter: Untersuchungen zur Geschichte der Folter.* Thomasiana, 4. Weimar: Böhlau.

—— (1984). Die französischen Kultureinflüsse auf den deutschen Frühaufklärer Christian Thomasius. *Wissenschaftliche Zeitschrift der Universität Halle* 33: 63–73.

LINDEBOOM, G. A. (ed.) (1958). *Haller in Holland: het dagboek van Albrecht von Haller van zijn verblijf in Holland (1725–1727).* Delft: Gist- en Spiritusfabriek. Repr. Amsterdam: Rodopi, 1979.

—— (ed.) (1962). *Boerhaave's correspondence*, i. Leiden: Brill.

—— (1968). *Herman Boerhaave, the man and his work.* London: Methuen.

—— (1969). Het eerste lesrooster (1656) van de Kwartierlijke Universiteit te Nijmegen. *Numaga* 16: 395–401.

LOCKE, J. (1968). *Epistola de tolerantia: A letter on toleration.* Latin text ed. with a preface by R. Klibansky; English transl. with an introduction and notes by J. W. Gough. Oxford: Clarendon.

—— (1982). *The correspondence of John Locke*, ed. E. S. de Beer, vii. Oxford: Clarendon.

LOPEZ DE HARO (1985). *David en Felix Lopez de Haro (1627–1694) boekverkopers op het Rapenburg over de Academie: vijf bijdragen.* Leiden: Bibliotheek der Rijksuniversiteit and Sir Thomas Browne Institute.

LUIG, K. (1977). Der Geltungsgrund des römischen Rechts im 18. Jahrhundert in Italien, Frankreich und Deutschland. In: *La formazione storica del diritto moderno in Europa: Atti del terzo congresso internazionale della Società italiana di storia del diritto.* Florence: Olschki. ii: 819–45.

—— (1977*b*). Christian Thomasius. In: M. Stolleis (ed.), *Staatsdenker im 17. und 18. Jahrhundert: Reichspublizistik—Politik—Naturrecht.* Frankfurt/Main: A. Metzner: 228–47.

MACCORMACK, G. (1983). Juristic use of the term dolus: contract. *Zeitschrift der Savigny Stiftung für Rechtsgeschichte, romanistische Abteilung* 100: 524.

MCGAHAGAN, T. A. (1976). *Cartesianism in the Netherlands, 1639–1676:*

The new science and the Calvinist counter-reformation. Xerox University Microfilms.

Maffei, D. (1968). *Gli inizi dell'umanesimo giuridico*, 2nd imp. Milan: Giuffrè.

Maris, A. J. (1981). Prins Willem III en het provisionele regeringsbestel in Gelre en Zutphen van 1674. *Bijdragen en mededelingen Gelre* 72: 139–74.

——(1984). Prins Willem III en het provisionele regeringsbestel in Gelre en Zutphen van 1674: De benoemingen in de hoofdstad Nijmegen. *Bijdragen en mededelingen Gelre* 75: 124–31.

Maris, A. J. and Driessen, H. L. (1978). *Het Archief van het Hof van Gelre en Zutphen (1543–1795) het Hof van Justitie (1795–1802) en het Departementaal Gerechtshof (1802–1811)*, i. Inleiding/Een geschiedkundig overzicht etc. Arnhem: Rijksarchief in Gelderland.

Martens van Sevenhoven, A. H. (1977). Leur. In: his *Een keuze uit zijn geschriften*. Werken Gelre, 35. Arnhem: Vereniging Gelre: 137–43.

Mayer-Maly, T. (1979). Kinderaussetzung. In: *Kleine Pauly* 3: 214.

Medicus, D. (1986). Entdeckungsgeschichte der culpa in contrahendo. In: *Iuris professio; Festgabe für Max Kaser zum 80. Geburtstag*. Vienna–Cologne–Graz: Böhlau: 169–81.

Meijers, E. M. (1954–5). *Verzamelde privaatrechtelijke opstellen*, 3 vols. Leiden: Univ. Press.

Meyer, T. J. (1971). *Kritiek als herwaardering: het levenswerk van Jacob Perizonius*. Leiden: Univ. Press.

Meylan, P. (1937). *Jean Barbeyrac, 1674–1744, et les débuts de l'enseignement du droit dans l'ancienne Académie de Lausanne: Contribution à l'histoire du droit naturel*. Lausanne: Recueil de travaux de l'Université de Lausanne.

Miscellaneae observationes: see van de Water, J., 1733.

Moerkerk van Steel, C. B. A. (ed.) (1856). Foreword to L. A. Warnkönig, *Regtswijsgeerte of natuurlijke regtsleer*. Utrecht: Kemink.

Mommsen, T. (1899). *Römisches Strafrecht*. Anastatic repr. Graz: Akademische Druck- und Verlagsanstalt, 1955.

Montaigne (1962). *Œuvres complètes*. ed. by Albert Thibaudet and Maurice Rat; introduction and notes by Maurice Rat. Bibliothèque de la Pléiade. Paris: Gallimard.

Moorman van Kappen, O. (1983). Het habeas corpus-beginsel in het oud-Nijmeegse recht. *Numaga* 30: 76–85.

Morel, H. (1970). La Place de la Lex Regia dans l'histoire des idées politiques. In: *Études offertes à Jean Macqueron*. Aix-en-Provence: Faculté de droit et des sciences économiques: 545–55.

Mulder, G. E. (1984). *Om het recht: Verzamelde geschriften*. Arnhem: Gouda Quint.

Neck, J. van (1770). *Specimen historico-iuridicum, quo inquiritur, quamdiu antiquitus apud Romanos obtinuerit ius necandi et exponendi infantes*. Leiden.

Nelissen, A. P. L. (1880). *Huur en vervreemding*. 's-Hertogenbosch: Lutkie & Cranenburg.

Neocorus, L. and Sikens, H. (1697–9). *Bibliotheca librorum novorum*, 5 vols. Utrecht.

Neustetel, L. J. (1818). *Bonae fidei negotia dolo inita non esse nulla*. Heidelberg: J. Engelmann.

Nève, P. L. (1972). *Het Rijkskamergerecht en de Nederlanden: Competentie—territoir—archieven*. Assen: van Gorcum.

Nicéron, R. P. (1729–45). *Mémoires pour servir à l'histoire des hommes illustres dans la République des lettres*. Paris: Briasson. [Noodt: 1731, xvi: 303–20].

Nicholas, B. (1962). *An introduction to Roman law*. Oxford: Clarendon.

Niellius, J. (1597). *Controversiae juris feudalis disputationibus XI enucleatae* . . . 2nd edn. Marburg: P. Egenolphus.

Noodt, G. (1674). *Probabilia juris civilis liber primus*. Leiden: Felix Lopez.

——(1784). *Redevoering over het regt der opperste magt* . . . Amsterdam: J. Weppelman.

Noodt, W. (1921). *Geschichte der Familie Noodt von 1540 bis 1920*. Altona.

Oldewelt, W. F. H. (ed.) (1945). *Kohier van de personeele quotisatie te Amsterdam over het jaar 1742*. Amsterdam: Genootschap Amstelodamum.

Olivier-Martin, F. (1948). *Histoire du droit français des origines à la Révolution*. Paris: Domat Montchrestien.

Org (1984). J. Zandstra, Deventer. In: M. A. M. Franken and R. M. Kemperink (eds.), *Herstel, hervorming of behoud? Tien Overijsselse steden in de Patriottentijd 1780–1787*. Overijsselse Historische Bijdragen; Verslagen en Mededelingen Vereeniging tot beoefening van Overijsselsch Regt en Geschiedenis 99: 32–46.

Osler, D. J. (1983). Humanist philology and Justinian's Digest. Ph.D. thesis Univ. of Cambridge.

——(1985). Budaeus and Roman law. *Jus commune* 13: 195–212.

Otte, G. (1971). *Dialektik und Jurisprudenz*. Ius commune Sonderhefte, 1. Frankfurt/Main: Klostermann.

——(1983). Leibniz und die juristische Methode. *Zeitschrift für neuere Rechtsgeschichte* 5: 1–21.

Otto, E. (ed.) (1733–5). *Thesaurus juris Romani continens rariora meliorum interpretum opuscula in quibus jus Romanum emendatur, explicatur, illustratur, itemque classicis aliisque auctoribus lumen accenditur*, 5 vols. 2nd edn. Utrecht: Broedelet.

Oven, J. C. van. (1933). Le Droit romain aux Pays-Bas. *Atti del congresso internazionale di diritti romano, Bologna 1933*. Pavia, 1934. ii: 25–55.

——(1953). D 4.3.7 pr.: Contribution à l'histoire du dol dans les conventions. *Studi in memoria di Emilio Albertario*, i. Milan. Giuffrè: 275–92.

Palazzini Finetti, L. (1953). *Storia della ricerca delle interpolazioni nel Corpus Juris giustinianeo*. Milan: Giuffrè.

Paquot (1760–70). *Mémoires pour servir à l'histoire littéraire des Pays-Bas*. Louvain: Imprimerie académique. [Noodt: 1760, i: 181–92].

Pater, C. de (1979). *Petrus van Musschenbroek (1692–1761), een Newtoniaans natuuronderzoeker*. Leiden: Museum Boerhaave.

Pauw, W. (1964–72). *Observationes tumultuariae novae*, ed. H. F. W. D. Fischer *et al.* 3 vols. Haarlem: Tjeenk Willink.

Peckius, P. (1647). Tractatus de testamentis conjugum. In: his *Opera omnia*. Antwerp: H. Verdussen.

Piano Mortari, V. (1978). *Diritto logica metodo nel secolo xvi*. Naples: Jovene.

P[ilato] de T[assulo] (1774). *Traité des loix civiles*, 2 vols. The Hague and London: P. F. Gosse and Société typographique.

Pithou, P. (1656). *Mosaycarum et Romanarum legum collatio . . . ex Bibliotheca P. Pithoei . . .* Heidelberg: S. Braun.

Poel, J. van der (1942). *Rondom compositie en compromis (fiscale studie in bestuurs- en strafrecht)*. Utrecht: Kemink.

Poelhekke, J. J. (1973). *Geen blijder maer in tachtigh jaer: Verspreide studiën over de crisisperiode 1648–1651*. Zutphen: Walburg Press.

——(1975). Gelderland van 1609–1672. In: J. J. Poelhekke, G. J. Mentink, W. Jappe Alberts, and H. K. Roessingh (eds.), *Geschiedenis van Gelderland 1492–1795*. Zutphen: Walburg Press. ii. 133–210.

——(1978). *Frederik Hendrik, Prins van Oranje: Een biografisch drieluik*. Zutphen: Walburg Press.

Poll, L. van de (1700). *De exheredatione et praeteritione Romana atque hodierna liber singularis*. Amsterdam: F. Halma. 2nd imp., Utrecht: W. A. van Poolsum.

Popkin, R. H. (1967). 'Skepticism'. In: P. Edwards (ed.), *The Encyclopedia of philosophy*. New York and London: Macmillan. vii: 449–61.

Précis (1810): *Précis des discussions et des deliberations du Conseil d'état sur le code criminel traduit de l'originel hollandois*. Amsterdam: van Esveldt and Holtrop.

Puchta, G. F. (1847). *Cursus der Institutionen*, 2 vols. I used the 10th imp., ed. P. Krüger. Leipzig: Breitkopf & Härtel, 1893.

——(1877). *Pandekten*. I used the 12th edn., ed. Th. Schirmer. Leipzig: J. A. Barth, 1877. (1st edn., 1838.)

Putschius, H. (ed.) (1605). *Grammaticae latinae auctores antiqui*, ed. H. Putschius. Hanover: Typis Wechelianis, Apud Claudium Mamium et haeredes Joannis Aubrii.

Putte, P. C. A. van (1978). Twee brieven van Joan Dullaert met den aankleve van dien. In: *Nieuwe tegenstellingen op Nederlands taalgebied*, ed. B. van den Berg. Utrecht: 108–29.

Raab, C. (1729). Chr. Raabius, *Jurisjurandi verus ac legitimus usus, ejusque ecclesias protestantium devastans abusus, dissertatione theologica, praeside Chr. Raabio, respondente Joanne Friderico Scheffero Berleburgensi, . . . Juncto ei ejusdem argumenti sermone academico habito cum a.d. 17 cal. Nov. 1729 Fasces Academicos secundum susciperet, cum necessariis supplementis nunc edito*. Duisburg: Joh. Sas; also sold by S. Luchtmans, Leiden.

Radelant, W. (1637). *Decisiones posthumae curiae provincialis Trajectinae*. Utrecht: I. a Doorn.

Rademaker, C. S. M. (1967). *Gerardus Joannes Vossius*. Zwolle: Tjeenk Willink.

Regneri ab Oosterga, C. (1638). *Demonstratio logicae verae juridicae*. Leiden: Justus Livius.

——(1640). *De iniustitia quarundam legum Romanarum libri duo: Contra Jacobum Maestertium Jctum*. Leiden: Justus Livius.

Rechtsgeleerde (1767–72): *De regtsgeleerde in spectatoriale vertogen*. Amsterdam: Houttuyn.

Reibstein, E. (1972). *Volkssouveränität und Freiheitslehre: Texte und Studien zur politischen Theorie des 14.–18. Jahrhunderts*, ed. C. Schott. 2 vols. Fribourg and Munich: K. Alber.

Reiffenstuel, A. (1864–70). *Jus canonicum universum*, 7 vols. Paris.

Reinold, B. H. (1755). *Opuscula juridica adhuc rariora, recensuit illa, notulis instruxit, in Praefatione Vitam auctoris clarissimi exposuit, ac Dissertationem singularem de insignibus Germanorum in jurisprudentiam elegantiorem meritis praetermisit J. F. Jugler*. Leiden: Luchtmans.

Reynolds, L. D. and Wilson, N. G. (1974). *Scholars and scribes: A guide to the transmission of Greek and Latin literature*, 2nd imp. Oxford: Clarendon.

Riccobono, S. (1947). Interpretatio duplex del Fr. 2 D De transactionibus II, 15. *Bull. dell' Ist. di diritto romano 'Vittorio Scialoja'* NS 8–9: 6–29.

Ridder-Symoens, H. de (1985). L'Aristocratisation des universités au xvie siècle. *Zesty naukowe uniwersytetu Jagiellonskiego*, 761. Prace historyczene Z, 79: 37–47.

Rietbergen, P. J. A. N. (1983). Lambert Biesman, de eerste Nijmeegse Indievaarder (1595–1597) en wereldreiziger (1598–1601). *Numaga* 30: 18–22.

Rizzo, S. (1984). *Il lessico filologico degli umanisti*, 2nd imp. Rome: Edizioni di storia e letteratura.

Roberti, F. (1968). Aborto, diritto canonico. *Novissimo digesto italiano*. Turin: Unione tipografico-editrice torinese. i: 87.

Roberts, A. A. (1933). *A guide to Vœt including the life of Johannes Vœt with portraits, particulars of translations, and detailed index to the Commentarius ad Pandectas*. Pretoria (by the author).

Rodenburg, C. (1653). *Tractatus de jure conjugum . . . cum tractatione praeliminari de jure quod oritur ex statutorum, vel consuetudinum discrepantium conflictu*. Utrecht: G. Zyl & Th. v. Ackersdijck.

Roelevink, J. (1986). *Gedicteerd verleden: Het onderwijs in de algemene geschiedenis aan de universiteit te Utrecht, 1735–1839*. Amsterdam and Maarssen: APA Holland Univ. Press.

Rogier, L. J. (1954). De Ware Vrijheid als oligarchie. In: *Algemene geschiedenis der Nederlanden*. Utrecht and Antwerpen: de Haan and Standaard. vii: 195–212.

Rompaey, J. van. (1961). Het compositierecht in Vlaanderen van de veertiende tot de achttiende eeuw. *Legal History Review* 29: 43–79.

Roukens, Th. L. (1767). *Oratio scholastica in laudem Gerhardi Noodt . . . accedit ejusdem Gerhardi Noodt Oratio funebris in obitum . . . Petri de Greve*. Nijmegen.

——(1769). *Oratio de academia Neomagensi, publice dicta in templo academiae Groningo-Omlandicae*. Groningen.

Saint Genois, J. de (1849–52). *Catalogue methodique et raisonné des manuscrits de la bibliothèque de la ville et l'université de Gand*. Gent: Annoot and Braeckman.

Sassen, F. L. R. (1955). De kwartierlijke hogeschool te Nijmegen: Bij de 300ste verjaring van haar stichting, 1655–1955. *Numaga* 2: 57–67.

——(1962). Levensberichten van de hoogleraren der kwartierlijke hogeschool te Nijmegen. *Numaga* 9: 123–5.

Savigny, F. C. von (1840–9). *System des heutigen römischen Rechts*, 8 vols. Berlin: Veit & Comp.

Saxe, F. (1787). *Oratio de utilitate et jucunditate historiae juris civilis*. Utrecht: Paddenburg.

Schama, S. (1977). *Patriots and Liberators: Revolution in the Netherlands, 1780–1813*. New York: Knopf.

Scheltema, H. J. (1970). *L'enseignement de droit des antécesseurs*. Byzantina Neerlandica, Ser. B, fasc. 1. Leiden: Brill.

Schevichaven, H. D. J. van (1896). *Oud-Nijmegens straten, markten, pleinen, open ruimten en wandelplaatsen*. Nijmegen: ten Hoet.

Schneppen, H. (1960). *Niederländische Universitäten und deutsches Geistesleben von der Gründung der Universität Leiden bis ins späte 18. Jahrhundert*. Münster: Aschendorf.

Scholten, P. (1934). C. Asser's Handleidung tot de beoefening van het Nederlandsch Burgerlijk recht. *Algemeen deel*, 2nd imp. Zwolle: Tjeenk Willink.

——(1945). *Zakenrecht*. Asser's Handleiding tot de beoefening van het Nederlands burgerlijk recht, vol. 2. 8th imp. Zwolle: Tjeenk Willink.

Scholtens, J. E. and Feenstra, R. (1974). Hugo de Groot's De aequitate: Tekstuitgave en tekstgeschiedenis met bijdragen over Nicolaas Blanckaert en over de voorrede tot de Inleidinge. *The Legal History Review* 42: 201–42.

SCHOOCK, M. (1661). *De figmento legis regiae epistola ad . . . Antonium Schoockium*. Groningen: J. Cöllenus.

SCHORER, W. (1777). *Vertoog over de ongerymdheid van het samenstel onzer hedendaagsche regtsgeleerdheid*. Middelburg and Amsterdam: P. Gillissen and Yntema & Tieboel.

SCHRÖDER, J. (1979). *Wissenschaft und Lehre der 'praktischen Jurisprudenz' auf deutschen Universitäten an der Wende zum 19. Jahrhundert*. Jus commune Sonderheft, 11. Frankfurt/Main: Klostermann.

SCHUBART-FIKENTSCHER, G. (1970). Untersuchungen zur Autorschaft von Dissertationen im Zeitalter der Aufklärung. *Sitzungsber. Sächsischen Akademie der Wissenschaften*. Phil.-Hist. Kl. Bd. 114, Heft 5. Berlin: Akademie-Verlag.

——(1977). Christian Thomasius: seine Bedeutung als Hochschullehrer am Beginn der deutschen Aufklärung. *Sitzungsber. Sächsischen Akademie der Wissenschaften*. Phil.-Hist. Kl. Bd. 119, Heft 4. Berlin: Akademie-Verlag.

SCHÜLING, H. (1969). *Die Geschichte der axiomatischen Methode im 16. und beginnenden 17. Jahrhundert: Wandlung der Wissenschaftsauffassung*. Studien und Materialien zur Geschichte der Philosophie, 13. Hildesheim: Olms.

SCHULTING, A. (1720). *Enarratio partis primae Digestorum seu Pandectarum D. N. Justiniani, sacratissimi principis*. Leiden: J. van der Linden.

——(1717). *Jurisprudentia vetus ante-justinianea*. New edn. by G. H. Ayrer. Leipzig: Weidmann, 1737.

——(1738). *Thesium controversarum juxta seriem Digestorum decades centum*. Leiden: S. Luchtmans.

——and SMALLENBURG, N. (1804–35). *Notae ad Digesta seu Pandectas*, 7 vols. Leiden: Honkoop (later, Luchtmans).

SCHULZ, F. (1916). *Einführung in das Studium der Digesten*. Tübingen: Mohr.

——(1963). *History of Roman legal science*, 2nd repr. Oxford: Clarendon.

——(1969). *Classical Roman law*. (1st edn. 1951) Oxford: Clarendon.

SCHUTTEVAER, H. (1982). *Vijftien generaties, de geschiedenis van een Nederlands geslacht (1480–1980)*. Arnhem: Gouda Quint.

SIMON VAN DER AA, J. (1914). Uit de opleiding van de juristen aan de Groninger Hoogeschool in vroeger tijd. In: *Academia Groningana MDCXIV–MCMXIV: Gedenkboek ter gelegenheid van het derde eeuwfeest der universiteit te Groningen*. Groningen: Noordhoff: 347–83.

SIMPSON, A. W. B. (ed.) (1984). *Biographical dictionary of the common law*. London: Butterworths.

SINNINGHE, J. R. W. (1944). *Hollandsch sagenboek: legenden en sagen uit Noord- an Zuid-Holland*. The Hague: A. Storm van Leeuwen.

SLEE, J. C. VAN (1916). *De illustre school te Deventer 1630–1878: Hare geschiedenis, hoogleeraren en studenten, met bijvoeging van Album studiosorum*. The Hague: Nijhoff.

SMITSKAMP, H. (1953). Perizonius en de crisis der geschiedeniswetenschappen in de 17e eeuw (het historisch Pyrrhonisme). *Bijdragen en medelingen Historisch genootschap* 68: 47–70.

SMITS-VELD, M. B. (ed.) (1983). *Een baljuw in opspraak: twee toneelteksten van Goudanus*. Muiderberg: Coutinho.

SOLAZZI, S. (1928). Note esegetico-critche di diritti romano. *Archivio giuridico* 100: 3–18.

SOLLNER, A. (1969). Zu den Literaturtypen des deutschen usus modernus. *Jus commune* 2: 167–85.

——(1977). Die Literatur zum gemeinen und partikularen Recht in Deutschland, Österreich, den Niederlanden und der Schweiz. In: Coing, 1977.

SOUBIE, A. (1960). *Recherches sur les origines des rubriques du Digeste*. Tarbes: Saint-Joseph.

SPANGENBERG, E. (1817). *Einleitung in das römisch-justinianeische Rechtsbuch oder Corpus Juris Civilis Romani*. Hannover: Hahn. Repr. Aalen: Scientia, 1970.

——(1822). *Jacob Cujas und seine Zeitgenossen*. Leipzig: J. F. Hartknock. Repr. Frankfurt/Main: Sauer & Auvermann, 1967.

SPIEGEL, L. P. VAN DE (1777). (Anon.), *Gedagten over het samenstel onzer hedendaagsche burgerlijke regtsgeleerdheid*. Goes and The Hague: J. Huysman and J. A. Bouvink.

SPRENGER (1898). Ueber dolus causam dans und incidens. *Archiv für die civilistische Praxis* 88: 359–91.

STAR NUMAN, O. W. (1869). *Cornelis van Bynkershoek: Zijn leven en zijne geschriften*. Leiden: Hazenberg.

STEIN, P. (1958). *Fault in the formation of contract in Roman law and Scots law*. Edinburgh: Oliver & Boyd.

——(1980). *Legal evolution, the story of an idea*. Cambridge: Univ. Press.

STINTZING and LANDSBERG *Geschichte der deutschen Rechtswissenschaft*, i–ii by R. Stintzing, Munich and Leipzig, 1880–4; iii. 1 by E. Landsberg, 2 vols., Munich and Leipzig, 1898; iii. 2 by E. Landsberg, 2 vols., Munich and Berlin, 1910.

STOLLEIS, M. (1980). *Arcana imperii und ratio status: Bemerkungen zur politischen Theorie des frühen 17. Jahrhunderts*. Göttingen: Vandenhoeck & Ruprecht.

STOLTE, B. H. (ed.) (1979). A legal opinion by Johan Vœt and Gerard Noodt. *Acta juridica*: 421–7.

——(1981). *Henrik Brenkman (1681–1736) jurist and classicist: A chapter from the history of Roman law as part of the classical tradition*. Groningen: Bouma's Boekhuis.

STOLTE, B. H. (1984*a*). The partes of the Digest in the codex florentinus. *Subseciva groningana* 1: 69–91.

——(1984*b*). Did Paul and Ulpian disagree? Dig. 22.5.15 vs. 28.1.20.5. *Mnemosyne* 37: 152–4.

TEITLER, H. C. (1983). *Notarii en excerptores: Een onderzoek naar de rol en betekenis van notarii en excerptores in dienst van overheid en kerk in de Romeinse keizertijd (tot ca. 450 A.D.).* Utrecht: Hes.

TEX, C. A. DEN (1839). Over wetenschap en wetgeving in derzelver noodwendig verband. *Ned. Jaarb. voor Regtsgeleerdheid en Wetgeving* 1: 1–34.

TEX, J. DEN (1926). *Locke en Spinoza over de tolerantie.* Amsterdam: Scheltema & Holkema.

THIBAUT, A. F. J. (1834). *System des Pandekten-Rechts,* 2 vols., 8th imp. Jena: F. Mauke.

THIJSSEN-SCHOUTE, C. L. (1954). *Nederlands Cartesianisme.* Verhand. Kon. Ned. Akademie van Wetenschappen, Afd. Letterk. NR 60. Amsterdam: Noord-Hollandse Uitgeversmij.

TIMPANARO, S. (1971). *Die Entstehung der Lachmannschen Methode.* Hamburg: Buske.

TROJE, H. E. (1970). Die europäische Rechtsliteratur unter dem Einfluss des Humanismus. *Jus commune* 3: 33–63.

——(1971). *Graeca leguntur: Die Aneignung des byzantinischen Rechts und die Entstehung eines humanistischen Corpus iuris civilis in der Jurisprudenz des 16. Jahrhunderts.* Cologne and Vienna: Böhlau.

——(1972*a*). Zur humanistischen Jurisprudenz. In: Festschrift für Hermann Heimpel. Göttingen: Vandenhoeck & Ruprecht: 110–39.

——(1972*b*). Humanistische Kommentierungen klassischer Juristenschriften. *Jus commune* 4: 51–72.

——(1977). Die Literatur des gemeinen Rechts unter dem Einfluss des Humanismus. In: Coing, 1977: 615–795.

TROTZ, C. H. See Hugo, 1738, and Wächtler, 1733.

TULLY, J. (1980). *A discourse on property: John Locke and his adversaries.* Cambridge: Univ. Press.

TYDEMAN, M. (1787). *Oratio de caussis quibusdam corruptae jurisprudentiae.* Harderwijk: J. Moojen.

ULLMANN, W. (1975). *Law and politics in the Middle Ages: An introduction to the sources of medieval political ideas.* London: Sources of History Limited.

Utrechtsche consultatiën: Utrechtsche consultatiën, dat is decisoire ende andere advisen, instructien ende advertissementen van rechten, gegeven ende gemaeckt by de vermaerste rechtsgeleerden . . . der stadt Utrecht, ed. L. van Lanckeren, 4 vols. (Various edns., see Roberts, 1942: 180 f., for vol. iii I used the edn. of Utrecht: A. Schouten, 1700.)

VANGEROW, K. A. VON (1856). *Lehrbuch der Pandekten*, 3 vols., 6th imp. Marburg: Elwert'schen Universitätsbuchhandlung.

VEEN, T. J. (1976). *Recht en nut: Studiën over en naar aanleiding van Ulrik Huber (1636–1694)*. Zwolle: Tjeenk Willink.

——(1978). Naturrecht und praktische Philosophie. *The Legal History Review* 46: 151–60.

——(1982). Van Vranck tot Kluit: Theorieën over de legitimatie van de soevereiniteit der Staten Provinciaal (1587–1795). In: *Freonen om. ds. J. J. Kalma hinne*. Leeuwarden: de Tille: 302–24.

——(1985*a*). De lege regia: Opmerkingen over de interdependentie van geschiedbeschouwing, politieke theorie en interpretatie van Romeins recht bij Ulrik Huber. In: G. Th. Jensma, F. R. H. Smit, and F. Westra (eds.) *Universiteit te Franeker: Bijdragen tot de geschiedenis van de Friese hogeschool*. Leeuwarden: Fryske Akademy: 321–34.

——(1985*b*). Interpretations of Inst. 1.2.6, D 1.4.1 and D 1.3.31: Huber's historical, juridical and political–theoretical reflections on the *lex regia*. *The Legal History Review* 53: 357–77.

——(1985*c*). Harderwijkse promoti en Nijmeegse studenten. In: *Sine invidia communico*, essays for A. J. de Groot. Nijmegen: Gerard Noodt Instituut: 243–58.

VEENENDAAL, A. J. (1958). Gisbert Cuper 1644–1716. In: *Overijselse portretten: Jubileumbundel, uitgegeven ter gelegenheid van de viering van het honderdjarig bestaan van de Vereeniging tot Beoefening van Overijsselsch Regt en Geschiedenis*. Werken Overijselsch regt en geschiedenis, 30. Zwolle: 79–94.

VIORA, M. (1927). Un parere inedito dello Schulting, del van Noodt e del Vitrarius. *Rivista italiana per le scienze storiche*, NS 2, fasc. iv: 1–49.

VITRIARIUS, J. J. (1734). *Oratio funebris in obitum Antonii Schultingii*. Leiden: Luchtmans. (For other edns. see Ahsmann–Feenstra, 1984: nr. 986–7.)

VLUGT, W. VAN DER (1916). *Twee Nederlandsche meesters in de rechtsgeleerdheid* [Huber and Noodt]. Leiden: Brill.

VOGT, W. (1971). *Franciscus Duarenus 1509–1559: Sein didaktisches Reformprogramm und seine Bedeutung für die Entwicklung der Zivilrechtsdogmatik*. Beiträge zur neueren Privatrechtsgeschichte, 4. Stuttgart: Kohlhammer.

VOLTERRA, E. (1971). Il problema del testo delle costituzioni imperiali. In: *La critica del testo: Atti del secondo congresso internazionale della Società italiana di storia del diritto*. Florence: Olschki. ii: 821–1097.

——(1978). Le notae di Cujas ai tituli ex corpore Ulpiani. In: *Festschrift für Franz Wieacker zum 70. Geburtstag*. Göttingen: Vandenhoeck & Ruprecht: 296–307.

VOORDA, B. (1762). *Oratio de arte legislatoria ex Tabulis Romanorum decemviralibus comparanda*. Franeker: Coulon.

VOORDUIN, J. C. (1837–40). *Geschiedenis en beginselen der Nederlandsche Wetboeken*, 9 vols. Utrecht: Natan.

VORSTERMAN VAN OIJEN, A. A. (1885–90). *Stam- en wapenboek van aanzienlijke Nederlandsche familiën: Met genealogische en heraldische aanteekeningen*, 3 vols. Groningen: Wolters.

VOSSIUS, G. (1606). *Oratoriarum institutionum libri sex*. Leiden: Clouck. (Several later edns.)

VRIEMOET, E. L. (1763). *Athenarum Frisiacarum libri duo, quorum alter praeter historiam academiae, quae est Franequerae, elogia ephororum alter professorum . . . complectitur*. Leeuwarden: Coulon and De Chalmot.

VRUGT, M. VAN DE (1982). *Aengaende criminele saken: Drie hoofdstukken uit de geschiedenis van het strafrecht*. Deventer: Kluwer.

WÄCHTLER, C. (1680*a*). *Disputatio inauguralis de gradibus culpae in contractibus quam . . . praeponit ad D XII octob. MDCLXXX*. Wittenberg: M. Henckel.

——(1680*b*). *Notae ad Gerardi Noodt Probabilia juris, ubi textus aliquot juris Romani tanguntur*. Wittenberg: M. Henckel. Also in Wächtler, 1733.

——(1681). *Notae ad Gerardi Noodt Probablium juris civilis libri tres*. Wittenberg: J. Wilkius.

——(1733). *Opuscula juridico-philologica rariora in unum volumen collecta . . . cum praefatione C. H. Trotz*. Utrecht: J. van Lanckom.

WACKE, A. (1977). Circumscribere, gerechter Preis und die Arten der List (dolus bonus und dolus malus, dolus causam dans und dolus incidens) unter Berücksichtigung der §§ 138 Abs. II und 123 BGB. *Zeitschrift der Savigny Stiftung für Rechtsgeschichte, romanistische Abteilung*, 94: 185–243.

WAL, G. DE (1825). *Oratio de claris Frisiae jureconsultis: Accedunt annotationes de vita, fatis ac scriptis jureconsultorum*. Leeuwarden.

WAL, J. DE (1852). Oratio altera de detrimento quod neglectum historicum juris nostri studium patriae disciplinaeque adtulit [8 Feb. 1851]. In: his *Orationes academicae de historico neerlandici studio*. Leiden and Amsterdam: Gebhard: 72.

WAL, N. VAN DER and LOKIN, J. H. A. (1985). *Historiae juris graeco-romani delineatio: Les Sources du droit Byzantin de 300 à 1453*. Groningen: Forsten.

WARMELO, P. VAN (ed.) (1979). Cornelis van Bijnkershoek notae selectae ad Pandectarum libr. XII Tit. 1–XXXV Tit. 2. *Acta juridica*: 225–77.

WATER, J. VAN DE (1713). *Observationes juris Romani libri tres in quibus multa juris civilis capita emendantur et explicantur ac nonnulla aliorum auctorum loca illustrantur*. Utrecht: W. van de Water.

[WATER, J. VAN DE] (1733) [Anon.] Gerardi Noodtii Liber quartus Probabilium juris civilis a Christfridi Waechtleri notis vindicatus. In:

Miscellaneae observationes in auctores veteres et recentiores ab eruditis Brittannis anno MDCCXXI edi coeptae, cum notis et auctario variorum virorum doctorum. iii. 1: 110–30; iii. 2: 271–301.

WEBER, W. (1959). *Wirtschaftsethik am Vorabend des Liberalismus: Höhepunkt und Abschluss der scholastischen Wirtschaftsbetrachtung durch Ludwig Molina SJ*. Münster: Aschendorffsche Verlagsbuchhandlung.

WERTHEIM-GIJSE WEENINK, A. H. (1972). *Democratische bewegingen in Gelderland 1672–1795*. Amsterdam: van Gennep.

——(1975). Gelderland van 1672–1795. In: J. J. Poelhekke, G. J. Mentink, W. Jappe Alberts, and H. K. Roessingh (eds.), *Geschiedenis van Gelderland 1492–1795*. Zutphen: Walburg Press: ii: 211–330.

WEST, M. L. (1973). *Textual criticism and editorial technique*. Stuttgart: Teubner.

WIEACKER, F. (1960). *Textstufen klassischer Juristen*. Göttingen: Vandenhoeck & Ruprecht.

——(1967). *Privatrechtsgeschichte der Neuzeit, unter besonderer Berücksichtigung der deutschen Entwicklung*. 2nd imp. Göttingen: Vandenhoeck & Ruprecht.

WIELING, A. (1727). *Iurisprudentia restituta sive index chronologicus in totum iuris iustinianaei corpus*. Amsterdam: Janssonio-Waesbergios.

——(ed.) (1758). *Alexandri Chassanaei Paratitla Institutionum juris civilis, accedunt Anonymi Protheoria Institutionum, Alex. Chassanaei Index et epitome obligationum et actionum, Anonymi Flores sententiarum juris*. Utrecht: G. Mulder.

WINDSCHEID, B. (1891). *Lehrbuch des Pandektenrechts*, 3 vols., 7th edn. Frankfurt/Main: Literarische Anstalt.

WISSENBACH, J. J. (1736). *Emblemata Triboniani* and Joannis Wybo, *Tribonianus ab emblematibus Wissenbachii liberatus*. Preface by J. G. Heineccius. Halle: Impensis Orphanotrophei.

WOHLHAUPTER, E. (1940). *Die Kerze im recht*. Weimar: Böhlau.

WOLF, R. (1859). *Biographien zur Kulturgeschichte der Schweiz*, 4 vols. Zurich: Orell, Füssli & Co., 1858–62. [Bernoulli: vol. 2, 1859].

WYBO, J. see Wissenbach, 1936.

ZILVERBERG, S. B. J. (1980). Kerk en verlichting in Noord-Nederland. *AGN* 9: 318–30.

ZWAGER, H. H. (1980). *Nederland en de Verlichting*, 2nd imp. Haarlem: Fibula-van Dishoeck.

Index of Names

The appendices (pp. 334–43) are not indexed

Index of Subjects

Index of Sources

1. Ancient Legal Sources

A. Pre-Justinianic Sources

B. Corpus Juris Civilis

2. *Ancient Literary Sources*

3. *Later Sources*